Oxford India Studies In Contemporary Society

SERIES EDITOR
SUJATA PATEL

OXFORD INDIA STUDIES IN CONTEMPORARY SOCIETY is a new series of interdisciplinary compilations on issues and problems shaping our lives in twenty-first century India. The Series appears at an opportune time, when the boundaries of social science disciplines are being redefined, and theories and perspectives are being critically interrogated. Using the frameworks developed by social science interdisciplinarity, this Series captures, assesses, and situates social trends in contemporary India. It affirms the necessity of analyzing issues and themes that have a direct bearing on our daily lives, and in doing so, brings fresh perspectives into play, integrating knowledge from a variety of unexplored sources in conventional social science practice in India. The Series aims to introduce to a wider audience the central importance of interdisciplinarity in contemporary social sciences. It presents novel themes of investigation and builds a fresh approach towards the longstanding debates on methodologies and methods. With its emphasis on the debates on and about 'society' rather than 'social sciences', this Series should find an audience not only among the students and scholars of conventional social sciences, but also among the students, researchers, and practitioners of fields such as law, media, environment, medicine, policy studies, and business studies.

The series editor would like to acknowledge the help of University of Hyderabad's UPE II (C1.2) grants for the support of this work.

Sujata Patel is Professor, Department of Sociology, University of Hyderabad.

OTHER BOOKS IN THE SERIES

Rowena Robinson (ed.)
Minority Studies

Ravi Sundaram (ed.)
No Limits
Media Studies from India

Sanjay Srivastava (ed.)
Sexuality Studies

Oxford India Studies in Contemporary Society

FIRST CITIZENS
STUDIES ON ADIVASIS, TRIBALS, AND INDIGENOUS PEOPLES IN INDIA

edited by
Meena Radhakrishna

OXFORD
UNIVERSITY PRESS

Oxford University Press is a department of the University of Oxford.
It furthers the University's objective of excellence in research, scholarship,
and education by publishing worldwide. Oxford is a registered trademark of
Oxford University Press in the UK and in certain other countries.

Published in India by
Oxford University Press
YMCA Library Building, 1 Jai Singh Road, New Delhi 110 001, India

© Oxford University Press 2016
The contributors retain copyright to their individual essays.

The moral rights of the authors have been asserted.

First Edition published in 2016

All rights reserved. No part of this publication may be reproduced, stored in
a retrieval system, or transmitted, in any form or by any means, without the
prior permission in writing of Oxford University Press, or as expressly permitted
by law, by licence, or under terms agreed with the appropriate reprographics
rights organization. Enquiries concerning reproduction outside the scope of the
above should be sent to the Rights Department, Oxford University Press, at the
address above.

You must not circulate this work in any other form
and you must impose this same condition on any acquirer.

ISBN-13: 978-0-19-945969-8
ISBN-10: 0-19-945969-X

Typeset in 10.5/12.5 Adobe Garamond Pro
by The Graphics Solution, New Delhi 110 092
Printed in India by Rakmo Press, New Delhi 110 020

Contents

List of Abbreviations   vii

Acknowledgements   ix

Introduction   1
Meena Radhakrishna

I CATEGORIES AND IDENTITIES AS HISTORICAL PROCESS

1. Formation of Adivasi/Indigenous Peoples' Identity in India   33
   Virginius Xaxa

2. Primitive Accumulation, Labour, and the Making of 'Scheduled Tribe', 'Indigenous', and Adivasi Sensibility   53
   Savyasaachi

3. 'Hindus Have to Be Born as Hindus': The Magic Wand of Brahminical Hinduism and Conversions   77
   Biswamoy Pati

4. Peoples, Power, and Belief in North-East India   97
   David Vumlallian Zou

5. The Adivasi Other: Ethnicity and Minority Status   126
   Rudolf C. Heredia

6. Denotification of the Rathvas as Adivasis in Gujarat   151
   Arjun Rathva, Dhananjay Rai, and N. Rajaram

II DESTRUCTION, LOSS, DISLOCATION

7. In the Name of Sustainable Development: Genocide Masked as 'Tribal Development'   159
   Felix Padel

8. Unfree Mobility: Adivasi Women's Migration   178
   Indrani Mazumdar

9. Tribal Labour in the Tea Plantations of West Bengal: Problems of Migration and Settlement   207
   Sharit K. Bhowmik

10. Urban Housekeepers from Tribal Homelands: Adivasi Women Migrants and Domestic Work in Delhi   228
    Neetha N.

III NEGOTIATIONS AND REDRESSALS

11. Shifting the Terrain of Struggle: Critically Evaluating the Forest Rights Act   255
    Sudha Vasan

12. Retrieving Ancestral Rights: The Making of the Forest Rights Act   278
    Madhu Sarin

13. 'Adivasis' and the Trajectories of Political Mobilization in Contemporary India   307
    Archana Prasad

14. Conservation and Rights in India: Are We Moving towards Any Kind of Harmony?   337
    Ashish Kothari and *Neema Pathak Broome*

Epilogue: Violence of 'Development' and Adivasi Resistance—An Overview   370
Meena Radhakrishna

Appendix: A Brief Review of Laws Impacting Adivasis   409
Meena Radhakrishna

Index   422

About the Editor and Contributors   443

Abbreviations

ASC	Adivasi Solidarity Council
BAMCEF	Backward and Minority Communities Employees' Federation
BJP	Bharatiya Janata Party
CCA	community-conserved areas
CEC	Central Empowered Committee
CFR	community forest resource
CNTA	Chota Nagpur Tenancy Act
CPI(M)	Communist Party of India (Marxist)
CRPF	Central Reserve Police Force
CSD	Campaign for Survival and Dignity
CWDS	Centre for Women's Development Studies
DPA	Dooars Planters' Association
FRA	Forest Rights Act
IDCO	Industrial Infrastructure Development Corporation of Orissa Limited
ILO	International Labour Organization
IPT	Indian People's Tribunal
JFM	Joint Forest Management
JMM	Jharkhand Mukti Morcha
LAA	Land Acquisition Act
MoEF	Ministry of Environment and Forests
MoU	memorandum of understanding
NACDIP	National Advocacy Council for the Development of Indigenous People
NBSAP	National Biodiversity Strategy and Action Plan

NGO	non-governmental organization
NP	national park
NREGA	National Rural Employment Guarantee Act
NSS	National Sample Survey
NSSO	National Sample Survey Organisation
NTFP	non-timber forest products
NWAP	National Wildlife Action Plan
OBC	Other Backward Classes
PA	protected area
PESA	Panchayats (Extension to Scheduled Areas) Act
PLA	Plantation Labour Act
PVTG	Particularly Vulnerable Tribal Groups
PWD	Public Works Department
RTI	Right to Information (Act)
SC	Scheduled Caste
SEZ	special economic zone
SHGs	self-help groups
SPO	special police officer
ST	Scheduled Tribe
TDLA	Tea Districts Labour Association
UN	United Nations
UNESCO	United Nations Educational, Scientific, and Cultural Organization
UNWGIP	United Nations Working Group on Indigenous Populations
VHP	Vishva Hindu Parishad
WGIP	Working Group on Indigenous Populations
WLPA	Wild Life (Protection) Act
WLS	wildlife sanctuary
WWF	World Wide Fund for Nature

Acknowledgements

My first acknowledgement is to my family, without whom this volume would probably still exist, but a far lesser and poorer one. To Nasir, fellow traveller (and fellow reader committed to reading at least once all words which I write for the public domain), for advice and support during the longish gestation period preceding this volume's birth. To my daughters—Shirali who tracked with unshakeable pride and enthusiasm the tardy progress of this project, and Rushika who has joined it by nonchalantly agreeing to 'lend' the image of one of her sculptures for the cover of this volume. And to my very elderly mother, who generously put the deadlines related to the volume above her own pressing needs, and frequently chose to redirect my attention to the volume, instead.

My deepest gratitude is also to all the contributors to this volume for their faith, resilience, and solidarity, and for standing firm with me as a community during the travails this volume went through, as is in the nature of most edited volumes.

The anonymous referees' suggestions have added substantially to the final version, and I thank them sincerely for their painstaking critiques of the original manuscript.

And lastly, I would thank the team at Oxford University Press for providing continuous support through the process of publication.

Introduction

Meena Radhakrishna

The old discourse on 'who is a tribal?' was foregrounded again a few years ago by the Gujjars agitating and demanding to be included in the Scheduled Tribe (ST) category. This single event sharply brought into focus the curious fact that in post-independence India, the concept of 'tribe', in itself a beleaguered one, is treated almost completely synonymously with the ST category.

It is important to clarify at the very outset that the ST category is not inclusive of a number of very similarly placed communities who were not given this post-independence constitutional protection and designation. The constituency of people who are the subjects of this volume's focus, then, comprises a much larger number than the population of STs would imply, which by itself is a very large section of the Indian population.[1]

It is in this context that the title of this book needs a bit of an explanation. A number of similarly situated communities may prefer to identify themselves with specific nomenclatures—as 'tribes', 'adivasis', 'indigenous people', or even STs, among others.[2] However, they have shared with each other, for centuries, the painful predicament of

---

[1] Just the ST population, according to the 2011 census, is 8.6 per cent of the total Indian population. According to the census, this percentage translates into 104,281,034 people (GoI 2013).
[2] Some of these labels have been taken up for extensive discussions in this volume, as also the reasons for different communities' preference for one marker or the other.

being subjected to disparate, inimical historical processes which have led to their destitution. In the recent decades, these diversely named communities, with all their unique historical trajectories, have joined hands with numerous other nameless ones to demand to be recognized *first and foremost as citizens*, both as a common identity and as a right. The protest movements they have created all over India are poised to, finally, wrest this from an unwilling Indian state.

The main title—'First Citizens'—locates this ongoing process in a global context. In different regions of the world, notably North America, South America, and Australia, analogous communities consciously choosing to be called First Nations or indigenous people or aborigines have also been successfully leading remarkable political campaigns to reclaim lost land and citizenship rights. It is not an accident that the words 'indigenous', 'aborigine', and 'adivasi' all literally mean an original inhabitant. The phrase 'First Citizens' derives from the understanding that all such communities, including in India, are amongst the world's *first, original people*, and so by definition, the world's first citizens. Terms like 'tribe', 'adivasi', and 'indigenous' have genealogies which arise from specific historical–political Indian contexts. Historicizing and contextualizing these terms is the only way to understand the significance of nomenclatures current at particular periods of time. The next few pages will attempt that difficult task, as a way of introducing the precise constituencies of people with which this volume is concerned.

This is all the more important since the constitutional, administrative category of 'Scheduled Tribes'[3] has now become the staple of anthropological studies all over the country, which implies that even contemporary disciplinary boundaries have been drawn with state-given categories. In reality, these social formations are dynamic, and the defining characteristics of communities and groups have been changing all this time. The administrative categories have frozen them over decades, and do not adequately recognize their vitality or the porous boundaries which they share with other social formations.

An immediate, related concern out of which this volume was thus conceptualized, then, is the troubled history of disciplines like anthropology. Just as the British invented the category of 'tribe', their

---

[3] The Indian state's parameters for defining an ST, quite questionable in themselves, were, and remain: (*a*) primitive traits; (*b*) distinctive culture; (*c*) geographical isolation; (*d*) shyness of contact with the community at large; and (*e*) economic backwardness (GoI 2013).

administrative practices constituted the discipline of anthropology, both past and present. Since disciplinary boundaries have remained firmly drawn according to the administrative criteria, it has resulted in a travesty of sound anthropological as well as historical research as far as these communities are concerned. Contributors to this volume have avoided conflation of analytical/sociological categories with administrative/constitutional ones, which have followed a certain pattern from colonial times. The understanding that administrative categories—past and present—are not autonomous and have their roots in hegemonic state practices has informed all related research questions in this volume.

TRIBE

The British categorized the Indian people arbitrarily into castes and tribes, apart from groups based on religion. From the second half of the nineteenth century onwards, a number of volumes with titles including the words 'Castes and Tribes…'of a particular region were produced, pertaining to different Provinces and Presidencies (for example, *Castes and Tribes of Southern India* by Edgar Thurston; *The Tribes and Castes of Central Provinces of India* by R. V. Russell; *The Tribes and Castes of Bengal* by H. H. Risley; *Mysore: Tribes and Castes* by L. K. A. Iyer; and *A Glossary of the Tribes and Castes of the Punjab and North-West Frontier Province* by H. A. Rose). The British started this exercise in the aftermath of the 1857 rebellion, in order to map and govern India more effectively, to understand turbulent India and its people better. The census of 1881 and the accompanying District Handbooks and District Gazetteers originated from a similar impulse, and historical records show that classifications and categories were a new administrative obsession in the late nineteenth century.

Hence, the basis for the British classification of the Indian people into castes and tribes is not very helpful in understanding what a caste is, or a tribe, as the purpose of the classification was a political/administrative one. In fact, nowhere have the authors of 'castes and tribes' volumes clearly differentiated between these two categories, and it appears that anyone who did not belong to the hierarchy of the Hindu *varna* or caste system, or did not practise an identifiable mainstream religion, was classified as a 'tribe'. Thus, it is more by a process of elimination that this category seems to have been arrived at, and then endowed with some sociological features. Moreover, the word 'tribe', used over the centuries by colonial authorities, did not usefully suggest communities with distinct cultures and practices—distinct both to the colonizers and to the mainstream mainland communities—but almost always insinuated backwardness and savagery.[4]

In fact, it is becoming increasingly evident that states can create new categories of 'undesirable' people altogether—'tribes', 'primitive tribes', 'wild tribes', 'wandering tribes', 'aboriginal tribes', and 'criminal tribes' were some of the creations of the British, and 'Scheduled Tribe', 'Primitive Tribal Groups', and 'Denotified Tribe' are categories concocted by the post-independence Indian state.

It is thus important to point out that some communities who are the subjects of our study in this volume may also belong to the ST category, but what we are concerned with here is a reassessment of the earlier anthropological definitions and taking cognizance of empirical realities. The presence or absence of these communities in the ST category is not germane to the concerns of this volume. The judiciousness of this position is eminently borne out by an important chapter in this collection by Rathva et al.: communities declared STs decades ago can be taken off the list at any point in time at will by the state if this act serves its stated or unstated political purposes. The contributions by some authors in this volume—Xaxa, Savyasaachi, Heredia, and Prasad in particular—help the reader reach conceptual clarity about these terminologies. While debating the taxonomies, and specifically the question of 'who or what is a tribe', it has been suggested that given the immense diversity and complexity of the many social systems which exist in India, with their distinctive cultures and separate economies, a single definition of the word 'tribe' is not possible within the Indian context. Moreover, as implied earlier, like all societies these formations too are dynamic in nature, thus defying a single definition true for all time. The concerned people did not call themselves tribes, or identify with any other comparable term, but did define what an 'outsider' was.

Heredia and Xaxa make several useful points in this context. Outsiders who worked with these communities variously termed them as adivasis, *adimjati*s, *vanyajati*s, *vanvasi*s, *girijan*s, *pahadia*s, etc. The idea of the backward and the primitive with respect to these communities is embedded in the understanding of social workers, reformers, missionaries, as well as Indian administrators, and has a long

---

[4] However, it must be stated straightaway that for their own good reasons, in the north-eastern region of the country, today this term of address is still preferred by the concerned tribal communities over all other terminologies. These issues are explained in the course of this volume.

history from the colonial period onwards. Moreover, the idea of the 'primitive' referred not to a single aspect, but to the entire universe of these groups, to their very mode of living: social, cultural, economic, and technological. As both Xaxa and Heredia point out, this was as true of the Gandhians who called them *adimjati* (*adim* = primordial, primitive, primeval) as of pre- or post-independence administrators. The Gandhians also coined terms like *ranipaja*, *vanyajati*, and *girijan* (jungle, forest, and mountain dwellers, respectively).

According to Heredia, the 1931 census separated out these groups under the category of 'primitive tribes' instead of 'forest tribes' as in the 1891 census, or 'hill tribes' as in subsequent censuses. He also suggests that in the pre-British period, the forest people served as 'bridge and buffer communities between kingdoms', which made it possible for them to remain autonomous and preserve their distinct identities. The Sanskrit word *jana* referred to non-monarchical societies outside the jati system, and the British called those people 'tribes' who retained their distinct culture and identity, especially in isolated and remote areas, and could not be absorbed into the rigid jati hierarchy or into Christianity, Islam, or other mainstream religious orders.

Given the preceding discussion, initiated by authors in this volume, the category of 'tribe' is clearly a contested one today from the point of view of academic enquiry. Moreover, just as there are generic differences between the two entities called 'castes' and 'tribes', so can we sometimes see some similarities between these two sets of people. Research points to the possibility of a tribe–caste continuum rather than these remaining discrete and separated entities for all times to come, and about a 'tribe' beginning to present itself as a 'caste' over a period of time (Vidyarthi and Rai 1985: 455). However, where this has happened, it was in specific historical circumstances, and caution is needed in putting this idea forward as a historical necessity or inevitability.

As a corollary to the point about the tribe–caste continuum, it can also be argued that over time, conversions by members of both 'tribes' and 'castes' into major religious groups may show the disappearance of earlier, generic cultural differences that existed between them as members of specific tribes or castes. Here, the chapters by Zou and Pati redraw our attention to the fact that, historically, the religions to which adivasi communities converted included Islam and Buddhism.

Further, through conversion or cultural assimilation, the differences between at least some members of such 'tribes' and other, *non-tribal* members of their adopted religion may also begin to vanish. This process is particularly expected to become evident when such converted communities become Hinduized. Pati's chapter shows how, in Odisha (formerly known as Orissa), around the beginning of the twentieth century, the varna system opened up a space for 'integration' by incorporating a large section of the non-*pahadia* (hill dwellers) or plains adivasis as Khandayats/Kshatriyas, and adivasi society itself adopted conversion as a part of a broad survival strategy, including conversion to Christianity.[5] In the context of Naga conversions, Zou too perceptively suggests that Christianity was found to be 'irresistible' because of not spiritual but pragmatic, social, and survival reasons for the women as well as slave girls and boys. These examples anticipate the possibility that conversions may not significantly alter either the belief systems or the social life of the converts in accordance with the demands of the adopted religion.

Pati records in the case of Odisha that while 'the converts to the varna order ... participated in the Hindu as well as tribal festivals, the converts to Christianity [also] observed certain customs and beliefs that were antithetical to the basic tenets of Christianity. They participated in tribal festivals and, when asked about their identity, mentioned their tribe, suppressing the Christian connection.' Similarly, Zou's research into Khasi-Jaintia conversion to the Welsh Calvinistic faith shows that 'despite the condemnation of social practices such as alcoholic drinks and use of opium, the preservation of (a marriage related) core social code... enabled the Khasi-Jaintia to convert without a sense of identity conflict.'

Questions about the erosion of 'tribal' characteristics can thus be raised only after due research in the field about the precise nature of shifting identities. In contemporary India, a number of adivasi communities have been displaced, and have migrated from their traditional habitats to join the informal sector of the urban or semi-urban economy. Further research would be required before one can speculate as to whether this absorption into the labour force has significantly modified their lived social and cultural life, as well as their self-image or identity as distinct adivasi communities. It would be interesting, too, to research how those numerous adivasi communities perceive themselves who first converted to Christianity decades ago, and then, treated by fanatics as lost ground,

---

[5] Guha (1999) quotes the *Report on the Territories of the Rajah of Nagpur*, where it is stated that because the Gonds had been Rajahs of 'Nagpur country' for long, in the 1820s they were allowed to join the Kshatriya caste by the compliant Mahratta officers.

were recovered through 're-Hinduization' (that is, inducted into the Hindu religion through what Pati calls *shuddhi karan* or rituals of purification). These are political as much as anthropological questions, yet to be answered satisfactorily. The degree of retention of earlier distinct community cultural practices as well as self-image and identity could point to incomplete answers to the vexed question of 'who is still a tribal', but a sounder anthropological assessment of such communities is needed through further theorizing and research.

Further, there still exist innumerable communities which did not have 'tribal characteristics', or were not 'tribes' in the sense in which the term came to be defined, but who were also outside the varna system. These were itinerant people, some of whom were also forest-dependent but were only partially forest dwellers—these groups moved in or out of the forests in pursuit of their livelihoods. There were also pastoral nomads, similarly dependent on the forests, but who travelled much beyond those spaces with their herds. In fact, many itinerant groups had nothing whatsoever to do with forests, but were called nomadic 'tribes' because they did not fit into the caste system or any mainstream religion—important parameters for the British to define a community as a tribe—and they still continue to be called so by the Indian state.

The most interesting aspect, however, is that a number of these nomadic 'tribes' were put in the Scheduled Caste (SC) category after independence, showing how tenuous administrative categories and official parameters are. However, there is a sociological explanation for this curious fact. The independent Indian government revised the British category of Scheduled Caste created in 1935 which the British drew almost entirely from the Hindu caste system, but which also included what were then seen to be marginalized sections, and initially put into the category 'depressed classes'. Many of these marginalized communities were also victims of untouchability by high caste Hindus.

The explanation for nomadic 'tribes' belonging to the SC category is also borne out by field research. When some of these nomadic communities became sedentary, they began to be treated as belonging to the lowest rung ever of the existing caste hierarchy. Their extreme social and cultural marginalization, as well as the untouchability practised against them by surrounding communities, seems to have been the reason for administratively clubbing them together with the outcastes of the caste hierarchy. Some further investigation and anthropological explanation is required for understanding the fact that these nomadic 'tribes' even today are at the bottom of the social hierarchy created by the caste system, and that even the erstwhile untouchable communities treat these so-called tribes as untouchables. All this points as much to permeable boundaries within anthropological (and administrative) nomenclatures as to the immense complexity surrounding state-given labels.

In the post-independence context, the term 'tribe' has become largely identified with those targeted for welfare policies, that is, STs, but Zou in his chapter offers critical inputs for understanding how complex the histories of the diverse peoples in the north-eastern region are. Among its many insights, the chapter contributes to our understanding of the immense diversity of people inhabiting the term 'Scheduled Tribes'. Savyasaachi (this volume) suggests that this category was created by the 'colonial determination to counter insurgencies against primitive accumulation'. He explains that in the last quarter of the eighteenth century, the commercial exploitation of forests led the East India Company to expand its territory to areas inhabited by forest dwellers. All these insurgent people had to be pulled out of the forests for the social production and reproduction of capital, and finally suppressed and co-opted. In this sense, the ST category has served important counter-insurgency functions in independent India.

In an attempt to trace the trajectories of terminologies, the volume tries to study the intersections of these various terms, particularly 'tribe', with other groups with distinct cultures. This is essential because the term 'tribe' not only dominated colonial deliberations, but has an unrelenting presence in the independent Indian state's administrative vocabulary as well. By squarely placing this term in a historical context, the volume tries to explore a set of important complexities: the divergences as well as intersections between the so-called tribes and other groups of people in India on the one hand, and between the self-designated adivasis and indigenous people on the other.

ADIVASI

While use of the word 'tribe' may denote deep imperial prejudice, 'adivasi' (literally *adi* 'earliest' + *vasi* 'inhabitant') has come to embody protest and assertion.[6] At the outset, it is useful to keep in mind the

---

[6] It is not the literal meaning of the term which is significant here: the term Dalit (Sanskrit: broken, cracked, split) too signifies a compelling political presence that terms like 'Scheduled Caste', 'untouchable', or 'Harijan' do not.

distinction made by Prasad (this volume) between 'the adivasi politics of communitarian elites', who were formed as a result of the process of affirmative action and are in competition for political power, and 'the adivasi politics of working-class led movements', which is rooted in a different material reality. It has been suggested by Heredia, in this volume, that the term adivasi 'refers to a wide variety of communities which before had remained relatively free from the control of outside states, but were eventually subjugated during the colonial period and brought under the control of the state'.

Generally, authors in this volume remind us that the native equivalent 'adivasi' has a long usage, especially in eastern, central, western, and southern India. There are, of course, legitimate objections by scholars that all adivasis are not original inhabitants of the regions in which they currently live, and might be migrants from neighbouring or faraway regions. Xaxa discusses the complexity of this issue in some detail in the context of India: groups may be original inhabitants of the country as a whole, though not original inhabitants of the current region within India to which they may have historically migrated, raising the question as to whether such groups are to be considered original inhabitants/indigenous or not. The term 'adivasi' is widely used by those very communities to describe themselves who are generally described as 'tribes' by outsiders.

The term adivasi, according to contributors in this volume, was first used in the Chota Nagpur region of Bihar in the 1930s, and was extended to other regions in the 1940s by A. V. Thakkar, who worked among the concerned communities. Xaxa suggests that the idea underlying the term adivasi did not have its origin amongst the concerned communities themselves. Rather, it originated from British administrator-scholars, ethnographers and, more importantly, Christian missionaries. The administrators and ethnographers invariably described the communities as autochthonous or aborigines, terms that carry the same meaning as 'original inhabitants'. With this, the idea of these people being of a different racial, linguistic, and cultural stock emerged, and it was the Christian missionaries who made them aware of this description. This idea of being not primitive but autochthonous or aboriginal shaped the consciousness of these communities and became a marker of self-identity, first among their educated elite. Xaxa further suggests that it was the consciousness of being exploited and dominated which sharpened this consciousness of being different. Such a process and such an awareness did not take shape in north-east India, as communities there did not live in close proximity with the Indian civilization and thereby escaped its influence. More importantly, they did not experience the process of colonization that communities in mainland India had already begun to experience even before the coming of British rule. The coming of the British rule only hastened and intensified a process that was already at work.

Interestingly, according to Xaxa, the usage of the term adivasi is markedly absent in northern and north-eastern India, where over 11 per cent of India's so-called tribal population lives. (In this region, communities preferring to call themselves tribals use the term adivasi to refer to those people who migrated from other regions during the colonial period to work in the tea plantations.[7]) Here, according to Xaxa, the term tribe is preferred by the communities for themselves, and adivasi is used more as a frame of reference than the aspect of indigeneity that the term implies. Burman (2009), in fact, objects that the adoption of the term adivasi jeopardizes the legitimate rights of the tribes dwelling in all regions beyond the Hindi heartland. Like the imposition of Hindi as an official state language, he argues, the term adivasi 'smacks of North Indian chauvinism'. He feels that communities in the south would find it offensive to be called adivasi.

It is thus instructive to note the recent use of the terms 'adivasi' as well as 'indigenous' by the communities in the south of India.[8] It is perhaps the strategic connection between the terms 'adivasi' and 'indigenous' which has led to this adoption, not just in the five southern states of India, but in the rest of India as well. It has been suggested in the context of Kerala that 'the discourse of tribals as indigenous people only became explicitly politicized in the 1990s, partly under the influence of

---

[7] There is also an implicit hierarchy involved in the use of these terms in this region. Because the migrants are not considered to be tribes, their claim to be included in the ST category is seen to be illegitimate as well.

[8] A newly formed Adivasi Solidarity Council (ASC), on its website, informs us that it has over 50 grassroots organizations as members of its network. 'ASC is now functioning in all five southern states namely Tamilnadu, Pondicherry, Kerala, Karnataka and Andhra Pradesh state. ASC associates with 15 states of adivasis through the National Advocacy Council for the Development of Indigenous People (NACDIP).... The mission of ASC network is promoting a collective forum of adivasi organisations to create a united voice to uphold the sustainable development of indigenous communities of India' (Website of the Adivasi Solidarity Council, http://ascsouthindia.org/about.html [accessed 16 May 2015]).

the international indigenous movement. The term adivasi ... enabled activists to connect to the global discourse on indigenous rights despite the Indian government's insistence that India ... has no indigenous people' (Steur 2009: 28).

The preceding discussion leads directly to the question of whether adivasi people are the Indian counterparts of indigenous or aboriginal peoples elsewhere. Though the Supreme Court cannot be an arbiter of history, it is important that in a little-noticed judgment, it ruled very recently that adivasis are the original inhabitants of India, and that the other 92 per cent of communities have come in waves of migration over the centuries:

> Among the disadvantaged groups, the most disadvantaged and marginalized in India are the Adivasis (STs), who, as already mentioned, are the descendants of the original inhabitants of India, and are the most marginalized and living in terrible poverty with high rates of illiteracy, disease, early mortality.... they have been victimized for thousands of years by terrible oppression and atrocities. They were deprived of their lands, and pushed into forests and hills where they eke out a miserable existence of poverty.... And now efforts are being made by some people to deprive them even of their forest and hill land where they are living, and the forest produce on which they survive.[9]

INDIGENEITY

Karlsson (2003: 407) notes that one of the most important goals of Indian delegates to the United Nations Working Group on Indigenous Populations (UNWGIP) between 1985 and 1990 was 'to make the term "tribal peoples" and the Indian term "*Adivasis*" (original inhabitants, a Sanskrit derivation) equivalent to the new international term "indigenous peoples"'.

Though the United Nations (UN) recognizes no formal definition of indigenous people, it follows the following working definition:

---

[9] Supreme Court of India, Criminal Appellate Jurisdiction, Criminal Appeal No. 11/2011 (Arising out of Special Leave Petition (Crl) No. 10367 of 2010), *Kailas & Others versus State of Maharashtra*, judgment dated 5 January 2011. Available at: http://www.thehindu.com/multimedia/archive/00351/Full_Text_of_SC_jud_351589a.pdf (accessed 16 May 2015). This statement entails an implicit and important recognition of the rights of these communities to the ancestral lands that they lost.

Indigenous populations are composed of the existing descendants of the peoples who inhabited the present territory of a country wholly or partially at the time when persons of a different culture or ethnic origin arrived there from other parts of the world, overcame them, by conquest, settlement or other means, reduced them to a non-dominant or colonial condition; who today live more in conformity with their particular social, economic and cultural customs and traditions than with the institutions of the country of which they now form part, under a state structure which incorporates mainly national, social and cultural characteristics of other segments of the population which are predominant. (Cobo 1986)

In the process of tracing the history of the term indigenous, Xaxa argues that concepts of 'race' and 'minority' have shaped the concept as well as identity of indigenous people. Once discrimination against racial and minority groups was acknowledged and a case for recognition of their rights was made in the various conventions of the International Labour Organization (ILO) and the UN, the internationalization of this issue was accompanied by an evolving definition of indigenous people.

Three criteria, in Xaxa's words, are critical to the definition of the term indigenous:

- First, 'the indigenous are those people who lived in the country to which they belong before colonization or conquest by people from outside the country or the geographical region'.
- Second, 'the people govern their life more in terms of their own social, economic, and cultural institutions than laws applicable to the rest of the society or the country at large'.
- And third, 'this category of people was progressively being marginalized and dispossessed from their sources of livelihood and was vulnerable to cultural shock as well as loss of their collective identity'.

As far as the idea of indigeneity is concerned, Xaxa points out that what seems to be critical to the shaping of this identity is the aspect of experience of domination through colonization.

Savyasaachi in his chapter too traces in some detail the trajectory of the term 'indigenous' in various international conventions and treaties. The historical injustices were to be done away with, but prescriptions for relieving the suffering of these peoples remained heavily weighted against cultural plurality: they were designed to facilitate these communities' integration and assimilation into the mainstream. With key terms like nation building, equity, development, and diversification of industrial production, *productivity* was the most important determinant of this discourse. By the 1980s, it was the concerned communities' own struggles and protests against invasions, genocide, militarization, racism, labour exploitation, and forced sales of land which helped to develop, not just the term 'indigenous', but a genuine indigenous perspective on critical issues which affected them. There was, on the one hand, resistance to being marginalized in the name of being assimilated into a modernized, industrialized world, and on the other, the emergence of an understanding of cultural distinctiveness and the legitimacy of cultural plurality. All these aspects were captured in the word 'indigenous'. According to Savyasaachi, since 'history for the indigenous people has its origins in dispossession' it was an engagement with another notion of not just history, but a worldview, a perspective, an alternative way of being, which the term indigenous represented to the people concerned. In the light of being dispossessed, recovery of origins became one of the major constituents of their struggles, a struggle also for identity. The term indigenous, then, has come to signify an ongoing process of internationalization of demands for territorial and cultural rights by analogous communities across the world.

It is important to note here that it was the ILO, born in 1919, which first used the term indigenous and conducted one of its first studies on 'indigenous workers'. Savyasaachi (this volume) convincingly argues that it was in fact an impulse for 'primitive accumulation' by means of the law or the gun—which took the form of the genocide of as many as seven million people in what are now the United States and Canada alone—that led to the ILO taking up the cause of the colonized peoples in these continents. By 1957, the ILO had adopted a treaty dealing with the original inhabitant populations, including aboriginal people predating colonization or conquest, but also 'tribal' groups irrespective of whether they could be considered indigenous or not. This extended to people from America, Australia, the Near and the Middle East, and the African continent. These measures were designed to facilitate the absorption of these peoples into the mainstream.

This discussion of indigeneity also gives an insight into the debates regarding assimilation, integration, or isolation, which probably had their origins in the aforementioned worldview represented by the ILO and the UN. With a wider-ranging sweep, on 13 September 2007, the UN General Assembly adopted the historic Declaration on the Rights of Indigenous Peoples, which recognizes indigenous people's rights to self-determination, traditional lands and territories, traditional languages and customs, natural resources, and sacred sites. This is an extremely important declaration, as it recognizes the historical injustice of dispossession as well as the communities' cultural distinctiveness, thus laying the grounds for integrating them into the mainstream, rather than advocating isolation in order for them to preserve their culture. Implicitly, it also rejects the homogenization of cultures implied in the notion of assimilation. In this volume, Heredia engages with these questions in detail in the Indian case, making out a strong case for integration as well, as opposed to assimilation.

It has been argued that indigenous identity is not a 'primordial given' with an uncontested substantive meaning, but rather a 'product ... of the later half of the twentieth century' constructed precisely in struggles over different visions of development (Steur 2009: 28). In that sense, this identity is a relatively recent phenomenon. The UN Declaration apart, Native American people have been able at least to nominally retrieve, through a sustained political campaign/movement, some of their rights, which other extremely disadvantaged people with similar histories, for instance the aborigines of Australia, have not been able to do. Such communities, by and large, do not yet refer to themselves as 'indigenous'.

The need to understand these differences is as compelling as mapping political and other commonalities of struggles by indigenous people in the rest of the world. Clearly, lessons can be learnt from other parts of the world about how indigenous people's struggles are shaping public policy. In the case of India, the communities in question have been waging their own struggle for several decades, which over the last decade have become more intensified, and also became wider in their aims as well as issues, thus involving communities other than tribal, adivasi, or indigenous ones. Radhakrishna's contribution in this volume, the Epilogue, deals at length with these struggles, and the alliances which these movements have tried to forge. It is for all these reasons that what our constituency of people *called* is much less important than tracing the social and economic processes which affect analogous communities, on the one hand, and the measures these communities take to politically address their increasingly common problems, on the other.

At the same time, this volume, consciously and in a considered way, largely adopts the term adivasi as opposed to tribal or indigenous. It is evident from several contributions on this debate in the present volume that the term 'tribe' has historically carried, and still carries, considerable colonial baggage. It must be noted here again, however, that communities in the north-east, who were not subjected to British colonization in the way mainland India was, seem to readily accept the term tribes or tribals to identify themselves, and also use it to distinguish themselves from the 'adivasi' plantation workers, as well as those who are not in the ST category.

Lastly, the adoption of the term adivasi as opposed to indigenous is also important for another significant reason. There are other Indian contestants for the identity connected with the word 'indigenous' whose histories, political concerns, and struggles are quite different from those with which this volume is concerned. James Massey (2001; see also 1994) asserts that 'the Dalits indeed are one of the earliest settlers or indigenous communities of India'. Karlsson (2003: 408) noted that the Dalit delegation participated at least four times in the UNWGIP's annual sessions, claiming that they, the former 'untouchables' who now call themselves Dalits, should be regarded as India's indigenous people. With a population of 250 million people, the Dalits may thus consider themselves to be the largest indigenous population in the world. Another researcher has also argued that Dalits are the indigenous people of India just like the Australian Aborigines were the first people of their continent (Rathna 2014).

The contemporary adivasi has taken up cudgels against the Indian state, and the term now carries a certain political connotation for the concerned communities, for all those who are supporters of their rights, and even for the Indian state. The term has evolved in direct proportion to the evolving consciousness of these communities with regard to very specific historical injustices, and increasingly has a pan-Indian appeal and usage by the communities themselves. As evident from several contributions in this volume, 'adivasi' captures the multiple facets of a politically active section of people in the Indian context much less imperfectly than other terms, and thus is the preferred editorial term for this volume. However, individual authors who have contributed to the volume may or may not share this view, and use the terms 'tribe', 'adivasi', and 'indigenous' as they deem fit.

FORCED MIGRATION AND DISPLACEMENT: ENTRANTS INTO THE INFORMAL ECONOMY

An extremely important set of issues which this volume addresses has to do with the onslaught on the life situation and livelihoods of adivasis during the colonial and post-independence periods. This process led to the large-scale migration of whole communities from their homelands, and to a continuing process of integration into the developing labour markets through absorption into the informal economy. Two chapters (Mazumdar, Bhowmik) explicitly explore important issues relating to the historical causes for large-scale adivasi migration, and some deal with contemporary livelihood issues, again leading to forced migration (Padel, Mazumdar, Neetha).

Mazumdar's contribution shows the diverse locations existing as sources and destinations and also the myriad occupations in which the migrants engage. She discusses the reasons for the historical exodus of adivasis from the Chota Nagpur plateau and the Central Provinces (present-day Madhya Pradesh, Chhattisgarh, and Odisha) for work in the Bengal and Assam plantations, in Bengal and Bihar indigo production, and for 'coolie' work in wet rice fields, factories, road building, and land reclamation in several regions during the colonial period. Bhowmik discusses historical migration from the Chota Nagpur region of Jharkhand and Chhattisgarh for work in the tea plantations in Bengal and Assam from the mid-nineteenth century onwards. These contributions are important because they show how forced migration for the adivasi is a historical phenomenon, and not just a consequence of the recent policies of the Indian state.

Mazumdar's chapter in particular, with its focus on women, shows how from the late nineteenth century migration has remained an evil necessity, and not a choice, for the adivasi communities as a whole. However, the intensity of this process has varied from region to region. By the first quarter of the twentieth century, a number of adivasi villages had been completely bought over by non-adivasi proprietors of land, converting the former into tenants or sharecroppers or landless labourers. Extension of arable land into forests, colonial land tenure arrangements, and the exploitation of forests for timber and plantations through reorganized forest administration in the latter half of the nineteenth century, all pushed forward the conversion of the hitherto largely autonomous adivasis into a subordinate 'coolie' labour force. The conversion of the adivasi peasantry into migratory labour and the transformation of adivasi-dominated regions into labour catchment areas—processes set in motion by colonial rule and its practices—were repeated across a large number of tracts and regions. Left to cultivate the worst-quality soils, plagued by lack of irrigation and drainage facilities, and reduced to indebtedness and penury, a large number of adivasi groups became 'the most heavily coerced elements in the migrant workforce and the first resort of nearly every recruiting agent' (Bates and Carter 1992, cited in Mazumdar, this volume), including for the Assam and Bengal tea plantations.

What was equally catastrophic, in addition to the factors just described, was an inordinately heavy tax system under the British, and the vagaries of nature. In Chota Nagpur region, for instance, 'five famines, three major floods, seven scarcities lie squeezed into the history of a little above a hundred years' (Singh 1975: 30, quoted in Bhowmik, this volume). All these factors squarely set the stage for large-scale migration: the adivasi was not just impoverished, but, Bhowmik argues, 'the entire adivasi agrarian system was being destroyed, shaking the very basis of the old society'. These adivasis found their way into the tea plantations, where they were subjected to the harshest of working and living conditions. They remained unorganized till long into the twentieth century, only to watch their progeny again being subjected to migration to any place which will find them work, as there is no more work on the plantations. Mazumdar remarks in her chapter that, regardless of the diversity of communities which were affected—Gonds, Baigas, or Bhils, all belonging to different provinces—'the broad contours of the story followed similar trajectories'.

There are profound differences, however, in the reasons for adivasi migration under colonial rule, and in contemporary times. A very important concern of this volume which addresses large-scale adivasi migration is the issue of 'development'-related displacement and dispossession under an Indian state committed to liberalization. A number of authors engage with this theme in great detail at different levels (see the chapters by Padel, Savyasaachi, Radhakrishna, and Prasad). Padel, for instance, eloquently sets out the larger canvas of disaster and adivasi dispossession precipitated by neo-liberalization: 'Adivasis, through invasions of their land by dam and mining projects, face a situation of genocide: every aspect of their social structure is severely disrupted, and people witness the death of the communities, cultural security and ecosystems that they and their ancestors had always carefully maintained.'

Paramount among the reasons for forced migration of adivasi populations all over India is the entry of corporate giants in the garb of development of the area, particularly in the mineral-rich states of Andhra Pradesh, Odisha, Jharkhand, and Chhattisgarh. Padel and Radhakrishna have explored at length the destructive effects of mining on the habitats, livelihoods, and community life of the concerned peoples.

CONSERVATION-RELATED DISLOCATION

One of the most critical reasons for adivasi dispossession (which has not been given sufficient academic attention so far) has been the policies relating to conservation, which, in the name of environmental/wildlife protection, have led to a systematic ouster of a very large number of people from their habitats and resource bases. It has also led to the destruction of what Padel in his chapter calls 'the ancient symbiosis which maintains the forest as a community resource, shared with wildlife'. Kothari and Pathak Broome in their contribution eloquently describe the dislocation of adivasis as directly related to these policies.

It is a fact that the conservation policies of governments all over the world, but especially in South America, Africa, and Asia, are affecting forest-dwelling people in cruel, unimaginable ways. Many planners worldwide assume that a people-free wilderness is the best way of conserving biodiversity. The establishment of wildlife sanctuaries, reserved forests, and protected areas has thrown out innumerable forest-dependent communities from their homes, snatched away their livelihoods, and made them vulnerable to intense exploitation by mainstream communities. Exploring the global commonalities between analogous habitats, livelihoods, and living conditions of similarly placed people all over the world may be a strategic way of protecting these groups from displacement and forced migration/forced resettlement.[10]

In this volume, a number of authors engage with the dispossession of the adivasi in contemporary times through a set of government conservation policies (see the chapters by Sarin, Kothari and Pathak Broome, Vasan, and Radhakrishna).

Clearly a direct consequence of such policies and processes in contemporary India, adivasi migration takes place as a result of

---

[10] For example, the Commission for Human and Peoples' Rights in Kenya has ordained that the informed consent of indigenous people is necessary before wildlife sanctuaries are established. This, if treated as a precedent, has tremendous political potential for groups—whatever the nomenclature used to describe them—affected by comparable forest policies of their governments. In India, a law to give some autonomy to forest-based communities in decision-making, namely the Panchayats (Extension to Scheduled Areas) Act (PESA), 1996, has existed for two decades, and the Scheduled Tribes and Other Traditional Forest Dwellers (Recognition of Forest Rights) Act, 2006 to give rights over forest resources, has existed for almost a decade, but the situation has not improved much on the ground. The former Act is described in the Epilogue to this volume, and the latter is discussed in detail later in this chapter.

displacement from an astonishingly large number of regions. As far as their large-scale absorption into the informal sector is concerned, Mazumdar shows that adivasi women migrate mainly for agricultural work, the brick kiln industry, and for casual construction work. They migrate to not just villages and towns of their own state, but often to other far-off states for informal work. In her chapter, Neetha is concerned with contemporary adivasi women's migration from the states of Jharkhand, Chhattisgarh, Odisha, Assam, and West Bengal into the informal workforce in metropolises such as Delhi, Mumbai, and Bengaluru.

While discussing the factors involved in female adivasi migration, Neetha writes that for adivasi male migrants, construction is the major sector for employment, followed by mining. However, the volatility in employment in these sectors and the adverse nature of working conditions limit the possibility of these sectors becoming 'the economic backbone' of adivasi societies. In other words, from the point of view of adivasi families, there are sectors where both men and women could potentially be absorbed, but wherever male migrants are not able to find sufficient employment in these sectors, female migration accelerates to other forms of informal work, including domestic work in large cities.

The transformation in the lives and identity of migrant workers who become a part of the informal working class is explored by Bhowmik and Neetha in different ways in their respective chapters. They show how adivasi identity gets severely challenged in these circumstances, and how immense negotiation by individuals is necessary to balance the two different worlds they come to straddle. In the case of adivasis for whom their only home coincides with their workplace, the group or individual identity has to be renegotiated in the setting of a trade union. In the case of single, migrant adivasi women who seek domestic worker employment in metropolises, and who go back and forth between their home village and the city, there is the more difficult task of balancing the two different universes which they now inhabit.

THE FOREST RIGHTS ACT, 2006

Law is one of the most contentious domains as far as adivasi rights are concerned, and it is in the lower courts, the high courts, and finally in the Supreme Court where repeated representations are made by contesting parties, including the adivasis, who have been increasingly using the courts to safeguard their rights under the constitution. The adivasis are particularly impacted by those specific pieces of legislation which are opposed to their continued presence in the forest, and their use of the resources therein. In an important study, Sarin shows in the volume how insufficient recognition of communal tenures in Indian statutory law has decimated forest-dependent communities' economies and cultures, and how the immense legal expansion of the 'national forest estate' in Schedule V areas after independence has violated all constitutional provisions. Sarin and Radhakrishna both highlight the adverse impact of post-independence conservation laws on the adivasis. Kothari and Pathak Broome in their chapter eloquently describe the impact of wildlife conservation laws and policy on both conservation and the communities. Radhakrishna discusses in detail the land acquisition legislation and its uses for corporate entry into mineral-rich areas. The discussions by Sarin and Radhakrishna in this book clarify which parts of the violence committed upon adivasi communities by the state machinery are 'legal', so to speak, given that endemic aggression towards them is often dictated by the spirit and content of some of these laws, both new and old. The Appendix at the end of this book briefly discusses several of the potentially enabling pieces of legislation, themselves a result of long struggles by the communities and civil society activists, and the proposed dilutions therein.

However, the most controversial and important piece of legislation, taken up for detailed study in this volume, is the Scheduled Tribes and Other Traditional Forest Dwellers (Recognition of Forest Rights) Act, 2006, popularly known as the Forest Rights Act (FRA). This Act, in principle, has significant implications for other similarly placed communities all over the world, as it was supposed to set out for policymakers a framework which discussed the issues of conservation from the point of view of the adivasis rather than environmentalists. It was supposed to recognize forest dwellers' rights (individual rights to cultivated land in forestlands, and community rights over common property resources), aiming to make conservation strategists more accountable. Because this legislation was a result of prolonged struggle for livelihoods, homelands, and dignity, it could have set a precedent for forest-based communities all over the world both in terms of movements for democracy as well as the recovery of vanishing ways of being.

However, this piece of legislation has not delivered in actual practice because, on the one hand, the forest bureaucracy is hostile to the very aim of rights being given to communities under this Act, and on the other, there is a yawning gap between the intent and actual functioning of the Act. Several authors who take up the FRA for serious scrutiny in this volume, particularly Sarin and Vasan, point to the grossly inadequate implementation of the few enabling clauses of the FRA on the ground, and gaping holes in the legislation itself. Significantly, Vasan goes much further, arguing that FRA legitimizes 'a historical land grab of the state', shifts focus away from the discourse on adivasi autonomy, and establishes the state as a legitimate 'ruler' of the forests that is now dispensing 'forest rights'.

While discussing the provisions under the FRA, Sarin documents a number of struggles all over the country for community rights under the Act. Radhakrishna, on another note, highlights the fact that the environment movement in the country is sharply divided over the FRA. Powerful sections of the conservation movement in India have been extremely hostile to the institution of the FRA for conservation reasons. At the same time, a number of national and international conservation-related organizations recognize adivasis' traditional knowledge systems as conservationist in both spirit and practice. (Some of these community efforts at conservation are documented by Kothari and Pathak Broome in their contribution.) Such organizations support the FRA as a part of their vision of inclusive conservation. Whether this rift within the environment movement will narrow or widen will partially depend on whether this piece of legislation is allowed to function in actual practice.

There are misrepresentations, perhaps inadvertent, of facts about the Act's adverse impact on the environment. A recent satellite-assisted study undertaken by the Forest Department in Maharashtra, for instance, holds the FRA responsible for contributing to the loss of forest cover and escalation of greenhouse emissions, and recommends that the Ministry of Tribal Affairs should 'revisit' the FRA (Pinjarkar 2014). However, details about this phenomenon gleaned by this author from informed sources within the Maharashtra bureaucracy tell a different story. It appears that the exponential increase in cultivated land area since the institution of the FRA, indeed leading to loss of forest cover, is in fact due to new encroachments by *non-forest dwellers and non-ST individuals*. According to these sources, a very large number of illegitimate 'forest rights' have been gifted away to local bigwigs who have now put these patches of land under cultivation, and these lands have been regularized under the FRA by the concerned bureaucracy without any verification of credentials.

Immense political will is needed to not just honestly verify unwarranted claims and to weed out these unscrupulous elements so that the FRA and forest communities are not maligned for the destruction of forests, but also to put a committed bureaucratic machinery in place for a fair implementation of the Act. A number of factors seem to have led to the anomalous situation just described: use of muscle and political pressures on the forest rights committees by local influential individuals; absence of coherent and effective systems to implement FRA on the ground; lack of proper training of the concerned personnel in the administrative machinery; the pressure of reaching state quotas for clearing FRA cases by a certain date; and so on.

When studying related documents, one finds that the Ministry of Environment and Forests (MoEF), which is in letter and spirit totally opposed to the FRA, is predictably at constant loggerheads with the Ministry of Tribal Affairs, which pressed for the Act's institution. The two bodies have a different and almost opposing mandate, though they are dealing with the same jurisdiction—the forest spaces come under the former, and the people inhabiting those very spaces under the latter. Since the Forest Department, which vigorously participates in the implementation of the FRA, is under the MoEF, a large part of the problem of implementation originates here.

With all the imperfections in the conception as well as implementation of the FRA, however, it is worth noting here that after many years of adivasi struggle to oust the Vedanta Aluminium Mining Company from the Odisha forests in 2013, what carried the day in the end in the Supreme Court was a critical provision in the FRA. The bench foregrounded the fact that *gram sabha*s (village assemblies) under FRA are to play a critical role in protecting the rights of the forest-based communities (including how forest land and resources under their jurisdiction are to be used).[11]

---

[11] The gram sabha and the FRA were invoked literally dozens of times by the bench while giving its opinion on the Vedanta case. Supreme Court of India, Civil Original Jurisdiction, Writ Petition (Civil) No. 180 of 2011, *Orissa Mining Corporation versus Ministry of Environment & Forest & Others*, judgment dated 18 April 2013. Available at: http://www.indiaenvironmentportal.org.in/files/Niyamgiri%20April%202013.pdf (accessed 18 May 2015).

What is most educative and interesting in this judgment is the fact that with all the arguments available to the bench against mining in the region by Vedanta Aluminium, including arguments on ecological damage, infringement of Schedule V area laws, duties of the state towards its Particularly Vulnerable Tribal Groups (PVTGs), impending loss of traditional livelihoods, and human rights violations, what the judgment strategically chose to flag was the right of the communities themselves to hold consultations in their gram sabhas, in the process reiterating that all gram sabha decisions were binding under the FRA. Predictably, all the concerned gram sabhas voted against the mining on grounds of cultural and religious rights, and this is what led to the ousting of Vedanta.

The potential of this Act, then, to deliver rights for forest dwellers may be limited, but because of its now proven ability to keep corporate interests out of the forests, there are moves to dilute it by the new government which came to power in May 2014.[12]

These developments, as well as insights by the authors in this volume, give rise to some significant debates about the FRA. Is the FRA an instrument of struggle, or an instrument of new forms of domination by the state? Has it made adivasis and forest communities more dependent on the state, in the process undermining adivasi autonomy, or has it helped healthy, however partial, integration of a hitherto isolated people? Has the FRA led to weakening or strengthening of the rights of the forest people? Does the FRA undermine collective rights in favour of private property rights? Are the concerns of the environment movement in harmony with or opposed to the interests of forest-dependent communities? These are some of the germane questions addressed by a number of authors in this book (see chapters by Vasan, Sarin, Prasad, Kothari and Pathak Broome, Savyasaachi, Padel, and Radhakrishna).

STRUGGLE AND RESISTANCE

It is obvious that communities which constantly face an onslaught on the very bases of their existence—the forests—would resist their oppressors, and would also press for implementation of any legislative measures instituted for their rights. Ironically but predictably, while the FRA claims to protect adivasi rights, there has been a violent administrative response to the communities attempting to procure those very rights. Sarin documents a number of struggles waged by adivasis all over the country for community rights under this piece of legislation.

Radhakrishna documents in the Epilogue other pieces of legislation which too are in principle enabling ones for the adivasis, like the PESA, 1996, which gives considerable powers to the concerned gram sabhas, or laws applicable to Schedule V areas which are aimed at preventing

---

[12] 'Tweaking' of the FRA is also being mooted in mineral-rich areas on the grounds that Maoist-controlled areas need more development to wean away the local communities from Maoist influence. According to this logic, there is a need for quicker clearance of industrial projects in these areas, including what is termed as 'restricted' mining (ignoring that indiscriminate entry of mining companies in the forests is the very reason why the Maoists have got a strong base in these areas) (see *Times of India* 2014).

land alienation in 'tribal'-dominated areas. However, what stands out in her discussion are not the legal means available to the adivasis for protection of their rights, but 'legitimate' means of violence available to the powerful corporate mining groups, via the armed state machinery, to suppress protests by adivasis.

The most important point for our purposes here is that while adivasi communities do use every available means to fight back, it is increasingly becoming clear to them that legislative means by themselves are unlikely to deliver. In recent times, a number of social movements have emerged all over the country, particularly in the mineral-rich areas, where there is evidence of full-scale mobilization of the adivasis around issues of forced land acquisition, destruction of habitats in the name of development, unequitable terms of development policy, displacement without rehabilitation, and so on.

The challenge on the ground to non-inclusive policies is likely to intensify in the near future. The movements which the adivasis and their allies have created on the ground do not just have the potential and the ability to conserve the forests; with their wide support base and manifold concerns, they have the potential to recast existing debates on multiple social, economic, and political fronts. Radhakrishna's overview of resistance movements makes this point amply clear.

Rebellions by forest-based communities throughout the period of colonial rule are well known and copiously documented. Adivasi movements in contemporary India are not just sparsely recorded, but less noticed and less understood as well. Just like 'adivasi' is not a homogeneous category, so will their mobilizations and movements not be similar or comparable over historical periods, or even within a given historical span. Prasad (this volume) makes a distinction between various class-based and non-class, identity-based political mobilizations of adivasis in post-independence India. She argues that these two kinds of mobilizations, respectively, arise from the simultaneous, twin impacts of historical dispossession on the one hand, and the affirmative action policies of the state on the other. The latter has spawned an adivasi elite, competing for political power and leading movements of a different kind to those led by 'working-class adivasis'.

The character of these resistance movements in contemporary India also vary according to the nature of the participants' aims as well as the means to achieve them, for instance, those under the tutelage of Naxalites or Maoists and those independent of them. While the Naxalite/Maoist mobilizations have got a lot of attention, all resistance movements by adivasis have been clubbed together by the state under the category of Naxalite or Maoist insurgency. Not only did the former prime minister Manmohan Singh treat this insurgency as the 'greatest internal security threat' to India, but for his government as well as for the subsequent administration, anyone in the forests who fights for their rights under the FRA, or simply refuses to part with their land for the corporates, is treated as a Maoist. This has made it extremely dangerous and difficult for adivasis to form a coherent movement around their demands.

The commentators in the media too tend to make the same error, namely of treating all adivasi resistance as necessarily being led by Maoists. As the Epilogue by Radhakrishna shows, the Naxalite and Maoist excuse has been used extensively by the state to vacate thousands of hectares of mineral-rich adivasi land for corporate groups on the one hand, and to legitimize its excessive use of force on adivasis, on the other. In the process, fraudulent acquiring of adivasi lands by corporate groups becomes a familiar occurrence. It is a most serious situation for a democracy to encounter when a state acts so contemptuously and violently against a vulnerable section of its citizens in order to push forth its 'development' agenda.

In contemporary India, a number of social movements have emerged both to challenge the development and conservation policies of the government, and to resist forest land acquisition by the government and corporate groups. These protests are localized, but their spread is pan-Indian in nature.[13] In the process of building their movements, the adivasis have gathered wider support from other marginalized and even relatively better-off sections, who are also adversely affected by state policies. The nature and success of these movements will be determined by the breadth of their demands, as well as by the support they are able to get from a wider section of society.

However, this raises the complex question of strategic alliances for those who are convinced that their concerns and the interests of adivasis are not coterminous. While most conservation activists support the adivasi protests, an influential section of the Indian environment movement continues to oppose adivasi rights to the forests on the ground of conservation. These questions are addressed by several authors

---

[13] From Kashmir to Kerala, from Gujarat to the north-east, 'protests against the undemocratic imposition of the so-called development projects are spreading far and wide in the country' (Thakkar 2012).

in this volume (see the chapters by Kothari and Pathak Broome, Sarin, and Radhakrishna). Radhakrishna examines these specific issues in the context of adivasi protest movements in the last decade, particularly in mineral-rich areas, and speculates at some length on the dilemma this poses for the environment movement.

Essentially, those in the environment movement who oppose forest rights for communities are not convinced that the environment movement cannot hope to preserve India's forests all by itself. Nor do they agree that joining the forest communities in their struggle to safeguard their habitats from the depredations of these companies is the only way to attain even the limited goal of conservation. On the ground, an attack on adivasi habitats and livelihoods has given rise not just to what Sarin calls 'creative grassroots assertion of their rights', but also to people-based initiatives to conserve their own resources. Some of these initiatives have been documented in some detail, with rare, relevant, state-based data in this volume (see the chapter by Kothari and Pathak Broome).

The 10-year old battle by the adivasis against the Vedanta group, which wished to mine in the Niyamgiri Hills of Odisha, attracted international attention. Like many similar movements all over the country, this struggle had the support of a disparate set of people: marginalized communities including Dalits dependent on the land acquired for mining, with no prospect of compensation; fisherpeople who stood to lose their livelihood in case the rivers and streams got polluted or dried up altogether; anti-land acquisition groups; human rights groups; civil liberty organizations; anti-globalization organizations; anti-special economic zones groups; farmers concerned about the diversion of irrigation water for industrial uses; women activists; health activists; legal activists, and many others also joined, showing how much that was precious was at stake, apart from the environment.

The movement against indiscriminate industrial projects in the forests is multifaceted and for a more just and democratic, inclusive India. There are a number of such campaigns to save the forests all over the country where women are often in the lead, not least because what is at stake is that bit of scant autonomy in their families which they have laboriously earned through independent livelihoods connected with the forests. No compensation package recognizes this, nor are these women any more prepared to give up their forest-based livelihoods in exchange for grossly exploitative informal labour in the brick kilns, sugarcane fields, or the construction industry in faraway towns and villages.

The development-or-conservation dilemma, never a very serious one even for the earlier government, may be an absolute non-issue for the new government at the centre. Rathva et al. in this volume reveal perhaps the first ever incident of its kind in Indian legislative history, of the Modi state government in Gujarat removing adivasi communities from an existing list of STs, so that special legislation to prevent adivasi land alienation could be bypassed in order to accommodate mining corporates. This was an ominous sign, and evidence of cynical disregard for the constitution even before the same political dispensation (and individual) took power at the centre in May 2014. The Epilogue to this book documents the proposed changes mooted by the Modi government in existing legislation to remove 'hurdles' to development, and also explains the significance of existing legislation for the protection of adivasi rights.

Some generalized, critical issues of insurgency, organization, and politicization are included in this volume (see the contributions by Prasad, Savyasaachi, and Sarin). Radhakrishna, however, discusses alliances forged by adivasi movements, and the nature of state responses to this resistance. The state seems to have on record broadly two sorts of responses: violent repression through armed forces, or different strategies to splinter communities and their unity so as to vacate mineral-rich land for corporate projects. Some of these state practices, including the Salwa Judum phenomenon, are discussed by Radhakrishna, and the virulent communalization of communities by bodies like the Vishva Hindu Parishad (VHP) is studied by Pati. Pati notes that in Odisha in particular, divisions among marginalized sections such as 'Christian Dalits' and 'Hindu adivasis' had reached such aggressive proportions by 2008 that it led logically to the Kandhamal communal violence, described as a massacre of Christians. It is not accidental that the Christian community, comprising both Dalits and adivasis, is at the forefront of resistance, and that in Odisha the adivasi resistance movements against the state as well as corporate groups are among the strongest.

Apart from these major issues, tangentially, there are other tracks in this volume which authors have explored like aspects of ethnicity (Heredia, Zou) and shifts in 'adivasi sensibility', identity, and consciousness (Prasad, Xaxa, Padel, Savyasaachi, Heredia, and Neetha). There are also explorations of the history and politics of religious change (Zou, Pati, Prasad) and of diversity and plurality among indigenous people (Zou).

Conceptual discussions on labels, nomenclatures, and terminologies, or identity, self-image, and consciousness, have thus been combined in this volume with a survey of hard, practical issues needing still more research and answers. What is the future of the development or conservation policies of the Indian government which have so adversely affected the adivasis and the regions inhabited by them? Is the distressingly insecure nature of occupations available to the displaced, dislocated, or migrant adivasis a necessary condition of growth? Can legislation affecting adivasis be shaped favourably through struggle, or are social movements for wholesale change the only possibility for the adivasi today? Have the contemporary adivasi protest movements come of age, judging from their strategies as well as wider alliances and aims? Has the political challenge to the Indian state posed by these movements led to any renegotiation of their position in Indian society, or has their association with the Naxalite movement further pushed them to the margins? A study of history reveals a powerful and consistent grassroots disavowal of elite structures of power. Does the resistance offered by these communities give us a glimpse of what has been termed as the 'politics of hope'?

This volume is meant to provide a sociological grid in which to catch some of these different strands while it tries to address a number of analytical questions, necessarily political in nature, at more than one level. The absence of a volume devoted exclusively to adivasi studies is a palpable gap in scholarly as well as activist circles today. This volume is intended to be a ready resource for understanding the Indian adivasi in as many disparate ways as possible. It has, as its subjects of study, those who historically shared different habitats from the rest of the population, and whose encounters and experiences with empire builders and independent state authorities have been distinct from those of other marginalized sections. For this very reason, the volume charts out for itself lines of enquiry which are quite distinct from those addressing other marginalized sections like Dalits or minorities. This volume, precisely because it attempts to trace the genealogies of disciplines, terms, and categories on the one hand and those of social processes and movements on the other, has to be firmly interdisciplinary in approach. Necessarily, then, the authors who have contributed to the debates in this volume are drawn from a number of disciplines. Firmly grounded in history, the volume is a first, faltering step towards a multidimensional understanding of India's First Citizens—the adivasis, tribals, and indigenous peoples.

November 2014

REFERENCES

ACHR (Asian Centre for Human Rights). 2008. 'Kandhamal Massacres: Where Is the State?' 8 August. Available at: http://www.indianet.nl/pdf/KandhamalMassacres.pdf (accessed 20 May 2015).

Bates, Crispin and Marina Carter. 1992. 'Tribal Migration in India and Beyond', in Gyan Prakash (ed.), *The World of the Rural Labourer in Colonial India*. New Delhi: Oxford University Press, pp. 205–45.

Burman, J. J. Roy. 2009. 'Adivasi: A Contentious Term to Denote Tribes as Indigenous Peoples of India', *Mainstream*, vol. 47, no. 32, pp. 14–17. Available at: http://www.mainstreamweekly.net/article1537.html (accessed 9 December 2015).

Cobo, Jose R. Martinez. 1986. 'Study of the Problem of Discrimination against Indigenous Populations', UN Special Rapporteur of the Sub-Commission on Prevention of Discrimination and Protection of Minorities, E/CN.4/SUB.2/1986/7/ADD.4.

Government of India (GoI). 2013. 'Tribal Profile at a Glance', Ministry of Tribal Affairs, May. Available at: http://tribal.nic.in/WriteReadData/CMS/Documents/201306061001146927823STProfileataGlance.pdf (accessed 15 May 2015).

Guha, Sumit. 1999. *Environment and Ethnicity in India, 1200–1999*. Cambridge: Cambridge University Press.

Karlsson, Bengt G. 2003. 'Anthropology and the "Indigenous Slot": Claims to and Debates about Indigenous Peoples' Status in India'. *Critique of Anthropology*, vol. 23, no. 4, pp. 403–23.

Massey, James, ed. 1994. *Indigenous People: Dalit Issues in Today's Theological Debate*. New Delhi: Indian Society for Promoting Christian Knowledge.

———. 2001. 'Movements of Liberation: Theological Roots and Vision of Dalit Theology', *CTC Bulletin*, vol. 17, no. 2. Available at: http://cca.org.hk/home/ctc/ctc01-04/ctc0104j.htm (accessed 16 May 2015).

Pinjarkar, Vijay. 2014. 'FRA Rights Have Destroyed Forests, Says Study'. *Times of India*, 19 September. Available at: http://timesofindia.indiatimes.com/city/nagpur/FRA-rights-have-destroyed-forests-says-study/articleshow/42838425.cms (accessed 18 May 2015).

Rathna, P. 2014. 'Tracing the Homogeneity between Dalit and Australian Aboriginal Communities: A Historical and Literary Perspective', *International Journal on Studies in English Language and Literature* (*IJSELL*), vol. 2, no. 2, pp. 20–5.

Singh, K. S. 1975. *Indian Famine 1967: A Study in Crisis and Change*. New Delhi: People's Publishing House.

Steur, Luisa. 2009. 'Adivasi Mobilisation: "Identity" versus "Class" after the Kerala Model of Development?' *Journal of South Asian Development*, vol. 4, no. 1.

Thakkar, Himanshu. 2012. 'Right Problems, Wrong Solution', *Hindustan Times*, 10 July.
Times of India. 2014. 'Centre May Tweak Forest Laws in Naxal-Hit States', 12 June. Available at: http://timesofindia.indiatimes.com/home/environment/developmental-issues/Centre-may-tweak-forest-laws-in-Naxal-hit-states/articleshow/36412743.cms (accessed 19 May 2015).
Vidyarthi, Lalita Prasad and Binay Kumar Rai. 1985. First published in 1976. *The Tribal Culture of India*. New Delhi: Concept Publishing Company.

I
CATEGORIES AND IDENTITIES AS HISTORICAL PROCESS

1

Formation of Adivasi/Indigenous Peoples' Identity in India

Virginius Xaxa

People have moved from one place to another through the centuries. The movement since the eighteenth century has been, however, somewhat unique. Not only has the movement since then been unidirectional but also the volume of migration has been phenomenal. The movement has invariably been from Europe and the direction has been towards the continents of Africa, America, Asia, and Australia, some of which were very sparsely populated. In fact, human settlements as they exist today in different parts of the world are products of this long chain of population movement. The movements to begin with were fluid and open, but they ceased to be so after territorial boundaries were drawn in the form of states, referred to more popularly as nations or countries. As said earlier, peoples inhabiting a country or nation made it their home or settlement in different phases. In general, the consequences of subsequent settlements for earlier settlers have been adverse; at least, this has been the case with European colonization.

As an example, one can take the case of Australia. Before the settlement of the whites about 200 years ago, the native population was described as small, dispersed, isolated, and homogeneous. European colonization led to a drastic change in the demography of the territory. In fact, with the onset of the white settlement, the aboriginal population is estimated to have fallen from 250,000 to less than 80,000, while the settler population estimated to have risen to about 11,500,000.

Such massive change in the population has also been witnessed in the Americas. In the rest of the continent such massive population change has been relatively absent (Béteille 1998).

TERMINOLOGIES: NATIVE, TRIBE, INDIGENOUS, RACE

Various terminologies have been used by the European rulers to describe the populations or peoples they subjugated. The terms used were either of a particularistic or of a general nature. The particularistic terms were generally ethnic or people-centred names, such as Zunis, Gonds, Kachin, or Shan. It is the terms that were of a general nature that are the concern of this chapter. Even when terms were of a general nature, some were confined to a given geographical region; the term 'Indians', for example, had wide usage in the Americas, while other terms gained wide currency across the world. Of the latter, some arose out of the need for the classification of populations as part of colonial rule and administration, and others emerged out of scholarly concern for understanding the population.

Of the terms used to describe the subject, one that has been widely in circulation is 'native'. The term 'native' is associated with the people/population born in a territory/region that constitutes a colony, irrespective of their ethnicity, language, creed, and colour. The 'native' was a man of the colony who carried his identity as a native even when he moved to the country of his respective empire (Béteille 1998). The term 'native', however, though used to refer to people of the colonies, is not identical with the term 'indigenous people' as it has come to be generally used in the literature. Whereas the terms 'native' and 'indigenous people' coincided in certain geographical regions or countries, such as North and South America, Australia, or New Zealand, the same cannot be said of countries in Asia and Africa, as there were groups and communities in these countries that did not share the features associated with indigenous peoples.

Interestingly, the features associated with the idea of 'indigenous peoples' come closer to the concept or category of 'tribe' that has widely been in use in anthropological literature. Though the term initially was used to refer to groups and communities with common ancestry, it came to be intricately linked with societal characteristics that have generally been described as *primitive* with the expansion of the colonial rule. In course of time, however, there has been a reconceptualization of the notion of 'tribe' among anthropologists. They view tribes not only as a group or community but also as a society. As a society, they are portrayed as characterized by a distinct territory, language, culture, laws, rules, and governing systems of their own. However, they are shown as distinctive kinds of society based on the characteristics of homogeneity or the lack of complex social differentiation, kinship-based social organization, and the lack of traditions of reading and writing. It may be noted that in the anthropological literature, the general conceptualization of the term 'tribe' has developed from the North American, the African, and the Melanesian experiences, omitting South Asia, even though ethnographically, communities in the latter region seemed to fit into the definition in all its richness. Thus, communities like the Crow, Omaha, Navaho, Arunta, Walbiri, Onge, Trobrianders, Nuer, Tallensi, Lozi, Toda, Santhal, Gond, Bhil, and Oraon, scattered across the length and breadth of the world, are all referred to as 'tribes' in the world of anthropologists (Béteille 1998).

The term 'tribe' has become a discredited concept across the world today. Scholars hardly use it in their writings, nor does it find a place in state administrative and policy documents. This is, however, not the case in South Asia in general, and India in particular. In India, the term is deeply entrenched in scholarly writings and in the legal and administrative structure of the state. Its use in state administration is partly a result of the colonial administrative structure that India continued with after independence. But more importantly, it is rooted in the state's concern to address the issues of the protection, welfare, and development of the 'tribal' population. Its rootedness also lies in the fact that the term 'tribe' in India has emerged not only in relation to social backwardness or stage of development, but also in opposition to a structure of society characterized by caste.

Linked to the concepts of 'native' and 'tribe' has been the concept of 'race'. Under colonial rule, it had been normal practice to classify a population in terms of racial categories. Whereas in some colonies, subjects were all classified as belonging to *one* racial category, in others such as India, they were classified as belonging to different racial categories. Since racial classification tends to cover the whole of the population, what were deemed to be tribes/indigenous peoples have also generally been placed in same racial category. However, certain racial categories were not necessarily treated as synonymous with tribes/indigenous peoples. In fact, even those identified and described as tribes/indigenous peoples were classified as belonging to *different* racial categories. Though the categories of race and tribe/indigenous peoples may overlap in actual empirical reality in some contexts, the two are conceptually distinct.

EVOLUTION OF INTERNATIONAL IDENTITY AS 'INDIGENOUS PEOPLE'

It is important to note that it was not the anthropological notion of 'autochthon' or 'aboriginal' that played a critical role in shaping of indigenous people's identity. This is not to deny the role of the concept of 'aborigine' in shaping this identity. The concept of 'aboriginal' or 'autochthonous' did point to the prior historical rootedness of certain people within a given geographical context. It refers to the original inhabitants of a given area as well as to the earliest people present at the beginning or 'sunrise' of human society, as Ajay Dandekar puts it (Padel et al. 2013: 25). The term 'aborigine', however, did not gain currency beyond the confines of the discipline of anthropology. Even in anthropology, the concept has not been so much in use as the term 'tribe'. The terms 'tribe' and 'aborigine', however, point to different ideas, though the two may overlap in actual social reality. Akin to the term 'aborigine' or 'autochthon' is the term 'indigenous population/people'. However, this has not been in wide currency until very recently.

The term 'indigenous' was first used in the late nineteenth century in an effort to separate the Europeans from the non-Europeans, and not to delineate the differences amongst the people in the colonies. However, it did not then gain the currency it now has. The wider currency of the term 'indigenous people' could be traced to the 1920s and 1930s, which is to do with the emerging concern about the welfare of these people (Baird 2008). In 1938, the term 'indigenous' took a significant turn after the Pan-American Union declared that 'indigenous populations, as descendants of the first inhabitants of the lands which today form America, and in order to offset the deficiency in their physical and intellectual development, have a preferential right to the protection of the public authorities' (Baird 2008: 201).

From the early 1920s, the International Labour Organization (ILO) had been studying the situation of indigenous people from the perspective of their participation in the labour market. As a result of the findings of a study titled *Indigenous Peoples: Living and Working Conditions of Aboriginal Populations in Independent Countries* (ILO 1953), the ILO adopted the first international instrument exclusive to indigenous peoples—the ILO Convention No. 107 on Indigenous and Tribal Populations (ILO 1957).

This convention was adopted in response to the challenge to protect indigenous peoples against discrimination and to ensure their continued existence. India was a signatory to that convention. The ILO later adopted a progressive instrument to replace the earlier convention, which had emphasized the need for indigenous people to be assimilated into the mainstream population. In contrast, the 1989 ILO Convention No. 169 emphasized the principle that indigenous peoples had the *right* to survive as separate peoples with their own cultures and traditions. Interestingly, India has not signed this convention till today.

What is important is that the aspect of race and racial discrimination has been an important factor leading to the shaping the category of 'indigenous peoples'. In fact, the entry of the term 'indigenous' in the discussion of international organizations such as the United Nations (UN) occurred via the concept of race, and the concern to eliminate all forms of racial discrimination in practice in the world. At the World Conference on Human Rights, Vienna, in June 1993, the international community made a commitment to the rapid and complete elimination of all forms of racism and racial discrimination, including racism and racial discrimination against indigenous peoples.

Equally important in sharpening the identity of 'indigenous peoples' was the category of 'minority', which the UN conceptualized primarily in terms of language and ethnicity. The overwhelming number of people brought under the umbrella of 'indigenous peoples', in fact, represent distinct ethnic minorities. It is in their capacity as minorities that the UN presented the problem of discrimination against indigenous people and their precarious condition. The UN organizations have been concerned with the rights of minorities to participate in the political, cultural, social, and economic life of the countries to which they belong. This concern has often been tied to the issues of race and racial discrimination. Tribes/indigenous peoples all over the world constitute a distinct minority and hence in the UN's deliberation on the question of minorities, the issue of tribes and indigenous people has come to be strongly figured. Minority groups have often been denied civil, political, and social rights. Moreover, often violence has been used against them to take away from them their resources that they have been traditionally and historically controlling. At least, this has been the case with groups popularly delineated as tribes/indigenous peoples.

In 1970, the UN Sub-Commission on Prevention of Discrimination and Protection of Minorities commissioned Special Rapporteur Martinez Cobo to undertake a study of the problem of discrimination against indigenous populations. This monumental study (known as the Cobo study), completed in 1984, carefully documented modern discrimination against indigenous peoples and their precarious situation. It concluded that the continuous discrimination against indigenous peoples threatened their existence.

The categories referred to above such as race and minorities that had a bearing on shaping the indigenous people's identity were invariably tied with the question of rights and it is the articulation of the rights and their entitlements that eventually led to shaping of the idea of indigenous people at the international level.

The establishment of the UN Working Group on Indigenous Populations (WGIP) in 1982 was a direct result of the Cobo study. Consisting of five independent experts, the WGIP has met annually in Geneva, which has been perhaps the only arena in the UN system where indigenous peoples can voice their views. In 1994, the WGIP adopted a Draft Declaration on the Rights of Indigenous Peoples, which emerged out of the active participation of indigenous peoples from all over the world. After prolonged discussions, the declaration was finalized and adopted as the Declaration on the Rights of Indigenous Peoples by the General Assembly of the UN in September 2006.

THE CONCEPT OF INDIGENOUS PEOPLES IN INTERNATIONAL ORGANIZATIONS: ILO AND UN

In the deliberations of international agencies, the term 'indigenous people/population' was used for the first time in 1957 at the ILO Convention No. 107. In an attempt to give a universal identity to the concept of 'indigenous people', several questions relating to historical continuity, distinctive cultural characteristics, traditional lands, non-dominance, self-identification, and group consciousness were discussed by the WGIP (Daes 2008).

The ILO convention in 1957 made a distinction between tribal and semi-tribal populations on the one hand, and indigenous tribal populations on the other. The former were described as populations who were at a less advanced stage of development than that reached by other sections of the national community, and whose status is regulated wholly or partially by their own customs and traditions. The latter (indigenous peoples) were, however, referred to as those categories of tribal or semi-tribal populations which traced their descent from the population which inhabited the country or geographical region at the time of conquest or colonization, and which, irrespective of their legal status, live more in conformity with the social, economic, and cultural institutions of that time than in conformity with the institutions of the nation to which they now belong (Daes 2008; ILO 1989; Roy Burman n.d.).

What the ILO convention adopted in 1989 was different in substantive terms from that in 1957 in respect of its conceptualization. It speaks of, to begin with, (*a*) tribal/indigenous *peoples* instead of tribal/ indigenous populations and explicitly states their distinctiveness from other sections of the national community in the social, cultural, and economic domains; and (*b*) makes a distinction between tribal peoples and indigenous peoples (Xaxa 2008). In general, however, people including scholars, activists, and others continue to use the term 'tribal' along with term 'indigenous'. The term 'indigenous people' gained wider currency after 1993 with the declaration of that year as the international year of indigenous people.

It is also pertinent to note here that in 1957, the ILO had proposed the integration of tribal and indigenous peoples as a desired objective, but this was no longer seen as appropriate by 1985, when the ILO felt the need to revise the convention on account of worldwide changes in attitudes and approaches towards these peoples. This was so because international organizations and an increasing number of governments were moving toward greater recognition of the rights of indigenous and tribal peoples to retain their specific identities and to participate fully in the planning and execution of activities affecting their way of life. Accordingly, the ILO adopted a revised convention in 1989 in consultation with other international bodies (ILO 1989).

The UN WGIP[1] had already begun to employ the working definition of 'indigenous peoples' developed in 1972 by Martinez Cobo. The definition was reworked in 1986 by Cobo in his final report, titled 'Study of the Problem of Discrimination against Indigenous Populations', as follows:

> Indigenous communities, peoples and nations are those which, having a historical continuity with pre-invasion and pre-colonial societies that developed on their territories, consider themselves distinct from other sectors of the societies now prevailing in those territories, or parts of them. They form at present non-dominant sectors of society and are determined

---

[1] As mentioned earlier, this body was set up in 1982 by the Sub-Commission on Prevention of Discrimination and Protection of Minorities of the UN Commission on Human Rights.

to preserve, develop and transmit to future generations their ancestral territories, and their ethnic identity, as the basis of their continued existence as peoples, in accordance with their own cultural patterns, social institutions and legal systems. (Daes 2008; Roy Burman n.d.)

To rephrase then, the ILO convention referred to above and Cobo Report of UN both speak of two aspects that are central to the conceptualization of indigenous peoples. First, the indigenous are those people who lived in the country to which they belong before its colonization or conquest by people from outside that country or geographical region. Secondly, that the people govern their life more in terms of their own social, economic, and cultural institutions than by laws applicable in the rest of the society or in the country at large. What is important here is that the notion of indigenous peoples, despite sharing attributes in common with peoples described as 'tribal' and 'semi-tribal' populations, are different from the latter in the sense that indigenous peoples are invariably marked out as distinct international entities. The indigenous are invariably victims of conquest and colonization from outside. Furthermore, the outsiders are easily identifiable. Being the descendants of peoples who lived in their territory before conquest or colonization is the most important criterion in the definition of 'indigenous peoples', but it is not the only criterion. This category of people has progressively been marginalized and dispossessed of their sources of livelihood, and are vulnerable to cultural shock as well as the loss of their collective identity.

NATIONAL GOVERNMENTS AND INDIGENOUS PEOPLES

The terminologies used to denote peoples or populations are a separate matter in itself. The label used often becomes an issue in the politics of identity. The term 'primitive', for instance, lost its use and importance after the Second World War, and the communities came to be termed as 'disadvantaged' rather than primitive. This term is completely independent of the diverse socio-economic and geographic conditions each community hails from. The identification of a population as 'indigenous' occurs when there exists another population in the region that can be termed as 'settlers'. In many countries, this has been at the root of serious differences over the use of the term 'indigenous peoples'.

Although the term 'indigenous peoples' is widely in circulation in the New World, along with other terms such as 'Indians' (in the Americas) or 'natives', several countries including the USA, Canada, Australia, and New Zealand have not ratified either ILO convention 107 of 1957 or 169 of 1989. Several of these countries have even declined to be signatories to the UN Declaration on the Rights of Indigenous Peoples. Of countries from South America, only nine had ratified the ILO convention 169 of 1989. Of the African countries, where the applicability of the concept of 'indigenous peoples' is shrouded in controversy, none of the states has signed ILO Convention No. 169. And so has been the case with Asian countries. In fact, India and China have been consistently questioning the applicability of the category of 'indigenous peoples' in international fora. The view held by these states is that all people inhabiting their territories have been indigenous. Interestingly, despite this reservation, most countries in Asia and Africa have signed the UN Declaration on the Rights of Indigenous Peoples.

THE 'INDIGENOUS' QUESTION AND THE GOVERNMENT OF INDIA

The objections raised by the Indian government through its delegations at UN bodies, stemming from the writings of scholars, have been twofold. One objection is that tribal people in India do not have distinct social, economic, political, and cultural identities. To make this argument, delegates draw upon observations made by anthropologists, social reformers, and government officials like census commissioners. In particular, they draw on G. S. Ghurye's observation that religion, occupation, or racial features have proved inadequate when attempting to distinguish tribal people from the non-tribal population in India (Prasad 1992). The same point is further articulated by dwelling upon the conceptual problem in defining tribal communities in India. Béteille's observation, where he states that tribal populations show, in varying degrees, elements of continuity with the larger society in India, serves to substantiate this argument (Prasad 1992). In the same paragraph, the observation made by Béteille that 'groups which correspond closely to the anthropologists' conception of tribe, have lived in long association with communities of an entirely different type' is conveniently overlooked (Béteille). And so has been the case with Ghurye's observation where he treats adivasis as the original inhabitants of India.

There is still another argument which has been put forward by government delegates in international fora. It has been argued by them that the category 'tribe', and more specifically 'scheduled tribe', with which indigenous people are associated is a politico-administrative category and not a historical category as the idea of 'indigenous people' suggests. It is said that the identification of groups as scheduled tribes has to do with the administration of social welfare measures to ameliorate the condition of tribal people. The point made is that the terms 'tribe'/'scheduled tribe' and 'indigenous' are not synonymous and thus cannot be equated. They see no congruence between the two (Prasad 1992). Interestingly, however, the considerations or criteria based on which scheduled tribes have been defined by the government, clumsy and esoteric though they may be, are concealed in the making of this argument. The scheduled tribe is not the only category to which social policy measures have been directed. There are other categories too, such as scheduled castes and other backward castes, which have also been brought under the ambit of social welfare policy. The grounds needs to be explored on which certain groups of people are declared as scheduled tribes and others as scheduled castes or other backward classes. If one delves deeper into it, one will realize that certain people are defined as tribes precisely because they are socially, culturally, linguistically, and economically different from the dominant segments of the population, and to that extent they represent a set of distinct social groups vis-à-vis the larger society. This has generally been the sense in which tribes have been historically delineated. In fact, considerations such as a definite geographical area, distinctive culture, and primitive traits adopted by the Indian state for the delineation of groups as scheduled tribes in the post-independence period emanate from the earlier-mentioned definitional characteristics of 'tribal society'.

Notwithstanding such objections at international fora, India has been a signatory to the UN Declaration on the Rights of Indigenous Peoples, though within the country the state provides for no such recognition of any communities, except as scheduled tribes.

EMERGENCE OF ADIVASI/INDIGENOUS PEOPLES' CONSCIOUSNESS

The idea of 'adivasi', or its equivalent 'indigenous peoples', has now become a part of the consciousness of tribal people in India. The idea expressed by the term 'adivasi' is an expanded identity cutting across tribes bearing different names, speaking different languages or dialects. It also goes beyond the groups and communities, or parts thereof, that are listed in the constitution. It is to be noted that there is an important gap in the sense in which the term 'tribe' is used and understood by the adivasis, and the sense in which it is understood by others, especially administrators, lawyers, and academicians. For the latter, communities are tribes only if they are listed in the constitution. Adivasis, on the other hand, do not view 'tribes' in the sense of a politico-administrative category. Rather, they view a 'tribe' as a set of people belonging to the same community, irrespective of whether a group, or a segment of it, is listed or not listed in the constitution.

Although the term 'indigenous peoples' is a new coinage, its native equivalent 'adivasi' (*adi* = original + *vasi* = inhabitant) has a long usage in India, especially in eastern, central, western, and southern India. The word is widely used to refer to communities generally described as tribes. Interestingly, such usage is markedly absent in northern and even in north-eastern India, where over 11 per cent of India's tribal population lives. In fact, in north-east India, the term 'adivasi' is restricted to communities who were brought in as indentured labour by British tea companies to work on the tea estates that had begun to be opened up in Assam from the middle of the nineteenth century. These groups mostly belong to communities referred to as adivasis in their places of origin. This is not to say that tribal communities in north-east India do not identify themselves as indigenous peoples. They do, and many organizations representing them have been participating in international events concerned with indigenous peoples. However, such identity and articulation among tribes of the north-eastern region is a phenomenon which has emerged with the internationalization of issues of the tribal peoples. In fact, some tribal community groups and leaders in Assam, where most of the adivasis live, have questioned the indigenous status of the adivasis (who were brought in by the British for labour in the plantations in this region). They have raised objections to the government's initiative to grant these adivasis scheduled tribe status, which may entitle them to certain constitutional privileges. They have challenged this initiative on the ground that they are not indigenous to the region, thereby opening up new grounds than the ones which have been accepted for determining scheduled tribe status. It is obvious that that the term 'adivasis', which is the equivalent of the term 'indigenous peoples' and has been in use in mainland India for a long time, has a different meaning in north-east India.

As observed earlier, the term 'adivasi', meaning original inhabitants, has a wide currency in mainland India. It is not clear as to when, where, and how this term originated and how it travelled across the length and breadth of mainland India. The historian David Hardiman (1987) traces the origin of the term to the 1920s in Jharkhand. If this had its origin in Jharkhand and in 1920s, then it is very likely that the term was coined by the concerned communities themselves, mark themselves off from 'non-tribals' and was thus a product of modern education. It was not something imposed on them by outsiders and which later the communities appropriated for themselves as a marker of their self-identity, as I had stated in an earlier publication (Xaxa 1999). It is to be noted that the educated intelligentsia among indigenous people had just begun to emerge in Jharkhand in the 1920s as a result of modern education, which Christian missions had introduced among them along with their missionary work. Christianity had already brought them within the ambit of a congregational life that went beyond their individual 'tribal' identities. Though the congregation gave rise to an identity that was religious, it also opened up a space for a larger and wider identity. The modern education introduced by the Christian missionaries only accelerated this process, except that the associational life that emerged later was non-religious in nature. This associational life gained momentum on account of their shared historical experience of domination and exploitation by the colonial state and by non-indigenous outsiders. It was this stirring of self-consciousness among educated 'tribal' elites in Chota Nagpur that opened up the space for adivasi identity.

However, the idea underlying the concept of 'adivasi' or 'indigenous peoples' did not have its origin amongst the concerned communities themselves. It originated from British administrator-scholars, ethnographers, and more importantly Christian missionaries (Sengupta 1988a, 1988b). In their writings on tribes, two perspectives had been simultaneously at work. First, as the term 'tribe' itself indicates, they were considered to be 'primitive' people. This idea of their being primitive was based on their modes of living, which hinged primarily on their economic practices and the technology in use among them, but it also referred to their social and cultural life. Non-tribals including scholars and social workers such as Gandhians primarily identified and addressed them as primitives. The Gandhian social workers named them *adimjati*, and the organization formed for their development and welfare was named Adimjati Sewak Sangh. Alongside the process of such description, the British administrators-scholars and missionaries invariably described them as 'autochthonous' or 'aboriginal', terms which carry the same meaning as 'original inhabitants'. With this, the idea of these people as being of a different racial, linguistic, and cultural stock emerged.

However, while administrator-scholars and ethnographers described them as such, Christian missionaries made them aware of this description. This identification became increasingly sharper with increased interaction between 'tribals' and 'non-tribals', which was far from symbiotic and harmonious. Rather, the interaction and relation were marked by exploitation and domination. This situation was instrumental in shaping the new consciousness of indigenous peoples. It was not the idea of the 'primitive' but of 'aborigines' and 'autochthons' (which is how scholars, administrators, and missionaries referred to them) that the educated elite among these communities internalized and chose to mark themselves off from others. Since then, this idea has become an important marker of self-identity. Even outsiders today identify and address the concerned people as adivasis. In fact, the idea of 'adivasi' has taken precedence over the idea of primitiveness that had prevailed earlier. Such a process and such an awareness did not take shape in north-east India, as communities there did not live in close proximity with the Indian civilization and thereby escaped its influence. More importantly, they did not experience the process of colonization that indigenous communities in mainland India had already begun to experience, even before the coming of British rule. The coming of the British rule only hastened and intensified a process that was already at work.

ADIVASIS/INDIGENOUS PEOPLES' IDENTITY IN THE NATIONAL AND REGIONAL CONTEXTS

The thinking and writing on indigenous peoples have proceeded at different levels in India. One level is that of the country as a whole. Articulation of their identities and entitlements by indigenous peoples at international fora such as the WGIP or the UN's Permanent Forum on Indigenous Issues falls within this level, as does the state's articulation of its responses at the international level. Other than this, the Indian state hardly ever articulates the issue of adivasi people in the mode and language of 'indigenous peoples' at either the national or the state level. Indigenous peoples, however, through their organizations and fora such as the Indian Confederation of Indigenous and Tribal Peoples with its different zonal branches, articulate the issues of their indigeneity in reference to the country as a whole. They do not articulate their indigenous status with reference to a given state or a given region within the country, though they might be physically located within specific states or regions.

In short, they assume that they are the original people of the *country in which they live*, and do not formulate the problem of indigeneity at the local or regional levels. Issues articulated by the confederation at the international level are primarily concerned with rights and entitlements, which are then taken up at the national and zonal levels and vice versa. Indigenous people's organizations conceptualize and address the issue of indigeneity at the level of the country or the national level, no matter which part of the country they inhabit.

Though the question of indigenous people has generally been discussed in the context of the country as a whole, the discussion has also been conducted in relation to regions or territories within the country, as well as in relation to different populations living there acontiguously. Social scientists, in particular, have raised the issue along these lines (Béteille 1998: 189; Hardiman 1987: 15–16). Often they straddle the arguments made at the national and the regional levels, and extend arguments pertaining to one level to the other. For example, some tribes in the north-east are said to have a much shorter history of habitation in the *country* than communities which have a longer history and yet are not considered indigenous peoples. However, as a matter of fact, these communities are original inhabitants as far as the *regions* of their current habitations are concerned. These regions became part of India only with the advent of British rule. Prior to that, they were not even a part of India, in both the politico-administrative and the cultural sense. In the light of situations such as these, questioning the indigenous status of the tribal people of north-east India tends to be problematic. To judge their indigenous status, in terms of historicity and territory of which they had not been part until about two hundred years ago seems to be misplaced.

In discussions on indigenous people in India, it is important that we do not mix the issues obtaining at the two different levels. Often the problem at the level of the country is used to make a case against communities being indigenous even at the regional/local level, and vice versa. Posing the question of indigenous people in relation to dispersed territories within the country indeed gives rise to problems of a somewhat different nature. The movement of a population belonging to a particular race, ethnicity, and linguistic group, including those described as indigenous, from one place to another has been in process within India over centuries. This process was most pronounced under British rule, when communities, either in part or in toto, were pushed to regions inhabited historically or originally by other communities, including other indigenous communities. Due to this historical process, the status of their 'indigeneity' is questioned by scholars. However, if their status as the original people of the region where they are presently located is in doubt, this is hardly so if the country or the nation is taken as the reference point.

In India, then, the issue of indigenous peoples has come to be raised at various levels. In this context, broadly two patterns can be discerned. First, there are groups who may be indigenous with respect to the country as a whole, and may also be indigenous with respect to the region or territory of their existing settlement. The Oraons, Mundas, and Kharia, for instance, in what is known today as Jharkhand or Chhattisgarh, may fall in this category. The second group consists of those who may be indigenous with respect to the country as a whole, but may not be indigenous in respect of their present settlement in a given territory or region. Thus, it may so happen, as is usually the case, that the group may be indigenous and 'not indigenous' at the same time. The Oraons, Mundas, and many other communities living in the Jharkhand region, for example, may have a legitimate claim to be called 'indigenous people' in respect of their settlement in the country called India, or even in respect of their settlement in Jharkhand. But it is not clear if they can claim to be indigenous in Assam or Bengal, where they have moved in the course of the last century or so. Indeed their claim of being indigenous is strongly contested in these places. Nowhere is this truer than in Assam, where the migrant adivasis' claim to be indigenous people is being disputed by communities such as the Bodos and others (the original inhabitants of the region), who have a much longer history of settlement in the region than those of the communities from erstwhile Bihar, Madhya Pradesh, Odisha, and so on. If, however, one takes India as a whole, then these migrant groups have a much longer history of settlement than those in the north-eastern region. Thus, the Oraons, Mundas, and others are indigenous in some contexts, that is, in the context of their claim to have lived in India before the Aryan invasion, and also in the context of their being the first settlers of Jharkhand. However, their claim to being indigenous becomes doubtful in places and territories outside the Jharkhand region.

On the other hand, groups in the north-east region may be original inhabitants of the area they have been inhabiting, but if the country in its present form is taken as the unit of reference, then many tribes in the region may not be considered to be original people, since their presence in the country might be traced to later dates than that of communities who are not considered indigenous. This aspect has already been referred to earlier in the discussion. Even within the same region, there have been movements of communities from one place to another either out of choice or compulsion. Such process has also been at work in the regions inhabited by indigenous people as well. This has given rise to the problem of indigeneity in the sense of local versus migrants even among groups who are otherwise regarded as indigenous peoples of the country. Nowhere is this more visible than in the north-east region, where it has taken various forms of expression. The demand for autonomy or greater control over resources for the local indigenous groups is one of such expressions. In contrast, non-local indigenous groups have been articulating demands of certain basic rights and entitlements in the place of their existing settlements. Important instances of this situation in the north-east are those of the Chakma community in Arunachal Pradesh and adivasis in Assam, whose articulation of demands for certain rights and privileges is resisted by 'local indigenous people' on account of the former's migrant status.

IDEAS AND PROCESSES SHAPING ADIVASI/ INDIGENOUS PEOPLES' IDENTITY

An interesting question to pose is how people at the grass root construct their identity as indigenous peoples. What are the ideas around which they have built this identity? Are the ideas underlying the identity same or different among educated, articulate and non-educated and non-articulate indigenous people? Are the ideas more or less the same among different adivasi communities, or within a particular region? Of the ideas around which they have built their identity, which ideas are more critical? Of the ideas critical to the understanding of indigenous peoples' identity, the aspect of historicity seems to be of paramount importance. The question is how indigenous people conceive of this aspect. Do they conceive it in relation to the country as a whole, or in relation to a given state or territory or locality? Or do they conceive it in relation to certain groups or communities, and, if so, who are the groups in question? Such are some of the issues which need to be explored in concrete, empirical situations. The aspect of historicity is critical to understanding the identity of indigenous peoples and the educated among them do tend to articulate it in reference to history that traces their settlements to a time prior to the coming of the Aryans, the dominant population in India.

However, is this the way people at the grass-roots level think when they address and identify themselves as 'indigenous peoples'?

Although some idea of historicity seems to be critical, it is not clear if indigenous people think in terms of very distant history. What seems to be critical to the shaping of this identity is the *aspect of experience of domination through colonization*. That explains as to why the idea of indigenous peoples is so deep and well entrenched in the consciousness of these groups in eastern, central, western as well as southern India. The aspect of colonization is seen in terms of their economic, social, cultural, and political domination by the non-indigenous population at a certain time in history. That is, history is traced to the phase and experience of colonization and not as far back as the history of the coming of the Aryans. It is the aspect of colonization that has shaped and sharpened their identity as people distinct from the colonizers. This identity cannot be understood outside of this historical experience, coupled with their identity as people who are socially and culturally distinct from those identified and represented as the dominant population. In mainland India, such processes had already begun much before the coming of the British rule. However, it got accelerated and entrenched during the colonial rule.

In the north-eastern region, such processes had just begun to take shape during British rule, but did not get entrenched partly due to the British policy adopted in the hills of the region, and partly due to the resistance to colonization which was just beginning on the eve of independence. In fact, this resistance brought to a halt the process of colonization in the hills. The hilly regions of the north-east are thus marked by the absence of large-scale settlers. Hence, there has been no erosion of control over land, forest, and other resources by indigenous communities. These communities still maintain control over these resources and have autonomy of governance in the form of autonomous councils. They enjoy economic and political power (however limited may be) and determine their social and cultural life in their own way. This partly explains why the idea of 'original people' or 'indigenous peoples' is not so strong among the hill tribes of the region. The same, however, was not the case in the valley or the plains areas of the north-east.

The plains areas of the region are marked by tension and cleavage between the original inhabitants and migrants. The original inhabitants in this context are, however, not necessarily and exclusively identified with the 'tribal' population. The 'non-tribal' population, which had settled in the region prior to the arrival of colonial rule, has also not been generally described as settlers or migrants by the local groups of the region. The markers of 'local' and 'migrant' have thus come to be articulated in the region in reference to the movement of populations with the advent of British rule, no matter whether the migrants came as peasants, plantation workers, or other workers, and whether the relationship between them was one of exploitation or non-exploitation. However, the process of settlement was such that the newcomers did not dominate the region and its inhabitants economically, politically, socially, and culturally, as had been the case in mainland India. No doubt, movement and settlement in course of time have given rise to tensions and conflicts between the migrants and local inhabitants, but the relations between the two groups, with some exceptions, at certain levels has not in general been characterized by aspects of domination and subjugation. Rather, they are characterized by competition, which has assumed different forms and may be seen in play at different levels. 'Local versus migrant', or 'national versus foreigners' are the two major forms in which these tensions have been most generally articulated.

The local and migrant distinction, though it overlaps with indigenous and non-indigenous distinction, is not the same. Indigenous and non-indigenous distinction is invariably tied up with 'tribal/semi-tribal' and 'non-tribal' populations, and is intricately linked not only with their distinct social and cultural life but also their social, political, and economic marginalization by the migrant population. In the case of the local–migrant distinction, such marginalization may not necessarily have occurred, but even if it has, it is far from total as in the case of indigenous peoples. More often than not, the distinction between locals and migrants has not moved beyond certain legal entitlements, such as the rights to residence, employment, and other related issues. In short, the local versus migrant issue has not been articulated in terms of the relation between indigenous and non-indigenous peoples.

The invocation of the distinction between indigenous and non-indigenous peoples is a recent phenomenon, and is confined to certain groups with whom migrants, especially 'adivasis' from central India, have entered into conflict because of their demand for scheduled tribe status under the Indian constitution. The local groups are opposed to this demand of the adivasis, as it would drastically curtail the size of benefits the existing scheduled tribe groups have been enjoying. In their opposition to the demands of the adivasis, the concerned groups have been invoking the dimension of indigenous and non-indigenous in support of their argument.

In short, the articulation of their rights and entitlements in their capacity as indigenous peoples has been rather weak in the north-east region. It was only after the internationalization of the idea of 'indigenous peoples' that this articulation has gained some momentum among a few groups of the region.

MARGINALIZATION AND THE ARTICULATION OF RIGHTS

Indigenous and tribal peoples all over the world, including India, are marked by extreme marginalization in the economic, political, social, and cultural domains. As noted previously, the validity of the category of 'indigenous peoples' has been put to serious challenge in the Indian context. The challenge has come precisely because it is loaded with rights claim over land and territory with which they are intricately linked. This jeopardizes the rights and privileges that the dominant section of the society as well as the state have so far maintained and enjoyed. Now, whereas such privileges and rights are recognized in respect of the dominant linguistic communities, the same has been denied to the indigenous communities in India. The result is that they are progressively getting dispossessed from their control over land, forest, water, minerals, and other resources and in the process getting subjected to inhuman misery, injustice and exploitation. It is in the absence of such powers and rights that a new form of identity, namely the identity of 'adivasis' or 'indigenous people', is crystallizing among the communities of mainland India. It has long been an important marker of identity in what is known as the Eastern India but this is also catching up in other regions. A large number of adivasi organizations that have emerged in recent years both at the local/regional and at the national level are a pointer to their growing consciousness.

REFERENCES

Baird, Ian G. 2008. 'Colonialism, Indigeneity and the Brao', in Christian Erni (ed.), *The Concept of Indigenous Peoples in Asia: A Resource Book*, IWGIA Document No. 123. Copenhagen: International Work Group for Indigenous Affairs and Asia Indigenous Peoples Pact Foundation.

Béteille, A. 1960. 'The Definition of Tribe', *Seminar*, vol. 14, pp. 15–18.

―――. 1998. 'The Idea of Indigenous People', *Current Anthropology*, vol. 39, no. 2, pp. 187–91.

Cobo, Jose R. Martinez. 1984. 'Study of the Problem of Discrimination against Indigenous Populations', Final report submitted by the Special Rapporteur, Mr José Martinez Cobo to the United Nations Permanent Forum on Indigenous Issues, UN Doc. E/CN.4/Sub.2/476.

———. 1986. 'Study of the Problem of Discrimination against Indigenous Populations', UN Special Rapporteur of the Sub-Commission on Prevention of Discrimination and Protection of Minorities, E/CN.4/SUB.2/1986/7/ADD.4.

Daes, Erica-Irene A. 2008. 'On the Concept of Indigenous People', in Christian Erni (ed.), *The Concept of Indigenous Peoples in Asia: A Resource Book*, IWGIA Document No. 123. Copenhagen: International Work Group for Indigenous Affairs and Asia Indigenous Peoples Pact Foundation.

Hardiman, David. 1987. *The Coming of the Devi: Adivasi Assertion in Western India*. New Delhi: Oxford University Press.

ILO. 1953. *Indigenous Peoples: Living and Working Conditions of Aboriginal Populations in Independent Countries*. Geneva: International Labour Office.

———. 1957. Indigenous and Tribal Populations Convention (No. 107), ILO, Geneva.

———. 1989. Indigenous and Tribal Peoples Convention (No. 169), 76th ILC session, ILO, Geneva, 27 June.

Padel, Felix, Ajay Dandekar, and Jeemol Unni. 2013. *Ecology, Economy: Quest for a Socially Informed Connection*. New Delhi: Orient BlackSwan.

Prasad, Jayant. 1992. 'Statement Made on Behalf of the Delegation of India in the Working Group on Indigenous Population at Geneva', Samata.

Roy Burman, B. K. No date. 'Indigenous and Tribal Peoples and the U.N. and International Agencies', mimeograph, Rajiv Gandhi Foundation, New Delhi.

Sengupta, Nirmal. 1988a. 'Reappraising Tribal Movements I: A Myth in the Making', *Economic and Political Weekly*, vol. 23, no. 19, pp. 943–5.

———. 1988b. 'Reappraising Tribal Movements II: Legitimisation and Spread', *Economic and Political Weekly*, vol. 23, no. 20, pp. 1003–5.

Xaxa, Virginius. 1999. 'Tribes as Indigenous People of India', *Economic and Political Weekly*, vol. 34, no. 51, pp. 3589–96.

———. 2008. 'The Concept of Indigenous Peoples in India', in Christian Erni (ed.), *The Concept of Indigenous Peoples in Asia: A Resource Book*, IWGIA Document No. 123. Copenhagen: International Work Group for Indigenous Affairs and Asia Indigenous Peoples Pact Foundation.

2

Primitive Accumulation, Labour, and the Making of 'Scheduled Tribe', 'Indigenous', and Adivasi Sensibility

Savyasaachi

This chapter discusses labour potential in the context of the history of primitive accumulation of capital, which extends from feudalism to contemporary neoliberalism (Perelman 2007; von Werlhof 2000). From this history we know two interrelated attributes of primitive accumulation, namely the necessary use of force to divorce the producer from the means of production,[1] and the necessary struggle against 'natural economy' that totally disregards nature, the lives of the people and their rules, laws, customs, and practices prevalent in places outside Europe. History has shown that the force of revolution, war, and oppressive taxation have been used to pull people out of the 'state of nature'.

[1] In 1867, Marx (*Capital*, Vol. 1) pointed out that

> the so-called primitive accumulation, therefore, is nothing else than the historical process of divorcing the producer from the means of production.... In the history of primitive accumulation, all revolutions are epoch-making that act as levers for the capital class in course of formation; but, above all, those moments when great masses of men are suddenly and forcibly torn from their means of subsistence, and hurled as free and unattached proletarians on the labour-market. The expropriation of the agricultural producer, of the peasant, from the soil, is the basis of the whole process. (Marx 1974: 668–9)

A study of the origin and development of the category 'scheduled tribe' in the first section of this chapter shows that primitive accumulation eats into labour potential. In the second section, the study of the origin and development of the 'indigenous' perspective shows that, as long as labour is constituted in a relation of alterity to nature, which is an aspect of primitive accumulation, labour potential cannot be realized. The third section shows that the adivasi sensibility has not been determined by the processes of primitive accumulation, and it says 'no' to this process. In this capability lies the possibility of realizing labour potentiality.

From the discussion in these three sections, it becomes clear that the potential of labour to realize itself by its own effort emerges in the act of saying no to the historical formations created by primitive accumulation.

THE COUNTER-INSURGENCY CATEGORY: 'SCHEDULED TRIBES'

The category 'scheduled tribes' was created by the colonial determination to counter insurgencies against primitive accumulation, pull insurgent forest dwellers and peasants out of 'natural economies', and bring them within the fold of irreversible universal time for the social production and reproduction of capital. Rosa Luxemburg pointed out that James Mill's argument in his *History of British India*—that under primitive conditions land belongs to the sovereign—was based on dubious historical evidence and distortions of practices in India (Luxemburg 1951: 352n1). This argument determined the directive principle of primitive accumulation that legitimized the territorial sovereignty of the state, namely that all land unknown or known, used or unused, belongs to the state, and land that does not give revenue is wasteland (Baden-Powell 1974, vol. 2:379). The teleology of this directive was to convert all wasteland into revenue land. Thus, all the forest and land used for subsistence by forest dwellers and peasants was classified as 'wasteland' because it did not give revenue.

This principle legitimized, in the period between the mid-eighteenth century and the mid-nineteenth century (between 1760 and 1860), aggressive primitive accumulation by commercial forestry and large-scale single crop commercial agriculture. Grove (1995: 386–92) points out that under the East India Company regime in the 1760s, there was timber shortage because of reckless extraction to provide for constructing railway tracks, developing the ship-building industry, making furniture, and a continuous supply of firewood. In both Bengal and Bombay Presidencies between 1760 and 1790, this led the company to expand its territory to get resources from areas inhabited by forest dwellers and peasants. This was the beginning of forestry in irreversible linear time, because the extraction of timber was determined not by the capacity of the forest to regenerate, but by commercial demand. As regards agriculture, the Permanent Settlement of 1793 initiated commercial large-scale agriculture.

The commercial necessity to not misuse resources and to have enough to meet the demand gave legitimacy to the idea of conservation of forest resources, and prepared the ground for the creation of 'reserves of nature'. This economic necessity for conservation was the basis of the Dalhousie Memorandum of 1855, which prepared the ground for centralized forest management policy to be adopted in India after 1860 (Grove 1995: 460–1). The institutional set-up to enable conservation for commerce was inaugurated in 1864, when Dietrich Brandis was given the post of the first inspector general of forests to the Government of India. In this year, the Forest Department of Bengal was set up and a conservator of forests was recruited. This idea and institution were given legitimacy by the first Indian Forest Act of 1865. The Act was modified in 1873–4, 1878, and in 1924, when a new Forest Act was implemented replacing the Act of 1865 (Ghosal 2011: 111).

This forest regime was designed for primitive accumulation. The expansion of forest territory after 1800 (Grove 1995: 390) to include remote areas as 'reserves of nature' for commercial use was not possible without forcibly taking away from forest dwellers and peasants the forest and land that was their means of production. During these years of commercial expansion, there were at least 110 known instances of insurgency over a period of 117 years from 1783 to 1900 (Guha 1983: 1–2). Shachi Arya (1998: 216–20) chronologically records the history of insurgency from 1778 onwards. The labour teleology underlying the primitive accumulation of capital legitimized measures to counter insurgency, not just to get timber without difficulty, but, more importantly, to pull forest dwellers and peasants out of the 'state of nature'.

The formulation of Warren Hastings's cultural policy of 1773, and the Queen's Proclamation of 1858, prepared the ground, in accordance with this teleology, for constructing appropriate counter-insurgency measures. This cultural policy advocated informed, culturally sensitive governance. It stressed the need to know and understand the social and cultural life of the people. In keeping with this policy, the Queen's Proclamation stated that

We declare it Our royal will and pleasure that ... none be molested or disquieted, by reason of their religious faith or observances, but that all shall alike enjoy the equal and impartial protection of the law; and We do strictly charge and enjoin all those who may be in authority under Us that they abstain from all interference with the religious belief or worship of any of Our subjects on pain of Our highest displeasure. (Quoted in Belmekki 2008: 117)

The recognition of ancient rights by the Queen's Proclamation was not intended to restrict the expansion of forest territories. On the contrary, it legitimized administrative arrangements for taking away from forest dwellers and peasants' their means of subsistence of land and forest. Areas inhabited by unreconciled forest people were maintained under military control and were known as non-regulated areas. In other areas, civilians were employed to look after the administration, and these were known as Regulation districts. In these districts, the ancient rights of people were recognized by the Scheduled Districts Act of 1874 and the Agency Tracts, Interest, and Land Transfer Act of 1917. These acts protected limited rights of forest dwellers to use forest materials for their subsistence by declaring them as inalienable and non-transferable. The Census of India of 1931 used the two categories of 'caste' and 'tribe' to divide insurgents. These categories were created by ethnological inquiries of India under the direction of J. H. Hutton, one of the Cambridge anthropologist-administrators who had served the colonial state. Soon after, under the Government of India Act of 1935, the 'unrestricted' and 'restricted' areas became known as 'excluded' and 'partially excluded' areas.

With the construction of this category, insurgents were suppressed and co-opted. Suppression clamped down on the forest time and space that was the basis of ancient (customary) rights, and co-option brought them into the frame of linear irreversible productive time. Both suppression and co-option are now integral to post-colonial governance and have become part of the modern worldview.

In 1950, the Constitution of independent India designated these areas as the fifth and sixth scheduled areas, respectively. The 73rd amendment to the Constitution in 1992, the Panchayats (Extension to Scheduled Areas) Act (PESA) of 1996, the carving out of new adivasi states like Chhattisgarh and Jharkhand in 2000, and the Forest Rights Act (FRA) of 2006 have not undone this structure. For instance, in these legislations, the recognition of customary rights is a continuation of the 'recognition of ancient rights' by the Queen's Proclamation of 1858, and not its critique.

This contemporary legal regime continues to pull adivasi people out of the 'state of nature' and bring them, as well as nature, into the fold of the non-cyclical linear time of production and reproduction of commodities and capital accumulation. Are the struggles to implement PESA and FRA against the neo-liberal programs for economic development? Are these Acts not instruments to counter insurgency and facilitate the primitive accumulation of neoliberal capital? The teleology of land and forest revenue legislation underlying these legislations is directed by capital's struggle against 'natural economy' and the 'state of nature'.

The category 'scheduled tribe' now has four counter-insurgency functions—a political function, an economic function, a security function, and an information function. Its political function is reconciliation and reform of governance. Its economic function is to provide essential services and stimulate long-term economic growth, build confidence in the government, and reduce the pool of frustration amongst the landless and the unemployed youth. Its security function is to develop legal frames, civilian oversight mechanisms, and judicial systems. Its information function is to bring on record essential information of the condition of people that is necessary for governance.

The legal regimes of the category 'scheduled tribe' determine the post-colonial politics of recognition and development (Kapila 2008). Who is a tribal, eligible to be included in this category? What notion of identity is at the basis of this recognition? Any claim to a scheduled tribe status today is measured against the following criteria: cultural or social identity; demarcated occupation and use of primitive technology; lack of relationship to the majority community; of marriage payments; an animist or totemic religion; and practice of endogamy. It is necessary to reflect on why has there been no discussion on the criteria? What implication has this on the notion of identity and on the people's self-perception that has been conditioned by this notion?

Today, counter-insurgency measures continue to determine the dynamics of state power and cultural classifications. An important aspect of these measures is that they discourage a discussion on the validity of such criteria and thus freeze 'identity'. This prepares the ground for the unfolding of industrial labour teleology: while, on the one hand, there are constitutional rights to customary practices of livelihood (granted by PESA 1996 and FRA 2006), on the other hand, according to the criteria of Tribe, these communities are backward and primitive and live on the margins.

This absurd juxtaposition of progressive and backward elements frames the ontology of labour. In the counter-insurgency discourse, the present of these people is determined by annihilating their past; this is done by conceptualizing it as labour in the the 'state of nature'. Thus, no value is accorded to the labour of the ancestors of those adivasis who have included themselves and those who have not been included but have the desire to be included in the category 'scheduled tribes'.

The historical sense of people in this category strives to preserve a sense of what it has lost and to not lose whatever remains. For these communities, their sense of their presence in the world today, in relation to other communities and to the state, is embedded in their past labour, which for them is not in the 'state of nature'.

When the historical sense of the people becomes assertive, and they make efforts to bring this sense of the past in a constructive relation with labour, the teleology of primitive accumulation works immediately to suppress it. For instance, the provisions of PESA 1996 and FRA 2006 have deprived these communities of the time and space necessary for their traditional practices. With the land and forest available under these acts, it not possible to conserve the diversity of the forest through customary practices such as shifting cultivation.

It is important to see that these acts pretend to empower adivasis, but they in fact empower the state even more. It is equally important to see that communities which have benefited from being categorized as 'scheduled tribes' have progressively lost touch with the forest— only few of them are willing to live in or around the forest. They have internalized the state's view, that is, to give the forest a foundational position in their worldview is to want to stay in isolation, underdeveloped and deprived of the benefits of modern development.

The ratification of these acts may at best be a legislative victory, but these legislations are in fact instances of political defeat, because they have undermined and put an end to debate and negotiation. The discussion is not any more about the value of the forest, the forest worldview, its traditions, and the customary practices of caring for nature. Only a handful of people, approximately 20 per cent, are well versed in these ideas. The handful of acres of land made available by these acts has prepared the ground for the mass migration of people in the third if not in the second generation. The forest has been displaced from its foundational position in the worldview of the adivasi people; it is no longer a living space.

This process is embedded in the understanding that, so long as labour and economy are in the 'state of nature', they cannot have exchange value. The teleology of this exchange value of labour is to counter insurgency, pull people out of the 'state of nature', and 'civilize' them. This eats into labour potential.

THE 'INDIGENOUS' PERSPECTIVE AND LABOUR ALTERITY

First, the International Labour Organization (ILO) used the term 'indigenous'. Over time, an indigenous perspective has evolved against primitive accumulation.

The colonization of what is now the United States and Canada is dated to 1492.[2] Here, primitive accumulation by means of law and gun took the form of the genocide of a substantial population, of approximately as many as seven million people who had settled in these continents. This population was diverse in culture, economy, and social organization. There were 12 distinct language groups each embracing numerous individual tribes with differing economies—some depended on hunting game and gathering food from the forests and meadows; others cultivated maize, beans, squash, melons, and tobacco.

The effort to do justice to and address the suffering of tribal people in these continents began after the First World War. In the treaty of Versailles, the creation of the ILO was suggested for the protection of workers. The ILO was born in 1919, and one of its first studies was concerned with indigenous workers. In 1926, the governing body created a committee of experts on native workers. The social ethos made it necessary to initiate steps globally to combat the injurious effects of industrialization, as an important precondition for peace was social justice for all workers.

In 1957, the ILO adopted Convention 107—the first treaty dealing with indigenous and tribal populations. This convention included not only aboriginal people pre-dating settlement or conquest, but also tribal and semi-tribal groups irrespective of whether or not they could be regarded as indigenous in this sense. It included people from America, Australia, the Near and the Middle East, and from the African continent (Barsh 1986; Savyasaachi 2004; Yupsanis 2010).

These measures were designed to facilitate integration and assimilation into the mainstream. The key terms for discourse now were: nation building, equity, development, and diversification of industrial production. Productivity, which shaped the relation between land, labour, and capital, was the most important determinant of this discourse. Technology that

---

[2] See Mann (2006).

mediated productivity, equity, and development laid down standards that opposed modernity to tradition. Accordingly, adivasi people's social and cultural traditions of work (which linked their knowledge systems to their ways of life) were considered obstacles and marginalized, since cultural perceptions of productivity differed from those of industrial production.

With the emergence of the human rights movement during the 1970s, social and cultural factors became important for industrial production and development. It was argued that culture mediates technology and labour. The culture of the workplace was defined not by technology alone, but also by the social–cultural background of labour; thus, attitudes and dispositions of labour could not be understood without taking into account people's social and cultural practices. It was clear that social and cultural perceptions of work and of worker identity determined the social dynamics of the production process and of the workplace. Thus, the social-cultural framework of production became important. The social and cultural integration of a large mass of marginalized wage labour became an important component of the process of nation-building. Adivasi people were seen to be at a less advanced stage of development largely because their social life was regulated wholly or partially by their own customs or traditions, and not by rational thinking.

A major change occurred in 1981 with the UN Educational, Scientific, and Cultural Organization (UNESCO) Declaration on Ethnocide and Ethno-development. The post-First and Second World War efforts of reconstruction played an important role in the formulation and acceptance of this declaration. On the one hand, the UN inherited a series of political instruments signed after the wars. These contained special measures for the protection of ethnic, religious, and linguistic groups, and referred to minorities in Poland, Austria, the Serbo-Croat-Slovenic state, Czechoslovakia, Bulgaria, Romania, Hungary, Albania, Lithuania, Greece, Turkey, Estonia, and Iraq, among others. On the other hand, the sordid story of Nazi genocide made it more than clear that all genocide begins with cultural aggression. The UNESCO declaration thus recognized that a fundamental component of modernization and development was intolerance of social-cultural diversity in the external as well as internal environment. From here emerged the indigenous perspective that the ground for alternative development is pluralism, and that this ground could not be prepared without including indigenous people, not only because they were the first to suffer and point towards the intolerance and violence inherent in the culture of modern man, but also because they in fact constituted this plurality.

During the 1980s, indigenous peoples all over the world were engaged in struggles against invasions and genocide, militarization, the formation of nuclear states, mining, large dams, reckless commercial forestry, pollution, missionizing, modern education, racism, exploitation of labour, sterilization of women, prisons, tourism, and forced sales of land (Moody 1988). Towards the end of the twentieth century, these struggles multiplied and became more articulate, as in a standpoint. These enriched the indigenous perspective. From the late 1980s onwards, environment and ecology became important factors of production. Technology and finance were directed towards the preservation and conservation of the environment and of ecology. Control over natural resources gradually became 'monopolistic', denying access to indigenous people. This added to subsistence problems and brought about further marginalization. Indigenous people were concerned with finding an alternative to this 'mainstream' way of being part of the world order and of acquiring a sense of belonging. Their struggles highlighted that in addition to genocide, ecocide was also at the foundation of modernization and development.

These understandings cleared the way for indigenous struggles to assert in the political arena that their cultural perception of the notion of origins is at the basis of their sense of history. This assertion dispelled the fuzziness created by the use of several terms to refer to indigenous people: 'natives', 'aboriginal', 'autochthonous', 'ethnic minorities', 'tribal people', 'first nations', and 'fourth world'. 'The most undisputed criterion is that indigenous peoples are the descendants of the original inhabitants of a territory taken over through conquest or settlement by aliens' (Khan and bin Talal 1987: 6). To capture the sense of 'being original inhabitants', Roger Moody (1988) uses the expression 'species of origin', and suggests that indigenous people's struggles are concerned with 'conscientisation and the recovery of origins'. History for indigenous people has its origin in dispossession. In the light of 'being dispossessed', the meaning of 'species of origin' and 'recovery of origins' is defined by the substantive concerns of their contemporary struggles. For indigenous peoples, 'origins' are not dated; they cannot be determined in a frame of linear time. Origins articulate a sense of belonging that sees in natural space and the passage of time the presence of larger life processes that create the potential for labour.

The frame of reference had changed. The process of industrial modernization was no longer conceptualized in terms of the opposition between the traditional and the modern. In its place, a discourse of opposition between the marginalized and the dominant forces emerged. The dominant forces totalized the process of modernization. They monopolized the definitions, standards, and norms of social and economic life, by taking control of the terms and categories of cultural and intellectual discourses. Consequently, people's sense of their own identity, their capability, and confidence was undermined.

With all these struggles in the background, in 1989, ILO Convention 107 was criticized for emphasizing integration and assimilation, and a revised version was formulated as Convention 169. This new convention stipulated that 'self-identification as indigenous or tribal shall be regarded as a fundamental criterion for determining the groups to which the provisions of this Convention apply'. This convention drew attention primarily to the endogenous efflorescence of human potential. In turn, this allowed for the definition of 'indigenous' in a historical-axiological sense and not in a purely chronological sense. The emphasis was on plurality in the relation between social formations and a sense of identity. This allowed for the inclusion of indigenous people from all countries in Asia and Africa, while the purely chronological criteria applied to North and South America and Australia.

By the beginning of the 1990s, the ground had been prepared for pursuing the question of alternatives in a pluralist framework. The suffering of indigenous peoples showed that the processes of mainstream industrial modernization had continuously unleashed social forces that had undermined the support systems that sustain life itself.

The Economic and Social Council by consensus established the UN Permanent Forum on Indigenous Issues on 28 July 2000, at its 45th plenary meeting. The forum's mandate was to discuss and advise on indigenous issues relating to economic and social development, culture, the environment, education, health, and human rights within the council on the one hand, and to promote the integration and co-ordination of activities relating to indigenous issues within the UN system on the other. However, it was clarified that 'the Permanent Forum is not specifically given any mandate to set new standards in international law' (Lile 2006: 24–5).

In 2005, Victoria Tauli-Corpuz was unanimously elected chair of the UN Permanent Forum on Indigenous Issues. The volume *Paradigm Wars* (Mander and Tauli-Corpuz 2006) published the following year showed that the process of primitive accumulation was continuing unabated, in fact with greater force, and that there was equally strong resistance from indigenous people across the world:

No communities of peoples on this Earth have been more negatively impacted by the current global economic system than the world's remaining 350 million indigenous peoples. And no peoples are so strenuously and, lately, successfully resisting these invasions and inroads.

It is the first purpose of this book to describe the nature, breadth and ferocity of the assaults upon native societies that are ongoing today, and the global institutions and corporations that drive them, while desperately seeking access to their own lifeblood—the planet's fast disappearing resource supply.

But it is also our purpose to convey the impressive energy, scale, and clarity of purpose of a global indigenous resistance. It is growing increasingly broad, powerful, well organized, and effective in both domestic and international contexts. Indigenous peoples are demanding respect, recognition and codification of their 'prior rights' to live where they have always lived, in the manner they choose, and with control over all decisions about their ancestral lands, and what is on them and in them. (Mander and Tauli-Corpuz 2006: 3)

In an article in this book, Tauli-Corpuz argues that traditional economic practices are the basis for the 'right to remain separate and distinct'. The traditional practices, she points out, are in conflict with economic globalization, and were for this reason labelled as obstacles to progress. This is a progress that depends upon the destruction of peoples' lands and resources, even of the genetic materials of human beings and plants. She provides a full discussion of how these assaults play out through global bureaucracies, and what is being done to reverse this trend. As 'species of origin', indigenous people share a view of work, nature, and productivity that is differently institutionalized in different communities, allowing for plural work cultures.

These interventions contributed to the further enrichment of the indigenous perspective. The contours of this perspective are as follows. According to the indigenous perspective, the politics of alterity that is embedded in the teleology of industrial labour is manifested as genocide. Here, labour is determined in alterity to nature. The difference from earlier genocides is twofold. On the one hand, this politics of alterity is based on the view that certain peoples' cultural values foster laziness, rendering them incapable of the labour necessary for the accumulation of capital, and that these people had to be exterminated.[3] On the other

---

[3] 'Among American Indian people, centuries of genocidal child removal policies remain fresh in our minds. We remember our children were taken away from us by white society to facilitate assimilation and because we are

hand, it prepared the ground for the emergence of a subjugated European subjectivity (see Popke 2003) unsettled by the imperatives of capitalist penetration. This particular subjectivity mapped the 'Other' not only in the outside world (Africa, America, and so on), but also internally in Europe and its neighbourhoods (for instance, the Jews).

The indigenous perspective, which argues for a relationship between technology, culture, environment, ecology, human rights, productivity, equity, and work culture, is directed toward recovering and restoring ecological balances, arresting environmental destruction, enriching the productive capacities of labour, and preventing the violation of the right to means of subsistence. It emphasizes that land, water, and forest are common resources, and that this is a precondition for security and certitude. It upholds democratic spaces where plural production norms are grounded in plural perceptions of work, nature, and productivity. Further, it holds that life support systems can be enriched when an economy ensures plural livelihoods to all. Decentralized social organization ensures human rights and equity, taking into account people's social and cultural traditions and practices. The history of marginalized peoples suggests that different and new methodologies be acquired to create plural livelihoods.

With this perspective, the ground is being prepared for a fresh constitution of the meaning of enlightened being-in-the-world, one that is caring, secure, and certain of continuities in the life-world. The transition from the twentieth to the twenty-first century is a transition from being and living 'of the world' to being and living 'for the world'. 'Being of the world' emerges from the destructive process of globalization, and 'being for the world' emerges from care for the life-world. Life support systems for 'being of the world' are discontinuous with the production system. In 'being for the world', production and reproduction systems are contiguous with the life support systems and are governed by the regenerative, creative components of a living process.

---

viewed as essentially inferior, lazy, alcoholic, and inherently unable to care for our children' (Poupart 2003: 94). The Germans viewed the 'Nama to be lazy good-for-nothing. Hence, they devised a deportation scheme and aimed at the eventual extinction of the Nama' (Berat 1993: 23n110). 'It was a cornerstone of the Nazi demonization of Jews that they were essentially a parasitic class, incapable of "honest" work and thus driven to usury, lazy cosmopolitanism, and criminality' (Jones 2010: 265).

In 'being of the world', the relations between the three aspects of the process of living—political economy, social structure and culture, and science and knowledge—are asymmetrical and fragmented, because of which processes of production are discontinuous with the life process. The production process exists 'of' the life-world, taking from it without taking care to not diminish and damage it. Articulation between the production process and the life process, for this reason, is one-directional and not reciprocal, that is, its aim is to conquer nature and subjugate it to the advantage of human beings. This is destructive of life support systems.

In 'being of the world', production processes transgress the limits of life processes. In this way, they move towards capital accumulation and the generation of surplus. The conceptual apparatus of this science cannot satisfactorily address questions of human rights, cultural plurality and identity, and ecological and environmental viability. The processes of material production and distribution are unrelated to the reproduction of social and cultural capital (symbolic goods). For this reason, the life support system is destroyed.

A caring mode of 'being-in-the-world' builds reciprocity between the three aspects of the process of living mentioned earlier: political economy, social structure and culture, and science and knowledge. Here, 'being for the world' is concerned with ensuring the continuity of living processes. From this perspective, life support systems cannot be defined satisfactorily either by the market or by the state, or by both of them put together. The state and the market perpetuate and deepen the contradiction between equity and development. The relations between labour, technology, culture, environment, ecology, human rights, productivity, equity, and work culture are important for the production and reproduction of material and symbolic goods that ensure the necessary conditions for the recovery of the human capacity for self-regeneration. For this, adivasi people need to be engaged not only as numbers, or as cultural identities alone, but also as persons with knowledge and skills. Culture includes the experiments undertaken by people to create conditions for self-determination and to correct the asymmetry between equity and development.

THE ADIVASI SENSIBILITY AND LABOUR POTENTIALITY

Agamben (1999) argues that the structure of potentiality is both potentiality and impotentiality (that is, the potentiality not to). According to Gulli (2005),

[the] potentiality not to, the ability to say no, to withdraw, is freedom itself.... If all concrete labors do not spontaneously make use of their ability to not pass into actuality, it remains the task of a radical ontology of labor to show the viability of such an option, at least at the level of theory; and show that other and better worlds are indeed possible once the logic of exploitation is destroyed, as well as show once again that it is on the shoulders of labor that the global machinery of capital rests... [p. 6]

... what remains to be ascertained is whether there is an outside to subsumption and globalization—but this outside does not have to be spatial in character, it is of an ontological and political outside that we are speaking here [p. 7].

The suggestion here is that 'once the logic of exploitation [of the process of subsumption and globalization of capital] is destroyed', then the 'not-spatial ontological and political outside' will become a meaningful 'other and better world'. Further, labour's ability to say 'no' makes this possible. The 'saying no' is not a negation; rather, it simultaneously creates time and space for 'other and better worlds'. This seems to be Gulli's idea of a radical ontology of labour.

In his discussion on this subject, however, Gulli does not give sufficient attention to the foundation of the process of subsumption, namely primitive accumulation. The process of accumulation of capital continues to take from people their means of subsistence. This taking away is the means to universalize labour teleology, that is, pulling human beings out of the state of nature and annihilating their sense of belonging. This process universalizes the European culture of modernity by means of three sets of separations: the separation of consciousness from conscience, fact from value, and lexical truth from applied praxis.[4] The forcible separation of people from their means of production is not possible without effecting these three sets of separation. The teleology of labour maintains these separations by reproducing them each time the extracted surplus value is reproduced. Thus, the teleology directs labour to generate surplus value, accumulates it, creates capital on the one hand, and drives all classes of society—the rich, the middle class, and the labouring poor—to internalize these separations.

The ability of labour to say 'no' needs to be read in relation to these separations and their universalization. The way labour can say 'no' is

[4] These separations are discussed in Uberoi (2002).

The Making of 'Scheduled Tribe', 'Indigenous', and Adivasi Sensibility 67

by creating a dialogue between consciousness and conscience, bringing together fact and value, and lexical truth with applied praxis.

What is the bearing of adivasi sensibility on the teleology of labour of primitive accumulation? A close 'listening to' makes it clear that adivasi sensibility resists and says 'no' to these separations. Ranajit Guha's (1983) study of accounts of insurgencies reported by the British over a period of 117 years from 1783 to 1900 gives an idea of the 'elementary aspects' of adivasi sensibility. Some of these aspects, selected from the point of view of our discussion, include discrimination and negation, inversion and ambiguity, the communal process of mobilization, the sparing use of violence, and territoriality. Guha's interpretation of these accounts is textual, 'decontextualized' as it were. These accounts could also be read with reference to the nature of the process of primitive accumulation.

According to Guha (1983),

> ... negations characteristic of insurgency in our period were worked out in terms of two sets of principles. The first, which we shall call discrimination, was realized in its most explicit form in the violence selectively directed by peasants at particular targets [p. 20] ... demonstrated how clearly the peasant distinguished between enemies and allies. The definition of friend and foe could of course vary from one insurrection to another [p. 21].... The logic of this extension applies to people as much as to things [p. 25].... The other modality of negation characteristic of insurgency consists of the peasants' attempt to destroy or appropriate for themselves the signs of the authority of those who dominate them [p. 28].

The communal process of mobilization occurs in the sequence—'confer, plan, assemble, attack' (Guha 1983: 116). Peasants sparing in their use of murder is on account of 'two aspects of rebel consciousness—namely its inertia and its negativity' (Guha 1983: 164). The rebel consciousness that is 'bitterly denounced by revolutionaries as a limiting factor of peasant insurgency' is 'in its Indian form, a sense of of belonging to a common lineage as well as to a common habitat' (Guha 1983: 279).

About the principle of discrimination, Guha says that 'it was a *negative class consciousness* in that the definition of class which was involved was that of their enemies rather than of themselves; in other words, the nobility' (Guha 1983: 20; emphasis in original). About inversion, Guha says there is an

> imprint of a consciousness trying to identify some of the basic elements of economic exploitation and the political infrastructure.... However, ... it is still a rather ... disjointed perception ... [which] falls far short of

conceptualizing the structure of authority which made such conditions possible. 'The only form in which the State is perceived', one could say after Gramsci, is in terms of officialdom. (Guha 1983: 28)

About the sparing use of murder as a kind of violence, Guha says:

> The answer must be sought in two aspects of rebel consciousness—namely, its inertia and its negativity. It was not a liberated consciousness. On the contrary, ... it was still trapped in the old culture. That culture imbued the peasant with a sense of reverence for the body of anyone ranked as his superior. For the form of the human body is a symbol, as Hegel said, and its symbolism in the highly semioticized world of traditional India was very potent. (Guha 1983: 164)

Finally, about territoriality, Guha says, 'What is this consciousness which is so bitterly denounced by revolutionaries as a limiting factor of peasant insurgency? It is made up, in its Indian form, of a sense of belonging to a common lineage as well as to a common habitat—an intersection of two primordial referents, which ... we shall call territoriality' (Guha 1983: 279).

To frame these accounts of insurgency, Guha creatively interweaves ideas that evolved from the revolutionary left (Kosambi, Engels, Gramsci, Lefebrev, Mao, and others) with social anthropology. The balance is tilted towards the former. What is noticeable is a discussion of the absence of the works of Rosa Luxemburg, who discussed at length the aspects of primitive accumulation and anthropological fieldwork. These are significant absences.

Two very important elements seem to be missing from Guha's frame. The first is the backdrop: the description of the historical landscape created by primitive accumulation, and the people and events to which these insurgents are responding. The second element is a sense of the insurgent's social structure, labour, and existence. The insurgent adivasi sensibility as it emerges from Guha's frame has the following elementary aspects. It is negative class consciousness, in that the definition of 'class' identifies their enemies rather than themselves. It is based on a 'rather disjointed perception', because it falls short of conceptualizing the structure of authority. It is imbued with inertia and negativity. It is not a liberated consciousness. It has a sense of reverence for the body of anyone ranked as its superior, and its sense of territoriality is bitterly denounced by revolutionaries.

There is a question here: is the revolutionary sensibility party to the ploy of primitive accumulation of pulling people out of the state of nature? The works of social anthropologists, some of which have been used by Guha, suggest that there is no such thing as the 'state of nature'. Guha seems to hold the position that a revolutionary consciousness rooted in the necessity of conceptualizing the structure of authority would break out of its inertia and negativity, and create the ground for a liberated consciousness that would transcend the limits of territoriality marked by the sense of belonging to a particular lineage and habitat.

Are these not attributes of the sensibility of primitive accumulation and its underlying teleology of labour? Primitive accumulation express a negative class consciousness more focused on its enemies rather than on the self. This may be seen as an instance of the separation of consciousness from conscience. It is based on a rather disjointed perception of authority, where there is separation of fact from value, and for this reason it falls short of conceptualizing its structure. It is unable to reflect on its self and for this reason; it shows high-level inertia and concomitant negativity. Another instance of its inability to conceptualize is its failure to see that the sense of reverence for the body of those who are ranked superior is not possible without a sense of reverence for everyone's body. The insurgents' sense of belonging and territoriality, 'so bitterly denounced by revolutionaries', reflects that theirs is not a liberated but a grounded consciousness. This denouncement emerges from the separation of lexical truth from applied praxis. That is to say, the theory of revolutionary consciousness is not linked with the practices (embedded in the social structure, work, and existence) of the insurgents.

It is worthwhile considering a different way of reading the insurgents' sensibility. The ability to differentiate between enemy and friend demonstrates that consciousness and conscience are in dialogue and not separated. Consciousness of their enemies is not possible without a clear understanding of themselves. The clarity of perception of the relation between fact and value that underlies structures of authority informs 'inversion'; without such clarity, inversion would not be possible. The sparing use of murder as a kind of violence does not show inertia and negativity; rather, it demonstrates a sense of restraint. Adivasi territoriality is embedded in their sense of belonging, which is different from the sense of territoriality of primitive accumulation that murders recklessly and indiscriminately and destroys any sense of belonging. Further, the revolutionary denouncement of the insurgents' sense of territoriality begs the question of the nature of a revolutionary consciousness that is uprooted, that has no sense of belonging.

It is important to draw attention to adivasi insurgents' relation to revolutionaries. In post-independence India, revolutionary political forces of diverse persuasions have endeavoured to provide leadership to the adivasi people. Alongside, there has been a very strong current amongst adivasis to say 'no' to any form of assimilation or openness to solidarity with other peoples. Sanjay Munda and Bosu-Mullick (2003: 269–70) point out that the people have

> successfully nullified the predictions of both the bourgeois and classical Marxist schools of thought that 'the aboriginal's last act will be squalid, instead of being tragic. What will be seen with most regret will be, not his disappearance, but his enslavement and degradation' and that 'such national groups (are) non-historic ... who were lacking national vitality and condemned to disappear or prone to be denationalised'....
>
> [in] years of struggle against different forms of colonial forces the people have experienced all the three options: negation-isolation-tragedy, surrender-assimilation-squalid and equilibrium of rejection-accommodation-symbiosis-integration....
>
> The people have always remained open to direct change but what they have opposed is assimilation.... Their age-old wisdom, manifested in their daily practices even today, upholds the human approach of integration with other peoples within the same political and social framework.... In early days, every lineage group separately fought against the alien forces. Later on different combinations of joint efforts emerged and very soon there evolved a pan-indigenous unity. And finally, a broad-based unity of indigenous peoples, peasantry, and artisan communities was reached at.

Adivasis have resisted assimilation by left revolutionary politics as much as right-wing and liberal politics, but have remained open to issue-based alliances. What has held them back is their restraint concerning violence in politics, their sense of belonging to lineage and habitat, and their understanding of the state political structures they are struggling against. The left is no different from the right or liberal political forces with respect to its policies on minerals, forests, and other natural resources, or on the question of militarization and industrial development.

This mode of adivasi insurgency is not about the 'negation' of revolutionary politics, but about saying 'no' to absolute inclusion in parliamentary political processes, saying 'no' to armed political struggle, and to development processes that undermine the gifts of nature. Adivasis are opposed not to modernization, but to subordination to the rationale of the dominant systems in the world.

The adivasi sensibility of refusing assimilation has been described as a 'sense of autonomy' and 'self-rule'. The insurgency that comes from this sensibility seeks broad-based alliances with the working class and with people who respect nature's gifts and seek friendships across inequalities. Adivasi insurgency is grounded in a sense of belonging to lineage and habitat.

The formation of the state of Jharkhand in the year 2000 is an expression of this sensibility. Other instances are to be found in experiments in 'autonomy and self-rule'. Three examples are briefly described here.

Hebbar (2011: 202–4) describes how the Ho people of Mirra village in West Singhbhum district, Jharkhand, took the responsibility of looking after the forest:

> Some of the young villagers ... were upset by the idea of hiring outsiders for a job that could be performed by villagers. In retaliation, they cut down trees, which were marked out for the purpose of silkworm rearing. So, the concern over forest involved introspection on such acts of violence against the forest, wherein villagers were involved in aggravating the problem of degradation by cutting forest. They found themselves behaving like the forest department by disrespecting the forest and setting an aggressive relation with it.... They expressed distress over the rate of degradation and felt that not only will the villagers of Mirra suffer if this continues, but so will the villagers around it....
>
> The formation of VRDs (Van Raksha Dals/Forest Protection Groups), then involved a reflection on two important aspects regarding the forest: (a) control, i.e., who should be in charge of the forest and (b) what should be the methods and techniques that should be employed to restore the forest ... whether the forest should be rejuvenated along the principles set around tradition by respecting the boundaries of spirits ... or should they adopt modern principles of forest rejuvenation whereby the rates of reproduction of forest is sought to be altered by introducing fast growing trees, hybrid seeds, etc?

Hebbar points out that a significant point of contention between three Van Raksha Dals was whether or not to establish a relation with Tata Steel Rural Development Society; whether taking help from the body would involve finally compromising their independence. The coexistence of these *dals* (groups) kept the tension in the village alive. Each point of view was provided with space for contestation within the dynamics of day-to-day life. 'Differences, in this sense, are a field for contest and transgression. Thus, it is through transgression that villagers experiment with self-rule to constitute themselves as "subjects" and at the same time, to restore the forest' (Hebbar 2011: 206). The 'self' and the 'other' are constituted within the village space not only at the level of personal differences and village politics, but also at the level of their understanding and management of the forest (Hebbar 2011: 208).

Mendha-lekha are Gond villages in the Maoist-infested district of Garchiroli, Maharashtra. Here the people of the village have organized themselves to regenerate and protect their forest in accordance with their tradition (Tofa and Hiralal n.d.). Their efforts preceded the FRA of 2006. And this was the first village to be granted community rights over the forest under FRA 2006.

To take another instance, Claus and Hartig (2011) report on adivasi struggle against the Koel Karo hydroelectric project. A hydel project was proposed on the rivers Koel and Karo, about 80 kilometres south-west of the capital Ranchi in the state of Jharkhand. The project area lies at an average altitude of 480 metres and includes the districts of Singhbhum, Gumla, and Ranchi, mainly inhabited by the adivasi Mundas and Oraons. The hydel project was intended to generate 710 megawatts of electricity via different constructions distributed throughout these districts. The survey work carried out by the Bihar State Electricity Board had already commenced in 1956–7. According to the Koel Karo Jan Sangathan, 256 villages with a total population of 150,000, primarily adivasis, would have been affected by the project.

Further, Claus and Hartig point out, the people of the Koel Karo area had been living under constant threat and insecurity since the beginning of the project in the 1950s. This pressure resulted in lack of investment in land because of the fear of losing their property to the dam. People concentrated their energies in compelling the government to abandon the dam project. The period of resistance was very difficult. For instance, younger people did time-consuming work in the resistance movement as well as supporting their families financially.

The announcement of the closure of the project motivated the people to be autonomous, to form co-operatives for collective decision-making, and create the opportunity to design and implement their own plans for development in the area in the domains of education, health, agriculture, sustainable forestry, and fishery. They had plans for irrigation systems, water reservoirs, and the construction of small hydroelectric projects without displacing the population. In addition, a Munda school was set up, along with vocational training institutes, and the cultivation of fruit-bearing trees and other economically productive plants began. There were plans to provide special attention and assistance for development to support victims' families. All this has contributed to the strengthening of solidarity among the village community, and has also inspired other villages to join the development strategies of the Koel Karo Jan Sangathan.

The adivasi sensibility in India has emerged from the hard work of insurgency over two hundred years. It gives expression to the creative potential of 'insurgent energy'. It is grounded in the active principle of labour, namely its ability to say 'no', to withdraw, and to reflect on the conditions of its possibility.

ON LABOUR POTENTIAL

The indigenous perspective and the adivasi sensibility have each emerged in different historical contexts, but they share a common concern, namely to explore the human labour potential outside the frame and processes of the primitive accumulation of capital. The primitive accumulation of capital continues to determine the conversion of use value into exchange value. To convert use value into exchange value, it is necessary to use force to pull labour and the economy out of the 'state of nature'. When a thing is taken out of the state of nature, it becomes a commodity and has two sets of attributes: natural attributes (which make it useful), and those attributes that have been added by labour, because of which it can be consumed and has exchange value.

The primitive accumulation of capital determines the attributes of labour—its capacity for work that enables the production and reproduction of goods and services, and the potential of its identity and being (Marx 1974: part viii and chapter 1, sections 1, 2). Capital shapes the capacity for work as well as the possibilities of production and reproduction in particular historical conditions. From this, labour acquires its teleology—its direction, purpose, and meaning. Labour 'has to' serve capital, it is subsumed under it, and it is directed by the economy of rates of profit. Over time, the rates of rates of profit increase, and, in direct proportion, the rates of extraction of natural resources also increase. The rate of extraction is several times higher than the rates at which these resources can regenerate.

Consequently, labour and economy are progressively disembedded from nature. This shapes the ontology of labour: it continues to acquire a consciousness of itself as well as of its being-in-the-world as part of the process that transforms use value into exchange value. And the agency of labour is impaired because it has no control over the means of subsistence.

Under these circumstances, labour consciousness is dislocated from its conscience. The formation of the exchange value of its identity and of its being-in-the-world does not correspond to what labour is in itself, its potential (its ontology).

The indigenous perspective and the adivasi sensibility argue that the potential of labour comes forth in experiments with saying 'no' to primitive accumulation, and prepares the ground for embedding economy in the rhythms of nature. This process simultaneously embeds labour in its own nature, which is more than the metabolic process of human biology and industrial productivity. These experiments are testimony to the fact that the capacity to think itself 'over and over again' (to self-correct its course, and reflect on itself and its foundations) on which labour 'rests' is the gift of nature. Rest is not just the ability to retreat and be in a state of repose; it is an attribute of labour time for determining care as a mode of being-in-the-world.

REFERENCES

Agamben, Giorgio. 1999. *Potentialities: Collected Essays in Philosophy*, trans. Daniel Heller-Roazen. Stanford: Stanford University Press.

Arya, Shachi. 1998. *Tribal Activism: Voices of Protest*. Jaipur: Rawat Publications.

Baden-Powell, B. H. 1974. First published in 1892. *Land Systems of British India: A Manual of Land Tenure and Systems of Administration Prevalent in Several Provinces*, 3 vols. Oxford: Clarendon Press.

Barsh, Russel Lawrence. 1986. 'Indigenous Peoples: An Emerging Object of International Law', *American Journal of International Law*, vol. 80, no. 2, pp. 369–85.

Belmekki, Belkacem. 2008. 'A Wind of Change: The New British Colonial Policy in Post-revolt India', *Atlantis: Journal of the Spanish Association of Anglo-American Studies*, vol. 30, no. 2.

Berat, Lynn. 1993. 'Genocide: The Namibian Case against Germany', *Pace International Law Review*, vol. 5, no. 1.

Claus, Martina and Sebastian Hartig. 2011. 'The Koel Karo Hydel Project: An Empirical Study of the Resistance Movement of the Adivasi in Jharkhand/India'. Available at: http://www.adivasi-koordination.de/dokumente/Diplomarbeit_KoelKaro_summary.pdf (accessed 4 June 2015).

Ghosal, Somnath. 2011. 'Pre-Colonial Forest Culture in the Presidency of Bengal', *Human Geographies: Journal of Studies in Human Geography*, vol. 5, no. 1.

Grove, Richard. 1995. *Green Imperialism: Colonial Expansion, Tropical Island Edens and the Origins of Environmentalism, 1600–1800*. Cambridge: Cambridge University Press.

Guha, Ranajit. 1983. *Elementary Aspects of Peasant Insurgency in Colonial India*. Delhi: Oxford University Press.
Gulli, Bruno. 2005. *Labor of Fire: The Ontology of Labor between Economy and Culture*. Philadelphia: Temple University Press.
Hebbar, Ritambhara. 2011. *Ecology, Equality and Freedom: The Engagement with Self-Rule in Jharkhand*. Navi Mumbai: Earthworm Books.
Jones, Adam. 2010. *Genocide: A Comprehensive Introduction*, 2nd edn. Oxford: Routledge. Available at: http://www.genocidetext.net/gaci_holocaust.pdf (accessed 2 June 2015).
Kapila, Kriti. 2008. 'The Measure of a Tribe: The Cultural Politics of Constitutional Reclassification in North India', *Journal of the Royal Anthropological Institute* (n.s.), vol. 14, pp. 117–34.
Khan, S. A. and H. bin Talal. 1987. *Indigenous Peoples: A Global Quest for Justice—A Report of the Independent Commission on International Humanitarian Issues*. London: Zed Books.
Lile, Hadi Khosravi. 2006. 'A New Era for Indigenous Peoples: The United Nations Permanent Forum on Indigenous Issues', *Galdu Cala: Journal of Indigenous Rights*, no. 2.
Luxemburg, Rosa. 1951. *The Accumulation of Capital*, trans. Agnes Schwarzschild, with a new Introduction by Tadeusz Kowalik. London: Routledge and Kegan Paul.
Mander, Jerry and Victoria Tauli-Corpuz (eds). 2006. *Paradigm Wars: Indigenous People's Resistance to Globalization*. San Francisco: Sierra Club Books.
Marx, Karl. 1974. *Das Capital*, vol. 1. Moscow: Progress Publishers.
Mann, C. Charles. 2006. *1491: New Revelations of the Americas Before Colombus*. New York: Vintage.
Moody, R. (ed.). 1988. *Indigenous Voices: Visions and Realities*, 2 vols. London: Zed Books.
Munda, R. D. and Sanjay Bosu-Mullick (eds). 2003. *The Jharkhand Movement: Indigenous People's Struggle for Autonomy in India*. Copenhagen: International Work Group for Indigenous Affairs.
Perelman, Michael. 2007. 'Primitive Accumulation from Feudal Times to Neoliberalism', *Capitalism, Nature, Socialism*, vol. 18, no. 2.
Popke, E. Jeffery. 2003. 'Managing Colonial Alterity: Narratives of Race, Space and Labour in Durban, 1870–1920', *Journal of Historical Geography*, vol. 29, no. 2, pp. 248–67.
Poupart, Lisa M. 2003. 'The Familiar Face of Genocide: Internalized Oppression among American Indians', *Hypatia*, vol. 18, no. 2.
Savyasaachi. 2004. 'Indigenous Peoples and Their Life Support Systems: A Perspective on Production Processes', in Eleonora Barbieri-Masini (ed.), *Quality of Human Resources: Disadvantaged People, Encyclopedia of Life Support Systems (EOLSS)*. Oxford: UNESCO, EOLSS Publishers.

Tofa, Devaji and Mohan Hirabai Hiralal. No date. 'Mendha (lekha): The Village That Declared, "We Have Our Government in Delhi and Mumbai but in Our Village We Ourselves Are the Government', published by Hirabai Hiralal, Chandrapur Maharashtra.

Uberoi, J. P. S. 2002. *European Modernity: Science, Truth and Method*. New Delhi: Oxford University Press.

von Werlhof, Claudia. 2000. '"Globalization" and the "Permanent" Process of "Primitive Accumulation": The Example of the MAI, the Multilateral Agreement on Investment', Special Issue: Festschrift for Immanuel Wallerstein, Part II, *Journal of World-Systems Research*, vol. 6, no. 3. Available at: http://www.jwsr.org/wp-content/uploads/2013/05/jwsr-v6n3-werlof.pdf (accessed 1 June 2015).

Yupsanis, Athanasios. 2010. 'ILO Convention No. 169 Concerning Indigenous and Tribal Peoples in Independent Countries, 1989–2009: An Overview', *Nordic Journal of International Law*, vol. 79, pp. 433–56.

3

'Hindus Have to Be Born as Hindus'

The Magic Wand of Brahminical Hinduism and Conversions

Biswamoy Pati

It is difficult for most of us to accept that originally we were all adivasis. Another related problem is the manner in which Hinduism is located as a religion wherein the concept of conversion does not exist. Traditionally, it is said that one cannot *become* a Hindu by conversion, since one has to be *born* a Hindu.[1] However, as this chapter, which draws upon my research in Odisha, will attempt to show, the ground realities of social

---

[1] Innumerable tracts have been published to justify this either directly or indirectly. Lamb and Bryant (1999: 1, 3) raise the question: 'Is there conversion to Hinduism?' They leave this question unresolved when they state that 'ethnic religions like Hinduism ... seem less concerned with conversion except in so far as it is a negative force they have to confront'. In the same volume, Taylor (1999) argues that conversion is not a burning issue within Hinduism and becomes one only when Hindus come into contact with other religions. The traditional conservative Hindu—whom he identifies as members of the Rashtriya Swayamsevak Sangh or the Arya Samaj—would not accept that a non-Hindu can convert to Hinduism. As Taylor (1999: 43) puts it: 'According to their way of thinking a person must be born a Hindu.' He finds this reasoning 'quite logical'. This is perhaps the most illogical argument seen in the context of South Asian history.

dynamics would appear to suggest something different, and this premise (that one cannot *become* a Hindu) may, in a profound sense, be open to contestation. After all, the history of the adivasis and the social process leading to their absorption into Brahminical Hinduism would, in fact, point to the gaps and contradictions existing between this kind of received wisdom (regarding the impossibility of 'conversion' to Hinduism) and the complexities of actual cultural practice on the ground. In other words, I would argue that the history of the tribal people would instead seem to suggest that, in an important sense, Hinduism did 'convert', and the chapter further goes on to raise the question whether adivasis and untouchables were/are Hindus in the first place.[2]

'Common sense' dictates that this absence of a system of conversion within Hinduism makes it, by implication, more humane, tolerant, and perhaps superior to proselytizing religions like Islam and Christianity. This, in fact, may be said to be one of the subtexts of the political discourse especially over the last two decades or so. However, it needs to be pointed out that the roots of such a perception, that proselytizing faiths are the 'Other', go back a longer way. While colonial exploitation and its association with Christianity have, among other features, contributed to the creation of this idea, colonial and post-colonial communal politics and, more recently, Hindu fundamentalism have sustained it. Here we should mention the stereotypical images of Christianity as fiercely proselytizing that one encounters in parts of India, more specifically in urban/coastal Odisha in the recent past. In fact, this has been the argument drawn upon to justify the violence directed against and the massacre of Christians under the aegis of the fascist, right-wing groups in Kandhamal in 2007 and 2008.

Interestingly enough, however, while the idea of conversion is presumed to be an impossibility in Hinduism, the concept of 're-conversion'—or *shuddhi*, as it has been defined since the nineteenth century—is considered acceptable by most scholars (Oddie 1977).[3] What is in fact striking is the order of purificatory rites and rituals associated

---

[2] Most of the materials on this subject—especially the articles and some of the books— are of very poor quality. A very long list of books and articles talk of conversions mostly to Christianity, but also to Buddhism, and are centred on case studies of individuals. I would like to mention two scholars who look at adivasis as non-Hindus in the pre-colonial period: Bhairabi Prasad Sahu (1986, 1987), and Richard M. Eaton (2000).

[3] In fact, J. T. F. Jordens (1977) accepts this unquestioningly.

with re-conversion in the way that it exists even today. In contemporary India, for instance, we witness a great deal of fanfare and media reports on the occasion of the 're-conversion' of adivasis to Hinduism.[4] What is lost sight of here seems to be the fact that adivasis were never Hindus to begin with. After all, can we locate adivasis as those who are 'born as Hindus'? This implies that, at least in this case, re-conversion is actually conversion. However, there is in general an unquestioning acceptance of their 're-conversion' to Hinduism—which goes hand in hand with an unquestioning acceptance of their original Hindu identity. In other words, their Hindu identity is taken for granted, which makes the notion of re-conversion perfectly possible, acceptable, and even justifiable.[5] One finds in all this a set of contradictions, which homogenizes all sections of adivasis and outcastes as Hindus.

Further, in the case of the adivasis and the outcastes, this process of 'Hinduization' or 'integration' into the varna order involves complex shifts in their identities. The question is whether it is possible for outcastes to be actually seen as Hindus, while being simultaneously located as the outcaste 'Other'.[6] More importantly, it needs to be emphasized that this process of 'integration' into the caste order involves a silent process of change, through which power is established over the adivasis and outcastes in order to exploit them.[7]

Consequently, this chapter interrogates the way conversion has been understood. It acknowledges that Hinduism does not convert in the same way as perhaps some other religions do. However, some process of 'conversion' can be traced among the adivasis and outcastes. I draw upon my research related to colonial/post-colonial Odisha to highlight how this process was marked by the interplay of a host of complex features,

---

[4] Interestingly, although they are defined as Hindus, Dalits (the exploited untouchables) are not allowed entry into the temple of Jagannath. 'They are'/'they are not' is a logic that is invoked to explain many things in the strangest possible ways. Thus, as argued by the Puri Sankaracharya some years ago, Harijans need not go into the temples since God himself will come to them (interview in the *Illustrated Weekly of India*, 24 July 1988).

[5] Oddie (1977: 1) refers to 'tribal' or 'primitive' religions within Hinduism, along with those influenced by beliefs and practices more characteristic of the 'brahminic tradition'. A rather crude homogenization results in such assertions.

[6] See, for example, Ilaiah (1996), to get an idea of this dimension.

[7] In fact, Weber (1967: 11–12, 16–17) speaks of how, in this manner, power and control were established over these people. He calls it 'discriminatory integration' in the social and economic sense, when it comes to the adivasis.

rooted in shifting material conditions and identities. Nevertheless, many of the problems highlighted in this chapter are applicable to different parts of this diverse country.

EXISTING STUDIES AND METHODS

Without going into too much detail, one can point to the focus of some scholars on individual converts.[8] Such efforts tend to individualize the experience, besides externalizing the process of conversions. They also tend to blur the internal dialectics of a colonial society. After all, religious conversions did not begin only with the advent of colonialism. Moreover, the economic dimensions associated with colonialism, and the manner in which they marked shifts and changes in a society which had a pre-colonial past, are not clearly delineated.

While dealing with conversions, the relevance as well as limitations of the concepts of Sanskritization and Hinduization should perhaps be delineated. Sanskritization was a route through which low castes were able to rise—over one or two generations—to a higher position in the hierarchy by adopting vegetarianism and teetotalism, and by sanskritizing their ritual and pantheon. One can agree with this argument as long as it is accepted that such shifts were linked to some degree of upward economic movement, and were not a one-way process involving the Hinduization of tribal beliefs (Srinivas 1952: 30–1).[9] Another problem inherent in this formulation is that it abstracts caste from deeper economic processes, and does not see the level of violence inflicted on adivasis and their ideas while negotiating this process. In fact, even sensitive socio-anthropological studies sometimes

---

[8] Oddie's *Religion* is a classic example. Scholars like Meera Kosambi (*Pandita Ramabai's Feminist and Christian Conversions: Focus on Stree Dharma-Neeti*), Uma Chakravarty (*Re-writing History: Life and Times of Pandita Ramabai*), and Gauri Vishwanathan (*Outside the Fold: Conversion, Modernity and Belief*) are more nuanced and accept the pluralities/complexities associated with the conversions to Christianity, Buddhism, and so on, which coexisted with a shift towards questioning Hindu patriarchy and caste oppression.

[9] As Srinivas (1952: 30) puts it, such movement was possible especially for those in the middle regions of the hierarchy. This perhaps implies some degree of affluence, which needs to be stressed. I would also like to refer here to Weber (1967) and his 'diffusion model'. The basic problem with this model is that it locates this movement as a one-way process involving the Hinduization of tribal beliefs.

categorically assert that Hindu civilization did not on the whole seek to convert or displace tribals, although they agree that conflicts were frequent, and that tribes were forced to retreat to the 'remotest areas'— namely the forests and mountains (Padel 1995: 17). Taken together, these arguments contradict the 'civilizational' claims of Hinduism.[10] In fact, if anything, the opposite seems to be the case. Thus, what has been witnessed is a process of hegemonization through which Brahminical Hinduism actually operates. Its exploitative content vis-à-vis those who were incorporated and hierarchized, while being 'Hinduized', should not be overlooked.[11] Similarly, Brahminical Hinduism was/is marked by a high degree of exclusiveness, involved in the very idea of keeping the order of varna 'clean' and 'pure', especially when it comes to those who are located as outcastes, as also sections of adivasis. It also needs to be mentioned here that this process was not a one-way affair. It was/is not only contested and interrogated, but has also changed and evolved. It was/is marked by a host of complexities which have to be taken into account by any social historian.

THE BACKGROUND

Talking specifically about pre-colonial, but especially early medieval Orissa (now known as Odisha), scholars like Bhairabi Prasad Sahu highlight the dynamics of the feudalization of this region. The manifestations of this process included, at one extreme, the emergence of intermediaries and superior landlords, and at the other end the reduction of peasants and artisans to the position of semi-serfs. As suggested, the caste system developed late in Orissa, and when it did (over the tenth–eleventh centuries AD), it was marked by certain features and points of difference in comparison to the Indo-Gangetic plains model (Sahu 1986, 1987). This was primarily because of the preponderant tribal population and the geographical variations in the region, with its coastal tract and hilly/

---

[10] A major exponent of this 'civilizational' character of Hinduism is Ravinder Kumar. I am not aware of any serious work by him on the subject, though he has published short newspaper pieces. This right-wing position veils the basic components of terror and violence directed against adivasis and outcastes by Brahminical Hinduism.

[11] While disagreeing with most of what Dumont (1980) says, I find his assertion that Brahminical Hinduism incorporates and hierarchizes very valuable.

forested interior. As a result, the land grants to Brahmins and the extension of agriculture implied the conversion of most of the tribes into Sudras, which converged with the process of their peasantization. Alongside this, their chiefs were absorbed as Kshatriyas into the varna system. This implied the absence of any rigid polarization. The classic fourfold varna system continued to remain largely notional, as in practice the two-tier structure with numerous intermediary occupational castes constituted the functional reality. Consequently, we see the evolution of two clearly identifiable varnas—the Brahmins and the Sudras. The Vaishyas were not really visible in society, though men of substance appropriated this status for themselves. This implied that the Vaishyas surfaced in epigraphical sources only occasionally in times of trade. Similarly, the Kshatriyas never had local roots, and were created in this period of state formation (from clan to caste society) that saw shifts in the identity of adivasi chieftains, who invented this category for themselves. The rise of the Kshatriyas/Karanas was a feature associated with the emergence of feudalism. As delineated, the varna system was a major legitimizing force in this process of state formation.[12]

The research of Richard M. Eaton (1993, 2000) on the Bengal frontier for a slightly later period demonstrates the way in which agricultural expansion involved the process of Islamization of the adivasis. What is

---

[12] See Sahu (1986, 1987). Datta (1989) does refer to the phenomenon of land grants to Brahmins; what one needs to emphasize here is that they also emerged from within stratified adivasi society. Kulke (1976) focuses on the issue of Kshatriyaization in the context of medieval Orissa, and extends its relevance up to the seventeenth–eighteenth centuries AD. He emphasizes this process as more useful/relevant than Brahminization and the functional reality. Sinha (1995) feels that the diffusion of the Rajput model of the state and indigenous developmental processes could gain ground only among those tribal groups who had attained the technological level of settled agriculture. Thus, as he puts it, we do not find shifting cultivating groups like the Juangs or the Hill Bhuiyas of Orissa developing a kingship supported mainly by their primitive technique of cultivation. However, Sinha (1995: 335) makes it clear that the use of the plough was not essential to determine the rise of kingship. Guha (1999: 110–16) also refers to certain aspects of 'Rajputization' affecting some of the adivasi communities. Interestingly, Beverley (1872: 193) mentions the absence of a 'pure' Kshatriya caste in Orissa and refers to the Khandaits (swordsmen) who formed the erstwhile militia and who took their caste from their profession, which corresponds to the military class in the fourfold division of northern India.

fresh about these two approaches is their openness and the way they engage with a reality that saw various shifts. Whereas in pre-colonial Orissa it meant Hinduization, in the case of the Bengal frontier it was associated with Islamization. In both cases, one sees the way the non-Hindu adivasis were integrated into the process of feudalization with the expansion of agriculture.

Colonialism reinforced the existing situation through various interventions, but most significantly through land settlements and the commercialization of agriculture. One obviously important point was a sharpening of the caste/class polarization, which had a clear association with agrarian interventions, irrigation, commercialization of agriculture (howsoever limited), and an increasing degree of monetization.[13] In fact, a very superficial survey of some of the available land settlement reports of the Temporarily Settled Areas of Cuttack, Puri, and Balasore, the princely states, and some of the major zamindaris illustrates the rather serious fallout of the agrarian interventions and the expansion of cultivation, especially the way they polarized social relations centred around caste (Pati 1993: chapter 1, pp. 1–60).

These processes had a bearing on the question of conversion, since the land settlements entailed a set of complex negotiations with the adivasis. Certain features of the context are perhaps reflected in the way the Rana tribes of Jeypore wore the 'sacred thread' and believed that they had bought the right to do so from the Maharaja of Jeypore (Senapati and Sahu 1966: 110). What deserves emphasis is the significance of this language of exchange that was applied to the sacred realm. We also witness the Gonds of Sambalpur inventing new legends to relocate themselves within the framework of Hinduism, and the Gond zamindars wearing the 'sacred thread' (O'Malley 1932: 70).[14] These practices not only implied a degree of Hinduization, but also a strategy to cope with the agrarian interventions. Thus, the Kandhas of Ranpur (a princely state) preferred to be identified as 'Oriya Kandhas'—indicating thereby an allied component of this process, namely Oriyaization (Singh 1963: 10).

---

[13] One has to be very cautious in accepting the variations between the erstwhile Mughalbandi (coastal tract) and the western interior. For details, see Chaudhury (1991), Rout (1986), and especially Padhi (1999) for the variations between the coastal and the western tracts.

[14] Senapati and Mohanty (1971: 117) refer to Gond zamindars wearing the 'sacred thread'.

It needs to be pointed out that the importance of the Kshatriyas continued—perhaps even more so now. After all, the colonialists needed to have 'settlements' with 'rulers'—especially the princes and the landed zamindars. Here the classic varna system was invoked to get legitimacy for alliances with the Kshatriyas who were 'rulers'. Starting from the Raja of Puri—who was 'a king without a kingdom'[15]—this interaction reinforced the pre-existing order of things we have already encountered, along with Orissa's colonization. The other vital component included the relatively affluent agriculturists, including a section of the adivasis. Many from this section emerged as 'rich' peasants over the nineteenth century. Here one is talking about those who did well in the new 'production for the grain market' environment and claimed Khandayat (the Oriya variant of Kshatriya) status. *Khanda* means a sword, and Khandayat means 'sword wielder'. In fact, this caste accommodated a wide variety of the prosperous section of the adivasis as well. This implied a level of Rajputization/Kshatriyaization that converged with Hinduization, and affected the affluent sections of the adivasis.[16]

Some of the references in the census reports also offer clues to understand this process. For example, the first census report mentions

---

[15] After all, the Raja of Puri was actually the Raja of Khurda, which was taken over by the British. The Khurda raja was, in fact, reinvented as the Raja of Puri—and Orissa—and compensated as the superintendent of the Jagannath temple; for details, see Kulke (1987).

[16] Leading anthropologists like F. G. Bailey (1996) also see the Oriyas as migrants to the Kandha hills. As he puts it, in the 1950s, Oriyas were about three in every eight of the population, and he feels that they were probably fewer at the beginning of the century (1996: 3). Although the question of Oriya migrants cannot be disputed, Bailey cannot conceptualize their emergence from among the Kandhas itself. Thus, the hillman/plainsman dichotomy is a feature haunting even sensitive scholars like Bailey. What needs to be also borne in mind is a complexity where 'Oriyas'—besides being migrants—emerged from among the adivasis in the pre-colonial and colonial period, as we have sought to demonstrate. Thus, castes like the warrior caste that Bailey refers to (Paikas or Khandayats) also emerged from among the Kandhas and other adivasi groups. This in fact illustrates the process of conversions of adivasis via Hinduization/ Kshatriyaization/Oriyaization, and Bailey's reference to the Oriyas should also be seen as an extension of this process that was perhaps 'happening' even while Bailey was doing his fieldwork in the area. Weber (1967) in fact mentions how those who sought assimilation got integrated with the Hindu community, and through this the 'barbarians' who formed the ruling stratum 'secured their superiority over the subject classes'.

the presence of 'numerous' Savaras (adivasis) in the Cuttack and Puri tracts (Beverley 1872: 191). At the same time, a very superficial survey of the tribal population shows a decline between 1891 and 1941 in some parts of Orissa, although there is no serious reason to explain this. One also sees a very large increase in the Khandayat population—45.4 per cent (the largest for any caste)—between 1901 and 1931 in the Orissa division and the Orissa states (based on Lacey 1933: 267). It is important to grasp that a large number of adivasis identified themselves as Khandayats. Consequently, the connection between a decline in the adivasi population and the phenomenal increase of Khandayats should be borne in mind while discussing the question of conversions and Hinduization in Odisha.

Shifting identities marked the phenomenon of conversion. For example, according to a legend of the Binjhals (adivasis) of the Sambalpur region, the mother of the first Chauhan Raja of Patana had taken shelter in the hut of a Binjhal. Here she gave birth to Ramai, who became the king of Patana and made the Binjhal the chief of Borasambar. We also come across some 'advanced' Binjhals claiming Rajput status and adopting the 'Hindu' practice of burning (instead of burying) their dead (Senapati and Mohanty 1971: 118; Senapati and Sahu 1968: 103).[17] The emulation relating to the disposal of the dead symbolized an attempt to get incorporated into the Brahminical order.

Given this complexity, it is in fact quite usual to come across innumerable references to a fractured adivasi reality, which speaks of two chief categories of adivasis—the plains people and the *pahariah* (*pahar* = hill) or *dongariah* (*dongar* = shifting cultivation) adivasis, with the colonial establishment clearly admiring the former.[18] Most adivasis who converted to Hinduism, at least in the initial years—via the varna system—retained their specific social and religious customs. The Brahminical order was quite comfortable with this aspect. After all, they were 'ancient people' who had to maintain their customs. This process implied that while being integrated into the Brahminical order, they were also being hierarchized. Thus, it would, for example, be difficult to talk about adivasis gaining acceptance as Brahmins in

---

[17] O'Malley (1932: 70) refers to 'rich' Binjhals being burnt.
[18] Lieutenant Elliot (Deputy Commissioner of Raipur), 'Report on Kalahandi State, 28 July, 1856', cited in Senapati and Kuanr (1980: 473); hereafter Elliot's Report.

any major way.[19] In fact, the Rajputization scheme and categories like '*haliya* Brahmins' (*hala* = plough; Brahmins who were agriculturists) have to be borne in mind while explaining the limits up to which such transgressions could be normally accepted.[20] These were perhaps the most common routes through which the process of conversion seems to have been channelized. Thus, the adivasi chiefs and the affluent sections got linked to the caste system through these routes. Nevertheless, what is observable is their 'acceptance' into the system, albeit with clear boundaries and hierarchization. Thus, the Hinduized Kandhas of Puri, for example, employed Brahmin priests. More significantly, given their position in the hierarchy of caste, they had to employ 'low Brahmins' from among low-caste Hindus, who were elevated as a consequence as well (O'Malley 1913: 235). These aspects illustrate a process where class and social position mattered.

As mentioned earlier, social position was closely related to the question of conversions of the adivasis. This was also a vital reason why the landless outcastes were kept out of this process. If anything, their position became further marginalized with the polarization of the caste system. They were distinctly classified as the 'Other'. This meant that whereas some of the adivasis were forced to shift over (via the caste formation process) to Hinduism, the landless outcaste was considered to be a major threat not only to the 'purity' of the varna system, but also to the colonial system, as it were. Thus, whereas some of the 'animists' were 'civilized', the landless outcaste had to be 'tamed' and negotiated as 'criminal classes'.[21]

Consequently, there appears to have been a shift from the pre-colonial times in the way the adivasis were relocated. This was the result of a very complex dialectical process involving the varna system, which

[19] Some scholars tend to overemphasize the 'openness' of the caste system in Orissa; see, for example, Dash (1989: 16–17).

[20] Haliya Brahmins included those who took to agriculture mostly in the coastal tract. Most probably the category included some who desired upward social mobility, or sections of Brahmins who faced marginalization.

[21] Clarke (1908) indicates a classification strategy that incorporated this thrust. In fact, Clarke's idea was to rehabilitate the adivasis in Angul by giving them 'good' land and loans. Needless to say, the ideas related to the outcastes were most clearly influenced by the upper-caste tradition of Orissa. References to the common Oriya saying *chora chandala* (a thief and an outcaste), which suggests an interchangeability between the two, should be borne in mind in comprehending the way the varna order locates the outcaste.

seems to have opened up a space for 'integration' by incorporating a large section of the adivasis as Khandayats/Kshatriyas, and by adivasi society itself negotiating the new context and adopting conversion as part of a broad survival strategy. Among the several complex features of this situation, one notes that most of the big zamindars and especially the princes—many of whom were literally colonial constructs—went all out to prove their association with the adivasis. This was vital to prove their ancientness. Many folktales that were invented to establish this also served the purpose of securing legitimacy and exercising power over the adivasis.[22]

These features were intimately associated with the popularity and expansion of Jagannath worship, and coexisted with drives to build Hindu temples in parts of western Odisha. Thus, the temple-building project of the tahsildar Dinabandhu Patnaik involved building a Shiva *mandira* (temple for Shiva) in 1855 at Bisipara. This was Patnaik's headquarters. In fact, it was not built only by the people of Bisipara, but by people of the Kandhamal region through *bethi* (forced, usually unpaid, labour) (Bailey 1996: 18–19).[23] In this way, Hinduization made deep inroads into western Odisha.

Thus, what can be seen is the emergence of a system—however invisible it might have been—to direct the conversions to Hinduism. This entailed mainly two methods. The first was comparatively non-violent and long-drawn, and, in this sense, a hegemonic process. Although it had pre-colonial roots, it was substantially altered over the nineteenth century.[24] The second method included a set of terror campaigns unleashed by

---

[22] Even a cursory look at most of the revenue settlement reports illustrates this aspect. One may also cite here 'The Brief Histories of Each of the 24 States (1909)', R/2 (285/1), Crown Representative Papers, India Office Library, London. The importance of the tribal population can also be grasped from the fact that the head of a particular Kandha family (Pat Majhi) made the young prince of Kalahandi sit on his lap during his coronation. Such features not only reveal the complex process of the peasantization/Hinduization of the tribals, but also the pre-colonial ruling class' attempt to seek legitimacy from the tribals, especially the Kandhas who formed a major component of the tribal population; for details, see Elliot's Report, pp. 478–9 (457–82).

[23] The practice of bethi or forced labour coexisted with the drive to build Jagannath temples.

[24] As long as one sees things in the perspective outlined in this chapter, one can agree up to a point with Srinivas (1952: 31) regarding the role of caste in enabling Hinduism to proselytize without the aid of a church.

colonialism and the privileged tenure holders in the hills.[25] These were marked by sudden disruptions. What is, of course, clearly observable is the relative unity of the different constituents involved in the conversion of the adivasis—the Brahminical order, the internal exploiting classes, and, last but not least, colonialism. Compared to the pre-colonial context, this process saw continuities as well as shifts and changes. Thus, the Kshatriyaization component seems to have continued on a much wider scale, incorporating the non-pahariah adivasis into the 'order' of Hinduism, unlike in the early medieval period, when most of them were sought to be 'integrated' as Sudras. In fact, the nineteenth century saw a toning down of this process, unlike what has been observed by Sahu (1986, 1987) for early medieval Orissa. It was largely inclusive vis-à-vis the already peasantized adivasis, or those who—with the exception of the pahariah folk—opted to work as settled agriculturists.

CONVERSIONS TO CHRISTIANITY

We next take up the question related to conversions to Christianity. This was rather nuanced, and not as simple as it is normally made out to be either in the missionary tracts or in the Oriya press.[26] Moreover, it should be made adequately clear that the magnitude of conversions to Christianity was hardly felt in the region, in spite of the projections. The association of Christianity with colonialism was a major stumbling block, and this perhaps explains why it was never seen as a serious option, although considerable efforts were made in this direction and many outposts were created for the purpose.

However, certain complexities associated with the shift to Christianity should be delineated here. In a context of uncertainties and insecurities, the Oraons, for example, felt that Christianity protected them from

---

[25] As pointed out by Weber (1967: 18), this process was marked by a certain degree of internalization of the caste hierarchies of the Hindu order by the underprivileged strata. I have discovered this particular aspect in parts of coastal Odisha during my own fieldwork in the 1990s.

[26] A typical example of the thinking on missionary tracts may be found in Anon (1858), which refers to Gunga Dhor (one of the early converts) testing the divinity of Jagannath by abusing 'him' and scratching 'his' back with a pointed iron, since he had not responded to his petition. Oriya newspapers like the *Utkala Dipika* (9 February 1867, 23 February 1867) projected the activities of the Christian missionaries in the context of the 1866 famine.

witches and *bhoots* (ghosts) who were powerless against this system (Dalton 1872: 247). Perhaps these beliefs need to be located as metaphors signifying the intrusion of Brahminical Hinduism that spelt doom in the form of dispossession. Moreover, like the converts to the varna order who participated in Hindu as well as tribal festivals, the converts to Christianity observed certain customs and beliefs that were antithetical to the basic tenets of Christianity. They participated in tribal festivals and, when asked about their identity, mentioned their tribe, suppressing the Christian connection (Senapati and Sahu 1966: 121–2).

THE GANDHIAN PHASE AND HINDUIZATION

The Indian national movement seems to have made a distinct mark on the process of conversion.[27] In the specific context of Odisha, Gandhian politics were indeed very influential. Nevertheless, this would have not been possible if Hinduization and the process of conversions, along with other associated complexities, had not prepared the background for Gandhian politics. In fact, Gandhian politics saw the advent of a new phase in the history of conversions. Adivasis and outcastes in large numbers gave up beef and liquor.[28] The Gandhian idea of renaming the outcastes 'Harijans' (children of God) created a certain level of 'respectability' for these discriminated sections. Even though limited, since the issues affecting the outcastes were never taken up for any questioning, this inclusive component of Gandhian politics made deep

---

[27] Historians seem to be taking note of the possibilities of conversions in Hinduism, specifically in the context of the development of Gandhian nationalism. See, for example, Sarkar (1985), who does not consider the possibility of conversion in Hinduism. In contrast, see an updated version of this article in Sarkar (2011: 65), where she begins by referring to Jitu Santal (the leader of the tribal movement she examines) being converted to Hinduism by Congressmen in 1926. The nuances and fluidities of this shift are subsequently developed in the chapter.

[28] See, for example, All India Congress Committee Papers, File no. P20/1940, Private Papers Section, Nehru Memorial Museum & Library, New Delhi. I am not for a moment discounting the pluralism associated with the perceptions of Gandhian calls for solidarity that also included 'distributing' opium after 'looting' them from shops that we see in the context of Koraput during the 1942 Movement; for details see Pati (1988: 195–7). However, at this point I am examining the issue from the side of the people who accepted vegetarianism and gave up beef and liquor.

inroads into different parts of the region and connected the socially discriminated to the national movement.[29] What developed was the extension and the coexistence of the process of Hinduization with a social-reformist current under the aegis of the Gandhian-led national movement. The dialectics of these processes worked to harmonize the 'integration' of the adivasis and the outcastes with the anti-colonial struggle, without confronting the Brahminical order in any way.

It is very important to emphasize here that for the adivasis and the outcastes, vegetarianism was a major sacrifice, especially for those who were not settled agriculturists, and who did not have any stable source of income. After all, it meant giving up readily available food from the forests and rivers, or beef when someone's cow in the village died.[30] Gandhism reworked the logic of Hinduization by providing a space and a possibility—howsoever limited—to outcastes and adivasis to get limited access, especially in terms of gaining some self-respect in their immediate environment, and through this it incorporated a large number of them into the struggle against colonialism.

At the same time, given the nuances and complexities of Gandhian nationalism in Odisha, it also reinforced both Hinduization and the conversion of adivasis and outcastes along with its inclusive and 'integrative' character. This entailed a new thrust when it came to the question of conversions in the post-1920s period.

POST-COLONIAL ORISSA

Like many other features, the process of conversions and the Hinduization associated with it continued after India became a free country. The compulsions of the new state and its efforts to establish itself saw a new thrust. The administration in Odisha stuck to symbols that had made

---

[29] One may cite here the surname 'Harijan' adopted by Dalits in western Orissa—a feature I have encountered during fieldwork.

[30] Bailey (1996: 39) in fact refers to the Panas and the idea of enjoying a meal when someone's cow died. Amin (1995: chapter 15, 101–6) touches upon the issue of vegetarianism and abstinence from liquor. However, what eludes him is the fact that this was a very major sacrifice for the marginalized adivasis, low castes, and outcastes. Besides animal flesh and fish, it meant giving up *salapa* and *tari* that could be tapped from the trees in the forests, or *handia* that could be made at home. And, taken together, it meant giving up major constituents of their diet.

deep inroads in the region, like Jagannath. One is reminded here of the Bondas—an adivasi community of Koraput—who had to go through revenue settlements in the 1950s and 1960s. A method that clearly harked back to the colonial past saw the district administration selecting the oldest-looking man in the village, who was 'declared' to be the maharajah, through whom the settlement was apparently negotiated. He was given a rusty sword and a wooden chair as his throne. And, although he complained to me that he was among the poorest people in the village—worse than 'the king without a kingdom'—the administration had managed to achieve its mission.[31] After this, the process of imposing the new 'gods' and the Brahminical order began in the region, which had remained somewhat isolated from the process of Hinduization.

In the absence of colonialism, the situation with regard to opting for Christianity also changed. In the 1950s, some Kandhas, for example, adopted Christianity, which was no longer identified with the government and offered a defence against Hindu exploitation (Padel 1995: 10), and the process of Hinduization. However, this was/is far from being uniform.

The situation has indeed altered since the late 1980s, with an unprecedented level of homogenization and religious polarization.[32] The way the post-Ayodhya polarization has impacted the adivasis can be judged from the manner in which the Kandhas in Phulbani clashed with Panas (low castes/outcastes) in 1994, denying them entry into a Hindu (Shiva) temple.[33] This is indeed an irony since, as discussed earlier, Brahminical Hinduism extracted the forced labour of adivasis—who may have very well included some Kandhas of the region—to set up a Shiva temple in the 1850s. Thus, whereas some Kandhas have perhaps been integrated into the varna order over these years, some others who may have technically remained outside its fold see themselves as Hindus today. Communalism and divisive politics have entered Orissa and have attained

---

[31] I have seen both the sword and the 'throne' (wooden chair). Personal interviews in the Bonda hills, Koraput.

[32] There have been quite a few writings on this subject; see especially Panikkar (1999).

[33] This was a fallout of a Pana youth entering the Shiva mandira in the village of Khudutentuli (Phulbani district) on 14 January 1994; the conflict that this episode triggered lasted till June. Oriya dailies like *Samaj* and *Prajatantra* reported the clashes and the subsequent mobilization; see Mohapatra and Bhattacharya (1995).

a high level of aggressiveness. This has been legitimized not only by the political process, but also by the electronic and the print media, and by scholars and intellectuals.[34] Alongside, the middle class has earned for itself some degree of respectability. This has assumed alarming proportions with anti-Christian mobilization of adivasis by fascist outfits associated with the 'Sangh Parivar' (the fascist family of the Rashtriya Swayamsevak Sangh) to target Dalit converts to Christianity over 2007–8, features that pose a serious threat to the very existence of civil society (Pati 2008a, 2008b).

POSTSCRIPT

Odisha was in the news in 2008. Unlike the rumours that were manufactured and circulated in December 2007, the news of Swami Laxmanananda Saraswati's death in 2008 was real. Nevertheless, very much like the previous time, the Vishva Hindu Parishad (VHP) had gone berserk again. Political murders, the killing of Christians (as 'imagined murderers'), and the vandalization of churches assumed monstrous proportions in the Kandhamals. The violence inflicted was meticulously planned and executed over two to three days, during which the Odisha government and its affiliated agencies seemed overwhelmed by what was going on.

When Mahatma Gandhi visited coastal Orissa in 1921, he said: 'I was prepared to see skeletons in Orissa but not to the extent I did. I had seen terrible pictures but the reality was too terrible' (*Young India*, April 1921). In fact, if he had visited western Orissa or the Kandhamal region today, he would have perhaps repeated this sentiment. After all, communalized perceptions do seem to cloud the real world of poverty, hunger, and unemployment, which is indeed a cruel joke considering the fact that we are talking about a region that has a predominantly tribal and Dalit population, where more than 55 per cent of the people and 89 per cent of families live below the poverty line. In fact, in the present context, Orissa seems to pose a serious set of problems for the very existence of 'civil society'. And going by Saraswati's murder and the subsequent killings, political scientists may well argue that what is being witnessed today indicates the breakdown of civil society. However, the deeper question is: has this tract ever seen civil society?

[34] Here I have in mind a large number of studies that project the Jagannath 'cult' as 'Orissa's cult'; I would include the Eschmann et al. edited *The Cult of Jagannatha* (1978).

This question needs to be located in a context where the government has virtually abdicated its responsibility of providing the basic features of civil society, including the possibilities of basic livelihood, education, and health. In the absence of any land reforms or governmental interventions designed to improve the condition of the poor, the schools and ashrams provide meagre alternatives, along with institutions run by the VHP, the Christian missionaries, and non-governmental organizations (NGOs).

Ironically, the activities of the VHP correspond to what they accuse the Christian missionaries of doing in western Odisha. Both work to attract and convert people to their respective faiths—something that is allowed under the Indian Constitution. Moreover, both have access to resources—internal and external—to be used towards the uplift of the poor. But then, how does one explain the way in which the term 'conversion' appears to be synonymous with Christian missionaries? This might appear to be a profound question. But this is precisely where the 'Sangh Parivar's' majoritarian and hegemonic hold needs to be grasped. This hold is sustained by poverty, lack of land struggles and reforms, and the virtual non-existence of either civil society or the state in this area. It is further clothed by a finely crafted 'reality' created by the VHP. One could cite two clear examples to illustrate this point: (*a*) the idea that tribals are Hindus and Christian missionaries are villains who are spreading Christianity through inducements and converting poor and ignorant tribals; and (*b*) the claim that the VHP has the right to re-convert them to their original faith. It is indeed amazing that most of the reports on Kandhamal wrongly assume that tribals are Hindus. In fact, what the 'Sangh Parivar' has been attempting in Odisha their post-Gujarat laboratory—is the large-scale conversion of tribals to Hinduism. This is skilfully combined with terrorizing sections of Dalits, who had opted to convert to Christianity after suffering social discrimination and exclusion, to re-convert to Hinduism.

This 'common sense' makes the conversion of tribals appear as 're-conversion'. This has been skilfully woven with terror directed against Dalit Christians over quite some time. More significantly, the majoritarian orientation of such conversion drives and their ancillaries—namely the ghee-burning *shuddhi karan* (re-conversion) rituals, as seen through the electronic media—hides the real agenda. It is this 'common sense' that has enabled the VHP to make serious inroads into Odisha, even as the world debates the conflicts among Dalit (Panas) Christians and the adivasis (Kandhas) over diverse issues. The real problem in Kandhamal is related to the aggressive drives to convert tribals to Hinduism, including terror directed at Dalit Christians, who are the stumbling blocks in the path of the 'Sangh Parivar' and the VHP.

REFERENCES

Amin, Shahid. 1995. *Event, Metaphor, Memory: Chauri Chaura, 1922–1992*. Berkeley and Los Angeles: University of California Press.
Anon. 1858. *A Brief Sketch of the Rise and Progress of the Baptist Church Orissa Mission*. Cuttack: Mission Press.
Bailey, F. G. 1996. *The Civility of Indifference: On Domesticating Ethnicity*. Ithaca: Cornell University Press.
Beverley, H. 1872. *Report on the Census of Bengal, 1872*. Calcutta: Bengal Secretariat Press.
Chakravarty, Uma. 1998. *Re-writing History: Life and Times of Pandita Ramabai*. New Delhi: Kali for Women.
Chaudhury, Pradipta. 1991. 'Peasants and British Rule in Orissa', *Social Scientist*, vol. 19, no. 7, pp. 28–56.
Clarke, R. 1908. 'Panas of Orissa', in M. Kennedy, *Notes on Criminal Classes in the Bombay Presidency with Appendices regarding some Foreign Criminals Who Occasionally Visit the Presidency including Hints on the Detection of Counterfeit Coin*. Bombay: Government Central Press, pp. 324–9.
Dalton, E. T. 1872. *Descriptive Ethnology of Bengal*. Calcutta: Government Press.
Dash, Gaganendra Nath. 1989. *Hindus and Tribals: Quest for a Co-existence (Social Dynamics in Medieval Orissa)*. New Delhi: Decent Books.
Datta, Swati. 1989. *Migrant Brahmanas in Northern India: Their Settlement and General Impact c. A.D. 475–1030*. New Delhi: Motilal Banarsidass.
Dumont, Louis. 1980. *Homo Hierarchicus: The Caste System and Its Implications*, trans. Mark Sainsbury, Louis Dumont, and Basia M. Gulati. Chicago and London: Chicago University Press.
Eaton, Richard M. 1993. *The Rise of Islam and the Bengal Frontier, 1204–1760*. Berkeley: California University Press.
———. 2000. 'Who Are the Bengali Muslims? Conversion and Islamisation in Bengal', in *Essays on Islam and Indian History*. New Delhi: Oxford University Press, pp. 259–75.
Eschmann, A. Hermann Kulke, and Gaya Charan Tripathi (eds). 1978. *The Cult of Jagannatha and the Regional Tradition of Orissa*. New Delhi: Manohar.
Guha, Sumit. 1999. *Environment and Ethnicity in India, 1200–1991*. Cambridge: Cambridge University Press.
Ilaiah, Kancha. 1996. *Why I Am Not a Hindu: A Sudra Critique of Hindutva, Philosophy, Culture and Political Economy*. Calcutta: Samya.
Jordens, J. T. F. 1977. 'Reconversion to Hinduism, the Shuddhi of the Arya Samaj', in G. A. Oddie (ed.), *Religion in South Asia: Religious Conversion and*

Revival Movements in South Asia in Medieval and Modern Times. London: Curzon Press, pp. 145–69.
Kosambi, Meera. 1995. *Pandita Ramabai's Feminist and Christian Conversions: Focus on Stree Dharma-Neeti.* Mumbai: SNDT Women's University.
Kulke, Hermann. 1976. 'Kshatriyaisation and Social Change: A Study in Orissa Setting', in S. D. Pillai (ed.), *Aspects of Change in India: Studies in Honour of Prof. G. S. Ghurye.* Bombay: Popular Prakashan, pp. 398–411.
——. 1987. 'The Struggle between the Rajas of Khurda and the Muslim Subahdars of Cuttack for the Dominance of the Jagannath Temple', in A. Eschmann, H. Kulke, and G. C. Tripathy (eds), *The Cult of Jagannath and the Regional Tradition of Orissa.* New Delhi: Manohar, pp. 345–57.
Lacey, W. G. 1933. *Census of India, 1931,* vol. VII: *Bihar and Orissa,* part I: *Report.* Patna: Superintendent Government Printing.
Lamb, Christopher, and M. Darrol Bryant. 1999. 'Conversion: Contours of Controversy and Commitment in a Plural World', in Christopher Lamb and M. Darrol Bryant (eds), *Religious Conversion: Contemporary Practices and Controversies.* London: Cassel, pp. 1–19.
Mohapatra, Bishnu, and Dwaipayan Bhattacharya. 1995. 'Politics in Phulbani, Orissa: The 1995 Assembly Election'. Unpublished report presented at a workshop on Assembly Elections and Democracy in India, School of Social Sciences, Jawaharlal Nehru University, New Delhi, 22 April.
Oddie, G. A. (ed.). 1977. *Religion in South Asia: Religious Conversion and Revival Movements in South Asia in Medieval and Modern Times.* London: Curzon Press.
O'Malley, L.S.S. 1913. *Census of India, 1911,* Vol. V: *Bengal, Bihar and Orissa and Sikkim, Part I, Report,* Calcutta: Superintendent Government Printing.
——. 1932. *District Gazetteers: Sambalpur.* Patna: Superintendent of Government Press.
Padel, Felix. 1995. *The Sacrifice of Human Being: British Rule and the Khonds of Orissa.* New Delhi: Oxford University Press.
Padhi, Shakti Prasad. 1999. *Land Relations and Agrarian Development in India: A Comparative Historical Study of Regional Variations.* Thiruvananthapuram: Centre for Development Studies.
Panikkar, K. N. (ed.). 1999. *Concerned Indian's Guide to Communalism.* New Delhi: Viking Penguin.
Pati, Biswamoy. 1988. 'Storm over Malkangiri: Laxman Naiko's Revolt (*1942*)', in Gyanendra Pandey (ed.), *The Indian Nation in 1942.* Calcutta: K. P. Bagchi and Sons, pp. 185–205.
——. 1993. *Resisting Domination: Peasants, Tribals and the National Movement in Orissa (1920–50).* New Delhi: Manohar.
——. 2008a. 'Re-convert or Die', *Tehelka,* 19 January. Available at: www.tehelka.com/story_main37.asp?filename=Ne190108re_convert.asp (accessed 31 August 2015)

———. 2008b. 'In a crucified state', *Hindustan Times*, 2 September. Available at: http://www.hindustantimes.com/columnsothers/in-a-crucified-state/article1-335316.aspx (accessed 31 August 2015).

Rout, Sanjib. 1986. 'Rural Stratification in Coastal Orissa, 1866–1900', *Social Science Probings*, vol. 3, no. 1, pp. 136–50.

Sahu, Bhairabi Prasad. 1986. 'The Brahminical Model Viewed as an Instrument of Socio-cultural Change: An Autopsy', in *Proceedings of the Indian History Congress 1985*. New Delhi: Indian History Congress, pp. 180–92.

———. 1987. 'Orissan Society: Past and Present Manifestations', Paper presented at the Training for Development of Scholarship Society, Pune.

Sarkar, Tanika. 1985. 'Jitu Santal's Movement in Malda: A Study in Tribal Protest', in Ranajit Guha (ed.), *Subaltern Studies*, vol. IV. New Delhi: Oxford University Press, pp. 136–54.

———. 2011. 'Rebellion as Modern Self Fashioning: A Santal Movement in Colonial Bengal', in Daniel J. Rycroft and Sangeeta Dasgupta (eds), *The Politics of Belonging in India: Becoming Adivasi*. Oxford: Routledge, pp. 65–81.

Senapati, Nilamani, and B. Mohanty (eds). 1971. *Orissa District Gazetteers: Sambalpur*. Cuttack: Orissa Government Press.

Senapati, Nilamani, and D. C. Kuanr. 1980. *Orissa District Gazetteers: Kalahandi*. Cuttack: Orissa Government Press.

Senapati, Nilamani, and N. K. Sahu. 1966. *Orissa District Gazetteers: Koraput*. Cuttack: Government Press.

———. 1968. *Orissa District Gazetteers: Balangir*. Cuttack: Orissa Government Press.

Singh, G. N. 1963. *Final Report on the Original Survey and Settlement Operations of the Ranpur Ex-State Area in the District of Puri 1943–1952*. Berhampur: Sarada Press.

Sinha, Surajit. 1995. 'State Formation and the Rajput Myth in Central India', in Hermann Kulke (ed.), *The State in India, 1000–1700*. New Delhi: Oxford University Press.

Srinivas, M. N. 1952. *Religion and Society among the Coorgs of South India*. Oxford: Clarendon Press.

Taylor, Donald. 1999. 'Conversion: Inward, Outward and Awkward', in Christopher Lamb and M. Darrol Bryant (eds), *Religious Conversion: Contemporary Practices and Controversies*. London: Cassel, pp. 35–50.

Viswanathan, Gauri. 1998. *Outside the Fold: Conversion, Modernity and Belief*. Princeton: Princeton University Press.

Weber, Max. 1967. First published in 1958. *The Religion of India: The Sociology of Hinduism and Buddhism*, trans. Hans H. Gereth and Don Martindale. New York: The Free Press, and London: Collier-Macmillan.

4
Peoples, Power, and Belief in North-East India

David Vumlallian Zou

Tribal indigenous peoples have a dominant presence in the highlands, and an undeniable existence in the lowlands of the north-east in contemporary India. Since the dawn of historical time, paddy states[1] in the river valleys expended much effort on devising handles by which to grab various stateless populations. At once described as 'shy' and 'wild', these peoples had a long history of evading different state regimes—pre-colonial paddy state, colonial state, or nation-state. The nature of their interaction with state polities was premised on the ecological niches and the livelihood patterns that prevailed among different local communities. In fact, the writ of the pre-colonial states had little effect on hill populations till the British Raj fought its way into the hills to incorporate one 'tribe' after another. Exposure to colonial contact produced different outcomes for hill tribes with distinctive memories and local cosmologies.

---

[1] Paddy or *padi* states in Asia were political systems formed around core areas of irrigated agriculture in the river valleys. Culturally more inclusive than Buddhist *madala* states in Southeast Asia, the term 'paddy state' is applicable to pre-colonial state formations in north-east India influenced by Sanskritic cultural models. Such states were characterized by staple wet-rice cultures (as different from dry-rice varieties grown on the hillsides), the concentration of human resources accessible to state-builders, the emulation of classical Indic or Islamic cultural patterns, and the use of literacy for limited functions. See Scott (2010).

From the early nineteenth century, such encounters resulted in religious change that gained momentum in the mid-twentieth century in many hill areas. Forged by the educated elite, a colonial modernity emerged from this historical process under colonial conditions. Having dislodged the old chiefdom, the new elite have been slowly coming to terms with an overlapping 'tribal' peoplehood and state citizenship. Struggling for a perspective on the tribal question, this chapter hopes to unpack certain critical ingredients that went into the making of histories and peoples in north-east India.

From a historical point of view, there are broadly two kinds of peoples—people with history and people without history. By definition, indigenous tribal communities belong to the latter category, because history-writing has been intimately connected to state-making. According to James C. Scott's (2010: xi) anarchist formulation, 'Ethnicity and "tribe" begin exactly where taxes and sovereignty end.' Although 'tribes' are non-state peoples, their pasts are knowable only in relation to projects of rule by state-builders. In north-east India, people without state contended with three major trajectories of the state: the pre-colonial paddy state, the British colonial state, and the Indian nation-state. Apart from Kon-baung Burma (the regional hegemon), Ahom Assam, Ningthouja Manipur, and the 'Hidimba'[2] state (in present-day Cachar) were other pre-modern states that immediately preceded the British Raj and republican India. An appraisal of the relation between these state-builders and the hill peoples will put the 'tribal question' in colonial and post-independence India in clearer perspective. Our knowledge of the hill people during the pre-colonial past comes from mediated sources such as royal chronicles and inscriptions produced by the states themselves. In this sense, alternative pasts of non-state peoples were silenced. In such early modern registers, the hill people appeared either as dreaded marauders or as hill levies allied with state-builders at different points of time.

This chapter is not meant to be a comprehensive survey of the literature on tribal studies in north-east India. It is a synthetic essay that looks at

---

[2] The Sanskritizing princes of Cachar, who built the so-called Hidimba state from the 1750s, claimed their descent from the son of the epic hero 'Bhim… through Hidimba' (Bhattacharjee 1977: 5). And older paddy states such as the Koch and Tripura no longer mattered much when Kon-baung Burma and British Bengal entered the political scene of today's north-east India at the start of the nineteenth century.

the role of religious change in state formation as a vantage point for mapping a complex borderland history. It focuses on multiple linkages connecting pre-colonial state projects, contemporary nation-building, the process of religious change, and the emergence of colonial modernity. The relationship of pre-colonial paddy states in the Irrawaddy, Barak, Brahmaputra, and Imphal valleys with the surrounding hill peoples often contributed to either the durability or vulnerability of their projects of rule. By striking a fine balance between punishment and persuasion, capable Ahom or Meitei princes won over many hill peoples against outside invaders such as the Mughals or Burmese. Tribal hill peoples asserted their independence whenever the authority of paddy states waned. The balance of power sometimes tilted in favour of hill chiefs. Throughout history, the presence of a 'persistent tribal factor' (Guha 1984: 76) had been a powerful check on the expansion of centralized states and sedentary populations—sometimes halting and even reversing the progress of the Leviathan. But by virtue of superior arms, the British Raj stepped into the shoes of pre-colonial Ahom rulers and other lesser princes in the region. The Raj perfected the imperial repertoire of indirect rule in the tribal hill areas where they identified or invented traditional institutions of chieftainship or its equivalents. In the pre-colonial era, top-down religious change from local to Indic belief systems was mostly confined to settled wet-rice cultivators and Sanskritizing elites in the irrigated valleys of the Brahmaputra, the Barak, the Gumti-Haorah, and the Imphal rivers. Under colonial rule, bottom-up conversion to the Judeo-Christian faith largely occurred among *jhum* ('swidden' or shifting cultivation) cultivators (especially among slaves, women, and the youth) in the hill areas, such as the Naga, Jaintia-Khasi, Garo, and the Lushai hills.

RELIGIOUS CHANGE, PADDY STATES, AND SANSKRITIZATION

Proselytizing religions often acted as powerful catalysts of social change and new political possibilities. Two missionary sects—popular Vaishnavism and Protestant missions—left indelible marks in the valley and the hill societies, respectively. Whereas religious change in the pre-colonial period assisted the process of Sanskritization in sixteenth-century Assam or eighteenth-century Manipur, Christian conversion of the hill peoples in the colonial and post-independence periods spoke the idiom of modernization.

The oldest varieties of religion in north-east India consisted of animistic rituals and goddess cults worshipped with either animal or human sacrifices, or both. Goddess Kesai Khati of ancient Sadiya in Upper Assam was allegedly 'the eater of raw flesh' (Eliot 1910: 1157). Similar fertility goddesses of fierce description had existed among the Tripuris, Kacharis, Koches, Jaintias, and others. The headhunting ritual in the hills was in many ways associated with fertility cults and beliefs. The encounter of tribal religions in Assam and Bengal with Indic religions appears to have taken the form of late Tantric Buddhism[3] and Shakta Hinduism. Historian S. K. Bhuyan asserts that Hindu and Buddhist advocates not only tolerated, but legitimized 'the rites of aboriginal tribes, read an esoteric meaning in them, and absorb[ed] them' (Bhuyan 1974: 190). Tribal fertility goddesses came to be identified with the dark aspects of Shiva's wife. As in Shivite Hinduism, goddesses were much revered in Tantric Buddhism beyond Assam. In Nepal, the goddess Hariti was believed to have possessed women curers and mediums of Newar Buddhism (Gellner 1993: 330). And Bodhisattva Tara became the patron goddess of Tibet (Eliot 1910: 1158; Harvey 2004: 137).

Perched on the Nilachal hill on the banks of the Brahmaputra, the shrine of Kamakhya (the goddess of sex) was the centre of Shakta Brahminism in Assam. The local goddess Kamakhya was incorporated into Shakta worship. Invoked by traditional healers (*ojas*) in medieval Assam, Kamakhya was identified by the Bodos with their chief goddess, Kharia Brui (Datta 1995: 52). The prominence of female deities in no way corresponded to the actual position of women. What mattered most was that various chiefs and princes embraced the Shakta form of Brahminical religion, and Shakta Brahmins returned the favour by supplying local chiefs and princes with unblushingly fabricated genealogies. Therefore, Shaktism offered a legitimizing formula to local rajas on their way to Sanskritization. Even in pre-Ahom Kamarupa, Shiva had been 'the most significant deity' (Lahiri 1991: 124), variously called Rudra, Sambhu, and Samkara. The Koch kings followed the Shivite path; and in 1515, they were declared to be the sons of the Puranic god Shiva himself (Eliot 1910: 1160). The genealogy of the Ahom Swargadeos was tracked back to the Indo-Aryan god Indra (Bhuyan 1974: 21). The Ahoms embraced Shaktism and 'considered Vaisnavism to be too passive and mild to be suitable for a ruling class who had to maintain their domination by the force of arms' (Bhuyan 1974: 18). Shaktism superbly suited the needs

---

[3] There is little consensus among historians on the coming of Buddhism in north-east India. For a discussion of Buddhism in Assam and Arunachal Pradesh, see Bhattacharyya (1995).

of the elite Ahom militia, and it enabled them to exclude or include outsiders as required, and legitimize their alien rule over their caste-differentiated subjects. The fierce and violent aspects of Shakti goddesses might have served to exclude and warn potential enemies or rebellious tribes. Nevertheless, the image of a benign Vaishnavite god was hardly suited to produce such an impression of power.

In medieval Assam, Shaktism did a better job at winning the favour of princes than the hearts of the people. This left ample room for the emergence of popular religiosity and a missionary sect that would meet the needs of the lower orders. During the sixteenth century, a serious rival of aristocratic Shaktism had risen in the form of popular Vaishnavism preached by Sankardev (1449–1568). He had his work cut out to tame and purge 'the rude and manly savagery of Tantric worship and animism' (Sarkar 1932: 12) that lurked behind Shaktism in Assam. Unlike Shaktism, which was tied to its royal patrons, Vaishnavism was a proselytizing religion with its arms open to all caste groups. A Sudra named Anirudh became Sankardev's disciple, and founded a new Vaishnava sect whose adherents came to be known as Moamarias (Eliot 1910: 1169). They turned into a political force that struck the Ahom state with fatal consequences during the eighteenth century. Coming to terms with new political facts, the persecutor Ahom state soon pragmatically turned into a Vaishnava patron.

Beyond the Brahmaputra valley, Vaishnava Brahmins fanned out into the courts of Manipur and Cachar throughout the eighteenth century. Vaishnavism turned full circle; a sect that had originated as a popular movement in the Brahmaputra valley ended up as the religion of royalty in the Imphal and Barak valleys. Vaishnava Brahmins traced back the pedigree of Ningthouja princes in Manipur to the epic hero Arjun. Likewise, the Cachar raja was announced in 1790 as the descendant of Bhim, the hero of the Mahabharata. After the conversion of the first Meitei king to Hinduism in 1704, Indo-Persian and Indo-Aryan surnames such as Singh, Chandra, or Garibniwaz became all the rage in Manipur. Even as the hill peoples of Manipur came under tighter state control in the eighteenth century,[4] the process of Sanskritization in the Imphal valley appeared to widen the cultural distance between the caste-acquiring valley people and the 'polluted' hill people on the one hand, and religious tension between Vaishnava Hindu converts and

---

[4] The process of Sanskritization in Manipur accelerated under King Garibniwaz (ruled 1709–48).

adherents of the old Meitei religion (Sanamahi) on the other hand. Like their Tai-Ahom counterparts in Assam, princes in Manipur used a well-established device for claiming high-status identity through genealogical fictions with imagined Indo-Aryan ancestors. The royal titles of Meitei kings mirrored shifts in cultural orientations from Sinic to Indic influences. Names of Meitei princes used to evoke Southeast Asian connections. King Kyamba, for instance, meant 'conqueror of Kyam', a Shan principality in Upper Burma. This cultural pattern among the Ningthouja princes equally applied to the Ahom Swargadeos.[5] Historian Jayeeta Sharma (2011: 59) rightly points out, 'By asserting their status as historical Indic migrants, these elites aggressively denied kinship with Assam's [or Manipur's] lower castes and hill groups, who ranked low in the Sanskritic ritual hierarchy.' All origin myths of elite warriors either from north India or Southeast Asia sought at once to distance as well as elevate the local ruling regimes in the valleys of Assam, Manipur, Cachar, and Tripura from the surrounding hill groups.

Meitei kings before Garibniwaz had professed various Hindu beliefs, and practised them as an additive component without giving up the old ancestral religion of Manipur called Sanamahi. The *Cheitharon Kumpapa* (Court Chronicles of the Kings of Manipur) (2005: 114) registers that King Charai Rongba had already taken 'the name of a Hindu *lai*' or god (*laiming louba*) before Garibniwaz. 'To take the name of a god'—or a different god—is a pre-modern way of understanding 'conversion'. A Brahmin from Puri initiated him into the new faith. Though Charai Rongba professed Vaishnavite beliefs, he practised them as an additive component without giving up his old ancestral religion, Sanamahi. For Garibniwaz, however, Vaishnava Hinduism was *the* religion—worthy of state patronage. Won over by the guru Shanti Gopal Das, King Garibniwaz converted to Vaishnavite Hinduism in 1717. This ignited a missionary enthusiasm directed at the old Meitei religion. The outcome of the tension between the two belief systems varied over time.

Abodes of some gods or goddesses were destroyed, others retained distinct local identities as forest deities (*umang lai*) (*Cheitharon Kumpapa* 2005: 133), and yet some others came to be identified with Hindu deities

---

[5] Swargadeo (literally 'lord of heaven') was the title adopted by the Tai-Ahom kings who arrived in present-day Assam from Upper Burma during the early thirteenth century AD. This title reflects the divine ancestry claimed by the ruling dynasty. This mythical origin was narrated first by the Ahom Deodhai priests and later modified by the Brahmin genealogists.

(Kabui 2003: 255). As tropical forests receded before an expanding agrarian frontier at Imphal and Samsok (in the Kabaw valley), the forest spirits increasingly appeared remote to the concerns of sedentary souls. If Brahmin migration served as an external stimulus, agrarian expansion at the cost of forests, and the need of the Ningthouja dynasty for political legitimacy, provided the immediate contexts for Meitei conversion to Vaishnavism in the eighteenth century. In the forested hills, however, no Brahmin ventured; jhum cycles enabled the renewal of forest covers that embodied forest spirits; and tribal chiefs could just get by without deep genealogies. For the moment, the freshly titled maharajas revelled in their acquired distance from their rustic hill neighbours as a means of gaining more social respectability. Consequently, hill resentment would later turn this attitude on its head; but that was still in the future.

However significant the conversion of 1717 may be as a historical moment, the path towards religious change in Manipur was a long-drawn-out process. The Meitei king was the recognized head of the priests of the umang lais and of Vaishnavite Brahmins. Both religions enjoyed varying degrees of royal patronage. There is no consensus about the degree and depth of Vaishnavite conversion in Manipur. In the 1910s, two colonial ethnographers debated on this question. Hodson (1913) argued that Meitei Hinduism was an outward veneer masking an inner animism. But Shakespear (1913) maintained that the best-informed Meiteis may pass off easily as Hindu, as distinct from animists in the surrounding hills. The concerns of this debate shifted to a new terrain when the erstwhile animists of the hills embraced Judeo-Christian beliefs under colonial rule.

The rise of Burma's last dynasty (the Kon-baung) in Upper Burma had serious repercussions for Southeast Asia and the north-east of British Bengal. Upper Burma shared a long history of interaction with present-day north-east India during the pre-colonial and early colonial eras. Kon-baung Burma (1752–1885) had been a regional hegemon in Arakan (Rakhine), Assam, and Manipur (Kathe). Rebelling against the Ahoms, Moamarias (a sect of popular Vaishnavism) sought the help of Burma. General Bandula, 'the greatest of all Burmese generals' (Bhuyan 1974: 490), defeated the ruling Ahom king in 1822. And it 'marked the extinction of Ahom authority in Assam' (Bhuyan 1974: 492).

'WILD TRIBES', THE COLONIAL STATE, AND IMPROVEMENT

An expanding East India Company in Bengal frequently clashed with Kon-baung Burma, which wielded enormous influence in what is today north-east India.[6] The British stepped into the shoes of the Kon-baung after Burma's prestige took a beating at the end of the first Anglo-Burmese War. The discovery of the tea plant and the subsequent formation of the Assam tea company in 1839 attracted British commercial interests in the region. Indentured labour from Chota Nagpur (in present-day Jharkhand), Bihar, Ghazipur, and Benaras was transported here to lessen the planters' dependence on local labour (Sharma 2011: 81). It was estimated that there were 1,200,000 time-expired coolies[7] in Assam by the 1920s (Sharma 2008, 2011: 13, 18). Because the plains ryots were seen as 'lazy natives' and the hill groups as 'wild tribes', indentured labour from outside served as the foot soldiers for improving the empire's garden estates (Sharma 2011: 87).

When the extractive plantation economy moved right up to the foothills of upland tribal peoples, tension developed between British (read Scottish) tea planters and shifting cultivators who resented intruders into the forest commons, clan lands, or hunting grounds. The fact that the last Ahom rulers wielded an increasingly weak influence on the hill peoples did not help their British successors. The writ of the paddy states had little effect on hill peoples until British Bengal closed an expanding state frontier. Pre-modern powers such as Ahom Assam, Konbaung Burma, and Garibniwaz's Manipur had, at best, a tenuous hold on the hill peoples that surrounded their principalities in the agrarian cores. Becoming more independent of plains dominance in chaotic times, upland communities such as the Naga and the Lushai (Mizo) were all too ready to 'raid' the tea gardens within striking distance; they made slaves of revenue-paying ryots within British territories. The British continued the Ahom policy of paying a share of the revenue (*posa*) to hill tribes such as the Aka and the Dufla on the northern fringes

---

[6] At the dawn of British colonial takeover, a number of irritants arose between the English East India Company and Kon-baung Burmese rulers, since anti-Kon-baung rebels sought refuge in British territory. Conflict resulted whenever Kon-baung troops pursued rebels across the Arakan into British Bengal. The first Anglo-Burmese War (1824–6) that ensued changed the fate of India's north-east, whose political history decisively gravitated towards British Bengal (and later republican India) while moving away from its historical connections with Southeast Asia.

[7] Between the 1860s and 1920s, tea planters in Assam recruited labour from different tribal belts of British India under a contract system called indenture. Lured by surplus to agricultural land, workers who stayed on after the expiry of the contract were called 'time-expired' coolies.

of Assam. Whereas posa was paid in kind earlier, the British commuted it into cash payment, disbursing Rs 360 per annum to the Aka in 1842, and increased it to Rs 668 fifteen years later (Mackenzie 1884: 21–3). Likewise, the British compensated 238 Dufla chiefs for loss of posa to the tune of Rs 2,543. This arrangement worked fairly well, but troubles erupted from time to time. Colonial officials talk about 'Duphla's love for troubles' or their 'troublesome character' (Mackenzie 1884: 27, 29). Thus, the colonial stereotype of 'wild tribes' was born, best seen in the representations of Naga headhunters and Lushai head-cutters.[8] (In fact, certain colonial ethnographers claimed that the name 'Lushai' itself meant 'to cut off head', which, of course, was a doubtful proposition [Shakespear 1912: 59]). Much of the 'wildness' and 'tribalness' were colonial constructs, although there existed usable pre-colonial pasts to draw on.

A historian of the Subaltern School, Ajay Skaria (1999: 35), has drawn attention to the complex process involved in 'being Dangi, being wild' in colonial western India. He insists that organized raids were rational pursuits enabled by 'alliance among rajas of different dangs' (Skaria 1999: 142). They were premised on the shared sovereignty of several Bhil rajas as opposed to the exclusive sovereignty claimed by the British Raj. The Bhil chiefs of western India and the Lushai chiefs in north-east India seem to have arrived at two different, yet equally rational, ideas of the best season for conducting raids in the neighbouring plains. The Lushai (Mizo) on the border of the tea plantations in the Cachar plains preferred post-monsoon September, when there was a short respite before the next harvest began (Jones 1998: 70). The Bhils favoured the month of May when food became scarce and the monsoon deluge rendered their hill tracks virtually inaccessible for outside forces because of swollen rivers, spread of malaria, and thick undergrowth (Skaria 1999: 142).

The protection of British commercial interests in Assam tea called for tighter control and eventual occupation of the hill countries. Since the end of the first Anglo-Burmese War in 1826, the Raj had fought its way into the hills to incorporate one hill area after another. The Raj expanded into the hill areas in three distinct phases in less than one century: first, the Jaintia-Khasi hills and Cachar in the 1830s; second, the Garo hills and Naga hills in the 1860s; and finally, the Lushai hills and Manipur in the 1890s. Present-day Arunachal Pradesh and Hill Tripura escaped formal annexation by the Raj. The colonial incorporation of indigenous tribal peoples in Africa and India was known as 'indirect rule' via both

---

[8] For a detailed discussion on headhunting, see Zou (2005).

traditional and 'invented' tribal chiefs. It was a project of rule over vast territories; it was cheaply and lightly performed through a white resident official, assisted by minimal junior staffs and native interpreters.

In colonial language, the legal foundation and basis for indirect rule in north-east India were Regulation X (1822), the Inner Line Regulation (1873), and the Excluded and Partially Excluded Areas (1936).[9] Authored by a Scottish official, David Scott, Regulation X pre-dated the colonial occupation of Assam to introduce a special judicial system 'to conclude engagements with the independent Chiefs' (Mackenzie 1884: 253) and 'rude Tribes' on the north-eastern parts of Rungpore. In 1823, Scott became the agent to the governor-general of the North-Eastern Frontier, and the first chief commissioner of Assam when it was separated from Bengal in 1874 (Bhuyan 1974: 458). Scott has been regarded as a paternalist who fought against the spirit of 'regulation' and sought 'to work through native institutions in evolving an administration for the newly annexed Assam' (Barooah 1969: 181). In the preamble to Regulation X, Scott criticized the zamindars for exploiting 'savage tribes' such as the Garo and the failure 'to reclaim the tribes to civilized habits' (Mackenzie 1884: 251). In 1825, Scott also blamed the Christian missionaries for 'directing their attention to the polished natives instead of rude tribes who are still in the state of national childhood which enable the stranger priest to enact the schoolmaster and to teach what he likes' (Mackenzie 1884: 253–4). Unlike the more polished caste societies, Scott expected 'rude tribes' to be more receptive to schemes of improvement. Guided by the spirit of paternalism, colonial policy towards the tribal hill peoples in British Assam was intent on a cartography of inner lines dividing hills and plains, and a legal exceptionalism that excluded most parts of the hill areas from laws passed by the Indian legislature. While this was conducive to border security and sound finance, it would mean virtual economic blockage to the plains bazaars for the hill people. In cordoning off 'rude tribes' (seen as schoolchildren) from the plains, there was a punitive element meted out by the paternalist Raj acting like a schoolmaster. Musing on the frequency of Garo raids in the 1850s, Lord Dalhousie wrote, 'I consider that further Military operations would be a

---

[9] Excluded areas included the North-East Frontier Tract (present-day Arunachal Pradesh), the Naga Hills District, the Lushai Hills District (Mizoram), and the North Cachar Hill Sub-division. Partially excluded areas were the Garo Hills District, the Mikir Hills in the Nowgong and Sibsagar Districts, and the British portion of the Khasi and Jaintia Hills Districts.

waste of life uselessly. It is possible that the *exclusion of the Garos from the plains* will be effectual' (Mackenzie 1884: 257; emphasis added).

In spite of the strategic location, the hill areas of British Assam were less attractive in terms of their capacity to generate revenue. These tribal hills were cordoned off since 1873 from the plains administration by a special regulation called the Inner Line. Even without this regulation, colonial surveyors in 1872 had demarcated undefined boundaries between the south Garo hills and plains Goalpara with 87 pillars. In the process, both the Garo hills and Goalpara became discrete units of colonial governance, and got 'separated from several areas with which it [they] shared a pre-colonial connected history' (Misra 2011: 85). Gunnel Cederlöf (2009) has recently argued that early colonial rule in the north-east of Bengal created dual polities under one Company Raj—one for the agrarian lowlands under direct rule and the other for indirectly ruled or 'unadministered' highlands. Cederlöf (2009: 537) insists that such a dual fiscal regime had implications for the colonial ruler–subject relation in ways that were disruptive of the older economy of hill–valley exchanges. This is not to say that the British actually invented such a hill–plains duality. However, the territorial thrust of colonial policy reinforced the internal differentiation and caste hierarchy already initiated by Sanskritizing elites of the pre-colonial era, especially the Tai-Ahom Swargadeos, Ningthoujas of Manipur, Manikyas of Tripura, and the Rajas of Cachar.

Various Christian missionaries followed the British flag in its ascent into the hills. The colonial state and the Christian missionaries shared a 'civilizing mission' even if they differed on how to bring about the desired 'improvements' for their subjects or converts. While colonial indirect rule expended its energies on law and order, the missionaries were entrusted with schools, health care, and proselytization. The frontiers of the state and of religion tended to converge here throughout the nineteenth century. The history of Christian conversion is at the heart of the unprecedented transformations that convulsed various communities across the region. At the start of colonial contact, Sanskritic and later Islamic religious frontiers had been moving eastward for several centuries in what is now north-east India. Both these world religions attracted adherents in the lowlands, especially among the builders of paddy states in the Brahmaputra, Barak, Imphal, and Gumti-Haorah valleys based on wet-rice cultivation. While Hindu Shakta cults had suited the political needs of pre-colonial rulers in plains Assam, the Vaishnavite sect under Shanta Das had outclassed both its Shiva rivals and the local Sanamahi worship in the valley of Imphal by 1720.[10] Neither Indic nor Islamic civilizations managed to climb up the hills where people practised the ubiquitous monsoon religion of spirit cults and subsisted on clearing hillsides of inferior soil.

Following the British occupation of Assam, the Serampore Mission initiated mission work at Gauhati in the late 1820s, but soon abandoned their schools at Gauhati and Cherrapunji. As the Serampore Mission failed to strike root in the north-east, two Protestant mission societies appeared on the scene—first, the American Baptists in the 1830s, and then the Welsh Calvinistic mission in the 1840s. In the 1850s, three Roman Catholic missionaries from Paris established a base in Assam with a view to entering Tibet. En route to Tibet, two ill-fated missionaries, Father Krick and Father Bourri, were murdered in 1854 by a Mishmi chief named Kaisa. The prestige of the white man was at stake. In an earlier report, Father Krick himself had alluded to the local conflation of all white peoples: 'In their [tribal] opinion, any white skin, any nose somewhat protruding is of English make.'[11] Therefore, to avenge the murder of the two white men—irrespective of their nationality—the British hanged Chief Kaisa at Dibrugarh. The sole surviving missionary narrowly survived the Revolt of 1857 on his way to Simla, from where he made another abortive attempt to reach Tibet. Because these early French missions eyed the north-east merely as a transit point to Tibet, they left no enduring institutional legacy in British Assam.

Up to a point, it was the endeavours of two Protestant sects that made present-day Meghalaya, Nagaland, and Mizoram predominantly Christian belts. Of course, there were other missionary players in the region such as the Roman Catholics, the Anglican Church, the British Baptists, the New Zealand Baptists, the Gossner Lutherans, the Salvation Army, the Seventh Day Adventists, and the United Pentecostals. But viewed solely in terms of cultural impact on local societies, two Protestant missions, namely the American Baptists and

---

[10] King Garibniwaz (Pamheiba) converted to the Ramanadi cult of Vaishnava Hinduism propagated by Shanta Das. Whereas S. N. A. Parratt (see *Cheitharon Kumpapa* 2005: 125) maintains that 'Gopal Das was also known as Shanti Das', G. Kabui (2003: 251–3) treats Gopal Das and Shanti Das as rival Brahmins from Sylhet (Bengal).

[11] Father N. M. Krick, 'Account of an Expedition among the Abors in 1853', trans. Father A. Gille, *Journal of the Asiatic Society of Bengal*, vol. IX, 1913, p. 108, reproduced in Becker (1989).

the Welsh Calvinists, and the Roman Catholic mission stood out from the rest.

The earliest writings on the church in north-east India appear as celebratory accounts of particular sects among different peoples connected with their mission. Perhaps one of the earliest extant studies in this vein was done by J. H. Morris in 1910. He wrote a triumphal account of the doings of the Welsh Calvinistic Methodists in the Khasi-Jaintia hills, the Lushai hills, the plains of Cachar and Sylhet, and among the 'ignorant and superstitious peasants' (Morris 1910: 249) of Catholic Brittany in north-western France. The Welsh Calvinists established their mission headquarters in the Khasi hills because of the location's relative proximity to the Calcutta port. From this hill base, they hoped to work their way into China (Morris 1910: 44). Such stories were recounted for donors at home in the West and for prospective readers within the confessional community in the mission field. This genre of mission history continues to be written today for internal consumption during special occasions like jubilee or centenary celebrations. *Harvest in the Hills*, penned by the Welsh missionary chronicler J. Meirion Lloyd (1991a), is a recent case in point within the context of Mizoram. Using a horticultural metaphor, Lloyd stresses retrospectively how an initially unpromising field in the Lushai hills came to yield an abundant harvest of souls for the parent Welsh Calvinistic mission.

Another major missionary venture, the American Baptists, produced their own version of mission history on the occasion of their centenary celebration. Victor Hugo Sword authored *Baptists in Assam* (1935), and the subtitle of the book captures its spirit: 'A Century of Missionary Service'. The American Baptists met with little success in the Brahmaputra valley and the Barak valley; their initial dream of expanding from their base at Sadya (Upper Assam) into the Shan area and thence to China was shattered. But they had pleasant surprises in the Naga hills, from where they fanned out into the hill areas of Manipur, first among the Thangkhul Nagas and later among the Thado-Kuki of present-day Senapati district.

If the Welsh Calvinists claimed the Khasi-Jaintia and the Lushai hills, the American Baptists were still left with the plum valleys of Assam, Cachar, and Sylhet along with the Naga hills. By the latter half of the twentieth century, the American Baptists came to regard their initiatives among the hill peoples a great success. This perception is reflected in F. S. Downs's (1971) celebratory history of the Baptist churches in the north-east, titled *The Mighty Works of God*. But the religious outcome of their civilizing mission in the Assam plains was far from mighty.

Thus far, the mission histories of particular sects had been written by missionaries themselves for the consumption of donors and church members. But from the 1970s and especially in the 1980s, a handful of scholars attempted to explain Christian conversion among the hill peoples by being more attentive to the social context and to historical contingencies. In a perceptive but neglected piece, Gordon E. Pruett (1974) engages with non-Naga intellectuals and the concerns of Indian officials about Naga conversion to Christianity. While some of these non-Naga writers showed a bias due to their preoccupation with Indian national security, many observers had genuine concern for Naga cultural integrity and the disorienting impact of missionaries.

Pruett, however, accents the need to consider the point of view held by Naga intellectuals, informed by their historical pasts, that is as much Naga as Baptist. After all, the reasons for Baptist success in the Naga hills 'are not wholly on the side of missionary insight and vigour' (Pruett 1974: 60). Even from its origin, the Naga mission was an indigenous venture undertaken by an Assamese Christian, Godhula Brown. The Naga churches ceased to depend on foreign mission support as early as the 1930s, and became even stronger after they severed the final ties in 1950. The Ao Naga converts, rather than the American Baptists, became the chief agents for the spread of the new faith. This indicates that the Naga indigenous church has deeper roots than many non-Naga intellectuals allow. This local form of Christianity 'cannot be now conceived as an outer skin of the native culture, to be sloughed off with the departure of Western influence'(Pruett 1974: 62). The compatibility of Baptist polity and Naga polity might have proved attractive to the earliest Ao Naga converts. Pruett points out, 'The Baptist polity meshes happily with Naga tribal polity.... Both polities are "congregational" and solidly committed to the concept of local autonomy' (1974: 60). Enquiry into the organizational or associational aspects of missionary societies is a promising direction for students of church history in the north-east. The term 'Christian conversion' is loaded, and it needs a bit of unpacking. In the Naga hills, the Christian message arrived through a specifically mediated form and associational norms—the American Baptist mission and its congregational polity. Would there have been a differential outcome if a Calvinistic or Catholic mission had landed in the Naga hills instead of congregational Baptists? Jayaprakash Narayan, who went to Nagaland as part of a three-member peace mission, wrote, 'I am of the view that if Roman Catholics or priests from the Church of England had gone to Nagaland, perhaps the sentiment of separation may have diminished. The missionaries [American Baptists] who went there did not intensify this feeling, nor did they reduce it' (Narayan 1965, cited in R. Guha 2010: 430). But would the Naga have expressed the same degree of enthusiasm for either Catholicism or Anglicanism as they did for the radical Protestant sect, American Baptist congregationalism? What were the mechanisms of a cultural process at once as personal and political as religious conversion? Some of these questions have been resolved by Richard M. Eaton (1984) in his influential article on Naga conversion. With a breadth of intellectual outlook, Eaton considers conversion to be an aspect of cultural change that ensued from the expanding frontiers of agrarian states from the Gangetic core into the jungles of eastern Bengal and western Punjab. In the east, indigenous populations of Bengal had been incorporated into the lettered religious traditions we now call Hindu, Buddhist, or Islamic. Yet there still remained certain interior pockets that succumbed to colonial conquest and a literate religion. For Eaton (1984: 2), a study of Naga conversion may suggest 'how previous aboriginals of India might, in earlier epochs, have acculturated to Hinduism, Buddhism, or Islam'.

In explaining Naga conversion, Eaton (1984: 19) shows statistically that conversion 'cannot be explained in terms of the number of distribution of foreign missionaries' (see Table 4.1). A contrast of missionary outcome between the Sema Naga and the Angami Naga illustrates this point. By the mid-1950s, when foreign missionaries left the Naga hills, Christianity had struck deep roots among the Sema, but failed to make much headway among the Angami. Employing only two missionaries, proselytization among the Sema started as late as 1948 in the post-independence era, and continued only for seven years. In contrast, seven missionaries laboured among the Angami as early as 1880, and continued for as long as 74 years. Now this is the outcome of

TABLE 4.1

Name of Community	No. of Missionaries	Duration (in Years)	Baptized Membership by 1961	Baptized Membership by 1971
Sema	2	7	18,626	23,000
Angami	7	74	4,653	7,000

Sources: These statistics are compiled from two unpublished sources: Philip (1972) and Sema (1972). The same data is reproduced in Eaton (1984: 19).

missionary labour in terms of baptized converts: 18,000 converts for the Sema and 4,653 for the Angami by the end of the year 1961.

In this context, the intensity of missionary labour alone fails to explain Naga conversion. The focus has to shift from the missionaries to the converts themselves. According to Richard Eaton (1984: 20), 'Religious change in Nagaland ... cannot be explained in strictly nonreligious terms. Rather, the key to these changes is to be found in the particular forms of interaction between the Nagas' religious cosmology and their social relations, each of which influenced the other.'

The slow rate of conversion among the Angami Naga has been put down to factors such as local agricultural and religious systems. The Angami, alone among the Nagas, built elaborate systems of terracing. Corresponding to their permanent cultivation of hillsides, the Angami developed a relatively more stable religious system than other Nagas. They had a democratic polity controlled by a council of elders. With such a democratic polity, the Angami cosmology had no supreme male deity. Therefore, the first Bible portion printed in Angami in 1890 adopted a Hebrew derivative, 'Ihova', for the generic term 'God'—thus imposing a foreign word on Angami cosmology. The Baptist missionary Sidney W. Rivenberg spent five years in Kohima without producing a single convert.

In contrast to the Angami, the Sema were the most migratory of all Nagas; and the polity was characterized by despotic chiefs who belonged to a single dominant lineage. The centralizing tendency of the Sema socio-political system was consistent with Sema attention to a supreme god Alhou, who 'had already become important for the Sema even before the British arrived on the scene' (Eaton 1984: 38). It was precisely this god Alhou that missionaries identified with the Judeo-Christian deity. Acting like intellectual engineers, the missionaries tinkered with Sema cosmology, and fitted their own system into the Sema's. Moreover, the strains of generation and gender had particular relevance for explaining religious change within patriarchal hill societies. Based on census figures of 1891, 1901, and 1911, a recent study estimates that most of the Naga 'converts to Christianity came approximately from below the age of 35 years, especially within the age group of 25 to 30 ... the younger generation increasingly felt the need to move beyond the existing community norms and structures, and to explore and experiment what the new dispensation had to offer' (Thomas 2010: 99; see also Thomas 2012). But we are less sure about the receptiveness of colonial Naga women to the Christian message.

In the Lushai hills, *bawih*s (domestic slaves of chiefs) (Nag 2012) and *khawhring*s (women accused of the evil eye) were particularly receptive to Christian conversion. Folk belief in khawhring was widespread and resilient: that certain women with a malignant spirit could cast the evil eye to harm or even kill another person. Before colonial rule, suspected women either found no husband or often faced the death sentence (Shakespear 1912: 111). Such victims existed in the average Lushai village, and they found spiritual salvation and social respectability within the missionary fold. No wonder that many khawhring women became 'wives of Christian workers and they are none the worse' (Lloyd 1991b: 223). There was widespread—but not universal—belief in the evil eye among the Jaintias and Kuki-Chins, including the Mara or Lakher.[12] Whereas the evil was gender-neutral in other cases, the exclusive female association of khawhring made the Lushai women vulnerable. Unless the evil eye is gender-biased, the mere existence of this folk belief complex is not enough to explain why certain social groups left an old belief system to embrace religious change.

Slave girls and boys fled their masters to the Welsh missionary headquarters at Aizawl, and they represented a large section of the early Christian converts. A bawih census report in 1923 arrived at the figure of 1,426 slave households in the Lushai hills.[13] Dr Peter Fraser was a medical missionary at Aizawl who championed the cause of bawih abolition. He paid dearly with his missionary career for this initiative. Between 1909 and 1912, slave girls who sought his support complained of sexual harassment and elderly women were vulnerable to physical violence from bawih-owning Lushai chiefs.[14] The bawihs were the most likely persons to see a prospect for spiritual and social redemption in the egalitarian message of Christian missionaries. Many slave boys availed of missionary schools and transformed themselves into respected leaders

---

[12] A comparable folk belief in *ka taroh* (an envious she-devil) existed among certain clans of the Jaintia (Meghalaya), the Mara (Lakher) of southern Mizoram, and the Kuki people. Unlike the Lushai idea of khawhring owned only by women, the Jaintia's taroh, the Mara's *ahmaw*, and the Kuki's *kau* were believed to be possessed by both men and women (Gurdon 1907: 107–8; Parry 1976: 462–3).

[13] Statement of J. E. Webster, Commissioner, Surma Valley and Hill Division, dated 1 February 1923, cited in Bezbaruah (2008: 225–47).

[14] National Library of Wales, Calvinistic Methodist Archives (Aberystwyth), 27, 318, File V: The 'Bawi' System in Lushai—Dr. Fraser's Case.

of the Christian Mizos and even of the whole Mizo community. As a young bawih, Dohnuna escaped from his chief's village to urban Aizawl, where he attended the missionary school and earned enough cash wages to redeem himself. He converted to the new faith, became a successful shopkeeper, a church elder, an entrepreneur who invested in a weaving machine, and later a salaried missionary to southern Manipur (Jones 1998: 87).

A popular Mizo Christian hymn composed by an educated ex-bawih, Thanga (born 1883), is dedicated to the praise of abolitionist Pathian, the pre-Christian Mizo deity who came to be identifed with the Judeo-Christian God:

> Aw Lalpa, Chungnung ber, kan fak hle a che!
> Pathian Nung leh Engkimtithei I ni e;
> Hnehchhiahte, bâwih, riangvaite, mi sualte thian;
> Fahrahte, retheite Lal, Pa leh Pathian.
> —*Kristian Hla Bu* (2010),
> Hymn no. 434

Free translation:
Oh most exalted Lord, we praise you!
You are the Living and Almighty Pathian;
The friend of the oppressed, bawih, sufferers and sinners;
The Chief, Dad and Pathian of orphans and paupers.

The ex-bawih composer represents the Judeo-Christian God as an exalted abolitionist, suggesting that he is none other than Pathian (the clan deity of the powerful Sailo chiefs) and a *lal* (chief) who owns no slaves. Such an ally and protector would have been irresistible to the first bawih converts to the new faith community.

Eaton (1984) draws heavily on the seminal articles of Robin Horton on the rationality of 'African conversion' published in the journal *Africa* (see Horton 1971, 1975, 1993). Here conversion is perceived in terms of cognitive adjustment to changing material circumstances, rather than as the outcome of encounter between two belief systems. External forces, such as missionaries, might merely serve as catalysts to the process of religious change. Missionaries facilitated the transition from primal religions of local or ancestral spirits to monotheistic world religions that better captured their experience of imperial integration. The Africans, or the Nagas, for that matter, responded to the problem by modifying their local cosmology in two ways: first, by elaborating their traditional belief in the Supreme Being, and then ignoring the importance or presence of lesser jungle spirits. The strength of this intellectualist explanation lies in its recognition of local agency in the process of conversion. But, according to J. D. Y. Peel (2000: 4; see also Fisher 1973), this explanation tends to downplay 'the distinct cultural dynamics of the world religions themselves, which produce real effects even when their initial adoption has a strongly local rationale'.

A church historian by training, O. L. Snaitang (1993) stresses the distinctive forms of Khasi-Jaintia conversion to the Welsh Calvinistic faith since the 1840s. Departing from the earlier focus on the story of foreign missions, Snaitang examines how Calvinistic Christianity and the local culture, embodied in the tradition of *tipkur tipkha* (know clan, know father's clan), interpenetrated each other. This process of religious change actually resulted in the forging of a new Khasi-Jaintia identity under colonial conditions. Old tradition had it that god in heaven gave the Khasi-Jaintia a social code: tipkur tipkha. Translated into customary practice, this means that marriage within the mother's clan is incest. The vitality of the tipkur tipkha solidarity depends on the relationship of three persons, namely the ancestress, the ancestor, and the maternal uncle. Snaitang observes that the Anglican missionaries initially failed to realize the centrality of this kinship institution for the Khasi-Jaintia. This cultural insensitivity compelled some converts to revert to the old belief system. But the Welsh Calvinists affirmed the tipkur tipkha code and prohibited marriage within the same clan. To enforce this customary code, they created a special committee called Ka Komiti Sang (Committee for the Prohibition of Incest). The members of this incest committee included the white missionaries and the Khasi-Jaintia converts. Despite the condemnation of social practices such as alcoholic drinks and the use of opium, the preservation of the core social code of tipkur tipkha enabled the Khasi-Jaintia to convert without a sense of identity conflict.

SCHEDULED TRIBES, NATION-STATE, AND MODERNIZATION

If colonial indirect rule patronized hereditary and territorial chiefdoms as 'traditional' leaders of the local society, missionary schools openly provided the intellectual skills necessary for the emergent 'ethnic' leaders in the twilight of the Raj. Most of the plains tribes of the Brahmaputra valley and the hill tribes of the Khasi-Jaintia hills, Naga hills, and Lushai hills embraced Western education to fulfil their modern aspirations in the late colonial era. It was not the tribal commoner, but rather young men with modern education and urban exposure who developed the sharpest sense of ethnic consciousness. Students of ethno-genesis know that ethnicity and 'tribalism' are diachronically mutable and synchronically heterogeneous.[15]

Change of guard in the hill areas came not with the transfer of power in 1947, but with the exit of Assam's premier and first chief minister, Gopinath Bordoloi, who had headed the sub-committee on tribal affairs that drafted the Sixth Schedule of the Indian constitution. Bordoloi's successor, Chief Minister Bishnuram Medhi, was of the view that 'the integration of the hills with the plains needed to be brought about immediately, if necessary by force' (Rustomji 1983: 36). Looking at this decisive moment, Charles Pawsey, deputy commissioner of the Naga Hills, also agreed that 'a change in policy came with a change of Chief Minister and Governor. Hill officers were replaced by plainsmen'.[16] Here it may be recalled that the assertion of 'Assamese' identity itself gained momentum from the state imposition of Bengali as the official language in colonial Assam. Since colonial times, state pursuit of one official language in a multilingual Babel had always spelt disaster for Assam. By the 1950s, the quest for Assamese self-respect 'turned into one of building a Greater Assam by an Assamisation of the hills' (Franke 2009: 69). The educated Naga leadership resented such developments, and protested with placards when the chief minister visited the Naga hills. The Assam government retaliated by posting the state police at Mokokchung; this marked a clear departure from the colonial practice of 'indirect rule'. This further alienated the Naga public from the post-independence state, which was soon trapped in a cycle of violence.[17] Unfortunately, the new political masters of Assam showed little restraint or sensitivity in addressing tribal concerns, especially in the Naga hills and the Lushai hills. Smarting under the rule of the new brown masters,

---

[15] The words 'tribalism' and 'ethnicity' made their debuts in the *Oxford English Dictionary* in 1886 and 1953, respectively. In the context of north-east India, pre-colonial clans and lineages gave way to colonial 'tribes'. In the post-independence era, a handful of tribes successfully transformed into ethnicities or ethnic nations such as the Naga, Khasi, Garo, and Mizo. Tribalism mutated over time: non-state *clans* became administrative *tribes*. At its core, ethnicity is void of cultural content; rather, it is defined by the boundaries it draws and maintains. This is what renders ethnicity so heterogeneous.

[16] Private Papers of Charles Pawsey, 1965, p. 8, Centre for South Asian Studies, Cambridge.

[17] Private Papers of Charles Pawsey, 1965, p. 8, Centre for South Asian Studies, Cambridge.

the proverbial last straw for the hill peoples came in 1962 with the imposition of Assamese by the Assam legislature as the official language for the entire state—a state well known for its linguistic diversity. It led to disastrous outcomes and troubled legacies that eventually led to the partition of British Assam.

The Sixth Schedule laid the foundations for administering most of the tribal hill areas of north-east India in the post-independence period. According to S. K. Chaube, 'The most remarkable thing about the Bardoloi Report was the skill with which the subcommittee sought to reconcile the hill people's demand for "political" autonomy with Assam government's drive to integrate them with the plains' (Chaube 1999: 100). But the Constituent Assembly did not extend the Sixth Schedule to the tribal hill peoples in the princely states of Manipur and Tripura. Because of its all-India dimension, the problems of the princely states and their tribal populations 'missed special attention needed in the north-eastern region'. The tribal hill areas of the two princely states did not figure in the list of 'backward tracts' of Assam notified in 1929. Six years later, the 'backward tracts' became 'excluded' and 'partially excluded areas'. When republican India renamed them as 'tribal areas' under the Sixth Schedule, the hill tribes of Manipur and Tripura were left out by default. Given the demographic deluge, constitutional safeguards under the Sixth Schedule were extended to Tripura as an afterthought in 1985. The case of the hill tribes in Manipur remains the only exception in north-east India (Zou 2010).

The hill–valley tension was just one aspect of the struggle for power; another dimension was the fault line dividing the old chiefs and the new elite within the tribal hill societies. The Sixth Schedule retained aspects of colonial legal traditions, while trying to meet the democratic aspirations of the educated 'tribal' elites through its provision for the Autonomous District Council. The contest for power between the traditional leaders and educated elites played out in the making of the Sixth Schedule. On the whole, this post-independence arrangement tilted power in favour of the new council against the old chiefs. In Mizoram, the triumph of the middle class over the slave-owning lals (chiefs) was decisive. The council dealt a death blow to the lal, and eventually abolished this traditional institution. Late colonial Mizoram was already a highly stratified society where the traditional elite consisted of old hereditary chiefs and new administrative chiefs: the British merely recognized the privileges of the former chiefs, but the latter type was purely their own invention to suit colonial needs. Popular leadership for the council (as distinct from the hereditary offices) emerged from the educated elites (middle class) who entered the professions as clerks, schoolteachers, doctors, nurses, contractors, pastors, salaried Bible women, press compositors, and postmen. Latecomers to the colonial professions, budding tribal politicians cut their teeth at council meetings against British-backed old privileges represented by the chiefs.

In Meghalaya, the old chiefly group was variously represented by the *syiem* in the Khasi hills, the *doloi* in the Jaintia hills, and the *nokma* in the Garo hills. Here, the council–chiefs contest was resolved through an uneasy compromise. Reverend J. J. M. Nicholas Roy of Shillong was 'a vocal critic and bitter enemy of the Khasi *syiems*, whom he managed in the end to marginalize through his new administrative design' (Karlsson 2011: 256–7). In fact, Roy was a Congressman, Khasi politician, and an architect of the Sixth Schedule. Another member on the Sixth Schedule sub-committee was a graduate named Aliba Imti Ao, the son of a Naga Baptist pastor. In the Naga hills, the distinction between the traditional and modern elite was blurred; chiefdom was either weak or non-existent in most parts of the Naga hills. Since colonial indirect rule required chiefly institutions, the Raj had created administrative chiefs (*gaonburas*) and interpreters (*dobasi*s) simultaneously. Clothed with 'scarlet jackets and blankets as signs of their office' (Franke 2009: 56), both groups were stakeholders in colonial indirect rule. The traditional vision of 'Naga raj' conceived by Zadonang posed an alternative to colonial modernity and Christian conversion, but it did not represent any chiefly reaction to the middle-class challenge. Among the Kuki-Chin hill groups of Manipur, violent conflict ensued in 1960 between the traditional Haokip chiefs and modernizing Hmar elites in the Tamenglong district. The Kuki chiefs emerged stronger from this conflict. In the absence of safeguards for tribal land provided by the Sixth Schedule, many hill people in Manipur began to see the otherwise hated chiefs as a rallying point against the dominant plains community. The hill–valley tension and Naga–Kuki inter-tribal rivalry in Manipur have overshadowed the chief–council struggle witnessed among the rest of the hill groups governed by the Sixth Schedule.

ETHNICITY AND 'TRIBE'

An enumerable category of colonial governance, 'tribe' is a modern construct rather than an anachronistic artefact. To make the innumerable clans and lineages more governable, the Raj spoke in the idiom of tribes and chiefs. Early access to missionary education and the birth of articulate ethnic ideologues transformed colonial tribes into larger ethnicities or ethno-nations, such as the Naga, Mizo, Khasi, and Garo, during the post-independence era. African or Asian ethnicity has been an inexhaustible source of strength as well as strife. The 'tribal' was an ethnographic and bureaucratic construct of the colonial state; and, up to a point, the 'Scheduled Tribe' of the post-colonial Indian state is a derivative discourse. Likewise, ethnicity served as a language of victimhood in which postcolonial minorities addressed the nation-state. Ethnicity is Janus-faced: empowering and oppressive. While the justness of 'ethnic premises' (Wilmsen and McAllister 1996) is contested, it would be premature to dismiss its ideological power in north-east India.

In north-east India, the terms 'tribe' and 'tribal' are not regarded as politically incorrect. Public discourse in north-east India is familiar with three categories of tribal populations: hill tribes, plains tribes, and tea tribes. Being recognized as a member of the ST community is 'seen as a badge of honour' (Sharma 2011: x) against the backdrop of 'caste' societies. To many of the hill peoples in north-east India, asserts political scientist Sanjib Baruah, 'the English term tribe is consistent with the assertion of their modernity, as well as their cultural distinctiveness from mainland India. If anything, the Sanskritic term adivasi (literally "earliest inhabitants") has the opposite effect' (Baruah 2010). The indigenous hill peoples constituted the bulk of the official ST population in the region. Apart from the official vocabulary, the distinction between 'plains tribe' and 'hill tribe' has had a certain currency since the late colonial period. The term 'plains tribes' was introduced by a colonial ethnographer as a generic term for 'the tribes of the Brahmaputra valley as distinct from the tribes who lived in the hills' (Pathak 2010: 62), such as the Kachari (Bodo), Mikir (Karbi), Miri (Mishing), Lalung (Tiwa), and Rabha. Fostered by associative tribal conventions called *mels*, the plains Tribal League was established in 1933 as 'a mode of organised tribal politics' (Pathak 2010: 61).

In the north-eastern region, the Sanskritic term 'adivasi' refers to the 'tea tribes' who came to work in the Assam tea plantations as indentured labour. In the local Asomiya language, they are known as *baganiya* ('people of the garden') (Sharma 2008: 1321). The pejorative identity of 'coolie' has been officially discarded in favour of new names such as 'tea tribes' and 'adivasis', but this 'could not conceal workers' continued existence as an economically disadvantaged and racially stigmatized people' (Sharma 2011: 235). In recent years, the tea tribes have worked for their recognition as an ST within the state of Assam in the hope of enjoying certain benefits. But other plains tribes such as the Bodos have opposed such demands, because they threaten to reduce the small affirmative action pool (Sharma 2008: 1321). Since Bodo activists see the adivasis as interlopers, ethnic clashes locally reported as 'tribal–adivasi' conflicts have erupted between the two communities in the Bodoland Territorial Council areas (Baruah 2010). The birth of armed groups such as the Adivasi Cobra Force and Birsa Commando Force has fed into the spiral of violent reprisals. These outfits struggle for state recognition of the adivasi community in Assam as ST, against opposition by other tribal groups such as the Bodo. Their existence surfaced during the unruly Guwahati rally on 24 November 2007, in a brutal confrontation with the police. They have occasionally indulged in spells of violence—the so-called 'Bodo–adivasi clashes' in Assam (Misra 2007: 13). These are clear signals that the adivasi struggle for identity has entered a militant phase.

As far as the state is concerned, as a whole, the educational level of the ST population in north-east India is on a par with the most advanced social groups in the region, and far ahead of other STs in the entire country. National Sample Survey Organisation (NSSO) data indicates that in north-east India, 'being an ST is not as big a disadvantage as in the country as a whole' (Dubey and Pala 2009: 90). Christian STs are more likely to be literate than any other religious groups in the region, but the Christian factor plays a negligible role as far as achievements in secondary or higher education goes.[18]

Baruah (2010) claims that protected enclaves and differentiated citizenship 'provided incentives for a style of politics that privileges ethnicity and places indigenes and interlopers in a situation of structural conflict'.

* * *

In this chapter, I have not treated religious ideology as a determined superstructure that merely reflects a determining material base. Although

[18] Breakdown of the NSSO data for three religious communities (Hindu, Muslim, and Christian) also shows interesting results. Both in the 1983 and in the 1999–2000 surveys, Christians led all the rest for primary education, but Hindus consistently outperformed other groups at the level of secondary and higher education. Likewise, Christians showed the least number of illiterate persons in both NSSO surveys, while Muslims accounted for the largest number of illiterates in the north-east region.

religious change is not an autonomous agent, it sometimes served as a catalyst for new political possibilities. Over the long term, unique historical constellations converged to establish the dominance of particular belief systems for various social groups. Since the seventeenth century, the Ahom state had patronized and harnessed Shakta Brahmins who legitimized their political power by assigning them a correspondingly respectable pedigree in the caste hierarchy. Later, in the eighteenth century, Vaishnava Brahmins bestowed similarly noble pedigrees and legitimacy to the then promising princes of Manipur and Cachar. By claiming to be the offspring and protectors of sovereign deities, human kings asserted and displayed their rule over human subjects (Appadurai 1981: 51). Religious change was not simply a tool of political legitimacy for Sanskritizing princes; it can equally carve out new political pathways for dominated social groups. This was borne out by the political role of the Vaishnava sect of Moamarias in the downfall of the Ahom state, and also in the rise of a predominantly Christian educated elite which effectively challenged hereditary or nominated chiefs in the Sixth Schedule areas of republican India.

In core areas of state-building—both paddy and colonial states—Sanskritization and modernization did not necessarily lead to the secularization of minds or the retreat of religion. Even today, when organized religion has tactically moved out of secular public space, bourgeois spirituality and new-style faiths are making new conquests in the age of globalization. Varieties of rationalist thought (including the secularism of Nehru) hoped to dislodge religiosity from the Indian mind as the nation progressed linearly. But social reality proved a lot messier. Given the adaptability of proselytizing belief systems, it would be a mistake to write off religious change as a social force. Indeed, this cultural process deserves better understanding even by secular publics. Instead of discretely studying particular religious changes as bounded isolates, a synthetic gaze can reveal broader patterns of connected changes. This chapter is a small step in that direction. In the past, surely traditional religions, or rather older forms of religiosity, often lost out to new world religions such as Hinduism or Christianity. If Koch and Ahom princes sought to legitimize their militarized state through Shakta Brahminism, the rising state-builders of eighteenth-century Manipur and Cachar turned to a revitalized Vaishnavism. Likewise, educated tribal elites under colonial rule enthusiastically embraced Christianity, informed by Protestant confessional biases. Here, new forms of piety and respectability went together (Bayly 2004: 325). New belief systems flourished only by working with the grain of social and political changes in new locales (Bayly 2004: 335). Although indigenous tribal religions lost out to world religions, they still left residual traces in the form of Tantric rituals in Hinduism or the enthusiasm for post-harvest feastings on animal meat (read Christmas feasts) among tribal Christians of the north-east India. If the Ahoms converted to Shaktism without dispensing with their traditional Deodhais, the Meitei community in Manipur also embraced Vaishnavism while retaining their old Sanamahi worship.

Throughout history, tribal hill peoples had successfully evaded the paddy states in the lowlands, but the colonial state managed to incorporate local chiefs into the body of the Leviathan through a system of indirect rule. In the post-independence period, modernizing tribal elites vied for a role in the post-colonial nation-state. The new elite stood their own ground against older indigenous chiefs, foreign missionary tutelage, and majoritarian politicians in the plains. Within the hill groups, the struggle between traditional chiefs and modernizing elites played out in the overlap of authority between the district council and the cornered chiefs. Political outcomes varied from abolition to tolerance of chiefdom by democratizing councils under the Sixth Schedule. The tribal peoples in contemporary north-east India constitute a heterogeneous body with distinct historical lineages and divergent political trajectories. While the term 'tribal' is a politically privileged identity in the post-independence era, plains tribes have not been prepared to share the benefits of being 'STs' with Assam's tea tribes, also known as adivasis. The hill tribes and plains tribes had differential experiences of relating to the dominant peoples of the valley, the site of pre-colonial state-builders, the hub of British Assam, and the political seat of nation-builders in republican India.

REFERENCES

Appadurai, Arjun. 1981. *Worship and Conflict under Colonial Rule: A South Indian Case*. Cambridge: Cambridge University Press.

Barooah, Nirode K. 1969. 'David Scott and the Question of Slavery in Assam: A Case Study in British Paternalism', *Indian Economic and Social History Review*, vol. 6, pp. 179–96.

Baruah, Sanjib. 2010. 'Indigenes and Interlopers', *Himal Southasian*, July. Available at: http://old.himalmag.com/component/content/article/213-indigenes-and-interlopers.html (accessed 17 July 2015).

Bayly, C. A. 2004. *The Birth of the Modern World 1780–1914*. Malden and Oxford: Blackwell Publishing.

Becker, C. 1989. *Early History of the Catholic Missions in Northeast India*, trans. F. Leicht and S. Karotemprel. Shillong: Vendrame Institute, Secret Heart College.

Bezbaruah, Ranju. 2008. *North-East India: Interpreting the Sources and Its History*. New Delhi: Indian Council of Historical Research.

Bhattacharjee, J. B. 1977. *Cachar under British Rule in North East India*. New Delhi: Radiant Publishers.

Bhattacharyya, N. N. 1995. *Religious Culture of North-Eastern India*. New Delhi: Manohar.

Bhuyan, S. K. 1974. *Anglo-Assamese Relations 1771–1826*. Gauhati: Lawyer's Book Stall.

Cederlöf, Gunnel. 2009. 'Fixed Boundaries, Fluid Landscapes: British Expansion into Northern East Bengal in the 1820s', *Indian Economic and Social History Review*, vol. 46, no. 4, pp. 513–40.

Chaube, S. K. 1999. *Hill Politics in Northeast India*. Hyderabad: Orient Longman.

Cheitharon Kumpapa (The Court Chronicles of the Kings of Manipur). 2005. Vol. I, trans. S. N. A. Parratt. London: Routledge.

Datta, Birendranath. 1995. *A Study of the Folk Culture of the Goalpara Region of Assam*. Guwahati: Gauhati University Publication Department.

Downs, Frederick Sheldon. 1971. *The Mighty Works of God: A Brief History of the Council of Baptist Churches in North East India: The Mission Period, 1836–1950*. Guwahati: Christian Literature Centre.

Dubey, Amaresh and Veronica Pala. 2009. 'Role of Christianity in Fostering Literacy and Education in North-eastern Region: Statistical Evidence', in T. B. Subba, et al., *Christianity and Change in Northeast India*. New Delhi: Concept Publishing Company, pp. 80–1.

Eaton, Richard M. 1984. 'Conversion to Christianity among the Nagas, 1876–1971', *Indian Economic and Social History Review*, vol. 21, pp. 1–44.

Eliot, Charles N. E. 1910. 'Hinduism in Assam', *Journal of the Royal Asiatic Society of Great Britain and Ireland*, October, pp. 1155–86.

Fisher, H. J. 1973. 'Conversion Reconsidered: Some Historical Aspects of Religious Conversion in Black Africa', *Africa*, vol. 43, pp. 27–40.

Franke, Marcus. 2009. *War and Nationalism in South Asia: The Indian State and the Nagas*. London and New York: Routledge.

Gellner, David N. 1993. *Monk, Householder, and Tantric Priest: Newar Buddhism and Its Hierarchy of Ritual*. New Delhi: Cambridge University Press.

Guha, Amalendu. 1984. 'Pre-Ahom Roots and the Medieval State in Assam: A Reply', *Social Scientist*, vol. 12, no. 6, pp. 70–7.

Guha, Ramachandra. 2010. *Makers of Modern India*. New Delhi: Penguin Viking.

Gurdon, P. R. T. 1907. *The Khasis*. London: David Nutt.

Harvey, Peter. 2004. *An Introduction to Buddhism: Teachings, History and Practices*. New Delhi: Cambridge University Press.
Hodson, T. C. 1913. 'The Religion of Manipur', *Folklore*, vol. 24, no. 4, pp. 518–23.
Horton, Robin. 1971. 'African Conversion', *Africa*, vol. 41, pp. 85–108.
———. 1975. 'On the Rationality of Conversion', *Africa*, vol. 45, pp. 219–35.
———. 1993. *Patterns of Thought in Africa and the West: Essays on Magic, Religion and Science*. Cambridge: Cambridge University Press.
Jones, D. E. 1998. *A Missionary's Autobiography*. Aizawl: H. Liansailova.
Kabui, Gangmumei. 2003. First published in 1991. *History of Manipur: Pre-Colonial Period*. New Delhi: National Publishing House.
Karlsson, Bengt G. 2011. *Unruly Hills: Nature and Nation in India's Northeast*. New Delhi: Social Science Press and Orient BlackSwan.
Kristian Hla Bu (Christian Hymnal). 2010. 18th revised edition, 4th reprint. Aizawl: Synod Literature and Publication Board.
Lahiri, Nayanjot. 1991. *Pre-Ahom Assam: Studies in the Inscriptions of Assam between the Fifth and the Thirteenth Centuries AD*. New Delhi: Munshiram Manoharlal.
Lloyd, J. Meirion. 1991a. *Harvest in the Hills: History of the Church in Mizoram*, Gospel Centenary Series No. 1. Aizawl: Synod Publication Board.
———. 1991b. *History of the Church in Mizoram*. Aizawl: Synod Publication Board.
Mackenzie. 1884. *Relations of the Government with the Hill Tribes of the North-East Frontier of Bengal*, Calcutta: Home Department Press.
Misra, Sanghamitra. 2011. *Becoming a Borderland: The Politics of Space and Identity in Colonial North-Eastern India*. New Delhi: Routledge.
Misra, Udayon. 2007. 'Adivasi Struggle in Assam', *Economic and Political Weekly* vol. 42, no. 51, pp. 11–14.
Morris, J. H. 1910. *The History of the Welsh Calvinistic Methodists' Foreign Mission*. Wales: Carnavon (reprinted by North-Eastern Hill University, Shillong, 1996).
Nag, Sajal. 2012. 'Rescuing Imagined Slaves: Colonial State, Missionary and Slavery Debate in North East India 1908–1920', *Indian Historical Review*, vol. 39, no. 1, pp. 57–71.
Narayan, Jayaprakash. 1965. *Nagaland ka Saval* (The Question of Nagaland). Varanasi: Sarva Seva Sangh Prakashan.
Parry, N. E. 1976. First published in 1932. *The Lakhers*. Aizawl: Tribal Research Institute.
Pathak, Suryasikha. 2010. 'Tribal Politics in Assam: 1933–1947', *Economic and Political Weekly*, vol. 45, no. 10, pp. 61–9.
Peel, J. D. Y. 2000. *Religious Encounter and the Making of the Yoruba*. Bloomington and Indianapolis: Indiana University Press.
Philip, Puthuvail T. 1972. 'The Growth of the Baptist Churches of Tribal Nagaland'. MA thesis, Fuller Theological Seminary.

Pruett, Gordon E. 1974. 'Christianity, History and Culture in Nagaland', *Contributions to Indian Sociology* (n.s.), no. 8, pp. 51–65.
Rustomji, 1983. *Imperilled Frontiers: India's North-Eastern Borderlands.* Delhi: Oxford University Press.
Sarkar, Jadunath. 1932. *Chaitanya's Life and Teaching.* Calcutta: M. C. Sarkar & Sons.
Scott, James C. 2010. *The Art of Not Being Governed: An Anarchist History of Upland Southeast Asia.* New Delhi: Orient BlackSwan.
Sema, Najekhu Y. 1972. *A Study of the Growth and Expansion of Baptist Churches in Nagaland with Special Reference to the Major Tribes.* M.Th thesis, Bethel Theological Seminary.
Shakespear, Lt Colonel John. 1912. *The Lushei Kuki Clans.* London: Macmillan and Co. Ltd.
Shakespear, J. 1913. 'The Religion of Manipur', *Folklore,* vol. 24, no. 4, pp. 409–55.
Sharma, Jayeeta. 2008. '"Lazy" Natives, Coolie Labour, and the Assam Tea Industry', *Modern Asian Studies,* vol. 43, no. 6, pp. 1287–324.
———. 2011. *Empire's Garden: Assam and the Making of India.* Ranikhet: Permanent Black.
Skaria, Ajay. 1999. *Hybrid Histories: Forests, Frontiers and Wildness in Western India.* New Delhi: Oxford University Press.
Snaitang, O. L. 1993. *Christianity and Social Change in Northeast India.* Shillong: Vendrame Institute.
Sword, Victor Hugo. 1935. *Baptists in Assam: A Century of Missionary Service* (reprinted by Spectrum Publications, Guwahati and Delhi, 1992).
Thomas, John. 2010. *Missionaries, Church and the Formation of Naga Political Identity 1918–1997*, PhD thesis, Centre for Historical Studies, Jawaharlal Nehru University, New Delhi.
———. 2012. 'Sending Out the Spears: Zeliangrong Movement, Naga Club, and a Nation in the Making', *Indian Economic and Social History Review,* vol. 49, no. 3, pp. 399–437.
Wilmsen, Edwin N. and Patrick McAllister (eds). 1996. *The Politics of Difference: Ethnic Premises in a World of Power.* Chicago: University of Chicago Press.
Zou, David Vumlallian. 2005. 'Raiding the Dreaded Past: Representations of Headhunting and Human Sacrifice in North-East India', *Contributions to Indian Sociology* (n.s.), vol. 39, no. 1, pp. 75–105.
———. 2010. 'A Historical Study of the "Zo" Struggle', *Economic and Political Weekly,* vol. 45, no. 14, pp. 56–63.

5

The Adivasi Other
Ethnicity and Minority Status

Rudolf C. Heredia

If fundamental questions of adivasi identity and dignity are to be faced, we must go beyond such 'vague' descriptions of them as 'indigenous peoples', or treat them merely as colonial administrative categories, or identify them as a contemporary ideological category.[1] A historical-evolutionary approach takes us beyond such pragmatic operational definitions. Here I argue that to preserve the identity and dignity of these threatened people today, adivasi ethnic identity needs to be mobilized to overcome their minority status, so that in their integration into the national mainstream, the distinctive contribution they make will be appreciatively acknowledged, and the incisive challenge they pose will be honestly faced by the larger society. However, to do this effectively, we must take into consideration the class dimensions of ethnicity.

The term 'adivasi', meaning 'original inhabitants', was first used in the Chota Nagpur region of Bihar in the 1930s, and was extended to other regions in the 1940s by A. V. Thakkar, who worked among these communities. The Gandhians popularized other polite equivalents such as *ranipaja*, *vanyajati*, and *girijan* (jungle, forest, and mountain dwellers,

---

[1] This chapter draws on my earlier work in *Tribal Identity and Minority Status: The Kathkari Nomads in Transition* (with Rahul Srivastava), Concept Publishing, New Delhi, 1994.

respectively). In the historical Indian context now 'adivasi' refers to a wide variety of communities which before had remained relatively free from the control of outside states, but were eventually subjugated during the colonial period and brought under the control of the state. Today they are classified as 'Scheduled Tribes' by the Indian Constitution, and more generally they are known as tribal or indigenous peoples.

IDENTIFYING OUR 'TRIBALS'

In attempting a definition of a 'tribe', we must be sensitive to the diversity and complexity of adivasi society in our country. There are many adivasi systems with their distinctive cultures and separate economies. In fact, we need to be aware of intra-adivasi differentiation as well, since, but for a few isolated and small communities, no adivasi community in India today subsists on a single mode of production. Surveying the present literature, Susana Devalle (1992: 33) writes that from the earliest studies by colonial administrators and other pioneers to 'the bulk of contemporary writings on adivasis, the term "tribe" has remained vague, not adequately conceptualized and, consequently, of weak methodological value.... Most Indian "tribal studies" have remained synchronic and descriptive, ignoring the economic and political transformations that affected the populations studied.'

The etymological origin of the word 'tribe' goes back to the Latin *tribus*, which referred to the three original divisions of the early Romans, and which has then been extended to any similar division whether of natural or political origin. Today the ordinary meaning of the word in the *Oxford Dictionary* is a 'group of people in a primitive or barbarous stage of development acknowledging the authority of a chief and usually regarding themselves as having a common ancestor'. More recently, the *International Encyclopedia of the Social Sciences* suggested that 'the unnecessary moralistic overtones that this usage implies can be minimized by the use of the expression "tribal society"' (Lewis 1968). The *Dictionary of Anthropology* defines the word more neutrally, but rather restrictively, as 'a social group, usually with a defined area, dialect, cultural homogeneity, and unifying social organization' (Winick 1960: 546).

However, in ancient Indian literature there is really no equivalent word. The early Sanskrit references are to *jana*s, or 'people'. Jagannath Pathy writes that 'prior to the British annexation, most of the presently called tribes were unselfconscious of their ethnic distinctiveness and referred to themselves as "people", vis-a-vis outsiders, in their own distinctive speech' (Pathy 1984: 2). It was the British who designated these people as tribes, to distinguish them from Hindus and Muslims, since they were considered to be 'animists'. The other indigenous terms in use today are all of Sanskritic origin and were coined rather recently by outsiders who worked with these communities, variously called adivasis, *adimjatis*, *vanyajatis*, *vanvasis*, *girijans*, or *pahadias*.

The veteran anthropologist Stephen Fuchs categorically affirms that 'in fact, there exists no satisfactory definition of the term "tribe" anywhere' (1974: 24). Since there is no common agreement on a substantive definition, anthropologists and others have fallen back on listing group characteristics to identify a people as 'tribals'. But more often than not, these lists themselves serve better to illustrate the prejudices and presumptions of the compilers, than to make any but a very tenuous and sometimes even arbitrary delineation between tribals and non-tribals in this country.

An Administrative Category

But then, urgent administrative requirements do not wait for the leisurely resolution of scholarly controversies. Already in 1916, the Indian Legislative Council had decided that 'criminal and wandering tribes', 'aboriginal tribes', and 'untouchables' would be included in the term 'Depressed Classes'. The 1931 census separated out the tribals under the category of 'primitive tribes' instead of 'forest tribes' as in the 1891 census or 'hill tribes' in subsequent ones. In 1941, the census used just 'tribes', and today the Constitution of India refers to them as 'Scheduled Tribes'. This list, notified in 1950, was revised in 1956 by the Backward Classes Commission following the reorganization of the states, and has been subjected to periodic revisions since.

The Constitution nowhere attempts a substantive definition of the term 'tribe'. But it did try to set down a method and a machinery for designating tribals. However, what the Commissioner for Scheduled Castes and Tribes underlined in 1952 still remains true:

> No such uniform test has however, been evolved for classifying Scheduled Tribes with the result that in view of the divergent opinions held by Census authorities and public men from time to time, difficulties have been experienced in determining as to which tribe can rightly be included or excluded from the Scheduled Tribes. I consider that some definite criteria for this purpose must also be devised so that full justice is done

at the time of respecification of the 'Scheduled Tribes'. (Government of India 1952: 77)

Yet no such 'just criterion' has been devised, and it is political pressures rather than social justice that has been at work in the revisions of this schedule. Thus, in 1950 there were 212 STs; by the 1981 census, after two revisions of the list in 1956 and 1976, there were 427, comprising 7.76 per cent of the population, or 51.6 million people. By the time of the 2011 census, 705 tribes were notified, comprising 8.2 per cent of the population or 105.3 million. However, as yet ethnographic data on a number of adivasi communities are lacking.

An Ideological Concept

In other words, 'tribe has clearly become an ideological concept, a concept which fails to recognize the reality it expresses' (Pathy 1988: 25). As such, it could be expected that like 'race', as a concept, 'the tribe would become redundant in academic discourse', except where it has remained politically 'useful to the powers that be to manipulate divisions and rule over their subjects' (Pathy 1988: 20).

Today, 'for almost all Indian researchers a tribe is a tribe which is included in the list of Scheduled Tribes' (Pathy 1988: 22). But such a reduction of the term to a political-administrative category leaves out the socio-cultural dimensions, not to mention the economic one as well. This amounts to a fatal truncation for any relevant perspective on the adivasis. Obviously another approach is called for. We believe the historical evolutionary one to be more promising.

A HISTORICAL PERSPECTIVE

The importance of a historical perspective in adivasi studies has not always been conceded. Too easily this has been dismissed because the documented referent was missing. Due to their isolation, the limited worldview of the adivasis was said to be characterized by lack of historical depth, where history merged into mythology. Unfortunately, little effort has been made to use oral history, mostly because of ignorance on the part of the historian-ethnographer in interpreting folklore metaphors and symbols for tracing the past of the people.

This has led to a static view of adivasi society, which gets increasingly out of sync as the pace of change among these people quickens. For no society can be completely static, and adivasi society has a dynamic of its own. More recently, the study of these communities as changing aggregates has become an important departure from earlier research, and a much overdue one too. In fact, in the rapid transition that all such communities are undergoing, each has its own history and stage of evolution, from food gatherers and hunters, to shifting and settled cultivators, from pastoral nomads to urban-industrial workers. Any study of the adivasis, then, must situate the group within the context of its evolutionary history.

The Sanskrit word 'jana' referred to non-monarchical societies outside the jati system. Yet some would insist that the 'Hindu mode of absorption' is an inadequate explanation, since it characterizes the direction of adivasi change unidirectionally towards jati characteristics. Surely, 'tribes' have been transformed into castes in many varied situations. D. D. Kosambi (1975: 49) insists that 'the entire course of Indian history shows tribal elements being fused into a general society'. But then these people cease being 'tribal'. Yet at the end of this period, the British still found communities outside the caste system, though mostly isolated ones in more remote areas, whom they called 'tribes'. For the janas that retained their culture, and consequently their adivasi identity, could not be absorbed into the rigid jati hierarchy. Probably their geographic isolation did help as well.

Representation Technology

When the colonialists first discovered oral cultures, they rather patronizingly assumed that if language distinguished men from beasts, it was writing that distinguished the civilized from the savages! In the ultimate analysis, writing as a representational technology was a decided advantage in such an encounter. And when these pre-literate people did begin writing, it was often the 'others' who wrote about them and seldom in their own language. This could not but alienate them further from authentic self-representation.

The underlying ethnocentrism and chauvinism of such a presumption served the political purposes of the dominant colonizers, to the point where their treatment of such pre-literate peoples, mostly adivasis, would make one wonder, as Montaigne did in his *Essays*, who really are the more barbarous, the colonized or the colonizers! But what is more significant is why writing gave such an overwhelming advantage in this clash of cultures. Why could not an oral tradition cope with this encounter as effectively as the literate one did? This is surely a pertinent question for any venture in oral history.

Writing has always marked a quantum jump in the history of a human community. Tzvetan Todorov, commenting on the clash of cultures in the New World, concludes that 'the absence of writing is an important element of the situation, perhaps *the* most important' (1984: 80). Interestingly, the absence of writing did not lead so much to 'a loss of the past', for the formal discourse in an oral culture was in fact dominated by memory. It was 'rather a fatal loss of manipulative power in the present.... The culture that possessed writing could accurately represent to itself (and hence strategically manipulate) the culture without writing, but the reverse was not true' (Greenblatt 1991: 11).

Oral History

Moreover, too easily have adivasi societies been considered as societies without a history. Such recollections as they do have of their past are recorded in their oral traditions, grouped together under the overriding rubric of 'myth' and 'legend'. What would qualify as their history is by and large what has been recorded by other communities, and that in relation to the others', that is, these historians' own past. This yields only a reflected history, constructed through the perspective of others, and for these others. Certainly this is a great cultural deprivation, since we know how important historical memories are in the construction of community identities, certainly no less important than personal memories are for personal identities. Such an understanding of history deprives adivasi societies of an important cultural resource, namely the mobilization of their past to cope with the present.

Recording the oral history of such people, where they will speak for themselves, is but a small attempt to redress this huge disadvantage. For adivasi societies do have a rich oral tradition in which their collective memories are recorded. It is a living tradition and a changing one, precisely because it is still alive today. However, if historical constructions are to privilege written documents and dismiss oral history, then these oral traditions stand devalued.

And yet we know that every 'text', whether written or oral, must be read in its 'context'. And it is precisely this dialectic between text and context that can authenticate an oral historical tradition. A narrow positivist understanding of history in search of 'objective facts' does not recognize this. In such a perspective, oral traditions can yield merely a 'mythic history' with only a tenuous grounding in objective fact. This perspective obviously privileges literate society over oral ones, and all too readily condemns the latter to the eternal return of the seasonal cycle, without a chance of development and progress through time.

Once such a self-understanding is internalized by a community, it cannot but lead to its progressive marginalization in the larger society in which it is placed, left behind by the progress and development of other communities around. However, if we contextualize oral traditions within the adivasi societies that have given rise to them, then we can use them to attempt an authentic reconstruction of their past. In distancing ourselves from the positivist prejudice that privileges the objectivity of written documentation, we do not want to fall into the opposite extreme of the subjectivism of an oral tradition. Rather, the more sources we can use to set the context, the richer will be our interpretation and understanding of the text, whether it is oral or written.

Traditional Sources

What these peoples do have in common is a vibrant oral culture expressed in their language and symbols, their myths and rituals, their legends and sagas. However, given the scarcity of written resource material on these peoples, one may be tempted to discount their unwritten history, or worse, to consider them to be an ahistorical people! Certainly no history in the positivist sense of objective history can be effectively put together for the pre-colonial period of adivasi history, since there are few historical records that would meet the test of positivist criteria. However, to conclude from this that the adivasis had no history until it was recorded by others is totally unwarranted. It is tantamount to assuming that a people do not exist until others 'discover' them! In fact, many adivasi peoples have evolved a complex cultural heritage of their own. Writing about the Warlis in coastal Maharashtra, Hardiman (1987: 13) rightly concludes: 'the fact that they practised so many different methods of cultivation, that they are known to have migrated from one area to another, and that they were in some cases a regionally dominant power—all indicate that their history was every bit as full and complex as that of the rulers whose deeds fill medieval ballads and chronicles.' This is true of many large adivasi communities in other geographic areas. Rather, the way they recorded their own history and preserved their culture was quite different from that of their colonial 'discoverers'!

There are oral sources of tradition in these societies that are not strictly religious or even mythic. These are the legends and songs and sagas that are part of the collective memory of the adivasis. It is here that their experience of change in time is recorded, as one can see from the way in which these stories evolve and develop over time. These two types of traditions are not entirely separate, for they do indeed overlap; however, they are distinct both in the purposes they serve as also the objects they refer to.

Thus we have legends of origin, and also narrations of encounters with the environment as well as with outsiders. These give us an understanding of the identity and self-perception of these people, how they position themselves with regard to their natural environment, as well as how they respond to the encroachment of outsiders into their geographical and social space. Mythomoteurs, or myths of origin, among these people are scant and sketchy. They may have felt no strong need to identify themselves thus as long as they were isolated from outsiders and secure within their forest dwelling. Most of these outsider intruders became landowners, cultivators, timber merchants—in short, people who lived off the forest and not in it. As outsiders penetrated into their territory, settling in small habitations and opening up the forests, the adivasis tended to withdraw more and more into the interior, until the limits of their forest habitat were reached. The inevitable cultural clash was disastrous for the adivasis, and this is reflected in their collective memory, which must be a critical source for a reconstruction of this encounter. For too long has this been recorded only through the perceptions of the outsider. Now a subaltern sensitivity is required to remedy this. But this will demand a deconstruction of the earlier perspectives, their prejudgements and presumptions, particularly the ones from the colonial past that still impinge on our perception of adivasis, as also their own self-perceptions.

In fact, all through the pre-British period, the forest people served as bridge and buffer communities between kingdoms. It was this role that made possible the autonomy needed for the preservation and persistence of adivasi communities as distinct entities. But with the coming of the British all this changed.

The Colonial Penetration

In attempting to reclaim these 'primitives' for modern civilization, the colonial administration introduced private property rights in land, which led to a breakdown of the communal mode of production and control of common resources among these people. Processes of 'peasantization' and 'depeasantization' became inevitable, with the large-scale transfer of land from adivasis to non-adivasis. Further, the commercialization of the forests saw an alienation of traditional adivasi rights in their familiar habitat. The gradual but relentless monetization of the adivasi economy replaced the earlier, more personal barter economy with an impersonal medium of exchange.

The cumulative effect of all these changes was the gradual disappearance of the non-market mechanisms of social control of resources and allocation of goods. This resulted in further alienation, bewilderment, poverty, and confusion among adivasis. For now their non-competitive, non-accumulative, egalitarian ethos was distinctly to their disadvantage. In other words, the unequal exchange relation between the adivasis and the outsiders deteriorated dramatically into an oppressive exploitation of the adivasi community.

It is not surprising, then, that these adivasi people were among the earliest communities in India who resisted the British. Stephen Fuchs (1965) offers an impressive catalogue of these adivasi movements in his study *Rebellious Prophets*. Certainly, the overall impact of the colonial period was to effect a profound and unenviable transformation of adivasi dignity and identity in this country. This could be called the 'colonial mode of absorption', certainly more aggressive and penetrating than the earlier Hindu one, and it was the smaller and the less remote communities who were the most vulnerable to these changes, which they were unequipped to resist.

Earlier rulers had given the adivasis usufruct rights which provided all the produce they required for domestic and agricultural purposes from the forests. This provided a crucial safety net, allowing the forest dwellers to subsist off the commons when their survival was threatened in times of scarcity. However, colonial penetration into adivasi society was much more acute and comprehensive than earlier regimes. For, the exigencies of the colonial state dictated its policies, and in this cruel venture the government had more than eager collaborators in the region.

Moreover, the strong negative perceptions of these peoples by outsiders only served to strengthen and legitimize government policies that adversely affected these adivasis. They became the 'other' whose economic non-conformity was more than just a nuisance; it came in the way of the exploitation of natural resources on which their way of life so intimately depended. As they were increasingly alienated from their life-supporting environment, they became destitute, sometimes reduced to a lumpen and criminalized proletariat.

The colonial period thus witnessed a progressive and aggressive monetization of the economy of the adivasi region for revenue generation, making dependence on the forest ever more precarious and destroying adivasi self-reliance. Moreover, as the forests were taken over by government agencies and commercial interests, the adivasis were forced more and more to live from farming the land, where they were progressively forced into bonded labour by exploitative landlords, moneylenders, government officials, and other outsiders.

Moreover, the creation of private property rights in land was an equally disastrous break with adivasi tradition, in which land had always been held by the community even when it was assigned to private use. The unrestricted freedom to use and transfer land was intended to create an independent class of proprietors who would work the land productively. The upper castes, forest contractors, and others were the first to gain an advantage from this. They already possessed large landholdings which now became the base for expropriating the adivasis further.

But this had devastating effects on the adivasi population, who now were progressively dispossessed. For across the land,

> the adivasi peasant proprietor was soon turned into a tenant. He depended on the new settlers for his requirements of seed, consumption loan, money to pay the state revenue and for drink; the last becoming an instrument of exploitation for the settler and a form of escape for the adivasi, whereas it was earlier an expression of the solidarity and freedom of the adivasi collective. (Saldanha 1984: 175)

The squeeze on the adivasis between the zamindar, the *saukar*, and the *sarkar* (landlord, moneylender, and government) could not have happened without a collusion between these actors, each with their own agenda. The exigencies of revenue generation and commercialization of the regional economy needed an intermediary class owing allegiance to the colonial state, whose land and forest policies were so successful precisely in facilitating this. The result was the expropriation and pauperization of the adivasis by a class of expropriators who outlasted the colonial government, reducing the adivasi homeland, here as elsewhere, to 'a world where only unimaginable misery, poverty, destitution, degradation, disease, death and exploitation, flourish' (Parulekar 1947: 4).

Evolutionary Patterns

Not all ethnologists would concede an evolving pattern in adivasi society. For some, tribalism can be viewed as a defensive reaction to the formation of a complex society rather than a necessary preliminary stage in evolution. They appear as primitive enclaves in juxtaposition to highly organized cultures. But this is a static view, if not a reactionary one, of adivasi communities.

Other anthropologists have been more adept at enumerating stages in the development of such communities, than at indicating the dynamics of their evolution. Thus, L. P. Vidyarthi (1975) identifies six occupational groups among adivasis today: hunters and food gatherers, hill cultivators, plains farmers, simple artisans, cattle keepers, and industrial-urban workers. But this is more a descriptive than an analytical categorization.

Gadgil and Guha (1992: 14), in their presentation of *An Ecological History of India*, 'from the long sweep of human history' that they 'can distil four distinct modes of resource use: gathering (including shifting cultivation); nomadic pastoralism; settled cultivation; industry'. They provide an elaborate comparison of the features of these four major modes and their ecological impact. At any given time, human societies will be at different stages along this evolutionary path, and they can enact their social drama only in the context of the historical processes and circumstances which set the stage for them. The better these are understood, the more effective the interventions of the actors will be.

From a Marxist perspective, M. Godelier (1977: 87) distinguishes 'between the two uses of the term tribe, seen as a *type of society* and as a *stage of evolution*', by emphasizing how 'each stage of evolution is characterized by a specific mode of social organisation', 'as the mode of production changes the organisation of class in the evolution from tribe to chiefdom'. But this leaves out the question of multiple modes of production. Moreover, in considering a tribe to be a 'completely organised society', Godelier seems to be assuming identifiable boundaries for such communities. But this is not very helpful in distinguishing adivasi from non-adivasi societies, especially in the context of adivasi absorption in India.

Search for Identity

In the rapid and radical changes that are sweeping through India, the adivasis are clearly a very vulnerable group. Their identity as adivasi people is in effect negated, and their dignity as human persons all too often violated. Obviously, there is a connection between these two aspects of adivasi life today: their marginalization from the benefits of development, and their relegation to the bottom of the social hierarchy. For it is the same process of change that first isolates adivasis, negating their identity and denigrating their dignity, and then integrates and assimilates them in a 'forced division of labour', to use this phrase in the Durkheimian sense, into the lowest social strata, as alienated, anomic, violated persons, without rights or dignity in our society. Efforts to reverse this process have often been ineffective or even counterproductive.

In 1959, Nehru in his foreword to Verrier Elwin's *Philosophy for NEFA* set out the basis of the national policy on tribal development. This has remained its Magna Carta, its 'Panchsheel' till today:

(a) People should be allowed to develop on the lines of their own genius and nothing should be imposed upon them,
(b) tribal rights on land and forests should be respected,
(c) induction of too many outsiders into tribal areas should be avoided,
(d) there should be no over administration of tribal areas as far as possible, and
(e) the results should not be judged by the amount of money spent but by the quality of the human character that is involved.

Unfortunately, in the hurly-burly of electoral politics, such noble ideals tend to be honoured more in the breach than in actuality. However, in this contemporary scene it is not just governmental policies and their implementation that need to be taken into account. Equally, if not more important, are the adivasi initiatives and responses, if indeed we consider them to be active subjects of their history and not passive objects of change.

The Anthropological Survey of India in 1976 identified as many as 36 ongoing adivasi movements.

Behind all these movements lie the tribal's interminable search for identity and his urge to secure a better deal for himself.... Like peasant movements the tribal movements at this stage of social formation are bound to remain local, limited, restricted to dominant tribe or a group of tribes. This however does not minimize their importance, or detract from the issues they seek to highlight. (Singh 1982: 1344)

APPROACHES TO ETHNICITY

In the 1970s, 'a vast range of phenomena formerly subsumed under tribal, cultural, linguistic and religious differences, became increasingly identified with the term *ethnicity* despite some initial resistance' (Devalle 1992: 31). But theoretical perspectives were slower to change. Thus, in the Indian situation Surajit Sinha already in 1965 spoke of 'tribes' as 'certain ethnic groups' (Sinha 1965), and S. C. Dube introduced the idea of 'tribal ethnicity' in 1977 (Dube 1977: 1–5). More recently, others have used the term more analytically. Here we will first try to clarify the discourse before proceeding with our analysis.

In trying to reach the substantive core of 'ethnicity' and to set it in our adivasi context, we must at the outset realize that 'there never has been a single discourse of ethnicity. Rather there have been a *plurality of discourses*' (Devalle 1992: 16). Our purpose, however, is not to deal with just 'the *theoretical construct* created by social theorists to catalogue phenomena and social groups', but rather to 'encounter ethnicity as actually *lived*, as a dynamic process with a specific present, entailing a particular mode of social experience' (Devalle 1992: 18). Ethnicity, then, is here treated as a dynamic historical phenomenon, not a static conceptual category.

Hence we will not enter some of the overly theoretical debates: between the 'primordialists', for whom the ethnic group is based on a natural, primordial bond, and the 'instrumentalists' who stress its utilitarian and rational basis; or the 'survivalists', who see ethnic forms changing but not disappearing, and the 'evolutionists', who hold that these will eventually yield to a more democratic, socialist participation; or the 'maximalists', who limit ethnicity to strong and violent manifestations, and the 'minimalists', who include weak and symbolic expressions as well (Pathy 1988: 4–5).

Constructed Identities

Broadly speaking, ethnicity refers to a collective identity based on some common characteristics. Lists of these characteristics have been made to arrive at some kind of common substantive core. But as with the concept of 'tribe', here too much overlap and even arbitrariness is apparent in these listings. Obviously, any collective identity will have some content to it. But what this content will be, and how the group comes to an awareness of it, will depend on who is defining this identity and how it articulates it to others in that society. For besides the objective basis, as important if not more so for ethnic identities is the subjective construct. It is this which can create and legitimize such ethnic groups, as in the case of 'imagined communities' (Anderson 1983) and the 'invention of traditions' (Hobsbawm and Ranger 1983). Moreover, 'as collective identities practiced in everyday life' (Devalle 1992: 18), these ethnic identities must change as the group evolves.

Thus, while the objective features constitute a basis for an ethnic group, the boundary is delimited by the group's changing subjective consciousness. Hence, for our purposes here, an 'ethnic group is a historical entity whose members in large part conceive of themselves as being alike by virtue of certain common stable features located in language, culture, stereotypes, territory, ancestry—real or fictitious—specific nomenclature and endogamy and are so regarded by the members of other ethnic groups' (Pathy 1988: 19).

Now while none of these features are by themselves indispensable, the operative ones add up to what has been variously called 'primordial sentiments' (Geertz 1963), 'core values' (Barth 1970), 'symbolic estates' (Lyman and Douglas 1973), and 'corporate holdings' (Handelman 1977). However basic or primordial these core features may be, in so far as they are part of a 'constructed identity', they are never immutable or static, but always responsive to the eco-political and socio-cultural context in a concrete historical situation. It is only when ethnicity is conceptualized in such a relational context that it can be a useful analytical tool. But unfortunately not all approaches to ethnicity have been sensitive to this.

The earliest attempts at constructing ethnic identities for the adivasi world were usually by outsiders imposing ethnocentric stereotypes that were largely negative and/or patronizing, as for instance the 'noble savage' or 'the primitive tribal'. This reflected more the West's need to come to terms with the 'other', the non-Western world, than the historical reality and experience of these people. In fact 'the de-historization and deculturation of subordinate peoples and the imposition of constructed identities have helped in the process of economic and political domination' (Devalle 1992: 28).

Ethnicity, Class, and Caste

In classical Marxism, ethnicity was subsumed under class divisions that are essentially economic differences, which have political consequences. But soon it became apparent that the capitalist state, rather than homogenizing ethnic differences within it, on the contrary 'produces the condition for the rise of ethnic self-consciousness and accelerates parochial loyalties' (Pathy 1988: 3). Later, with neo-Marxism, ethnic differences are seen to be reinforced and to become 'a mechanism for the recreation of hegemony and the reproduction of socio-economic inequality' (Devalle 1992: 43). However, the Marxist approaches still 'leave ethnicity unexplained, or explained as a vague superstructural phenomenon serving ruling class interests, ... to keep the workforce divided and preclude the development of class consciousness' (Devalle 1992: 44).

The more recent civilizational or ethno-national approach developed in Latin America and Africa is opposed to both extremes: 'to perspectives that maintain the autonomy of ethnicity and to economistic reductionism' (Devalle 1992: 45). Rather it emphasizes both economic and socio-cultural domination, that gives rise to ethnic formations among the oppressed, who are now 'emerging peoples', and who will have 'a central role in the forging of a new society' (Devalle 1992: 45).

However, this approach remains somewhat weak in locating ethnic movements within the class structure. Hence, the distinction between an ethnicity that supports the dominant class hegemony, as in populist nationalist politics, and one that opposes this from the counter-hegemonic subalterns, is blurred if not lost. For ethnicity and class generally reinforce each other, for better or worse. In India such multiple disadvantages most often add up to a 'cumulative backwardness' (Galanter 1984: 249). But such a 'system of cumulative inequalities' does not automatically transform itself into one of 'dispersed inequalities' (Dahl 1961). In fact, 'industrialization did not so much transform cumulative distribution of inequalities as intensify it' (Dahl: 1972: 109).

Our understanding of ethnicity cannot remain preoccupied with delimiting its substantive core but must comprehend how an ethnic group articulates with the wider structures of social stratification, and how the group in turn gets stratified by these. For an ethnic group cannot be studied as an isolated, autonomous sub-system. This is certainly true of adivasis in India today.

Now, adivasi society is not hierarchically segregated. There is no sacred principle of ritual purity/pollution that stratifies, inter- or intra-adivasi societies. The 'homo hierarchicus' of Louis Dumont is very far from 'tribal man'. Yet it is an illusion to think of adivasis as homogeneous peoples any more. They were always segmented into various 'tribes' and clans. Today adivasi society is increasingly stratified by class. With a capitalist model of development, it would be hard to see how adivasi society could resist the forces of class formation. Thus, Pathy (1988: 29) affirms that 'without any exaggeration one can say that over 90 per cent of the so-called tribes are actually class societies inextricably intertwined with the Indian political economy as a whole'. In practice, 'class consciousness develops out of the collectively experienced everyday reality' (Devalle 1992: 238). A class-in-itself is not translated into a class-for-itself by some abstract discourse, but by lived common experiences. And 'when ethnic ascription and class situation correlate, ... both ethnic and class consciousness may develop in unison' (Devalle 1992: 238). This can provide a powerful strategic basis for group mobilization. But when a big ethnic community is stratified by class divisions, or a large social class is segmented into many ethnic groups, then the contradictions between class and ethnic interests can be manipulated and mobilized by vested interests.

ADIVASI MINORITIES

The Indian Constitution recognizes only linguistic and religious minorities, and the courts have defined a 50 per cent limit for a group to be considered a minority in a state. However, the term 'minority group' as it is used today in the social sciences does not refer to relative numbers. To quote the *International Encyclopedia of the Social Sciences*:

> Contemporary sociologists generally define a minority as ... a group of people differentiated from others in the same society by race, nationality, religion or language who both think of themselves as a differentiated group and are thought of by the others as a differentiated group with negative connotations. Further, they are relatively lacking in power and hence are subjected to certain exclusions, discriminations and other differential treatment. (Rose 1968: 365)

Pathy rightly insists that 'the Scheduled Tribes undisputedly possess all the properties of ethnic minorities' (1988: 194). But since we are referring to adivasi ethnicity, we would prefer to be more specific with the term 'adivasi minorities'. Whatever the terminology, the insistence on the class dimension of ethnicity is precisely to ensure that ethnic identities are not manipulated in favour of dominant group interests.

Thus, just as the better-off adivasis are mobilized by the non-adivasis for their own class interests, though they may later try to restrict or deny the adivasis their share in the pay-offs, so too are the poorer adivasis mobilized by the better-off ones. This is possible precisely because

> the poor Adivasis are mobilized in politics by the vocal tribal on tribal and non-tribal rather than on class lines. Moreover, the vocal strata of the

tribals instil 'tribalness' in terms of tribal culture which tranquilizes the poor. But the vocal tribals themselves discard the so-called 'tribal culture' in their day-to-day life because it is against their own aspiration and interests. (Pathy 1988: 194)

Thus, class inequalities of the larger society are reproduced within an adivasi people through the use of ethnicity.

Now, whether these ethnic groups are mobilized to change or preserve the status quo would depend on whether they have subordinate or dominant social status. When an ethnic group is subordinate, then it can be called an 'ethnic minority'. Here there is an overlap between an ethnic identity that is socio-culturally subservient and a class status that is eco-politically subordinate. With ethnic communities in India, especially the smaller ones, this coincidence of negative identity and low status is not unusual.

The essential features, then, are not just some objective characteristics, but a subjective construct consisting of a set of attitudes: self-definition from within and prejudice from without; and a set of behaviours: self-segregation from within and discrimination and exclusion from without.

IDENTITY AND INTEGRATION

Adivasi minorities, as we have explained, are distinctive ethnic groups in a subordinate class position. The issue to be addressed in their regard is one of overcoming their minority status and of affirming their adivasi identity, or rather remedying the first by mobilizing the second—in other words, integrating adivasi people into a culturally pluralist, economically egalitarian society, and not assimilating them into an ethnically uniform, class-stratified state. But integration has not always been the official policy with regard to our adivasis, nor has it been understood in the same way at different times or by all concerned.

Gadgil and Guha (1992: 109) indicate varying responses to the clash of cultures involved, when different modes of resource use come into competitive contact. One resolution to the conflict has been 'the *path of extermination*.... In this scenario, the earlier modes are more or less wiped out'. This has generally been the path of Europe, and its encounter with the non-European peoples.

In the Indian experience, 'two complementary strategies, of leaving some ecological niches (hills, malarial forests) outside the purview of the peasant mode, and reserving certain niches within it for hunter-gatherers and pastorals, helped track a distinctive path of inter-modal cooperation and coexistence' (Gadgil and Guha 1992: 109). Here, the less resilient modes survived but were subordinated to the more dominant ones. In traditional Indian society, such institutionalized hierarchy was acceptable to all groups. But as this changes, another more democratic basis for cooperation and coexistence must be found, unless we want to perpetuate 'homo hierarchicus' into the present millennium.

The historical syncretism that developed in the subcontinent across ethnic and religious divides produced a composite culture for a segmented society within a hierarchical structure. Remarkably, it reproduced this hierarchy within the assimilated groups, even as it found a niche to encapsulate them in the overall system. However, the encounter with modernity that came with colonialism deeply disturbed this arrangement.

Today the clash of adivasi and non-adivasi cultures in our country is harsher and deeper because the changes people are undergoing are more rapid and comprehensive than ever before. Robert Goodland (1982: 25) shows that these 'major and rapid social changes are associated with:

a. loss of self-esteem;
b. increase in actual and perceived role conflict and ambiguity;
c. increase in the perceived gap between aspiration and achievement.'

The resulting anomie has precipitated reactionary and revivalist responses in many sections of our society. The aggressive fundamentalist religious movements sweeping the subcontinent today are evidence of this. Surely the adivasis are the more vulnerable to rapid social change and so the more susceptible to a self-destructive anomie.

Efforts to mitigate and buffer the negative consequence of developmental change have certainly been made. 'India is one of the few countries in the world with elaborate systems of preferential treatment for ascriptively defined groups' (Pathy 1984: 163), especially for the scheduled castes and tribes. But after more than half a century of independence, they still have a long way to go to catch up with the mainstream, especially the smaller, weaker adivasi communities.

Isolation and Assimilation

In the colonial period there was a policy of isolation, but this was not in fact effective. The needs of the colonial state, its paternalism notwithstanding, were often satisfied at the cost of the adivasis. The many adivasi revolts, and even more so their forcible suppression, are ample evidence of this. The deteriorating terms of exchange between the adivasis and the outside world epitomize the relationship between the two, that is, neither autonomous isolation nor egalitarian integration, but a de-culturated assimilation at the lower end of the class strata that were being formed wherever the colonial political economy penetrated. Today it is no longer possible for adivasis to retreat into isolation, even if this were desirable, which we think not. For this approach to the adivasis seems to assume a static identity, often idealized by non-adivasis.

Some adivasi communities have over time been Sanskritized into the jati system. In this context it makes sense to speak of a 'tribe–caste continuum'. This of course assumes an assimilationist model. But for those communities which have kept their adivasi identity and stayed out of the jati hierarchy, this does not apply. Among the Indian anthropologists who urged the adivasis' entry into the national mainstream, many have advocated their assimilation into non-adivasi society, much the same way as the 'Hindu mode of absorption' had done earlier. Thus, G. S. Ghurye in his study *The Scheduled Tribes* (1963: 211) wanted an 'integrative assimilation' that would make the adivasis 'part and parcel of the Hindu Indian polity that is slowly but surely arising', and he wanted adivasi languages, which tend 'to counter-balance to some extent the speeding up of the process of assimilation' (Ghurye 1963: 152), to be replaced by the Indo-Aryan languages (Ghurye 1963: 190). The Sangh Parivar today has an aggressive programme for such a 'Hinduization' of the adivasis, while there are others who think of helping the adivasis to 'detribalize' themselves so as to be indistinguishable from other people in the region.

What the assimilationists seem to suggest, then, is overcoming adivasi minority status by sacrificing their ethnic identity. But experience in the field is contrary to this. For one thing, the potential of a positive identity to mobilize the group is lost, and the process of assimilation leaves the adivasis with a negative self-image and a deteriorating socio-economic status.

Since independence, the Government of India's adivasi policy has not been assimilationist, but it has tried to follow the 'Panchsheel' proposed by Nehru in 1959. However, the development it pursued has been more disintegrative for the adivasis than a genuine integration, with internal autonomy and economic equity. For, as a group of eminent scholars at a seminar on 'The Tribal Situation in India' asserted in their concluding statement: 'integration must be sharply distinguished from assimilation which means complete loss of cultural identity for the weaker groups...

integration is a dynamic process which necessarily involves mutual give-and-take by the various sections of the national community' (Singh 1992: 631–2).

Integration, then, depends very much on what kind of society our adivasis are being integrated into. Is it the caste hierarchy of our traditional culture, or the class stratification precipitated by our present political economy, or the pluralist-secular, democratic-socialist ideal sketched in our Constitution? It is only this last that can accommodate the kind of adivasi integration we must envisage, one which will salvage both their identity and their dignity. For while in the caste hierarchy, integration must mean a loss of their adivasi identity, in a class system they are only confirmed in their minority status. And yet, since caste is very much a factor to be reckoned with in our culture, just as class is in our economy, any realistic approach to integration must take cognizance of both these.

Contribution and Responses

Hence, a dynamic process of adivasi integration must not only preserve their cultural autonomy, but also mobilize them to participate in their own development, which in turn must be both equitable and sustainable. Needless to say, it is the smaller, poorer adivasi communities that are most in need of such development and most deprived of it too. But, if dynamic integration is also to be a two-way process, in which adivasi identity and dignity are respected and preserved, then it must be sensitive to their contribution to the larger society as well. This has not always been conceded, so here we mention only a few convincing instances.

With regard to sustainable development of forests and other eco-sensitive regions, Gadgil and Guha (1992: 52) point out that the people who live close to and accept their dependence on the environment are better able to live in harmony with it, than those who want only to exploit it from a distance for commercial purposes. Robert Goodland writing for the World Bank confirms this. In marginal lands, 'unlike tribal societies, both agro-industrial groups and peasant farmers have shown themselves almost totally unable to manage sustainably and produce effectively in such environments' (1982: 13). Further, he adds that in preserving the precious and precarious biodiversity of the planet, 'indigenous knowledge is essential for the use, identification, and cataloging of the biota' (Goodland 1982: 14). What our adivasis do represent, therefore, is a *significant economic opportunity for the nation*, not a luxury. They are at the forefront of knowledge of the management of marginal environments and can contribute to the national society. Sustainable exploitation of eco-systems often considered marginal is becoming increasingly necessary for national societies and the world as a whole. Capitalization on these unique strengths is highly desirable for economic development. (Goodland 1982: 15)

It might seem ironic, but it is now becoming more apparent, though still somewhat reluctantly admitted in conventional circles, that given their accumulated experience and collective traditions, adivasi 'religion and custom as ideologies of resource use are perhaps better adapted to deal with a situation of imperfect knowledge than a supposedly "scientific" resource management' (Gadgil and Guha 1992: 53). Our frantic pursuit of an ever higher 'standard of living' has not led to a corresponding improvement in our 'quality of life', but has rather compromised and even undermined it. Such contradictions challenge us to a new understanding of development in which we have much to learn from adivasi societies, especially with regard to a cultural basis for a sustainable relationship to our environment.

Stephen Fuchs distinguishes three responses of the adivasis to their critical situation in developing India. The response of rejection and regression into isolation will only leave them 'practically condemned to total extinction' (Fuchs 1992: 50). Only a few of the nomadic forest communities would opt for this. However, by far the largest portion are 'ready to change their tribal ways of life and to go along with the national mainstream' (Fuchs 1992: 50). But they would not want to lose their adivasi identity. What they do seem to want is integration, and not assimilation, as explained earlier. But there are also adivasis who look 'for another alternative, in the hope of saving their tribal identity and independence' (Fuchs 1992: 50). These are generally from among the larger, more geographically concentrated communities. Some of these movements have even sought to secede from the Indian union, as in the north-east, while others have fought to express their solidarity in an adivasi state within it, as in Jharkhand in Chota Nagpur and in the north-east of the country.

These movements are of course only the extreme expression of what many more adivasi communities experience, though they are unable to mobilize themselves in response to it. The major roots of adivasi solidarity movements may be traced to their ecological-cultural isolation, economic marginalization, and a feeling of relative deprivation vis-à-vis mainstream society. What our adivasis, then, seem to be looking for is an integration into our national society, which will respect their 'cultural autonomy' even as it gives them their economic and political place under the sun. Surely this is not an illegitimate or an unreasonable demand.

The Constitution (74th Amendment) Act, 1992, mandated devolution of governmental power to local village panchayats to facilitate effective local governance and self-reliant local communities. This legislation was extended by the Panchayat (Extension to Scheduled Areas) Act (PESA), 1996. The synergy created, with state governments providing the funding and local panchayats setting priorities and enforcing accountability, has great promise for local adivasi communities. But unfortunately, this is often stymied in the scramble for mining and forest resources in these scheduled areas, led by corporations and largely with the connivance of state and central governments. This has now precipitated a violent resistant movement in adivasi areas led by the Maoists, the Communist Party of India (Marxist-Leninist), or the CPI(ML).

The Adivasi Challenge

It is not only at the margin or the periphery of a society that adivasis have an important and valuable contribution to make, for adivasi non-consumerist solidarity provides an alternative to the competitive consumerism of the non-adivasi world. This is a moral challenge we can ill afford to ignore, in view of the pervading crises which have riddled our society.

Often enough, it is these marginal groups that have posed a substantial challenge for a revitalization and regeneration of the larger society. Here it may well be the distinctive cultural traits of an adivasi group rather than its relative size and influence that may pose the more incisive question, the moral challenge to the 'other' in us, in the search for an alternative way of life. For in spite of the apparent difference and distance between these two worlds, there is the real possibility of creative communication. As Robert Redfield and Milton Singer have observed: 'in every tribal settlement there is civilization; in every city is the folk society' (1971: 343). Indeed, at a deeper level, the adivasi nomad in the forest-hills may have more relevance to George Simmel's 'stranger' in the metropolitan cities than may appear superficially at first.

If we assimilate the adivasis into our society, we do away with any possible contribution or challenge they may be able to make to our society as adivasis, and though we may devalue their contribution now, are we sure we will never be in need of it in the future? And if we leave them isolated, 'natural, wild and free', are we not freezing them into a time-warp as 'objects' to be 'used' by us, if and when we need them? The response we are urging here is to reject both these alternatives, for we do value the contribution and challenge they represent to us already in the present. Our unsustainable, polluting, consumerist society needs this constructive critique from a counter-cultural 'other'. Assimilation or isolation of our adivasis cannot do this.

What we must struggle for together with our adivasis, then, is to achieve an integration that will address the fundamental issues of the adivasi question, issues that affect ethnic minorities in our society more acutely, but must be the concern of all in our country as well: social equity, ecological sustainability, people's participation, cultural autonomy, and democratic integration, to mention but a few. If we are pointing to a utopia, which is many giant leaps out of our reach just yet, then we can at least begin to grasp what small steps we must take now to make an integrative response to the larger adivasi dilemma.

REFERENCES

Anderson, Benedict. 1983. *Imagined Communities: Reflections on the Origin and Spread of Nationalism*. London: Verso.
Barth, Fredrik (ed.). 1970. *Ethnic Groups and Boundaries: The Social Organisation of Culture Difference*. London: George Allen and Unwin.
Dahl, Robert A. 1961. *Who Governs? Democracy and Power in an American City*. New Haven: Yale University Press.
———. 1972. *Authority in a Good Society: After the Revolution*. Bombay: Allied.
Devalle, Susana B. C. 1992. *Discourses of Ethnicity: Culture and Protest in Jharkhand*. New Delhi: Sage.
Dube, S. C. 1977. *Tribal Heritage in India*, vol. I: *Ethnicity, Identity and Interaction*. New Delhi: Vikas.
Elwin, Verrier. 1959. *Philosophy for NEFA*, 2nd edn. Shillong: Government of Assam, pp. 4–5.
Fuchs, Stephen. 1965. *Rebellious Prophets: A Study of Messianic Movements in Indian Religions*. Bombay: Asia Publishing House.
———. 1974. *The Aboriginal Tribes of India*. Delhi: Macmillan.
———. 1992. 'The Religion of Indian Tribals', in Buddhadeb Chaudhuri (ed.), *Tribal Transformation*, vol. V. New Delhi: Inter-India Publication, pp. 23–51.
Gadgil, Madhav and Ramachandra Guha. 1992. *This Fissured Land: An Ecological History of India*. New Delhi: Oxford University Press.

Galanter, Marc. 1984. *Competing Equalities: Law and the Backward Classes in India*. New Delhi: Oxford University Press.
Geertz, Clifford (ed.). 1963. *Old Societies and New States*. New York: Free Press.
Ghurye, G. S. 1963. *The Scheduled Tribes*, 3rd edn. Bombay: Popular Prakashan.
Godelier, M. 1977. *Perspectives in Marxist Anthropology*. London: Cambridge University Press.
Goodland, Robert. 1982. *Tribal Peoples and Economic Development: Human Ecologic Considerations*. Washington, D.C.: World Bank.
Government of India. 1952. *Report of the Commissioner for Scheduled Castes and Tribes*. New Delhi: Government of India.
Greenblatt, S. 1991. *Marvelous Possessions: The Wonder of the New World*. Chicago: University of Chicago Press.
Handelman, D. 1977. 'The Organisation of Ethnicity', *Ethnic Groups*, vol. 1, no. 3, pp. 187–200.
Hardiman, David. 1987. *The Coming of the Devi: Adivasi Assertion in Western India*. New Delhi: Oxford University Press.
Hobsbawm, E. J. and T. O. Ranger (eds). 1983. *The Invention of Traditions*. Cambridge: Cambridge University Press.
Kosambi, D. D. 1975. *An Introduction to the Study of Indian History*. Bombay: Popular Prakashan.
Lewis, I. M. 1968. 'Tribal Society', in David L. Sills, ed., *International Encyclopedia of the Social Sciences*. New York: Macmillan, vols 15, 16, 17, pp. 146–50.
Lyman, S. and N. A. Douglas. 1973. 'Ethnicity: Strategies of Collective and Individual Impression Management', *Social Research*, vol. 40, no. 2, pp. 344–65.
Parulekar, S. V. 1947. *Revolt of the Warlis*. Mumbai: Peoples Publishing House.
Pathy, Jagannath. 1984. *Tribal Peasantry: Dynamics of Development*. New Delhi: Inter-India Publications.
―――. 1988. *Ethnic Minorities in the Process of Development*. Jaipur: Rawat Publications.
Redfield, Robert and Milton B. Singer. 1971. 'City and Countryside: The Cultural Interdependence', in Teodor Shanin (ed.), *Peasants and Peasant Societies: Selected Readings*. Middlesex, UK: Penguin.
Rose, Arnold M. 1968. 'Minorities', in David L. Sills (ed.), *International Encyclopedia of the Social Sciences*, vol. 10. New York: Macmillan, pp. 365–70.
Saldanha, D. 1984. 'A Socio-Psychological Study of the Development of Class Consciousness'. Unpublished PhD. thesis, Department of Sociology, University of Bombay.
Singh, K. S. 1982. 'Transformation of Tribal Society: Integration vs Assimilation', *Economic and Political Weekly*, vol. 17, no. 34, pp. 1376–84.
――― (ed.). 1992. 'Statement Issued by the Seminar', in *The Tribal Situation in India: Proceedings of a Seminar*. Simla: Indian Institute of Advanced Studies, pp. 631–2.

Sinha, Surajit. 1965. 'Tribe-Caste and Peasant-Caste Continua in Central India', *Man in India*, vol. 45, no. 1, pp. 57–83.

Todorov, Tzvetan. 1984. *The Conquest of America: The Question of the Other*, trans Richard Howard. New York: Harper and Row.

Vidyarthi, L. P. 1975. 'Strategy for Tribal Development in India', Proceedings of the Seminar on Tribal Development, Bhubaneshwar.

Winick, Charles. 1960. *Dictionary of Anthropology*. London: Peter Owen.

6

Denotification of the Rathvas as Adivasis in Gujarat*

Arjun Rathva, Dhananjay Rai, and *N. Rajaram*

The Gujarat government recently issued an order denotifying the Rathvas as a tribe ostensibly because their school records show them to be Hindus. The government's argument is that the Rathvas cannot be adivasis if they are Hindus. What makes the move ominous is that the Chhota Udepur region inhabited by the Rathvas is mineral-rich, and laws that protect adivasi rights come in the way of corporate exploitation of these resources. The order could also set a precedent to threaten adivasis elsewhere who protest against the loot of natural resources in their areas.

A storm is thus brewing in the eastern tribal belt of Gujarat, which could have far-reaching political and social consequences for the state's marginal groups which constitute 15 per cent of its population. The recent order[1] by the state's commissioner, Scheduled Tribe Development Office, which denotifies the Rathvas of Chhota Udepur as a tribe, is a move that is bound not only to hamper the constitutional protection extended to the various adivasi groups across India, but also to pave the

---

* This chapter was previously published in *Economic and Political Weekly,* vol. 49, no. 6 (2014), pp. 22–4.

[1] See order no. AVI/TAS/O/F No 430/2013-14/2770 to 2783, dated 19 October 2013, by the commissioner, Scheduled Tribe Development Office, Birsamunda Bhavan, Sector 10, Gujarat, Gandhinagar.

way for further displacement and exploitation of natural resources in Chhota Udepur.

DENOTIFICATION AND ITS IMPLICATIONS

According to the 2011 census, adivasis constitute 8.6 per cent of India's total population, and in Gujarat they account for 14.79 per cent of the population. The Fifth Schedule of the Constitution categorically specifies the role of the state in respect of scheduled areas and STs. The governors of nine states listed under this schedule regulate land transfer, allotment, and business activities in the scheduled areas. The Scheduled Areas (States of Bihar, Gujarat, Madhya Pradesh, and Odisha) 1977 (CO 109) Order identifies various talukas in Valsad, the Dangs, Surat, Bharuch, undivided Panchmahal, undivided Vadodara, and undivided Sabarkantha districts as the scheduled areas in Gujarat.[2] The PESA of 1996 empowers adivasis through gram sabhas to manage natural resources at the village level.

The Gujarat government, through the recent order, has cancelled the status of 11 government employees who are from the Rathva community. This order is bound to invite serious implications at several levels. At present, the Rathvas can contest elections to all seats reserved for adivasis, ranging from the sarpanch to membership of the taluka, district panchayats, assembly, and Parliament. It is possible that the order will abolish this right. Once the process of cancelling the community's status as a tribe is completed, denotification becomes a matter of a single circular by the state government. This order also gives the state government further powers to denotify adivasi groups that take part in resistance struggles against corporate loot through undemocratic processes.

The Gujarat government also cancelled jobs offered to 25 persons from the Rathva community after due completion of the selection process. The reason cited was unavailability of the caste certificate,[3] since they could not produce these certificates during the caste verification process. For the same reason, two students from village Aniyadri in Chhota

---

[2] See http://www.tribal.gov.in/Content/ScheduledAreasinGujarat.aspx (accessed 4 December 2013).

[3] The term used is 'jati' certificate, which has been roughly translated to 'caste' certificate.

Udepur district could not join a medical course.[4] The state government's justification for the notice of denotification is superficial to say the least. Apparently the Rathvas categorically stated their religion as Hindu in the school registers. The argument is that the Rathvas cannot be Hindu if they are adivasis. Interestingly, this argument can be extended to other adivasis in Gujarat who declare themselves as Hindu in the school records. By implication, adivasis are not or cannot be Hindu.

The official letter further states that the information given in the school records is sufficient proof to declare the Rathvas as non-adivasis. However, it is silent on many other crucial issues. There is no examination of the adivasis' way of life and traditions. The fact that this makes them a distinct category seems to be immaterial for the state government. In Gujarat, as elsewhere, adivasis do describe themselves as Hindus. Moreover, following Independence, the state government described the Rathvas as 'Rathva (Hindu)' in its documents and in educational records through schools, and this has been an 'unwritten norm'. There is hardly any evidence to suggest that the adivasis asked the state to describe them as 'Rathva (Hindu)'. Besides, in the period soon after Independence, the adivasis showed a literacy rate of 0.5 per cent, thus making it clear that they had had hardly any say regarding the nomenclature to describe them.

HINDU VERSUS ADIVASI

It was the state's responsibility to clearly demarcate the two nomenclatures, that is, adivasis and Hindus, which in fact are distinct. There have been no legal guidelines in this regard either for schools or any other authorities since Independence. The category 'Hindu' should not have been used for the Rathvas for a number of reasons. The state government's specious plea that the term 'Rathva' is not found anywhere in the 1931 census does not hold much merit, since the subsequent census and other documents list the Rathvas as a sizeable group;[5] for instance, as per the records of the 2001 census, the Rathvas constitute the fifth largest group of STs in Gujarat, comprising 7.2 per cent of the total ST population.

---

[4] This information was collected from Chhota Udepur district.
[5] Available at: http://censusindia.gov.in/Tables_Published/SCST/dh_st_guj arat.pdf (accessed 7 August 2015).

In the neighbouring state of Madhya Pradesh, there is a provision to write 'adivasi' in place of 'Hindu'. The Rathvas of Madhya Pradesh exhibit the same cultural and traditional traits as the Rathvas of Gujarat, and share similar norms like mentioning the *gotra*, for instance Kanashya, Tadavala, Damariya, and Lohariya. The same adivasis in Gujarat mention or identify themselves as Rathva, Koli, or Rathva (Koli). This is clearly a case of 'invited misconstrual' by the Gujarat government. There is also no clarity regarding the ontic of words like 'Rathva' and 'Koli' for this area. Despite these ambiguities, the Gujarat government has gone ahead and taken a decision that will significantly affect the fate of 700,000 adivasis.

This leads us to arrive at the following conclusions: (*a*) the state government's action is not transparent; (*b*) the sudden denotification without authentic evidence will invariably lead to corporate loot of the mineral-rich Chhota Udepur region. According to one description Chhota Udepur encompasses 'a rich forest area of 75,704 hectares, 5.39 lakh tonnes of dolomite, 52,000 tonnes of fluorite, 90.77 lakh tonnes of sand, 4,000 tonnes of granite'.[6] The adivasi representatives in the Gujarat assembly and Parliament have maintained a stoic silence on this issue. They have clearly not transcended 'party lines' on this subject. The process of denotifying adivasis has begun with the Rathvas, but eventually could lead to many other adivasi communities suffering the same fate. This also has significance in the context of inter-religious dimensions. On a similar pretext, the state government may issue an order vis-à-vis those adivasis who have converted to Islam or Christianity or Jainism.

ARBITRATOR OR ENABLER OF RIGHTS?

Due to the constitutional protection and remoteness of many of the adivasi-inhabited areas, the renewable and non-renewable resources there have not yet been explored and exploited. However, due to the changed nature of the political economy, unexplored resources have

---

[6] Available at: http://archive.indianexpress.com/news/rich-in-mineral-reso urces-chhota-udepur-set-to-become-highest-revenueearning-district/1162154/ (accessed 7 August 2015); in the Gujarat government documents the figures are higher. For instance, the figure in 2003 is mentioned as 7,200 lakh tonnes for dolomite; 116 lakh tonnes for fluorspar. See http://imd-gujarat.gov.in/policy/ policy_36_eng_web.pdf (p. 20; accessed 4 December 2013).

been of serious concern for adivasis in Gujarat. In the adivasi areas, particularly in Chhota Udepur, investors are being invited to set up industries. The state government's promise to corporate entities for the usage of land, forests, mineral, and water is an indicator. In the absence of a strong 'enabler' state, adivasis easily become the soft and obvious target. This brand of development—the Gujarat brand—is a dark reality for adivasis.

The Rathva adivasis are also aware of the potentially disastrous results for the community. The denotification was taken up by the Adivasis Federation of Gujarat (Chhota Udepur and Vadodara districts), which called a protest rally on 10 November 2013 that was attended by nearly 35,000 people. Besides Rathvas, members of the Chaudharis, Vasavas, Gamits, and other adivasi communities also attended the meeting. Federation leaders like Pradeep Garasia, Shantikar Vasava, Dayaram Vasava, and Arun Chaudhari assured the gathering that they would take up the issue with the state government.

The secretary of the Adivasi Ekta Parishad,[7] Ashok Chaudhari, also participated in the protest and a memorandum was submitted to the government demanding cancellation of the order and issuing of caste certificates immediately (Table 6.1). The memorandum also said that the process of issuing certificates must be smoothened and simplified. The implementation of the Fifth Schedule of the Constitution, PESA, and usage of the forest labourers' cooperative land for adivasis were the other demands. The forest labourers' cooperative was created in order to fell trees in the adivasi areas soon after Independence. The land was acquired in the name of this cooperative so that the wood from the trees that were cut down could be supplied to the cities. However, this land is being encroached upon by mining companies.

This crucial issue has not yet caught the attention of the wider media and civil society. These institutions appear to be satisfied with the minimalist definition of democracy, that is, democracy as participants. Therefore, 'election' and 'stability' become the defining moments in democracy. What is missing in the discourse on Gujarat is the realization that democracy goes beyond election and stability. Therefore, these insidious attacks on the rights of the adivasis are hardly ever a part of the national debates concerning Gujarat. The relationship of adivasis and the

[7] The Adivasi Ekta Parishad has spread in four states—Gujarat, Madhya Pradesh, Rajasthan, Maharashtra—and also the Union Territory of Dadra and Nagar Haveli.

TABLE 6.1　Protest and Demand

Protest Areas	Participants' Numbers	Participant Adivasi Communities	Active Federations	Demands
Chhota Udepur	30,000–35,000	Rathva, Chaudhari, Vasava, Gamit, and others	Adivasis Federation of Gujarat, Adivasi Ekta Parishad	• Cancellation of the order and issuing of caste certificate immediately • Implementation of Schedule 5 of the Indian Constitution • Implementation of PESA • Usage of the forest labourers' cooperative land for the adivasis

Constitution is a complex one, and the latter's core demand goes beyond mere citizenship rights. While citizenship rights ensure the state's role as a guarantor cum sole arbitrator of rights, the tribal rights' discourse emphasizes the role of the state as an enabler of rights. The enabling is informed by incessant struggles and a collective epistemic whereby adivasis articulate their demands and press for their incorporation in the state policy. Although the Constitution has been reluctant about moving beyond the citizenship discourse, the various schedules and articles in it show the possibility of incorporating some of the adivasi demands.

The Indian state, and particularly the Gujarat government, is now creating legal ways to intervene in the scheduled areas to exploit natural resources. The Fifth Schedule and PESA are proving to be significant hurdles. Therefore, a new method is being embarked upon—that of denotifying communities from the list of adivasis as declared by the president and mentioned in the Constitution.

THE WAY OUT

The Gujarat government must take back the denotification order. This will not only ensure overall development but also protect the scheduled areas. The state must assume the role of enabler of rights instead of arbitrator of rights.

II
DESTRUCTION, LOSS, DISLOCATION

7

In the Name of Sustainable Development
Genocide Masked as 'Tribal Development'

Felix Padel

One aspect of adivasis' identity is that their cultures are highly developed in the principle of sustainability, meaning systems of cultivation and an economy or mode of production that does not destroy by overexploiting a community's natural environment. Restraint is built into the culture and religion, with conscious taboos on collecting bamboo and other seeds too early so as to allow a large proportion to regenerate, and sacred groves or forests on mountains being left undisturbed. 'Deep ecology' is embedded into adivasi consciousness, alongside the principle of sharing: in many ways, adivasi society is radically egalitarian and communist in the original sense of emphasizing community-based land ownership.

This is not to idealize adivasi societies. No one is saying they are perfect: they have a 'shadow' side, like any society, and a long history of being imposed upon, resulting in an often drastic undermining of ecological and egalitarian values. But it is sometimes hard to emphasize the positive features of an adivasi society without being accused of 'primitive romanticism', as much from the left as the right.

The value which adivasi societies place on community and sharing is in stark contrast to mainstream society's emphasis on private property, and its long history of an entrenched attitude towards nature of dominating and controlling it so as to maximize production and profit—even when this clearly depletes resources beyond a point of replenishment. This is evident when we compare cultural attitudes towards the forest and minerals in mountains, towards fish in the sea, and also towards water (damming rivers and extracting groundwater far beyond proper limits, vastly diminishing the water flow and lowering the groundwater table). What the mainstream society views in materialist terms as 'resources' to extract for profit, adivasi culture views as sources of life. This is in line with the consciousness of indigenous peoples in other countries also, who view other creatures as 'kin', and as being of equal standing to humans.[1]

Another aspect is that adivasi communities are rooted to the land, in terms of what is in effect an invisible umbilical cord. Displacement for adivasi communities means a severing of this cord: a psychic death that few non-adivasis have any conception of, since most families in mainstream society have had no roots in land they have worked for generations. This is the sense in which adivasis, through invasions of their land by dam and mining projects, face a situation of genocide: every aspect of their social structure is severely disrupted, and the people witness the death of the communities, cultural security, and ecosystems that they and their ancestors had always carefully maintained.

For most adivasis, as they often say, 'development projects' therefore constitute the opposite of real development. 'Development-induced displacement' is usually an absurd misnomer. They see themselves as 'flooded out by money'. A proper term for this kind of dispossession is 'investment-induced displacement'—also appropriate since, in many ways, capitalism is the arch-enemy of ecologically minded societies.

Talk of 'tribal development' often adds insult to injury. As P. Sainath shows in *Everybody Likes a Good Drought* (1996), sums earmarked for tribal development schemes are prone to exceptional levels of corruption. 'Development' originally referred to an organic process of change, guided by an intrinsic force, as in a plant's transition from seed to tree. Tribal development plans are rarely conceived and guided by adivasis themselves: more often, such plans are a mask for unasked-for, ruthlessly imposed changes, whose impact often amounts to genocide and ecocide.

---

[1] This was expressed in the 'Universal Declaration of the Rights of Mother Earth' or 'Rights of Nature', set in motion at an indigenous people's conference in Cochabamba, Bolivia, in April 2010, as a counterpoint to the spectacular failure of the Copenhagen Climate Conference to achieve any solid agreement on worldwide restraint in greenhouse gas emissions (*EPW* 2012).

THE AIM OF SUSTAINABLE DEVELOPMENT

Between the principles of long-term sustainability and 'development', as the term has come to be used, in the sense of basically increasing the material intensity of human life, there is tremendous tension. Jairam Ramesh (2010) puts this well in his essay published in *Economic and Political Weekly*, written while he was the environment minister. In this essay, he highlights environmental economics, otherwise known as 'green accounting', which is basically economists' attempt to place an economic value on natural resources. The trouble is, economists tend not to understand how ecosystems work and what they are, since it is not part of their curriculum, and they tend to be indoctrinated into the belief that the economy comes first.

Ramesh does not mention ecological economics at all, which works the other way around, examining flows of money and resources—'material flows' between regions and countries—to understand the overall system of resource use and impacts on ecosystems. In this, the economy plays a part—often a dominant part that has a multitude of unintended consequences for the environment that economists remain barely conscious of. In many ways, ecological economics—still a fringe subject that most economists are not trained in—actually corresponds much more closely to Aristotle's original definition of *oikonomia* than present-day economics, since it looks at the 'laws of housekeeping' as a whole. Modern economics, and the theories behind our modern financial system, correspond more closely to what for Aristotle is a much less important subject, *chremistike*—'the art of acquisition', or how to make a profit.

Oikologia was only formulated as a concept during the nineteenth century, by Ernst Haeckel, under the influence of Darwin's overall view of the interrelation of species in nature. In its Greek origin, the concept means almost the same thing as *oikonomia*—the logic or laws of correct housekeeping—correct 'use of resources' as we would say now. Yet there is little or no correlation between the disciplines. This is the point of Ramesh's essay: economists and environmentalists—or adivasi rights activists for that matter—adhere to completely different, often incompatible, belief systems (Padel et al. 2012).

So the two need to be brought into harmony. We humans, many as we are, have to survive now through a rational economics. We also need to recognize that our survival is dependent on healthy ecosystems. 'Sustainable development' is the concept used to square the circle—we all believe in both sustaining life and developing. The trouble is, can we agree on what we mean by 'development'?

The 'three pillars' of sustainable development, as defined by the Brundtland Report and the UN World Summit on Sustainable Development at Johannesburg (2002) are economy, society, and environment (Brundtland 1987; Kates et al. 2005; CEE 2007). This formulation essentially puts the terms the wrong way around, allowing a mining project to be termed 'sustainable' if it can make a profit for the next few years. If healthy ecosystems are the basis for life on earth, shouldn't environment come first? And shouldn't society come next? Human society existed long before 'economy' was defined as a separate domain, and long before 'markets'. For example, the first senior administrator of the Konds, the Hon. G. E. Russell of the Madras government, promoted markets among the Konds in 1837 on the principle that introduced 'wants' would gradually become 'necessities of life', giving government the surest means of controlling them, undermining their annoying tradition of independence (Padel 2010: 178–9).

Economists are not trained to study social structures, or to bring 'society' into their calculations, any more than they are trained to understand ecosystems. From the left as well as the right, the primacy given to the economy, and to economics, therefore allows 'market forces' to take over.

Real sustainability is the essence of adivasi societies—obviously, these are societies that have sustained themselves over hundreds of years without destroying their natural environment, living in balance with it. If one looks at adivasi knowledge systems, it is not just that they incorporate vast bodies of 'ethno-botanical' information about plant use; there are also very strong values about not taking too much, or too early in the season (Padel 1998). The first time I went to an adivasi village among Santals in 1980, a house owner offered me maize from another family's field, even though his own was ripe. When I asked why he didn't pick his own, he said '*Ham abhi tak puja nahi kiya*' (We haven't done the first fruits puja yet). Maize isn't even an indigenous crop, which tend to be much more ritualized, as are many wild products. The restraint of waiting to do puja before harvesting bamboo, mango, and many other plants gives time for regeneration (Ramnath 2004).

The Dongria Konds, in the Niyamgiri mountain range, have maintained a taboo on cutting forest on the mountaintops. They are one community whose preservation of their natural environment and attuning of economy to ecology are not in question. When their leader

Lado Sikoka called Vedanta and other invading companies *asurmane* (demons) at the Belamba public hearing in Lanjigarh on 25 April 2009, he spoke in a voice we rarely hear coming to the surface:

> We won't give up Niyamgiri for any price.... Niyamgiri is not a pile of money.... We won't tolerate Niyamgiri being dug up. They have bought Niyamgiri from the government, but it doesn't belong to the government, it belongs to adivasis.... How many lies they tell! We won't fear them, even though it seems that the demons of mythology (*asurmane*) have returned. (Dash 2009)

Just as Marshall Sahlins (1972) argued that Stone Age or hunter-gatherer societies, far from being impoverished and caught up in a struggle for existence, were the 'original affluent society', so anthropologists need to insist that adivasi ways of life are not 'uneconomic'. Perhaps we should start talking about adivasi economics both as an indigenous system, characterized by a subtle rhythm of work and leisure, including resource use and restraint, as well as the vast shifts this system has undergone as adivasi lands have been invaded or taken over. Nowadays, the number of communities that still have control over their environment and economy has declined dramatically, due to the system of endemic exploitation that has eaten away at adivasi land rights.

Various shifts can be discerned in adivasi economics during the twentieth century: hunting and gathering plays a less important role as forests decline or these activities are illegalized under forest laws introduced by the British; shifting cultivation, often on steep hill slopes, gives way in many places to fields, permanently removing the forest; millet has often given way to rice as a less nutritious staple; a largely subsistence economy has given way to an increasing tendency to cultivate cash crops; many families have lost their lands and become dependent on wage labour; even where they retain their lands, many are now forced to migrate for wage labour. Related to these shifts is the transformation from a little-monetized economy to an economy defined by money. Many of these changes are associated with a decline in the variety and nutritional value of the food crops cultivated.

For all these shifts, adivasi areas are still generally among the country's areas of greatest biodiversity. This is because adivasi economics is still firmly rooted in long-term symbiosis with the local ecology, enabling adivasi communities to live amidst biodiversity, and profit from it in their mix of cultivation, gathering, and hunting, without destroying it or even (until some years ago, at least) depleting it.

IN THE NAME OF TRIBAL DEVELOPMENT

The terms 'tribal' and 'adivasi' have a complex history. Which term is appropriate and politically correct is often highly debatable: 'adivasis', 'Scheduled Tribes', 'tribal people', 'indigenous people'—each of these terms has different connotations.

Obviously, the term 'Scheduled Tribes' is a colonial construct. Numerous communities have suffered a bureaucratic hell by being misclassified, from Gujjars in Rajasthan to Jhorias and Durvas in south Odisha. Whether a group is designated ST, SC, or as Other Backward Classes (OBC) has often been arbitrary, and a matter of intense dispute. While some groups suffer because they were denied tribal status, adivasis living in cities sometimes dislike negative associations that are often implicit in the term 'tribal'. Actually, *tribus* is a Latin word originally used to refer to divisions of mainstream society. One positive feature is that it emphasizes relationship, which is appropriate, since the concerned societies place a lot of emphasis on their internal relationships, as well as external ones, including a sense of kinship with other species.

The term 'adivasis', meaning 'original dwellers' or 'aboriginals', was first used in a major way during the Jharkhand movement in the 1930s by Jaipal Singh, when he formed the Adivasi Mahasabha. Though the term is in general use throughout peninsular India, in the north-eastern states it is mainly used for the communities brought from Bihar and Odisha to work on the tea plantations in British times, but not for local peoples indigenous to Assam, who were often displaced by the tea gardens—and so in effect by the central Indian communities. Tension between local 'tribes' such as Bodo or Karbi and central Indian adivasis has been rising (Dungdung 2012).

Each term also has an unfortunate history of being used derogatively, reflecting the depth of negative stereotypes that still overshadow attitudes towards adivasis. At the heart of this is *social evolutionism*, the idea that adivasi people represent a 'primitive' or 'less advanced' stage of development (Padel 2010: chapter 7). Since the 1950s, the concept of 'development' has been defined in relation to 'underdevelopment' and an extremely rigid conception of social evolution along set stages. 'Educated' people tend to take for granted the division of countries and regions promoted by the World Bank/International Monetary Fund into 'developed', 'developing', and 'underdeveloped'. As Gustavo Esteva puts it in *The Development Dictionary* (1992), the day that President Truman took office, 20 January 1949, he inaugurated the concept of 'underdevelopment' as a blueprint for the spread of America's development paradigm and influence.

> On that day, 2 billion people became underdeveloped.... [The concept] took on an unsuspected colonizing virulence.... Since then, development has connoted at least one thing: to escape from the undignified condition called underdevelopment....
>
> For those who make up two thirds of the world's population today, to think of development—any kind of development—requires first the perception of themselves as underdeveloped, with the whole burden of connotations that this carries. (Esteva 1992: 6–7)

Darwin's theory of evolution showed how thousands of species have developed on multiple interrelated yet separate paths. By contrast, when this theory was applied to society, by Herbert Spencer, Karl Marx, Friedrich Engels, and others, theorists from the left as well as the right laid down a uniform model of set stages of development, from 'primitive communism' to feudalism and capitalism. Development and underdevelopment are the key concepts used to impose a uniform model of rapid growth projects, culminating in today's 'new world order', characterized by extreme forms of exploitation and inequality. Can we move *Beyond Developmentality* (Deb 2009)?

As for 'tribal development', B. D. Sharma (1984) has questioned what this would really mean, and how it could be implemented. *The Web of Poverty*, according to Sharma (1989), enmeshes the rural poor in a system of endemic exploitation. Funds and programmes for 'tribal development' are flawed by exceptionally high levels of corruption, essentially because projects are conceived in a manner that is irredeemably top-down. Projects that involve displacing adivasis increasingly include a 'tribal development plan'. But it is an extreme misuse of language to call top-down models of imposed change 'development', especially when implementation is so systemically corrupt. 'Develop' is an intransitive verb, and as such, refers to an organic process of change, motivated indigenously rather than imposed.

When adivasi communities are displaced, they undergo a process that is the polar opposite of real development, especially because of a gulf between what is supposed to happen and what actually happens (Padel and Das 2008, 2011), which regularly includes violent repression, exposure to goondas and corruption, illegal liquor shops, and a rise in rapes and prostitution. For example, at least 500 sex workers are reported working in the Damanjodi area of Koraput, which is one of the poorest districts in India despite 30 years of 'tribal development' overseen by the National Aluminium Company (CSE 2008, Perry 2010).

Mainstream society's disconnect from displaced people operates at many levels. The neglect faced by displaced people represents a fundamental injustice, congruent with the historic racism and injustice towards adivasi people recognized by the Supreme Court judgment of 5 January 2011 (in the case of a Bhil woman beaten and paraded naked in Maharashtra), which affirms their status as indigenous people. India has not officially recognized adivasis as 'indigenous', partly because it may seem invidious to term 92 per cent of India's population as 'old immigrants' (referred to in the Supreme Court judgment). This non-recognition also has the effect of making it difficult to apply UN legislation protecting indigenous people in India.[2]

Seventy-five groups are still classified as Particularly Vulnerable Tribal Groups (PVTGs), (until 2010 classified as Primitive Tribal Groups), according to the Planning Commission (2010: 178–9). A report from the Ministry of Tribal Affairs titled *The Development of Primitive Tribal Groups* (2002) defines them using the concepts 'primitive' and 'backward', and the Planning Commission defined their customary practice of shifting cultivation as environmentally damaging. This classification was made supposedly in order to protect from exploitation groups that still maintain highly distinctive customs. Yet the social evolutionism inherent in terms like 'primitive' and 'backward' implies an agenda of trying to 'bring them into the mainstream', rather than a recognition of difference.

This has certainly been evident in the case of the Dongria, the PVTG who made international news for their resistance to Vedanta's planned bauxite mine on Niyamgiri's summit. Their administration is managed through the Dongria Kondh Development Agency, which has overseen an extensive road building programme funded through the Prime Minister's Sadak Yojana into the heart of the Niyamgiri range, in line with Vedanta's mining plans. Similar is the case with the Paudi Bhuiyas, a PVTG who live around Khandadhara, the mountain whose iron ore Posco and other companies seek permission to mine.

---

[2] Nevertheless, this issue of indigeneity has been taken up vociferously by organizations such as the Backward and Minority Communities Employees' Federation (BAMCEF), who promote the term *mulnivasis* to cover STs, SCs, and OBCs (BAMCEF 2012).

'Primitive' is basically a hangover from anthropology's primitive, colonial phase. Defining adivasi society and economy as 'primitive', 'backward', or 'underdeveloped' implies a programme of 'civilizing' or 'developing' these peoples. The implicit stereotypes are blind, ignoring that adivasis' symbiosis with their natural environment, that developed over many centuries. Adivasi societies, in other words, are highly developed. Uproot them from their niche in an ecosystem, and centuries of development are effectively undone.

ADIVASI VOICES AND REALITIES

Whatever term we use in various contexts, adivasis' point of view is too little heard. Since colonial times, adivasi people and their interests have been too much defined by non-adivasis, operating with a multitude of vested interests. This emerged in mid-2011 in a debate initiated by Gladson Dungdung over a Peace Award by the Gandhi Foundation, which was misleadingly advertised as 'to the Adivasis of India' when it was actually intended for Binayak Sen and Bulu Imam (Dungdung 2011b). Adivasis have been at the receiving end of unremitting violence and racism, with non-adivasis tending to try and define who they are as well as taking credit for adivasi movements, from colonial times to the extreme violence unleashed on communities in Operation Green Hunt right now.

> 'Operation Green Hunt' was launched with the clear intention to create fear, insecurity and livelihood crisis in the villages so that the villages [*sic*] would leave the vicinity. Consequently, the government can hand over the Adivasis' land to the corporate shark comfortably. The Jharkhand government has allotted iron-ore to 19 steel companies including Mittal, Jindal, Tata, Atro-Steel and Torian in Saranda Forest. Therefore, of course, they want to clear the land. (Dungdung 2011a)

Of course, adivasis speak with a multitude of voices, according to people's perceptions and place in an overall social structure that is becoming increasingly polarized: pro-mining company, anti-company, Maoist or member of the legislative assembly—each strand amplified by media that is jointly owned with mining interests, polarizing the population into often antagonistic camps. The raw voices of people who have been or are being displaced often get drowned out (Sahu 2010).

One of the most painful aspects of displacement is the delinking of people's economy from an all-round embeddedness in ecology. In the words of Bhagaban Majhi, a Kond adivasi and a leader of the Kashipur movement against the Utkal alumina project since the early 1990s:

> We have sought an explanation from the Government about people who have been displaced in the name of development: how many have been properly rehabilitated? You have not provided them with jobs; you have not rehabilitated them at all. How can you again displace more people? Where will you relocate them and what jobs will you give them?... We are tribal farmers. We are earthworms. Like fish that die when taken out of water, a cultivator dies when his land is taken away from him. So we won't leave our land. We want permanent development. (Bhagaban Majhi for the Kashipur movement in Odisha, in Das and Das 2005)

In this view, changes that are not guaranteed to benefit future generations cannot be called real development.

Discourse on adivasi poverty is too often couched in evolutionist/developmentalist terms, as a justification for imposing change. Baba Mahariya, an adivasi facing displacement by the Sardar Sarovar dam on the Narmada river, refuses to view his society as 'poor', and points out the poverty evident in the cities:

> You take us to be poor, but we're not. We live in harmony and co-operation with each other.... We get good crops from Mother Earth.... Clouds give us water.... We produce many kinds of grains with our own efforts, and we don't need money. We use seeds produced by us.... In the spirit of Laha (communal labour) we produce a house in just one day....
>
> You people live in separate houses. You don't bother about the joy or suffering of each other. But we live on the support of our kith and kin.... How does such fellow-feeling prevail in our villages? For we help each other. We enjoy equal standing. We've been born in our village. Our Nara (umbilical cord) is buried here. (Mahariya 2001)

FOREST RIGHTS AND COMMUNITY OWNERSHIP

As is often said, India has some of the best environmental and human rights legislation of any country, but implementation is often poor. One problem is that many laws seem to contradict each other, or contain self-contradictory clauses. This is particularly evident in the Forest Rights Act (FRA), which has been rightly celebrated as a milestone, granting adivasis and other forest dwellers their natural rights, long promised and overdue. There is also no doubt that the Act has proved to be effective for movements opposing dozens of destructive displacement projects that cannot go ahead until forest rights have been settled—in Niyamgiri, the

Posco area, villages in the Polavaram submergence zone, to name but a few.

But the final form of the FRA essentially marginalized community claims, making these much harder to implement, even though one essence of adivasi society is a strong tradition of community ownership. Given the system of exploitation that has long penalized adivasis due to lack of individual land rights (*patta*), it is hardly surprising that many adivasis have fixed their sights on getting these. But is this essentially 'privatizing the forest'? Will it hasten an undoing of traditional social structure, transforming social relations into the mould of capitalist competition promoted by the mainstream? Once thousands of families have established individual entitlement to pieces of forest land, will they preserve the forest, or will this hasten a widespread clearing of forest?

Profound dangers in the FRA are perceived by many who wish to see forests as well as adivasis continue to flourish, and who understand the act's implications for communities and wildlife at the ground level. In Savyasaachi's (2006) view, 'this Act turns forests into a service provider for capitalism'. Madhu Ramnath (2008) examines the act's details in relation to ground realities, which differ dramatically among different social groups and areas. Some adivasi groups now tend to clear the forest wherever they move, while others still live in symbiosis with the forest, but this involves hunting, which is explicitly banned in the Act. Fishing by contrast is allowed. Both hunting and fishing by traditional methods of bow and arrow or muzzle-loader and fish net or plant poison don't basically damage the ecosystem. Continuing the ban on hunting illegalizes a custom at the core of adivasi identity and territory, and thereby, in a sense, promotes illegal hunting, carried out with anger at the injustice. On the other side, as traditions have eroded, adivasi fishing nowadays too often involves tipping insecticide into a stream, killing a large cross-section of life forms. Also, the Act empowers the gram sabha in a context where panchayat raj is often in effect sarpanch raj: the same top-down model prevalent throughout capitalist democracy, where elections often depend heavily on funding, and elected representatives frequently make deals with vested interests outside the village and build up a top-down clique within it.

In effect, does the FRA complete the process of land privatization that started with the 'Permanent Settlement' in the 1790s?—a process begun, as in the FRA, with an avowed aim of giving permanent status to people's customary land rights! The FRA became law during the same year as the Wildlife Protection (Amendment) Act (no. 39 of 2006), known as the 'Tiger Amendment'. The complex process of compromise, involving often bitter warfare between social activists and conservationists, is discussed by C. R. Bijoy ('The Great Indian Tiger Show', 2011), who points out that 'what is often glossed over is that bigger forces, including the various arms of the State, have illegally encroached upon this common habitat of the tribals and the tigers'. Project Tiger started in 1972, when India's tiger population was estimated at 1,827. In 2011, after lavish funding, this number has come down to 1,411—a tragic decline aided by rampant corruption and a hunting mafia that spreads its tentacles throughout the subcontinent.

Disputes over the FRA have driven a wedge between conservationists and social/political activists—a case of 'divide and rule', since both confront basically the same nexus of vested interests. But the style differs. Conservationists often operate more top-down, with more funds, and don't seem to realize that when adivasis are displaced for tigers, they tend to turn against tigers. But will the FRA, in the name of correcting a historical injustice by giving forest dwellers full rights to their land, end up privatizing the forest, destroying concepts of communal ownership, in the process spelling death for an ancient symbiosis which maintains the forest as a community resource shared with wildlife?

CULTURAL GENOCIDE

For adivasis in particular, displacement usually means cultural genocide (Padel and Das 2008, 2010), since losing their lands and villages destroys every aspect of their social structure: their economy and identity because their status shifts from skilled, self-sufficient cultivators to that of 'unskilled labour'; their political structure because they lose control over their environment and are forced to become dependent on corporate and government hierarchies; their social structure because the ties that made them a cohesive community are frayed in many ways; their religion because 'even our gods are destroyed' when their villages and ancestral sites are bulldozed; and their material culture because the traditional village spatial arrangement gives way to 'colonies' of alien design.

The term 'genocide' was first used in 1944–5 to describe Nazis' treatment of Jews. The classic case of genocide, however, is what happened to countless indigenous peoples throughout America and Australia (for example, Brown 1975; Wilson 1998). Examining this latter process, it is evident that there are two levels to the killing: physical extermination, and the killing of cultures. Survivors from physical extermination were herded onto reservations and subjected to a policy of 'de-tribalizing' or 'forced assimilation', which included separating children from their families and forbidding them to speak their own languages or practise their traditional cultures (documented throughout Wilson 1998; referred to in Padel 2010: 240–1).

In popular usage now, 'culture' often just means 'the pretty bits', exemplified by adivasi dances or handicrafts. But its original meaning, from Latin *cultus*, refers to *cultivation* of the soil and *cults* of nature as well as the general traditions of society. In other words, political and economic systems are an integral part of culture, and what is special about adivasi cultures—alongside their emphasis on long-term sustainability—is that these three meanings are still interlinked. This means that when adivasi communities are displaced, indigenous systems of cultivation are erased, along with spiritual traditions linking to the ecology of fields and forests.

Publicized killings of adivasis, such as the Maikanch police firing that killed three adivasis opposing the Utkal aluminium project in Kashipur on 16 December 2000, or the Kalinganagar firing, when 14 adivasis protesting against a Tata steel plant died on 2 January 2006, have become symbolic of this genocide: the numbers killed may be small, but these events symbolize a wider, psychic annihilation of people's cultures and links with their land.

A similar process of cultural genocide is apparent from many of the world's surviving tribal cultures, or 'ecological peoples': for example, in Ecuador, Peru, Brazil, and many parts of the American continent; in Indonesia, Malaysia, and many places in Southeast Asia; also among Palestinian farmers displaced from their fields and villages by Israeli settlements; and among the Kurds in Turkey, several thousand of whose villages have been destroyed by the Turkish army, turning their inhabitants into refugees and ending a nature-based way of life that had existed over centuries (Öcalan 2012).

Adivasis' way of life under threat in central India is in many ways the antithesis of capitalism—which is partly why these cultures are under attack. An elder in a Kond village in Kandhamal once confronted my co-author, Samarendra Das: 'Where are the saints in your society? In this village we are all saints. We make do with little, share what we have, and waste nothing!' (Padel and Das 2010: 68–9 and 593). The value of sharing is in stark contrast to competition, and applies also to law: the aim of legal process, as reported in many adivasi societies, is not to make one party wrong and the other right, but to reconcile them, so that they can live in a community again. A fine is often imposed on both parties, that goes to pay for a feast of reconciliation.

It is fashionable to criticize the anthropology of Verrier Elwin, but in many ways his writing goes to the heart of adivasi cultures and describes them a lot more humanly and holistically than most anthropology since. The criticism often made of Elwin, that he wanted to preserve adivasi cultures as in a museum, is a crude parody of the protection he advocated, which was arguably a far-sighted attempt to prevent the cultural genocide whose seeds were sown in British times. If one looks at the adivasi museums that have been built since, these preserve beautiful cultural artefacts, but removed from their living context—in effect, dead. Making such museums has often formed an integral part of the cultural genocide process, with items acquired from villages about to be displaced. For example, the adivasi museum in Koraput was made by collecting items from villages being displaced by the Upper Kolab and other dams. Going around adivasi museums sometimes with adivasi friends, their sense of shock is palpable, at so many beautiful items and their own history in photographs, taken away and preserved in a completely alien environment, from bows and arrows to musical instruments, mute behind glass.

Another area where adivasi culture is extremely highly developed is in the culture of love—with a wealth of songs and poetry, and of subtle customs celebrating the art of love. Among the fullest, most sensitive studies are Elwin's *The Muria and Their Ghotul* (1947) and W. G. Archer's *The Hill of Flutes* (1974). This is a difficult subject, and Elwin's book on the Ghotul perhaps played some part in disseminating an idea that adivasis were sexually 'loose' and exploitable. One extraordinary feature of adivasi cultures such as the Muria Gond and Santal is the lack of double sexual standards applied to men and women, in terms of the idea that a woman getting married should be a virgin—double standards which plague almost all mainstream traditional societies, leading to many forms of oppression of women. However, if women generally have a higher status and are freer in traditional adivasi villages, this is not to deny the shadow side of adivasi societies today; a high incidence of 'witch attacks' is apparent in some regions, with women branded as witches becoming outcast or even being killed.

But perhaps nothing harms women's status more drastically than displacement. If displaced adivasis' standard of living declines drastically, this is especially so for women: without their own land, for example, they can no longer grow and sell their own crops. When Vedanta started constructing its alumina refinery at Lanjigarh, the invasion of an alien workforce had dramatic impacts on surrounding villages, and elders told us with tears in their eyes of women who had been raped, or had affairs with outsiders who subsequently abandoned them—situations almost unknown in the area before. The impact of illegal liquor shops and prostitution, ubiquitous in industrializing areas, has obvious negative impacts on women (Perry 2010).

These facts and trends need placing alongside development discourse that claims the opposite: Vedanta's annual *Sustainable Development Reports*, for example, claim to be raising women's status through self-help groups (SHGs) and teaching adivasis new agricultural techniques to make them 'more sustainable' (Padel and Das 2010). Microcredit loans in SHGs often isolate and deactivate families through a burden of debt, and have a highly questionable role in improving people's long-term living standards. Questioned at an annual general meeting in London about the complete contrast between the rosy picture painted in these corporate social responsibility reports and numerous accounts from the grassroots stressing dire pollution, a high rate of accidents among workers as well as on roads, and human rights abuses by goondas and police, Vedanta directors simply read out a list of huge sums paid out for SHGs and various 'tribal development' initiatives. This reveals the hierarchical model in the corporate social structure. Bhagaban Majhi in Kashipur relates how, when he said to the government authorities that they would like schools and hospitals, they told him, '*Company debo!*' (The company will give!): a model of 'largesse' under private, not public control, dependent on pleasing the corporate hierarchy.

It is not that hierarchy is completely absent in a traditional adivasi village. Several communities in central India made the transition towards 'tribal kingships', and communities such as the Konds have their own traditional aristocracies. But the tendency towards hierarchy was promoted by the British colonial tendency to try and find headmen to rule through—even though British officials often recorded the position of a headman as *primus inter pares* (first among equals). Even Hindu kings, such as the raja of Boad in central Odisha, until British times, were completely dependent on being acknowledged as rajas by their adivasi subjects. Unlike the European model of kingship, where a king often imposed religious rules on his subjects, kings in adivasi areas of central India gained their legitimacy by patronizing the cult of adivasi deities.

Adivasi society is radically egalitarian in many ways, and there can be no doubt that this represents a very old tradition. When Ashoka attacked

Kalinga in the third century BC, these people, who put up extremely strong resistance, were without kings. Almost certainly, the Kalinga were the Konds, whose name for themselves is Kuwinga, and who were still being ousted from east Odisha kingdoms during the nineteenth century by rajas coming under British influence who were trying to raise their revenue by bringing in more 'efficient' cultivators (Padel 2010, 2011). Ashoka recorded that his invasion of Kalinga killed 100,000 people in fighting, that 150,000 were enslaved, and many times these numbers died of famine and disease afterwards. The naming of Kalinganagar, as a complex of steel plants displacing thousands of adivasis, imposed through frequent violence, is therefore extraordinarily ironic. When Odisha's chief minister visited Kalinganagar for the first time since the 2006 firing, in December 2009, it was to inaugurate a new police station there, paid for by steel companies, for which he publicly thanked them (Padel and Das 2010: 55, 405–8, 417–18).

This example makes clear a collusion that is often concealed—that police, who are meant to be public servants dedicated to serving the people, are often in effect serving the corporations who are invading and taking over adivasi lands. Kalinganagar is one out of hundreds of adivasi areas in central India showing a similar pattern of enforced takeover.

To be real, 'tribal development' needs to be in the hands of adivasis. This is the intention underlying Panchayats (Extension to Scheduled Areas) Act (PESA), which followed an acclaimed commission into possibilities for self-governance in adivasi areas under Dileep Singh Bhuria. The Act is supposed to delegate power to gram sabhas and panchayats. Implementation in the various scheduled areas has been poor, and this failure to decentralize decision-making to the village level has been seen as a prime cause of the rising power of the Maoists, who can appeal to adivasis' justified sense of gross injustice and powerlessness in regard to official channels (Dandekar and Choudhury 2010). To counter the Maoists' appeal, the central government's Integrated Action Plan for Maoist-affected districts was initially formulated around the implementation of PESA (NDTV 2010). Since then, this emphasis on PESA has been neglected, and 300 million rupees have been allocated to nearly 200 districts for the twin goals of security and development, with key decisions remaining with the traditional 'triumvirate' of local power (collector, superintendent of police, divisional forest officer). The trouble is, in a context where 'development' has often been a euphemism for invasion and displacement by mega-projects, how can a genuine democratic process be allowed to rise and function in adivasi areas?

'Development'? As Gandhi said when asked what he thought of Western 'civilization': 'That would be a very good idea.' When equality before the law becomes a reality, and adivasis or dalits can go freely to the courts and expect justice, even when the perpetrator is a government servant or corporate executive, then real development is guaranteed, since the law would turn against the exploiters. It is hard to see this happening in the immediate future without confronting 'the most dangerous fundamentalism'—neoliberal economics—that is essentially displacing adivasis and causing their cultural genocide (Padel and Das 2010: 493). If humans are to survive, we may need to turn our back on capitalist models of growth, and relearn from adivasis the art of living with nature without over-exploiting it, and sharing what we have on a far more equal basis.

REFERENCES

Archer, W. G. 1974. *The Hill of Flutes: Love, Life and Poetry in Tribal India*. London: George Allen & Unwin.
BAMCEF. 2012. The All India Backward (SC, ST, OBC) and Minority Communities Employees Federation website. Available at: http://www.mulnivasibamcef.org (accessed 12 August 2015).
Bijoy, C. R. 2011. 'The Great Indian Tiger Show', *Economic and Political Weekly*, vol. 46, no. 4.
Brown, Dee. 1975. First published in 1970. *Bury My Heart at Wounded Knee*. London: Pan.
Brundtland, Gro Harlam. 1987. *Report of the World Commission on Environment and Development*. Oxford: Oxford University Press.
CEE (Centre for Environmental Education). 2007. *Sustainable Development: An Introduction*. Internship series vol. 1. Ahmedabad: South Asia Youth Education Network (SAYEN). Available at: http://www.sayen.org/volume-i.pdf.
CSE (Centre for Science and Environment). 2008. *Rich Lands, Poor People: Is 'Sustainable' Mining Possible?* Delhi: CSE.
Dandekar, Ajay and Chitrangada Choudhury. 2010. *PESA, Left-Wing Extremism and Governance: Concerns and Challenges in India's Tribal Districts*. Anand: IRMA (Institute of Rural Management at Anand). Available at: http://www.outlookindia.com/article/the-missing-prong/267052.
Das, Amarendra and Samarendra Das. 2005. *Matiro Poko, Company Loko* (Earth Worm, Company Man), documentary film in Odia with English subtitles and commentary.
Dash, Surya Shankar. 2009. *The Real Face of Vedanta*, documentary film. Available at: www.vimeo.com/11183545; see also http://www.youtube.com/watch?v=ipHmVee_uXw&feature=related (accessed 12 August 2015).

Deb, Debal. 2009. *Beyond Developmentality: Constructing Inclusive Freedom and Sustainability.* New Delhi: Daanish.

Dungdung, Gladson. 30 August 2011a. 'Killing, Denial and Manipulation in Saranda Forest', *Jharkhand Mirror*, available in Gladson Dungdung, *Whose Country Is It Anyway? Untold Stories of the Indigenous Peoples of India.* Kolkata: Adivaani, 2013, pp. 187–95.

———. 22 October. 2011b. 'Which Adivasi? What India?' *Tehelka.* Available at: http://realindianews.blogspot.in/2011/10/which-adivasi-what-india.html (accessed December 2011).

———. 2012. 'The State Sponsored Crime against Adivasis in Assam', *Jharkhand Mirror*, 12 March, available in Gladson Dungdung, *Whose Country Is It Anyway? Untold Stories of the Indigenous Peoples of India.* Kolkata: Adivaani, 2013, pp. 33–45.

———. 2013. *Whose Country Is It Anyway? Untold Stories of the Indigenous Peoples of India.* Kolkata: Adivaani.

Elwin, Verrier. 1947. *The Muria and Their Ghotul.* Bombay: Oxford University Press.

EPW (Economic and Political Weekly). 2012. 'If Mountains and Rivers Could Speak', Editorial, vol. 47, no. 2. Available at: http://www.indiaenvironmentportal.org.in/files/file/rights%20to%20Nature.pdf (accessed 12 August 2015).

Esteva, Gustavo. 1992. 'Development', in Wolfgang Sachs (ed.), *The Development Dictionary: A Guide to Knowledge as Power.* London: Zed, pp. 6–25.

Kates, Robert W., Thomas M. Parris, and Anthony A. Leiserowitz. 2005. 'What Is Sustainable Development? Goals, Indicators, Values and Practice', *Environment: Science and Policy for Sustainable Development* (e-journal), 47, no. 3 (April): 8–21. Available at: http://www.hks.harvard.edu/sustsci/ists/docs/whatissD_env_kates_0504.pdf.

Mahariya, Baba. 2001. 'Development at Whose Cost? An Adivasi on Dislocation and Displacement', in K. C. Yadav (ed.), *Beyond Mud Walls: Indian Social Realities.* New Delhi: Hope India.

Ministry of Tribal Affairs. 2002. *The Development of Primitive Tribal Groups.* New Delhi: Government of India. Available at: http://164.100.24.208/ls/CommitteeR/Labour&Wel/33.pdf (accessed 12 August 2015).

NDTV. 2010. 'Government to clear Integrated Action Plan for Naxal districts soon', 7 August. Available at: http://www.ndtv.com/article/india/govt-to-clear-integrated-action-plan-for-naxal-districts-soon-42801 (accessed 12 August 2015).

Öcalan, Abdullah. 2012. *Prison Writings III: The Road Map to Negotiations.* Cologne: International Initiative 'Freedom for Abdullah Öcalan—Peace in Kurdistan' and Mesopotamien Verlags (www.freedom-for-ocalan.com).

Padel, Felix. 1998. 'Forest Knowledge: Tribal People, Their Environment and the Structure of Power', in Richard Grove, Vinita Damodaran, and Satpal

Sangwan (eds), *Nature and the Orient: The Environmental History of South and Southeast Asia*. New Delhi: Oxford University Press.
———. 2010. *Sacrificing People: Invasions of a Tribal Landscape*. New Delhi: Orient BlackSwan.
———. 2011. 'Mining Projects and Cultural Genocide: Colonial Roots of Present Conflicts', in Biswamoy Pati (ed.), *Adivasis in Colonial India: Survival, Resistance and Negotiation*, pp. 316–37. New Delhi: Orient BlackSwan.
Padel, Felix and Samarendra Das. 2008. 'Cultural Genocide: The Real Impact of Development-Induced Displacement', in H. M. Mathur (ed.), *India: Social Development Report 2008: Development and Displacement*, pp. 103–15. New Delhi: Oxford University Press.
———. 2010. *Out of This Earth: East India Adivasis and the Aluminium Cartel*. New Delhi: Orient BlackSwan.
———. 2011. 'Resettlement Realities: The Gulf between Policy and Practice', in H. M. Mathur (ed.), *Resettling Displaced People*, pp. 143–80. New Delhi: Council for Social Research and Routledge.
Padel, Felix, Ajay Dandekar, and Jeemol Unni. 2012. *Ecology, Economy: Quest for a Socially Informed Connection*. New Delhi: Orient BlackSwan.
Perry, Kevin E. G. 2010. 'Secrets and Lies: Tackling HIV among Sex-workers in India', *Guardian*, 7 December.
Planning Commission. 2010. 'Social Justice', *Mid-term Appraisal of the Eleventh Five Year Plan 2007-2012*, chapter 8. Available at: http://planningcommission.nic.in/plans/mta/11th_mta/chapterwise/chap8_social.pdf (accessed 13 August 2015).
Ramesh, Jairam. 2010. 'The Two Cultures Revisited: The Environmental Development Debate in India', *Economic and Political Weekly*, vol. 45, no. 42.
Ramnath, Madhu. 2004. *Crossing Boundaries: Adivasi Women and Forest Produce—A Story from Central Bastar, Chhattisgarh, India*. Coonoor Press.
———. 2008. 'Between Scylla and Charybdis: Surviving the Forest Rights Act', *Economic and Political Weekly* 43, no. 9(1 March): 37–42.
Sahlins, Marshall. 1972. *Stone Age Economics*. London: Tavistock.
Sahu, Subrat Kumar. 2010. *DAM-aged*, documentary film in Odia with English subtitles and commentary.
Sainath, P. 1996. *Everybody Likes a Good Drought: Stories from India's Poorest Districts*. London: Penguin.
Savyasaachi. 2006. 'Forest Rights Act 2006: Undermining the Foundational Position of the Forest', *Economic and Political Weekly*, vol. 46, no. 15, pp. 55–62.
Sharma, B. D. 1984. *Planning for Tribal Development*. New Delhi: Prachi Prakashan.
———. 1989. *The Web of Poverty*. New Delhi and Shillong: Prachi Prakashan and North-Eastern Hill University.
Wilson, James. 1998. *The Earth Shall Weep: A History of Native America*. New York: Grove Books.

8

Unfree Mobility
Adivasi Women's Migration

Indrani Mazumdar

On a hot summer's day in 1982, while walking through a jungle path in Bankura, West Bengal, anthropologist Narayan Banerjee asked an old Santhal woman who was accompanying him to narrate her experiences as a migrant agricultural labourer. At this, she stopped and exclaimed, 'What a foolish question to ask! I have lost count of how many times I have gone to "your" village and of course you know how we stayed and worked there, what we gave and what we received. Even if you were young in those days, surely you noticed' (Banerjee 1989).

As Banerjee later wrote, 'she was right'—he had indeed noticed Santhal men, women, and children visiting his village in Barddhaman twice a year regularly to undertake agricultural work, when he was a child in the 1950s, a phenomenon that then 'never appeared strange to me in any way'. But 'she was wrong' when she assumed that he knew them. In his words,

> I never knew them individually, because they all seemed to look alike....
> I never bothered to ask why they looked tired on the date of arrival and departure, why there used to be more *kamin* than *Majhi* and why some kamin-mothers returned with empty backs and elbows.[1] ... I did not

[1] *Kamin* refers to a woman manual labourer—usually including a connotation of belonging to a low caste or adivasi, here the Santhal community. *Majhi* is the colloquial word used for Santhal men by non-Santhals, although

know them at all in spite of meeting them year after year in my own house, in my own village.

'Dwarfed and humbled' by his lack of knowledge, Banerjee wrote of that day in 1982 that

> a nameless tribal woman took me by the hand and helped me to see the strange world of their lives.... She told me frankly about many things—her childhood, the unhappy marriage, desertion, return to her own village and her everyday battle for two square meals. She had absolutely no feeling of guilt for whatever she had done to keep her body and soul together. As a young child she used to accompany her parents year after year. She used to be fascinated at first seeing new places. Gradually it became a monotonous journey and at the same time, an evil necessity. It was a labyrinth from which there was no way out. And in that labyrinth she was not alone. Suddenly she was narrating the story of thousands of women like her, women for whom intermittent migration was a way of life.

He goes on to quote the old woman's words, 'Can you tell me, we women being mothers, what kind of future we are giving to our children? Are we not passing on our past as their future? Have we undertaken these innumerable treks to do just that?' (Banerjee 1989).

Some 30 years later, after a series of surveys on gender and migration in different parts of India, a report on the key findings concluded that a large number of women from historically disadvantaged communities (SC/ST) were 'being corralled and condemned to a cycle of advance/debt based circulatory migration with little scope for social advance' (CWDS 2012). The question posed by the old Santhal woman in 1982 indeed has continuing relevance, even as her words contain an implicit challenge to common perceptions of a primordial and timeless compass to tribal women's sense of the world.

ADIVASI LABOUR MIGRATION IN HISTORICAL CONTEXT

In the districts of Bankura, Puruliya, and Medinipur (West), *namal jaoa* is the most commonly used term for seasonal agricultural migration. Its literal meaning in the local language is 'to go to the east'. It thus provides an apt description of the phenomenon of seasonal migration from the

---

in the Santhali language, it is the term for headman. The empty elbows, as elucidated later by Banerjee, indicate that the children carried on their elbows had died 'either of diarrhoea or unintentional neglect'.

south-eastern reaches of the rolling hills of the Chota Nagpur plateau located within the three districts just mentioned, to the plains of Bengal further east. While the source area for 'namal jaoa' is dependent primarily on rainfed agriculture in hilly terrain marked by overdrainage and soil erosion on its slopes, the destination areas are all located in fertile alluvial and irrigated plains. At the destination, migrants generally receive better wages and, more importantly, they find employment/income during their lean season. From periodic migration ranging from two to four times a year (in spells of two to four weeks each), they bring back not only cash but also some rice to supplement the inadequate amounts that are cultivated in their own area/land. As such, they are definitely better able to survive through seasonal migration.

Yet, in 1991, in a seminal study, Banerjee and Ray (1991) sensed that 'an undertone of misery ... anxiety, sadness and helplessness was intimately associated with the word [namal]'. They found a 'general consensus on certain issues' that the migrating women associated with their repeated treks every year. These were

> neglect of children's health and education, deteriorating health of family members, especially of women, unstable family life due to change of residence three or four times a year, increase in bigamy, divorce, desertion, indignity suffered by women at workplace as well as during travel, discontinuity in asset management such as livestock, house, backyard gardens, etc., fragmented and ad-hoc approach to social development of family, low, uncertain income, [and] a vicious cycle of indebtedness.

According to Banerjee and Ray, '*Namal* was originally restricted to a single community, viz. the Santhals and their brethren of Kherwar origin, such as Deshwali Majhis.'[2] Seasonal migration to the plains of Barddhaman originated in the colonial period, and, the authors argue, it continued thereafter with an expanding number of destination areas due to increasing degradation of the source region, as opposed to increasing industrial and agricultural development of the destination points,

---

[2] Santhals are the largest adivasi community in West Bengal (the third largest tribe in India). In 2001, Santhals, numbering 2.28 million, constituted 52 per cent of the ST population in West Bengal. Deshwali Majhis (a community of largely Santhal origin who underwent religious transformation during the Kherwar movements of the late colonial period and became more or less assimilated into Hinduism) are considered 'semi-tribal' by Banerjee and Ray (1991), although they are officially classified as OBC.

particularly due to improvement in irrigation facilities.³ As irrigation expanded, so also did intensive rice cropping, and the practice of agricultural migration by adivasi labour expanded further into the post-independence period. Banerjee and Ray (1991) calculated that the local agricultural labour force could not come anywhere near fulfilling the labour requirement for rice cultivation in the area, and estimated that seasonal migrants accounted for 40 to 60 per cent of annual agricultural labour days.⁴

The source region in the study had once been famous for its forest—in what the Mughals and the British called the Jungle Mahals. The particular blocks covered by Banerjee and Ray's (1991) study (Ranibandh block in Bankura, Manbazar/Banduan in Puruliya, and Binpur in Medinipur) were part of a compact forest tract inhabited mainly by the Santhals and Bhumij.⁵ The forest had provided the wherewithal, food, and land for subsistence agriculture as well as other forest produce for supplementing diets and incomes. This situation, however, changed dramatically from the late nineteenth century, when due to the rising value of timber with the opening of the railway in Bankura and Puruliya, large areas of forest were cleared of trees by several interest groups—the zamindars, timber contractors, and the people, both tribal and non-tribal—to meet the demand of the rail companies and particularly the spikes in demand

---

³ Banerjee and Ray (1991) point out that by the end of the nineteenth century, more than 20 per cent of Barddhaman district's population was supported by industry, commerce, and other service professions. A form of seasonal migration for coal mining is also referred to in Dagmar Engels's paper on adivasi women in Bengal (1993), where she mentions that Santhals and Bauris (Bauris are an SC, considered by colonial anthropologists to be a 'tribal caste', that is, as having been only 'tribal' till very recently) formed the bulk of the labour force from the beginnings of coal mining in Bengal. Many of these workers used to go back to their villages for agricultural operations, and in fact a substantial number were settled as agricultural tenants in nearby lands by nineteenth-century coal companies, thus maintaining an agricultural identity.

⁴ In 2001, Rogaly et al. made a calculation for the Barddhaman district as a whole and arrived at the figure of a requirement of half a million migrants for the *aman* harvest (November–December), and even more for transplanting.

⁵ The Bhumij are a semi-Hinduized community of Mundari origin autochthonous to the area, and even formed zamindaris (in the erstwhile estates of Manbhum, Barabhum, and Dhalbhum in present-day Puruliya and Bankura). In 2001, the Bhumij numbered 336,436 in West Bengal, constituting around 8 per cent of the ST population in the state.

during the two World Wars. Although officially declared 'protected forests', a second phase of devastatingly intensive deforestation came during the mid-1950s. This latter phase occurred during the interregnum between the demise of the private ownership claims of the zamindars over forest lands (with zamindari abolition) and before the government's Forest or Revenue Department established full control, a short period during which forest trees were open to anyone to fell.[6] The *longue durée* of erosion of the balance between the forest economy and cultivation that had marked the survival pattern of tribals in the area thus gave rise to and sustained the pressure for seasonal migration.

The specific tribal features of such seasonal migration are at the same time inextricably linked to the reconfiguration of land tenures/ ownership and agrarian relations in the Jungle Mahals during the colonial period. In pre-colonial times, much of the Jungle Mahals had remained inaccessible to the Mughal land surveyors, and under the Mughal zamindari system—in the area covered by the study—it was the autochthonous Bhumij who had first set up villages. These villages were largely rent-free or paid token rent (to the zamindar), under what was known as the *ghatwali* system. A stratified socio-political order thus emerged among the Bhumij, with the chiefs acquiring greater control over land and forest wealth. The Santhals, on the other hand, were not autochthonous to the area, and were associated with the *pradhani* or *mandali* system. In this system, a band of settlers led by a *pradhan* or *mandal* (headman) undertook to reclaim jungle land by paying a stipulated lump sum to the zamindar. The Santhal reclaimers were not, however, the virtual owners of the reclaimed land, as was the case for the Bhumij. Although pioneer tribals had reclaimed virgin lands in the area to make them arable, and were indeed encouraged to do so by both rent-seeking zamindars and the revenue-hungry colonial administration throughout the nineteenth century, most of the good land at the bottom of the valleys did not ultimately remain with them.

With the entry of colonial administration and its systems of land settlement, and with trading and commercial concerns like the British-owned Midnapur Zamindary Company making inroads into a developing local land market, vigorous measurement of landholdings, imposition of stiffer rents and revenues to be paid in cash, and the associated enlarged

---

[6] Later experiments in joint forest management from 1988 remained of an ad hoc nature and at the discretion of the Forest Department, for whom forest villages had become largely only a source of labour.

presence of non-tribal moneylenders/traders/peasants/artisans played havoc with the non-competitive mode of tribal existence.[7] Rampant indebtedness among the tribals and loss of land were the consequences. By the first quarter of the twentieth century, the pradhani/mandali villages were completely bought over by non-tribal proprietors of land, converting the Santhals into rack-rented tenants/sharecroppers or landless labourers, while even the Bhumij chiefs or zamindars and *ghatwals* became victims of moneylending *mahajan*s (usurious moneylenders), and finally lost their forests and surplus land following zamindari abolition. Boxed into agriculturally less productive land and with depleted access to forest produce, the tribal peasants and agricultural labourers were left without sustenance in their home villages for a large part of the year. The pioneer adivasi settlers were thus pushed into survival-oriented intermittent labour migration as a way of life that continues till the present.[8]

While there are indeed area- and tribe-specific features in this story of conversion of sections of the adivasi peasantry into migratory labour, its essential processes—set in motion by colonial rule and its practices—are repetitive across larger tracts and regions in middle India. Addressing questions of tribal social transformation at a wider level, K. S. Singh has argued that: (*a*) the British survey and settlement operations introduced in previously unsurveyed tribal regions acted as an instrument for the transformation of tribes into peasants; (*b*) the colonial system ended the relative isolation of the tribal society, brought it into the mainstream of a new administrative set-up, and put an end to the political dominance of the tribes in the forested territories they occupied; (*c*) tribal communities which had earlier been spared the strain of surplus generation were roped into a new system of production

[7] These were all areas where the Permanent Settlement (1793) was implemented by the British East India Company, whereby the former landholders and revenue intermediaries (zamindars) were granted heritable, rentable, and alienable proprietary rights (effective ownership) to the land they held, and the land tax was fixed in perpetuity. Under the Permanent Settlement, on one side the landlord class acquired greater power than earlier, while on the other the Company's policy of auction of any zamindari lands deemed to be in arrears created a market for land which previously did not exist. Intermediary rentiers proliferated, increasing the rent and debt burden on tenant cultivators who were also unprotected from eviction/replacement by others.

[8] The Bankura district *Human Development Report* of 2007 highlights the otherwise rapid development of the district, yet records the continuance of seasonal migration from the uplands (GoWB 2007).

relations; and (*d*) while following a policy of strengthening the feudal crust of tribal societies formed by the rajas, chiefs, and zamindars, the colonial regime simultaneously created conditions in which their economy and political system were undermined by 'rampaging market forces' (Singh 1982). Labour historians tracking the migration of labour drawn from the Chota Nagpur tribes (primarily Santhal, Munda, and Oraon) to the Assam tea plantations point to the continual decay of an agrarian economy characterized by monocrop rice cultivation, poor soil condition, lack of irrigation and drainage facilities, soil erosion, and deforestation that had made Chota Nagpur's 'peasants and tribesmen' into a reservoir of cheap labour and transformed the region into a 'labour catchment area' (Das Gupta 1986). Drawing on detailed crop and arable land data in some of the area's sub-regions (Ranchi, Hazaribagh, and Singhbhum), Mohapatra (1991) shows that extension of arable land in forested landscapes (albeit unevenly), demographic pressures, as well as colonial land tenure arrangements had also impacted the cropping patterns of the tribal economy, with rice gaining at the expense of more drought-resistant crops in many areas.[9] The shift in crop actually made local agriculture less resilient against failure of the rains and more susceptible to famines. The heaviest outmigration from Chota Nagpur in the late nineteenth and early twentieth centuries was actually from the areas where the most rapid intensification of arable farming had occurred (Mohapatra 1991). In general, there is agreement that arable expansion in tribal areas brought in a range of non-tribal rentier interests and their retainers, who were soon able to acquire land in the tracts that were earlier controlled by tribals. Resistance to such depredations through a spate of tribal rebellions was militarily crushed by the British, and 'pacification' policies led to the creation of an enormous population that had to move out of their regions in search of livelihood (Ghosh 1999). The colonial policy of 'pacification' through sedentarization of semi-nomadic tribes in defined areas and their actual expulsion from much of the better-quality lands thus both operated in tandem.

As the survival economy of tribal communities became more tenuous and fraught, perennial mortgage of their land and labour became a prominent feature of their integration into the broader agrarian economy under colonial rule. These features persisted into the twentieth century,

---

[9] It is of course well known that rice can support more people per unit of land than most other staples (see *Cambridge World History of Food* [Kiple and Omelas 2000]).

despite belated experiments in the protection of their 'customary' rights in some designated areas.[10] From the late nineteenth century onwards, the 'Agency system' was put in place by the British, whereby the normal operations of ordinary law were not applied in 'Scheduled Areas' to protect tribal lands from takeover by outsiders. Part of the 'pacification' drive in response to tribal rebellions, such an enclaving policy was based on the principle of supposed non-interference into the affairs of the tribals and their isolation. Yet, even where restrictions on alienation of tribal land to non-tribals were enforced, market forces remained at work, and while mortgage of land to non-tribals became impossible, intra-tribal stratifications and transactions in land between tribals and tribals emerged that spawned the emergence of a class of tribal or 'insider' moneylenders as well (Singh 1982). Further, exploitation of forests for timber and related plantations through reorganized forest administrations in the latter half of the nineteenth century effectively transferred much of the wealth of the forests out of the hands of tribal residents, and pushed forward the conversion of the hitherto largely autonomous tribal indigenes into a subordinate 'coolie' labour force.[11]

Historical researches for the colonial period, spanning the entire middle India girdle of tribal homelands, have documented the process of 'dissolution of entire economies that were nomadic or forest based, the conversion of land into a scarce commodity, and a growing ethnic cleavage in access to the means of production' (Bates and Carter 1992: 208). Beyond Chota Nagpur, in the Central Provinces (in present-day Madhya Pradesh, Chhattisgarh, western Odisha) too, adivasis were 'fairly consistently among the group who suffered expropriation' either during or shortly after the colonial settlement period.[12] Even when the

[10] K. S. Singh (1982) points out that it was in these enclaves that the concept of protection of the tribes as an ethnic community developed in stages.

[11] The Tana Bhagat movement among the Oraon, in fact, started with a refusal by one Jatra Oraon to accede to the demand by the local police for unpaid coolie labour by the Oraon tenantry. This was at a time when the Oraon of that area (Bishanpur in present-day Gumla district, Jharkhand) were being subjected to excessive requisition of labour for the construction of the summer residence of the lieutenant governor on the Neterhart plateau (Sinha 1993).

[12] In the Central Provinces, under the *malguzari* settlement system, ownership was conferred on those who had acquired a proprietary status on quasi-feudal conditions as *jagirdar* or *talukdar* (*malguzar*s), including some adivasi chiefs or their relatives, grantees of state revenue, and others, but in contrast to Bengal, some measure of tenant right was also included.

rate of expropriation slowed, they were left cultivating the worst-quality soils, resulting in their becoming 'one of the most heavily coerced elements in the migrant workforce and the first resort of nearly every recruiting agent' (Bates and Carter 1992).[13] Whether it was the Gonds and Baigas in the Central Provinces and Berar, or the Bhils of Khandesh (Maharashtra), Malwa (Madhya Pradesh), Mewar, and Wagad (southern Rajasthan), the broad contours of the story followed similar trajectories: as tribals lost their autonomous or semi-autonomous modes of existence, large numbers became indebted peasants and agricultural labourers; as their earlier survival patterns were eroded by deforestation and restricted access to the forest commons and its products, many of them were converted into subordinate 'coolie' labour and seasonal migrants. The first super-profits earned by the Europeans from indigo production in Bengal and Bihar were to a great extent dependent on the availability of cheap seasonal migrant labour from the Chota Nagpur area, as was the spread of intensively cultivated wet rice fields in the Bengal plains. Similarly, in the Central Provinces and Berar, agricultural development in the Narmada valley wheat zone and the Nagpur-Berar cotton zone was made possible by the seasonal migration of primarily Gond tribals from the upland regions, while Bhils were drawn upon to fulfil the seasonal demand for labour in the cotton-growing areas of Khandesh as well as the canal zones of the Bombay Deccan. It has been argued that such seasonal migrant labour in fact played a pivotal role in the continuing reproduction of agricultural underdevelopment in the upland areas of tribal concentration as well as the greater levels of development in the lowland areas that they migrated to (Bates 1985).[14]

[13] For example, Bates and Carter (1992: 213–14) show that the settlement regime in Mandla district granted proprietary rights to the Gond adivasis, who constituted over half the population in the 1860s, in only 432 out of a total of 11,430 villages. The Baigas, who were 4 per cent of the population, were granted only 20 villages. This pattern was repeated in all of the adivasi districts in the Central Provinces. In Betul, Seoni, and Chhindwara, where adivasis constituted 35–40 per cent of the population, less than one in seven villages were allowed to remain in adivasi hands. Within 20 to 30 years after these settlements, 270 villages were transferred in Mandla—mostly to Marwari moneylenders—while between 1869 and 1912, the number of Gond villages fell from 294 to 129 in Raipur.
[14] For the cotton zone across the districts of Nagpur, Wardha, Amraoti, Yeotmal, Buldana, and Nimar, based on cotton and other crop output data for 1890–1, Crispin Bates (1985) calculates that the labour requirements of cotton

In the first half of the nineteenth century, 'Boonooahs',[15] 'Dhangars',[16] or 'Hill Coolies' were the terms used by the British to refer to adivasi labour of Chota Nagpur (usually from Santhal, Munda, and Oraon tribes), who migrated seasonally during the winter months to various districts in Bengal (then including Bihar) for employment in the indigo plantations and factories (Van Schendel 2012), for harvesting of the winter rice crop, for road building, and land reclamation around Calcutta. 'Chaitharas' was the popular name for the adivasi seasonal migrants (predominantly Gond) in the wheat zone in the Central Provinces.[17] 'Dhangars' were among the first (if not the last) to be sent as indentured labour to foreign lands, when, following the abolition of slavery, the global colonial plantocracy was in search of pliable and controllable labour to replace their erstwhile slaves (Das Gupta 2012;

---

in the late nineteenth century exceeded the capacities of local agricultural labour, at a time when cotton accounted for 30 per cent of the gross cropped area. Bates argues that migrant labour must have become of even greater significance over the next few decades as cotton rose to cover 44 per cent of the gross cropped area in the same zone by the 1920s. For the wheat zone of the Narmada valley, Bates refers to specific contemporary descriptions of the intergenerational annual migration of Gond Chaitaharas from the Rewa hills for 1867, 1901, and 1911.

[15] Writing on indigo labour, Van Schendel (2012) describes 'Boonoah' workers as primarily seasonal labour, and quotes a nineteenth-century observer Machell as writing, 'the Boonooahs are the inhabitants of the Boons or the Jungles. . . . They are very ingenious in making mats, nets, baskets &c., and are supposed by some to be the aborigines of Hindoostan.'

[16] John Mackay, an indigo planter over a period of 28 years till 1836, with plantations in 'Jessore, Dacca and Nuddea in lower Bengal; Patna, Tirhut and Bhaugulpoor in the province of Bahar', claimed to have employed up to 500 'Dhangars' at a time. He described these workers in the following words: 'There are no mechanics among them, unless assistant brick makers may be so considered; many of them are good hands at mixing the clay for brickmakers, and expert in forming tanks, but I would consider the Hill Coolies as fittest to be employed as labourers of the ground . . . [they] will travel a distance of 500 miles in search of employment, and know the value of money, and carefully save the wages they earn to carry back to their country to spend with their families.' John Mackay, Minutes of Evidence on Indian and British Immigration, *House of Commons Papers, 1838*, vol. 22, p. 186.

[17] The term 'Chaitharas' comes from the season of Chait (March–April), when the wheat crop is harvested.

Ghosh 1999).[18] It was in the latter half of the nineteenth century that the infamous recruiters of indentured labour for Assam's tea plantations turned to the Chota Nagpur area as the 'favourite hunting ground' for the so-called jungly coolies who were their labourers of choice (Sen 2012),[19] later extending their field further south to the adivasi populations of the Central Provinces (Bates and Carter 1992). Tea plantation labour however, was different from the predominant pattern of circular migration of adivasi labour. Most migrants for tea plantations were permanently divorced from their areas of origin, and their descendants in Assam, now referred to as 'tea tribes', still constitute a major part of the tea plantation workforce both in Assam and the Dooars of West Bengal; they are still located within enclaves that combine agricultural and industrial characteristics, and are also still largely socially segregated from the rest of the local population.[20]

The indigo fields and factories have long disappeared, colonial-style land clearing/reclamation using adivasi 'coolie' labour has long reached its historical limits, and the migration stream of middle India adivasis to north-eastern tea plantations came to a close within a decade or so after independence, but the legacy of conditions and pressures that led to conversion of adivasi communities into a surplus labour force that is most easily corralled into and dependent on labour migration for survival, continues to operate in contemporary times. The adivasis still remain a significant social component of particularly the rural migratory workforce of twenty-first century India, concentrated in hard manual labour based occupations. They are today predominantly to be found in agriculture, construction, and brick kilns.

ADIVASI WOMEN'S MIGRATION IN CONTEMPORARY TIMES: A COMPARATIVE PROFILE

One of the distinctive features of adivasi labour migration streams has been the high participation of women. Significant numbers of women were involved in the more permanent migrations of adivasi labour to the

---

[18] For Dhangar and Hill Coolies, see House of Lords, Session Papers, Session 1837–8, vol. VIII, p. 44.

[19] Between 1879 and 1890, 53.36 per cent of workers in the Assam tea plantations were from Santhal Parganas and Chota Nagpur.

[20] Despite being adivasis, 'tea tribes' do not have ST status in Assam as they do in their states of origin.

tea plantations of Assam and north Bengal, as also in seasonal or circular labour migration across a wider set of regions and sectors from the nineteenth century onwards.[21] The habit of men and women migrating for work together in a family or even larger adivasi groups/gangs perhaps drew upon their heritage of moving together to reclaim land from the jungles for the establishment of new settlements whenever the need was felt, the practice of shifting cultivation, and nomadic/semi-nomadic ways of life. When transformed from autonomous indigenes and peasants into subordinate migrant wage labourers in a commercializing but colonized economy, many adivasis would still move or be recruited in bands that included women. A lack of any tradition of confinement/ seclusion of women indeed distinguishes adivasi society from other communities in India, among whom graded hierarchies are far more entrenched, and the seclusion of women has long been linked to higher social status. Nevertheless, women were and are not positioned as equals even within adivasi society (Prasad 2011; Sinha 2005). Further, in the wage economy, whether adivasi or non-adivasi, women workers were paid lower wages than men, and this was true for migratory labour as well. Still, the traditional lack of any severe internal restraints on women's labour and personal mobility in adivasi societies has been an important factor in maintaining the higher rates of female work participation among adivasis, and their relatively greater participation in wage labour based migration in comparison to other social groups in colonial as well as independent India.[22]

In general, female labour migration in contemporary India is poorly recorded by the official macro surveys, and it is difficult to derive a picture of adivasi women's work migration from these surveys. Since they define migrants as those who have changed their place of residence,

---

[21] Sugata Bose (1993) shows that in the Jalpaiguri tea gardens in 1921 (north Bengal Dooars), women in fact outnumbered men. In the Assam tea plantations too, women ultimately constituted the majority of the workforce. Similarly, Bates (1985) shows that in the cotton belt, seasonal migrants were largely women and children. Banerjee and Ray (1991) show that adivasi women clearly led the way for women from other communities in seasonal migration to the rice plains of Bengal.

[22] The National Sample Survey (NSS) 61st round employment survey for 2004–5 shows that female work participation rates among STs stood at 44.4 per cent in comparison to 30.8 per cent among SCs, 29.9 per cent among OBCs, and 21.4 per cent among others.

women migrants vastly outnumber men in macro surveys because of the widespread prevalence of village exogamy and patrilocal residence in marriage practices. Yet their estimates of female labour migration have remained notoriously lower than what field/ground experience/reports suggest. Since only one reason for migration is asked for, a significant amount of labour migration by women is camouflaged under other social reasons such as marriage or family movement. Further, the definitions followed by the official surveys have been slow to respond to the findings of micro studies that women's labour migration is predominantly short term and circular in nature, both of which tend to be poorly recorded in official surveys. Even when special efforts have been made to bring temporary or short-term migration within the ambit of macro surveys, as was done for 1999–2000 and 2007–8 by National Sample Survey Organisation (NSSO), changes of definitions between the two survey rounds have made for difficulties in trend analysis. Nevertheless, the three migration surveys conducted by NSSO between 1993 and 2007–8 do provide some indications that a more significant presence of women is still a distinguishing feature of adivasi labour migration, and also that adivasi women's migration for work is relatively temporary in nature and more concentrated in rural areas.

First, the three rounds of migration surveys (NSSO) just mentioned consistently show that the proportion of *migrant households* among STs is higher than among other communities. Since 'migrant households' here refer to households migrating within a reference period of only one year preceding the date of survey, we may safely assume that the higher proportion of migrant households among STs is because more adivasi women migrate alongside their menfolk in comparison to other social groups, among whom more women may be left behind by male migrant workers, or may migrate to join their menfolk only much later. This is notwithstanding the fact that the overall female migration rates (that is, proportions of the female population who have changed their usual place of residence) are lowest among ST women in comparison to women of other social groups. In other words, the NSS surveys indicate that relatively lower proportions of adivasi women effect more durable change of residence (whether due to marriage or employment reasons), but greater proportions of adivasi women tend to migrate with their households for employment.[23] The 1999–2000 survey further showed

---

[23] The lower migration rate among adivasi women is, however, changing at a rapid pace. Between 1999–2000 and 2007–8, the increase in the migration

that STs were the single largest group among female *temporary migrants for employment* in rural areas but not in urban areas. Unfortunately, the most recent migration report of NSS for 2007–8 does not give the proportions of STs among the newly defined category of short-term migrants for employment. We can, however, fill some of the gaps in the macro data by referring to the findings of a recent set of surveys that were conducted by the Centre for Women's Development Studies (CWDS) between 2009 and 2011 across 20 states in India, and have been consolidated to present a meso-level view of the broad patterns of women's labour migration in India (CWDS 2012). The CWDS surveys again provide evidence of the relatively greater involvement of adivasi women in female labour migration in contemporary times. They show that STs were over 26 per cent of the migrant women workers in rural destinations and 21 per cent in urban destinations, which is close to 3 times their share of the general female population in rural areas, and close to 10 times in urban areas.

With the application of a more nuanced typology of migration, some of the distinguishing aspects of adivasi women's migration that are only hinted at in the macro surveys came out very sharply in the CWDS surveys. They showed that the most distinctive feature of adivasi women's labour migration is their concentration in short-term and circulatory migration—that is, migrating and returning to their native villages every year or several times in a year. In comparison, relatively smaller proportions of adivasi women workers are involved in long-term or medium-term migration for settlement or more durable residence in urban areas. Table 8.1 presents the consolidated findings of the CWDS surveys in relation to the distribution of types of migration among women migrant workers from different social groups.

As the table clearly shows, among the types of migration, the weight of short-term migration, circulatory migration of longer duration, and circulatory migration of shorter duration is greater among ST women migrant workers than among all other communities/social groups. When taken together, it is most striking that the great majority (59 per cent) of migrant women workers from STs are involved in short-term and circulatory migration. This is a significantly greater proportion than the 41 per cent of such short-term and circulatory migrants among SC

---

rate was highest among adivasi women, having jumped from 35.7 per cent to 44 per cent, bringing it much closer than before to the national average of 47.7 per cent migration rate for the female population as a whole.

TABLE 8.1 Distribution of Women Migrant Workers by Type of Migration (%)

Type of Migrant	General	OBC	MBC	SC	ST
Long-term migrant	44.51	41.56	21.51	25.98	20.81
Medium-term migrant	30.02	22.98	30.11	17.36	10.48
Short-term migrant	3.93	11.91	10.75	14.54	25.16
Irregular short-term migrant	6.42	1.13	1.08	1.08	1.45
Circulatory migrant of longer duration	2.90	9.93	5.38	19.52	22.10
Circulatory migrant of shorter duration	4.55	6.95	4.30	6.06	10.00
Daily/weekly commuters	4.97	3.69	25.81	14.67	8.71
Migrant for family care	2.69	1.84	1.08	0.81	1.29
All	100	100	100	100	100
Short-term and circulatory combined	17.81	29.93	21.51	41.18	58.71

Source: CWDS (2012).

women migrants, almost double the 30 per cent among OBC women, and more than three times the proportion (18 per cent) among the general/upper-caste women migrant workers. Related to this high share of short-term and circulatory migration is another finding of the CWDS surveys, namely that the destination areas of a majority of the adivasi women migrant workers (56 per cent) are rural, in contrast to the majority of women migrant workers of upper-caste and OBC origin, among whom 71 per cent and 54 per cent, respectively, were found to be migrating to urban destinations. Only among migrant women workers of SC background is the 62 per cent share of rural destinations higher than among adivasis.

The CWDS study found that types of migration were very closely correlated with sectors and occupations. Service occupations (white-collared, intermediate combinations of mental and manual work, as well as menial services such as paid domestic work) and manufacturing (factory-based or home-based) are more linked with long-term and medium-term migration. On the other hand, heavy manual labour based seasonal occupations in the primary or secondary sector that are generally attached to the most degraded conditions of work, and where the figure of the labour contractor/recruiter/agent looms large, is more closely correlated with short-term and circular migration. At an overall level, the CWDS study showed that labour migration by women had led to limited occupational diversification, and in fact had propelled their concentration in a relatively narrow band of occupations. Within this overall picture, adivasi women were further concentrated in three sectors/industries, namely agriculture, brick kilns (in rural areas), and construction (in both rural and urban areas). These are the principal sectors/industries driving the short-term and circulatory types of migration by women in contemporary times, and for which recruitment, particularly in rural destinations, is often of male–female pairs or family units rather than individuals of any one sex (which partially explains why there are more migrant households among STs).[24] On the other hand, adivasi women were found to be virtually absent in textile/garment factories, which have otherwise drawn in women workers from all other social groups/communities. The CWDS surveys showed that among adivasi women migrants in urban India, it is not manufacturing but construction that featured as the most prominent employment, while in the feminized occupation of paid domestic work, adivasi women migrants were prominent among the 'live-ins', that is, those who resided in their employers' homes, but relatively insignificant in the larger sea of 'live-out' domestic workers who generally live with their own families in destination areas. Finally, although the small sample of mine workers in the CWDS surveys did not reveal much, it is perhaps significant that the few mine workers covered by the survey were predominantly of adivasi origin.[25]

A corollary of the high share of short-term and circulatory migration among ST women was the finding that white-collar services accounted for a mere 18 per cent of ST women migrant workers, among whom young women from the north-east were more prominent than the adivasis of middle India. The low proportion of ST women in white-

[24] The CWDS survey showed that 42 per cent of rural women migrant workers had been recruited as part of a unit of labour that was either a pair or family-based.

[25] Most of the women workers encountered in the mining areas of Jharkhand and Chhattisgarh during the fieldwork were, of course, descendants of earlier migrants like in the tea plantations, which are also not drawing any fresh migrants.

collared employment was roughly the same as that of SC women migrants (19 per cent), but contrasts strongly with 66 per cent of upper-caste women migrants and 36 per cent of OBC women migrant workers in white-collar employment.

Table 8.1 follows the legal definitions of social group categories. The ST category thus makes no distinction between different groups of tribes or their differing social and regional histories. To our minds, however, there is indeed a need to make some differentiation between migrants from the tribes endogenous to the north-east of the country and the adivasis from middle India, since their migration and employment patterns are quite different. The CWDS surveys found, for example, that women migrants from the north-eastern tribes were actually more concentrated in urban-ward medium-term migration for modern service sector employment that is salaried and requires relatively higher educational levels (sales girls, office workers, or beauticians).[26] Lack of opportunities in the north-eastern states has no doubt propelled the relatively recent but noticeable phenomenon of work/education-based migration by young women from the north-east to large cities in other parts of India. Studies have shown that their conditions of work are exploitative, stereotyped, difficult, and trying (Shimrah 2007) and often compounded by race- and culture-based targeting. Nevertheless, their relatively stronger educational backgrounds, their services-oriented occupational profile, and perhaps their initial context of exclusive rights over larger amounts of land and territory (relative to population) in their relatively more autonomous tribal homelands, has made for a qualitatively different social location from which women from the tribes of the north-east have made their entry into urban life in comparison to other adivasi migrant workers.

Migrant women workers from the middle India tribes in urban destinations are more concentrated in casual labour in construction and prominent among live-in domestics, and are even more concentrated in migration to rural destinations for agriculture, brick kiln work, and again, construction. Related to such a process of concentration are the other features of adivasi women's labour migration, namely circularity, a greater level of involvement of intermediaries such as labour contractors and recruiters, and a continuing living relationship with the agrarian adivasi social order that is rarely sundered by migration. These features

---

[26] Young women from the north-east were also working as beauticians in more organized beauty parlours.

were spawned by the particularities of development of commercialization and enclaved capitalist enterprise under colonial rule. Why they should persist more than 60 years after independence, in the specific role given to adivasi women's labour, and the differential manner in which they continue to be concentrated in the lowest echelons of the migratory semi-proletariat, are questions that cannot be answered without reference to continuities/changes in the sphere of labour processes and the impact of accumulation regimes on adivasi labour, as well as the particular location of adivasi populations in the broader agrarian economy and social order.

CIRCULATING AT THE BOTTOM OF THE ECONOMY

In contradistinction to the general short-term pattern of seasonal agricultural migration is that of sugarcane cutters in western India (Gujarat, Maharashtra, Karnataka),[27] where the annual spell of migration is of a longer duration covering the major part of the year—generally from November to June. The cane cutters move across a wider set of fields and, all-importantly, they are employed not by the farmers whose fields they harvest, but by the managements of sugar mills (cooperatives as well as others privately owned) through agents/contractors. Recruitment is not of individuals, but of groups or gangs of workers, but what distinguishes the particular pattern of recruitment is that the gangs are composed of units of pairs of workers (each comprising a male and a female, generally a husband-and-wife team) called *koyta*s.[28] Wages are piece-rated, that is, paid by the ton, and labour is mobilized through a system of advances that are given before the season begins. Advances effectively tie the gangs of koytas to particular factories/employers/contractors. The division of labour within koyta gangs assumes that the men cut the cane and clean the stalks of leaves, while the women arrange the cane in rows and make bundles that can be loaded, although it has been observed that women may also participate in the cutting of cane (Breman 1978; Teerink 1995). Output demands per day are particularly onerous, driven by the demand to keep the factory machines fully supplied.

---

[27] The other major sugarcane belt in north India (Uttar Pradesh) does not draw on female migrant workers, although during the CWDS migration survey it was found that some adivasi boys from the crisis-ridden tea plantations were being recruited for sugar cane in Uttar Pradesh.

[28] 'Koyta' is also the local name for the sickle-like implement used for cutting the cane.

As a distinctly post-independence phenomenon, seasonal migration for sugarcane has served the development of cooperative-based capitalism in agriculture and the emergence of a politically powerful agro-industrial capitalist class from among the landed cultivating castes/communities, particularly in Maharashtra and also in Gujarat. An insistence on hiring migrant workers for the cutting of cane and keeping local workers out has been a particular strategy of cheapening labour costs and exercising hegemony and control over both local agricultural labour as well as migrant labour (Breman 1978).[29] The sugar mills located near the source areas of such migration bring their workers from elsewhere rather than employing local workers. (In Nandurbar, Maharashtra for example, Bhil workers are brought from Madhya Pradesh, while Nandurbar Bhils are recruited for mills outside the district.)[30] Yet the recruiting system, based as it is on *mukaddam* (middleman) led community or village based gangs, foregrounds the tribe/caste boundaries of labour mobilization and associated catchment areas. The marginalized nature of the community base of sugarcane cutters (which includes adivasis and other dalit and OBC communities) has made for their being kept physically and socially isolated from the villages whose sugarcane they harvest. Their conditions of work and stay are notoriously subhuman. Inadequate shelter facilities or protection from the elements and marauding wildlife is particularly harsh on the women cane cutters. The nomadic form of labour in sugarcane, its long season of unsettlement and constant shifting, its intensive and long hours of work determined by industrial demand rather than the normal agricultural labour day, have all combined to prevent social, educational, or cultural advance for the families of cane cutters. Further, neo-bondage based on cycles of dependence on the advances ensures intergenerational continuity of unfree labour mobility. For the women, the nature of unfreedom is doubly predicated by the fact that the piece rate system ensures that their wage is subsumed in the koyta wage (generally paid to the male member), and they therefore receive no independent income for their labour.

As far as adivasi women's migration for non-agricultural occupations is concerned, the CWDS surveys particularly highlighted their present concentration in construction as well as in brick kiln work. In

---

[29] Breman (1978) points out that it is not shortage of local labour that has driven the use of migrant workers in cane cutting.

[30] This is discussed in detail by Teerink (1995), and was observed in the field by the CWDS research team as well.

construction, where the workforce is more male-dominated than in brick kilns, adivasis may actually constitute the largest social group in the sector's female workforce.[31] A high density stream of migration for construction in which women are particularly prominent is from the contiguous adivasi belt on the Gujarat, Madhya Pradesh, and Rajasthan borders, mainly to various parts of Gujarat and also to other parts of all three states. Brick kiln labour has a higher proportion of women as well as a wider set of labour catchment areas that can be found in practically every state. Nevertheless, mass migration of adivasis for brick kiln work has been observed in western Odisha, from where they migrate to the southern states of Andhra Pradesh and Karnataka and other parts of Odisha (Agnihotri and Mazumdar 2009). Similar mass-scale migration takes place from several districts in Jharkhand, from where they go to the brick kilns of Bihar, West Bengal, and Uttar Pradesh. While brick kiln work is definitively seasonal, with the kilns operating for around eight months in a year (generally October/November to June), adivasi migration for construction also tends to follow a seasonal pattern, with workers returning to their home villages in the rainy season to cultivate their increasingly fragmented plots of land. Migration for brick kilns and construction are no doubt interlinked, both having expanded as part of the real estate boom, particularly since the 1990s (although the NSS classifies construction as a separate industry, while brick making is put under manufacturing). However, while brick making has remained an unorganized industry with localized and dispersed patterns of ownership, the construction industry, although largely unorganized, has seen a rapid growth of a large, organized and corporatized segment on the capital side, even as its workforce remains virtually defined by its casualized nature.[32]

Illustrative of the weight and distinctive patterns of adivasi migration for construction, a survey/study of 42 Bhil villages in central western

---

[31] As per the 2007–8 NSS survey on 'Migration in India', women constituted just 10 per cent of the migrant workforce in construction, and a larger proportion of the female construction workforce were adivasis in comparison to the male construction workforce. The NSS 2009–10 employment survey shows that the share of women among construction workers has risen significantly to a little less than 15 per cent.

[32] The organized sector accounted for 48.7 per cent of what the National Accounts Statistics calls operating surplus/mixed income from construction in 2003–4. Its share had jumped to 71 per cent by 2007–8, dipped to 60 per cent in 2008–9, but again moved up to 66.4 per cent the following year.

India in the latter half of the 1990s (Mosse et al. 2005) estimated that the overwhelming majority of the 65 per cent of households involved in seasonal migration from these villages go for casual urban construction work. According to the authors of the study, construction work has become the primary source of cash for Bhil families. Of these migrants, 42 per cent are women, who tend to be poorer, older, and married with children. Mosse et al. argue that, whether migrating for work on construction sites, stone quarries, brick making, or digging cable trenches, the seasonal flow of Bhil casual labourers from upland villages has contributed directly to the physical expansion of the industrial growth poles in Gujarat, such as Surat, Baroda (now Vadodara), and Ahmedabad. For construction, some migrants travel on their own to nearby towns and cities, where they are recruited as daily wage labourers at *naka*s (informal labour *mandi*s or markets at streetcorners). Others travel in kin groups, including younger women having some direct contacts with builders/contractors. Still others are mobilized in their own villages by mukaddams, who in this case were identified as former adivasi labourers turned supervisors and village moneylenders, a few of whom had settled in town. Mukaddams arrange cash advances from contractors/employers (in the monsoon season) for tying the prospective migrants for work that is relatively long term. Mosse et al. argue that while 'the extent of the first kind of positive or opportunistic migration varies with the availability of household labour in any year/village (influenced by domestic cycles), the extent of the last, advance driven survival migration, is a factor of poverty' (2005: 3027). However, they also find that adivasi migrants are not to be found in the skilled segments of the construction workforce (masons, carpenters, and so on), which incidentally are completely male. They dig earth, mix the mortar, carry cement bags, while the women carry head-loads of bricks and other construction materials, and underpayment of wages is common.[33]

At a broad level, the study finds Bhils from eastern Gujarat villages mainly migrating to nearby Baroda city, their links to contractors established through repeated migration, while those from Jhabua or Ratlam (in Madhya Pradesh) travel to far-off Kota, Surat, or to Bhuj,

---

[33] Women head-loading broken stone are expected to carry 400 head-loads a day—each receiving a stone 'token' for every head-load. When the loads carried are fewer than the target, wages are reduced. Underpayment of wages is common, statutory minimum wages rarely applied, while naka workers often remain without work for 10–20 days a month.

and typically depend upon mukaddams. Mosse et al. (2005) argue that migration is associated with changes potentially disruptive of cooperative agricultural life linked to increased monetization and need for cash, the increase in wage labour occurring 'at the expense of systems of reciprocal exchange, a decline in joint cultivation or well management, and significant strains on intra-household relations (gender, marital and inter-generational)' (Mosse et al. 2005: 3028). And yet importantly, they also hold that since survival for rural households is increasingly dependent on seasonal labour migration to urban construction sites, such migration has become perhaps the only means to reproduce 'valued agricultural livelihoods'. For most Bhils, such migration is not an external factor engendering non-agrarian identities, but 'was integral to the reproduction of subsistence agriculture and village culture' (Mosse et al. 2005).

Brick kiln work, on the other hand, is concentrated in rural areas, and completely based on contractor recruitment. While a lower end of the tier of contractors may be from the adivasi community (mukaddams and sardars, for example), the CWDS migration survey found that many contractors, and particularly the big ones, are from outside both community and village. Such professional contractors are not workers themselves, and they operate through an army of small agents/musclemen who may or may not be from within the communities. Their primary mode of recruitment is through advances given for each *jodi* (pair).[34] At the time of the workers' journey to the brick kilns, contractors provide musclemen who ensure that the workers reach their particular destinations, but such escorts are singularly absent when thousands return from dispersed sites of work with one common destination— the labour catchment area. In the month of May 2010, at the station of Kantabanji, a small town with a population of less than 25,000 in Odisha's Balangir district, CWDS researchers observed over 300 men, women, and children carrying the clothes, pots and pans, and so on that they required for their seven to eight month stay at the brick kilns, alighting from just one train.[35] They had spent two days on the journey and were tired, yet eager to return to their village homes. Some were seeking out motorized transport tempos and bargaining over the rates.

---

[34] For such a small town, Kantabanji has a number of hotels and lodges where brick kiln owners, particularly from Andhra Pradesh come and stay while negotiating with the contractors.

[35] In 2001, the population of Kantabanji was 20,090.

Others just started off on foot, even though their trek might involve upwards of 40 kilometres. This was just the initial trickle that heralded the flood of thousands more over the next few weeks. Several such trains unload an estimated 200,000 brick kiln workers at Kantabanji in May–June, and almost every year some workers die on the journey due to overcrowding in the trains. Yet, even within that relatively small batch of first returnees, so many were angry and bitter at having been able to bring back so little of what they had earned from the hardest of labours, the bulk of their earnings having gone towards paying off their advances and for basic food supplies at the brick kiln sites.

The labour process in brick kilns involves softening of the soil/mud with water, digging the softened mud with a spade (generally done by males), packing the clay into moulds with the hands, emptying them on the ground in rows (done by men and women), then stacking them for further drying in the sun (done by women and children). These workers (*patheras*), who mould the raw bricks, are recruited in male–female pairs (jodis). Specialized firers of the kilns, on the other hand, are always male and generally different from all other categories of brick workers, and almost never from adivasi communities. Other categories of workers include (with some permutations and combinations) those who manually carry and arrange the green bricks at the kiln (*beldars*) and those who manually carry the fully baked and cooled bricks to storage points (*nikasis*)—mostly women. All functions involve hard toil out in the open all day. Payment rates are generally fixed per 1,000 bricks for all categories (although at different rates for the different categories of workers), except the firers who have time rated wages, and managerial personnel who are on monthly salaries. The manual workers stay on-site, at some distance from any village or other residential settlement, in rough temporary shacks, although some of the more long-standing and larger kilns have built single-room tenement lines. The workers are bonded to a brick kiln each year by advances paid by the contractors, often well before the work season begins.

One study of the brick fields of Hooghly district near Kolkata found adivasi women (of Oraon, Munda, Bhumij, and Kol tribes) migrating singly from Chakradharpur, Palamu, Ranchi, and Hazaribagh in Jharkhand. Their task was to carry 8 to 10 bricks weighing about 40 kilograms for a distance of 100 metres from the moulding department to the furnace (a total distance of 15 to 20 kilometres a day). These women, also known as 'coolies' (referred to as beldars earlier) had also to perform other jobs such as fetching water from a distance, carrying coal bags, and so on, and were generally managed by a *sardarin* (female sardar). Segmentation of labour followed 'ideas and myths about what each group are good at', largely based on ethnic and community identities. Thus, patheras tended to be non-adivasi family women from dalit and OBC families of Bihar and Bengal, while the firers were all from Uttar Pradesh (Ghosh 2009). Although the same principle of community and gender segmentation in allocation of jobs was observed by CWDS researchers in brick kilns across the country, the community composition of each segment varied. In another district of West Bengal (Medinipur), adivasi women (Santhal) from Puruliya were working in family units as patheras, while those from Jharkhand (Munda and Oraon, among others) were carriers of bricks. Similarly in western Odisha, many adivasi women (of Kondh, Gond, and Saora tribes) were a part of the jodi based pathera units. Like the sugarcane cutters, the jodi-based labour combined with piece rates has meant that women receive no independent income; the cycle of advance-based migration marks out their particular form of bondage; and the unsettlement of the annual trek that occupies the major part of any year ensures that there is little scope for educational, social, and cultural advance for either the women or their children. Indeed, the old Santhal woman's question regarding passing on the past to the future remains valid for the majority of adivasis involved in labour migration in contemporary India.

* * *

British administrative systems had ended the isolation and political autonomy of adivasi society, brought them into a system of production relations and surplus generation geared to colonial/feudal interests and extractive capital accumulation, and transformed even low population density adivasi areas into labour-surplus economies. In the process, large segments of adivasi populations faced resource dispossession, pauperization, and debt-based manipulation of their lives and labour. Increasingly confined as peasants to agriculturally poor lands with a single agricultural season, and with reduced access to forest resources, adivasis were the most easily drawn into mortgaging their labour and engaging in intermittent migration that enabled greater commercial agricultural development in areas other than their own. The broad contours of such a constrained and disadvantaged social and economic location of adivasi populations have persisted in independent India, providing a continued basis for the dominant pattern of survival-oriented migration as opposed to social-development-oriented migration. Labour migration by adivasi women in the post-independence decades has, however, served the interests of a wider range of classes than was the case in colonial India, enabling as well as pushing forward a greater level of class differentiation in Indian society since independence.

Adivasi community practices and cultures, particularly the lack of traditional restrictions on women's work and labour, have indeed been a significant factor in bringing larger proportions of adivasi women into more mobile forms of labour in comparison to other social groups in India. However, this chapter has shown that the long-standing and higher propensity to labour migration among adivasi women has not fundamentally altered their conditions of historical disadvantage in the agrarian economy, and in fact has integrated adivasi women in the developing labour market under capitalist development at several levels of additional disadvantage. It would appear that the predominantly survival-oriented circular and short-term pattern of contemporary adivasi women's migration predicates a regularized mobility for irregular employment that simultaneously constrains and constricts possibilities of social, cultural, and educational advance. Such constrictions additionally derive from the nature of the regimes of capital accumulation that draw on adivasi migrant labour, related forms and conditions of recruitment and labour mortgage, and the disproportionate targeting of adivasi communities and villages as labour catchment areas for the hardest of manual occupations. It is clear that several characteristics of unfree labour that characterized the deployment of adivasi labour under the colonial regime continue to persist in India, more than 60 years after independence.

The agricultural classes benefiting from seasonal agricultural migration by adivasi women include individual cultivating farmers (medium and large) at one end, and more organized agro-industrial capitalist interests at the other. The sector/case evidence cited in this chapter suggests that in more short-term migration streams for cultivating farmers, some of the earlier overtly patriarchal methods of recruitment of adivasi women have declined (sometimes as a consequence of political mobilization), as have gender-based wage inequalities. This is notwithstanding greater economic and even social compulsions to migrate periodically for survival, persistently harsh conditions of work, and even a growing competition from an expanding pool of agricultural labourers—men and women, local and migrant—as agrarian crisis has swept through agriculturally developed as well as underdeveloped regions.

Migration for non-agricultural employment of adivasi women has been concentrated in manual and 'unskilled' labour in construction and brick kilns. A third front has been opened for live-in domestic service, combining work and residence on employers' terms. Such a narrow field highlights the fact that little skill and occupational diversification has been achieved through migration. Further, the link between such occupations and temporary or circular types of migration vests the majority of adivasi women migrant workers with the dual characteristics of retaining their agricultural origins even as their occupation has become in great part industrial. Such a dual characteristic is partially linked to the value attached to agricultural livelihoods despite being unable to derive a living from such agriculture. At the same time, the particularly degraded conditions of adivasi women's migratory employment in agriculture and non-agriculture, the chronic cycle of debt/advance-based recruitment, low incomes, wage-reducing dependence on contractors, and related unfreedoms do not seem to be capable of providing any security of livelihood or settlement outside agriculture. Jan Breman's (1996) formulation that migration has engendered a shift from local feudal bondage to neo-bondage in the developing capitalist systems of production most appropriately applies to adivasi women's experience of labour migration in contemporary India.

REFERENCES

Agnihotri, Indu and Indrani Mazumdar. 2009. 'Dusty Trails and Unsettled Lives: Women's Labour Migration in Rural India', *Indian Journal of Gender Studies*, vol. 16, no. 3, pp. 375–99.

Banerjee, Narayan. 1989. 'Mills of Sustenance', *Lokayan Bulletin*, vol. 7, no. 1.

Banerjee, Narayan and Lokenath Ray. 1991. 'Seasonal Migration: A Case Study from West Bengal', mimeograph, CWDS, New Delhi.

Bates, Crispin. 1985. 'Regional Dependence and Rural Development in Central India: The Pivotal Role of Migrant Labour', *Modern Asian Studies*, vol. 19, no. 3, pp. 573–92.

Bates, Crispin and Marina Carter. 1992. 'Adivasi Migration in India and Beyond', in Gyan Prakash (ed.), *The World of the Rural Labourer in Colonial India*. New Delhi: Oxford University Press.

Behal, Rana P. 2006. 'Power Structure, Discipline and Labour in Assam's Tea Plantations', *International Review of Social History*, vol. 51, supplement S14, pp. 143–72.

Bhukya, Bhangya. 2010. *Subjugated Nomads: The Lambadas under the Rule of the Nizams*. New Delhi: Orient BlackSwan.

Bose, Sugata. 1993. *Peasant Labour and Colonial Capital: Rural Bengal since 1770*. Cambridge: Cambridge University Press.

Breman, Jan. 1978. 'Seasonal Migration and Co-operative Capitalism: Crushing of Cane and of Labour by Sugar Factories of Bardoli', *Economic and Political Weekly*, vol. 13, nos 31–3, pp. 1317–60.

———. 1996. *Footloose Labour: Working in India's Informal Sector*. Cambridge: Cambridge University Press.

Chandrasekhar, C. P. 2010. 'Liberalising Loot', *Frontline*, vol. 27, no. 14, pp. 3–16.

CWDS. 2012. *Gender and Migration: Negotiating Rights—A Women's Movement Perspective (Key Findings)*. Available at: http://www.cwds.ac.in/researchPapers/GenderMigrationNegotiatingRights.pdf (accessed 16 August 2015).

Das Gupta, Ranajit. 1981. 'Structure of the Labour Market in Colonial India', *Economic and Political Weekly*, vol. 16, nos 44–6, pp. 1781–806.

———. 1986. 'Popular Movements in Jalpaiguri District', *Economic and Political Weekly*, vol. 21, no. 47, pp. 2064–6.

Das Gupta, Sanjukta. 2012. 'Colonial Rule and Agrarian Transition in Singhbhum', in Sanjukta Das Gupta and Raj Sekhar Basu (eds), *Narratives from the Margins: Aspects of Adivasi History in India*. New Delhi: Primus Books.

Dhagamwar, Vasudha. 2006. *Role and Image of Law in India: The Adivasi Experience*. New Delhi: Sage.

Engels, Dagmar. 1993. 'The Myth of the Family Unit: Adivasi Women in Coal Mines and Tea Plantations in Early Twentieth Century Bengal', in Peter Robb (ed.), *Dalit Movements and the Meanings of Labour in India*. Delhi: Oxford University Press.

Ghosh, Kaushik. 1999. 'A Market for Aboriginality: Primitivism and Race Classification in the Indentured Labour Market of Colonial India', in Gautam Bhadra, Gyan Prakash, and Susie Tharu (eds), *Subaltern Studies X: Writings on South Asian History and Society*. New Delhi: Oxford University Press.

Ghosh, Swati. 2009. 'Fragmented Labour and Elusive Solidarity: The Brickfields of Bengal', paper presented at the Third Critical Studies Conference, mimeograph, Calcutta Research Group, Kolkata.

Government of India. 2009. *Socio-economic Conditions of Women Workers in Plantation Industry 2008–09*. Chandigarh: Labour Bureau, Ministry of Labour and Employment.

GoWB (Government of West Bengal). 2007. *District Human Development Report Bankura*. Available at: http://hdr.undp.org/en/reports/nationalreports/asiathepacific/india/Bankura_india_hdr_2007.pdf.

Janarth. 2005. *Sakri Survey Report*. Available at: http://www.janarth.org/Sakrireport.pdf (accessed 16 August 2015).

Kiple, Kenneth F. and Kriemhild Conee Omelas (eds). 2000. *The Cambridge World History of Food*. Cambridge: Cambridge University Press.
Kulkarni, S. D. 1974. 'Over a Century of Tyranny', *Economic and Political Weekly*, vol. 9, no. 10, pp. 389–92.
Lahiri-Dutt, Kuntala. 2001. 'From Gin Girls to Scavengers: Women in Indian Collieries', Resource Management in Asia-Pacific, Working Paper No. 28, Australian National University, Canberra.
Mishra, Deepak, Vandana Upadhyay, and Atul Sarma. 2012. *Unfolding Crisis in Assam's Tea Plantations: Employment and Occupational Mobility*. New Delhi: Routledge.
Mohapatra, Prabhu. 1991. 'Some Aspects of Arable Expansion in Chotanagpur: 1880–1950', *Economic and Political Weekly*, vol. 26, no. 16, pp. 1043–54.
Mosse, David, Sanjeev Gupta, and Vidya Shah. 2005. 'On the Margins in the City: Adivasi Seasonal Labour Migration in Western India', *Economic and Political Weekly*, vol. 40, no. 28, pp. 3025–38.
NSSO (National Sample Survey Organisation), various rounds (1993, 1999–2000, 2007–8). *Migration in India*. New Delhi: NSSO.
Prasad, Archana. 2011. 'More Marginal than the Marginalised', in *Against Ecological Romanticism*. New Delhi: Three Essays Collective.
Rogaly, Ben, Jhuma Biswas, Daniel Coppard, Abdur Rafique, Kumar Rana, and Amrita Sengupta. 2001. 'Seasonal Migration, Social Change and Migrants' Rights: Lessons from West Bengal', *Economic and Political Weekly*, vol. 36, no. 49.
Roy Burman, J. J. 2010. *Ethnography of a Denotified Tribe: The Laman Banjara*. New Delhi: Mittal Publications.
Sen, Samita. 2012. 'Kidnapping in Chotanagpur: Recruitment for Assam Tea Plantations in a "Tribal" Area', in Sanjukta Das Gupta and Raj Sekhar Basu (eds), *Narratives from the Margins: Aspects of Adivasi History in India*. New Delhi: Primus Books.
Shimrah, Singmila. 2007. 'North-East Women Workers in Delhi', mimeograph, CWDS, New Delhi.
Shyamala, B. Devi. 1984. 'Class and Caste Differences among the Lambadas in Andhra Pradesh', *Social Scientist*, vol. 12, no. 7, pp. 47–56.
Singh, K. S. 1982. 'Transformation of Tribal Society: Integration vs Assimilation', *Economic and Political Weekly*, vol. 17, no. 33 (14 August), pp. 1318–25.
Sinha, S. P. 1993. *Conflict and Tension in Tribal Society*. New Delhi: Concept Publishing House.
Sinha, Shashank Shekhar. 2005. *Restless Mothers and Turbulent Daughters: Situating Tribes in Gender Studies*. Kolkata: Stree.
Teerink, Rensje. 1995. 'Migration and Its Impact on Khandeshi Women in the Sugar Cane Harvest', in Loes Schenk-Sandbergen (ed.), *Women and Seasonal Labour Migration*. New Delhi: Sage.

Van Schendel, Willem. 2012. 'Green Plants into Blue Cakes: Working for Wages in Colonial Bengal's Indigo Industry', in Marcel van Linden and Leo Lucassen (eds), *Working on Labour: Essays in Honour of Jan Lucassen*. Leiden: Brill.

Venkateswarlu, Davuluri. 2007. 'Recent Trends in Employment of Child Labour in Hybrid Cottonseed Production in India', mimeograph, Glocal Research and Consultancy Services, Hyderabad.

———. 2010. 'Signs of Hope: Child and Adult Labour in Cottonseed Production in India', mimeograph. Available at: http://www.multiwatch.ch/cm_data/100620_Syngenta_seedsofhope.pdf (accessed 16 August 2015).

9

Tribal Labour in the Tea Plantations of West Bengal
Problems of Migration and Settlement

Sharit K. Bhowmik

This chapter deals with the migration and settlement of adivasis from the Chota Nagpur region of Jharkhand and Chhattisgarh in the tea-growing districts of West Bengal. The tea industry was started in the mid-nineteenth century in Darjeeling and in 1872 in Jalpaiguri district. Initially these were the only two districts engaged in tea cultivation. Later, a few tea gardens came up in Cooch Behar district, but after 1947. The two districts collectively produce 22 per cent of the country's tea even today. Jalpaiguri is the larger tea-producing district, and it produces approximately 17 per cent of the total production in India.[1] The labour in the Darjeeling hills is of Nepali or Gorkha origin, while on the plains (known as Terai), the labourers are from the same regions as Jalpaiguri.

---

[1] Assam is the largest tea producer in the country, producing around half of the country's total production. The state also engages half of the one million tea plantation workers in the country. The industry was established in 1837 in Assam, and the labour also originated from the same regions as in the Jalpaiguri district, namely the adivasi areas of Chota Nagpur and Santhal Parganas. Tea plantation labour in West Bengal has retained its tribe status while in Assam the same adivasis have been denied the status of STs. They were included as OBC 20 years ago.

In 2006, the total number of tea plantation labourers in Jalpaiguri and Terai was 168,867 and 39,680, respectively (Tea Board of India 2009: 158). Around 52 per cent of these workers are female (Tea Board of India 2009: 162–3). Besides these adivasi workers, the total number of bona fide dependents are 222,994 in Jalpaiguri and 35,887 in Terai (Tea Board of India 2009: 158). These figures do not show the actual number of dependents, because bona fide dependents include children of plantation workers who are less than 18 years of age and retired parents of the worker. Children above 18 are not included. Hence, the total number of adivasi workers residing in the plantations of Jalpaiguri and Terai would be much larger.

The tea-growing areas in Jalpaiguri district are known as the Dooars. The Tea Board of India has divided this region into three tea districts, namely the Dooars, the Terai, and Darjeeling. The first part of this chapter deals with the migration of the adivasis to the tea districts. The second part deals with their settlement in the plantations and the subsequent problems.

DATA COLLECTION

The fieldwork for this study was initially conducted in 1974–5 as a part of my doctoral research. Initially, I lived in the labour line of a tea plantation for over a year to interact with workers and observe their social and political interactions. My dissertation was completed in 1978 but I continued to visit the plantations and add on to my data. In 2011, I conducted a study on the recent developments in these areas. Data was collected through interviews with workers and through observation of their lives.

While tracing the history of the plantation workers in the Dooars, which includes their process of migration and their conditions of existence in the earlier days, one is handicapped by the lack of documentary evidence. The problem becomes more acute while trying to reconstruct their living conditions. One does not face the same problem in the case of Assam, as there is no dearth of printed material on tea plantation labour. While dealing with the Dooars, however, one finds an acute shortage of recorded evidence, even though most of the workers in both places had the same place of origin. There were annual reports on immigrant labour in Assam between 1878 and 1928–9, and two reports by labour enquiry committees, one in 1906 and the other in 1921–2. In addition, the conditions of the workers there attracted the attention of the nationalist movement. Nationalist leaders and the press made several exposés of the horrifying state of affairs among the labourers in Assam (Chandra 1964: 387).

The Dooars, on the other hand, was an isolated area, and it remained neglected by both the colonial government and the nationalist press. There were only two enquiry committees on the Dooars, one in 1911 and the other in 1936. Besides these, there were no regular reports on the conditions of labour there. Hence, it is difficult to get a systematic, chronological flow of information from these documents. Reports of the committees on plantation labour in general concentrated on Assam and devoted, at the most, a few pages to the Dooars.

Therefore, while dealing with these aspects of the workers, one has to rely on informal sources like the reminiscences of the older generation of workers, managers, and other employees, besides whatever bits and pieces one can pick up from the reports of the employers' organizations.

This method has its handicaps, as one cannot go too far back in time. Hence, while dealing with the conditions of existence of the workers, we have to limit our findings to a specific period. We shall deal with the period from the 1920s onwards.

EARLY 'PROBLEMS' OF THE PLANTATIONS

In founding the tea industry in eastern India, the planters faced two major problems. First, the areas most suited for tea cultivation were covered with thick, unhealthy forests, which had to be cleared. Second, there was an inadequate supply of labour. Low wages and hazardous conditions of work provided strong disincentives for the local population. The industry had to look elsewhere for its supply of labour.

The conditions of work were also far from attractive. Through the course of my interviews, a picture of the type of work performed emerged. There were no fixed hours of duty. Workers started work at sunrise and returned home at sunset. Plucking of tea leaves was not the only task the worker had to perform. Hoeing, weeding, pruning of bushes in winter, and other such agricultural activities were also a part of the work, as is the case at present. This type of work for a low pay provided strong disincentives for the local population to join the workforce.

RECRUITMENT OF ADIVASI LABOUR

This brings us to the question of how labour could be recruited, especially from Chota Nagpur, in spite of these hardships. Recruitment to Assam was done through the indenture system, where, once he or she had committed to working in the plantations, the worker was expected to work for a specific period of time (usually four years) under a contract. Under this system, the worker was expected to travel to work for a specific time in another place in exchange for expenses incurred on travelling to the place, food, and a place to stay. In the case of Assam, workers were recruited under the provisions of the Workmen's Breach of Contract Act (1858) that stipulated that a contract worker had to serve for a period of five years. The Act rendered the labourer liable to prosecution for any breach of contract, 'but gave him no protection against the employers and laid down no conditions with regard to the arrangements of his transit to the tea districts' (Griffiths 1969: 269).

In 1861, the government appointed a Committee of Enquiry into the Migration of Labour to Assam and Cachar. The state of affairs was found to be worse than expected (Griffiths 1969: 269). As a result, the Inland Emigration Act was passed in 1863. This marked the real beginning of the indenture system (Chandra 1964: 361). The Act provided that all recruiters should be licensed, that every intending emigrant should be produced before the district magistrate, that he should be medically fit, and that his contract should not exceed four years. The Act deplored the bad sanitary conditions and high mortality rates, but did nothing to improve them (Bose 1954: 71). Therefore, it is not surprising to note that out of 84,915 recruited between 1 May 1863 and 1 May 1866, 31,876 workers died (Bose 1954: 71; Griffiths 1969: 270).

The Act of 1863 was amended in 1865, granting a few concessions to the workers, like reducing their contract to three years and giving 'some kind of protection' to them (Griffiths 1969: 277–8). At the same time, it legalized punishment in cases of desertion or insolence. The planter could arrest any worker who was alleged to have left the estate (Bose 1954: 73; Chandra 1964: 361–2; Griffiths 1969: 277–8). This Act did not change the conditions of workers in any significant way. Workers continued to be deceived by false promises, now perhaps through licensed contractors (Hoffman 1964: 162). They were cruelly dealt with if they tried to leave after a period of disillusionment. 'The planter was bound by his contract to clear one-eighth of his land within five years and he could ill-afford to lose his labour.' He therefore showed no mercy to the workers, and 'short work was punished with flogging and absconders, when recovered, were also flogged' (Griffiths 1969: 270). A gruesome account of one such instance is given in Captain Lamb's diary (quoted in Bose 1954: 72). He came across seven men with marks on their backs that indicated that they had been mercilessly beaten. These men had been induced to run away because of inadequate rations, but they were caught. The assistant manager had caned them severely and later had oil and salt rubbed into their wounds.

In earlier years, recruitment was done through *arkatis*, or professional recruiters. Their modus operandi evidently was, as the *Assam Labour Enquiry Report* of 1906 indicates, deception and misrepresentation, by entrapping people on bazaar days when they had had something to drink and cajoling single women by offering various inducements (Das 1928: 65). But these could not be sufficient reasons for thousands of people to migrate over a long period of time. It is therefore necessary to enquire into the conditions of existence of these people at their place of origin.

MIGRATION TO THE TEA DISTRICTS

Adivasi society in Bihar (which includes Chota Nagpur) in the nineteenth century was in a state of turmoil. This is evident from the series of revolts and the general unrest prevailing in the area. The decay of their traditional society had started earlier, in the seventeenth century, when Hinduism crept into the ruling family. The adivasi raja of Chota Nagpur elevated his status through the process of Hinduizing himself. He no longer considered himself a Munda and traced his lineage to Nag Devata, the serpent god. The members of the princely family, after Hinduization, were able to intermarry with neighbouring Hindu princely families (Jha 1964: 31). This resulted in the alienation of the adivasi raja and his kinsfolk from the rest of the people.

Along with Hinduization came the *dikus* (aliens) who gradually expropriated adivasi cultivators of their land. These people were non-adivasis, mainly Hindus (Hoffman 1964: 1062), who were encouraged to settle in Chota Nagpur by the members of the princely family. They came primarily from neighbouring areas in Bihar. As most of these people had some rudimentary education, the ruling family encouraged them to take up administrative posts. Soon, most of the key posts in the administration had come under their control. Davidson, the governor-general's agent, noted, 'It became a great object with them (the princely family) to induce other Hindus to settle in Nagpore.' The royal administration came to be staffed not by the local adivasis, but by *kayastha*s from outside (Jha 1964: 31). These people used their wits to usurp the adivasi's property, which was not a difficult task for them.

The word 'diku', which at first meant a non-adivasi or a Hindu landlord (Hoffman 1964: 1062), came to be used as a word of abuse.

The Hinduized Nagvanshi rulers liberally donated land to the Brahmins 'whose influence over the new converts was very strong' (Jha 1964: 32). Muslims, Sikhs, and others who came as tradesmen dealing in horses, shawls, brocades, and other luxury goods 'fetched enormous offers for their wares from the Nagvanshi chiefs, and obtained farms or villages instead of cash' (R. D. Haldar, *Supplement to Calcutta [Government] Gazette*, December 1880, quoted in Jha 1964: 32). In this way, the adivasis were increasingly alienated from their lands, and a class of *jagirdars* (petty landlords) became firmly entrenched.

About the same time, while the adivasis were struggling with the unhappy effects of Hinduization came the British penetration into the area. Chota Nagpur, as a part of Bihar, was leased to the British East India Company in 1765. Both impacts, that of Hinduization and of British rule, were felt at the same time, as both thrust alien people and alien ideas on the adivasis 'in an influx which led eventually to the economic ruin of the people' (Jha 1964: 1).

The introduction of British rule resulted in a change of masters. The magisterial powers of the local raja were curtailed in the beginning and finally they were forfeited (Saha 1970: 37). Moneylenders and tradesmen poured into the area and cornered lands through trickery and connivance with the local authorities. As the population was sparse, land was available in plenty, but those virgin hilly tracts were difficult to level and cultivate, so the next best recourse was to grab the adivasi's land, which was already under the plough (Hunter 1872: 116).

It is now quite evident that the changes in the government had not been in any way beneficial to the adivasis; on the contrary, their conditions had worsened. 'The unfortunate simple adivasi races were neglected by their new masters, oppressed by aliens and deprived of the means they had formerly possessed of obtaining redress through their own chief' (Dalton 1882: 170). The deputy commissioner of Lohardaga district reported that the 'traditional authority of the Munda and Oraon chiefs had been entirely effaced by that of immigrant farmers'. In some villages the adivasis had lost all their lands to these aliens and had been reduced to the status of landless agricultural labourers (Saha 1970: 38).

The entire adivasi agrarian system was being destroyed, shaking the very basis of the old society. Never before had the sanctuary of adivasi society, secluded from the rest of the world, witnessed on such a scale this influx of dikus who were stubbornly lodged in their body politic, prospering and multiplying at their expense, giving rise to a new order. 'It was a hurricane that blew over their land' (Singh 1965: 7).

The simple-minded, illiterate, and ignorant adivasi was innocent of the system of complicated deeds and documents relating to the ownership of land, which was in contrast with the traditional, though unwritten, right to proprietorship. The new masters too were ignorant of these traditional rights and treated documents as the sole legal proof of ownership. The dikus could cleverly manipulate these documents to their advantage, and before the adivasi realized it he was relieved of his right to cultivation. He was therefore dispossessed by these aliens who even superseded the authority of the village headman who used to have the last say in matters regarding land. He found no solace with the civil authorities, as their offices were far away and he could not meet the expenses incurred in travelling. If someone was bold enough to reach the 'far-off station', he would find that the other party was well armed with a host of witnesses 'who would swear that he had not only no rights in the land, but was a turbulent rebel besides' (Dalton 1882: 170).

The notorious Permanent Settlement Act (1793), which gave legal sanction to the class of zamindars, was not applicable to Chota Nagpur initially, as the authorities feared adverse consequences. They could sense the hostility among the adivasis and felt that the revenue collectors would be met with resistance. A resolution to this effect was passed on 18 September 1789 (Jha 1964: 41). However, as if to rub salt into their wounds, this decision was revoked in 1823 and the Act came into force. Along with it came all its disastrous effects—rack renting, resumption, and subletting. The ancient tillage rights of the adivasi peasantry were now legally merged with the all-devouring power of the zamindar's permanent property rights. A series of taxes were imposed by the landlords and by the East India Company. Even the mahua tree, which was regarded by the adivasis as nature's gift, was taxed. Individually, these might seem as light measures, but when added up they were crushing (Jha 1964: 42; Saha 1970: 38; Singh 1965: 3–4).

ADIVASI UNREST

Unable to bear these tyrannies and the craftiness of dikus who had destroyed their land rights, and consequently their village system as the two were interlinked (Jha 1964: 10), the adivasis frequently rose in revolt. The entire nineteenth century was dotted with adivasi uprisings—1795–1800, 1811, 1820, 1831, 1858, and 1899. The unrest of 1831 was the first major revolt in the plateau against the dikus and the British and came to be known as the Kol insurrection. None of the earlier uprisings had been as broad-based as this one. All cultivating adivasis—Mundas, Kharias, Hos, and Oraons, among others—joined hands to fight their enemies (Jha 1964: 23; Singh 1965). It was 'the bursting forth of a fire that had long been smouldering' (Dalton 1882: 171).

The rest of the century was dotted with several such insurrections, reflecting the unhappy state of affairs of the adivasis, of which two achieved the magnitude of the Kol insurrection. They were the Santhal revolt of 1858, which created the legendary Santhal heroes Sidhu and Kanu. The Santhals under the leadership of Sidhu and Kanu reached as far as the outskirts of Calcutta. In 1899–1901, Birsa Munda led a militant protest movement which was known in Mundari as *ulgulan* (uprising). Like the Kol insurrection, these revolts were also directed against landlords, moneylenders, and traders (dikus) and the oppressive British rule. Birsa Munda's movement was, in addition, directed against the foreign missionaries. It was a reformist, or rather, a revivalist movement, which aimed at restoring to the Mundas their lost glory (Singh 1965: 8).

The final provocation, the figurative last straw, which gave rise to the ulgulan came in 1893–4 when 'all waste lands in villages, the ownership of which vested in the government, were constituted "protected forests" under the Indian Forest Act VII of 1878, subject to the raiyats' existing rights' (Singh 1965: 37). The adivasis were unable to understand this new restriction on what they considered their right to free fuel and grazing grounds. Petitions regarding the resumption of these ancient rights were sent to the authorities, some of them by Birsa himself, but no heed was paid (Singh 1965: 37). The adivasi cultivator had lost practically all his possessions to the hands of the landlords and the moneylenders.

In addition to the turmoil that alienated the adivasis from their lands and their traditional rights and increased indebtedness, the forces of nature also played havoc with their lives. Famines and floods plagued the area. The Indian Irrigation Commission of 1929 noted that Palamau in the Chota Nagpur area was 'the driest and probably the poorest district of the province'. Prior to 1859 there had been no information on famines, but after 1859 'five famines, three major floods, seven scarcities lie squeezed into the history of a little above a hundred years' (Singh 1975: 30). The first recorded famine occurred in 1868–9, followed by famines in 1873–4, 1893–4, 1897, and 1918. The severest was in 1897 when the death rate rose to 36.40 per mille (Singh 1975: 30–3). Major Archer, one of the members of the Enquiry Committee on Coolie Emigration from Bengal Presidency, noted that they are 'necessitated to subsist upon the products of the chase, reptiles, and insects ... to satisfy the cravings of nature and avert famine'. He further stated that nothing but acute necessity would induce these people to leave their country (Saha 1970: 41).

MIGRATION TO JALPAIGURI

The factors just mentioned collectively ruined the adivasis and uprooted them from their land. Deprived of their means of livelihood, the adivasis turned into pools of unemployment, which became a tempting target for the planters who were desperately seeking cheap labour. Furthermore, natural calamities and land alienation had turned the adivasi into a sturdy, hard-working person who could live at an almost subhuman level of existence. These were other points of attraction for the planter. We therefore find that immigration to Jalpaiguri district increased in leaps and bounds during the period from 1891 to 1914.

According to the 1901 census, there were 188,223 immigrants in the Jalpaiguri district as compared to 143,922 in 1891. Most of them were enumerated in the Dooars, and about half of the immigrants were tea garden coolies from Chota Nagpur and Santhal Parganas (Census of India 1901: 66). The migration statements show that 80,436 immigrants were from Ranchi district and 10,562 from Santhal Parganas (Census of India 1901: Appendix I, p. iii). According to the 1921 census report, the number of persons born in Ranchi who were enumerated in Jalpaiguri district at the 1911 census was 126,214 (Thompson 1923: 145). The report further stated that the most numerous community among the labour force were Oraons and Mundas who had migrated from Chota Nagpur. According to the 1921 census, 90,348 coolies had been born in Chota Nagpur and 20,018 in the Jalpaiguri district, and these were also children of 'imported coolies' (Thompson 1923: 389).

GROWTH OF TEA PLANTATIONS IN THE DOOARS

After the Dooars was annexed from Bhutan in 1865, the tea planters of Darjeeling explored the possibilities of growing tea there. 'Although Dooars was a most unhealthy district in which malaria and black-water fever were rife, climatically it had much to recommend it as a tea-growing area' (Griffiths 1969: 115). It was criss-crossed with innumerable rivers and impregnable forests containing valuable timber, and also fierce wild beasts, and as such it must have been attractive to only the 'boldest pioneers' (Griffiths 1969: 115).

The first tea garden was started in the western Dooars at Gazelduba in 1874 by a Darjeeling tea company (this garden was washed away by the river Teesta in a massive flood in 1952). Within two years, 13 gardens had sprung up around the Phulbari (now known as Leesh river tea garden) and Bagrakot area. Labour supply proved to be no problem in the tea gardens in the Darjeeling hills because economic pressure forced people from Nepal to flock to them (Griffiths 1969: 274). Initially, Nepali labourers settled in the Darjeeling plantations were employed here. However, they soon proved insufficient as the industry developed rapidly. The planters had thus to turn to the familiar recruiting grounds of Chota Nagpur and Santhal Parganas for their labour supply (DPA 1938: 111). The Revenue Department had demarcated large tracts of land in the Dooars especially for tea cultivation, known as the 'tea grant land'. The taxes to be paid on such land were lower than that on agricultural land. Therefore, the planters got land on favourable terms, and the growth of the industry in the 1880s was so rapid that the acreage under tea in 1892 was over six times that in 1881 (DPA 1938: 116). This trend of rapid development continued until the 1950s. During the period 1901 to 1951, the area under tea nearly doubled, and the labour force rose three times.

RECRUITMENT SYSTEM IN THE DOOARS

Labour recruitment to the Dooars was different from that in Assam. The labourers were never placed under any contract, and in that sense they were 'free'. The government also did not place any restrictions on recruitment. The reason for this difference between Dooars and Assam is not entirely clear, but Griffiths explains that it might be because 'Dooars was much nearer than Assam to its principal recruiting grounds' (1969: 284), and therefore the seemingly lesser degree of control. This is not exactly what the planters had in mind, however, because they insisted that their labour 'is obtained from a considerable distance' (DPA 1938: 111). The planters occasionally tried to opt for the notorious Workmen's Breach of Contract Act (1859), as is evident from the earlier Dooars Planters' Association (DPA) reports (1920, 1937), but never succeeded in doing so. Perhaps they were counselled that it would earn them the same notoriety from the nationalists as their counterparts in Assam, and hence they refrained from such open acts of coercion. Though the planters shunned naked oppression, subtle forms were widely prevalent and formal contracts were not necessary in such situations.[2]

Labour was recruited mainly from Chota Nagpur and Santhal Parganas in Bihar. Adivasis from Odisha, Madras (Tamil Nadu), and the Central Provinces (Madhya Pradesh) were also recruited later (DPA 1938: 111). A majority of the workers were 'drawn from the Oraon, Munda, Kharia and Santhal races [*sic*]', but there was also 'a sprinkling of the semi-Hinduised castes of Chota Nagpur, such as Lohas [*sic*— Lohars], Baraiks, Bhogtas [*sic*—Bhagats] and so on. The Santhals came not only from the Santhal Parganas, but also from the other branch of the race of Singhbhoom and Maha-bhung [Manbhum]'. (DPA 1920: 291).

Recruitment to the Dooars was done mainly through the garden sardars (gang leaders belonging to the same communities as the workers). This method was perhaps more successful in inducing new recruits to join. The arkatis had already earned a bad name among the adivasis. The sardars, on the other hand, were tea garden labourers and not local recruiters like the arkatis. They were sent to the recruiting grounds in the recruiting season, which generally began after the rains in October or November and ended in February. Once they returned to the garden they resumed their work (DPA 1920: 292). It was easier for these people to induce new recruits by showcasing all the advantages of the work and the prospects of ultimate settlement on independent holdings.

The Tea Districts Labour Association (TDLA), an organization formed by the Assam planters to coordinate recruitment, also supervised recruitment to the Dooars. The TDLA had its recruiting agents in the recruiting districts, to which the sardar would report for assistance. Before setting out for his village, the sardar would collect a pass 'containing his name, race [*sic*], and village' (DPA 1920: 292). This document was his identification, which would enable him to obtain advances from the recruiting agent from his area to transport the recruited coolies to the

---

[2] In Assam, there were formal contracts such as the Workmen's Breach of Contract Act (1858) and the Inland Emigration Act (1862) that formed the basis of the indenture system. Both acts provided that the worker had to complete his/her contract period. They gave planters the right to force the worker to return in cases of desertion. The Inland Emigration Act reduced the period of the contract to four years (against five years earlier), but gave the planter the right to arrest and punish the worker in case s/he left.

garden (DPA 1920: 292). The garden manager would advance the sardar his rail fare and expenses.

On returning to his village, the sardar would look around for anyone willing to go to 'Bhutan' for work. After collecting a few people, he would take them to the recruiting agent, who would advance him the necessary money to return with the 'coolies' (DPA 1920: 292). The sardars were usually accompanied by a garden supervisor who supervised the recruitment and also kept an eye on the sardars. This is not admitted in any of the documents or reports of the DPA, but during the course of my interviews with the managers, this point emerged. They feared that if the sardar were sent unaccompanied, he would never return.

The TDLA laid down rules for the Dooars, which permitted three types of recruitment, the most popular being the sardari system. The other two were the arkati system and recruitment through local agents in the recruiting districts. These two types were utilized by those gardens which had either no contact with the recruiting districts, or which did not want to send their sardars there as they could not spare their workers or other personnel (Griffiths 1969: 286). The sardari system may have been a more efficient method of recruitment, but often planters found it expensive as it meant that they had to send both sardars and someone from the management to supervise to the recruiting districts.

The Indian-owned gardens followed a slightly different system of recruitment, for they did not have the facilities of the TDLA. Recruitment was done through private agencies (Rege 1946: 76) with the help of arkatis. The manager of the garden generally sent a babu (clerk) to the recruiting areas who contacted these agencies and selected the workers. The agency would enter into an agreement with the workers and also with the garden, which made it responsible for the delivery of the workers to the garden concerned. The agency would then be paid by the garden. These workers were known as *girmitia*s (a corruption of the word 'agreement'). Sometimes, if the garden was unable to pay the agents or if the agents supplied more workers than needed, the girmitias would be left abandoned in Dooars. They were usually taken by some other garden that needed extra workers. That the workers while being recruited were given false promises by the recruiters became evident in the course of my interviews with them. They spoke of promises of light work and an abundance of cultivable land in the tea gardens. They were lured by these false promises made by the recruiters, and they had hoped to work for a few years so as to make some money and return to their homeland. But once they entered the gardens, they realized their mistake. They knew that returning to their homes with some wealth was a remote possibility. The pay was low and they could never save enough for financing their return journey.

At the same time, it would be incorrect to assume that all workers were recruited only through deception or because of poverty. Most of them migrated because of poverty and deprivation, but some came out of a spirit of adventure, some young boys ran away from home to seek better opportunities, and two persons I interviewed actually confessed that they came to the plantations in search of a mate.

Most of these workers interviewed were either first-generation or second-generation migrants. The third- and fourth-generation migrants, who formed the bulk of the labour force at the time of my fieldwork, did not seem to know of the situation back home. A large number of them did not even know the names of their villages.

ENTICEMENT

The recruited worker was usually given an advance of a few rupees to meet his immediate expenses, with the necessary utensils. The cost of recruitment for workers from Chota Nagpur and Santhal Parganas in 1944 was, according to the Rege Commission, 25 rupees per head before the Second World War and 36 rupees per head after the war. The sardar's commission was three rupees per recruited worker (Rege 1946: 76–7). The managers, on the other hand, held that recruitment costs were higher and that is why constant vigilance was kept on the workers by the garden *chowkidars* (watchmen) to prevent them from being taken away to other gardens. Any outsider visiting the labour lines was questioned by the chowkidars, and if there was a suspicion that the person had come to lure away workers to another plantation, they would beat him and throw him out of the plantation.

In spite of these preventive measures, workers would sometimes leave the gardens to seek work elsewhere because of better wages, much to the annoyance of the planters. In the 1920s, the Public Works Department (PWD) was often accused of inducing them to leave by offering higher wages (Griffiths 1969: 132). The Department of Forestry and railroad contractors were also constantly luring away workers from the tea gardens in the early twentieth century. The *Annual Report of Dooars Planters' Association* for the year 1920 contains pages of correspondence with the Department of Forestry and the deputy commissioner, protesting against this 'unfair' practice. While complaining to the Department of Forestry, the planters alleged that it had offered higher wages and cultivable land to tea garden workers so as to induce them to leave the gardens (DPA 1920: 380–7). The planter had the protection of the Dooars Planters' Rules to prevent other planters from taking away his labourers. However, in the case of the Forest Department and the PWD, he could do nothing, besides protesting in strong terms to these departments.

Though there was generally a shortage of labour in the pre-1947 period, it must be noted that this phenomenon was not uniformly present at all times. There would be times when gardens needed to decrease their labour population. When there was a slump in the tea market, tea gardens had to reduce production. This happened soon after the First World War and in 1931 as an effect of the Great Depression. At such times, labour would frequently be retrenched from the tea gardens. This 'surplus' labour would be given to the Forest Department, which would use their services and give them cultivable land in return. The release of tea garden labour for this form of employment gave rise to adivasi cultivators in the Dooars. The settlements they formed were known as bustees. A part of this surplus labour was also exported to Assam to be employed in sawmills and sugar factories. The annual report of the DPA for 1920 contains information on this in the section entitled 'Communications'. One gathers from the correspondence published in this section that the planters did not mind the use of their surplus labour by the Forest Department in the post-First World War period, as there was an understanding that the people who were given cultivable land would be allowed to work on the plantations as *bigha* (temporary) labour whenever the need arose. At the same time, as mentioned earlier, the planters were annoyed with the Forest Department for enticing their workers in normal times when the tea gardens needed the labour.

Migration to the tea estates was mainly family migration, and rarely individual. The adivasis were encouraged to take their families along. Planters wanted cheap labour, and the best way was to have families migrate to the region. Besides having a family labour force, there were two more advantages. First, the workers would not be keen to leave their work on the plantations and return to their places of origin. Second, labour could be reproduced, as the children of the plantation workers could become a part of the labour force, thus reducing the need for new recruitment.

Labour in the gardens was housed within the area of the estate. In the early years of the industry, the planters made no attempt to regulate the pattern of housing. The workers had to construct their houses in the way they thought best with little or no help from the management. When a worker arrived in the garden, his sardar was responsible for his housing. He would allot the worker his house site and give him the materials needed for construction.

It appears that the planters were keen on letting the workers live among their own adivasi communities with their own dwellings constructed according to their customs. 'Labourers of the same tribe naturally prefer to live near each other and permission to do so is appreciated' (DPA 1938: 112). Hence, adivasi workers who performed the same type of work on the plantation lived separate lives once they returned to their houses.

SOCIOLOGICAL CONSEQUENCES

By joining the ranks of plantation labour, the adivasi workers were engaged in economic activity which was different from their traditional mode of livelihood. The adivasis are not a homogeneous group, as they comprise different communities and artisan groups, including Oraons, Mundas, Kharia, Santhal, Lohar, Bariak, Ghasi, Mahali, and Turi. Lohars were ironsmiths, Baraiks (Chik Baraik) were weavers, Ghasis made musical instruments, while Mahalis played these instruments. They also wove baskets along with the Turis. These groups have been classified as ST in West Bengal. A hierarchy existed among them that was based on their traditional occupations. They could be placed in two categories, namely the cultivating communities and the non-cultivating artisan communities. The cultivating communities formed a common status group and claimed to be superior to the others. In order to assert its superiority, the common status group observed certain taboos and concepts of pollution and purity relating to marriage and commensality. These were enforced by the panchayat comprising mainly of common status group members. Besides claiming superiority as they were cultivators, the adivasis comprising the common status group were also in the majority. The district census handbook for the 1961 census (Ray 1964: 83) shows that Oraons formed 51.3 per cent of the adivasi population. Mundas came next at around 15 per cent. The Santhals too were at around 15 per cent, and Kharias around 8 per cent. Santhals were, and still are, a distinct group that has little social intercourse with the other adivasis. They also had their own body to decide on social issues in plantations where they were numerous (above 15 per cent of the population). Or Santhals from a group of plantations would form their own informal body for regulating their social life.

Though the concepts of purity and pollution seem similar to those in the caste system, there is no evidence that the latter had influenced the adivasis. Most of the older adivasis told me that these were practised in their places of origin as well. The cultivating communities had maintained social distance from the artisans even in Chota Nagpur. The artisans had migrated later and were economically dependent on the cultivators. For most adivasis, all outsiders were polluted. This included a Hindu Brahmin as well. If the polluted person entered the kitchen, the women would purify the place by coating the floor with cow dung (see Bhowmik 1981: chapter 3).

Till about half a century ago, the adivasis maintained strict rules regarding pollution, marriage, and commensality. 'Inter-tribal' marriage was taboo and so was interdining. Marriage within the common status group was frowned upon, but could be accepted after a feast was given for both groups. If a boy or a girl from the common status group married into the other adivasi groups, both would be excommunicated and the panchayat (comprising the common status group) would take them to the nearest highway with their belongings and ask them never to return. The adivasis would refer to this as 'PW *paar*' (moving across the PWD road).

Changes started taking place in the lives of the adivasis after independence in 1947. There were two major factors involved: first, the entry of trade unions, and second, the implementation of the Plantation Labour Act (PLA) of 1951. The new government, after independence, was not as hostile to the working class as its colonial predecessors. Acts were passed that gave protection to workers. These included the Industrial Disputes Act (1947) and Factories Act (1948), which were applicable to the plantation workers.

Among the legislations affecting the tea garden workers, the most important is the PLA of 1951. This Act makes some provision for the welfare of plantation workers. This was the first Act which sought to raise the living standards of plantation workers. It laid down that every year, 8 per cent of the houses in every plantation were to be converted into permanent structures (that is, houses with walls of bricks and mortar, with tiled roofs). The houses of the workers are traditionally built of bamboo walls covered with mud or clay with thatch roofs. These houses are known as *kuchcha*, or temporary, houses. They do not have proper ventilation, and they are subject to early wear and tear as they cannot always withstand heavy rains. Besides improved housing, provisions were made for sanitation and water supply to the labour lines. The Act also laid down that there should be primary schools in the tea gardens, a trained social worker, and crèches with trained nurses.

The provisions of the PLA, if implemented properly, could improve the quality of life of the workers. Unfortunately, the planters were not too keen to spend on labour welfare, and hence most of the provisions have not been implemented. However, even the little that was implemented helped in partially changing the social organization of the adivasis. The new housing pattern to some extent changed the household composition and at the same time helped break barriers between different adivasi communities. Earlier, workers used to live in proximity to their own particular adivasi community members, as this was how they had built their own huts. The new permanent houses were twin quarters with a common wall between the two. Allotments were usually made on the basis of random selection. Hence, quite often an Oraon family might have a Mahali as neighbour. This in fact helped in bringing different adivasi groups closer to each other.

Trade unions undoubtedly had the largest single impact on the lives of the adivasi workers. Trade unions entered the plantations at a fairly late stage, in 1946. For the first 60 years of its existence, plantation labour had been unaware of the methods of collective bargaining. In 1946, the Bengal Assam Railroad Workers Union came under the influence of the communists. Its organizers tried to make inroads into the plantations through the railway gangmen (the lowest category in the railways), who were from the same adivasi community origins as the plantation workers. They had to conduct their activities clandestinely because outsiders were not allowed in the plantations. Trade unions were formed in a few plantations situated near the railway stations. After independence, especially after the declaration of elections, trade union organizers could enter the plantations in the guise of doing election work. Soon after, from the 1960s, trade unions gained in strength. Almost all plantation workers were members of one of the major trade unions. Till around 2004, the main trade unions were the Centre of Indian Trade Unions, the Indian National Trade Union Congress, and the United Trade Union Congress. These unions are supporters of the Communist Party of India (Marxist), the Congress, and the Revolutionary Socialist Party, respectively.

Trade unions gave greater confidence to the workers and changed the existing relations between the planters and the workers to formal employer–employee relations. However, the influence of trade unions did not just end there. They entered into all aspects of the life of the worker. They became the organization that unified the workers. Workers belonging to different adivasi groups came together under the banner of a trade union. These workers would have to interact with each other during the course of trade union activity. Adivasi barriers started breaking down due to the unity of the workers in their fight for economic demands.

Today, in cases of 'inter-tribal' conflict, the trade union leader intervenes and negotiates a settlement. The local adivasi panchayat is at times replaced by the trade union committee, as workers expect it to discuss their social problems as well. The garden unit leader is also regarded as the mediator in social affairs by members.

At the conferences of the trade unions, where workers met and stayed together for a couple of days, orthodox concepts of pollution slowly started eroding. Workers belonging to different adivasi groups ate together as there were common dining facilities for all. These instances definitely indicated a change in the attitudes of the workers towards pollution and the relationships between different adivasi groups. Division among the workers into separate adivasi groups was an impediment for a trade union, which was trying to forge unity among all sections of the workers on a plantation. The union had to consciously fight against these community barriers.

Like the other provisions of the PLA, education too was implemented half-heartedly. Nonetheless schooling helped in creating a section of literate adivasis, some of whom studied up till high school or passed the board examinations. These young people would play an important role in the new adivasi movement. Further, improvement in communications in the area has broken down the isolation of the plantations. The adivasi workers are now exposed to the world outside the plantation. At the same time, despite these changes, the adivasis have sought to retain their identity as a separate group, distinct from the local Bengali population.

TRADE UNIONS AND ADIVASI LEADERSHIP

The trade union movement is well entrenched as almost all workers are unionized. Almost all the national trade union federations have their unions. Trade unions have undoubtedly contributed towards improving labour standards of living. However, their major drawback is that they have not promoted leadership from within the working class. The trade union leaders are non-adivasis, mostly middle-class Bengalis belonging to the political parties of the concerned trade unions. Moreover, they have made no conscious effort to understand the social life of the adivasis and, barring a few, most of them cannot speak the Sadri dialect, the lingua franca of the adivasis. They prefer to keep their distance from the workers and rarely consult them while framing demands or while negotiating with the management.

Trade unions operate at the district level. Almost all the central trade unions have their branches in the district. These unions have units at the plantations through which they operate. The union leadership at the plantation comprises mainly local adivasis. However, at the district level, trade unions rarely have adivasis as leaders. All important positions such as general secretary, treasurer, president, and vice-president are occupied by middle-class Bengalis, most of whom are full-time organizers. They are paid by the political party. Adivasis are included in the executive committees and other similar committees comprising large numbers of members. At the plantation, problems are tackled by the local union leaders. However, when important issues need to be discussed with management, the district-level trade union leader is called in to negotiate. Major industry-wide issues such as wage increase, bonuses, and issues regarding workload are discussed in Kolkata in tripartite discussions (government, trade unions, and employers' associations). The unions do not always consult workers while framing demands. The adivasi workers are hence alienated from major issues concerning their living and working conditions.

The backlash from this situation can be seen in the growing unrest among adivasis in recent years. Adivasi workers have started to mobilize through the educated adivasi youth. These people have revived a defunct non-governmental organization (NGO) known as Adivasi Vikas Parishad. In 2008, a group of young educated adivasis on the plantations started mobilizing the workers by articulating their interests. The underlying message was that only adivasis can solve the problems of adivasis. This initiative received a tremendous response from the plantation workers and those engaged in petty agriculture near the tea plantations. The adivasi leaders sent notices to the Labour Department and the associations of the planters saying that they would represent the workers. In 2010, the Adivasi Vikas Parishad registered a trade union known as the Progressive Plantation Workers Union. In fact, its impact has been significant. The union called for a movement to increase wages by 200 per cent. The other unions were on the defensive.

They could not oppose this demand and yet could not support it as this would appear as if the Progressive Plantation Workers Union had set the agenda.[3]

I have tried to examine the migration, settlement, and later progress of the adivasi tea plantation workers in West Bengal who are from the Chota Nagpur region. Though changes have taken place, they have proceeded at a slow pace. The workers and their families are isolated and insecure on the plantations. Their low educational levels keep them at a disadvantage as they cannot get employment outside the plantations, except as unskilled workers. Those within the plantation system have low wages, with a large number of dependents who have become pools of cheap labour for the planters. These unemployed dependents work as temporary workers when the need arises. This, in fact, is the sole source of income for the unemployed, and because of this the planters are able to negotiate low wages. When workers' representatives ask for higher wages in the wage committees, the managements counter by saying that they will pay higher wages but they will cut down on temporary employment. Since agreeing to this would reduce the family income of the worker, the worker is caught in a trap which in effect favours the planters.

The worsening conditions on the tea plantations have forced many unemployed youth to migrate out to distant places as unskilled labour. In my last phase of fieldwork in 2011, I found that these people had gone to distant places like Haryana, Bangalore, and Kerala to work as construction labour or other types of unskilled labour. I interviewed some who had returned, and they told me that wages in these places were fairly high and they could save money to send home. These migrants are again opening up to a new world, just as it was when their forefathers migrated to the plantations. The main difference is that in present migration, the adivasis drift from one place to another, wherever employment is available. There are contractors who take groups of unemployed adivasis to work sites. The situation seems to have come full circle.

---

[3] There is another issue that has prompted the adivasis to rally behind their own organization. The people of Nepali origin (known as Gorkha) have been demanding a separate state comprising Darjeeling and the Dooars. The movement is led by the Gorkha Jan Mukti Morcha. The adivasis have opposed this, as they feel that their identity would be lost to the Gorkha. This has resulted in tension between the two groups in the Dooars (see Bhowmik 2011).

REFERENCES

Bhowmik, Sharit K. 1981. *Class Formation in the Plantation System.* New Delhi: People's Publishing House.

———. 2011. 'Wages and Ethnic Conflicts in the Tea Industry in West Bengal', *Economic and Political Weekly,* vol. 66, no. 22, pp. 26–9.

Bose, Sanat. 1954. *Capital and Labour in the Indian Tea Industry.* Bombay: All India Trade Union Congress.

Census of India. 1901. *Bengal Report.* Calcutta: Government Printing Press.

Chandra, Bipin. 1964. *Rise and Growth of Economic Nationalism in India.* New Delhi: People's Publishing House.

Dalton, E. T. 1882 . *A Descriptive Ethnology of Bengal.* Calcutta: Government Press

Das, R. K. 1928. *Plantation Labour in India.* Calcutta: Thacker, Spink, and Co.

DPA (Dooars Planters' Association). 1920. *Detailed Report of the General Committee.* Jalpaiguri: Royal Printing Works.

———. 1937. *Detailed Report of the General Committee.* Jalpaiguri: Royal Printing Press.

———. 1938. *Detailed Report of the General Committee.* Kalimpong: Kalimpong Printing Press.

Griffiths, Percival. 1969. *History of the Indian Tea Industry.* London: Wiedenfeld and Nicolson.

Hoffmann, Rev. J. 1964. *Encyclopedia Mundarica* (reprint), Patna: Government of Bihar Press

Hunter, W. W. 1872. *Statistical Account of Bengal.* Jalpaiguri: Royal Printing Press.

Jha, G. C. 1964. *The Kol Insurrection of Chota Nagpur.* Calcutta: Thacker, Spink, and Co.

Ray, B. 1964. *Census of India District Census Handbook: Jalpaiguri.* Calcutta: Government Press.

Rege, D. V. 1946. *Report of an Enquiry into Conditions of Labour in Plantations of India and Ceylon.* Delhi: Government of India Press.

Saha, Panchanan. 1970. *Emigration of Indian Labour, 1834–1900.* New Delhi: People's Publishing House.

Singh, K. S. 1965. *Dust Storm and Hanging Mist: A Study of Birsa Munda and His Movement.* Calcutta: Firma K. L. Mukherji.

———. 1975. *Indian Famine 1967: A Study in Crisis and Change.* New Delhi: People's Publishing House.

Tea Board of India. 2009. *Tea Statistics 2005–2006.* Kolkata: Tea Board of India.

Thompson, W. H. 1923. *Census of India 1921,* vol. V: *Bengal,* part I: *Report.* Calcutta: Government Printing Press.

10

Urban Housekeepers from Tribal Homelands

Adivasi Women Migrants and
Domestic Work in Delhi

Neetha N.

Women have always been central to the adivasi economy with their important role in agriculture. With the penetration of modern economic values and ethos in adivasi social and economic life, agriculture is no longer the backbone of these communities. Acquisition of land for non-agriculture uses, expansion of mining operations, exploitation/ destruction of the natural flora and fauna, and the impact of these changes on adivasi lives are now widely acknowledged. Increasingly, small farmers and landless adivasi households have to depend on non-agricultural occupations which are available only in the urban centres. The most visible and affected victims of the 'modernization' process have been women in these communities. Thus, the increasing exodus of adivasi women to urban centres in the recent past needs to be understood beyond the typical phenomenon of rural–urban migration, as their socio-cultural contexts and migration particulars differ sharply vis-à-vis other migrant groups in the city.

Migration of adivasi women to urban centres to take up domestic work is an important development in the past few decades. The occupation is one of the major avenues of employment of adivasi women in cities. Against this backdrop, this chapter details the specificities of adivasi women's migration for domestic work, their employment, and their life in the cities, and discusses the larger gender and social consequences of the phenomenon. The analysis not only focuses on the linkage between adivasi migration and domestic work, but also provides an entry point to understanding the role and status of women in adivasi societies. To situate migration for domestic work within overall migration, the demographic and social profile of adivasi domestic workers and the particulars of migration, migration processes, and so on are elaborated in the light of existing literature. The role of middlemen and placement agencies and its interrelation to employment specificities are also examined using micro-level insights. The organization of live-in domestic work in urban areas and the associated employment relations are elaborated in order to situate the occupation in terms of labour rights. The subsequent section elucidates the influence of urban life on the socio-cultural ethos and lifestyles of adivasi domestic workers and highlights some of the anomalies arising out of this.

Finally, the dimensions of social/familial exclusion, often leading to decisions of return migration and the absence of married and settled lives in the home community, are outlined. Inability to fully participate in the urban society, together with the incapability of adjusting back to the socio-cultural settings of the home communities, puts female adivasi migrants in a dilemma. They are suspended between cultures, lacking in social and cultural identity—both in the cities and in their homelands. Women's entry into wage work and its impact on women's overall social status are debatable issues, especially in the contemporary context. The economic and social roles of women prior to wage work and the nature of their current employment are important parameters in delineating the overall impact of any such change. If new categories of wage employment are based on a regressive gendered ideology, or are extensions of existing social values, the overall impact of such changes on women are bound to be adverse. The transformation of adivasi women from their independent roles in agrarian societies to wage labour within a 'quasi-feudal-capitalist' system rooted in a gendered ideology of house work is bound to impact gender relations in these societies. Based on the findings, the chapter argues that entry of adivasi women into paid domestic work has resulted in a reconfiguration of their roles in their native societies, providing new foundations for gender differentials and inequalities, adversely affecting women's status.

ADIVASI FEMALE MIGRATION FOR DOMESTIC WORK: THE LARGER CANVAS

Migration of women and domestic work in urban areas are closely related. Both migration statistics at the macro level as well as field-level studies have clearly brought out this link. The process of concentration in paid domestic work is the most gender-distinctive feature of the labour migration of women. Rural-to-urban migration, which characterizes such mobility, cuts across all caste and community categories of women. However, there exists a distinct concentration within communities in terms of their share in such work, with significantly higher proportions of women from historically oppressed caste groups and adivasi communities engaging in paid domestic work (Raghuram 2001). The share of adivasi women in the total number of domestic workers, though, is not high compared to SCs at the macro level; their share among urban live-in workers is not only high but also increasing over time. Thus, for adivasi women migrants in urban areas (especially for single migrants), employment is often understood as almost synonymous with domestic work. The movement of women from adivasi pockets to cities for domestic work goes back to the late 1970s.[1] It witnessed an unprecedented increase in the 1980s and more so in the 1990s. The major source areas for adivasi women are the states of Jharkhand, Chhattisgarh, Odisha, Assam, and West Bengal. The big cities such as Delhi, Mumbai, and Bengaluru are the receiving places for adivasi migrants. Of the three, Delhi is the most attractive destination (TCSW 2008).

Migration of women to take up full-time domestic work is central to the survival of families in the adivasi areas. While micro studies to a large extent confirm this popular understanding, macro data on migration do not reveal such sharp concentration. Domestic work as per the 2007–8 migration data collected by the National Sample Survey Organisation (NSSO) shows only about 5 per cent of adivasi women migrant workers in urban areas undertaking domestic work.[2] Such low shares of domestic work in the overall employment of adivasi female migrants are indicative of the invisibility of domestic work in macro data in general. Ambiguities exist in the definition of domestic work and its categories adopted by the

---

[1] A few scholars argue that migration from Jharkhand to the metro cities started in the late 1960s with the displacement of adivasis as part of the planning and development process (ISI 1993).

[2] Data for the age group 15–60.

agency, which are bound to affect the quality of data collected and result in poor reporting of the number of domestic workers. Further, adivasi women domestics are largely live-in workers, whose enumeration thus would be purely dependent on reporting by the employer households, and this situation results in the under-reporting of many such workers.

In contrast to the macro data, a recent large sample survey of female migrant workers conducted by Centre for Women's Development Studies (CWDS),[3] which also included adivasi migration, found about 15 per cent of adivasi migrants working as domestic workers in urban areas. The macro data on domestic workers is not fully reliable, nor does it provide insights into various dimensions of occupations and the related migration. In the absence of macro data on the issue, micro-level studies are the only sources of information which provides insights into adivasi migration for domestic work. The outlining of the profile of these workers and the overall issues are thus largely based on micro-level studies.[4] Since most of the available studies are in the context of adivasi migration to Delhi, some of the generalizations based on these studies may not appeal to specific situations of other urban locations, though broadly the issues raised would prevail.

Adivasi domestic workers in urban areas are largely in the age group of 15–30, though child workers are also documented.[5] The data collected by the CWDS survey found 82 per cent of domestic workers in this age group. The largest concentration is in the age group of 15–25 years. Indicative of the age composition, almost 70 per cent of the workers are unmarried, single migrants. In contrast to the general status of illiteracy among domestic workers, a good proportion of adivasi workers can read and write their language and have completed primary schooling. About 60 per cent of the workers were literate, with 22 per cent having

---

[3] The research project on Gender and Migration conducted by the CWDS is based on a series of micro surveys conducted between 2009 and 2011 across 20 states. It also surveyed domestic workers in urban centres from tribal areas. For a detailed discussion on the methodology, see CWDS (2011).

[4] Current profiling is based on the CWDS survey. For the rest of the chapter, studies conducted by the author on domestic workers in Delhi in 2000 and 2008 are the main sources. A wide range of oral communications and discussions with domestic workers, placement agencies, organizers of domestic workers, and so on are also drawn on.

[5] In contrast, a large segment of part-time workers are from the age group of 30–40 years, and are part of family migration.

attended high school or above. The higher education level could be attributed to the spread of education institutions run by Christian missionaries in the source areas, and may also be an indication of the relative non-discriminatory nature of these societies. A large section of adivasi domestic workers belong to the Oraon, Munda, Santhal, and Ho communities.

One of the key reasons for migration and entry into domestic work is the economic pressure, though other factors such as attraction to the city and the urge for autonomy are also noted. Poverty, lack of local employment, possibilities of better employment in the cities, and so on are major reasons for such an exodus of women from these regions. The significant push factors for adivasi female migration identified by a study conducted for the Planning Commission are: very low rates of local wages; unemployment; and land alienation along with poverty and indebtedness (TCSW 2008). Male migration is also common from these areas, but the scale of such migration is smaller, largely owing to the nature of occupations for which men migrate for work. Construction is the major sector, followed by mining, in the context of adivasi male migration. The volatility in employment in these sectors and the adverse nature of the work and working conditions involved limit the possibility of these sectors being the economic backbone of these societies. Taking up domestic work is thus often seen as a necessity by young adivasi women migrants—they are burdened with the cultural expectations imposed on daughters by their families. Though most families of domestic workers own land, and also possess other supporting resources such as livestock, the family incomes are often below subsistence level due to low productivity of agricultural land. This has led to large-scale borrowing to finance daily expenses as well as contingencies. Borrowings to meet expenses related to social events and festivals (such as Christmas or Karma[6]) are also common. The expansion of education among the households has also meant increased demand on family income for education, which involves additional resources. One of the most common practices that is prevalent in these families is the taking up of domestic work by elder sisters to sponsor the education of younger siblings, mainly boys.

Apart from financial considerations, changed gender relations are also central to the migration of adivasi women. For many, migration to urban

---

[6] Karma is one of the most important festivals of many tribes, especially among Oraons in Odisha, Chhattisgarh, and Jharkhand, and is celeberated in the months of autumn.

areas also means a rite of passage that provides status, independence, exposure, training, savings, and self-advancement. Further, the search for personal freedom and the accompanying rejection of traditional gender roles were also found to be important. Living in cities is seen as a step forward in social mobility and status. A few domestic workers also pointed out that home visits by friends/relatives working as domestic workers in Delhi tempt the aspirants. Some women were lured by the success of their predecessors in migration, who visited the village well dressed, well fed, and dignified, and who could also support the family. This is reflected in the increased flow of new migrants following the early migrants, leading to chain migration from a particular area. The migration of men, the option of men having more than one wife, and the absence of women's rights over land and other productive resources, all have combined to create an environment where the desertion of women by their husbands is extremely common. Thus, for another set of women, migration for domestic work is the only way to support their nuclear or extended family. (In such cases, children are often left with their grandparents.)

The fact that many workers continue in domestic work for many years merely for income benefits is indicative of the ongoing demand for cash income in these societies. The initial plan for many workers is to work for a shorter span, usually a year or more, earn some cash, and then return. However, many soon realize that with the poor salaries, their savings in the city are insufficient to meet the financial needs of their families. Further, the expectations or demands on them from their families also increase, which leaves them trapped for many years. The other attraction of self-advancement and independent living, if it exists, takes a back seat. Almost 60 per cent of the workers studied as part of the CWDS study reported working as domestic workers for 5 years or more, with 23 per cent having experience of more than 10 years.

The state of Jharkhand is the source of a large number of adivasi domestic workers, followed by Chhattisgarh, Odisha, and Assam and other north-eastern states.[7] However, within these broad geographical areas, the supply is maintained through a regular flow of distress migrants of varied and shifting rural origins and economic conditions. Ownership of land among worker households is reported as high, with an average of

---

[7] In Delhi, part-time domestic workers are mostly from the states of Uttar Pradesh, Bihar, and West Bengal, and are largely SCs.

1–2 acres of land. However, output from agriculture is meagre, with no facility for irrigation and poor quality of land.[8]

Migration from adivasi areas to urban centres for domestic work is channelized through previous workers, agents, or labour contractors. Many have migrated to the city for the first time with a small group of two to three other migrant women, or with a relative or friend. Once the migrant worker gets settled in an urban area, further rounds of migration are generally more independent in terms of movement into the city. However, for placement, many have to depend on agents or on informal channels such as kith or kin. Relatives and friends are very important networks that workers use in knowing about the possibility of migration, and in some cases for placement too. The decision to migrate for domestic work is largely a family decision (CWDS 2011; Neetha and Mazumdar 2009). The decisions are driven by the experiences of families in the neighbourhood or known people such as relatives and friends. However, many are also lured by the promise of advances and monthly salaries offered by the labour contractors. The church also assumes a key role in the migration of women for domestic work. The church not only works as an agent of organized mobility and employment as domestic workers, but as an institution which has to a larger extent given social sanction in adivasi pockets to migration for domestic work.

The way in which religious institutions are implicated in the process of migration is clearly evident when one looks at the evolution of domestic work in Delhi. The prominence of Christians among domestic workers has a strong link to the initiatives by local parishes to provide employment to poor, adivasi women with the help of their counterpart organizations in the cities. The first set of adivasi migrant domestic workers in Delhi were drawn by church-based institutions for housekeeping and cooking activities. This was largely seen as a measure of charity which helped adivasi households to find productive employment for their young women. With the increase in unemployment among the adivasi population, largely on account of poor development programmes in these areas, the church expanded its operation. This was done by recruiting domestic workers who were known to the church for urban households, ushering in a chain migration of young women to the city. With chain migration, the number of migrants outside the boundary of

---

[8] Many workers also reported financial constraints in cultivating agricultural land.

the church also increased, though they were largely from the Christian community. This resulted in a demand for an increased role of the church in protecting adivasi migrants in the city, especially their 'morals', which led to the setting up of the first placement organization under the Religious of Mary Immaculate in 1976. A sister concern of this organization was established in 1987. The involvement of the church as a mediating and supportive institution increased the credibility of the service, and also the social status of the workers in their native places in the beginning. This along with the comparatively better wages and working conditions of domestic workers placed through these voluntary agencies seems to have led to the creation of a religious identity in this occupation. This is evident in the composition of the workers. Among the community groups, Oraons are found to be the prominent group among those from the Chota Nagpur belt, among whom the missionary influence is high (ISI 1993).

The organizations just mentioned are even now the most reputed organizations facilitating the placement of about 1,500 workers per year. At present, there are many organizations which are under the church directly or indirectly facilitating such migration. Migration for domestic work is not discouraged within the institution, especially if it is routed through the church. The acceptance of a gendered division of work, with household work earmarked as women's work, underlies such passive routing of adivasi women to domestic work. Further, aspects of charity and voluntary work associated with missionary work also do seem to influence this process. The role of the church in formally organizing recruitment and placement of adivasi domestic workers needs to be seen in such a context.

PLACEMENT AGENCIES: THE INEVITABLE EVIL

The role of networks and agents/labour recruiters is important in the process of adivasi migration and entry into live-in domestic work. They act as coordinators between the employer households and the domestic workers. Single adivasi migrants depend on these channels/networks for migration as well as employment, as they are unfamiliar with the city and the dispersed opportunities. The linguistic barrier for the migrant is another factor, which makes the mediator inevitable. Thus, apart from independent migration, agents/recruiters also mobilize workers from adivasi belts to meet the rising demand for domestic workers in the city.

The adivasi pockets (of the states of Jharkhand,[9] Chhattisgarh,[10] Odisha,[11] and the tea belt of Assam[12]) are often hubs of recruitment, from where large number of women (especially unmarried girls) are mobilized.

The last two decades have witnessed a proliferation of placement agencies that supply live-in domestic workers in the cities, especially Delhi. These agencies are very heterogeneous in scale, operation, and the lines of services offered, and most are highly informal. Organizational patterns range from trade-union-initiated agencies (such as Self Employed Women's Association (SEWA) in Kerala) to purely commercial establishments operated by a single person.[13] Owing to these diversities, it is extremely difficult to arrive at a reliable estimate of the number of agencies that currently exist. The more formal placement agencies have a legal or socially approved framework that guides their existence as service providers of domestic workers to urban households. They may be registered as, or backed by, an NGO/trust/union. They work with a definite organizational set-up and try to enforce more or less defined terms and conditions of placement.[14] While a few placement

---

[9] The major pockets of tribal female migration for domestic work are Simdega, Gumla, Ranchi, Dumka, and Pakur.

[10] Raigarh district is the major 'feeding pocket' in Chhattisgarh.

[11] The major feeding pockets are Sundergarh and Rayagada districts.

[12] In Assam, domestic workers are mobilized from the tea plantations of Kokrajhar and Darrang.

[13] The extent of informality is evident from the following case: X had migrated to Delhi from Jharkhand looking for a job. Through some contacts, he found work in a canteen which provided door-to-door delivery of food. As he was from Jharkhand, the person who owned the canteen asked him whether he could get a girl from Jharkhand to work as domestic help for someone known to him. He was also promised a commission. X got a girl (a relative of his). Slowly, he realized that placing girls in domestic work was a lucrative business. Initially, his circle was limited to relatives or neighbours or known people, but now he has started mobilizing though extended contacts. He started initially with a small commission of Rs 1,000. But now his commission ranges from Rs 4,000 to Rs 7,000. The commission varies depending on the requirement of the employer, and the age and work experience of the domestic worker. He runs this business purely through his contacts and has no office. The whole business is run through his two mobile phones.

[14] Apart from placement, other services are sometimes provided to domestic workers, including board and lodging until they are placed; vocational skill training (for example, literacy classes, basic hygiene and cooking, handling of household appliances, attending phone calls, and so on); socializing through

agencies have established office set-ups, most of them usually function in small rooms which are normally located in lower-middle-class localities. These offices often have limited furniture and a signboard indicating their 'registered' status. In contrast to these, many agencies are functional without any office space, operating through individual contacts over the phone. The agencies frequently change their identities, location, and phone numbers—in some cases, because of their intermittent engagement in the business and, in most cases, to avoid the authorities and previous clients (both employers and workers).

The involvement of the church provides some degree of security and acceptability to this form of rural–urban migration as well as creating a sense of obligation. Due to this, many commercial placement agencies (including those that do not have any connection with the church) use symbols of the cross, Jesus, and so on and name their agencies after saints, giving a false image of their closeness to the church. The degree of commercial interest is another difference that marks these agencies. The majority of these agencies are purely commercial, guided largely by profit considerations, and working conditions do not find any mention in their objectives. The profits made by placement agencies are attractive compared to the cost involved. The cost of running a placement agency comprises the cost of office space (if the agency has one) and payments to recruiting agents.[15] All the agencies[16] charge a registration fee from the employer, which ranges from Rs 7,500 to Rs 20,000 for a contract of 11 months.[17] It is also reported that a few agencies even take a repayable security deposit from the employer. The security amount is equivalent to two to three months of wages, and is taken by the agency to ensure that workers are not sacked by the employers on their own at any stage.

---

weekly meetings; periodic excursions; and celebration of regional festivals. Entries to such organizations are restricted to manage the food, accommodation, and training of the new entrants. Entry to the organization is limited largely to the network of kinfolk, and recommendations from the church are important in getting placements through such voluntary agencies.

[15] On average, the commission given to a labour agent or middleman is Rs 1,000–3,000 per head.

[16] Except for the two mentioned earlier, which have been operational for many years and are directly under the church.

[17] In many cases, agencies frequently shift the workers from one employer to another to maximize commissions, even without consulting the worker.

Though there is a definite and marked difference in terms of conditions of placement across agencies, the processes of recruitment of workers show considerable similarity. Most of the agencies rely on middlemen or agents—some agencies have up to 10–12 agents attached to them. The peak recruitment period for many placement organizations is during January to March. Fresh workers migrate under the influence of old workers who visit their native places during Christmas and other adivasi festivals.

Apart from this peak period, middlemen or agents also make visits to adivasi areas every month or once in two months and look for possible families/individuals who can be persuaded to send their girls to work as domestic workers.[18] Apart from recruitment agents, current workers and religious networks are also used. Workers who are placed through the organizations are encouraged to bring new members to the organization.

The existence of various layers of recruitment agents and the system of advance payments adds to the complexity. Broadly, the adivasi female migration process for domestic work can be categorized into four types: (*a*) those whose decision to migrate is 'independent' but who use the services of the agent in the migration process as well as for placement; (*b*) those who are organized and mobilized by agents who may or may not pay the migrant household an advance; (*c*) those who migrate in a group under the leadership of a known adivasi person (either engaged in domestic work or other work in the city), who then puts them in touch with agencies in urban areas; and (*d*) those who migrate with older workers/kith or kin on an individual basis, and who would be either placed by the worker herself or by the agency through which she is employed. The divisions across these categories are not rigid, and in many cases old domestic workers could also become agents for recruitment and placement as well. Interestingly, all those working at the lower level in the recruitment chain are mostly adivasi men or women, though the agencies in the city for which they are recruiting workers are mostly managed by non-adivasi persons.

A form of migration which is on the decline with the increase in agency-initiated recruitment drives in adivasi pockets is the group migration of adivasi girls. Girls organize themselves into groups led either by a domestic worker or by someone who has some information

---

[18] Agents often give incomplete or false information about the terms of employment and create debt bondage with prospective domestic workers or their family members by providing some advance amount in the form of loans.

about the city and its employment opportunities. Such groups board the trains to Delhi during the months of January to March. Agents approach these migrants at the railway platforms through intermediaries who are from adivasi areas. Adivasi intermediaries are important, as knowledge of their language is crucial in winning acceptance among fresh migrants. Migrants who are new to the city and unaware of the employment opportunities and the geographical location of their distant kin or kith (if they have any) often depend on these intermediaries.

It is widely documented that a large number of agencies take undue advantage of the illiteracy and ignorance of migrants, leading to non-payment of wages and prevalence of forced/bonded labour situations (Neetha 2004, 2009). Most agencies do not share information regarding negotiated wages with the workers. Most of the workers are not aware of the employment terms. In many cases, the salary is directly collected by the placement agency from the employer. A considerable proportion of the domestic worker's salary is adjusted towards brokerage expenses, travel costs, boarding, and so on. Yet, the agencies usually take little responsibility for the worker and her working or living conditions. Nor do they make an extended commitment to the worker, such as support during illness or provision of interim stay and so on. Cases of denial of wages, virtual incarceration in the employer's home, refusal of leave because of payments made by the employer to the agent, as well as sexual abuse by the agent or in the employer's household are issues that are documented. There were no regulatory mechanisms that ensure the accountability of placement agencies till 2013. There are regular traumatic incidents of exploitation of adivasi domestic workers in the cities by agencies as well as employers. Trafficking for domestic work and the possibility of sexual exploitation of domestics (by middlemen, agents, and employers) are among the concerns often raised in this context.

The working of the placement agencies, especially those who claim association with the church, often leads to the construction of regional and religious identities as far as live-in domestic workers are concerned. The ways in which placement agencies match suitable employees to jobs reinforce stereotypes pertaining to the natural qualities of women of different regions. These regional identities signify a group's supposed proclivity to domestic work as well as the quality of care they are able to provide. The submissiveness and docility of adivasi women are assumed to be natural traits, and are central to understanding the increasing demand for adivasi women for live-in domestic work.

ON CALL '24 × 7': WORK ORGANIZATION AND EMPLOYMENT RELATIONS

As mentioned previously, adivasi women are largely live-in workers. This is understandable because of the single migrant status of these workers and the lack of any residential possibility for such migrants in urban areas. On the demand side, there is also an increasing demand for full-time live-in workers, with many women from middle-class households joining the workforce.

Domestic service in general is distinct from other wage-earning occupations in terms of wage payments, working conditions, and work relations, with informality being a dominant feature of domestic work (Neetha 2009). The modern system of domestic labour relations of live-in workers is comparable to the earlier version of domestic work, where the worker was attached to a single household. Workers are responsible for multiple tasks depending on a variety of factors. While the traditional system was based on feudal relations, where caste status did matter for the tasks performed and rewards offered, the modern domestic service combines elements of feudal and capitalist labour relations. The market and the language of contract explicitly frame the terms of employment, since monetary wage rates are central in the negotiation. The wages of live-in workers range between Rs 1,000 and Rs 6,000 per month (in 2009), depending on the worker's experience and the specific tasks to which they are assigned.[19] All these factors being equal, wages differ across workers depending on the recruitment contract. Board, lodging, clothes, and other articles of daily use are usually provided by employers. Such unquantified perks in kind are a supplement (albeit important), rather than central to the payment as was the case earlier (Neetha and Palriwala 2011). However, the personal relation remains significant,

---

[19] Only in few states in the country is domestic work included under the list of scheduled employment in the Minimum Wages Act, 1948. The denial of this basic labour right leaves domestic workers outside the purview of all labour legislations in the country. There have been many attempts in the past to bring about a national legalization, but due to counter-political pressures none of these were passed (for details see Neetha and Palriwala 2011). The National Commission for Women in 2008 framed the Domestic Workers (Registration, Social Security, and Welfare) Bill, which also lapsed due to lack of political support. At the time of writing, the first-ever national policy for domestic workers is awaiting approval of the union cabinet, but the future of this policy is also uncertain.

because of the intimate nature of the work or because the workers stay with the employers, but also because of their extreme dependency on the employer. While employer–worker relations in the past have been based on shared cultural norms and values, adivasi domestic workers and their employers in most cases represent different social and cultural ethics (which inter alia is one of the reasons for their being preferred workers, as explained in the next section).

Despite the specification of their work, the workers often have to undertake additional multiple tasks, though the intensity of their involvement may vary. They are on call 24 hours a day. The basic wage, perks, and benefits, such as festival bonus, loans, medical costs, and gifts, all differ as a result of the length of service of the worker and the personal ties that have formed between them and their employers. Length of service does not always guarantee increased payment, as wages often tend to stagnate after a short period of employment. Apart from the unduly long hours of work and poor wages, there is a lack of standards in terms of working hours, leisure, holidays, and so on. Sick leave is not granted in normal cases for live-in workers as they stay with the employers. Apart from this, in many cases, workers also face cuts in wages as they may not have performed all the agreed tasks or some of these tasks partially during periods of ailment or if the employer meets her medical treatment expenses.

IDEAL HOUSEKEEPER: DISSECTING THE PREFERENCE

Domestic work assumes importance in women's employment in urban areas largely owing to the ease with which poor migrants can enter this occupation. The assumption is that the skill to perform domestic work is present in every woman, gained in the process of her social upbringing. It is also believed that the occupation does not demand any capital, making it easier for asset-less women to enter. Thus, it is the feminized nature of the occupation, coupled with the migrant status of adivasi workers, that is generally highlighted in explaining their concentration in the occupation. Security considerations of the household, with increased incidents of crime involving male domestic workers, are also found to influence the gendering of live-in domestic workers. Apart from this overall picture, stereotyped assumptions regarding adivasi women's cultural and social life, however, are central in understanding their concentration in this occupation.

Apart from the devaluation and feminization of domestic service and the variety in the nature of the labour market for this service, an important aspect that needs elaboration is the nature of domestic labour relations. In the erstwhile aristocratic set-up, the work relationships were based on unwritten agreements and expectations, in a paternalistic mode. Current situations show that there are many instances of coexistence of patronage and contract-based relations, which may differ across societies and regions. Work relations, thus, are the products of both economic and cultural factors. The work relations in these occupations cannot be captured in purely economic terms, as a considerable amount of subjectivity and personal dealings define the employment relations. The nature of contracts is mostly oral and informal, and heavily dependent on personal relationships. This makes the understanding of the socio-economic and cultural context of these workers equally or more critical.

To understand employer preference for adivasi domestic workers, one needs to understand the skills involved in domestic work. The understanding of household work in terms of physical tasks that demand knowledge of the activity as well as related aspects needs to be exposed. Household work in the context of paid domestic work, apart from actual tasks, also entails some notion of the personal characteristics of the worker. Apart from the social background of the worker such as gender, caste, and age, the qualities of a good domestic worker are often framed as 'honest, reliable, polite, docile, and efficient'. The employer preference for adivasi workers is largely due to their assumption that adivasi workers fit into their notion of a good worker perceived thus. This is evident in the Institute of Social Studies Trust study (ISST 2009), where employers showed a preference for young adivasi workers because they were more reliable, obedient, and efficient and preferable for childcare and elder care. Their religious identity as Christians and their association with church-based institutions also play an important role in their being seen as reliable and honest (Neetha 2003, 2004). These qualities are regarded as essential especially for those who stay with the employers on a 24-hour basis—with part-timers these qualities are not so central. Docility is also sometimes related to the lack of command over the local language, which restricts their socialization process. This increases the possibility of staying with one employer for longer periods, agreeing to work for lower wages, and easy control of the worker.

Yet another factor that adds to the preference for adivasi girls for domestic work is the absence of caste-informed notions of household work (Kasturi 1990). Adivasi women are preferred over SC women for house work, especially for cooking, with broad notions of purity slowly emerging in the urban contexts. Further, the readiness to undertake all kinds of domestic tasks, even those marked as undignified, makes this category the most in demand. Since adivasi societies are outside the frame of caste-based division of work and purity considerations, cleaning tasks, especially those which are generally resisted by other caste groups, are often accepted by adivasi workers without any negotiation.[20] Though domestic workers from some SC subcategories are also ready to take up all cleaning operations, there is still an aversion among many employers to entrusting cooking and related tasks to these workers. The caste non-identity makes the adivasi worker the most preferred category, allowing for any combinations of tasks as per the household's requirements. Further, adivasi migrant workers are considered less of an intrusion into the employer's family life because of their unfamiliarity with local language or network associations.

Hidden under these lists of preferred qualities is also the tension around the moral and sexual aspects of young and unmarried domestic workers. The sexual appeal and the related vulnerability are possibly the only factors that go against the preference for adivasi domestic workers. In many houses, domestic workers are prohibited or restricted from wearing make-up, jewellery, nail polish, or perfume. Dress codes prescribe a dupatta to suppress their femininity, thereby checking any threat, indicating the tensions that surround the employment of young domestic workers in general. The insistence on a 'simple and clean' dress code by some agencies and employers is also in tune with such considerations.

CHANGING VALUES AND LIFESTYLES: HOPES FOR A BETTER LIFE

Adivasi women migrants tend to reside between two cultures. They are transplanted into another society where they are expected to assimilate or integrate into the new culture, complete with a new status, role, and responsibilities. The exposure to urban life does have a significant imprint not only on their lifestyles but also on their understanding of family life and social relations. Migration often reconfigures or renegotiates familial

---

[20] For instance, workers from other regions and social backgrounds have been known to refuse to undertake 'polluting' work such as cleaning toilets, seeing this as 'undignified' work (Kaur 2006; Palriwala and Neetha 2009).

and gender roles, as migrants encounter potentially competing values and demands.

Their exposure to middle-class life in the city in terms of lifestyle and values does influence these workers. Their spending habits and change in outfits suggest their aspiration to imitate the lifestyle of the middle class. Western outfits, which are a recent entry even among middle-class women, are the most imitated dressing style—trousers, pants, jeans, and tops are the most accepted among the young workers. Such outfits clearly clash with the orthodox image of poorly clothed adivasi women and also of the domestic worker. Dress could probably be an important and easy way to transcend their stigmatized social position in urban locations. The craving for the latest expensive mobile phones, even though the use of many of their elaborate functions may be unknown and possibly beyond comprehension, suggests the extent of these workers' middle-class aspirations. These are indications that these workers do cultivate and actively practise lifestyles associated with cosmopolitanism, urbanity, and femininity to counter the stigma of being adivasi and to promote the image of a modern service-class woman. These changed lifestyles, however, are not accepted so easily by employers, and tensions around dress code and conduct inside as well as outside the employer's home are common. This even affects their employment prospects—cases of counselling, warnings/ scolding, cuts in wages/holidays, and even termination of employment are commonly reported. Many placement agencies try through their weekly meetings to check such changes in lifestyle, thereby reinforcing the workers' adivasi/religious identities. This contradiction between the middle-class employer's *image* of an adivasi domestic worker and an 'actual adivasi worker', however, does not seem to have affected the preference for adivasi domestic workers, which is often evident in the employer's substitution of one adivasi worker for another.

Domestic workers' aspirations of individual and family life are also influenced by the gender relations in the houses that they work in. Their new ideals of housewifery and motherhood no longer fit into their traditional framework after being exposed to city life. The everyday struggle to earn a livelihood and the intensity of physical labour which is a part of every woman's life in the adivasi pockets no longer belongs within their mental framework. Non-working women are idealized as successful women who have adequate time to spend in taking care of their husbands and children. Women who are employed also constitute a section of the employer class. Even in such cases, the patriarchal norms implied in the woman accompanying her husband well dressed to a party or on social visits often get foregrounded more than their economic independence. Women employers' dressing styles and jewellery collections are also common areas of desire. With many of them being childcarers, the detailing of childcare tasks and the finer features of childcare along with the notion of quality time influence the adivasi women's framework of ideals of motherhood.

Migration for domestic work not only exposes these workers to the lifestyles of the city, but also to some of the possibilities of job mobility. This is facilitated by the opportunity to get lettered, pursue an education, and learn new vocational skills. Some of the placement organizations, especially those with a missionary association, hold weekly classes for reading and writing English and Hindi, and/or offer vocational skills training such as artificial flower making, stitching and embroidery, and so on. Such vocational engagement is also a source of additional income for some of the workers and, for many, a matter of empowerment. Though the number of workers who have actually moved up the ladder are only a few, many do look forward to such mobility.

Adivasi girls are often victims of sexual exploitation either by organized or individualized networks. Alongside this, a few workers see this as an opportunity to earn quick money. When asked about the sexual exploitation of girls from the community, one of them said, 'many do opt for it because of its financial attraction. When we work for a month we will get only Rs 2,500–3,000. But if someone is ready to compromise on their morality, they earn close to 20,000 a month—almost equal to what we earn in a year.' The practice of adivasi women combing full-time domestic work with occasional sex work is also noted. The anonymity that the city offers is clearly a determining factor. But many who are now willing entrants into sex work were once victims of sexual exploitation, and in most cases placement agencies and particularly agents were involved. The image of 'Delhi girls'[21] in adivasi communities to some extent is an outcome of migrants returning either pregnant or diagnosed with sexually transmitted diseases.

HOMECOMING AND FAMILY LIFE

The larger urban middle-class notions of women's position in the family have thus penetrated these societies, impacting overall gender relations

---

[21] The term is used among the local communities to denote all girls who have migrated to Delhi for domestic work. It is a derogatory usage that stereotypes migrant women as immoral and dishonest.

in these communities. In this context, their social status in the home community is always a concern for adivasi women migrants. This is especially true for young migrants, with the growing negativity around 'Delhi girls' in these communities. The flow of money from the migrants to their home communities ensures that their social standing at home is validated even while they are absent. Their exposure to a different set of social values and gender ideology could be explained in terms of the entry of organizations, either religious or development based, and by male migration for work (largely for construction). The concern for status is also consistent with decisions on how wages are spent. A considerable proportion (and in many cases even the full amount) of their earnings is sent to support the family in the rural areas. This income, apart from meeting the daily expenses of the family, is mostly used to settle debts or for the education of siblings. A major expenditure goes towards annual visits to their homes. Domestic workers prepare for these trips by going on major shopping sprees to buy clothes for themselves and to get gifts for various relatives. With these material markers, they try to project an urban, fashion-conscious, sophisticated, and feminine image back in the rural areas. After all these expenses, even for those workers who have worked for many years in the city, the savings are normally none or negligible, leaving no money for any productive investment for a better future.

Single domestic workers negotiate their gendered responsibility to their families and the possibilities of establishing their own families. The continuous demand for money from her parents and brothers is a constant source of tension. To quote one domestic worker who is unmarried, in her late twenties, and has been working for almost eight years in Delhi:

> My father, my brothers, they always ask me to send more money. They ask me why I don't send all the money home. I used to send all the money earlier. But I now send only half of my salary—I have to leave some for myself. I also dream of having a family when I am not under any pressure to earn for some one.

Uncertainty regarding the number of years of future engagement as a domestic worker plagues many workers. Though this uncertainty is partially determined by the financial dependency of the family on their earnings, it is also related to the anxiety of finding a suitable bridegroom.

Some domestic workers decide to remain single because of a perceived incompatibility between the life of working in the city and the notion of family life in their societies. When asked about marriage, a domestic worker from Jharkhand, who had worked in Delhi for eight years since the age of 20, shook her head and said in a determined voice,

> No need to get married. There are no good men back home—they are all drunkards and unemployed. I see my sister's life after getting married. I don't need that. Unlike the city where men take up the task of earning, there it is the woman who finally has to toil to run the household. So being single is better. Now I have to do only domestic work—I am paid for it. After marriage I may have to do both.

Her remarks pinpoint the structural difference in women's role across communities, clearly bringing out the continuity between unpaid household labour and paid domestic work.

Though many adivasi women, after working for many years, have left Delhi for good, some of them return after a gap. Yet another group is ready to leave the city if suitable bridegrooms are found. In some cases, this is largely on account of the issues related to finding a suitable husband or the difficulty of adjusting back to family life in their societies. The general assumptions surrounding 'Delhi girls', which largely relate to the issue of perceived sexual morality as explained earlier, makes it difficult to find appropriate bridegrooms. Further, given the practice of girls getting married while still in a lower age bracket, the fact that many returnees are above the marriageable age makes marriage more complicated. The possibility of returnees' preference for a husband (moulded by their life in the city), though not explicitly expressed, also seems to play a role in delaying their marriage.

The return of women to take up domestic work in the city after a break-up in their marriage or otherwise is much more complex. In some cases, the marriage did not go smoothly, while in other cases it is the difficulty of adjusting to married life and the lifestyle of adivasi societies that prompt many to return. After working in a modern kitchen using cooking gas and gadgets such as pressure cookers and automatic grinders, some women clearly express their dissatisfaction with cooking the traditional way using firewood. Apart from this, their regular cash income as workers had facilitated independent decisions on expenditure, especially spending related to clothing, jewellery, and so on. The dependence on others for such expenditure is also a factor that favoured their return to domestic work in the city. A few workers also reported loss of dignity in the absence of earning a cash income—both at home as well as within the community. The sudden unwanted feeling within their home and community was recollected by many re-entrants with much emotional pain. This has also made many realize the need to save money for their future, resulting in their declining remittances to families. Aversion to manual agricultural work, with no possibility of using their newly acquired skills back home, are also issues that underlie the return to domestic work. Economic necessity, the need to earn for the survival of the family—sometimes the new family after marriage—all trigger return.

EMPOWERMENT OR SOCIAL ISOLATION?

Though the possibility of economic empowerment is a debatable attribute, at least for a few domestic workers the access to a cash income is a reality. Wages are not substantial, with variations across workers, the average income being around Rs 3,000 per month (Neetha and Mazumdar 2009). Since accommodation and other living expenses of the worker are met by the employers, the cash income supports the family back home. Even in the case of 'independent migration', the dependence on recruitment agents and the resultant exploitation calls into question the notion of autonomy involved in such migration. The urge to change the conditions of their lives and work is evident in the increasing number of migrants who declare that they themselves had decided to migrate. These factors do indeed indicate a wave of social assertion and aspirational motivation. However, the larger question is whether domestic work as an employment option provides any scope for challenging and transforming gender relations.

More than the economic aspect of domestic work, it is the social aspect of this occupation that needs exposition in this context. Domestic service has long indicated class and racial hierarchies in the private domain (Kaur 2006). Interactions between social groups do not always undermine, but often enhance, the boundaries that divide them. Migrant domestic workers are the perfect example of the 'intimate other'—they are recruited by urban households as substitutes for women in house work. Though they are termed as 'part of the family' by their employers, they are excluded from the 'heart' of the family. Many live-in workers desire more personal contact with their employers, viewing personalism as an avenue for employers to show respect for them as people.

Spatial difference is clearly displayed in the employer households (Kaur 2004). Often there is a clear-cut earmarking of space and other facilities. Migrant adivasi workers eat separately—at different tables or in different rooms, from different plates, or after the employers finish.

This indicates a prejudice that views adivasi migrants as uncivilized and unhygienic; eating separately also represents a daily ritual to symbolize an employment relation that is feudal—the 'master–servant distinction'. In general, other than her bedroom (if she has one[22]), the deemed appropriate spaces for a domestic worker to occupy include the kitchen, the balcony, and sometimes the children's playroom. By contrast, the living room is normally reserved for the social activities of the employer's family. Many workers have to rely on 'public spaces' to expand their life domains. The tendency to attach themselves to church-based institutions, even if one is not religious in everyday life, is an outcome of this desperation for personal space and social identity. For those who manage to go to church or get a day out on Sunday, it is often a day of meeting their friends and other community women who share similar social and economic backgrounds, and an opportunity for speaking their language. Since there is a restriction on dress and appearance at the employer households, when going out on Sundays there is a tendency to dress up in a different way.[23]

The nature of domestic work and the workers' social and economic vulnerabilities alongside their isolation leave many of them outside the purview of any organization. The organization of adivasi domestic workers is largely under the umbrella of NGOs or religious trusts, which do not approach issues from the point of view of workers' rights and interests but rather from a social welfare or charity angle. Many of these organizations are also placement agencies, which limits their objectives and functioning and confines them largely to the short-term and direct issues of wages and employment. These organizations, especially those which claim association with the church, are increasingly facilitating the construction of regional and religious identities. Moreover, the way in which such agencies match 'suitable' employees to jobs reinforces stereotypes pertaining to the so-called natural qualities of women of different regions. These regional identities are seen as signifying a group's proclivity to domestic work, as well as the quality of care they are able to provide.

On the whole, from the foregoing discussion, it is evident that the entry of adivasi women into urban domestic work has led to a transformation

---

[22] The servants' quarters or the servant's room, if it exists, is in contrast to the spacious house of the employer. They are inevitably small rooms with bad ventilation, and are located normally in the attic or basement.

[23] Along with modern dress, these workers also wear the prohibited make-up, nail polish, and dangling earrings.

in their roles and status in the home community, alongside changes in their values, lifestyles, and perceptions. This reconfiguration provides new foundations for gender differentials and inequalities. Migration for domestic work does not yield empowerment to these women. Stereotyped and gendered notions of docility become the primary axis for their preference for household labour and in the social reproduction process. The confinement of adivasi women strictly within the realm of reproductive labour (though paid) contributes to the devaluation of women's economic status in the urban, host society. Their status and roles become akin to the larger and general social understanding of women's role—underlined by confinement to reproductive labour and the resultant subordination. Quite often, the altered norms of socialization and familial relations acquired from the city life make these women incompatible in their own societies, leading to situations of social exclusion. Trapped between distinct societies and cultures, they live through situations of acute identity crisis and social isolation.

REFERENCES

CWDS (Centre for Women's Development Studies). 2011. 'Gender and Migration: A Women's Movement Perspective', mimeograph, CWDS, New Delhi.
ISI (Indian Statistical Institute). 1993. 'The Tribal Domestic Workers at the Cross Roads: A Search for Alternatives—A Report of the Status of Tribal Delhi Domestic Working Women in India', ISI, New Delhi.
ISST (Institute of Social Studies Trust). 2009. 'Domestic Workers in Urban Delhi', unpublished report, ISST, New Delhi.
Kasturi, Leela. 1990. 'Poverty, Migration and Women's Status', in Vina Mazumdar (ed.), *Women Workers in India: Studies on Employment Status*. New Delhi: Chanakya Publications, pp. 3–169.
Kaur, Ravinder. 2004. 'Empowerment and the City: The Case of Female Migrants in Domestic Work', *Harvard Asia Quarterly*, vol. 8, no. 2, pp. 15–24.
―――. 2006. 'Migrating for Work: Rewriting Gender Relations', in Sadhna Arya and Anupama Roy (eds), *Poverty, Gender and Migration: Women and Migration in Asia*. New Delhi: Sage, pp. 192–212.
Neetha, N. 2003. 'Migration, Social Networking and Employment: A Study of Domestic Workers in Delhi', NLI Research Studies no. 37, V. V. Giri National Labour Institute, Noida.
―――. 2004. 'Making of Female Bread Winners: Migration and Social Networking of Women Domestics in Delhi', *Economic and Political Weekly*, vol. 39, no. 17, pp. 1681–88.

———. 2009. 'Contours of Domestic Service: Characteristics, Work Relations and Regulations', *Indian Journal of Labour Economics*, vol. 52, no. 3, pp. 489–506.

Neetha, N. and Indrani Mazumdar. 2009. 'Conditions and Needs of Women Workers in Delhi', unpublished research report, Centre for Women's Development Studies, New Delhi.

Neetha, N. and Rajni Palriwala. 2011. 'Why the Absence of Law? Domestic Workers in India', Special Issue on Decent Work for Domestic Workers, *Canadian Journal of Women and the Law*, vol. 22, no. 2, pp. 97–119.

Palriwala, Rajni and Neetha, N. 2009. 'Paid Care Workers in India: Domestic Workers and Anganwadi Workers'. Unpublished report, The Political and Social Economy of Care, UNRISD, Geneva.

Raghuram, Parvati. 2001. 'Castes and Gender in the Organisation of Paid Domestic Work in India', *Work, Employment and Society*, vol. 15, no. 3, pp. 607–17.

TCSW (Tirpude College for Social Work). 2008. 'A Research Study on Migrant Tribal Women Girls in Ten Cities: a Study of their Socio-Cultural and Economic Reference to Social intervention', report submitted to the Planning Commission, Tirpude College for Social Work, Nagpur.

III
NEGOTIATIONS AND REDRESSALS

11

Shifting the Terrain of Struggle
Critically Evaluating the Forest Rights Act

Sudha Vasan

THE FOREST RIGHTS ACT: BREAKING THE TRADITION

The Scheduled Tribes and Other Traditional Forest Dwellers (Recognition of Forest Rights) Act, 2006, popularly known as the Forests Rights Act (FRA), is a remarkable piece of legislation in the socio-legal history of India. It not only aims to undo the 'historical injustice' to Scheduled Tribes (STs) and other traditional forest-dwelling communities, but also aims to empower communities with 'responsibilities and authority for sustainable use, conservation of biodiversity, and maintenance of ecological balance' (MoLJ 2007). In spirit, it represents a paradigm shift in thinking about forests and forest dwellers. It explicitly recognizes the injustices of earlier practices of forest management and attempts to shift the discourse on forest dwellers from dealing with them as 'encroachers' to seeing them as 'right holders'. Finally, in FRA 2006, we have a legislation that sees the forest as it is—as a resource which has multiple users and varied uses, including as an ecological resource and, most significantly, as an important source of livelihood for adivasis and other traditional forest dwellers.

The FRA recognizes and vests forest dwellers with different types of rights. The right that generated the most public discussion and debate, and has since been highlighted the most to claim success for FRA, is the right given to eligible individual forest dwellers to live in and cultivate forest land. The currently cultivated land should have been occupied before 13 December 2005 in the case of an ST individual and occupied for at least three generations for other forest dwellers. A maximum of four hectares may be given for use, and the land cannot be sold or transferred to anyone except by inheritance. The second type of right provided is to use and/or collect non-timber forest produce like tendu *patta* (leaves), herbs, medicinal plants, and so on that have been traditionally collected. It also ensures rights to traditional grazing grounds and water bodies, including traditional areas of use by nomadic or pastoralist communities. Third, FRA vests rights in the community to protect, regenerate, conserve, or manage any community forest reserves. This is significant since such management and conservation rights have earlier been the monopoly of the Forest Department. Section 3(1)(i) provides a right and power to conserve community forest resources, while Section 5 gives the community general power to protect wildlife, forests, and so on. Finally, FRA also concerns itself with rehabilitation in the case of unavoidable displacement from forest areas for development or conservation. It requires free prior informed consent to be taken from forest dwellers in cases of displacement and requires rehabilitation in case of eviction.

The FRA is equally significant for what it leaves unsaid. In a backhanded way, it has recognized that what is classified as 'forest' by the state—even through its own long-standing Indian Forest Act—may not be a forest at all. It is a law that explicitly recognizes and legislates on areas defined as 'forests' that have been cultivated by adivasis and forest dwelling communities for generations. In this sense, the law itself has noted indirectly that what has been classified as forest may have been cultivated for 75 years or more. However, this legal recognition of an incorrect classification does not seem to affect the flawed forest governance structures in any substantial manner. Given the hegemony of an environmentalism that refuses to see ground facts, there has been no call to re-evaluate the legitimacy of state claims to conservation. While the question of whether tribals or forest dwelling communities can manage a forest sustainably has been a matter of much debate, drawing forth both romantic visions of unchanging forest symbiotic communities as well as imageries of short-sighted, self-destructive ignorant 'natives' who need to be controlled for their own good, the same questions have not been asked of the state bureaucracy. Can a state and its institutions that, for over a hundred years, cannot even define a forest that needs to be conserved be given legitimacy for conserving our natural resources? The structural legacy of environmentalism in India, as elsewhere, is that the legitimacy of different social groups' claims to conservation is entirely delinked from their actual practice and history. This is also reflected in the public discursive struggles around the FRA discussed later in this chapter.

The FRA has come about at a particular moment in the social history of India—a moment when there was and is considerable unrest in the adivasi regions of India, particularly in central India. The fact that modern forest law and management have brutally affected tribal livelihoods and are in no small part responsible for adivasi alienation has been widely recognized. Tribal disenchantment with forest law and management practices has manifested itself in several ways since colonial times. In many tribal regions, forests have been the material and symbolic terrain where contestations over different worldviews have materialized. In areas where the Forest Department has been the main face of the state in everyday life, setting fire to the forest has also been seen as a form of symbolic protest against state property. State forest law and management practices in both colonial and independent India have involved unrelenting appropriation of forest and resources from forest dwellers. Both 'conservation' and 'development' agendas have meant the expropriation of forest land and even use rights from adivasis, often displacing entire populations and in other cases making them 'encroachers' on their own lands.

In May 2002, in response to a decision by the Supreme Court, the Ministry of Environment and Forests (MoEF) issued a directive to state Forest Departments to evict all encroachments from forest land within a fixed time. The letter estimated the forest area under encroachment to be 1,250,000 hectares (in eight states), and asked the states to remove all encroachments which were ineligible for regularization in a time-bound manner by 30 September 2002, explaining that such encroachments 'cause great harm to forest conservation [and] ... are also seriously threatening the continuity of the Wild Life corridors between various National Parks and Sanctuaries' (Bose 2010). Evictions of many millions of forest dwellers suddenly labelled as 'encroachers' were attempted in many states. According to the Campaign for Survival and Dignity (CSD), more than 300,000 families were driven into destitution and starvation. In Madhya Pradesh alone, more than 125 villages have been burned to the ground (CSD n.d.).

Ultimately, evictions had to be stopped, at least partly because of widespread mass agitation. This direct threat to life and livelihood resulted in widespread protests and also the formation of CSD, a loosely united campaign of civil society activists and 150 mass organizations. This forging of coalitions demanding forest rights for forest dwelling communities built pressure through rallies and campaigns at the local, regional, and national levels. This force, built with the support of middle-class opinion and policymakers, came at a time when the existing forest governance regime was already at a crossroads. There was increasing public recognition of the failure of many earlier laws, policies, and projects, including the realization that crores of rupees poured into regimes like Project Tiger had not really yielded proportional results (MoEF 2005). The FRA thus came at a moment when there were multiple crises pressuring the state—the obvious failure of earlier forest governance regimes, disaffection and various forms of struggles in adivasi regions against forest (mis)management, and a concerted coalition with a mass following demanding forest rights that was gathering support from the opinion making classes. With approaching general elections, the groundswell demanding rights for forest dwellers also gained support within sections of political parties. In this scenario, the government took the first step towards a forest rights bill. The Prime Minister's Office asked the Ministry of Tribal Affairs to prepare a draft bill, and the ministry produced a draft forest rights bill in two months, closely based on the demands drafted by the popular campaign.

However, the progress from initial draft of the forest rights bill prepared by the Ministry of Tribal Affairs in 2005 to the actual passing of the law in January 2007 and its subsequent implementation was not easy. It was fraught with contestations that provide a glimpse into the social relations embedded in the forests of India. For the first time in the legal history of India, there was public lobbying and use of popular media such as television to influence public opinion around a bill. Unexpected coalitions formed in favour of and against the law, drawing together groups that had appeared disparate till then. A strong lobby of the entrenched forest bureaucracy and an influential section of the environmentalist/conservationist movement fought a prolonged and vitriolic battle against the loss of control of the Forest Department over classified forest land. Several cases were filed in courts by a few stakeholders, including, significantly, retired forest officials, arguing that this law would destroy all forests in India and would spell environmental catastrophe. For the first time, open lobbying around a law in India utilized the media, attempting to create public opinion against the law. Television spots created a picture of pristine forests with clear streams and tiger cubs that would be destroyed for 'our' future generations if FRA became a law. A single aspect of the proposed law—the regularization of cultivated land, subject to a maximum of 4 hectares, when the cultivator can provide evidence for continuous cultivation for a period of 75 years—became the central point of the debate. This was portrayed as giving away pristine forests for cultivation to a large number of encroachers. The bill, even before it was placed in both houses of Parliament, was enmeshed in a series of legal battles.

Fissures appeared within the state mechanism. The Ministry of Environment and Forests emerged as the chief spokesperson against the implementation of the Act, seeing it as a threat to forests. The Ministry of Tribal Affairs, which was made the nodal ministry for this law, was the spokesperson for tribal welfare and therefore for the Act. The former presented scenarios where the implementation of FRA would result in increased encroachment and large-scale cultivation in forests. The forest bureaucracy emerged as the champion of forest protection and strongly opposed FRA, as it claimed it would destroy forests. However, with democratic pressure through large rallies and representations, intense lobbying by middle-class activists who championed forest dwellers rights, and the impending general elections, a much-modified version of the initial forest rights bill was passed by Parliament in January 2007. The final version diluted many crucial sections of the forest rights bill demanded by popular movements and activists. The CSD, the coalition that had spearheaded the movement for FRA, welcomed the law, calling it a 'victory and a betrayal' (CSD n.d.). One crucial and particularly contentious change that is of particular relevance is the distinction made between STs and other forest dwelling communities. Ground-level coalitions that were built across such distinctions and divisions were crucial in building the pressure that eventually resulted in enactment of the law. Hence, the division that the law sought to emphasize had particular political relevance. While an intermediate version of the bill sought to restrict rights to only STs, the final version included 'the Scheduled Tribes and Other Traditional Forest Dwellers'. This change was also a small but significant victory for people's movements.

The struggle over forest control did not end with the enactment of FRA. Given the substantive change that FRA brought in, it is perhaps unsurprising that it took another year of active campaigning before the government promulgated the rules under this Act, making it finally active. However, even after the actual implementation of FRA began, reports of gross violations of the Act and concerted violence by the state, particularly through the agency of the state Forest Departments, have poured in from all parts of India. Reports of government-commissioned committees (Government of India 2010; Joint Committee Report Alternative Version 2010;[1] MoTA 2012), research conducted or sponsored by non-governmental organizations (NGOs) and think tanks (AITPN 2012; CSD 2010; Vasundhara and Kalpavriksh 2012), or by individual research scholars (Aggarwal 2011; Kashwan 2011) all show that there are serious problems in the implementation of FRA. More specifically, they all suggest that there is clear violation of the law by state agents.

In April 2010, the Ministry of Environment and Forests and the Ministry of Tribal Affairs jointly constituted a 20-member National Forest Rights Act Committee to look at the various issues relating to the implementation of FRA and sustainable forest management. The committee submitted its report in December 2010. The overall finding of the committee is that, with notable exceptions, the implementation of FRA has been poor, and therefore its potential to achieve livelihood security and changes in forest governance along with strengthening of forest conservation has hardly been achieved (Joint Committee Report Alternative Version 2010).

The forest rights bill was enacted by the government in power with one arm of the state—MoEF and the Forest Department—kicking and screaming in protest. But in a democratic state, the expectation is that when a law is finally enacted by government, the entire state machinery is obliged then to implement it. After all, the Forest Department is an agency of the state, and its primary raison d'être is to implement the laws and policies of the government of which it is a part. However, this basic principle of the rule of law in a democracy is evidently being violated in the case of FRA.

THE STATE OF IMPLEMENTATION OF THE STATE'S LAW

The Ministry of Tribal Affairs of the Government of India is the state agency that is mandated to provide status reports on the implementation of FRA. It therefore collects information from different states on the status of implementation and publishes this on its official website: 'As per the information collected till 30th September, 2012, 32,31,078 claims

---

[1] This is an alternate version of the official Report of the National Committee on Forest Rights Act. It was endorsed by 10 members of the committee and widely circulated online. It is currently available from Academia.edu as uploaded by one of the endorsing members, Sharatchandra Lele.

have been filed and 12,72,076 titles have been distributed. Further, 14,248 titles were ready for distribution. A total of 27,84,382 claims have been disposed of (86.17%)' (MoTA 2012). This is only marginally different from the data provided in June 2012 on the same website (32.22 lakh claims have been filed and more than 12.63 lakh titles have been distributed). A total of 2,756,827 claims had been disposed of (85.53 per cent) (MoTA 2012). A majority of these claims were rejected, and the rest (39.37 per cent) were accepted and titles distributed. A state-wise break up shows that Uttarakhand rejected 100 per cent of the claims, followed by Himachal Pradesh (99.62 per cent), Bihar (98.12 per cent), Karnataka (95.66 per cent), and Uttar Pradesh (80.48 per cent). The rejection rate of 11 states is above 50 per cent. These official statistics provide a mixed picture of FRA implementation. While some states still continue to ignore the FRA, a number of states have also rushed to distribute titles. Qualitative studies also provide a number of case studies of success, where marginal forest dwellers have claimed and obtained legal rights to forests they have been using for generations. However, a closer analysis of the processes followed to implement FRA reveals a different picture, often one that violates the FRA, both in word and spirit.

As just mentioned, official data show that the rejection rate in 11 states is above 50 per cent. A closer look at who is rejecting these claims shows that the legal requirement of gram sabhas, which are aware of and close to the ground situation and in a position to ascertain the validity and fairness of claims, has been dispensed with in most cases. The Forest Department, which opposed this law tooth and nail for years, is now closely involved in the decisions to reject these claims. Unreasonable conditions not required by law are made on the claimants; for instance, claimants have been asked to produce fine receipts or primary offence reports from prior to 1980, or to show that their names are on the Forest Department 'encroacher lists'.

The FRA assumes that the Ministry of Tribal Affairs would play a major role in monitoring the implementation of this law. Remarkably, this ministry has shown no seriousness in taking up this responsibility, in spite of repeated pressures to do so. It has also clearly stated that it has neither the will nor the resources to do so. The Standing Committee on Social Justice and Empowerment (2011: 32) stated that they are 'of the view that with the kind of staff the Ministry have at their disposal at present it is practically impossible to monitor the Act'. Yet so far no alternative arrangement has been proposed or made.

The reasons for rejection are most often simply not provided or not communicated to the applicants, although rules 14(1) and 15(1) of FRA presume that the resolution of the gram sabha and the decision of the subdivisional-level committees are communicated immediately to the claimant, and that he/she has the right to appeal the decisions within 60 days. The National Committee on FRA found that 'in an overwhelming majority of cases, the rejections are not being communicated to the claimants and their right to appeal is not being explained to them and its exercise facilitated' (Government of India 2010: 14). In cases where reasons are given, they are based on procedural technicalities, with no opportunity given to claimants to present their side of the case. Even in cases which have been counted as 'successes', the amount of land given is arbitrary and dependent on the Forest Department's whims; titles that have been given in some instances are vague about boundaries, and their legal validity, which is yet to be tested, appears dubious.

Decentralization of the entire forest management process is an idea that emerged in the legal arena with another progressive legislation that died an untimely death. The Panchayats (Extension to Scheduled Areas) Act (PESA) introduced this through the formation of village-level gram sabhas. In this tradition, FRA also relies on a village-level general body that makes decisions about not only land rights but also forest management. The forest rights committee was envisaged as a very local-level autonomous body independent of the Forest Department. Section 6(1) of FRA clearly makes the gram sabha level committees the decision-making authority on all claims. Unlike various committees formed under earlier government schemes, which were often controlled by the respective state departments, the forest rights committee was created at the village level, where people were most likely to know one another, and the role of state departments in these committees was removed. Section 6 further stipulated that the resolutions of the gram sabha would be reviewed by subdivisional-level committees, which would adjudicate in the case of any grievances. The decision of the district-level committee would be final and binding.

The National Committee on FRA, set up as a joint committee of MoEF and the Ministry of Tribal Affairs, found that in most states no committees existed at the hamlet or revenue village level, that is, no gram sabha level committees existed. Committees were often made at the panchayat level, which consists of many gram sabhas, making local verification of claims very difficult (Government of India 2010: 40). The subdivisional-level committees and the district-level committees have also made decisions without any reference to gram sabha level committees. In some cases, Joint Forest Management (JFM) committees created and controlled by the Forest Department have been used in place of gram sabha level FRA committees. It is widely recognized, even by government-appointed committees, that there is gross violation in this respect. The domination of forest officials in the entire process and obstructions caused by them have been noted by the National Committee on FRA (Government of India 2010: 43). Thus, even where there is some implementation of this law and forest rights have been registered, the procedural requirement which alone can guarantee actual management rights over forests to adivasis has not been successful.

The other aspect of FRA that could have resulted in a fundamental transformation of the forest management regime was the collective rights that were given to forest dwelling communities to manage forests. The entire vocal opposition to the enactment and the attention from the media focused almost exclusively on one of the rights recognized by this legislation—the provision of private individual land titles to small areas of land that had already been cultivated for long periods of time. The urban public furore and the anxiety of environmentalists were all focused on this aspect of the law.

What is remarkable is that this is only one of the rights recognized by FRA amongst many others, and at least in one sense the least radical of them. FRA, apart from these non-transferable but inheritable individual ownership rights to land pattas (to land already farmed by tribals or forest dwellers as of 13 December 2005, subject to a maximum of four hectares), also recognized user rights to certain forest products, relief and development rights (rehabilitation in case of illegal eviction or forced displacement and basic amenities, subject to restrictions for forest protection), and forest management rights vested in communities. The silence over all these other rights guaranteed by FRA has continued.

Individual pattas are significant to the extent that they recognize the existing mis-classification of forests. FRA neither attempts to, nor should it, embark on creating new individual property rights in forests. Community forest management rights, in contrast to recognizing individual land rights, represent a significant shift in the power to manage forests, which currently rests exclusively with the Forest Department, which is the largest single land manager in India. While it is possible to read this shift in power into FRA, it is noteworthy that this is the most neglected aspect of its implementation.

Reports from across India clearly indicate that the enactment of a historic legislation has not transformed relations of power on the ground. In fact, what is evident is the concerted effort to undermine the law. Starting with the inordinate delay in formulating rules and promulgating the law, to attempts at misinterpreting the law, to completely ignoring the law, the Forest Department has attempted to subvert the law in every way possible.

How do we understand this gross failure by the state to respect its own laws in adivasi regions? One way of understanding this disjuncture between the historic promulgation of the law and its dismal implementation has been to blame the incompetence and incapacity of the implementation structures. Most readings of FRA take this more benign view that assumes that this is an implementation problem that can be fixed through reforming institutions. Another view sees the Forest Department as the sole villain within an otherwise benign state. Evidence for this is provided by the protracted battles between state institutions that accompanied debates over FRA. However, the failure of FRA can itself be read as the success of certain ideological frameworks. Law performs a hegemonic role in setting the terms of the debate, and the success of FRA needs to be understood in terms of its role in changing the terms of discourse regarding the relationship between adivasis and the modern state.

The implementation issues faced by FRA on the ground reveal a continuity in the working of the law in central India. It shows the relative weakness of the basic tenets of rule of law—an ideological frame necessary to establish the legitimacy of a liberal democratic state. Legitimacy of any law in society is premised on the presence of the rule of law that makes a particular law appear neutral, unbiased, and for the greater common good. The power of eminent domain, which has always been selectively utilized by the Indian state, appears legitimate only in the presence of rule of law. Hence, it is significant that eminent domain has been used and continues to be used extensively in adivasi areas, while the rule of law is marked by its absence.

ADIVASIS AND THE RULE OF LAW IN INDIA

Rule of law, the idea that the law is above all and applicable to all, as E. P. Thompson (1975) points out, is an unqualified social good. In a modern capitalist society, it serves the important function of limiting the excessive misuse of power by the ruling elites and the state. While the rule of law historically appears to provide an ordered capitalist workforce, by its very nature it also orders the ruling classes. The significance of the rule of law to a capitalist ruling class is the legitimacy it provides to its rule. Unlike earlier ruling regimes that required continuous armed violence to maintain kingdoms, rule of law provides a legitimate force that reduces the need for continuous costly armed wars. It is both less expensive and provides a more stable environment for the rule of capital.

Rule of law is the ideology that 'the law' exists above all and for everybody, and that no one, not even the state or the ruling class, is above the law. While critical theorists have pointed out that this idea was always a myth, as social location is never completely irrelevant and there is no neutral position in a hierarchical social space, it has allowed us to move away from the conspiratorial image of the state and develop a nuanced understanding of the role of ideology and hegemony in the establishment of liberal rule.

Rule of law is the idea that the legitimacy of rule for the ruling class comes from a framework of abstract rules that applies to everyone equally, unlike previous eras when the legitimacy of rule depended on the dynasty or on God's word or simple might. The rule of law creates an environment where everyone is willing and eager to follow the law, since there is general acceptance that no one is above the law, that the law applies to everyone including the ruling powers, and that law is more important than any other source of power in society. While this is probably never achieved in totality, it appears to be the norm in liberal democratic societies. It helps to justify and therefore legitimate those who wield power in these societies, since this power is gained entirely through legal means available to everyone.

What is missing in this image is the brute fact that in adivasi regions of India, rule of law simply does not exist. The everyday interaction of the adivasi with any facet of the state is significantly and qualitatively different from middle-class interactions with the Indian state. The non-existence of rule of law can be traced not to any essential cultural difference of the adivasis, but instead to a systematic and wilful abrogation by the state of any principles of rule of law with respect to adivasis.

The Forest Department in central Indian adivasi regions is the primacy face of the state, in competition only with the police, and perhaps increasingly now various versions of the armed forces. In the interaction of the Forest Department with the adivasis lies the crux of how the rule of law is constructed. While the idea of law, and the breaking of law, particularly the idea of state property encroached upon by adivasis, is often used in public discourse to justify Forest Department activities, the same concept is not applied with respect to the working of the Forest Department. This historical and ongoing disrespect of the state and its own legal frameworks and selective application of law in adivasi India erodes the imagination of the rule of law. Systematic reports of how FRA has been ignored, misread, and violated by the Forest Department are in continuation and reinforcement of the general weakness of the rule of law in these regions.

EMINENT DOMAIN AND ILLEGAL DISPOSSESSION

It is almost impossible to argue that there is no dispossession of adivasi land in central India, although there might be debates on the exact processes through which this process has played itself out historically and is occurring presently. Eminent domain is a legal weapon that refers to the inherent power of the state to seize citizens' property without their consent, but usually with some compensation. The concept of eminent domain in modern legal systems is an important element of the capitalist rule of law, where the idea of private property can be violated through state intervention without challenging the very legitimacy of capitalist rule that thrives on the myth of fair play. The discourse of a rational, systematic, modern legislative process through which the modern state acquires proprietary rights in forests is critical to the mythology of modern law. It is only on the basis of this that the 'encroachment' of original settlers on a land can be categorized as illegitimate, since proprietary rights were settled through a process of consent if not consensus. Pre-modern states did not have or require this condition for their existence and legitimacy. Rulers could establish their legitimacy through a variety of other means, such as natural superiority, hereditary leadership rights, gerontocracy, hegemonic systems such as caste, or divine representation. In contrast to this, modern states derive their legitimacy almost entirely through the rationality of legal process. Thus, the modern state at least needs to create the myth of following a legitimate process in the transfer of property to itself. Forest laws enacted in the late nineteenth and early twentieth centuries were designed precisely to provide such a legitimate framework.

Significant in this context is the Indian Forest Act of 1927, which has been adopted almost unchanged and still continues to be the foundation of all forest legislation in India. This law actually establishes the basis for defining forests in terms of property rights. Prior to the colonial interest in forests, actual forest tenures remained diverse and varied in most parts of the subcontinent. While they continued to remain diverse in practice (Vasan 2007), the Indian Forest Act of 1927 was the first successful effort in standardizing forest tenures. The main thrust of the 1927 Act is to identify and demarcate government forests. This is in many ways a watershed moment, where the idea of eminent domain comes into play over such vast land areas in India. All forests where 'rights' in the particular ways delineated in colonial law could not be established, the state appropriated through the Indian Forest Act of 1927 as state forests. It then classified these as reserved or protected forests, based on the level of pre-existing tenurial claims that the state had to concede. A forest where almost all rights are vested in the state becomes a reserved forest, and an area where there are claims of non-state groups to an extent become protected forests. In practice,

> areas were often declared to be 'government forests' without recording who lived in these areas, what land they were using, what uses they made of the forest and so on. 82 per cent of Madhya forest blocks and 40 per cent of Orissa's reserved forests were never surveyed; similarly 60 per cent of India's national parks have till today (sometimes after 25 years, as in Sariska) not completed their process of enquiry and settlement of rights. (CSD n.d.)

As the Tiger Task Force of the Government of India put it, 'in the name of conservation, what has been carried out is a completely illegal and unconstitutional land acquisition programme' (MoEF 2005).

A crucial element of establishing legitimate legal rights of the state in forests is the forest settlement procedure. This provides a visible public process that is supposed to involve all legitimate stakeholders and thereby create a legitimate framework of legal rights in forests. In many regions of India, clearly defined property rights as required by the provisions of the Indian Forest Act did not exist prior to the efforts of the British colonial government. Adivasi tenurial understandings were and often still are qualitatively different from the property tenures recognizable under modern English (and now Indian) law. Collective ownership, community property, use rights without ownership, seasonal and partial ownership, and other such adivasi practices were often unfathomable and invisible under the new property regime.

Modern law is premised on set procedures, which is critical to the establishment of rule of law. It is only by following these procedures that the state can differentiate between eminent domain and illegal confiscation or land grabbing. There is clear evidence that the procedures for setting up reserved and protected forests within the English law were not followed in many regions such as Jharkhand (Vasan 2009). For instance, the forest settlement officer is required under Section 6 of the Forest Settlement Act to publish a proclamation 'in the local vernacular in every town and village in the neighbourhood of the land' notified to be settled, requiring every person claiming any right in the land to present his/her claims to the forest settlement officer within a specified period. The sheer immensity of this task if followed in word or spirit is worth noting, given the linguistic diversity of India. Yet this clause is significant to establish a property rights regime where local people with prior rights in lands declared as state forests are given a legitimate opportunity to enter into negotiation for settlement of rights. While this is by no means unique to Jharkhand, it is worth reiterating this in the context of current public debates that address the question of *adivasi* 'encroachment' on government forests and its consequences.

The illegal creation of legal state property in forests in central India has not only been noted by local activists, but also by colonial and Indian settlement officers. In the Singhbhum region of Jharkhand, for instance, adivasis had specific and extensive rights in lands declared as protected forests. Several old abandoned village sites and burial grounds (*sasandaris*) found inside reserved forests indicate that adivasis lived here prior to state reservation (Areeparampil 1988; Haines 1904, 1910; Phillips 1924; Schlich 1885). Yet, no inquiry was undertaken to record these rights, nor was there any vernacular notification before declaration of these areas as reserved or protected forests.[2] Areeparampil (1988: 7–8), who has worked systematically to record the forest settlement process in this region, notes that there has been no proper demarcation in this region, and forest owner and right holders received no compensation for rights in forests taken over by the state to create protected forests. A settlement officer in Singhbhum noted that 'reservation was one great encroachment on khuntkatti [original settler] rights in Khas Porahat' (Macpherson 1908: 160). He also states that

> in an overwhelming proportion of cases the forests are the property of a Mundari or Ho group, which has always possessed full rights within the village. This being so, the government and its successor-in-interest cannot conceivably have any rights in the waste or forest land in

---

[2] Patna High Court Judgement, Mansid Oraon vs the King, AIR, 1951, Pat 380: PLT 128 (cited in Areeparampil 1988) (also see Majumdar 1950: 12).

these villages, unless, as in some khuntkatti villages in Ranchi, he has forcibly acquired them by seizure, followed by a long period of peaceful possession. Whether such a description is applicable to reserved jungles it is unnecessary to discuss. Government certainly never has any rights in the unreserved jungles and wasteland. (Macpherson 1908: 146)

Colonial settlements also record that an actual demarcation of protected forests was done only with the support of the armed forces (Macpherson 1908: Appendix VII).

The nature of eminent domain, and reparation for colonial excesses, has never been a part of our public discourse. Hence, lands which were illegally appropriated by the colonial state become the legitimate property of the independent state. The fact that these lands were illegally appropriated under violent colonial rule becomes irrelevant to the new ruling elite. Moreover, the record of the state in independent India has not been any better. State violation of its own legal procedures and creation of protected forests through sleight of hand and blatant violent repression of protest have continued in this region. In overt violation of its own laws, the state has over time converted private and community property into protected forests with no negotiated settlement or compensation. Over 20,000 square kilometres of protected forests have been created after independence in undivided Bihar, most of it in Jharkhand. Much of this was done through nationalization of a category called private protected forests, which was zamindari land in this region on which tenants also had rights. Again, as in the case of protected forests created in the colonial era, the procedure elaborated in the Indian Forest Act was violated in the acquisition of these private lands, and classification as protected forests violated legal procedures laid out in the Indian Forest Act (Vasan 2009). This form of 'illegal' appropriation also transformed another customary tenurial regime in the Chota Nagpur region of Jharkhand where the Munda tribe was predominant. The Chota Nagpur Tenancy Act (CNTA), 1908, clearly defines Mundari *khuntkattidar*s as a special category of right holders who are descendants of the original settlers of the land.[3] These customary tenurial regimes were ignored

---

[3] Section 7 of the CNTA describes raiyats having *khuntkhatti* rights as being 'a raiyat in occupation of, or having any subsisting title to land reclaimed from the jungle by the original founders of the village or their descendants in the male line, when such raiyat is member of family which founded the village or a descendant in the male line of any number of such family: provided that no raiyat shall be deemed to have khuntkhatti rights in any land unless he and all

and the forests were treated as zamindari forests and appropriated. Roy Burman (1986) reports on the significant extent of appropriation: 140 out of 203 units of private protected forests in one thana (subdistrict unit) alone were of Mundari khuntkattidar' status. Some Mundari khuntkatti forests have been reclaimed through filing cases in the Bihar High Court,[4] arguing that the Mundari khuntkattidars under customary law were not zamindars, only trustees managing land on the community's behalf. This tradition of illegal appropriation of adivasi forest rights by the state and use of legal loopholes and ambiguities to restrict existing rights continues. Each consecutive land settlement in the region increasingly consolidates all rights in the state. Legal guarantees have little value in a context where the state wilfully and systematically destroys them through contravening laws or bureaucratic and political process.

The CNTA and the Santhal Parganas Tenancy Act reflect the history of adivasi revolts to protect their forest rights and livelihood. They provide legal protection to customary law and practice. For example, Chapter XI (Section 76) of the CNTA establishes precedence of custom, usage, or customary right even over the Act; Chapter XII allows for the preparation of a record of rights (*khatian*), recording all pre-existing conditions such as

> the existence, nature and extent of the right of any person (landlord, tenant or other) to take forest-produce from jungle land or wasteland, or to graze cattle on any land, or to take fish from any water, or any similar right, in any village in the area to which the record-of-rights applies; and the right of any resident of the village to reclaim jungle land or wasteland, or to convert land into korkar.[5]

---

his predecessors-in-title have held such land or obtained a title there by virtue of inheritance from the original founders.' Section 8 of CNTA describes a Mundari khuntkattidar as 'a Mundari who has acquired a right to hold jungle land for the purpose of bringing suitable portions thereof under cultivation by himself or by male members of his family, and includes the male heirs in the male line of any such Mundari when they are in possession of such land or have any subsisting title thereto, and as regards any portions of such land which have remained continuously in the possession of any such Mundari and his descendents in the male line.'

[4] Bihar Gazette Extraordinary Notification (P-61), Patna, 9 July 1956 cancelled 300 earlier notifications of MK as protected forests.

[5] *Korkar* refers to wasteland settled and converted into cultivable land.

The record of rights for land in Jharkhand thus consists of a section called 'Khatian Part II' that records the rights of the village collectively, and details of customary rights of individual tenants in forests and common lands of the village. Unfortunately, Khatian Part II are systematically disappearing. While a few villages have their own personal copy of the *khatian*, often people claim it is difficult to retrieve such records from government offices. Existing records are getting destroyed and new land settlements ignore such records. These are often the only documentary evidence of some forms of customary rights to forest produce and grazing, recording various forms of user rights and collective rights. Commentators who have followed the more recent land settlement process record the systematic loss of local rights (Upadhya 2009). Moreover, any area declared as reserved forest after the last land settlement is seen as entirely outside the scope of the land survey and settlement procedure (Prasad 1970), and rights in these areas are not recorded. Even in protected forests,

> Under the government notifications, authorizing survey and settlement in the district, the existence, nature and extent of the right of any person, whether a landlord or a tenant or others, to take forest produce from jungle land or wasteland or to convert land into Korkar, were not to be recorded in respect of any area which have been declared to be Protected Forests, under the Indian Forest Act, 1927. Accordingly, such rights, in respect of protected forests have not been recorded in the present settlement in respect of any village. (Prasad 1970: 48)

Adivasi rights are simply not recorded in lands managed under the Indian Forest Act, and reserved and protected forests are left outside the scope of legal rights settlement processes. In Singhbhum, the chief conservator of forests even objected to protected forests being included in the last cadastral survey and settlement (Prasad 1970: 48). However, it was finally included in the survey without recording any people's rights in these forests. Although a Khatian II was prepared during this settlement, this includes only customary rights in village forests. The legally recorded forest rights of adivasis are thus being appropriated without compensation through procedural sleight.

Where settlement has not extinguished rights, Supreme Court orders that were given with entirely different situations in mind are applied here with disastrous results for adivasis. Uncultivated land in this region, which includes land put to a wide variety of uses including roads, water bodies, grazing areas, and occasionally land with trees, is classified in the land records under two categories: *gairmazrua khas* or *gairmazrua aam*. The former is land that belongs to the government, but in which local residents may still have customary rights of use. The latter are uncultivated lands that belong collectively to the inhabitants of the village. *Saranas/ jaherthans*, which are areas of worship or sacred groves as well as other lands which may have scrub forests (*jhadi/jhanti*), and small areas of sal forests (*sakhu*), are also categorized as 'gairmazrua aam'. These and many Mundari khuntkhatti lands discussed earlier are described as 'forests' in colonial land records. Such lands only occasionally have trees, and have been used and controlled by local communities for long. Gairmazrua aam lands in the Santhal Parganas could be cleared and settled by the village headman, according to the Santhal Parganas Tenancy Act.

The much-discussed 1996 Supreme Court Interim Order in the Godavarman case (202/95) declared that all lands recorded as 'forest' in government records should fall under the purview of the restrictive Forest Conservation Act, 1980, and be brought under Forest Department control. These lands that were earlier not under the control of the Forest Department were brought under its jurisdiction. Collective tenurial systems were destroyed in one stroke and customary rights of inhabitants were brought under the restrictive control of the Forest Department.

Thus, state forest property in this adivasi region of central India rests on an ambiguous legal foundation. Most of the state's own legal requirements were not met in the creation of these forest property regimes. Thus, while national-level debates on issues such as encroachment and tribal forest rights assume the legitimacy of status quo conditions, this is not in the least a clear or settled question at the ground level. Moreover, it is important to note that current state policy, law, and practice, particularly issues such as legal guarantees provided by the state, are perceived and processed by local people in the context of this history.

The FRA of 2006 needs to be located in this political-economic context. While FRA refers to a vague notion of historical injustice, it remains silent on the legitimacy of currently existing state forest tenures. By ignoring this question and focusing only on the legitimacy of adivasi cultivators, it shifts the frame of the discussion to one where the state is the benevolent giver of rights to adivasis in these forests. So FRA focuses on specific minimum rights of adivasis, indirectly legitimizing the vast tracts of forest land that have been illegally and illegitimately appropriated by the state. The tragedy is perhaps that this Act, which is so crucial, given the abject condition of adivasis in this region, is also legitimizing a historical land grab by the state.

This fact needs to be highlighted also in the context of court cases against FRA. Many of the specific cases that have been accepted by the courts against FRA make the argument that the colonial process of land and forest settlement was complete, legal, and adequate, and even perhaps 'fully sensitive to the needs of forest dwellers'.[6] The case of Jharkhand shows that this was clearly not the case. Within a perspective of legalism, it can be argued that since the state, and the Forest Department, in particular has violated the provisions of the Indian Forest Act, its legitimacy to now enforce this legislation is compromised. The positive transformation that occurs with FRA is that the future use of eminent domain is slightly regulated, since FRA requires the consent of gram sabhas. But eminent domain and the notion that any land appropriation by the state always implies 'public good' needs to be challenged.

SUCCESSES AND FAILURES OF FRA: SHIFTING THE TERRAIN OF STRUGGLE

Ferguson (1994) in his seminal work on the consistent and systematic 'failures' of development in Lesotho, argues that this often unintended consequence of development—that it expands bureaucratic state power in people's lives—is in fact its main achievement. The development apparatus can only comprehend problems that accept a development project as their solution. Rather than ask if development can ever help the poor, Ferguson asks what development does besides failing to help the poor. This critical perspective is useful to understand what appears as a conundrum in the case of FRA—why does the state enact a law and not invest in its implementation? Explanations that focus on the poor implementation of FRA as an aberration are important, but paint an incomplete picture. Looking at the historical continuity of the adivasi experience with the law, it is clear that the problem in adivasi access to and control over forests is not the absence of law, but the presence and then selective irrelevance of the law. Adivasi struggle for forest rights in India has to continuously engage with the limits of legalism, in a situation in which, on the one hand, law enters their life space riding on the notion of 'eminent domain', while on the other, legally mandated state institutions are often the principal violators of the 'rule of law'.

---

[6] For more details see 'Court Cases against the Forest Rights Act', available at: http://www.forestrightsact.com/court-cases (accessed 19 August 2015).

The FRA is successful precisely because it is able to frame public discourse in specific ways. The overwhelming conclusion around FRA is that it is a relative success, but the crucial devil is in the details. The FRA shows progress on the ground in precisely those aspects that encourage the discourse of demanding rights from the state, particularly individual rights. Its 'failures' are those aspects that promote the autonomy of forest dwellers in managing forests, thereby reducing the role of the state in these regions. The FRA also promises much more in terms of transforming institutional structures to devolve decision-making rights to the lowest-level body, the gram sabha. However, these aspects have been uniformly and systematically ignored in the actual implementation of FRA. Accessing some of these rights requires more than just a statement in a law, given the gross asymmetries in power. In the implementation of FRA, there is a clear emphasis on individual rights and least attention to the institutional processes that favour autonomy. The shift away from the framework of autonomy can be seen at every stage of this law and its development. From the first drafts circulated by activists working with adivasis on the ground, to the bill, and to the Act itself, the law has gradually but definitively moved towards an emphasis on ownership rights. The entire public media debate around the law focused on land pattas. And finally, in its implementation, what is counted as success is the number of individual claims granted. While these are important gains in the fast-eroding rights of the adivasis, it is worth noting the discursive shift that FRA establishes. Collective or community rights come with their own set of problems in that they reproduce structures of hierarchy and inequality that exist within any community. However, the fundamental difference in the case of the adivasis of central India is their specific relationship to the modern state and mainstream Indian society. In this context, the demand for community rights serves as a challenge to property regimes mandated by the modern state.

In many instances where FRA has given both community and individual rights, it is clear that processes involving devolution of power to the gram sabha have been violated. Moving further in this direction, new amendments to FRA passed in 2012 further erode the provisions strengthening autonomy, as they 'make a mockery of the powers of the gram sabha' (CSD n.d.). This amendment claims to empower the gram sabha by requiring the forest official to consult the gram sabha at the time of compounding offences, that is, to decide on the quantum of punishment. This implies that the gram sabha has no role in managing, protecting, and making decisions on who, how, and when forests are used, but only has an advisory role in deciding the fines once an offence has been filed by a forest official. It conveniently neglects the fact that FRA and earlier PESA actually give the gram sabha the legal authority to manage forests. If these laws were to be followed in word and spirit, the gram sabha may consult the Forest Department on these issues and not the reverse. While appearing to give rights to the gram sabha, this amendment to FRA denies the autonomy of the gram sabha.

One of the 'successes' of FRA from the perspective of the state is its ability to transform the discourse of autonomy into one of demanding rights. The latter provides a legitimacy to the Indian state that it has not enjoyed so far. The FRA also needs to be seen in the context of greater integration of adivasi populations into the Indian nation through increased migration, education, and employment. Further, qualitative expansion of state and market processes into adivasi regions and increasing land alienation and appropriation of natural resources also erode the material basis for a discourse of autonomy.

The 'success' of FRA then needs to be seen in terms of its success in emphasizing individual private property rights in forest land, and in shifting the focus away from collective rights and further away from autonomy where the state becomes irrelevant. The 'rights' discourse establishes the state as a legitimate ruler, and the needs of adivasis can now be spoken about as a demand addressed to the Indian state. The argument here is not that community autonomy based on an imagined or historically constructed 'adivasi' identity is unproblematic. The inequalities embedded in all community identities, hierarchies, exploitation and oppression on the lines of gender, class, clan, and other ascriptive identities, exist in adivasi communities as in others. And modern universal identities such as 'citizenship' have the potential in theory to create less exploitative societies. However, in the historico-political context of forest-dwelling peoples in central India, it is useful to critically engage with the content of citizenship offered to them by the Indian state. And implementation of FRA becomes a critical moment to understand contemporary transformations in adivasi–state relations.

REFERENCES

Aggarwal, Ashish. 2011. 'Implementation of Forest Rights Act, Changing Forest Landscape, and "Politics of REDD+" in India', *Resources, Energy, and Development*, vol. 8, no. 2, pp. 131–48.

AITPN (Asian Indigenous and Tribal Peoples' Network). 2012. *The State of the Forest Rights Act: Undoing of Historical Injustice Withered*. Available at: http//www.aitpn.org/Reports/Forest_Rights_Act_2012.pdf (accessed 10 May 2012).
Areeparampil, M. 1988. *Forest Reservation and Denial of Tribal Rights in Singhbhum*. Chaibasa: Tribal Research and Training Centre.
Bose, I. 2010. *How Did the Indian Forest Rights Act, 2006, Emerge? Improving Institutions for Pro-poor Growth*. Discussions paper series 39, Department for International Development. Available at: http:// www.ippg.org.uk/papers/dp39.pdf (accessed 19 August 2015).
CSD (Campaign for Survival and Dignity). 2010. *Summary Report on the Implementation of the Forest Rights Act* (September 2010). Available at: http://www.forestrightsact.com/component/k2/item/15 (accessed 20 August 2015).
———. n.d. 'The Forest Rights Act'. Website maintained by CSD. Available at: http://www.forestrightsact.com/home (accessed 20 August 2015).
Ferguson, James. 1994. *The Anti-Politics Machine: Development, Depoliticization, and Bureaucratic Power in Lesotho*. Minnesota: University of Minnesota Press.
Government of India 2010. 'Manthan'. Report by the National Committee on Forest Rights Act (A Joint Committee of Ministry of Environment and Forests and Ministry of Tribal Affairs), December 2010.
Haines, H. H. 1904. *Working Plan for the Reserved Forests of Singhbhum of Bengal Forest Circle*. Calcutta: Bengal Secretariat Press.
———. 1910. *A Forest Flora of Chotanagpur including Gangpur and the Santal-Parganas*. Calcutta: Bengal Secretariat Press.
Joint Committee Report Alternative Version. 2010. *Report of the National Committee on Forest Rights Act*, December 2010. Available at: Academia.edu.
Kashwan, Prakash. 2011. 'Democracy in the Woods: The Politics of Institutional Change in India's Forest Areas', PhD thesis, Indiana University.
Macpherson, T. S. 1908. *Final Report of the Operations for the Preparation of a Record of Rights in Pargana Porahat District Singhbhum 1905–1907*. Calcutta: Bengal Secretariat Book Depot.
Majumdar, D. N. 1950. *The Affairs of a Tribe*. Lucknow: Universal Publications.
MoEF. 2005. *Joining the Dots: The Report of the Tiger Task Force*. New Delhi: Ministry of Environment and Forests (Project Tiger), Government of India.
MoLJ (Ministry of Law and Justice). 2007. 'The Scheduled Tribes and Other Traditional Forest Dwellers (Recognition of Forest Rights) Act, 2006', *Gazette of India*, Ministry of Law and Justice. Available at: http://tribal.nic.in/writereaddata/mainlinkFile/File1033.pdf (accessed 15 November 2012).
MoTA (Ministry of Tribal Affairs). 2012. *Status Report on Implementation of the Scheduled Tribes and Other Traditional Forest Dwellers (Recognition of Forest Rights) Act, 2006*. For the period ending 30 September 2012, available at:

http://tribal.nic.in/writereaddata/mainlinkFile/File1450.pdf (accessed 19 November 2012). For the period ending 31 May 2012, available at: http://tribal.nic.in/writereaddata/mainlinkFile/File1400.pdf (accessed 22 June 2012).

Phillips, P. J. 1924. *Revised Working Plan for the Reserved Forests of Saranda and Kolhan Division in Singhbhum District, Bihar and Orissa Circle*. Patna: Government Printing Press.

Prasad, C. B. 1970. *Final Report on Survey and Settlement Operations in the District of Singhbhum (1958–65)*. Ranchi: Secretariat Press.

Roy Burman, B. K. 1986. *Historical Ecology of Land Survey and Settlement in Tribal Areas and Challenges of Development*. New Delhi: Council for Social Development.

Scheyvens, Henry (ed.). 2011. *Critical Review of Selected Forest Related Regulatory Initiatives: A Rights Perspective*. Kanagawa: Institute for Global Environmental Strategies.

Schlich, W. 1885. *Report of the Forest Administration in the Chota Nagpur Division*. Calcutta.

Standing Committee on Social Justice and Empowerment. 2011. *Eighteenth Report, Fifteenth Lok Sabha*. Lok Sabha Secretariat, New Delhi. Available at: http://164.100.47.134/lsscommittee/Social%20Justice%20&%20Empowerment/18th_Report_22-12-11.pdf (accessed 3 September 2015).

Thompson, E. P. 1975. *Whigs and Hunters: The Origin of the Black Act*. New York: Pantheon.

Upadhya, Carol. 2009. 'Law, Custom, and Adivasi Identity: Politics of Land Rights in Chotanagpur', in Nandini Sundar (ed.), *Legal Grounds: Natural Resources, Identity, and the Law in Jharkhand*, pp. 30–55. New Delhi: Oxford University Press.

Vasan, Sudha. 2007. *Living with Diversity: Forestry Institutions in the Western Himalaya*. Shimla: Indian Institute of Advanced Study.

———. 2009. 'Forest Law, Ideology and Practice', in Nandini Sundar (ed.), *Legal Grounds: Natural Resources, Identity, and the Law in Jharkhand*, pp. 113–31. New Delhi: Oxford University Press.

Vasundhara and Kalpavriksh. 2012. *A National Report on Community Forest Rights under Forest Rights Act: Status and Issues*, Oxfam. Available at: http://www.fra.org.in (accessed 5 August 2012).

12

Retrieving Ancestral Rights

The Making of the Forest Rights Act

Madhu Sarin

Poor recognition of customary communal tenures and resource rights in the private-property-based system of revenue administration introduced by the British is at the root of the poverty and marginalization of India's adivasi and indigenous communities. Superimposition of exclusionary forest and wildlife conservation laws on forested landscapes inhabited by them has criminalized their holistic natural resource use traditions and livelihoods systems.

Present centre–state–local relations concerning forests and forest land management, and how these impinge on tribal areas and other common lands, are riddled with acute conflicts due to unaddressed contradictions in the constitutional, legal, and policy framework. These are rooted in a history of massive misclassification of diverse kinds of land as 'forest' without following the due process of law, and often, even any ecological rationale; the superimposition of contradictory and increasingly stringent forest laws and centralized management control in tribal areas governed by Schedules V and VI of the Constitution; unaddressed anomalies between customary, state, and central laws aggravated by Supreme Court orders under two public interest litigation cases;[1] continuing conversion

---

[1] *T. N. Godavarman Thirumulpad vs Union of India*, W.P. (C) No. 202 of 1995; and Centre for Environmental Law, *WWF vs Union of India*, W.P. (C) No. 337 of 1995.

of non-forest common lands and customary community lands into state forests through dubious legal processes lacking transparency and local consultation; and the progressive dilution, erosion, and/or deprivation of the resource and livelihood rights of local communities resulting in their increasing marginalization and alienation. The Scheduled Tribes and Other Traditional Forest Dwellers (Recognition of Forest Rights Act [FRA]) 2006, has emerged as a legislative instrument to rectify some of the major contradictions resulting from ancestral tribal and other forest dwellers' lands being classified as state forests. The FRA has the potential for democratizing forest governance and making it compatible with the constitutional provisions of Schedules V and VI[2] governing tribal majority areas.

BACKGROUND

The Indian forestry estate has a long history, starting in the colonial period and continuing after independence, of a massive misclassification of large areas of ecologically diverse lands, including community common lands under diverse customary tenures and multifunctional uses, as government forest lands or 'waste' lands. During the colonial period, while valuable natural forests were notified as 'reserve forests' for commercial exploitation of timber, vast areas of both cultivated and uncultivated commons were declared state forests not because of the quality of forests they harboured, but as a means of asserting state proprietorship over non-private lands. Many such lands were also labelled 'the wastes', mainly because they did not yield land revenue. Declaration of these lands as wasteland or state forests[3] was often done without any ecological surveys or settling the rights of their pre-existing users and occupants. During the survey and settlement of revenue villages, however, significant areas were recorded as *nistari*, *gramya*, *khesra*, and so on, forests for meeting the villagers' bona fide needs. In undivided Madhya Pradesh, for example, at the time of independence, 9,478,000 hectares consisted of such common lands and forests in which the villagers had extensive recorded common property rights (Garg 2005).

---

[2] This chapter does not deal with the more complex situation prevailing in Schedule VI areas.

[3] The overlap between the two is also evident from the fact that the Indian Forest Act, 1927, empowers the government to notify any wasteland as a reserve or protected forest.

Post-independence India failed to review colonial forest policy in light of the new mandate of an independent, democratic nation; instead, it pursued, with even greater vigour than the colonizers, policies of state appropriation of the commons for commercial exploitation. As a result, state–community conflicts in forest areas intensified greatly. Between 1951 and 1988, the national forest estate was enlarged from 41 million hectares to 67 million hectares (Saxena 1995, 1999),[4] largely through sweeping notifications declaring constitutionally protected Schedule V tribal areas as state forests. In most cases this was done without recognizing pre-existing rights mandated even by the colonial Indian Forest Act, 1927. This resulted in vast areas of such lands being brought under the control of the forest department or the revenue department, riding roughshod over long-established rights, community institutions, cultural traditions, and livelihood systems. Recognized rights were converted into 'privileges' or concessions, and large forest areas were handed over to industry and private contractors for commercial exploitation. This led to the destruction of sizeable areas of biodiversity-rich natural forests and their replacement with commercial monocultural plantations, in the process depriving forest dwellers of major livelihood resources. The post-independence reservation of Schedule V tribal areas as state forests violated all the constitutional provisions for safeguarding tribal well-being, making the state the biggest encroacher on tribal lands (rather than vice versa) (Sarin 2003, 2005).

Despite protests and rebellions in Bastar, Jharkhand, Uttarakhand (the famous Chipko movement), and elsewhere from the 1970s onwards by forest-dependent communities against such wanton forest destruction, it was exclusionary forest and wildlife conservation rather than forest tenure reform that gained prominence. This ignored India's rich cultural heritage of community conservation respecting the vital interconnectedness of all forms of nature, including humans, wildlife, forests, mountains, and rivers. Enactment of the Wildlife Protection Act, 1972, led to the further curtailment of rights, and the Forest

---

[4] India's 'recorded forest area', over which Forest Departments exercise management control, is now 76.9 million hectares, which is 23.4 per cent of the country's geographic area. This is despite the fact that 17.3 per cent of the recorded forest area has not been legally notified as forest (FSI 2005: 5) and has diverse owners and tenures, the largest percentage consisting of customary shifting cultivation land in the north-eastern states protected under Schedule VI of the Indian Constitution.

Conservation Act, 1980, centralized the power to permit non-forest uses of forest land in the central Ministry of Environment and Forests (MoEF).

Under civil society pressure, the 1988 forest policy attempted to restore balance by proposing respect for tribal rights and greater involvement of forest dwelling communities in environmental protection and forest management. A major outcome of this policy, however, was non-statutory Joint Forest Management (JFM) based on administrative orders. JFM skirted around conflicts over tenure and forest boundaries by soliciting community participation in state forest protection on the promise of a share of regenerated forest produce; it did not involve any recognition of rights or devolution of authority to communities. Instead of community empowerment, donor-funded JFM evolved during the 1990s into an instrumentalist approach, enabling the forest bureaucracy to extend its control *within* villages through co-opted local leaders and to expand forest boundaries to cultivated and common lands by claiming such lands to be 'recorded' as forests. Indeed, while there has been little of the promised sharing of benefits with communities, or any 'joint' management, JFM committees today are often used by the forest department to evict forest dwellers labelled as encroachers on forest land.

DISSONANCE BETWEEN TRIBAL AND CONSERVATION LAWS

Due to repeated tribal rebellions against forest reservation and the establishment of intermediaries in their homelands during colonial rule, even the British and princely states were compelled to grant tribal areas considerable political autonomy in continuing with their traditional governance systems. Some tribal areas were 'partially excluded' from normal administration and were governed by an agent of the Crown, whereby tribal local self-governing institutions were left fairly undisturbed. In the fully 'excluded' (from normal administration) tribal areas in the north-east, there was even less interference by representatives of the Crown, and tribal chiefs or tribal councils continued to function in accordance with customary laws.

The Indian Constitution continued similar protection for the partially excluded and excluded areas through Schedules V and VI of the Constitution under Article 244. Any government interventions in tribal areas need to be in harmony with the constitutional provisions and other policy directives for safeguarding the culture, resource rights, and livelihoods of tribal communities. Schedule V of the Constitution empowers the state governor, after consulting the Tribes Advisory

Council, and subject to the assent of the president of India, to withhold laws considered detrimental to tribal interests from Schedule V areas for maintaining peace and good government.[5] Article 338(9) of the Constitution requires that the National Commission for Scheduled Castes and Scheduled Tribes (now bifurcated into separate commissions for SCs and STs) must be consulted by the union and state governments on all major policy matters affecting SCs and STs.

Yet, massive legal expansion of the national forest (and revenue 'wasteland') estate in Schedule V areas after independence violated all the constitutional provisions just cited. Due to the poor recording of adivasis' customary rights and tenures, Schedule V areas bore the brunt of the post-independence statization spree. By extending all its coercive laws to them, the state has been the biggest violator of the spirit of the Constitution through 'vesting' huge areas of customary tribal lands in itself as state 'forests', protected areas (PAs), or 'wastelands', without recognizing their ancestral rights. At best, rights were recognized only over lands under settled cultivation, largely leaving out shifting cultivators and nomadic and extremely vulnerable pre-agricultural hunting-gathering communities. The poor recognition of communal tenures in Indian statutory law[6] has decimated their economies and cultures. Instead of the Land Acquisition Act (LLA), 1894, the Indian Forest Act, 1927, the Wild Life Protection Act, 1972, and the Forest Conservation Act, 1980, being withheld or adapted to accommodate the adivasis' customary tenures and governance systems, their indiscriminate application in Schedule V areas has progressively negated even the hard-won rights the tribals had gained during colonial rule. These have been converted into fast-vanishing 'concessions' and 'privileges', with even their legally

---

[5] Prior to independence, no general laws could be extended to partially excluded areas without the permission of the agent of the Crown. Post-independence, this was reversed. All laws automatically applied to Schedule V areas unless specifically withheld by the governor. No state governor is known to have exercised this power till now. According to Dr B. D. Sharma, the ex-Commissioner for SCs and STs, instead of heralding freedom, the customary governance systems of adivasis in Schedule V areas were criminalized with the adoption of the Indian Constitution on 26 November 1949, with the automatic extension of the administrative and legal regimes of the states to Schedule V areas as a routine matter (Sharma 2010: 14–15).

[6] The apparently constitutionally protected communal tenures under customary laws even in Schedule VI areas in the north-eastern states are easily overruled by statutory laws and Supreme Court orders.

recognized rights in national parks and wildlife sanctuaries often being extinguished illegally. Loss of their customary resource rights, holistic land use systems without rigid forest–non-forest boundaries, and a rich diversity of resource management traditions and institutions has pauperized and disenfranchised tribal communities and led to their being labelled 'encroachers' on their ancestral lands. Most of Odisha's 'forest' land, for example, lies in Schedule V areas where lands with an over 10-degree slope were categorized as state-owned during the survey and settlement process, even though these were used for shifting cultivation and in many cases even terraced permanent cultivation by adivasi communities. Land below a 10 per cent slope was often not settled with the tenants if it was fallow at the time of settlement. Clan- and lineage-based territories of the tribes were not recognized in the settlement processes. The communal nature of ownership of land, especially swidden land amongst tribes like the Juangs and Kutia Kondhs, was totally ignored, and such areas were classified as government land (Padel 1995 quoted in Kumar et al. 2005: 45; Rath 2005). Consequently, three-fourths of the land in Odisha's scheduled areas is owned by the state, and in districts like Gajapati and Kondhmal, less than 10 per cent land is owned by tribals, with the vast majority of them being left legally landless. Hundreds of adivasi villages on lands declared to be state forests have never been surveyed, depriving them of access to basic development facilities, and effectively depriving them of their citizenship rights. A similar situation prevails in Andhra Pradesh where over 60 per cent of Schedule V areas have been declared reserved forests, although the final notification of almost a million hectares after the settlement of rights is yet to be done even after two decades of the preliminary notification.

Implementation of the provisions of Panchayats (Extension to Scheduled Areas) Act (PESA) has met the same fate. The PESA, 1996, makes the gram sabha (the body of all adult voters of a self-defined community) 'competent to safeguard and preserve the traditions and customs of the people, their cultural identity, community resources and the customary mode of dispute resolution' (clause 4d). Every gram sabha is also empowered to approve the plans, programmes, and projects for its social and economic development before their implementation, besides having ownership of minor forest produce. Thus, PESA effectively mandates community-based management of their customary forests by gram sabhas. Yet, due to MoEF claiming exclusive jurisdiction over forest lands even in scheduled areas, it has continued to enforce its unilateral interpretations of PESA in the absence of any other agency forcefully protecting tribal interests.

A FRAMEWORK FOR RESOLVING TRIBAL–FOREST CONFLICTS

In his 29th report (1987–9) to the President of India, the Commissioner for SCs and STs brought to the government's notice the disquiet in tribal forest areas resulting from tenurial conflicts, and recommended a framework for resolving disputes related to forest land between tribal people and the state. Based on the Commissioner's recommendations, MoEF issued a set of six circulars on 18 September 1990,[7] less than four months after it had issued its first JFM circular ignoring issues of rights and tenure.

Only the first of these six circulars related to regularizing pre-1980 'encroachments' on forest lands. The second circular required resolution of disputed claims over forest land between tribals and the forest department arising out of incomplete, faulty, or non-existent forest settlements. Given the abysmal state of government land records, particularly for the vast areas vested in the state after independence, jurisdictional disputes between revenue and forest departments are widespread across the country. Under earlier land redistribution policies, the revenue department has issued pattas and leases to lakhs of farmers on land which is also recorded as forest land in forest department records. Instead of penalizing villagers for the government's own failures, the third circular required recognition of such pattas/leases issued under due legal authority by a government department. The fifth 1990 circular

---

[7] Circular No. 13-1/90-FP of Government of India, Ministry of Environment and Forests, Department of Environment, Forests and Wildlife, dated 18 September 1990 addressed to the secretaries of Forest Departments of all states/union territories. The six circulars under this were:
FP (1) Review of encroachments on forest land
FP (2) Review of disputed claims over forest land, arising out of forest settlement
FP (3) Disputes regarding pattas/leases/grants involving forest land
FP (4) Elimination of intermediaries and payment of fair wages to the labourers on forestry works
FP (5) Conversion of forest villages into revenue villages and settlement of other old habitations
FP (6) Payment of compensation for loss of life and property due to predation/depredation by wild animals

required conversion into revenue villages of an estimated 2,500 to 3,000 'forest villages',[8] created by forest departments themselves in the past (for ensuring availability of what constituted, in effect, bonded labour) for forestry operations. This has been Government of India policy since the mid-1970s. On paper, the land of forest villages continues being recorded as 'forest'. On the ground, these are legally constituted villages whose residents have no titles to their land, cannot obtain domicile certificates, or benefit from social welfare programmes as other departments cannot work on 'forest' land. This leaves them at the forest department's mercy for most of their basic needs.

No state government took meaningful action on these circulars, leaving millions of forest dwellers trapped in a state of semi-non-citizenship, ever vulnerable to rent seeking, brutal eviction, and displacement without entitlement to compensation or rehabilitation. The MoEF pursued enforcement of only one of the six circulars— the one for regularizing 'encroachment' on forest land. It made no distinction between encroachers and those whose rights had not been recognized. Indeed, the ministry admitted the same in an affidavit filed in the Supreme Court in July 2004, where it stated that 'the State/UT governments could not maintain a distinction between the guidelines for regularization of encroachments and the settlement of disputed claims of tribals over forest lands ... the state/UT Governments have mixed up the whole issue.' Not surprisingly, all forest dwellers with long-pending disputed claims have become equated with 'encroachers' on forest land in the public mind, reflected in the vitriolic attack on the FRA by elite wildlife conservationists and MoEF itself (see later in this chapter).

As mentioned earlier, Schedule V areas have suffered the most acute violation of the constitutional protection for tribal rights and traditional institutions through the indiscriminate declaration of vast areas as state forests or revenue wastelands without proper recognition of customary tribal rights. Further notification of large tribal areas as wildlife sanctuaries and national parks through a totally non-consultative process has aggravated the problem. Instead of protecting tribal lands, both the centre and the states have permitted disproportionate tribal displacement, largely without any rehabilitation, through land acquisition and/or diversion of forest land for large development projects. The Forest Conservation Act, 1980, is inherently undemocratic, as it has no requirement for consulting or compensating those with customary

[8] Unofficial estimates suggest their number to be much larger.

or even statutory forest rights or dependent on forest lands prior to diversion of forest land for non-forestry uses.[9] Similarly, the Wild Life Protection Act (WLPA), 1972, has no provision for soliciting the affected people's views before the notification of a PA. All these have been major factors responsible for the progressive impoverishment of tribal communities and the growth of Naxalism in tribal areas.

IMPACT OF ENVIRONMENTALISM AND JUDICIAL INTERVENTIONS

The growing middle-class environmentalism in India, essentially rooted in exclusionary forest and wildlife conservation in which tenure reform has no place, manifested itself in multiple Supreme Court orders in the two still ongoing public interest litigation cases filed in 1995. These court orders further narrowed the ecological focus to protecting *trees*, *wildlife*, and forest *land*, and the administrative focus to central control (rather than recognizing rights and democratizing forest governance). Thus, the Supreme Court ordered the settlement of rights in all PAs (covering 4.75 per cent of the country's land area) within a year, without defining rights or providing clear guidelines for recognizing the complex diversity of pre-existing customary tenures. A subsequent court order was interpreted by MoEF as banning the collection of non-timber forest products (NTFPs) in all PAs. This exacerbated the already acute livelihood crisis among an estimated three to four million PA inhabitants, many of whom depend on NTFPs for both income and subsistence, while increasing their vulnerability to eviction and relocation. The court order with the most far-reaching consequences extended application of the Forest Conservation Act, 1980, not only to lands recorded as 'forest' in any government record but also to the 'dictionary definition of forest', irrespective of ownership. This brought several million hectares of community-owned forested landscapes in the north-eastern states and other forested community lands under the forest department's management and control without following any legal procedure.

---

[9] The FRA of 2006 has finally changed this with the MoEF being compelled to issue an order in July 2009 that no forest clearance shall be granted unless gram sabha resolutions certifying that the process of recognition of rights has been completed and that they give their informed consent to diversion accompany applications for forest diversion (see later sections of this chapter).

The Supreme Court orders under the two ongoing public interest litigation cases have effectively rewritten forest law by extending forest boundaries to all forested landscapes irrespective of ownership, ignoring even legally and constitutionally protected customary tenures and designating the forest bureaucracy as the sole agency competent to manage forests. They have also reduced space for resolving centre–state–local frictions related to forest land through negotiations, totally negating the role of panchayati raj institutions/gram sabhas/traditional institutions in local forest governance, and the state/panchayat and panchayat/community relationships. Bringing non-notified lands under diverse ownerships due to their conforming to the dictionary definition of forests under the purview of the Forest Conservation Act, 1980, has resulted in extending central control over forested lands earlier under the control of local institutions or state governments.

The cumulative impacts of these processes on the citizenship and survival rights of already marginalized STs and other forest dwelling communities have been devastating. Today, India's central forested tribal belt, which is also rich in mineral resources, has the country's highest concentrations of poverty as well as significant left-wing militancy.

ORIGINS OF THE FOREST RIGHTS ACT

The FRA is the outcome of a unique historical conjuncture. It brought centre stage in Indian national politics the historical injustice of the non-recognition of the rights of adivasi and other forest dwelling communities over their ancestral lands during the process of consolidation of state forests. Matters reached a flashpoint with an MoEF circular of 3 May 2002,[10] asking all states and union territories to summarily evict all forest 'encroachers' within five months, citing the Supreme Court's concern over growing forest encroachments in its 23 November 2001 order. The ensuing spate of brutal evictions, including the use of elephants to destroy the huts and crops of impoverished tribal communities during a drought year, caused an uproar and led to protests across the country (CSD 2004). In a matter drastically impacting millions of tribals, the chairman of the ST commission (the constitutional authority for STs) wrote to the prime minister objecting to not even being informed,

---

[10] Ministry of Environment and Forests, Government of India, 2002, Eviction of Illegal Encroachment of Forest Lands in Various States/UTs Time Bound Action Plan, No. 7-16/2002-FC dated 3 May 2002.

leave aside being consulted by MoEF and the Central Empowered Committee which had made draconian recommendations to the court for ordering eviction of forest 'encroachers'. With forest rights becoming a major national political issue due to the evictions, an informal alliance of grassroots movements, rights activists, and academics came together under the umbrella of the Campaign for Survival and Dignity (CSD).[11] Together with left-wing political parties and other rights movements, the CSD undertook nationwide political mobilization with mass protests, rallies, public hearings, and conventions aimed at members of Parliament, state legislatures, and political parties.

The MoEF was compelled to issue a clarification order in October 2002 that the 1990 circulars remained valid, and that not all forest dwellers were 'encroachers'. Despite this, by MoEF's own admission in Parliament on 16 August 2004, just between May 2002 and August 2004, evictions were carried out from 152,000 hectares of forest land.[12] The court itself has remained silent on the issues of disputed claims over forest lands and non-recognition of rights, while staying the regularization of even pre-1980 occupation of forest lands.

In February 2004, just before the parliamentary elections, MoEF issued two new circulars: one titled 'Regularisation of the Rights of the Tribals on the Forest Lands', which extended the date for regularization of forest land occupation by tribals to December 1993 (instead of October 1980 under the first 1990 guideline), and the other titled 'Stepping Up of Process for Conversion of Forest Villages into Revenue Villages'. These were promptly stayed by the Supreme Court in response to an intervention filed by the amicus[13] to the effect that these were a violation of the earlier court orders staying both regularization and de-reservation of forest land. The court's stay on the conversion of forest villages into revenue villages was particularly ironic as this has been the Government of India's stated policy since the 1970s. In its July 2004 affidavit to get the court's stay vacated, MoEF admitted that during the consolidation of state forests, 'the rural people, especially tribals who

---

[11] See the CSD website available at www.forestrightsact.com (accessed 20 August 2015).

[12] Although the number of people evicted is unavailable, assuming the cultivation of one hectare by each household, an estimated 150,000 households, or 750,000 forest dwellers, were evicted.

[13] An amicus, literally meaning 'friend', is often a senior lawyer appointed by a bench of the court to advise the judges on legal matters.

have been living in the forests since time immemorial, were deprived of their traditional rights and livelihood and consequently, these tribals have become encroachers in the eyes of law', and that 'it should be understood clearly that the lands occupied by the tribals in forest areas do not have any forest vegetation'. It further asserted that its February 2004 circulars 'do not relate to encroachers, but to remedy a serious historical injustice', and that '[this] will also significantly lead to better forest conservation'.

With the new United Progressive Alliance central government in 2004 having made a commitment to stop forest evictions, the initial demand of the CSD and other mass movements was for the implementation of the 1990 circulars of MoEF. However, this soon transformed into a demand for a comprehensive law for the statutory recognition of pre-existing rights, not only over cultivated lands but also over forests and customary community forest resources (CFRs), and for the empowerment of village assemblies to protect, conserve, and manage forest resources.

KEY PROVISIONS OF THE FOREST RIGHTS ACT[14]

The FRA is a milestone in Indian law making because it acknowledges the historical injustice done to India's tribal and other traditional forest dwellers by the failure to recognize their rights to ancestral lands during the consolidation of state forests. By declaring in its preamble that rights recognized under the Act include the 'responsibilities and *authority* for sustainable use, conservation of biodiversity, and maintenance of ecological balance thereby strengthening the conservation regime . . . while ensuring livelihood and food security' (emphasis added), the FRA questions the very basis of current state-controlled, exclusionary forest management.

The Act has three major provisions: on the rights to be recognized and vested in all categories of forest lands, including PAs; on the authorities and democratic procedures for receiving and verifying claims; and on the empowerment of rights holders and/or their gram sabhas for the conservation of forests, wildlife, and biodiversity while protecting their natural and cultural heritage from destruction. The FRA bars the eviction

---

[14] The following sections of the chapter are a marginally adapted and updated version of 'Case Study of India's Forest Tenure Reform, 1992–2012', written by the author in May 2012 as a background paper for the Rights and Resources Initiative, Washington, D.C.

of claimants from forest land until the completion of an investigation into their claims to rights. To reinforce the idea that most lands that have been declared state forests are tribal homelands, the nodal ministry for implementing the law is the MoTA, rather than MoEF.

The FRA is among the most contested laws to be passed by the Indian Parliament. Powerful elite conservationists and the forest bureaucracy launched a tirade against it, contending that it would lead to the destruction of the country's forests and wildlife. In particular, they wanted PAs to be kept out of the FRA's ambit, asserting that the three to four million people living within them needed to be relocated. Other areas of contention were whether only STs should be eligible to claim rights, or whether other traditional forest dwellers should also be included, and the cut-off date for proving occupation of forest land to be eligible to make a claim. Concerted lobbying of a joint parliamentary committee constituted to examine the initially weak draft law tabled in Parliament in December 2005 led to the substantial strengthening of the draft before it was passed by Parliament in December 2006. Even so, the bureaucracy subverted some of the committee's recommendations at the last minute, as it wanted to restrict the FRA's mandate to recognizing the rights of only STs, and those too over only small pieces of cultivated land (seeing the law purely as a tool for reducing unrest in tribal areas).

AUTHORITIES AND TRANSPARENT PROCEDURES FOR RECOGNIZING RIGHTS

The gram sabha is the authority for initiating the process to determine the nature and extent of forest rights claimed under the Act. This is a major departure from typical bureaucracy-controlled procedures and is designed to ensure transparency and accountability in the claim-making process. The claims verified and approved by the gram sabha are to be consolidated, examined, considered, and approved by committees at the subdivision and district levels consisting of representatives of the revenue, tribal, and forest departments and three elected local government representatives at those levels. A state-level monitoring committee chaired by the chief secretary with similar multi-departmental and political representation is to monitor implementation of the Act in each state. Although represented in the higher-level committees, forest officials must share decision-making authority with the elected representatives and officials of other departments.

THE RIGHTS TO BE RECOGNIZED UNDER THE FOREST RIGHTS ACT

The Act specifies 13 claimable rights providing individual and/or community tenure. Claimable community forest rights include rights to *nistar* (usufructs); NTFPs; water bodies; community tenure over customary habitat in the case of pre-agricultural communities; seasonal resource access for nomadic and pastoral communities; other traditional rights; and, most importantly, the 'right to protect, regenerate or conserve or manage any CRF which they have been traditionally protecting and conserving for sustainable use'.

COMMUNITY EMPOWERMENT TO PROTECT AND CONSERVE

The rights provided by the Act over CFRs, combined with the power to protect adjoining forests, wildlife, and biodiversity and to prevent destruction of cultural and natural heritage, in effect reinforce the empowerment of gram sabhas to manage community resources also mandated by PESA and enshrined in Schedule V of the Constitution. By creating space for statutory community forest governance (in contrast to forest department–controlled JFM), the FRA challenges the forest bureaucracy's hegemonic control over the country's forested landscapes.

TRANSPARENCY AND ACCOUNTABILITY ESSENTIAL FOR RELOCATION FROM PROTECTED AREAS

The FRA is also unique in making wildlife authorities accountable for decisions related to the relocation of communities from PAs. The modification of recognized rights in PAs is permitted only in 'critical wildlife habitats' identified within them through a transparent and consultative process. Relocation from such habitats can take place only after all rights have been recognized, after it has been established that coexistence could lead to irreversible damage to threatened species or their habitats, and with the free and informed consent of the concerned gram sabhas. A resettlement package must ensure a secure livelihood and be acceptable to the concerned communities, and land allocation and the development of facilities in the new location must be complete before relocation.

WHICH COMMUNITIES CAN BENEFIT?

Sixty per cent of India's forest cover falls in 187 tribal majority districts spread over only 33 per cent of the country's geographical territory. The FRA has particular significance for the forested, tribal-inhabited, and mineral-rich but mostly impoverished belt of central and eastern India, where constitutionally protected ancestral tribal lands have largely been declared state forests or PAs without following due legal process. This population of the country's poorest people, numbering perhaps 100 million, suffered institutionalized disenfranchisement during colonial rule and after independence, and it stands to benefit most from implementation of the FRA in its true spirit.

The individuals and communities eligible for claiming rights under the FRA must be STs or other traditional forest dwellers, the latter needing to prove residence in the forest area for three generations or 75 years. With 170,000 villages estimated to be in the vicinity of forests or having forest as a land use, the law can potentially benefit several million marginalized, forest-dependent communities who have been deprived of their rights to forest land and resources, whether for cultivation, grazing, NTFP collection, or management as per their own priorities.

OFFICIAL IMPLEMENTATION OF THE LAW TILL MID-2012: PROCEDURAL SUBTERFUGE

The intensity of bureaucratic and conservationists' resistance to the radical mandate of the FRA became evident in the concerted efforts made to stall the implementation of the Act soon after it was passed unanimously by both houses of Parliament and finally brought into force on 1 January 2008, more than a year later. Many state and non-state actors attempted to undermine the FRA by ignoring it or subverting it through wilful misinterpretation. Within India's federal structure, although the law was enacted by the Parliament, its implementation lies with the state governments. The central nodal Ministry of Tribal Affairs provided poor leadership, including by notifying rules for implementation that lacked clear procedures for recognizing the diversity of claimable rights. The ministry monitored only the number of claims received, rejected, or accepted, without any attention to compliance with gram sabha–centred procedures or to the diversity of rights claimed. The Prime Minister's Office exhorted the states to start time-bound implementation as soon as the FRA came into force, without ensuring that potential claimants and the officials responsible for implementation were fully informed about the law's provisions. Statements from the Prime Minister's Office, the Ministry of Tribal Affairs, and the office of the President of India referred only to the individual land rights claimable under the FRA, ignoring the diverse *community* forest rights and gram sabha empowerment also provided for. Central government statements also conveyed the impression that the FRA was meant only to recognize the rights of STs and not those of other traditional forest dwellers, despite the law providing otherwise.

Taking a cue from the central government, the states started implementation with a primary focus on recognizing only individual land rights and only those of STs, with almost blanket rejection of claims by other traditional forest dwellers. While some states are yet to begin or have been slow starters, others, which had upcoming state elections, initiated rapid, time-bound, and haphazard implementation with the intent of gaining electoral benefit. In Gujarat and Himachal Pradesh, implementation is being extended to non-tribal majority districts five years after the FRA came into force. Most states identified gram sabhas at the level of multi-village panchayats (instead of at the hamlet or village level, as required by the law), in which marginalized claimants had little voice. Odisha was an exception in its early notification that gram sabhas are to be called at the individual village level, and in issuing guidelines explaining the correct procedures to be followed, although the majority of the implementing field officials as well as villagers remain unaware of these guidelines. States like Chhattisgarh, with one of the largest forest dwelling tribal populations, refused to distribute or accept claim forms for community forest rights and permitted lower-rung field officials to accept, reject, modify, or reduce claims as they liked, tossing aside all specified procedures. The rules permit rejected claimants to appeal, but this has been denied in most states. In almost all states there has been little generation of awareness or dissemination of information about the law's provisions among potential claimants or implementing officials.

Central and state governments even attempted to declare implementation complete by the end of 2009, despite the law having no such provision. In addition to the flagrant violation of the procedures laid down in the law, the forest departments of most states have illegally taken effective control of implementation, even though the state tribal departments are the nodal agencies. The Ministry of Tribal Affairs remained a mute spectator to all this, despite being flooded with complaints. The state forest departments have been unilaterally rejecting claims without authority, or demanding evidence not required by the rules. Even before the FRA had come into force, evictions and/or the forced establishment of plantations on cultivated forest lands were undertaken to prevent cultivators from claiming rights over the land. In many states, the widespread use of forest department-constituted JFM committees for evictions to enable the establishment of plantations on cultivated lands continues to be reported. In many areas, JFM committees have been made into forest rights committees to receive claims, with state forest departments controlling the claim-making process through them. New JFM committees are being formed for areas being claimed as CFRs. Conditions are being inserted in the titles issued for CFRs requiring compliance with JFM guidelines, and not obstructing the implementation of forest department working plans in the CFRs even after the recognition of rights over them. Forest departments have also been spreading misinformation about the FRA—that it is not applicable to reserve forests and PAs and that only STs are eligible for claiming rights. On the faulty interpretation that the FRA would not be applicable to already notified critical tiger and wildlife habitats, elite conservationists pressurized the government to delay the act's being brought into force by an year. During this period, over 30,000 square kilometres of forest were hurriedly notified as critical tiger habitats without following the specified legal processes (Thapar 2012). The villagers living within these critical tiger habitats are now being pressured—again illegally—to relocate without meeting the FRA's conditions that the recognition of their rights has been completed, it has been concluded that coexistence will lead to irreversible damage to wildlife habitats, that their free and informed consent has been obtained, and that all facilities for improved livelihoods are in place at the new site prior to relocation.

OFFICIAL IMPLEMENTATION ACHIEVEMENTS

The statistics of official achievements need to be seen in this context of systematic subterfuge. According to the website of the Ministry of Tribal Affairs, as of 31 March 2012, 3.175 million claims had been received, 1.25 million titles had been issued over an area of 1.76 million hectares of forest land, and 2.736 million of the received claims had been 'disposed of'.[15] This implies that 54 per cent of the total claims processed so far

---

[15] For an update up to 31 December 2012, see http://tribal.nic.in/writereaddata/mainlinkFile/File1507.pdf (accessed January 2013).

(that is, 1.486 million of the 2.736 million claims disposed of) have been rejected. The majority of the claims filed and titles issued are for individual land rights over forest land under occupation, which is only one of the 13 rights claimable under the FRA. Many of the individual titles issued are faulty because they do not show the location of the land or are for areas far less than the area claimed. Accurate data about the number of claims received or titles issued for genuine community forest rights, particularly CFR rights to protect, conserve, and manage community forests within customary boundaries, are unavailable because data from the Ministry of Tribal Affairs does not distinguish between the various forms of community rights and the provision for the diversion of small areas of forest land for development facilities in villages. The present number of CFR titles issued in the country probably does not exceed 3,000 (when there are 170,000 forest-fringe villages), and the vast majority of even these titles suffer from illegal restrictions that nullify the rights afforded. In any case, these official figures are a poor reflection of the situation on the ground.

On the positive side, states such as Odisha, Andhra Pradesh, and Madhya Pradesh have issued instructions to extend regular development programmes such as subsidized housing, wells or water tanks for irrigation, agricultural inputs, and insurance against crop loss to forest lands over which rights have been recognized under the FRA. Odisha and Andhra Pradesh have also ordered withdrawal of forest offence cases against those granted titles. Despite all the shortcomings of implementation, about one million households—approximately five million people—have already benefited from increased tenurial and livelihood security from the recognition of individual rights over forest land.

CREATIVE GRASSROOTS ASSERTION OF RIGHTS

Grassroots movements, however, have maintained sustained pressure for the proper implementation of the FRA and have been challenging and protesting the illegalities being committed. In states and regions where such movements have a strong presence, mobilization and awareness among communities has been increasing, with the widespread filing of both individual and community claims. Through networking, experience sharing, media coverage, and political mobilization, this awareness is beginning to reach new and distant areas.

The arbitrary time limit imposed on implementation has been withdrawn, and some states that had stopped accepting claims have reopened their processes. In some states, inquiries into reasons for the excessive rejection of claims have been ordered, and attention is finally also being given to the recognition of community forest rights. Using the FRA as a weapon, sustained protests are being organized against the MoEF for continuing to divert forest land to non-forest uses, such as mining and dams, without recognizing forest rights. A significant milestone resulting from this was the denial of forest clearance in Odisha to enable Vedanta Alumina Ltd to mine bauxite in the sacred hill of the Dongria Kondh community. Also in Odisha, villagers resisting the allocation of their forest land to Pohang Steel Company Ltd (POSCO) for a major steel plant are challenging the permission for forest clearance granted to the company by MoEF on the grounds that their forest rights have not been recognized.

The growing political importance of the FRA finally compelled the MoEF to undertake the first important complementary reform in the procedure for diverting forest land under the Forest Conservation Act, 1980. On 30 July 2009, the ministry issued an order to all state governments that no permission for forest diversion would be granted without evidence that the process of recognition of rights, particularly of the habitat rights of pre-agricultural communities and CFR rights in the concerned forest area, had been completed. Gram sabha resolutions certifying the recognition of rights, and giving informed community consent for use of the forest for a non-forest purpose, must now be attached with each application for forest diversion. The MoEF has blatantly been violating its own order in permitting the large-scale diversion of forest land, but this order has helped assertions at the grassroots. Many villages to be affected by the large Polavaram Dam in Andhra Pradesh protested against the granting of forest clearance without recognition of their rights or their consent; this led the federal minister of environment to seek an explanation from the state government.

In Gujarat, close to 90 per cent of claims were rejected initially without informing the claimants of the reasons for rejection or providing them with an opportunity to appeal. Using the Right to Information Act, the Gujarat Adivasi Mahasabha, a network of grassroots organizations working with forest dwellers, compiled a list of the illegalities committed in the process of recognizing rights and filed a public interest litigation case in the state's high court. After the first hearing, although the authorities challenged the case's contentions, there was a flurry of hearing pending appeals and the rejected claims for several areas were approved. Even some CFR claims have reportedly been approved, although titles are yet to be issued. In other states, rejected claimants have also mounted challenges, and rectifications are beginning to be made.

THE ONGOING STRUGGLE FOR COMMUNITY FOREST RESOURCE RIGHTS

Andhra Pradesh

On paper, the largest number of CFR titles (1,970 titles over 379,000 hectares of forest land) have been granted in Andhra Pradesh to villages with 100 per cent ST populations. However, the completion report (July 2010) of a World Bank-funded forestry project in the state indicated that instead of these titles being claimed by gram sabhas based on their customary boundaries, as required by the FRA, the titles were granted (illegally) to JFM committees by 'invoking' the FRA. The state government had made a commitment that the Andhra Pradesh Forest Act would be amended to provide legal status to JFM committees before the World Bank project ended. Since the Act had not been amended, the Andhra Pradesh Forest Department decided to abuse the FRA for the purpose, even though JFM committees are not even eligible to claim rights under the FRA. A condition was inserted in the CFR titles that the JFM committees would continue functioning in accordance with the Andhra Pradesh Forest Department's JFM order. Through this coup of sorts, the department attempted to bestow legal status on its JFM programme, a status which the programme currently lacks, while retaining control over village institutions. Strong protests by organized villagers about their CFR claims being ignored in favour of JFM committees have compelled the Andhra Pradesh Scheduled Tribes Department to permit the gram sabhas of these villages to file fresh claims based on their customary forest boundaries. The titles issued in favour of JFM committees have been held back and, so far, 324 villages/hamlets mobilized by Adivasi Aikya Vedike, a local tribal movement, have submitted their genuine CFR claims as per their customary boundaries.

A review undertaken by state authorities in January 2011 following the critical observations of two high-level committees revealed that as many as 71 per cent of the villages/habitations with a forest interface had been left out of the first, hurried phase of implementation of the FRA; fresh claims have since been invited from both new and old villages. The state has also permitted the reconstitution of forest rights committees at the hamlet level in place of those formed for large, multi-village panchayats.

Odisha

About 300 CFR titles have been issued in Odisha, where the state's forest department has tried to use the same trick as the Andhra Pradesh Forest Department in the Mayurbhanj and Gajapati districts. Although the titles there have not been awarded in the name of JFM committees, the areas over which rights have been recognized are the smaller areas assigned by the Odisha Forest Department for JFM, and not for the area falling within customary village boundaries required under the Act. These titles also impose the condition of the continuation of JFM, even in CFRs. Despite a joint FRA committee of the federal MoEF and Ministry of Tribal Affairs pointing out the illegality of this in 2010, these titles are yet to be withdrawn. A recent campaign by Orissa Jungle Manch (a state-level platform of community forest management groups) to increase awareness about community forest rights is beginning to change the situation. Some villages in Kalahandi district, which have received CFR titles for their JFM areas, have passed resolutions dissolving the JFM committees formed by the Odisha Forest Department in their villages. One village has harvested bamboo from its CFR, with several others planning to do so. Four villages in Mayurbhanj district have stopped the forest department from implementing an ecotourism project designed to fence off the forest they have been protecting for 25 years and over which they have claimed CFR rights. The mobilization and awareness generated by protests against this ecotourism project are motivating surrounding villages to also claim and assert their CFR rights. Even before they have filed their claims, several villages in Kandhamal district have successfully prevented the Orissa Forest Development Corporation from harvesting bamboo in their customary forests for a paper company, which the villagers assert they now own.

Maharashtra

Gadchiroli district in Maharashtra represents a microcosm of the potential and pitfalls entailed in the struggle for the recognition of CFR rights. With a network of struggle-based and civil society organizations active in the district, Mendha and Marda villages were among the first in the country to receive CFR titles for their customary forests. Now, an estimated 400 villages in the district have received CFR titles for a forest area of over 350,000 hectares. Receiving the paper titles, however, meant little at the time because the Maharashtra Forest Department insisted that under the Indian Forest Act, 1927, bamboo was classified as timber (over which villagers do not have explicit ownership rights under the FRA). The Maharashtra Forest Department refused permission to Mendha's gram sabha to harvest and transport bamboo from its CFR outside the village. The federal minister of environment, the state's chief minister and forest minister, and other high-ups needed to go personally to the village to force the Maharashtra Forest Department to hand a transit passbook over to the gram sabha, after firmly conveying to the department that the FRA overruled the older Indian Forest Act. Once authorized, the village earned, in 2011, about Rs 10 million from the harvesting and sale of bamboo, with a large percentage of the money going to villagers as wages.

With the high availability of bamboo in 76 per cent of the district's area under forests, the Maharashtra Forest Department earns considerable revenue from leasing the bamboo forests to a paper company. Although many villages have been issued CFR titles for the leased areas, and despite their demands, the department has been reluctant to revoke the paper company's lease or to permit rights-holding villages to issue their own transit permits. Some villages have resorted to physically stopping the company from harvesting bamboo in their CFRs, leading to situations of conflict. With persistent struggle and lobbying, more villages are being authorized to issue transit permits to transport their bamboo harvests to the market.

More than 70 villages organized by the grassroots organization Bharat Jan Andolan in the Dhanora, Chamorshi, and Armori talukas of Gadchiroli district are also moving to establish control over their forest resources. Four of these villages expect to earn Rs 75.5 million from their bamboo harvest during 2012–13, of which 40 per cent will be paid as wages to the local harvesters. The villages plan to spend the remaining 60 per cent on new schools, health care, and legal education to strengthen community control. Of the remaining 66 villages, all but one also expect to begin their bamboo harvests this year and are planning to use the income in similar ways.

Community harvests of bamboo in Gadchiroli district provide a glimpse of the potential extent to which the FRA can restore forest-based livelihoods and income flows to communities. Gram sabhas in Gadchiroli district are also struggling to get the illegal conditions inserted into many CFR titles revoked—such as not preventing the Maharashtra Forest Department from implementing its working plan in their community forests.

West Bengal

In many states, although few community rights have been recognized to date, organized and aware communities have started asserting their authority over customary forests granted by the FRA by preventing forest departments from undertaking tree felling or other activities in them. In the north of West Bengal, several villages have put up boards outside their customary forests announcing that no one may undertake activities in them without permission from the gram sabha; they have not permitted the West Bengal Forest Department to undertake felling in their customary forests. In about 30 villages, the local movement has initiated community institution building by encouraging the gram sabhas to elect forest governance committees, which are evolving rules for regulating forest use. The gram sabhas have sent notices to the relevant authorities informing them of the constitution of their forest governance committees under the FRA rules for asserting their powers of protection and management. In one area, where there was a problem with the police over the assertion of local rights, the police backed off after being shown a copy of the FRA.

Jharkhand

Jharkhand is a forested state with a large tribal population that had compelled even the colonial government to recognize its extensive customary rights. It is the latest state in which tribal communities have decided to assert their rights under the FRA, irrespective of formal recognition. Eighteen panchayats mobilized by the Jharkhand Jungle Bachao Andolan in Ranchi district filed CFR claims, essentially to reclaim their recorded rights over large forest areas under the Chota Nagpur Tenancy Act (CNTA), 1908. These forests were vested in the Jharkhand Forest Department by executive fiat after independence without due legal process. The district collector agreed to approve their claims, but the Jharkhand Forest Department raised spurious objections, arguing that NTFP ownership rights could not be recognized until the state government withdrew its monopoly control over two commercially valuable NTFPs. The department also argued that local communities were responsible for forest degradation and could not be trusted with forest protection. Angered by this, all 18 panchayats have decided to assert their authority over their CFRs on the grounds that their rights stand recognized from the day the FRA came into force.

Assertion of Rights by a Pastoral Community in Gujarat

The Maldhari pastoral community in the non-tribal Kutch area of Gujarat has rejected the Gujarat Forest Department's working plan, which aimed to exclude the pastoralists from their customary pasture land. The Maldharis have started mapping their seasonal use areas to make a collective claim for community rights over 2,500 square kilometres of the Banni grasslands misclassified as forest. In response to massive protests by the Maldharis, the Gujarat government has finally had to extend FRA implementation to non-tribal areas of the state. Shaken by the Maldharis' protest against its working plan, the Gujarat Forest Department wants to initiate a dialogue with them. Pastoral communities in other states are also beginning to claim their customary grazing rights.

Pre-agricultural and particularly vulnerable tribal communities are similarly beginning to claim their habitat rights over large territories. Forest villages and unsurveyed settlements in forest areas in Uttar Pradesh, Uttarakhand, and Odisha are demanding the conversion of their settlements into revenue villages.

Other States

The Soliga tribal community in Karnataka has received community titles over three of the five forest ranges within the core area of the BRT Tiger Reserve, covering a number of forest and cultural rights. The community has also restarted NTFP collection, earlier banned by the Karnataka Forest Department (although they still have to deal with the department's resistance). In Uttar Pradesh, land titles have been awarded to the tribal residents of a forest village (which the Uttar Pradesh Forest Department had been trying to evict) in the core area of another tiger reserve. A total of 4,833 titles have been issued to the residents of 29 forest/*taungya*[16] villages spread over five districts in Uttar Pradesh, and the process of converting them into revenue villages has started.

[16] Under the taungya system, the forest department used to permit temporary labour settlements on forest land for planting trees and taking care of them for 3–4 years before moving them to a new location. During this period, the labourers were permitted to cultivate food crops between the plants for their subsistence needs. Once the taungya system was stopped, the labourers were left where they were without any rights on the land they lived on. These taungya villages are now to be converted into revenue villages.

In the Nilgiris in Tamil Nadu, 59 gram sabhas have put up boards outside their demarcated CFRs and banned the Tamil Nadu Forest Department and police from entering them without gram sabha permission. In most of these areas, in confrontations with departmental staff, it is the foresters who have had to back off due to the FRA.

Although uneven across the country, such grassroots assertion of rights under the FRA is spreading, with a discernible transformative impact on the balance of power between forest departments and forest communities. Unlike in the pre-FRA days, brutal evictions, beatings, arrests, and the burning of houses and villages by forestry staff have now become rare, although they are still continuing mostly in areas where people are not organized. In areas with strong grassroots movements, day-to-day rent seeking and harassment by forest staff have declined. If a forest department continues with illegalities, villagers are now able to implead the nodal tribal department or the district administration to hold it accountable; many have submitted complaints about violations to state-level monitoring committees constituted under the FRA. With elected as well as multi-departmental representatives in the higher-level committees responsible for recognizing rights, these committees can be mobilized by communities to exert pressure on forest departments to conform with the new law. Despite the shortcomings in implementation to date, the very existence of a law recognizing forest rights has diminished the forest bureaucracy's exclusive dominance and control over forest lands, and there has been a perceptible shift in the balance of power between communities and the forest bureaucracy. The FRA has created space for democratic control over forests, which communities have started using in creative ways to assert their rights.

With a new minister being appointed in July 2011, the Ministry of Tribal Affairs accepted many of the substantial recommendations lobbied for through the then National Advisory Council (which advised the central government on policy matters) to ensure that implementation conforms with the law's provisions by issuing new guidelines and amending the rules.

RISKS OF PUSHBACK

The forest bureaucracy and the federal MoEF remain the biggest pushback risks to forest tenure reform in India. They continue resisting complementary institutional reform by amending or withdrawing existing forestry laws and regulations which contradict the FRA. On the contrary, the forest bureaucracy has been attempting to argue the opposite—for instance, by asserting that NTFP ownership rights over bamboo could not be recognized because the Indian Forest Act, 1927, treated bamboo as timber. The ongoing policies and programmes of MoEF still fail to acknowledge the existence of statutory CFR rights and the fact that they supersede forest department–controlled JFM. The forest bureaucracy is making every effort to subsume CFR management within its JFM framework. Forest departments in Odisha, West Bengal, and Maharashtra have already issued new JFM guidelines with this intent. The massive funding for forestry projects from international donors and the central government continues to be routed through JFM committees. This is enabling forest departments to confuse and divide communities that are claiming forest rights and to foist JFM even in areas being claimed as CFRs. Despite complaints and protests against such violations of the FRA, the Japanese International Cooperation Agency continues to lend huge amounts of money for such forestry projects in several states. In Odisha, Uttar Pradesh, and Gujarat, protests against plantations being established under such projects on cultivated lands and forests claimed under the FRA are leading to conflicts, as organized communities fight to protect their hard-won statutory rights.

In the same vein, the National Tiger Conservation Authority and the National Board of Wildlife continue to pursue policies and implement management plans for tiger reserves and other PAs as if the FRA does not exist. Major conflicts are emerging in tiger reserves due to the illegal relocation of villagers without recognizing their rights, establishing that coexistence is not viable, or seeking their free and informed consent, as now required by law. The MoEF continues to violate its own July 2009 order requiring gram sabha certification of completed rights recognition and informed consent for any diversion of forest land. Since the FRA came into force in January 2008, over 200,000 hectares of forest land have been diverted for development projects without any recognition of forest rights. Some conservation organizations and retired forest officers have challenged the FRA in the courts on environmental grounds, and unfavourable judicial orders on their pending petitions remain a potential pushback risk. Three state high courts had initially stayed the granting of titles under the FRA: these were subsequently withdrawn in Odisha and Andhra Pradesh but remain in force in Tamil Nadu, and for this reason no titles have yet been issued in that state.

The stalling of the large Vedanta and POSCO projects due to the assertion of forest rights has made state agencies and private corporations apprehensive about the FRA's implications for their access to forest land for development projects. This has already increased the resistance of the Odisha government to the recognition of community forest rights—an unanticipated pushback effect of the successful assertion of rights. With increasing demand for the diversion of forest land for mining, dams, and other development projects, and forest rights movements demanding that such diversions conform to the order of the MoEF requiring recognition of rights and informed community consent, corporate pressure on the government to dilute FRA provisions has emerged as the latest pushback risk.

Finally, there is the possibility that the MoEF will sign international agreements related to climate change without a democratic or consultative process, with negative impacts on people's forest rights. The ministry has already formulated an ambitious 'Green India Mission' for mitigating climate change by improving or increasing forest/tree cover over 10 million hectares in the next 10 years, at an astounding cost of Rs 46,000 crores. Primarily aimed at attracting international funds for Reducing Emissions through Degradation and Deforestation (REDD+), this plan attempts to subvert the FRA by subsuming it within JFM. Although organized communities with recognized rights will be in a stronger position to challenge such impositions, scattered and remote communities remain highly vulnerable.

* * *

The outcome of a prolonged struggle, the FRA represents a milestone in Indian legislative history, with radical provisions for major reforms in tenure and forest governance. Acknowledging historical injustices, it challenges the misclassification of ancestral lands as state forests and provides for their extensive restoration to rights-holding communities. Perhaps for the first time in Indian law, the FRA clearly recognizes the concept of common property resources by providing for a range of community forest rights and powers. By stating that empowered rights holders vested with the '*authority* for sustainable use, conservation of biodiversity and maintenance of ecological balance' (emphasis added) will strengthen the conservation regime while ensuring livelihood and food security, the FRA questions the colonial principle of eminent domain and the very rationale of current state-controlled, centralized, and unifunctional forest management.

Evidence about implementation to date suggests that the state—at both the federal and state levels—is attempting the narrowest possible interpretation of the law's provisions, with the Ministry of Tribal Affairs doing little till recently to prevent blatant violations and attempted subversion by most state governments. Forest departments, in particular, are being permitted to subvert the law. But this is not going unchallenged.

Grassroots movements continue to mobilize communities and lobby political parties and parliamentary bodies, demanding proper implementation of the FRA as per its spirit. The very enactment of the law has become a weapon in their hands to challenge illegalities and the authority of forest departments in many creative ways. The assertion of rights by organized communities, even where these are yet to be recognized formally, is changing the balance of power between communities and the forest bureaucracy. Over one million households are already enjoying tenurial security over their cultivated lands obtained under the FRA, while community control over forests is beginning to expand to areas beyond the pockets in which it was achieved initially. With villagers beginning to receive income flows from resource control, they have also begun to strengthen their institutions for equitable and sustainable forest management and to invest in strengthening community control and benefits.

Major challenges remain, however. These emanate both from the limitations of the FRA as a pro-people law and the political context in which it is being implemented. Despite the unanimous passage of the FRA through the Indian Parliament, the Indian government has been unable to muster the unequivocal political will needed for its full implementation—as that would undermine its ability to support extractive industries and similar interests by manipulating the hegemonic control of the forest bureaucracy over the country's forests. Complementary institutional reform, such as the order of the MoEF making the diversion of forest land subject to the recognition of rights and the consent of rights-holding communities, needs to be extended to other areas and implemented. An inherently dichotomous legal regime, in which the existence of contradictory forestry, wildlife, and other laws impedes the implementation of laws like the FRA, needs systematic reform to ensure the unambiguous recognition of rights and the transfer of democratic control over forests to communities.

The most significant change that the struggle for the FRA has brought about in recent years has been the removal of the blind spot whereby authoritarian forest policies are considered to be 'natural'. The fundamental questions of who owns the country's forests, and by whom and for what objectives they should be governed and managed within the country's democratic and constitutional framework, are now at centre stage. Neither political parties nor policymakers can afford to dismiss forest dwellers as encroachers or to take for granted the centralized diversion of forest land for other uses, as they once did. This change in the terrain of the debate is spreading and gaining depth, as forest communities and struggle organizations take up new and creative ways of defining democratic control over forests.

REFERENCES

CSD (Campaign for Survival and Dignity). 2004. *Endangered Symbiosis: Evictions and India's Forest Communities*. New Delhi: Campaign for Survival and Dignity.
FSI (Forest Survey of India). 2005. *State of Forest Report 2003*. Dehradun: FSI.
Garg, A. 2005. 'Orange Areas: Examining the Origin and Status', Working Paper Series no. 21, National Centre for Advocacy Studies, Pune.
Kumar, K., P. R. Choudhary, S. Sarangi, P. Mishra, and S. Behera. 2005. *A Socio-Economic and Legal Study of Scheduled Tribes' Land in Orissa*. Bhubaneswar: Vasundhara.
Padel, F. 1995. *The Sacrifice of Human Being: British Rule and the Konds of Orissa*. New Delhi: Oxford University Press.
Rath, B. 2005. *Vulnerable Tribal Livelihood and Shifting Cultivation: The Situation in Orissa with a Case Study in the Bhuyan-Juang Pirh of Keonjhar District*. Bhubaneswar: Vasundhara.
Sarin, M. 2003. 'Bad in Law', *Down to Earth*, 15 July 2003.
———. 2005. 'Laws, Lore and Logjams: Critical Issues in Indian Forest Conservation', *Gatekeeper Series*, no. 116. London: International Institute for Environment and Development.
———. 2012. 'Case Study of India's Forest Tenure Reform, 1992–2012', Background paper for Rights and Resources Initiative, Washington, D.C.
Saxena, N. C. 1995. *Forests, People and Profit: New Equations for Sustainability*. Centre for Sustainable Development and Natraj Publishers, Dehradun.
Saxena, N. C. 1999. *Forest Policy in India*. New Delhi: WWF-India and International Institute for Environment and Development.
Sharma, B. D. 2010. *Unbroken History of Broken Promises: Indian State and the Tribal People*. New Delhi: Freedom Press and Sahyog Pustak Kuteer.
Thapar, Valmik. 2012. 'Tourism Did Not Kill the Tiger', *Indian Express*, 29 August. Available at: http://www.indianexpress.com/news/tourism-did-not-kill-the-tiger/994472/ (accessed 21 August 2015).

13

'Adivasis' and the Trajectories of Political Mobilization in Contemporary India

Archana Prasad

Contemporary India is seeing the unfolding of the conflict between local people and state-backed corporations in resource-rich, thickly forested regions. A majority of these people consist of dalits, adivasis, and other weaker sections of society who have borne the brunt of corporate capitalism. Though the roots of this conflict are not new, its form and character have changed with the transformations in the nature of capitalism.

This chapter traces the roots and multiple trajectories of political mobilization and conflict between the state and the 'adivasis' in the post-independence era. It analyses the forms of political mobilization and the practices that have come to characterize adivasi rights-based movements and politics in the tribal areas of contemporary India. Conceptually, the chapter distinguishes between the categories of 'tribal' and 'adivasi' on the basis of their relationship with political power and the state. Here, the term 'tribal' largely refers to a state-recognized identity which has existed since colonial times. The 'tribes' were social groups that were socially, economically, and culturally 'primitive'.[1] These groups existed

---

[1] The idea that tribes were primitive has been central to the colonial and official understanding of a tribal society and formed the basis of the paternalistic civilizing mission. The origins of the classification have been discussed in Savyasaachi (1998).

outside the fold of caste Hindu societies; rather, they were historically exploited by them and thus needed protection. The categorization itself was influenced by the European experience in Africa and formed the basis of the understanding that the 'tribes' were pre-class, kinship-based societies which needed to be modernized. They were also social groups that were concentrated in highlands and forested areas through a process of historical oppression, and thus needed to be protected from their caste Hindu brethren.[2] In this way, the institutionalized tribal identity came into existence in the late nineteenth century when the first tribal areas (scheduled areas) were demarcated by the colonial government. These state-recognized tribal groups came to be recognized as 'scheduled tribes' in the Indian Constitution and were defined as people with 'indications of primitive traits, distinctive culture, geographical isolation, shyness of contact with the community at large, and backwardness'.[3]

On the basis of such a definition, the state formulated its hegemonic, paternalistic role which structured the class- and community-based mobilizations in contemporary India. In its essence, this policy was designed in a way to appropriate surplus from resource-rich regions, and compensate the resource-using communities through social welfare measures. Hence, processes of dispossession and class formation coexisted with processes of affirmative action that reproduced non-class, community-based self-expressions. Thus, the term 'tribe' or 'scheduled tribes' came to denote a state-driven and institutionalized identity.

In contrast, the term 'adivasi' largely refers to forms of self-expression that have arisen in opposition to the state-led processes of dispossession. While such an identity has its material basis in the impacts of state-led development, its political expressions are largely concentrated in demystifying and opposing hegemonic developmental processes that have been epitomized in the tribal identity to some extent. In this sense, the 'adivasi' represents a political identity of protest whose character is determined by the social relations in which it is embedded (Prasad 2012). For example, the adivasi politics of communitarian elites is essentially divisive in character and largely based on a competition for political power. On the other hand, the adivasi politics of working-class movements has different structural characteristics, and is rooted

[2] This is one of the major arguments by Shereen Ratnagar in her book *Being Tribal* (2010), and also in her earlier work *The Other Indians* (2004).
[3] For the Nehruvian Panchsheel which structured the paradigm of tribal development, see Nehru (1972).

in a material reality that is not the same as that of the political elites (who were formed as a result of the process of affirmative action and reservations).

Yet the commonality between the two forms of adivasi politics is that they have been formed in opposition to the state-recognized identity whose reproduction is essential in order to maintain the system of affirmative action. In this generic sense, all self-expressions of 'being adivasi' are a form of politics, and the adivasi is essentially a continuously developing political identity that coexists with class differentiation within these social groups.[4] Who this adivasi political identity represents is determined by the class relations in which it is embedded. Such embeddedness also influences the way in which class- and community-based politics deals with adivasi politics in contemporary India. There is no one linear trajectory of adivasi politics. Rather, it has multiple forms and expressions.

This chapter is about the trajectory of adivasi politics in contemporary India. It uses the term 'adivasi' in a generic sense, that is, as a form of politics and an identity of protest. It refers to the 'adivasi' in the context of all struggles and movements even though the movements themselves may have used other terms (even at times the term 'tribal', as in the case of some north-easterners) for the same social groups. This is largely because the chapter identifies and locates the formation of an adivasi political consciousness in its relationship with state-driven hegemonic ideologies (the tribal identity being one such ideological instrument). Therefore, just as the term 'adivasi' is used for the politics of protest, which may or may not be counter-hegemonic depending on its class relations, the terms 'tribe' and 'tribal' are essentially used for state-recognized identities. As I will show, both these categories continuously transform themselves in their forms and expressions depending on their own social basis or the class positions of their protagonists. For this reason, the formation of a tribal or adivasi consciousness is not contrary to but rather related to its material reality in several complex ways. The continuous reproduction of the adivasi consciousness takes place simultaneously with the continuous class differentiation that is taking place within rural society.

It is pertinent to note in this context that today most adivasis are workers or people who sell their labour as a major source of their livelihood. Yet this was not always the case, and the forms of labour changed over time and formed the context of the long contemporary

---

[4] A similar argument has been made by Damodaran (2011).

history of adivasi politics. I will discuss the complex interplay of class forces and the transformations within adivasi politics during different stages and forms of capitalism within the country. I show that the development of the adivasi political consciousness has pluralistic ideological dimensions and is framed by the transforming relationship between state and capital.

THE BIRTH OF A COMMUNITY-BASED 'ADIVASI' POLITICAL CONSCIOUSNESS

The first articulation of the adivasi political community can be traced to the 1930s when adivasi elites responded to state-driven tribal identities by expressing their ambitions for autonomy and independent political rights. This put pressure on mainstream nationalist leaders to negotiate with these groups on the threshold of independence. This negotiation was done in the context of two major developments during colonial capitalism. The first was the proposal for the creation of partially excluded and excluded areas which had been mooted by the British in the Government of India Act, 1935. The practice of scheduling tribal areas had already started under the Scheduled Areas Act, 1874, and this itself had created a space for the formation and articulation of tribal identity (Savyasaachi 1998: Introduction). The second was the process of primary accumulation which led to the alienation of resource-dependent people from their own conditions of production and brought about a considerable displacement of livelihoods. This trend not only led to the migration of several adivasi families but also resulted in their entry into the labour market. Thus, labour became the main mechanism by which these social groups continued to be integrated into the larger colonial capitalist system (Prasad 2010a). In such a scenario, the official discourse of 'tribal welfare' served as a hegemonic tool for centralized decision-making in natural resource management regimes that both structured and camouflaged this process.

The rise of adivasi autonomy movements in the late colonial period has to be seen in a context where a dispossessed leadership used communitarian politics to counter and demystify the state politics of tribal welfare. The most well-known struggles for political autonomy and rights were the Naga and Manipur demands for separation from India on the threshold of independence.[5] There were also demands for

---

[5] For illustrations of this, see the regional examples in Singh (2006).

regional autonomy, the earliest of which was the demand for a separate state of Jharkhand by the Adibasi Mahasabha led by Jaipal Singh. Such articulations took the form of a generic 'adivasi' identity which was identified with all forest dwelling people especially in central and eastern India. Here, specific communities presented themselves as the first inhabitants of their regions with natural rights over their historical homelands. This perhaps was the genesis of 'adivasi' politics in the country, especially in the wake of the Jharkhand Movement of the 1930s when the Adibasi Mahasabha was formed under the leadership of Jaipal Singh. Recounting the beginning of adivasi politics, Jaipal Singh said in 1948 that till then their 'initiative has been of making the primitive man conscious of his political rights. Adibasis have begun to realize that their salvation is in their own hands.'[6] This understanding laid the basis for the subsequent Jharkhand party and its demand for separate statehood that was achieved at the turn of the twentieth century. Writing about it, some activists opine that the creation of the state was a success of Jharkhand nationalism which was 'adivasi' at its core. Here, the term 'adivasi' implies communities of those people who were not integrated into the caste Hindu society of sedentary peasant cultivation (Nathan 2000). For example, it is argued that elites within adivasi societies were incorporated into the caste peasant society and made compromises with the ruling elites to maintain their zamindaris and chieftaincies. Such an understanding implies an overlap between class positions and ethnic political identities, which came to inform all forms of adivasi politics (see, for instance, Sinha 1995).

By the advent of independence, the institutionalization of the state-induced tribal identity was taking place through the debates on the fifth and sixth schedules, whose discourse was framed by the Government of India Act, 1935. The Act allowed for the formation of district and regional councils in order to incorporate the political ambitions of the emerging adivasi elites (see Savyasaachi 1998). Such measures were, however, opposed by many nationalist leaders who saw the demands for such institutions as a part of an isolationist tendency that would create enclaves of traditional life that were aberrations in a modern nation. They accused the drafting committee of imitating imperialist strategies and encouraging separatist tendencies. The nature

---

[6] Jaipal Singh, 'Jai Jharkhand, Jai Adibasi, Jai Hind', address to the All India Adivasi Mahasabha, 28 February 1948, reproduced in Munda and Bosu Mullick (2000: 11).

of opposition was both casteist and communal in nature. While the
north-eastern nationalists accused the Christian missions of instigating
separatist tendencies among the adivasis by helping in the consolidation
of their political identity, at another level the Hindu Mahasabha and
its ideologues questioned the use of the word 'adibasi' or 'adivasi', and
argued for the use of the term *banajati*. The main objection of leaders
like K. M. Munshi lay in the fact that the 'adibasi' did not exist as a
single community, and the differentiation between communities had
to be taken into account.[7] But this understanding was not merely an
analytical and empirical understanding of the formation of the adivasi
identity, but a political understanding which was meant to prevent the
consolidation of the politics of the 'adivasi'. It would also provide the
basis for the expansion of the social basis of Hindu nationalist politics,
a phenomenon that became evident in the post-1980s period with the
expanding work of the Rashtriya Swayamsevak Sangh.

This powerful perspective was countered by advocates of adivasi
rights and a newly emerging political elite. Jaipal Singh, the founder
of the Adibasi Mahasabha, saw the proposals for the fifth and sixth
schedules as a part of a larger process of negotiation with the tribal
people and their relationship with the larger Indian nation. From the
north-east, it was left to the premier of Assam, Gopinath Bordoloi,
and Rev. Nicholas Roy, a tribal member from the hilly areas of Assam,
to provide a more substantive argument against the assimilation of
tribal people. Replying to insinuations that the government had failed
to understand the need for assimilation of tribal people, Bordoloi
made his most passionate plea against assimilation when he stated that
'there are certain institutions amongst these hill tribes which, in my
opinion are so good that if we wanted to destroy them I consider it
to be very wrong'. Nicholas Roy went a step further and asked why
these communities should assimilate themselves into a higher culture
when they had a better culture than them.[8] The emerging political
elites thus articulated adivasi identity and its cultural differences in
opposition to two different hegemonies. The first was the concept of
the state-sponsored notion of the 'tribal', and the other the Hindu

---

[7] For a fuller discussion of this, see the exchange between K. M. Munshi
and Jaipal Singh in the Constituent Assembly on 5 September 1949, quoted in
Savyasaachi (1998).

[8] Constituent Assembly debates, 6 September 1949, quoted in Savyasaachi
(1998).

nationalist notion of the banajati, or what was later called *banvasi* (forest dwellers).

The conditions for the birth of adivasi political consciousness emerged in response to several competitive hegemonic influences at the time of independence. Adivasi demands were shaped by the need to counter the tools of ideological domination that were structured so as to strengthen the systems of primary accumulation in resource-rich regions. But the ideologies of domination did not emanate from the state alone, but also from socially and economically powerful classes whose interests were closely bound with trading and industrial capital. In this context, the politics of the 'adivasi' did not represent any specific ethnic or social group. Rather, it represented a new political community where sociocultural symbolism became the norm of expression. Such a cultural expression was shaped by both the processes of accumulation by the state as well as the institutionalization of the state-structured tribal identity in independent India. Independent India's new tribal policy recognized the culturally specific character of these social groups without giving adequate recognition to their ecological and economic specificity. This led to an overdeveloped identity which did not necessarily represent a direct relationship with its material basis. Though the Nehruvian state propagated programmes of tribal welfare, it also intensified the process of dispossession, which led to the formation of a labouring class. This was reflected in the Nehruvian policies of multipurpose block development programmes that invested heavily in social programmes but very little in productive resources (Prasad 2009). It was the impact of these programmes that influenced the development of an informed political leadership which saw itself with some access to political power but no access to its own natural resources. Hence the discourse of the adivasi was informed by the changing character of the independent Indian state, and the development of an adivasi consciousness was intimately linked with the character of state policies. This formative asymmetry was the defining fulcrum of class- and community-based politics in tribal regions.

CLASS-BASED POLITICS AND THE ADIVASI CONSCIOUSNESS

Independent India also saw another form of adivasi politics whose social basis lay in class-based political organization by the communists. Such political mobilization was largely a result of the revolts which occurred in the post-Second World War period, and carried on well into the

1950s and 1960s.[9] The most famous of these revolts were the Telangana, Tebhaga, and Warli struggles. However, one of the oldest communist-led tribal organizations was the Ganamukti Parishad in the north-eastern state of Tripura. Though the struggles were largely a result of the organization of landless agricultural workers, many of them led to the specific organization of 'tribal people' and also created alternative, open-ended identities. This was especially the case with the Warli struggle led by Godavari Parulekar, and the continuous organization of tribal people by the less-known movements of Tripura's Ganamukti Parishad and Kerala's Punnapra Vayalar revolt (see, for instance, Debbarma 1986; Namboodiripad 1952). The development of the Warli and the Tripura organizations in the post-independence period is especially interesting in helping to analyse the relationship between class and community structures. This relationship was mediated by the understanding that the organization of adivasi people would help in building a common understanding and strengthening the alliance between peasants and workers.

Communist work in these regions had already led to the formation of multiple political identities which were shaped by their own local contexts. However, there were some similarities in the methods of organization and mobilization that led to the articulation of an adivasi consciousness which was embedded in a perspective of working-class unity. This simultaneous articulation and existence of a non-class adivasi and working-class consciousness was an organized attempt, and not the natural outcome of larger changes in the adivasi social structure. For example, Godavari Parulekar's narrative *Adivasi Revolt: The Story of the Struggle of the Warlis* (1975) traces the existence of an adivasi consciousness to the process of accumulation that was born out of the penetration of colonial and national capital. Hence, the whole idea of the 'adivasi' was the result of a certain dispossession and was constituted in opposition to the concentration of capital and accumulation of surplus by the ruling classes represented by large landowners and traders (Parulekar 1975: 1–3). The processes of dispossession were multilayered and articulated themselves at several levels. In the first instance, there were struggles against the low wages and unpaid labour of the contractors working for large companies. Another level of articulation was achieved through land struggles, which acknowledged the historical land dispossession of the

[9] For details on the class-based struggles of the early independence period, see Desai (1979).

adivasis. These land struggles were essentially based on a redistributive agenda that organized adivasis to take over the surplus land of large landholders. By doing so, they strengthened the collective power of the small peasants and also protected their landholdings against the large landlords (Rasul 1974).

This meant that the articulation of an 'adivasi' consciousness by Warli tribals in Thane and of the *upjati* (tribal communities) consciousness in Tripura was not inimical to the idea of a larger class unity amongst all dispossessed people. It also aided the process of class formation of 'adivasis', as both peasants and agricultural workers, through a concerted sectional organization. In this sense, the adivasi consciousness articulated within and embedded in the communist movement was democratically constituted and transformative in character. It sought to organize adivasis as dispossessed peasants who would contribute to the larger fight for land reforms even while they also reproduced a historically constituted adivasi consciousness. This class based adivasi consciousness had multiple layers as it organized the adivasis for land, on the one hand, and for getting the benefits of state-led affirmative action, on the other hand. This complex phenomenon was, however, never theorized within the communist movement, as its primary aim remained the restoration of land rights and the organization of adivasis for higher wages.

It is interesting to note that different strands of the communist movement attempted to resolve the problem of the overlap between class positions and the articulation of non-class adivasi consciousness. In Thane district, the adivasi were organized primarily as dispossessed peasants even though their specific needs were sought to be addressed through the formation of a social service organization, the adivasi *mandal* (organization), which began to address the problems of tribal education. Even though the adivasis occupied land through their land struggles, the lack of a 'legal title' and recognition of their rights by the state structured the articulation of a specific adivasi identity. Further, the process of affirmative action put into place by the independent Indian state also ensured that the communist parties organized different sectional interests for their legitimate rights. Thus, the communist mass organizations organized SC and tribal students within the framework of the larger students' movement in states like Andhra Pradesh. In Dahanu taluka of Thane, they continued to struggle for legalization of land rights in fifth schedule areas and also organized adivasis for their own forest rights. That this consciousness was predicated on a perspective that the 'adivasis' themselves needed to be modernized is evident from the fact that the communists set up schools and colleges to organize neighbourhood tribal people. They were, however, forced to recognize some community characteristics of adivasi life which were being strengthened by competing organizations like the Kashtkari Sangathana. As a scholar writing the history of peasant organizations in Thane explains, the problem of bridging the gap between peasant consciousness and adivasi consciousness remains despite successful economic struggles that have given dignity to the Warlis (Brahme and Upadhyaya 2004).

In the north-eastern state of Tripura, the relationship between the communist movement and the adivasi consciousness has evolved along a different trajectory. The Ganamukti Parishad began as the Jan Shiksha movement in the hilly regions of Tripura and was formed much before the communist political organization. The Parishad was largely an organization of adivasi youth leadership which laid the foundations of the Ganamukti Parishad. The Parishad itself was a militant organization that started as a campaign for civil rights, political participation, and economic development of the tribal people living in the highlands in the early decades after independence. The Ganamukti Parishad leadership did not itself believe in an exclusivist adivasi consciousness, and tried to create a unity between the Bengalis and adivasis. The pro-tribal measures and the consistent advocacy and struggle for autonomous district councils revealed the communist-led Ganamukti Parishad's understanding of tribal exclusivism. It considered the sixth schedule as a way of transforming and democratizing the tribal societies themselves in order to develop leadership amongst working-class adivasis. It also saw the schedule as a measure to correct the political imbalances between adivasis and others, especially the Bengalis. Kokborok (the local dialect) was given due recognition (Bhattacharya 1998: 162–96). This was another way of accessing tribal people and transforming their consciousness. Thus, though the effort of the Ganamukti Parishad was specific to its context, it tried to mobilize adivasis around a mode of modern politics and to build their linkages with the larger movement. In the process, the Parishad attempted to organize working-class adivasis to intervene in their own situation and democratize their own societies.

There was also a third trajectory of the communist mobilization of adivasis in the form of the Naxalbari movement. Ideologues of the movement worked largely amongst the Santhal peasantry of West Bengal. It is well known that the effective implementation of land reforms was one of the main demands of the communist movement. Therefore, with the formation of the United Front government in West Bengal (with the communists as partners) in 1967, the Communist Party of India (Marxist) (CPI[M]) minister of land revenue, Hare Krishna Konar, announced the redistribution of surplus lands amongst the peasants. However, the process of implementation of land reforms was a difficult one, and the landlords took the help of the bureaucracy in order to resist the seizure of land. In addition, there was no legal provision for the confiscation of *benami* lands, or lands purchased in the name of others, which were occupied by the landlords. This accentuated the conflict between the landlords and the peasantry, and led to the organization of the Naxalbari uprising amongst the tribal peasantry of Jalpaiguri under the radical leadership of a faction of the All India Kisan Sabha (Sanyal 1978).

While building a non-exclusivist adivasi consciousness was the hallmark of a class based perspective, it must be borne in mind that the different strategies of communist-led adivasi mobilization were primarily a result of the way in which the different trends of the larger movement resolved the problems of relating the class position of the adivasis with the reproduction of a sectional political consciousness. The undivided communist party (and later the CPI and CPI[M]) recognized the strategic value of fostering a democratic adivasi consciousness which needed to be reproduced in order to avail of the benefits of affirmative action. Yet this consciousness would have little meaning if it was not grounded in the larger agrarian movement which would socialize the adivasis into class-based politics. The Naxal movement altogether ignored the existence of a community consciousness and saw the formation of a class consciousness as obliterating all forms of pre-modern community-based politics (Banerjee 1984; Singh 1995). In both cases, the underlying assumption appeared to treat the adivasi as a dispossessed peasant who needed to be organized around land rights. In this sense, the adivasi consciousness may have persisted in political practice, but was not reflected in the theoretical paradigm of communist thinking. Clearly, one strand of the communist movement considered the reproduction of a democratic adivasi consciousness as a political necessity. Yet this recognition did not reinterpret the way in which the sectional adivasi consciousness would continue to coexist and overlap with class-based politics within the framework of state capitalism. This ideological shortcoming ensured that the seminal struggles of the early independence period did not lead to a more generalized understanding of the adivasi question within Marxist thinking.

REGIONALISM, CULTURAL BOUNDARIES, AND THE APOGEE OF ADIVASI POLITICS

The resurgence of the 'adivasi' identity as a strategy of mobilization by the adivasi political elite was structured by some macro trends in the post-Green Revolution period. The material basis of existence and the uneven impact of state capitalism had led to a push towards the formation of a rural working class amongst the adivasis. The seasonal migration of tribal people largely consisted of inter-district movement by women, and migration for construction and other types of non-farm work by the men (Prasad 2009).[10]

The enactment of the Forest Conservation Act, 1980, accentuated the problems of dispossession and put forest lands under direct control of the central government. It also laid down the procedures for the diversion of forest lands for non-forestry purposes. It thus opened the door to the penetration of big capital into these areas. This was evident from the fact that the rate of diversion of forest lands between 1950 and 1980 was about 10,000 hectares per year and more than half of this was done for agriculture. In 1980–9, however, this rate of diversion went up by 60 per cent to about 17 lakh hectares per annum. What is more, the purpose of diversion was quite different: whereas more than half of the diversion in the pre-1980 period was for agriculture, after 1980 it was largely for big developmental and industrial projects. This legalization and facilitation of the diversion process was accompanied by the designation of many tribal and non-tribal settlers as illegal encroachers if they were unable to prove that they had occupied and resided in forest lands before the enforcement of the Act (that is, before 25 October 1980) (Prasad 2010c: 118).

The process of diversion had implications for the organization of tribal people. In the case of diversion for agriculture, the contradictions between tribals and non-tribals sharpened, but in the case of diversion for industry, the possibilities of unity between tribal and non-tribal people became greater. The 1980s also saw the emergence of the first foreign-funded social forestry projects that sought to manage the problem of fuelwood for industry. The implementation of the 1952 forest policy

---

[10] For the gendered impacts of these movements, also see the chapter 'More Marginal than the Marginalised' in Prasad (2011).

had made it amply clear that people's participation was necessary if plantations were to be successfully managed.[11]

The twin impacts of the emergence of a new, well-informed adivasi leadership because of affirmative action and the exploitative, uneven development arising out of the process of diversion led to the resurgence of adivasi identity politics. This politics became a part of a larger counter-hegemonic process that contested state capitalism on the question of rights and control over productive resources, on the one hand, and the assertion of cultural identity on the other (Heredia 2002–3). This politics of adivasi rights was accompanied and supported by local struggles centred on control over local resources and a radical critique of 'modern development' itself. Such a critique also distinguished itself from the earlier class-based struggles over land and forest rights and for greater social control over the public sector. Rather, it advocated community control over local resources, as it identified the 'modern' state as the main exploiter of the tribal people. In this situation, the nation-state was seen not as a site of struggle, but as an institution that had to gradually fade out from local management of resources and be replaced by the neo-traditional idea of the community (Prasad 2010b). In this sense, the post-Nehruvian capitalist regime structured its own brand of primordial oppositional politics, setting the stage for a qualitative shift in the resource management regime which began to use the vocabulary of identity politics. Finally, the identification of the 'adivasi' with 'indigeneity' was largely accomplished by the formation of the UN-sponsored Indigenous Peoples Working Group in which 'adivasi' elites were active (Roy Burman 1994).

The re-emergence of the movement for a separate Jharkhand state and its expanding discursive boundaries need to be seen in this context. The second phase of the movement began with a critique of the developmental approaches of Nehruvian state capitalism. The tribal regions were identified as the 'fourth world' which faced processes of internal colonialism from the non-tribal regions. The articulation of this deprivation was structured through a discourse of the community, even though several sections within the movement were attempting to organize the working classes within the community. Thus, leaders like

---

[11] One of the most successful projects was the social forestry project (a precursor of JFM) in Bengal, which was significantly different from others. See Prasad (2010b: chapter 3).

A. K. Roy and Shankar Guha Niyogi preferred the regional identities that displayed a sense of regional discrimination. While A. K. Roy as a member of the Jharkhand Party wrote and argued about a 'Jharkhandi identity', Niyogi wrote about the right of self-determination of the people of Chhattisgarh. For both, control over land and resources was crucially linked to the question of separate statehood. This approach was different from the tribal exclusivism that was displayed by the Jharkhand Mukti Morcha (JMM) and Jharkhand Party in the 1970s and 1980s, even though Roy the trade unionist backed the demand and joined the united struggle for a separate Jharkhand (Sengupta 1982; see also Kumar 2000; Roy 2000). In contrast, Shankar Guha Niyogi's Chhattisgarh Mukti Morcha explicitly stated that the Chhattisgarh state, as visualized by the tribal political elite, would not yield much benefit to the working classes amongst these social groups. This overlap between social group and class was rather understated and almost never expressed in terms of 'adivasi' or 'tribal identity' (Sadgopal and Namr 1993). Hence it needs to be contrasted with the traditional 'adivasi' identities that were created by the tribal political elites.

The political expression of the 'adivasi' has been linked to the idea of culture and place. Its critique of the modern world is predicated on two fundamental principles. The first is the idea that the 'adivasi' is the original inhabitant of her surroundings and the struggle for control over resources is born not out of dependence but a historical right to their original homelands.[12] This conception of a historical homeland is a part of the larger organic nationalism that considers control over resources as an essential part of self-determination and self-rule. Interestingly, it is not the political elites among the adivasis who have made this connection, but leaders like Guha Niyogi who linked the national question to the land question. Some scholars also term this struggle of the 'original' inhabitants 'ecological nationalism' (Cederlöf and Sivaramakrishnan 2005). While rule over their own lands is crucial to the core conception of the 'adivasi', it is important to underline that land not only refers to agriculture, but the links of agriculture with other resources, particularly forests.

Myths about the forests being the original abode of the 'adivasis' have been revived from the writings of anthropologists and have been used to normalize the idea that the 'adivasis' were the kings of the forests and had

---

[12] For an exploration and critique of this conception, see Prasad (2011: chapter 1).

always lived inside them. In this sense, the idea of the 'adivasi' reinforced the belief that they were people of the forests. This was also different from the understanding of the class-based movements which analysed historical displacement from agricultural land and the settlement of 'adivasis' in forests as a process of their marginalization. Significantly, such a process of marginalization in the pre-colonial period has been termed as 'adjustment and coexistence' by pioneer environmental historians in India (Gadgil and Guha 1992). The political motivation for such a construction, however, becomes clear when forest dwelling 'adivasis' rightly struggle for their legitimate rights over forest use at the height of state capitalism in forests after the decade of the 1970s. Hence the myth of the 'original inhabitant' is itself a creation of the process of primitive accumulation after the establishment of monopoly of control over forests.

The second core value of the 'adivasi' ideology is the idea of a moral superiority (in terms of egalitarian and democratic values) and the cultural practices that form an essential part of the identity. Of particular significance is the fact that the JMM under the leadership of Shibu Soren mobilized ordinary 'adivasis' for struggle by propagating the preservation of cultural values and practices that would act as markers of adivasi life. Hence, the political struggle for survival was seen as a cultural struggle to preserve the community. In this sense, the creation of cultural boundaries that determine the limits of the political community is an essential component of being adivasi. Documentation of language and practices and an attempt to create an exclusive mode of communication that bound together several cultures were instruments used by the adivasi leadership for achieving this.

However, such cultural symbolism almost always creates conflicts within the idea of the adivasi identity. Susana Devalle (1992) describes this process amongst the Hinduized adivasi communities and the Christian adivasis of Jharkhand. The sense of adivasi identity is much stronger amongst the Christian adivasis who have created their own literature and social spaces. In this regard, the reformist as well as missionary influences are well known. A good example of the protection of social spaces is the creation of *akhara*s or informal schools by the JMM in order to reproduce the practices and values that exemplified their identity. Similarly, the observance of Jharkhand Divas as a way of celebrating Jharkhand culture is again symbolic of the cultural protest that has come to represent the struggle for self-dignity and self-esteem.

Within this framework, egalitarian social codes and customs are posited as alternatives to the unequal exploitative relations created by the modern state. Thus, harmony with nature and with humans is an essential characteristic of the ideology of such politics. Of particular interest is the projection of the status of women within this society in order to prove the moral superiority and greater democracy among the adivasis. The idea that women have freedom of mobility, the right to multiple marriages, and co-equal powers within marriage has been suggested in several anthropological texts and reproduced within the adivasi image. Customary codes have been projected as being both prudent and egalitarian even with respect to nature. This has helped to position the adivasi politics and image as an alternative to state-driven and -controlled systems of conservation.

Thus, the use of 'adivasi' as a tool of mobilization and opposition to existing forms of domination has resulted in a cultural revivalism for facilitating the creation of a larger political community. The struggles for the creation of Jharkhand and Chhattisgarh in the last two decades of the twentieth century were a reflection of this effort. They also reveal the hegemonic implications of the imagery that was used to create the social basis of the struggles (Prasad 2011). It is well known that many of these struggles were led by the erstwhile ruling classes among the tribal people, and this was reflected in the nature of the symbolism itself. For example, the dominance of Mundari symbolism, Santhali vernacular vocabulary, and several other social customs of larger tribes tends to obfuscate the voices of smaller tribal groups. Further, the apparently egalitarian character of the adivasis also ignores and obfuscates the trials, tribulations, and burdens of adivasi women. Any acknowledgement of this would only expose the fault lines of the imagined adivasi community that has achieved its limited objective of getting a separate Jharkhand and Chhattisgarh state at the turn of the century.[13] These fault lines have become even more evident with the use of the 'community' metaphor by external funding agencies in order to drive policy reforms. It shows that the ideal of self-rule and management of resources envisioned by 'adivasi' politics is an agenda that can be incorporated into mainstream neoliberalism.

[13] For the perspective of an egalitarian community, see Kelkar and Nathan (2003). For its critique, see Prasad (2008a).

COMPLEMENTARY HEGEMONIES: HINDUTVA AND THE NEOLIBERAL ORDER

With all its limitations, the politics of the adivasi is counter-hegemonic to a limited degree, and has served as an important focal point of opposition to state capitalism. But the language and non-class, community character of this protest has faced severe challenges in the face of two dominant tendencies: the establishment of the neoliberal paradigm, and the expansion of Hindutva politics in the tribal region. These two tendencies are interrelated and reflect the crisis in the social welfare system that was crucial to the growth of an adivasi political leadership. As mentioned earlier, in contrast to an 'indigenous' adivasi identity, the Sangh Parivar stresses the identity of the 'banvasi' or primitive forest dwelling people whose modernization process would only be complete when they are assimilated into Hindu society. This process of assimilation intensified during the period of the National Democratic Alliance regime (Sundar 2002).

The second factor aiding the expansion of right-wing Hindu forces led by the arms of the Rashtriya Swayamsevak Sangh in the tribal areas is their linkages with mainstream nationalism. Ideologically, both social and political forces work on the assumption that the reform of 'Hindu' society would help in an effective integration of adivasis into the mainstream society. But there is one difference between the two forces. Most Gandhian social reform movements spoke not only of the need to uplift the tribal people, but also of the need to reform Hindu society itself so that they could be assimilated within it as equals. This alliance of mainstream nationalism with right-wing nationalists in order to edge out Christian missionaries has played an important role in the expansion of such organizations (see Prasad 2011: chapter 3). Hence, the 1970s saw the setting up of several mass social reform fronts like the Vanvasi Kalyan Ashrams, and their rapid expansion after the Emergency and the revival of the Jan Sangh. By the turn of the century, there were Vanvasi Kalyan Ashrams in 8,955 places in 312 districts of the country under the supervision of 1,203 full-time workers. The movement received a definite fillip after the Bharatiya Janata Party (BJP) came to power. The Tribal Affairs Ministry and the Khadi and Village Industries Commission were used by the government to dole out grants to those non-governmental organizations (NGOs) and voluntary sector organizations that were steadily implementing the BJP agenda in these regions. More than 85 per cent of the funds of the Schedule Castes and Tribes Commission were given to NGOs associated with the Sangh Parivar in Madhya Pradesh and Jharkhand (Prasad 2004).

However, it is important to unveil the relationship between the expansion of Hindutva forces and the social classes that formed the foundations for the opening up of the forest economies on which the 'adivasis' had become dependent. Aggressive Hindutva (in the form of reconversion campaigns) in the post-Mandal period and the initiation of policies aiding corporate capital exemplified the BJP rule at the centre. Its policies revealed that most of this opening up had taken place for the benefit of the traders, big companies, and foreign interests who funded the activities of the Vanvasi Kalyan Ashram and Saraswati Shiksha Sansthan (an umbrella organization of all Parivar educational institutions). It is no coincidence, then, that the Shishu Mandir Trust is headed by one of the largest Marwari traders of Kolkata, and its local branches are patronized by influential landholders and traders. Thus, the activities of the Sangh Parivar have ended up strengthening rather than dismantling the very forces that have been exploiting the tribal people since the advent of the British rule in these areas.[14]

The policies of the National Democratic Alliance government (1998–2004) strengthened and aided this process. Disinvestment of industries like BALCO, and the privatization of land, water, and forest resources as in the case of the Sheonath River, will only lead to further deprivation and unemployment among tribal people. The withdrawal of the state from key sectors has led to the reduction of state investment in infrastructure development. In this context, all attempts at the decentralized management of forests and forest produce collection have strengthened traders, industrialists, and multinational companies who are appropriating the knowledge, labour, and resources of tribal people for their own profit.

The second major characteristic of the neoliberal paradigm has been the withdrawal of the state from welfare services that have been crucial to the survival of 'tribal people'. The constricting of job and employment opportunities has created new types of conflict, evident in the Kandhamal riots of 2008 which took a communal turn through the formation of a 'Hinduized tribal identity' under the influence of Hindutva forces. The conflict between Christian dalits and the Kui and Kandh Hinduized tribals began with the Christian Pano demanding ST status. But the Kui Samaj opposed this and received the full support of the Sangh leader

[14] For the politics of reconversion, see Kumar and Sunny (2009).

Lakshmananda Saraswati. Inspired by this support, the Samaj called for a bandh on Christmas day, resulting in the riots of December 2007. The demand of the Pano assumes importance because Odisha Vishva Hindu Parishad (VHP) secretary Gauri Prasad Rath stated that the Parivar organizations would ensure that those who converted to Christianity would not get the benefits of any reservation and would lose both their SC and ST status. This demonstrated how right-wing forces can hamper the unity of the welfare-dependent tribal societies in their opposition to dominant and exploitative influences (Chatterji 2009; see also Prasad 2008b).

The third feature which is characteristic of this period is the changing relationship between adivasi politics and the state. Since corporate penetration in tribal areas is led and facilitated by the state, its power to negotiate with the adivasi political elite has decreased. Consequently, the repression of opposition to corporate capitalism has also increased manifold. However, in contrast to this tendency, there is also another apparently contradictory trend. The discourse of recognition of the legitimate rights of adivasi people has been incorporated within the neoliberal state to some extent, as illustrated by the enactment of the Scheduled Tribes and Other Traditional Forest Dwellers (Recognition of Forest Rights) Act, 2006. The Act not only revised the deadline for the settlement of rights from 1980 to December 2005, but also enumerated 13 types of rights over land and produce. It widened the scope of the rights to include people who were displaced and people living in national parks and sanctuaries. But above all, it attempted to democratize the rights settlement process by making the panchayats responsible for the initiation of the process. It also laid down stringent conditions for the diversion of forest lands that were settled under the Act. Some of these radical and important provisions were not mooted at the initiative of the state, but the result of the recommendations of the joint parliamentary committee. This committee opened up the process of legislation to public debate and negotiated changes by providing a platform to tribal rights organizations, democratic movements, and some political formations like the left. But on closer examination, it is evident that the neoliberal state has been able to make some fundamental changes in the Act by inserting some limiting provisions in the fine print. It has thus been able to use its state power to protect the interests of the forest bureaucracy, the conventional environmentalists, and industry.[15]

---

[15] One of the major changes was with respect to recognizing the rights of non-STs. While accepting the condition of residence in forests for three generations,

The impact of these three factors is further exemplified by a looming agrarian crisis that has dried up all employment opportunities for agricultural labour. There are serious implications and challenges posed to adivasi politics by these wide-ranging structural changes. In the wake of increasing landlessness and displacement, the 'adivasi' worker has increasingly entered the mass of the casual labour force, which is largely migratory and mobile in nature. At the same time, the disinvestment in state-led tribal welfare programmes and the intensification of the penetration of corporate capital has increased the likelihood of overlap between adivasi and working-class consciousness. Such an emerging trend is decidedly incompatible with the aggressive adivasi politics which is based more on a sharp critique of 'modern' development, and not of the capitalist form of modern development (Prasad 2010c: 112).

THE RISE OF MAOISM IN NEOLIBERAL TIMES

The last two decades of neoliberalism have seen the acceleration of corporate penetration into resource-rich regions. This paradigm is based on the understanding that the market is the best equalizer. The mushrooming of open market trade in forest produce with big industry resulted in both land alienation and livelihood dispossession, which in

---

the bill defined one generation as equal to 25 years. This meant that non-STs would have to prove that they have lived in the forests for at least 75 years or since 1930 if they were to benefit from that legislation. The second change made by the government was with regard to the definition and powers of the gram sabha. Now the definition of 'gram sabha' had been altered from a 'hamlet-based panchayat' to a revenue panchayat, which in many areas is dominated by upper castes in the non-scheduled areas. The government had also ensured that the gram sabha was no longer the final authority to settle rights (as recommended by the joint parliamentary committee) by giving the subdivisional committee this power. The third change that the government made was in the nature of rights granted under the bill. Fuelwood, bamboo, stones, and so on, were kept out of the definition of minor forest produce, and the bill was silent on the right of multiple land use by people practising shifting cultivation. Further, the right to transportation of produce from national parks and sanctuaries had also been tampered with. Finally, the clauses making the gram sabha's consent mandatory in cases of diversion of forest lands ensuring a minimum support price for minor forest produce had been deleted as they hindered the penetration of market forces into tribal areas. For detailed discussions of this, see the special issue on Forest and Tribals in *Seminar*, August 2005. Also see Prasad (2006a, 2006b).

turn resulted in the emergence of a tribal and dalit rural working class. This working class was largely employed as agricultural and casual labour in both government and private enterprises and farms. Such corporate capitalism has been marked by three significant features that characterize neoliberal reforms in tribal areas.

The first is the rapid pace of corporate penetration through land acquisition in tribal regions. Of particular importance is the qualitative change in the process of diversion of forest lands for big projects. Much of this diversion is a result of the increase in mining leases and infrastructural projects. In the first decade of reforms, the rate of the diversion of forests was approximately 21,000 hectares per year, but this figure went up to about 70,000 hectares in the second decade, especially from 2004 onwards. This diversion is largely for mining companies who are now forcing the corporate takeover of mining resources and creating serious social conflicts within these regions (Prasad 2010c: 118). Roads and electricity and other types of projects are essential to opening up markets for natural resources. This has been seen in areas like Bastar, which has one of the biggest markets for minor forest products. At the same time, the much-acclaimed Pradhan Mantri Gram Sadak Yojana in Jharkhand also opened up mineral resources to corporate capital, generating new types of conflicts.

While the development of infrastructure has given a comparative advantage to states to attract corporate investment, the tribal people continue to be bereft of basic facilities. Eighty-four per cent of them have no drinking water and 93 per cent lack any decent housing or toilet facilities. This shows that the entire diversion process is not aimed at the overall development of the tribal villages, but only at the opening up of natural resources to the unregulated market. All this has ensured that the primary conflict of interests is now between the adivasis and big capital. Similarly, where the interests of forest dwelling people have come into direct conflict with private corporate capital, the state has taken the side of corporate capital, often leading to large-scale police atrocities and violent suppression of adivasi protests.

The contemporary politics of the adivasi is defined by this context and has taken certain specific forms. The first thing to be noticed is the incorporation of adivasi elites within the framework of the neoliberal state. Thus, it is not surprising that some of the most aggressive policies for corporate penetration in resource-rich areas have been followed in Chhattisgarh, Jharkhand, and Odisha. The impact of such penetration has led to the semi-proletarianization of the adivasis and widened the class divide among adivasis. The rising influence of the Maoists in central India reflects the inability of adivasi elite politics to cope with the impact of corporate capitalism and effectively check its advance. While it is true that many local struggles have erupted against specific instances of corporate penetration, especially in the case of mining leases (for example, Vedanta and Posco in Odisha), these localized struggles have been overshadowed by the violent conflict between the 'Maoists'[16] and the Indian state. Though the impact and character of Maoism is debated in scholarly writings, there is no doubt that the uneven development of tribal areas has led to political domination by armed Maoist guerrillas in the forested tracts of central and eastern India. Because of this, scholars and activists find legitimacy for Maoists' activities in these root causes, and assume mass support by the adivasis for Maoist operations. Hence, the 'Maoists' represent the 'people' and have no option but to retaliate against the initiation of counter-insurgency tactics like Salwa Judum or the paramilitary force-led Operation Green Hunt.

However, this picture is a simplistic one, as it does not explain the differences between the emergence and strengthening of Maoism in areas where land reforms have occurred and in places where they have not occurred so far. Thus, the Maoist activity in West Bengal is propelled by factors that are different from those in the states of Jharkhand and Chhattisgarh. In this context, it is important to note that in West Bengal, about 20 per cent of the 29.88 million beneficiaries of land reforms belonged to the STs. In the three districts of the Jangal Mahal areas where the Maoists are now active, there were about 2.5 million tribal people who became title holders of surplus land, and about 40,000 got sharecropping rights.[17] But these factors do not mean that no more work is to be done in tribal areas. This is in sharp contrast to areas like Chhattisgarh and Jharkhand which have a history of tribal people losing their lands to non-tribal farmers, moneylenders, and traders. Hence, while the land factor may have played an important role in creating the space for the Maoists in Chhattisgarh and Jharkhand, the same cannot be said of West Bengal.[18]

In Bengal, Maoist violence and opposition has been structured by left politics, and the current dilemmas that it faces as a consequence of the

---

[16] Those belonging to CPI (Maoists) but not necessarily following the Chinese Maoist ideology.

[17] Government of West Bengal, *Economic Review 2009–2010*, calculated from appendix tables.

[18] For a critique of the Maoist strategy, see Grewal (2010).

neoliberal environment and the long-term impact of its three decades of rule. Despite the successes of land reforms and democratization of forest management, the relative gap between the tribal people and others persists within the state. These problems of uneven development are likely to get accentuated if a new egalitarian vision of tribal development is not developed by the larger democratic movement. The Maoist opposition in Bengal needs to be seen in the light of this larger challenge. It has been pointed out that this armed opposition is primarily aimed at stifling dialogue and debate and generating an anti-left and anti-democratic politics (AIDWA 2009). Such a politics relies less on opposition to neoliberalism and more on political violence, where the elimination of the organized left has become a precondition for its growth and expansion.

In contrast, Maoist expansion in Chhattisgarh and Jharkhand may be seen as the result of the failure of primordial and communitarian 'adivasi' politics to deal with the neoliberal challenge. This situation has arisen because of the way in which neoliberal ideology was able to coopt the vocabulary of community ownership and control into its own framework. It thus exposed the inadequacy of primordial identity politics to provide an alternative discourse of resistance. Moreover, the recent analysis of Maoist ideology and practice in these areas has also shown that they do not pose any real threat or challenge to the neoliberal resource management regime.[19] Though the Maoists may have used the strategy of building mass organizations around issues of daily importance, their practices changed radically once they established their control. This is clearly evident in Dantewada, where the establishment of a 'Maoist liberated zone' provided a safe military base to leaders and cadres who were facing action from the state police in Andhra Pradesh. Many of these cadres had also been politically dislocated from the tribal villages which they had once dominated in the agency areas, because their social base had shifted to other mainstream left political parties who had begun to challenge their politics. Hence, it is not surprising that the first forays of the Maoists were on the Andhra–Chhattisgarh border, and their guerrilla base has also been set up there.

At the same time, the absence of the state and its limited impact from the pre-reform days onwards has also influenced Maoist growth. The increase in the rate and intensity of penetration of global industrial

---

[19] For detailed analysis of the political and ideological practice of the CPI (Maoists) in Chhattisgarh, see Prasad (2010d).

capital has added to and matured this process. In the process, the Maoists have ended up using and manipulating both local villagers and the market forces to strengthen their infrastructure and forces through the extraction of surplus (Prasad 2010d). An analysis of the working of the guerrilla base shows that the Maoists tend to be a mirror image of the exploitative state where tactics of repression and taxation are concerned. In fact, their processes of attracting surplus labour and taxes do not spare even those people who are ordinarily outside the net of taxation in a mainstream policy regime. Hence, even though Maoists may appear to be expressing the aspirations of an ordinary tribal, in reality they cannot provide a credible opposition to neoliberal market forces on which they partly depend for their survival. Rather, the character of their control and politics has discredited other social and political movements in the region and made them, and the 'adivasi' society, more vulnerable to the violence of the current neoliberal state.

CLASS, COMMUNITY, AND ADIVASI POLITICS

Thus, the ideological and tactical failures of primordial and Maoist politics in dealing with neoliberalism pose a new challenge, where the differences between class-based politics and communitarian adivasi politics are becoming easier to resolve. This has been seen in the confrontations between corporate houses, the Indian state, and grassroots adivasi organizations in both the Vedanta and Posco cases. The first indications of such confrontation came from Odisha almost eight years ago when the Odisha government killed several adivasi protesters whose lands were being acquired by a Tata steel plant. This protest marked a watershed in the way in which neo-traditional movements coincided with other class-based adivasi struggles. The subsequent Posco and Vedanta struggles have been launched as rainbow coalitions between different class- and community-based organizations. They are born out of resistance to land acquisition and dispossession of tribal people from their own lands. The discourse of such protests has been diverse and overarching in character. It takes the form of legalistic as well as militant protest and expresses itself in diverse forms, some of which are communitarian in character while others emphasize modern democratic rights.

An example of such a protest was initially seen in the case of opposition to bauxite mining in Andhra Pradesh. Samatha, a local non-governmental group, approached the high court to stop mining without the consent of the local gram sabha in 1995 (Prasad 2010b). The court ruling (known as the Samatha Judgement) that the panchayat's consent was necessary for mining became one of the main instruments in the hands of the resistance movements. Another current example of sustained militant struggle is the anti-Vedanta movement, which was supported by both scholars and activists. The villagers argued that protecting Niyamgiri was not merely a necessity for economic survival but also a matter of their cultural rights. Hence, the trope of the Niyam Raja was used to mobilize all affected people of the area and also for appeal to the courts. The have once again ruled that the consent of the panchayats is needed before environmental and forest clearances are given to the Vedanta project (Prasad 2013). This victory led to the temporary stalling of the project despite police repression. In the case of Posco too, the state sided with the company, but the local coordination committee, Posco Pratirodh Sangram Samiti, worked with all democratic and left forces to wage a protracted and continuing struggle (see Padel and Das 2010). Once again, the state sided with the corporates and used repressive and intimidatory tactics to suppress the struggles. But the rainbow coalition between scholars, activists, mass organizations, and the local committee have helped to keep the resistance alive.

These are just some examples of the developing conflicts and struggles in the adivasi regions. These continuing struggles also show that the impact of neoliberal policies and the current form of corporate capital has widened the gap between the adivasi working class and the adivasi elites. But the proletarianization of the adivasis has also provided a window of opportunity to build a unity between community- and class-based struggles. This unity is essential to build an alliance against corporate capitalism.

* * *

This chapter has attempted to write a contemporary history of adivasi politics by focusing on the central question of reconciling the problem of class differentiation with the need to reproduce adivasi political identity and consciousness. The structural basis for this apparent asymmetry arises from the simultaneous impact of historical processes of dispossession and the development of affirmative action in independent India. The relationship and impact of these two processes form the basis for the multiple trajectories of political mobilization amongst the adivasis of the country. As this chapter shows, the multiple expressions of adivasi consciousness are a political response to the impact of the hegemonic processes of state-led tribal development. Apart from these structural factors, two other aspects need to be considered while analysing the multiple and diverse trends in adivasi struggles. The first of these depends on the nature of differentiation within and between particular adivasi groups. The character of the political construction of the adivasi community is particularly dependent on this factor. The second aspect relates to the competing forms of hegemonies that have structured the multiple forms of adivasi consciousness and determined their character. Of these, the state-led strategies of tribal welfare and the forces of Hindutva have acted as catalysts in the formation of this consciousness.

As this chapter has shown, there have been three dominant forms of adivasi politics that can be perceived in the history of independent India. The first relates to non-class-based adivasi identity mobilizations that were born out of the projections of a unified adivasi community. The social basis of these mobilizations was rooted in the impact of affirmative action and the emergence of a new social class of the intelligentsia amongst the adivasis. Their early pressure on the nationalist leadership resulted led to the negotiated settlements resulting in the formulation of the fifth and sixth schedules which were designed to accommodate the political aspirations of adivasi politics. For this reason, adivasi politics remained largely dormant (except for few struggles) till the post-Nehruvian period, when the impact of state capitalism became apparent. Patterns of uneven development, along with the emergence and consolidation of the adivasi intelligentsia, were reflected in the resurgence of separate state movements in Jharkhand and north-east India. These non-class mobilizations have been culturally exclusive in their character and also possess their own hegemonic content. Since the adivasis do not represent any particular ethnic group or class of people in this form of adivasi politics, the idea of being adivasi may be used to oppose processes of political, social, and economic dispossession, but may be limited by its social basis in terms of its potential to be a counter-hegemonic force. Its tendency to negotiate with and get incorporated into competing hegemonic tendencies only exposes its limitation in dealing with challenges as they emerge in the current scenario. Hence the discourses of communitarian control and conservative nationhood often succumb to both Hindutva as well as neoliberal politics.

The second form of adivasi politics is essentially class-based mobilizations, which attempted to socialize adivasis into a modern peasant consciousness. From the perspective of one strand of the communist movement, the adivasis were seen as dispossessed peasants whose deprivation could only be countered through broad-based class struggles. The Naxalbari struggles of the early post-independence period were examples which served as counter-points to state capitalism. But in the process they ignored the need to reproduce the adivasi consciousness in a manner that addressed the special sectional interests of adivasis. This in turn created the space for the mobilization of sectional interests on the basis of non-class adivasi politics.

The adivasis' aspiration for the creation of a multi-class united front has led to a serious attempt to negotiate the problem of adivasi consciousness as seen in a third trend of mobilization. Represented by organizations like the Ganamukti Parishad, the Adivasi Mahasabha, Girijan Sangham, and social welfare organizations like Adivasi Pragati Mandal, such mass politics is based on a perspective of working-class unity and a non-exclusive, democratic adivasi consciousness. Having an adivasi consciousness means fighting for the adivasi cause, but also struggling for the democratization of adivasi society itself. This would be achieved through a dialectical relationship with and the embeddedness of this consciousness in mass organizations spearheading a broader class struggle. (The explanation for this political strategy lies in the fact that capitalism itself is reproducing the hegemonic tribal identity, and as long as that identity exists, the need to reproduce adivasi consciousness will be a political contingency.) Such an adivasi consciousness can counter the hegemonies of a neoliberal state as well as an aggressive brand of right-wing Hindu nationalism. That it remains confined to certain pockets of historical influence is a question that such politics has to confront in terms of both the theory and the practice of the mainstream communist movement. And in the wake of such limitations, the Maoists have gained ground and are making attempts to fill a political vacuum that neither elite, communitarian-based adivasi politics nor pure class-based politics can achieve.

Finally, the reproduction of adivasi consciousness is an inevitable and necessary process as it enables the movement to organize these social groups to protect the benefits that they have acquired through their struggles. In this sense, the protection of land rights and the right to social welfare and security are demands which have the potential to reduce the influence of corporate capital. Hence, the adivasi consciousness is a political consciousness whose significance, function, and meaning are derived from both contemporary corporate capitalism as well as the need for an alternative political practice. The potential of adivasi politics to achieve this counter-hegemonic position will be determined by its social basis and its capacity to attain a broader working-class unity. Hence there is an urgent need to build a unity and an ideological cohesion between class-based struggles and the communitarian adivasi politics of adivasi workers.

REFERENCES

All India Democratic Women's Association (AIDWA). 2009. *Political Violence Against Women in West Bengal*. Delhi: AIDWA.
Banerjee, Sumanta. 1984. *India's Simmering Revolution: The Naxalite Uprising*. London: Zed Books.
Bhattacharya, Harihar. 1998. *Communism in Tripura*. New Delhi: Ajanta.
Brahme, Sulabha and Ashok Upadhyaya (eds). 2004. *Agrarian Structure, Movements and Peasant Organisations*. Vol. II: *Maharashtra*. New Delhi: Manak.
Cederlöf, Gunel and K. Sivaramakrishnan (eds). 2005. *Ecological Nationalism: Nature, Livelihoods and Identities in South Asia*. New Delhi: Permanent Black.
Chatterji, Angana. 2009. *Violent Gods: Hindu Nationalism from India's Present—Narratives from Orissa*. New Delhi: Three Essays Collective.
Damodaran, Vanita. 2011. 'Customary Rights and Resistance in Singbhum', in D. Rycroft and S. Dasgupta (eds), *The Politics of Belonging: Being Adivasi*. London: Routledge.
Debbarma, Dasaratha. 1986. *Gana Mukti Parishad in Building the Peasant Movement in Tripura*, Golden Jubilee Series no. 7. All India Kisan Sabha.
Desai, A. R. (ed.). 1979. *Peasant Struggle in India after Independence*. New Delhi: Oxford University Press.
Devalle, Susana. 1992. *Discourses of Ethnicity: Culture and Protest in Jharkhand*. New Delhi: Sage Publications.
Gadgil, Madhav and Ramachandra Guha. 1992. *This Fissured Land: The Ecological History of India*. New Delhi: Oxford University Press.
Grewal, Pushpinder. 2010. 'Indian Maoism: Flawed Strategy and Perverted Praxis', in Prasenjit Bose (ed.), *Maoism: A Critique from the Left*. New Delhi: Leftword Books.
Heredia, Rudolf C. 2002–3. 'Interrogating Integration: The Counter-Cultural Tribal Other', *Economic and Political Weekly*, vol. 37, no. 52, pp. 5174–8.
Kelkar, Govind and Dev Nathan (eds). 2003. *Gender Relations in Forest Societies in Asia: Patriarchy at Odds*. New Delhi: Sage Publications.
Kumar, Amit. 2000. 'Second Phase of Jharkhand Movement', in R. D. Munda and S. Bosu Mullick (eds), *The Jharkhand Movement: Indigenous Peoples Struggle for Autonomy*. Copenhagen: International Work Group for Indigenous Affairs.

Kumar, Dharmendra and Yemuna Sunny (eds). 2009. *Proselytisation in India: The Process of Hinduisation in Tribal Societies*. New Delhi: Aakar Books.
Munda, R. D. and S. Bosu Mullick (eds). 2000. *The Jharkhand Movement: Indigenous Peoples Struggle for Autonomy*. Copenhagen: International Work Group for Indigenous Affairs.
Namboodiripad, E. M. S. 1952. *On the Agrarian Question in India*. Bombay: People's Publishing House.
Nathan, Dev. 2000. 'Jharkhand: Factors and Future', in R. D. Munda and S. Bosu Mullick (eds), *The Jharkhand Movement: Indigenous Peoples Struggle for Autonomy*. Copenhagen: International Work Group for Indigenous Affairs, pp. 119–30.
Nehru, Jawaharlal. 1972. 'Approach to Tribes', in *Jawaharlal Nehru's Speeches, 1953–1957*, pp. 458–61. New Delhi: Nehru Memorial Fund.
Padel, Felix and Samarendra Das. 2010. *Out of This Earth: East India, Adivasis and the Aluminum Cartel*. New Delhi: Orient BlackSwan.
Parulekar, Godavari. 1975. *Adivasi Revolt: The Story of the Struggle of the Warlis*. Calcutta: National Book Agency.
Prasad, Archana. 2004. 'Can the BJP make tribal India shine?' *Peoples Democracy*, 4 April.
———. 2006a. 'Survival at Stake', *Frontline*, 30 December.
———. 2006b. 'Conservation and Development in the Tribal Bill', *Social Scientist*, vol. 34, no. 7 (July–August).
———. 2008a. 'Patriarchies of the Community: Women and Oral Traditions in Verrier Elwin's *Baiga*', *Indian Historical Review*, vol. 35, no. 2 (July).
———. 2008b. 'Kandmal: The march of Hindutva in tribal Orissa', *Peoples Democracy*, 20 October.
———. 2009. 'On the Margins of Indian Planning', in V. Upadhyay, Shakti Kak, Kaustav Barik, and T. Ravi Kumar (eds), *From Statism to Neoliberalism: The Development Process in India*. New Delhi: Daanish Books.
———. 2010a. 'Capitalism, Forestry and Tribal Labour in Central India', *Social Action*, vol. 60, no. 2.
———. 2010b. *Environmentalism and the Left: Contemporary Debates and Future Agendas in Tribal Areas*. New Delhi: Leftword.
———. 2010c. 'Neoliberalism, Tribal Survival and Agrarian Distress', in Alternative Economic Survey Group, *Two Decades of Neoliberalism*. New Delhi: Daanish Books.
———. 2010d. 'The Political Economy of Maoist Violence in Chhattisgarh', *Social Scientist*, pp. 3–24.
———. 2011. *Against Ecological Romanticism: Verrier Elwin and the Making of an Anti-Modern Tribal Identity*. New Delhi: Three Essays Collective.
———. 2012. 'Class, Community and Identity: Politics of Adivasi in Contemporary India', Paper presented at the International Conference on Marxism: Marx and Beyond, Centre for Marxian Studies, Jadavpur University, and Institute of Development Studies, Kolkata, 22–4 March.

———. 2013. 'The Vedanta Judgment: Significance and Implications', *Peoples Democracy*, 28 April.

Rasul, M. A. 1974. *A History of the All India Kisan Sabha*. Calcutta: National Book Agency.

Ratnagar, Shereen. 2004. *The Other Indians: Essays on Pastoralists and Prehistoric Tribal People*. Delhi: Three Essays Collective.

———. 2010. *Being Tribal*. New Delhi: Primus Books.

Roy, A. K. 2000. 'Internal Colonialism', in R. D. Munda and S. Bosu Mullick (eds), *The Jharkhand Movement: Indigenous Peoples Struggle for Autonomy*. Copenhagen: International Work Group for Indigenous Affairs.

Roy Burman, B. K. 1994. *Indigenous and Tribal People: Gathering Mist and New Horizon*. New Delhi: Mittal Publications.

Sadgopal, Anil and Shyam Bahadur Namr. 1993. *Sangharsh aur Nirman: Shankar Guha Niyogi aur Unke Naye Bharat Ka Sapna*. New Delhi: Rajkamal Prakashan.

Sanyal, Kanu. 1978. *Report on the Peasant Movement in the Terai Region*, reprinted in Samar Sen, Debabrata Panda, and Ashish Lahiri (eds), *Naxalbari and After: A Frontier Anthology* (Calcutta: Kathashilpa), Vol. 2, pp. 203–31.

Savyasaachi. 1998. *Tribal Forest Dwellers and Self Rule: The Constituent Assembly Debates in India*. New Delhi: Indian Social Institute.

Sengupta, N. (ed.). 1982. *Fourth World Dynamics: Jharkhand*. New Delhi: Authors Guild Publications.

Singh, K. S. (ed.). 2006. *Tribal Movements in India*, vols 1–2. New Delhi: Manohar.

Singh, Prakash. 1995. *The Naxalite Movement in India*. New Delhi: Rupa and Co.

Sinha, Surajit. 1995. First published in 1962. 'State Formation and Rajput Myth in India', in Herman Kulke (ed.), *The State in India*. New Delhi: Oxford University Press.

Sundar, Nandini. 2002. 'Indigenise, Nationalise and Spiritualise: An Agenda for Education?' *International Social Science Journal*, vol. 35.

14

Conservation and Rights in India
Are We Moving towards Any Kind of Harmony?*

Ashish Kothari and *Neema Pathak Broome*

Ecosystem dwellers of all kinds in India—wild plants and animals, adivasi and non-adivasi peasants, fishers, and pastoralists—are in serious crisis. The forces of rapid economic growth, cultural and demographic changes, and political expediency are all responsible for the widespread decimation of natural ecosystems and hundreds of species, as also for the uprooting and dispossession of millions of people. Development and economic policies and programmes appear to be in direct conflict with policies and programmes enacted for safeguarding species, ecosystems, and local people. Adding to the complications, policies and programmes meant to safeguard the interests of wildlife on the one hand and

---

* This is a shorter, updated, and revised version of the study published by the Rights and Resources Group, *Deeper Roots of Historical Injustice: Trends and Challenges in the Forests of India*, Rights and Resources Initiative, Washington, D.C., 2012. This article may not have very recent developments related to some of the laws mentioned as it was first written in 2009 and slightly modified in 2012. Much has changed related to land and forest rights since then with the implementation of Forest Rights Act (FRA) 2006. Many of the issues mentioned in the article related to the social dimension of conservation, however, have remained the same.

ecosystem people on the other also seem to be in conflict with each other. There is a desperate search for alternatives, ways to bring the interests of conservation and people's livelihood rights together, so that a united front can be put up against the forces threatening to engulf them both. A series of on-ground initiatives, coupled with a number of policy pronouncements till 2012 when this chapter was updated, have provided the hope that this may well be possible. This chapter assesses how realistic this hope is.

We briefly recount the historical, socio-political, and economic context of the conservation and human rights interface. This includes the conflicts engendered by conservation policy and paths of development, and attempts at resolving these conflicts. We then look at some policy measures that have a bearing on this situation, as also briefly at some on-ground initiatives. We examine the role of different actors in influencing or shaping conservation and human rights policies. Finally, we offer tentative projections on the shape of the conservation and rights interface in India in the next few decades, providing some possible scenarios.

Some sections are very sketchily developed here. This is because more detailed treatment of these is easily available elsewhere, for which we provide some references.

HISTORICAL ASPECTS OF CONSERVATION

It is believed by many scholars and historians that the oldest forms of conservation in India are not the ones ascribed to rulers like Ashoka (Gadgil and Guha 1992). Adivasi and other communities have practised conservation in various forms for several thousand years: sacred spaces (groves, ponds, rivers, even entire landscapes), sacred or culturally important species (langur *Semnopithecus* spp., *ficus* spp., elephant *Elephas maximus*, and nilgai *Boselaphus tragocamelus*, to name a few), deliberate restraints on the harvesting of plants and animals, conservation of water catchments, protection of nesting or roosting animal populations, and so on. Many of these traditional 'community-conserved areas and species' continue till today (though many have also disappeared), and have been added to by a range of more recent initiatives responding to water and resource scarcities, external threats by development projects, conservation concerns, political self-empowerment, and other motivations (Pathak 2009; also see the section on 'Measures to Tackle Threats by "Development"' later in this chapter).

Protection by rulers too is ancient, with the conservation edicts of Ashoka and the protection of hunting reserves by a number of rulers being well known (Rangarajan 2001). During colonial times, the government significantly extended its control over forests and other ecosystems, and expanded the number and size of areas set aside for conservation. It was, however, mostly after independence that a major thrust was provided to state-sponsored conservation, especially with the promulgation of the Wild Life (Protection) Act in 1972 (WLPA). The number and spread of protected areas (PAs), meant specifically for the conservation of wildlife, increased significantly (from about 100 in the early 1970s to 657 in 2008 [Kutty and Kothari 2001]). This, along with prohibition on hunting and trade in several threatened species across the country, was the most important step in slowing down the pace of decimation of India's wildlife.

However, the takeover of forests (and other common property resources) by the state, which expanded greatly in colonial and post-independence times, has also had a number of serious negative consequences. These are briefly reviewed in the context of the discussion of PAs in the next section.

IMPACTS OF OFFICIAL WILDLIFE CONSERVATION POLICY AND PRACTICE ON PEOPLE AND CONSERVATION

Unfortunately, official forest and conservation policies ignored two very important aspects that, if taken into account, would have led these policies in a very different direction. Firstly, they did not take on board the long-standing conservation traditions and practices of local communities (and thereby lost an opportunity to enhance, support, and revive community-conserved areas and species). Secondly, they ignored the significant economic and cultural dependence of people on the ecosystems and species sought to be conserved in PAs (and thereby set the stage for alienation of local people, and conflicts between them and official conservation agencies).

Till 2002, the WLPA provided for two kinds of PAs, wildlife sanctuaries (WLS) and national parks (NP). While by law certain human uses can be allowed in a WLS, no human use is allowed in an NP, although this is beginning to change now with local people claiming land and forest rights under the Scheduled Tribes and Other Traditional Forest Dwellers [Recognition of Forest Rights] Act, 2006, or the FRA (for details, see the section on 'Recent Policy and Legal Measures' later in this chapter). Two more categories were added in the amendment to the Act in 2002: conservation reserves and community reserves. As of 2009,[1] there were 661 PAs in India covering a total of 4.83 per cent of the total area of the country. These included 99 NPs, 513 WLS, four community reserves, and 45 conservation reserves. This number had increased to 689 PAs by 2012, with 102 NPs, 524 WLS, 4 community reserves, and 57 conservation reserves. Thirty-nine of these PAs had also been declared tiger reserves (MoEF 2008a). As stated earlier, such a designation has saved many ecologically critical areas and threatened wildlife species from being wiped out by dams, mining, cities, and agricultural expansion. What is important, however, is that nearly 5 per cent of this area is also inhabited by people, some of them ancient adivasi or tribal communities. Studies conducted by the Indian Institute of Public Administration in the mid-1980s, updated by the Centre for Equity Studies in the late 1990s, indicate the human population inside PAs to be between 2.5 and 3 million; this number is only likely to have gone up, both because of increase in population and increase in the number of PAs. The actual relocation of people has been a tiny fraction of this total number.[2] Most of these people belong to communities that have lived in these areas *before* the PAs were notified. These people (and many millions more who live in regions adjacent to the PAs) consider such areas their home, and are dependent on local resources for fuel, fodder, medicines, non-timber forest products (NTFPs), fish and other aquatic produce, livelihoods, water, cultural sustenance, and myriad other critical functions. Although located in areas often remote from urban markets, they have not remained away from the market economy, making cash income, even if at a bare minimum, essential. Collection of NTFP or aquatic resources contributes significantly to each household's cash earnings in many of these areas. These subsistence or small-scale market-based activities are often recorded in government documents as rights or concessions, but many are not recorded at all and hence considered illegal. In Odisha, villages and cultivated lands that have existed for generations are treated as illegal occupations or 'encroachments' because they were never surveyed and did not enter into the government records; in Andhra Pradesh, lands lying fallow under traditional shifting cultivation practices

---

[1] See http://www.wiienvis.nic.in/Database/Protected_Area_854.aspx (accessed 10 September 2015).

[2] This is a projection based on statistics contained in Kothari et al. (1989) and Centre for Equity Studies (2003).

were declared reserve forests without an enquiry into existing customary rights, or taken over for the forest department's plantation schemes (Saxena 2001). On the other hand, increasing human populations, lack of alternative livelihoods, displacement from their original homes because of development projects, or other reasons have also ensured that many ecosystem-dependent people have now become illegal occupants of lands on which they critically depend.

Till the enactment of the FRA, the only process towards settlement of land rights was as prescribed by the WLPA. As per this, before any PA is finally notified, a process of settlement of rights needs to be carried out, and either the livelihoods and habitation rights are allowed (in the case of sanctuaries) or acquired by providing compensation or alternatives. A number of factors (such as badly kept land records, or unrecorded rights of people who have inhabited these areas for generations) have prevented the completion of this process in most states in the country. This has meant that a majority of PAs in the country have till recently remained *intended* PAs rather than *finally notified* ones. In 1996, the World Wide Fund for Nature (WWF) India filed a plea in the Supreme Court asking all state governments to implement the WLPA, including the process of settlement of rights. The court ordered states to do this within a year, the consequences of which were complex. Many state governments quickly complied with the order without any comprehensive assessments of rights, hence depriving thousands of people of their due rights; or conversely, they allowed all rights in PAs (as in Rajasthan) without assessing the validity of the claims or impacts on the ecosystem; in still others, they recommended that large parts of PAs be denotified as the process of settling rights would be nearly impossible. These recommendations led to numerous conflicts on the ground, and many had remained unaccepted at the time of writing this paper in 2009, over 15 years after the initial court orders.

In some states, efforts have been made towards rehabilitation of villages from inside the PA to other areas. Though in a couple of cases these efforts have involved a relatively successful rehabilitation process, most have invited extreme criticism for a number of reasons (Rangarajan and Shahabuddin 2006). The fate of the people living inside the PAs has therefore remained undecided for several decades now. Living under the constant uncertainty of not knowing whether and for how long they would be living in the area, and constant harassment over collection of forest or aquatic produce, the local people have developed serious contempt for the PAs. Since the 2006 amendment to the WLPA to include the category of the tiger reserve, there has been a spate of relocation from the newly declared and/or expanded tiger reserves in the country. Many such relocations are taking place in violation of the procedures laid out in the FRA, including the violation of free prior informed consent by not providing complete information to the concerned communities (Guptabhaya and Pathak 2011).

Given the experience with the ground realities of the settlement of rights process, as also the social and financial complexities involved in rehabilitation of villages, there is an increasing realization that human habitation in WLS and NPs in India is a reality unlikely to change. Although this is clearly an understanding among actual practitioners on the ground, including both government officials and non-government agencies, this reality has not reached the policymakers (and the handful of conservationists influencing them). On the contrary, in 2002, an amended WLPA brought in much more severe restrictions. It mandated state governments to 'provide alternatives' for all resource use activities as soon as the intention was declared to notify an area as a sanctuary (thereby assuming that no rights could continue inside the PA, which actually contradicted another provision within the same Act which explicitly did provide for such continuation!). It also prohibited any form of extraction of resources for commercial use. This was necessary to stop industrial-level extraction (for example, of bamboo), but ended up bringing under its purview local subsistence livelihood activities such as removal of grasses, medicinal plants, and other NTFP for small-scale sale, as described in the what follows.

The Ministry of Environment and Forests (MoEF) and the Supreme Court of India have played a major role in further complicating this relationship between PAs and local people. In 2003, the MoEF declared:

> The Supreme Court has passed an order on 14.2.2000 restraining removal of dead, diseased, dying or wind-fallen trees, drift wood and grasses etc. from any national park or Game Sanctuary.... *In view of this, rights and concessions cannot be enjoyed in the Protected Areas (PAs)* [emphasis added].[3]

In February 2000, the Supreme Court had indeed passed such an order. But it had done so in the context of a proposal by the Karnataka and

---

[3] MoEF FC Division, Guidelines for diversion of forest land for non-forest purposes under the Forest (Conservation) Act 1980, F. No. 2-1/2003-FC, 20 October 2003, in MoEF (2004).

Uttar Pradesh governments to allow the removal of timber from PAs under the guise of it being dead, dying, or diseased. The court had as its intention the stoppage of some activities that were obviously destructive and intended for commercial profit. But the MoEF interpreted this as asking for the stoppage of *all* activities, including resource uses for survival and livelihood by local communities.

Matters were made worse when the Central Empowered Committee (CEC) of the Supreme Court, in a letter dated 2 July 2004 to senior administrative and forest officials of all states and union territories, stated the following:

> A number of instances have come to the notice of the Central Empowered Committee where felling of trees/bamboo, digging of canals, mining, underground mining, collection of sand/boulders ... cutting of grass, collection of minor forest produce, grazing, construction, widening of roads etc. have been allowed to be undertaken in protected areas without obtaining permission from the Hon'ble Supreme Court on the plea that these activities are part of the management plans.... You are requested to ensure strict compliance of the Hon'ble Supreme Courts' order so that none of the above prohibited activities are allowed to be undertaken in protected areas.

After this circular, many states (Odisha, Karnataka, Rajasthan, Maharashtra, Madhya Pradesh, among others), stopped the extraction of NTFP from PAs with immediate effect. For hundreds of thousands of people who had no other source of monetary income, this came as a big blow. Overnight, contractors (including government corporations) pulled out their collection centres. The government did not provide any alternative to this sudden loss of livelihoods, threatening already impoverished and marginalized communities with further displacement and dispossession.

Vasundhara, an NGO from Odisha, reports that tens of thousands of people inside the state's PAs, most of them adivasi, are faced with unemployment, destitution, and even starvation. Detailed studies done in PAs like Satkosia Gorge Sanctuary and Sunabeda Sanctuary reveal an alarming state of affairs, with mass outmigration having begun in search of jobs and sustenance (Vasundhara 2005; Wani and Kothari 2007a, 2007b). Grass removal from PAs like Kumbalgarh Sanctuary and Keoladeo (Bharatpur) National Park in Rajasthan has reportedly stopped, with serious consequences for villagers, especially those critically dependent on animal husbandry. These steps have resulted in an inevitable rise in trauma, hostility, resentment, desperation, and conflict.

A belief that wildlife can be protected in such circumstances is more likely to be a delusion than reality. Consequently, the last couple of decades have seen moves towards political decentralization gaining ground in India. Local communities have been organizing and trying to empower themselves. Protests against conservation policies in general and PAs in particular have gained ground. These situations of local discontent leading to conflicts have regularly been used by political and commercial vested interests. Demands for doing away with PAs, or with unpopular wildlife restrictions, are on the rise. Acts of subversion, of deliberate violation of conservation laws, and of quiet collaboration with poachers and timber thieves have also been evident. Demands such as those by Naxal groups (ultra-leftist armed groups particularly active in some eastern, central, and southern states) to abolish forest acts seen as draconian, spurred by the socially unjust way in which such laws have been implemented, are on the rise. How can inadequately staffed and funded Forest Departments, charged with protecting India's wildlife, possibly cope with this? Even if one ignores the issues of human rights and social justice, even from a purely conservation point of view, these recent moves appear suicidal.

Even the direct ecological impact of some of these steps can be negative in some situations. Kumbalgarh Sanctuary in Rajasthan has reportedly already been affected by severe fire because grass has not been cut. Keoladeo (Bharatpur) National Park, also in Rajasthan, had several years back actually introduced grass cutting to stop the wetlands from turning into grasslands (a threat that arose as a result of a previous mistaken decision to stop buffalo grazing); if this is now stopped, what will become of the wetlands that harbour one of the world's greatest water bird spectacles? Blanket bans such as this are not even based on sound ecological sense, since they mistakenly assume that all ecosystems and species everywhere respond in the same way to all human activities. This is of course not to imply that all human activities are compatible with conservation; on the contrary, many are not or may not be, but this is precisely why a uniform approach of any kind is scientifically dubious.

The Ashoka Trust for Research in Ecology and Environment in Bengaluru and other organizations have shown that at least in the case of three medicinal plants or NTFP in the Biligiri Sanctuary (Karnataka), collection by the local adivasis is not ecologically detrimental. This would be the case for many (but certainly not all) resource uses by local populations across India's PAs, so there simply is no justification for imposing such a blanket prohibition. A ban on extraction was issued in Biligiri in 2004, reportedly because Karnataka officials want a tiger reserve status for this sanctuary (using the relevant provisions of the WLPA as described earlier), though there is no provision in any law that requires tiger reserves to be free of human resource use, although this debate is subject to interpretation—while some contend that 'inviolate' mentioned in the Act means free of all human activities, others say it means 'non harmful human intervention'. The ban order was questioned by the then divisional conservator of forests in charge of the sanctuary, stating in no uncertain terms that this would create suffering and hostility and make conservation difficult; but he was overruled, and in 2006 the ban was actually strictly imposed. Several thousand Soliga adivasis suffered loss of livelihoods and income as a result of this. In a related incident, severe forest fires in 2007 were left unattended by the adivasis who would otherwise have helped the wildlife authorities to douse them (Kalpavriksh 2007).

DEVELOPMENT CONTEXT INFLUENCING CONSERVATION TODAY

Ironically enough, the very government which has taken such draconian steps against some of India's poorest communities in the name of conservation has no compunctions in giving up ecologically critical areas for so-called 'development' projects. In November 2004, for instance, clearance for the construction of the Lower Subansiri project in Arunachal Pradesh was given, despite strong evidence that this project will destroy crucial and irreplaceable wildlife habitat (Vagholikar 2008a, 2008b). In October 2004, 40 organizations from across India signed an open letter to the MoEF, expressing dismay at the ministry's continuing to sign away wildlife habitats to such projects on the basis of flimsy and often fraudulent environmental impact assessments.[4] Many PAs from where traditional communities are being moved out are being opened up for large-scale commercial tourism, called 'ecotourism', as if adding the prefix 'eco' would magically transform a destructive activity into a benign one!

An indication of the short shrift being given to the environment, in the current era of globalization, is the increase in the number

[4] See http://www.kalpavriksh.org/campaigns/campopenletter/campol.

of 'development' projects given environmental clearance, and the increase in the rate of diversion of forest lands for non-forest purposes. Documents obtained by Kalpavriksh from the MoEF by using the Right to Information (RTI) Act, and an analysis by Centre for Science and Environment, reveal that of the total forest land diverted since 1980–1 (when the Forest Conservation Act was brought in to make it mandatory for state governments to seek central permission for non-forest use of such land), about 50 per cent has been after 2001–2, and of the 1.5 lakh hectares of forest land diverted for mining in the same period, over half has been diverted between 2000 and 2010 (CSE 2011).

MEASURES TO ADDRESS CONFLICTS BETWEEN CONSERVATION AREAS/WILDLIFE AND PEOPLE

As the problems related to local community alienation from PAs became difficult to ignore, the government responded with ambitious *ecodevelopment* programmes. In these programmes, people's needs were sought to be met through ecologically sensitive developmental inputs. Since 1990, this has been a central government-aided scheme, meant for state governments to use for villages around PAs. By and large these have not been used for villages inside PAs, the assumption being that such villages have to be moved out anyway. During 1997–2002, the Government of India also got substantial assistance from the Global Environment Facility/World Bank for ecodevelopment in seven prominent PAs. Independent evaluations suggest that this project met with mixed success. In some PAs such as the Periyar Tiger Reserve (Kerala), it was successful in turning a conflict situation around into one of positive cooperation and providing enhanced livelihood, thereby helping reduce poverty in several villages on the periphery of the reserve. However, in many others such as Nagarahole National Park (Karnataka) and Pench National Park (Maharashtra), it either failed or created new tensions (Shahabuddin 2010; Woodman 2002).

One of the key conceptual problems with 'ecodevelopment' is that *it still treats local communities and conservation as being incompatible* and it does not address issues of forest rights and land tenure. Hence, the primary focus is on 'diverting' local 'pressures' through provision of alternatives. The alternatives themselves are envisioned and decided centrally and are very much mainstream rural development projects, with no clear logic on how they would lead to better conservation or indeed more enhanced sustained livelihoods. In almost no known case has 'ecodevelopment' created a greater involvement of local people in the management planning and decision-making of the PA. The model of 'ecodevelopment' prevalent in India is not one which takes people's access to natural resources a matter of customary right, nor is it one which moves the country towards a new paradigm of conservation. Such new paradigms are being now accepted worldwide (and indeed are required to be adopted by India as part of its commitment to implementing the Programme of Work on Protected Areas of the Convention on Biological Diversity),[5] but India is far from getting close to them in official policy and practice.

One policy-level move towards this was, however, taken in the making of the National Wildlife Action Plan (NWAP), 2002–16, and in the process of formulating a National Biodiversity Strategy and Action Plan (NBSAP). The NWAP explicitly recognized the need to involve local people in conservation including PA management, and suggests some steps towards this. These include formation of PA-level committees including local community representatives. The final technical report of the NBSAP goes further, advocating a central role for communities in the management of conservation sites, respect for their customary rights, integration of livelihood security and poverty eradication with conservation, recognition of their own conservation practices and community-protected sites, building on traditional knowledge relevant for conservation, and so on (TPCG and Kalpavriksh 2005). Unfortunately, the final NBSAP released by MoEF in 2008 contains very little of this orientation (MoEF 2008b; Kothari and Kohli 2009).

The National Environment Policy (NEP), 2006, in its preamble also stresses the need to recognize the vital role that natural resources play in providing livelihood and life support ecological services. It acknowledges that 'sustainable development concerns in the sense of enhancements of human well-being, broadly conceived, are a recurring theme in India's development philosophy.' The dominant theme of this policy is that while conservation of environmental resources is necessary to secure the livelihoods and well-being of all, the most secure basis for conservation is to ensure that people dependent on particular resources obtain a better livelihood from the act of conservation than from the degradation of resources. Thus, the policy clearly acknowledges the close link between

---

[5] See Convention on Biological Diversity, COP 7 Decision VV/28, available at: http://www.cbd.int/decision/cop/?id=7765 (accessed 24 August 2015). Also see Galvin and Haller (2008) and Lockwood et al. (2006).

peoples' livelihoods and conservation prerogatives. In the case of PAs, it states:

> Conservation of wildlife, accordingly, involves the protection of entire ecosystems. However, in several cases, delineation of and restricting access to such Protected Areas (PAs), as well as disturbances by humans in these areas have led to man-animal conflicts. While physical barriers and better policing may temporarily reduce such conflict, it is also necessary to address their underlying causes. These may largely arise from the non-involvement of relevant stakeholders in identification and delineation of PAs, as well as the loss of traditional entitlements of local people, especially tribals, over the PAs.

In its goals, the policy therefore talks about 'participation of local communities' and the need to 'harmonize ecological and physical features with needs of socio-economic development'.

The NWAP and the NEP, however, continue to remain unimplemented policies. The NBSAP in its final form was not even accepted by the government, which instead produced a significantly watered down policy that has no detailed recommendations on this issue. There are therefore very few official moves towards actual changes on the ground, especially in PAs, towards a new paradigm of conservation that holds livelihood and survival rights as central.

COMMUNITY-CONSERVED AREAS

There are numerous people's initiatives towards integrating conservation and livelihood. Most prominent are the hundreds, perhaps thousands, of examples of community-conserved areas (CCAs) (see Box 14.1). These still cover only a small proportion of India's countryside, but are significant in themselves and for the potential they represent.

But CCAs also face a host of problems. One of the greatest is that India has, till recently, not recognized these efforts and has a very inadequate supportive policy environment. A number of legal provisions do provide some space to give backing to CCAs, but all of them have limitations. For instance, the Forest Act of 1927 provided for the handing over of reserve forests to communities to manage as village forests, but this provision has hardly ever been used; where it has been used, it has only been after heavy curtailment of community rights, responsibilities, and authorities, for example, in Uttarakhand (Pathak and Bhatt 2003). In 2003, a category of 'community reserves' was added to the WLPA,

Box 14.1 CCAs in India

Sacred sites and species were once extremely widespread across India, according to one estimate covering perhaps about 10 per cent of many regions (Das and Malhotra 1998). These included forest groves, village tanks, grasslands, and individual species such as those named in an earlier section of this chapter. Unfortunately, the forces of commercialization, cultural change, population increase, and development projects have destroyed many of these sites. But though considerably less in number and coverage, they are still common; researchers estimate that there may still be between 100,000 and 150,000 (Das and Malhotra 1998; Gadgil 1995). Many of the sacred groves have preserved remnant populations of rare and endemic species, sometimes in their original and undisturbed form, that have been wiped out elsewhere. In general, such areas are quite small (sometimes only a handful of trees), but there are also large ones like the Mawphlang Sacred Grove in Meghalaya which covers 75 hectares. In fact researchers from the North-Eastern Hill University have recorded 79 sacred groves in Meghalaya, ranging in size from .01 to 1,200 hectares, of which about 40 range between 50 hectares to 400 hectares (Tiwari et al. 1999). Interestingly, in some parts of India, communities have designated new forest areas as sacred in order to protect them. For example, in Uttaranchal in the late 1990s, a number of village communities devoted parts of their forests to the goddess till such time as the forests were completely regenerated.

Dozens of heronries (roosting and nesting sites of migratory and local birds, particularly water birds) are being protected by communities that live around them. Trees in or near village ponds are often the favourite nesting and roosting sites for pelicans, storks, herons, egrets, ibises, and other water birds. Well-known examples include Kokkare Bellur in Karnataka; Nellapattu, Vedurapattu, and Veerapuram in Andhra Pradesh; Chittarangudi and Vedanthangal in Tamil Nadu; and many others (some of which have become officially protected sanctuaries). Many of these harbour globally threatened species like the spotted-billed pelican.

Wintering water bird populations also find a safe haven in many wetlands within or adjacent to villages whose residents zealously guard them. Mangalajodi village in Odisha, on the edge of the Chilika lagoon, harbours several hundred thousand migratory ducks and waders. From being a village full of bird catchers (with substantial income coming from selling these birds), the residents are now offering complete protection against hunting and other disturbances. In Uttar Pradesh, Amakhera village of Aligarh district is home to a large number of migratory birds,

(Cont'd)

Box 14.1 (Cont'd)

which the villagers are careful not to disturb even while withdrawing irrigation and drinking water. Patna lake in Etah district of the same state can support up to 100,000 water birds in a favourable season. The lake was declared a WLS in 1991 but has been protected for centuries by the locals as a sacred site. Sareli village in Kheri district of Uttar Pradesh supports a nesting population of over 1,000 open-bill storks, considered harbingers of a good monsoon. As they feed on snails, villagers also consider them useful in controlling the spread of diseases (Khan and Abbasi 2009).

In Odisha, Andhra Pradesh, and other states, tens of thousands of hectares have been regenerated and/or protected by village communities. This is usually on their own (including in many cases by setting up all-women forest protection teams, as at Dengejheri village in Odisha), or occasionally through government-supported programmes like JFM. The biodiversity value of these forests is considerable, including several threatened mammal and bird species. In some parts of Odisha, elephants are reported to frequent the community-conserved forests, having moved in here from their earlier ranges that have been disrupted by highways and railway lines and industries. In Odisha alone, there are believed to be more than 10,000 village forest protection committees. In the Ranpur block near Bhubaneshwar, 180 conserving villages (many of them adivasi settlements) have together created a federation. This is to enable combining their initiatives at a landscape level, to maximize harmony and reduce conflicts, and to provide a unified organization to dialogue with the government or outsiders.

In Nagaland, several dozen villages have, over the last decade or two, conserved natural ecosystems as forest or wildlife reserves, the latter dedicated exclusively or predominantly to wildlife conservation. One of the biggest is the Khonoma Tragopan and Wildlife Sanctuary, spread over 20 square kilometres, where hunting and resource extraction are completely prohibited; in another 50 square kilometres or so, very minimal resource use for home use only is allowed. Amongst the earliest initiatives were the forest and wildlife reserves set up by Luzophuhu village in Phek district, and the Ghoshu Bird Sanctuary declared by Gikhiye village in Zonheboto district, both in the 1980s. Many of these are recognized as Important Bird Areas. Given the indiscriminate hunting that this state has witnessed in the last three decades, these efforts are crucial in giving Nagaland's unique biodiversity a renewed lease on life.

(Cont'd)

BOX 14.1 (Cont'd)

In Uttaranchal, some of the state's best forests are under the management of *van* (forest) panchayats set up several decades back, mostly in the Kumaon area (though by no means are all van panchayats well conserved) (Kumar 2006; Sarkar 2008). Some of these are very large, for example Makku van panchayat that covers roughly 2,000 hectares. Of the 2,240 square kilometre stretch of the Gori Ganga river basin, 1,439 square kilometres are under the management of the village van panchayat. This area forms an important corridor between the Nandadevi Biosphere Reserve and Askot Wildlife Sanctuary, which are critically important for highland biodiversity. In addition, villages such as Jardhargaon, Lasiyal, and Nahin Kalan in Tehri Garhwal district, influenced by the Chipko movement, have regenerated and protected hundreds of hectares of forests and helped renew populations of leopard, bear, and other species.

In Bongaigaon district of Assam, the villagers of Shankar Ghola are protecting a few hundred hectares of forest which contains, amongst other things, a troupe of the highly threatened golden langur. At Khichan village (Rajasthan), villagers provide safety and food to the wintering demoiselle cranes, which flock there in huge numbers of up to 10,000. Several lakh rupees are spent by the residents on this, without a grudge or grumble. In Goa, Kerala, and Odisha, important nesting sites for sea turtles such as Galjibag and Rushikulya beaches have been protected through the action of local fisherfolk.

With help from the NGO Tarun Bharat Sangh, several dozen villages in Alwar district (Rajasthan) have reconstructed the water regime, regenerated forests, and helped revive populations of wild herbivores, birds, and other wildlife. The Bhaonta-Kolyala villages have even declared a 'public wildlife sanctuary' over 1,200 hectares. On 1,800 hectares of deciduous forest, Gond adivasis of Mendha (Lekha), Gadchiroli district (Maharashtra), have warded off a paper mill from destroying the bamboo stocks, stopped the practice of lighting forest fires, and moved towards sustainable extraction of NTFP.

Quite a few sites conserved by communities have been recognized to be of such wildlife value that they have been declared WLS or NPs by state governments. In Punjab, lands belonging to the Bishnoi with a considerable blackbuck and chinkara population have been declared as the Abohar Sanctuary. Several traditionally community-managed heronries in southern India, such as Nellapattu, Vedanthangal, and Chittarangudi, are now WLS. Many grassland areas which had traditional pastoralism

(*Cont'd*)

Box 14.1 (Cont'd)

that sustained threatened bird populations have been declared bustard sanctuaries (such as Karera in Madhya Pradesh). In some cases, this has helped to stave off outside threats, but in several cases, it has transferred the responsibility of conservation away from villagers to government agencies who do not always have the resources or the zeal to carry out their duty, as a result of which the areas have suffered neglect and decline. In the case of Karera, it even led to the complete disappearance of the Great Indian bustard. In most cases, the declaration of the sanctuary led to significant restrictions on the local people and consequent conflicts.

The range of mechanisms used by communities in CCAs is fascinating. At virtually all sites, the community has formed rules and regulations, and imposed penalties on anyone violating these. At some places the penalties differ depending on the nature of the violation, or even on the class of the offender, with poorer people being fined less! Usually also there is an institutional mechanism set up to protect the area, such as forest protection committees, youth groups, wildlife protection groups, women's committees, or even gram sabhas (village assemblies) as a whole. Security of tenure of the land/resources being conserved, or the confidence that the community could continue with its initiative irrespective of the legal ownership of the land, is key to a successful initiative. A strong leadership from within the community, and often a catalytic or supportive role by government agencies or civil society organizations from outside, is crucial to successful conservation.

Source: Unless otherwise stated, information in this box is from Pathak (2009).

and could have helped provide much-needed legal backing to CCAs. Unfortunately, community reserves can only be declared on 'community or private' lands, whereas most common lands where CCAs are located are under government jurisdiction! The Biological Diversity Act, 2002, could provide some support, if its category of 'biodiversity heritage sites' is appropriately implemented as per the guidelines issued to state governments by the National Biodiversity Authority. The most relevant and appropriate legal provision for CCAs, however, is the FRA of 2006. It recognizes and vests the right to protect forests as 'community forests', following local rules and management strategies. (The actualization of the potential of this Act is yet to be seen; as of 2012, relatively few communities had claimed community forest rights, and only a handful of these claims had been accepted and titles granted (see the section on 'Recent Policy and Legal Measures' later in this chapter).

Administrative programmes such as Joint Forest Management (JFM) schemes or ecodevelopment schemes are usually the only avenues available to government functionaries or communities to give governmental support to CCAs. However, these schemes have severe limitations: they may not be applicable to many CCAs; or the conserving communities may not wish to bring their areas under these schemes as it entails greater government control. In several instances, the imposition of these schemes has resulted in the breakdown of previously well-functioning community initiatives, especially where parallel institutional structures have been set up by the government. There was hope that a new scheme for wildlife conservation outside PAs, in the 11th Five-Year Plan, would provide sensitive support, if the guidelines prepared by a committee set up by the MoEF were adhered to. However, as of 2012, even as the 12th Plan is getting finalized, there is little evidence that this scheme has benefited CCAs.

Appropriate legal and policy support is urgently needed, especially for the many CCAs that are threatened by mining, hydro-electricity and irrigation projects, urban expansion, industrialization, special economic zones, and other so-called 'development' projects. The locally sustained economies of CCAs are not seen as contributing to the economic security of the country. For example, several forests conserved by communities in Odisha have been destroyed or are threatened by the furious pace of industrialization that the state government has imposed on its citizens.[6] Despite a widespread community forestry movement in states like Odisha, there is still no state level policy to facilitate or support these initiatives. These forests are either reserved forests under the Forest Department's control, or disputed forests which can be claimed by the government at any point in time.

The conserving communities are seriously impacted by neoliberal economic policies and open market systems. Most communities are now dependent on the markets and money. However, the markets with which these communities interface are often highly exploitative. Government policies often end up supporting the exploitation. For example, many villages surrounded by an abundance of NTFP would like to develop a sustainable market for these produce or items made from them. However,

---

[6] See the several case studies by K. C. Samal, P. K. Mishra, S. P. Pani, K. A. Pratap, and T. Das presented in Wani (2008).

tendu patta (*Disopyros melanoxylon*), mahua (*Madhuca indica*), and other NTFP that they collect have been nationalized by the government and cannot be sold in the open market. This makes collectors dependent on government-approved contractors or government-run purchasing centres. Neither of these gives the collectors desired prices. In most cases, this stranglehold has continued despite Panchayats (Extension to Scheduled Areas) Act (PESA) 1996, which provided for tribal ownership of NTFP, but it is possible that the FRA, 2006 will change this situation in times to come (this is discussed further later in this chapter).

Community-conserved areas are currently faced with many threats both from within and outside. Wider market forces and 'modern' lifestyles are changing aspirations and rendering traditional values less effective amongst the youth. These are not being replaced by effective newer ecological and social ethical and moral value system. The modern system of education does not inculcate a respect for local values, and ignores the knowledge systems that formed the basis of traditional conservation. The youth are getting more and more isolated from local realities and drifting away, threatening the human and institutional base of many CCAs. Often a great amount of effort and time is spent by the villagers in protection and patrolling of the forests. This is at the cost of wages that they could have earned. The 'remoteness' of the area means that other employment opportunities are not easily available. In some cases, because of appropriate support, the livelihoods of local people have been improved and strengthened. But in many cases the communities are still struggling to achieve this, and the youth in particular face serious employment challenges. It is only in a few CCAs that the youth are at the forefront of conservation and sustainable livelihood initiatives, but these few are signs of hope.

In order to overcome these constraints, CCAs need a number of supportive actions. Some policy-level support was recommended in the NWAP and the final report of the NBSAP, and a new programme was also initiated to support CCAs as part of the wildlife scheme in the 11th Five-Year Plan (and being continued in the 12th Plan) (MoEF 2009). However, these schemes have mostly remained on paper, without getting translated into actual action.

MEASURES TO TACKLE THREATS BY 'DEVELOPMENT'

Biodiversity and local livelihoods have been faced with severe natural resource-related conflicts, and threatened by 'development' policies and projects. Some of the greatest opponents of such destruction have been local communities, their collectives, and social movements. Their struggles to regain control over their lands and common property, and decision-making processes related to them, have been gaining strength for several decades. Human rights groups fighting against injustices are also talking about politically empowering local people not only to secure livelihoods but also to protect and conserve their surrounding natural resources. Historically as also in present times there are very many examples of natural ecosystems and wildlife populations having been saved by local communities and their resistance movements from destruction. As examples, several big dams that would have submerged huge areas of forest or other ecosystems have been stopped by people's movements. This includes proposed dams like the Bhopalpatnam-Ichhampalli in Maharashtra and Chhattisgarh, which would have submerged a major part of the Indravati Tiger Reserve. Others include Bodhghat in Chhattisgarh and Rathong Chu in Sikkim. Such movements are likely to have saved areas that are equal in size if not sometimes bigger than official PAs, though there is little documentation on this aspect.

Additionally, many civil society organizations have also taken the battle to the courts, or to political forums, though mostly with little success in the case of big industrial or infrastructure projects. Meanwhile some battles against destructive development are being strengthened by collaborations between local communities and civil society organizations. In the case of the struggle against proposed mining by the multinational corporation Vedanta, in the Niyamgiri hills of Odisha (home to Dongaria Kondh adivasis who consider the forested hills as sacred), conservation and social action groups in Odisha and Delhi haved helped the adivasis with legal battles and expert studies to show the biodiversity value of the area. Civil society organizations in Delhi, Pune, and elsewhere are providing crucial technical and advocacy support to local community groups in several states of north-east India and in the western Himalaya, where governments have initiated a massive number of large river valley projects with grave ecological and livelihood consequences.

Advocates of community rights assert that laws like the FRA can be powerful tools against destructive projects, though till the time of modifying this paper in 2012 the implementation of the Act was still very slow and tardy (Desor 2012). While it is too early to gauge the conservation impact of this Act, a significant new initiative that could strengthen community struggles against deforestation is a circular issued by the MoEF in mid-2009.[7] This requires state governments to provide proof, while applying for diversion of forest land under the Forest Conservation Act, that they have complied with the provisions of FRA, 2006. This includes having received consent from the relevant communities for the proposed diversion.

RECENT POLICY AND LEGAL MEASURES INFLUENCING THE SITUATION

As a result of social movements against injustice towards forest dwelling communities caused by forest and conservation policies, the year 2006 saw two legislative developments that have created the potential for democratizing forest and conservation management and providing greater benefits to local communities. However, their implementation faces many complex issues of social and political nature. Concerns are now being raised by some conservation groups about the local capacities, and impacts of asserting these rights on conservation itself. Exactly how this act will impact the rights based conservation discourse in India is yet to unfold.

The passage of the FRA is an important and welcome step towards reversing the historical marginalization of the tribal (indigenous) and other forest dwelling people of India. This Act mandates the vesting of 14 kinds of rights over forest land and forest produce on two categories of communities: STs (that is, indigenous people who are listed in a schedule of the Indian constitution), and 'other traditional forest dwellers', defined as those living in forests for at least three generations.

The provisions of the FRA relevant to PAs are of special interest. The Act specifies that all rights need to be identified and established regardless of the status of the forest, including inside PAs. Furthermore, it mandates a process for determining 'critical wildlife habitats' inside PAs, and assessment of whether people's activities within such habitats can be in consonance with conservation. If 'irreversible damage' is established, communities can be relocated with their informed consent, and after ensuring their readiness for relocation and rehabilitation. Of particular significance are provisions of the Act which not only empower the local communities to conserve wildlife and biodiversity themselves but also empower them to be part of decision-making processes and

---

[7] MoEFcircular dated 30 July 2009, available at: http://envfor.nic.in/mef/Forest_Advisory.pdf (accessed 26 August 2015).

projects impacting the local bio-cultural diversity and heritage (Tatpati 2013).

While the Act is certainly a significant step towards democratizing conservation practice and extending long-denied rights of livelihood to communities dwelling inside forests, as mentioned earlier some have expressed serious concern about its potential impact on conservation itself. In the context of PAs, for instance, conservation groups have raised concerns that the rights (for example, to forest resources) could override the steps necessary to achieve conservation, if no limits based on ecological criteria are set for the extraction of resources. Although it must be mentioned here that the FRA clearly mentions the responsibilities of the rights holders towards conservation of wildlife and biodiversity, as of now no systems have emerged for monitoring whether this responsibility is being fulfilled. The precise relationship with the WLPA 1972 (which governs PAs) is unclear, leading to possible confusion on the ground on what action can be taken if a right granted under the Act violates a provision of the WLPA. Concern has particularly been raised regarding section 3(2) of the Act, which states that 'not withstanding anything contained in the Forest (Conservation) Act, 1980, the Central Government shall provide for diversion of forest land for' development activities, specifying a list of 13 development activities, for each of which 1 hectare of land (without felling more than 75 trees) can be diverted. Conservation groups fear that this could cause fragmentation in deep forests, or be misused to create major infrastructure by vested interests.

In 2008, a number of petitions were filed in the Supreme Court and several high courts, challenging the FRA as being constitutionally *ultra vires* or in other ways detrimental to the environment and people of India. Some high courts have issued interim orders specifying that granting of *patta*s or felling of trees will require the Courts' permission, till the matter is disposed of; as of mid-2012, however, at least two of these (Andhra Pradesh and Odisha) had already lifted their restrictions.

On the other hand, activists supporting FRA argue that the provisions of community rights to manage and protect forests, and to safeguard habitat, along with greater tenurial security, could be powerful bases for enhancing community-based conservation. Unfortunately, till now implementation has mostly been of individual land rights, with relatively few claims relating to community forests having been made or admitted (Pathak and Bose 2009). Nevertheless, the potential is evident from successful claims and titling in some regions such as Gadchiroli in Maharashtra (where over 300,000 acres of CFR rights have been titled to village gram sabhas as of mid-2012), and Biligiri Rangaswamy Temple Sanctuary in Karnataka (where several adivasi hamlets have got CFR rights over a large portion of the sanctuary) (Vasundhara and Kalpavriksh 2012).

Interestingly, the second legislative measure is within the WLPA itself. In late 2006, the Wild Life (Amendment) Act was passed, setting up a National Tiger Conservation Authority. This was in response to a long-standing demand from conservation groups, made urgent by the disappearance of tigers from one of India's well-known tiger reserves, Sariska (Rajasthan). The amendment brought in processes for notification and management of tiger reserves (which makes them a fifth category of PA under the WLPA), and the setting up of a Wildlife Crime Bureau. It specifies (similar to the FRA mentioned earlier) that 'inviolate' areas need to be determined in a participatory manner, and that relocation from such areas needs to happen only with the informed consent of communities. In late 2006, a legal challenge was mounted by some conservation organizations against such provisions; as of mid-2012, this had not resulted in any orders staying the operation of the amendment. However, whether this provision would make declaration and governance of a tiger reserve a more inclusive and participatory process is yet to be seen.

These developments also need to be placed in the context of some other legal and policy measures that are potentially powerful tools for democratizing governance and making governments more accountable to both conservation needs and people's livelihood rights and needs. These include the RTI Act and the National Rural Employment Guarantee Act (NREGA). Many civil society organizations are already making good use of the RTI to obtain information related to conservation and environment that was previously difficult to obtain. Kalpavriksh, for instance, has filed over 100 applications for information on a range of subjects related to environmental clearance of development projects, biodiversity access approvals, critical wildlife habitats, and so on; it has also obtained significant orders from the chief information commissioner directing the disclosure of policy documents even when under formulation. Grassroots organizations are also attempting to combine NREGA with other laws and programmes to regenerate land and water resources.

Interesting possibilities exist of combining various laws and schemes at the village level to optimize the integration of conservation and livelihoods. For instance, a community could claim rights to forest resources and management under the FRA, or the powers to manage forests under the Forest Act, set up a conservation committee under the same Act, or a biodiversity management committee for village-level planning under the Biological Diversity Act, declare its area a biodiversity heritage site under the same Act, apply to the MoEF for funds under its scheme on conservation outside PAs, and use NREGA to generate livelihoods linked to conserving and using the forest. Some initial work towards such combined usage has been done in a few villages in Maharashtra and other states (Gadgil 2008).

ACTORS SHAPING CONSERVATION POLICY AND PRACTICE

Till very recently, formal conservation policy and practice in India have mostly been shaped by a small minority of politically or economically influential people, within and outside the government (Tucker 1991; Kothari et al. 1995; Rangarajan 1996). Conservationists (some of them former hunters, and/or from royal families; others serious naturalists from research backgrounds; some senior bureaucrats in relevant departments; others from civil society organizations) close to Indira Gandhi were instrumental in utilizing her own proclivity towards conservation to push through a series of radical measures in the 1970s, including the WLPA and Project Tiger. The dominance of the Congress as a political party in that period also ensured that these measures were accepted by state governments without much explicit resistance.

There has been a sea change in this situation in the last decade or so. Changes in centre–state politics brought about by the increasing ascendancy of other political parties, the growing power of state governments, and the lack of interest in conservation issues amongst a series of prime ministers after Indira Gandhi have been amongst the key factors in weakening central diktats on conservation. Simultaneously, the shift to a globalized economy has further diluted the focus on conservation, as described earlier. But equally important, a range of civil society actors have forced their entry into the conservation policy-making domain, and/or into on-ground processes. These include communities in areas where they have organized themselves or been helped by NGOs, social activists of various hues, independent researchers and academics, environmental groups with an unconventional view of conservation, and political parties (in particular the left). These actors have brought the social issues of conservation much more to the fore than ever before, and are increasingly forcing the establishment to not only take cognizance of such issues but to reflect them in policy. The enactment of PESA in 1996; inclusion of two new categories of PAs in the 2002 amendment of the WLPA, both with a much greater (though still very inadequate) role for communities; the NWAP and the Final Technical Report of the NBSAP; provisions relating to rights and consent in tiger reserves in the 2006 amendment to the WLPA; and the promulgation of the FRA in 2006, are all examples of their influence.

Undoubtedly too, this influence has been aided by officials within the conservation bureaucracy who think differently from their more conventional colleagues. Many such officers are now more aware of the ground realities and would like to move towards resolving some of the local conflicts for the greater good of conservation. Much feedback has also gone from ground staff, which is stuck in a situation of having to implement provisions of the WLPA but not being able to do so because of people's opposition. A number of such officials have shown different ways of doing things on the ground (for example, promoting tribal livelihoods linked to the Periyar Tiger Reserve in Kerala, or providing employment options to grazier communities in conservation areas of Sikkim), and have articulated policy-level changes with more conviction. Additionally, other wings of government, such as the Tribal Affairs Ministry at the centre in the case of FRA, have also taken a more proactive role in influencing conservation policy.

Another critical influence has been that of the judiciary. The Supreme Court has a three-decade old history of active interest in environmental matters (starting with some of the earliest public interest litigations, such as those on mining in the Doon Valley), but this interest has become decidedly more proactive and far-reaching in its impacts in the first few years of this millennium. Two cases in particular have impacted conservation and rights issues across the country: *T. N. Godavarman Thirumulkpad vs Union of India* (WP 202 of 1995) and *Centre for Environmental Law (CEL), WWF vs Union of India* (WP 337 of 1995). Virtually every aspect of forestry and wildlife in India, and virtually every bit of forest land in the country, has come under the purview of the court through these cases, to the extent that some legal analysts consider it a case of the judiciary far overstepping its constitutional limits (Rosencraz and Lele 2008). The court has often shown a strongly conservationist bent of mind, which has been useful in putting a check on destructive practices and projects; but simultaneously it has also often been biased against the livelihood concerns of people dependent on forests and other ecosystems. It will be interesting to see what view it takes on the petitions filed by NGOs against the FRA.

For the moment, the interplay of these various forces in the conservation–rights arena is extremely chaotic. On the one hand, actors with a predominantly social agenda have gained much greater influence. On the other hand, conventional conservationists have retained some of their stronghold on conservation policy. The former's role is witnessed in WLPA 2006 and the FRA; the latter's in the continued resistance to more democratic forms of PA management, the rush to notify tiger reserves without due consultative process, or the stalling of the rules to be notified under the FRA for several months. The latter have had a powerful official ally in the CEC. The CEC was established on 17 September 2002 through a *gazette* notification issued by the MoEF, under the directions of the Supreme Court.[8] The objective was to look into violations of forest related laws and processes. Since then CEC has investigated and often given clear advice against destructive projects to the Supreme Court (though it has been less sensitive to people's livelihood concerns, as we will see later) (Dutta 2008).

Peopled by a small handful of very strong conservationists, the CEC has played a significant role in stalling or stopping a number of destructive 'development' projects in sensitive ecosystems (and indeed has become one of the few remaining effective points of environmental resistance *within* the system), but it (like the Supreme Court) has also been clearly biased against the livelihood interests and rights of people dependent on such ecosystems (for instance in its advice to evict fisherfolk and remove all traces of settlement in Jambudwip island of the Sundarbans in West Bengal in 2003) (Das n.d.).

Conservation policy making is currently like a tug of war between those fighting for social justice and those straining to retain exclusionary conservation. Decisions swing back and forth, and often the final decision is a messy attempt at compromise which no one is happy with—but which everyone also uses to their own advantage. In all this, both genuine democratic functioning as also decision-making based on sound knowledge are casualties. Witness for instance the attempt by the MoEF to rush through a process of identifying and declaring 'critical tiger habitats' (under WLPA 2006), and listing the number of villages that will need to be relocated from these. This was done before the notification

---

[8] Notifications dated 9 May 2002 and 9 September 2002 in W.P. 202/95 and 171/96.

of FRA and its rules so that democratic processes mandated by it will not be applicable for declaration of these tiger reserves. Consequently, this and CTH declared subsequently are reportedly happening in the absence of a number of steps that are supposed to be taken, including the establishment of people's rights, the fresh notification of tiger reserves, public consultations on what should be critical habitats, and processes of seeking consent from affected communities. Guidelines issued by the MoEF to state governments for this purpose also contain a number of other serious deficiencies. (See, for instance, the critique by a number of organizations under the banner of the Future of Conservation in India network.[9]) Fortunately, at least in the case of 'critical wildlife habitats', states are going slow, so there is an opportunity to influence them into using due knowledge-based and democratic processes.

Several organizations that are alarmed by the increasing polarization between conservationists and human rights activists, and by the ad hoc and haphazard manner of decision-making that has characterized conservation policy in the last few years, have attempted to start a process of working out a middle path.[10] Starting with a national workshop on the 'Future of Conservation in India' in early 2006, followed up with another national workshop in early 2007, these groups have the key goal of trying to foster dialogues towards mutual understanding and joint action, and to work together towards a more knowledge-based, equitable, and democratic approach to conservation.[11] In response to what they see as both threats and opportunities from the recent legal changes, they have issued detailed notes on the suggested process for identifying critical wildlife habitats, for moving towards coexistence in areas where wildlife and people will continue to live together, and for a just process of relocation in places where inviolate wildlife areas need to be created.[12] In 2008, they organized a national workshop on critical wildlife and tiger habitats, and made detailed recommendations to the centre and states on following knowledge-based, democratic processes.

---

[9] Available at: http://www.atree.org/cth_cwh.html (accessed 10 September 2015).

[10] These attempts build on previous processes that were carried out in the 1990s, through a series of consultations called 'Building Bridges' anchored by Kalpavriksh with a number of organizations in different parts of India.

[11] See statements and reports from these workshops at www.kalpavriksh.org.

[12] See notes at www.kalpavriksh.org and at http://www.atree.org/cth_cwh.html.

Unfortunately, these groups could not build the advocacy strength and presence in the corridors of power to be influential in conservation decision-making.

A number of organizations and people are also working on the ground, towards more inclusive forms of conservation. For instance, the Nature Conservation Foundation, Snow Leopard Trust, and Snow Leopard Conservancy work with communities in Himachal Pradesh and Jammu and Kashmir (Ladakh) for conservation of various species.[13] Samrakshan is working with the Garo community in Meghalaya on elephant conservation.[14] The Bombay Natural History Society is working with fishing communities in the Lakshadweep Islands towards community-based lagoon conservation (Deri et al. 2008).[15] In parts of north-east India, WWF India, the Wildlife Trust of India, Aaranyak, Nature's Foster, and others are helping build community capacity to conserve threatened primates such as the golden langur and hoolock gibbon.

In all this, the influence of international agencies and processes is as yet unclear. Major multilateral or bilateral donors have been including more human rights and social justice components in their funding guidelines and policies, though this is not always necessarily reflected in the projects they fund. An example of this is the Government of India's proposal for funding from the Global Environment Facility for a project on 'Biodiversity Conservation and Rural Livelihood Improvement in Forested Landscapes'. In its project document (contained in the World Bank's Project Appraisal Document of March 2006), there is the usual rhetoric of participatory conservation and so on, but the operational components are more or less business as usual, with the Forest Department retaining all powers, and issues of rights within PAs being sidestepped.[16] This has been pointed out to the Bank, including in terms of the ways in which a conventional approach would not be in line with the Bank's own policies, but there has been little sign of the Bank reconsidering. Or if there is such reconsideration, the Bank has not been transparent enough

---

[13] See www.snowleopardconservancy.org; see also the Nature Conservation Foundation at www.ncf-india.org.

[14] See their website at www.samrakshan.org.

[15] Personal observations by authors.

[16] Comments on 'Biodiversity Conservation and Rural Livelihoods Improvement Project', World Bank Project Appraisal Document, 21 March 2006, by Ashish Kothari, 7 June 2006.

to indicate this to the critics. More recently a consultation organized by the Wildlife Institute of India and Kalpavriksh in the Askot landscape of Uttarakhand, one of the two sites chosen for funding under this project, showed that villagers were largely unaware of the project's dimensions and objectives, and that the decision-making institution being proposed mostly excluded community representation.

COMMUNITY-BASED CONSERVATION: THE INTERNATIONAL CONTEXT

The imperative of moving towards participatory conservation has been underlined by a number of recent international events. The World Parks Congress, held in Durban in September 2003, was the fifth of such congresses, organized every 10 years by the World Conservation Union. It was by and large the biggest ever gathering of conservationists, with over 5,000 participants. All its outputs strongly stressed the need to centrally involve indigenous peoples and local communities in conservation, including respecting their customary and territorial rights, and their right to a central role in decision-making. The biggest breakthrough was the recognition of indigenous peoples' and local communities' conserved territories and areas (ICCAs) as a valid and important form of conservation.[17]

The Seventh Conference of Parties to the Convention on Biological Diversity, held in Kuala Lumpur in February 2004, had 'protected areas' as one of its main topics. Since the Convention on Biological Diversity is a legally binding instrument, its outputs are of great significance for all countries. One of its main outputs was a detailed and ambitious Programme of Work on Protected Areas, explicitly urging countries to move towards participatory conservation with recognition of indigenous/local community rights.[18]

Due to these and other processes, all countries that are party to the biodiversity convention, including India, are now committed to:

- Conserving a fully representative set of wildlife habitats
- Ensuring community participation at all stages of PA planning, establishment, governance, and management

[17] For copies of these documents see www.iucn.org/themes/wcpa/wpc2003.
[18] The Programme of Work on Protected Areas is available at www.biodiv.org.

- Giving full recognition to rights and responsibilities of communities
- Promoting various PA governance types including CCAs
- Developing policies with full participation of concerned communities
- Ensuring prior informed consent before any relocation

In February 2004, the MoEF committed the Government of India to an ambitious target under the Convention of Biological Diversity: moving towards full participation of adivasis and other local communities in the management of wildlife conservation, and in receiving benefits from such conservation, by 2008. However, little has been done to fulfil this obligation subsequently. On the contrary the development agenda of the government has only led to more evictions of the local communities and deprivation of their rights and access (Shrivastava and Kothari 2012; Kothari 2014).

CONSERVATION AND RIGHTS EQUATION IN 2025

Given the complex interplay of actors and influences discussed in this chapter, there are multiple scenarios which can be projected for the future. However, in our view, the following state of affairs is the most likely in the next few years.

Given the current path of economic growth 'at all costs', there will be continued loss in substantial areas of conservation importance, and/or of importance to the livelihoods of tens of millions of people. Unless the current economic crisis puts paid to the rapid expansion of industry and commerce in India, this trend will continue for the next few years. More and more PAs, or CCAs, or other parts of the landscape that are biodiversity-rich, and more and more sites crucial for local biodiversity-based livelihoods, will be given up for dams, mining, ports, expressways, cities, sports and tourism facilities, and so on. An indefinite tug of war may go on as well, that is, a continued situation in which human rights and conservation groups fight against each other, and are able to influence the government and on-ground processes in different directions, resulting in messy, directionless policy and practice and continued conflict. We expect this to be situation for at least the next few years, because diverse influences are continuing to work strongly on the government, and the government itself is unable or unwilling to take any dominant line. This in itself may not necessarily be detrimental, so long as those with diverse viewpoints increasingly realize the need to arrive at some common positions; this will hopefully then lead to the situation we describe below. We feel that this will be the most likely scenario for the next decade or more.

Our hope, then, is that a middle path can be forged: a gradual paradigm shift to inclusive conservation that privileges both wildlife protection and people's livelihoods, resulting in the strengthening of both, building a larger public constituency for conservation, and, in the long run, greater ability to resist the destructive forces of unbridled economic growth and globalization while pointing to alternative forms of 'development'. This would then have to take into consideration planning at the landscape (and seascape) level, where natural resources and biodiversity outside of PAs are managed and used as effectively as the PAs are conserved. This would then bring a much larger area in the country under appropriate management, providing larger spaces for wildlife as well as ecosystem-dependent people. Our hope and expectation is that in the long run, it is this scenario that will prevail. Some initial moves towards this are visible in the very many community-led natural resource initiatives, and the fewer but nevertheless significant official efforts at convergence of conservation and livelihoods, mentioned in various parts of this chapter. But these are scattered and sporadic, and it will require many years, perhaps decades, for them to converge into a national (and global) alternative.

REFERENCES

Centre for Equity Studies. 2003. 'Survey of Wildlife Protected Areas in India', Unpublished report sponsored by MoEF, Government of India, New Delhi.

CSE (Centre for Science and Environment). 2011. 'Forest Clearance', *Public Watch* 07, CSE, New Delhi.

Das, K. and K. C. Malhotra. 1998. 'Sacred Groves among the Tribes of India: A Literature Survey of Ethnographic Monographs', Mimeograph, Integrated Rural Development of Weaker Sections in India, Semiliguda.

Das, N. No date. 'Believe It or Not: Jambudwip—An Untold Story'. Available at: http://www.dishaearth.org/Believe%20It%20or%20Not.pdf.

Deri, A., D. Apte, I. Babu, and K. Shahib. 2008. 'Conserving Giant Clams through a Community Reserve in the Lakshadweep Islands: 1 April 2005–30 April 2008', Final Report, LEAD International, Bombay Natural History Society, and Darwin Initiative, July.

Desor, S. (ed.). 2012. *A National Report on Communitiy Forest Rights under Forest Rights Act: Status and Issues*. Pune and Bhubaneshwar: Kalpavriksh and Vasundhara with Oxfam India.

Dutta, R. 2008. *Supreme Court on Forest Conservation*. New Delhi: Universal Law Publishing.

Gadgil, M. 1995. 'Traditional Conservation Practices', in A. N. William (ed.), *Encyclopedia of Environment Biology*, vol. 3. California: Academic Press.

―――. 2008. 'Let Our Rightful Forests Flourish', Working Paper Series no. 27, National Centre for Advocacy Studies, Pune, November.

Gadgil, M. and R. Guha. 1992. *This Fissured Land: An Ecological History of India*. New Delhi: Oxford University Press.

Galvin, M. and T. Haller (eds). 2008. *People, Protected Areas and Global Change: Participatory Conservation in Latin America, Africa, Asia and Europe*, Perspectives of the Swiss National Centre of Competence in Research North South, vol. 3. Bern: University of Bern.

Guptabhaya, S. and N. Pathak. 2011. 'Policy Brief on Status of Rights Recognition and Pre-conditions for Relocation in Critical Tiger Habitat as Specified by the Scheduled Tribes and Other Traditional Forest Dwellers (Recognition of Forest Rights) Act (FRA) 2006 (FRA) and Wild Life (Protection) Amendment Act (WLPA), 2006'. Kalpavriksh, Pune.

Kalpavriksh. 2007. 'Forest Fires and the Ban on NTFP Collection in Biligiri Rangaswamy Temple Sanctuary, Karnataka: Report of a Field Investigation and Recommendations for Action', Kalpavriksh, Pune.

Khan, A. and F. Abbasi. 2009. 'Community Conserved Areas in Uttar Pradesh', in N. Pathak (ed.), *Directory of Community Conserved Areas in India*. Pune: Kalpavriksh.

Kothari, A. 2014. 'A Hundred Days Closer to Ecological and Social Suicide', *Economic and Political Weekly*, 49, no. 39, pp. 10–13.

Kothari, A. and K. Kohli. 2009. 'National Biodiversity Action Plan', *Economic and Political Weekly*, vol. 44, no. 20 (16 May).

Kothari, A., N. Singh, and S. Suri. 1995. 'Conservation in India: A New Direction', *Economic and Political Weekly* (28 October).

Kothari, A., P. Pande, S. Singh, and D. Variava. 1989. *Management of National Parks and Sanctuaries in India: A Status Report*. New Delhi: Indian Institute of Public Administration.

Kumar, A. 2006. 'Van Panchayats in Uttaranchal', in N. G. Jayal, A. Prakash, and P. K. Sharma (eds), *Local Governance in India: Decentralisation and Beyond*. New Delhi: Oxford University Press.

Kutty, R. and A. Kothari. 2001. *Protected Areas in India: A Profile*. Pune: Kalpavriksh.

Lockwood, M., G. Worboys, and A. Kothari. 2006. *Managing Protected Areas: A Global Guide*. London: Earthscan.

MoEF. 2004. *Handbook of Forest Conservation Act, 1980: Forest Conservation Rules, 2004 and Guidelines and Clarifications*. New Delhi: MoEF, Government of India.

―――. 2008a. *Annual Report 2007–08*. New Delhi: MoEF, Government of India.

―――. 2008b. *National Biodiversity Action Plan*. Delhi: MoEF, Government of India.

———. 2009. *Report of the Committee for Looking into the Management and Funding of Community Conserved Areas in India*. New Delhi: MoEF, Government of India.

Pathak, N. (ed.). 2009. *Directory of Community Conserved Areas in India*. Pune: Kalpavriksh.

Pathak, N. and S. Bhatt. 2003. 'Forest Management: Colonised by Brethren'. *The Hindu Survey of the Environment*.

Pathak, N. and A. Bose. 2009. 'Rights and forests', *Frontline*, vol. 26, no. 5, 28 February–13 March.

Rangarajan, M. 1996. 'The Politics of Ecology: The Debate on Wildlife and People in India, 1970–95', *Economic and Political Weekly*, vol. 31, pp. 2391–409.

———. 2001. *India's Wildlife History: An Introduction*. New Delhi: Permanent Black.

Rangarajan, M. and G. Shahabuddin. 2006. 'Displacement and Relocation from Protected Areas: Towards a Biological and Historical Synthesis', *Conservation and Society*, vol. 4, no. 3, pp. 359–78.

Rosencraz, A. and S. Lele. 2008. 'Supreme Court and India's Forests', *Economic and Political Weekly*, vol. 43, no. 5, pp. 11–14.

Sarkar, R. 2008. 'Decentralised Forest Governance in the Himalaya: A Re-evaluation of Outcomes', *Economic and Political Weekly* (3 May 2008).

Saxena, N. C. 2001. 'Empowerment of Tribals through Sustainable Natural Resource Management in Western Orissa', Report prepared for IFAD/DFID, New Delhi, December.

Shahabuddin, G. Forthcoming. 'India Ecodevelopment Project: A Fragmented Legacy', in *Conservation at the Crossroads*. New Delhi: Permanent Black.

Shrivastava, A. and A. Kothari. 2012. *Churning the Earth: The Making of Global India*. Delhi: Viking/Penguin India.

Tatpati, Meenal (ed.). 2013. 'Assertion of Rights over Community Forest Resource'. Unpublished, Kalpavriksh and Greenpeace, Pune.

Tiwari, B. K., S. K. Barik, and R. S. Tripathi. 1999. *Sacred Forests of Meghalaya: Biological and Cultural Diversity*. Regional Centre, National Afforestation and Ecodevelopment Board, North-Eastern Hill University, Shillong.

TPCG and Kalpavriksh. 2005. *Securing India's Future: Final Technical Report of the National Biodiversity Strategy and Action Plan*. Delhi/Pune: Kalpavriksh.

Tucker, R. 1991. 'Resident Peoples and Wildlife Reserves in India: The Prehistory of a Strategy', in Patrick West and Stephen Brechin (eds), *Resident Populations and National Parks: Social Dilemmas and Strategies in International Conservation*. Tucson: University of Arizona Press.

Vagholikar, N. 2008a. 'Large Dams in North East India: The Politics of Environmental Governance', in *Green Governance Award Issue 2008*. Mumbai: Bombay Natural History Society.

———. 2008b. 'Lies Dammed Lies: Untruths Compromise India's Ecological Security', *Sanctuary Asia*, vol. 28, no. 4 (August).

Vasundhara. 2005. 'Impacts of Wildlife Policy on the Lives and Livelihood of Poor Tribal and Other Marginalised Communities Living in and near the Protected Areas', Unpublished report, Vasundhara, Bhubaneshwar.

Vasundhara and Kalpavriksh. 2012. *A National Report on Community Forest Rights under Forest Rights Act: Status and Issues*. Bhubaneshwar: Vasundhara and Pune: Kalpavriksh, in collaboration with Delhi: Oxfam. Available at: http://fra.org.in/new/document/A%20National%20Report%20on%20Community%20Forest%20Rights%20under%20FRA%20-%20Status%20&%20Issues%20-%202012.pdf

Wani, M. (ed.). 2008. *Nought without Cause: Almost Everyone's Guide to the Underlying Causes of Deforestation and Forest Degradation in the Era of Neoliberal Globalisation*. Pune: Kalpavriksh, Vasundhara, and Global Forest Coalition.

Wani, M. and A. Kothari. 2007a. 'Conservation and People's Livelihood Rights in India: Final Report of a Research Project Conducted under the UNESCO Small Grants Programme', unpublished report, Kalpavriksh, Pune/Delhi. Available at: www.kalpavriksh.org/f1/f1.2/UNESCO%20CNL%20project%20final%20report.pdf

———. 2007b. 'Protected Areas and Human Rights in India: The Impact of the Official Conservation Model on Local Communities', *Policy Matters*, 15 July.

Woodman, J. 2002. 'Ghosts in the Transmission: The Translation of Global Conservation Concepts to Local Scenarios—A Case Study of Ecodevelopment in Central India', paper submitted for the Ninth Biennial Conference of the IASCP: 'The Commons in an Age of Globalisation', Victoria Falls, Zimbabwe, 17–22 June.

Epilogue

Violence of 'Development' and Adivasi Resistance—An Overview

Meena Radhakrishna

It is increasingly becoming clear that for the large section of our citizens which adivasis constitute, all is not well. The essential problem which the adivasis face today is that of gradual and incremental loss of land, livelihood, culture, their very identity, and in extreme cases which are no longer rare, loss of life itself. The issues are complex and the players virtually uncountable. While writing about crises concerning the adivasi people over the last decade, it is important to disentangle the multiple strands or factors which impact their lives on a day-to-day basis.

A careful, scholarly study of the events of the last decade relating directly to the adivasis is hampered by the impossibility of systematic data collection from the field by any individual researcher. This author finally decided to try and reach some generic conclusions on the serious situation facing the adivasis today by analysing the extensive secondary sources available. These sources are in the form of reports written by civil liberty activists or human rights organizations (including international ones); accounts written by environmentalists or expert committees set up by the Ministry of Environment or the Supreme Court itself; intermittent press releases by NGOs working with adivasis and others; declarations, manifestos, statements, or demands by such organizations; editorials and opinions in the print media, regional, national, as well as international, on matters affecting the adivasis; reported news items in the national and international press about protests and violence of all forms involving adivasis; and coverage of various landmark judgments by courts, including the Supreme Court.[1]

A systematic, year-by-year, event-by-event, document-by-document study of the available material on the numerous players involved from the beginning of the twenty-first century uncovers a fascinating mosaic, and shows a criss-crossing of interests amongst different *dramatis personae*, so to say.

The analysis of the events in this chapter is entirely based on 'facts' as reported, but it raises larger, very serious issues about state policies and state practices on the one hand, and lack of state responsibility and accountability to its adivasi as well as non-adivasi citizens, on the other. Concretely, it raises crucial debates about notions of development held by the Indian state and followed by state governments; the grounds for the severe and militant opposition which has arisen to those notions; the role of the state in facilitating the so-called development projects; the conduct of the state if there is opposition to its cherished notion of development; and more recently, the nefarious role of the state in

---

[1] This chapter is thus entirely based on secondary sources. Individual documents were accessed by the author on the internet from a number of databanks available on different specialized sites (for example, conservation-related or human-rights-related sites). The most extensively used databank, however, is the official website of Mines and Communities, http://www.minesandcommunities.org/. Data compiled by the Human Rights Documentation Department of the Indian Social Institute, New Delhi, available at http://www.isidelhi.org.in/, has also been used frequently. A serious attempt has been made to cross-check the details in each and every document thus accessed from other internet sources as well. Wherever possible, the online version of the actual report, study, or news item quoted on these websites was accessed, and details taken from there. However, the corresponding databank website is always cited, as a way of acknowledging it as the original source of information, and also to make it easier for the interested reader who may want to access a particular document.

Though it is possible that a few details quoted in this chapter may be controversial, there is no doubt in this author's mind that the overall conclusions based on the investigation will still remain valid. The organizers to all the databanks, especially the two excellent databanks just mentioned, are sincerely thanked by the author. They are, however, in no way responsible for any deemed 'misrepresentation of facts'.

pitching adivasis against adivasis. Even if the adivasis agreed with the Indian state's notion of development, which they do not, the debate would still have to take place on how to make such development less destructive of not just human rights or liberties, but of human life itself.

There are also provocative questions raised by this data about what defines conservation when it begins to threaten the well-being of those humans who have lived for centuries in an 'environment' which they are now accused of destroying. It is critical to understand the role played by a section of the environment movement in this very specific context.

There are other concerns which will come up as the narrative unfolds of the devastation, misery, and pain of the adivasi people; their decades-old battles and struggles to end indiscriminate wreckage of their lives and livelihoods; their opponents and their allies; their defeats and their victories; and finally their hope and vision of a more just and inclusive India.

'DEVELOPMENT': THE SCOURGE OF ADIVASI LIVES

Poverty in Mineral-Rich States

A strong argument was put forward by policymakers in the earlier, Manmohan Singh–led government that in order to alleviate poverty in some of the poorest Indian states, coincidentally also the ones in which a large proportion of the populations lived in the forests, what was needed was a thorough exploitation of the natural resources of such states. These Indian states are endowed with an abundance of minerals, and allowing domestic and foreign mining companies to mine under detailed memorandums of understanding (MoUs) with the respective state governments was presented as a way out of poverty, and a road to development in step with the Indian state's economic policies of liberalization and globalization.

Odisha, for instance, has almost 60 per cent of India's known bauxite reserve, 25 per cent of its coal, 98 per cent of chromites, 28 per cent of iron ore, 92 per cent of nickel ore, and 28 per cent of manganese. Under the policy of economic reforms, creation of the Kalinganagar complex as an industrial park spread over 12,000 acres was conceived in the early 1990s.[2] As a prominent writer on aluminium mining in India has written,

---

[2] 'Police Firing at Kalinganagar: A Report', People's Union for Civil Liberties (PUCL) Orissa, 2 January 2006, available at: http://www.minesandcommunities.

The Orissa Government is… trying to set up a State-wide programme of rapid industrialization based on a vastly increased scale of mining projects—primarily bauxite, iron-ore, coal and chromite, along with aluminium refineries and smelters, steel plants, plus coal-fired power stations and hydro-electric dams to power them. The idea is that this will rapidly bring great wealth into the State in the form of Foreign Direct Investment, which will quickly pay off Orissa's Foreign Debt to the World Bank and other foreign institutions, at the same time as it promotes overall development in a State which has a high level of poverty and records of starvation deaths. (Padel and Das 2006)[3]

There are two more states which are particularly mineral-rich, which have been subjected to this development policy for a couple of decades now, namely the 'tribal states' of Chhattisgarh and Jharkhand, apart from Odisha. Chhattisgarh, carved out of Madhya Pradesh in November 2000, is India's richest state in terms of mineral wealth with as many as 28 varieties of major minerals, including diamonds. The world's best-quality iron ore is said to be found in the state's Bastar region, and it has almost a fifth of the country's coal deposits.[4] Jharkhand, earlier a part of Bihar, has deposits of uranium, mica, bauxite, granite, gold, silver, graphite, magnetite, dolomite, fireclay, quartz, feldspar, and iron. It has 32 per cent of the coal and 25 per cent of the total copper deposits of India.[5]

---

org/article.php?a=3094 (accessed 27 August 2015). See also 'Visit Report by Vidhya Das (based on her visit to Kalinganagar, first circulated on the Forestrights listserve)', available at: http://www.minesandcommunities.org/article.php?a=34 (accessed 27 August 2015).

[3] Also available at: http://www.minesandcommunities.org/article.php?a=40 (accessed 29 August 2014).

[4] 'Chhattisgarh to Be World's Diamond Bowl', Indo-Asian News Service, 13 February 2005, available at: http://www.minesandcommunities.org/article.php?a=852 (accessed 27 August 2015). According to this report, six companies were competing for a piece of the state's 'diamond pie', with South Africa's De Beers and Diamond Prospecting Pvt. Ltd carrying out surveys along the 3,975 square kilometre stretch in Kanker, Dhamtari, Durg, and Rajnandgaon districts. For a detailed account of diamonds, gold, and gems in Chhattisgarh, see the official website of the government, at http://chhattisgarhmines.gov.in/Other-Minerals.htm (accessed 27 August 2015).

[5] *Resource Rich Tribal Poor: Displacing People, Destroying Identity in India's Indigenous Heartland*, report by ActionAid, Indian Social Institute (New Delhi), and LAYA, New Concept Information Systems Pvt. Ltd, 2008, p. 19.

These percentages and figures are important, as they give some idea of the sheer extent of mineral wealth in these states in relation to the country as a whole. However, given the vision behind the development policy, and despite the vast natural resources of these states being exploited under this policy, the number of 'backward districts' in these three states, according to the government's own indices of what constitutes backwardness, is staggering: Jharkhand (19 districts out of 22), Odisha (27 out of 30), and Chhattisgarh (15 out of 16).[6] In other words, the envisioned development policy has not worked out from the point of view of the communities inhabiting these mineral-rich forested regions.

There are more serious issues. Not only have the populations of these resource-rich regions not flourished with mining activities and other development projects which have been in operation for years, much worse has happened. Literally hundreds of thousands of adivasis have been displaced, losing their land, livelihood, culture, and identity because of these measures to develop the region, without deriving any benefit out of the projects or industries.[7] 'Tribal communities are the worst affected by development projects. They constitute 8.2% of the total population yet they account for *40% of the total displaced population*', observe researchers who investigated Andhra Pradesh, Chhattisgarh, Jharkhand, and Odisha, all states rich in natural resources and home to significant tribal populations.[8]

Adivasis can see for themselves that those who were displaced have not been rehabilitated adequately, if at all, and often they can see that their erstwhile fellow adivasi cultivators have been reduced to casual

---

[6] This fact is borne out by studies. See 'Making Mining "Work" for "Development"', submission to the Group of Ministers by the Centre for Science and Environment, New Delhi, 26 June 2007, available at: http://www.cseindia.org/userfiles/Mining%20Presentation%20given%20by%20SN%20at%20Home%20Ministy%20on%20June%2026,%202007(2).pdf (accessed 27 August 2015).

Another study was conducted in 2007, in five districts of four resource-rich states of Jharkhand, Chhattisgarh, Odisha, and Andhra Pradesh. *Resource Rich Tribal Poor: Displacing people, Destroying Identity in India's Indigenous Heartland: A Report* by ActionAid, Indian Social Institute (New Delhi) and LAYA, New Concept Information Systems Pvt. Ltd., place of publication unknown, 2008. Henceforth, *Resource Rich Tribal Poor*.

[7] *Resource Rich Tribal Poor*, p. xiv.

[8] *Resource Rich Tribal Poor*, p. xiii.

labour, migrants, rickshaw pullers, or even beggars.[9] They notice that schools, hospitals, jobs, and other large compensatory packages promised by the government and the companies are not forthcoming. Instead, they find that there are more and more MoUs being signed between state governments and transnational mining companies which will allow forcible acquiring of their land for the projects. What will surely follow is not only the total wrecking of the ecology of the region, but permanent displacement from their homes, most often from the district, or even from the state itself. The despair and destruction imminent after summary displacement caused by these development projects, including mining, and the lack of even rudimentary rehabilitation has made the adivasi not just sceptical but hostile to any further intrusion into their lives by companies promising 'development'.

Pushed out of their land and having lost their traditional means of land (or forest) dependent livelihoods, large-scale migration is the only answer in the absence of any new industrial or other jobs. So sometimes able-bodied men or women, sometimes whole adivasi families, even whole adivasi communities, are forced to leave their devastated birthplaces, their homes and hearths, for regions unknown to them. They are easily deceived into entering the informal workforce via cold-blooded labour contractors, who begin by lending them money for rock-bottom subsistence. Ignorant of the ways of the world outside the one they have inhabited all their lives, ignorant also of the language of the inhospitable 'host' region, whole families, including children, end up in bonded labour-like working conditions in faraway brick kilns or sugarcane fields or in the construction industry.

Those who remain closer to what was previously their home, find it difficult to keep away company touts or human traffickers. The following extract most poignantly captures the destruction of those adivasi communities who stay behind after some sort of settlement with the corporate group which has entered the region.

> In terms of social anthropology, industrial projects imposed on a tribal area destroy the cohesive social structure of tribal society. They are dispossessed of the land that is central to their self-sufficient economy and production of food, as well as to their identity, and many shift closer towards a class of landless labourers. The factories, from the moment

---

[9] 'Orissa Farmers Protest Diversion of Irrigation Water to Industries', ANI, Bargarh (Orissa), 13 January 2007, available at: http://www.minesandcommunities.org/article.php?a=4291 (accessed 27 August 2015).

their construction starts, generally cause a considerable degrading of their remaining cultivated land through pollution and desiccation. Their religion and moral values receive a shock at the disrespect shown by company and Govt. people towards their mountains, forest and water-sources—as well as to themselves. In terms of kinship and the structure of social relations through kin groups, communities are torn apart when they are resettled, as well as from the variable, divisive treatment they receive from 'the company'. Mining companies have a strong tendency to divide people against each other. They bring a new spirit of competitiveness, and hierarchy into what have been markedly egalitarian societies. Those who hold out against company interests tend to get poorer, while those who serve its interests get chances for quick wealth. In other words, a corruption of values sets in, which goes hand in hand with mass poverty, prostitution and the breakup of families, and an assault on everything in their social as well as natural environment which traditionally they valued. (Padel and Das 2006)

Increasingly, however, those who stay back don't just stand and watch these projects destroy their lives—they discuss their situation, reach their conclusions, they organize, and they protest. The issues have to do with loss of livelihood, first and foremost. Then there is the loss of ancestral land they have cultivated, and of homesteads where they have lived for generations. This, to understate it, implies a total loss of identity, culture, and their very being—to protect which adivasis come out in large numbers against new projects and MoUs. They have been organizing opposition to these projects for years now.[10] They say they have nothing more to lose in any case: 'What will we do, how will we live in case our forests are lost?' they ask the government and the company managements again and again. Most overt are the protests against acquisition of land under threat or pressure, with inadequate compensation, and without clearance from the gram sabhas. (According to the Constitution of India, gram sabhas are the prime bodies which must give consent in Schedule V areas where adivasis constitute the predominant population.)[11]

---

[10] Campaign for Dignity and Survival is just *one* union of a large number of forest community groups and campaigns. See 'Thousands Protest for Rights over India's Forests', Planet Ark INDIA, 30 November 2006, available at: http://www.minesandcommunities.org/article.php?a=3713 (accessed 27 August 2015). There are a large number of localized adivasi people's organizations and anti-land acquisition groups in forest areas which are quite organized and articulate.

[11] According to the Ministry of Tribal Affairs website, the following are the criteria for declaration of a scheduled area: 'preponderance of tribal population;

Land Acquisition for Industrial Projects

To comprehend the intensity and content of adivasi protests, it is important to understand the process of land acquisition from adivasis. Land for all industrial projects is acquired from two sources: land under the ownership of the government, and that owned by private individuals. Industrial projects require at least a few hundred acres of land, often much more, depending on the scale of operations. Mining in particular can potentially spread over very large areas of land, as the extent of the deposits underneath would be the most important determining factor.

The government sells the land under its ownership at the rates it chooses to fix with a corporate group, or the company has to acquire land from private individuals. The government can also acquire land from the communities at a price fixed by itself, and then resell it to the companies as it wishes. It has been pointed out that

> one important aspect of land acquisition is that after the Forest Rights Act (FRA) has been instituted, the definition of 'government land' (as opposed to private land) changes, as much of the forest land which the government was earlier able to parcel out for mining as it 'owned' it, no longer belongs to the government in legal terms. This land now in principle belongs to forest dwellers, pending a permanent and legal recognition of tenurial rights through a settlement process under the rules of FRA.[12]

This can be, and is, a very important source of conflict on the ground between the state and the affected communities.

To understand clearly some other issues involved regarding land acquisition, let us look at the example of Kalinganagar in Odisha which has been in the news for almost two decades, because of vehement protests by communities inhabiting the region. Kalinganagar Complex is a massive industrial park with an area of over 12,000 acres. It was set

---

compactness and reasonable size of the area; under-developed nature of the area; and marked disparity in economic standard of the people.' See http://www.tribal.nic.in/Content/DefinitionofScheduledAreasProfiles.aspx (accessed 27 August 2015).

[12] 'Report by the Independent Fact Finding Team on Issues related to the Proposed Posco Project in Jagatsinghpur (Orissa), 19–22 April 2007', available at: http://www.minesandcommunities.org/article.php?a=4464 (accessed 27 August 2015).

up by the government body Infrastructure Development Corporation of Orissa Limited (IDCO) in the Jajpur district of Odisha, where a number of industrial units were allocated land. The area has a significant adivasi and dalit population. The ST population in the acquired area is also much higher than the block average.[13]

Land was first acquired in the area by IDCO through the then prevailing, archaic land acquisition legislation, and then sold to the companies for a large profit margin (allegedly at seven times the price paid to the original patta holders). Several industrial units came up here, including Neelachal Ispat Nigam, MESCO, and Jindal.[14] The Land Acquisition Act of 1894 (Amendment 1984) (LAA) did not give the owner of land, that is, the seller, the right to say 'no', as the land was supposed to be acquired for 'public interest'. The truth, however, was that the land acquired by the government under the LAA for 'public purpose' was actually meant for private companies.[15] Another common issue of grievance was that if the company was unable to use all the land it had acquired, the unutilized part was not returned to the government or to the original seller.

Moreover, the LAA had provisions only for providing compensation for patta land, and a miniscule plot of land for homesteads for the landless. It did not take into account the fact that the local adivasis and other marginalized communities had been mostly cultivating non-patta land due to non-regularization of land ownership. In Odisha, for instance, where land survey and settlement has not been done since 1928, this had disastrous consequences for a number of those who had been using the land without having any record of a patta in their names. Further, those who were sharecroppers were also outside the purview of the LAA.[16] Even though all these people were absolutely dependent on their lands for their livelihoods, they were neither offered compensation, nor given land in return for the land cultivated by them. Neither was any compensation given for lost homes or for

---

[13] The two blocks—Sukinda and Danagadi—under which the area falls have an ST population of 36.06 per cent and 28.19 per cent, and SC population of 11.89 per cent and 22.31 per cent, respectively. See PUCL, 'Police Firing at Kalinganagar', available at: http://www.pucl.org/Topics/Dalit-tribal/2006/kalinganagar.htm (accessed 27 August 2015).
[14] 'Visit Report by Vidhya Das'.
[15] PUCL, 'Police Firing at Kalinganagar'.
[16] PUCL, 'Police Firing at Kalinganagar'; 'Visit Report by Vidhya Das'.

'items' obtained from local common property resources.[17] Many of these cultivators who were dalit communities now had a large stake in any movement against land acquisition for mining or other projects along with the adivasis.

A working group on land relations was formed in 2006 at the instance of the then Prime Minister under D. Bandopadhyay, former land reforms commissioner of West Bengal. The recommendations of the group give a good indication of the issues involved, and possible solutions.[18] It gave far-reaching recommendations to revise the LAA in favour of the landless adivasis: that in case adivasis had 'encroached' on government land, it ought to be settled in their favour; that the exact extent of land required for projects ought to be reassessed by a neutral agency consisting of experts, along with representatives of the adivasi population; and that government land leased in adivasi dominated areas by the tribals for agriculture and homestead purposes ought to be more than proportionate to the percentage share of the adivasi population of the village. The group also recommended fixing of the price of land sold by adivasis to the companies by the government; it wanted to see greater transparency in the process of acquiring of adivasi land; and it advocated that common property resources, including grazing land, village forest, and water resources must not be acquired without providing alternative sources of equal or higher value.

Most significantly, the group recommended strict following of the rules under Panchayats (Extension to Scheduled Areas) Act (PESA)[19] in matters of land acquisition. It reiterated that the consent of the gram sabha was mandatory for minor and major exploitation of minerals, and, if necessary, mining concession rules ought to be modified to reflect the provision requiring consent of the gram sabha. The group gave a pre-eminent role to gram sabhas for approval of any compensation package and pointed out that even those adivasis who were not patta holders but were dependent on land-related livelihoods ought to be compensated. Compensation must

---

[17] 'Brakes on Industrialisation', *Dainik Statesman*, 23 August 2006, available at: http://www.minesandcommunities.org/article.php?a=4565 (accessed 27 August 2015).

[18] This group was formed after it became clear from the Planning Commission's estimate that 25 per cent of the country's mainland territory was 'being practically governed by extra legal and in some places illegal authorities' (that is, governed by Maoists or Naxalites in mostly adivasi-dominated areas). See 'Brakes on Industrialisation'.

[19] See Appendix for its implications in relation to land.

be calculated and given on the basis of calculation of a 20-year prospective income stream to adivasi families for loss of customary forest rights.

With regard to resettlement, the group recommended that not only ought efforts be made to ensure that all adivasi families were resettled to the extent possible, but that resettlement and rehabilitation ought to be completed prior to the project's commencement. Adivasis displaced by development projects must be resettled in a zone adjacent to the affected area in consonance with their social, ecological, linguistic, and economic affinities. One of the group's most significant recommendations was that the state must promote the concept of a land bank wherein adivasi land is purchased by the state and allotted to other deserving landless adivasi families in the same area.[20]

Many of these recommendations were soon reflected in the demands put forward by subsequent anti-land acquisition and anti-displacement protestors.[21]

CORPORATE GROUPS, LAND ACQUISITION, AND PRACTICES OF THE INDIAN STATE

The way land has been acquired in practice, and continues to be acquired, is not only through the obsolete and undemocratic LAA. It appears from a study of the available data that state governments have to deal with, broadly, at least three kinds of situations as far as land for mining projects is concerned. First, cases where mineral-rich land is still occupied by adivasis or other villagers while companies wait for that land to be made available for the mining project. Second, situations where land has already been acquired, and the work has started, but issues regarding non-fulfilment of promises with respect to compensation packages or other concerns lead to protests that prevent the work from continuing. Third, there is the situation of some land having already been acquired by companies waiting to start work, but not being allowed to enter. In the second and third sort of situations, the same company or similar companies may also be waiting to acquire more land in the same area. Sometimes, these situations might obtain simultaneously in contiguous areas in different permutations and

---

[20] 'Brakes on Industrialisation'.
[21] 'Land Acquisition Decried', Statesman News Service, Bhubaneswar, 26 September 2006, available at: http://www.minesandcommunities.org/article.php?a=2564 (accessed 27 August 2015).

combinations, and there might be many other scenarios. However, this section will try and grapple with the data to understand how the state responds to these three situations.

The 'Naxalite/Maoist' Adivasi in Mineral-Rich States: Jharkhand and Chhattisgarh

Maoists, in mineral-rich states, according to their own proclamations, oppose corporate entry into adivasi areas and land acquisition for industrial projects or special economic zones (SEZs). The association between Maoism and mining is strong even in the administrative mind.[22] The Maoists have been demanding and supporting exactly what the adivasis have been demanding as well. These armed groups have often opposed on their own the state's repressive machinery (including the Forest Department), which targets adivasis, or joined the struggles against land acquisition and mining. This has meant that a number of adivasis have turned into Maoist sympathizers or supporters, and sometimes they have actually joined the Maoists in their armed challenge to state authority in all its manifestations. However, in a number of other Maoist-occupied areas, adivasis remain ambivalent and do not necessarily support Maoist activities.

The important point for our purposes here, however, is that as far as the state is concerned, any adivasi who struggles for her or his rights under the FRA, or protests against the taking over of their land by mining companies, or in any way resists the government's plans for 'development' of their habitats is immediately declared as a Maoist and treated as such. It is thus difficult to estimate how widespread the reach and support base of the Maoists really are. At any rate, according to the states as well as the centre, there has been in the last decade tremendous growth in the influence of Naxalites and Maoist groups, armed with sophisticated weapons. This has happened to the extent that they have been named the biggest internal security threat by no less a person than the then Prime Minister Manmohan Singh. Chhattisgarh, Jharkhand, Andhra Pradesh, Odisha, and Bihar have been estimated to account for over 91 per cent of the Maoist violence in the country. Chhattisgarh and

[22] 'More Mining Means More Maoism, Says Jairam Ramesh', *Economic Times*, 29 February 2012, available at: http://articles.economictimes.indiatimes.com/2012-02-29/news/31110698_1_maoist-hit-areas-jairam-ramesh-iron-ore-mining (accessed 27 August 2015).

Jharkhand are said to account for about 70 per cent of the total Maoist violence.[23] It is important to remind ourselves here that the states just mentioned are mineral-rich states, needing to be cleared of populations from the point of view of both corporate groups and the state.

State targeting of Naxalites/Maoists in the mineral-rich forests of Jharkhand has been repeatedly alleged to be a way of providing land for mining corporates.

> The circumstantial evidences suggest that the anti-naxal operations have a clear mining interest.... 17 mining companies including Mittal, Tata, Jindal have been given mining leases in Saranda Forest. Therefore, the Center and state governments want to clear the land through the anti-naxal operations. The Adivasis are not yet given land entitlement under the Forest Rights Act 2006 though they are eligible for it and secondly, the land entitlement and other papers of 4 revenue villages were also destroyed by the security forces so that they would not be able to claim their rights over the land they have been cultivating for years. Hence, the mining companies would comfortably acquire the forest and environment clearance for mining.[24]

Saranda holds a quarter of India's proven iron ore reserves. Mining companies operate 50 mines in the region, including Tata Steel and the Steel Authority of India. The lethal Operation Anaconda in Jharkhand for armed action against the Maoists, reported from the Saranda forests, is allegedly also aimed at clearing the villages in the garb of 'combing' operations so that mines can be 'set up'.[25] A foreign reporter who visited the area of this operation quotes a development officer working in the Saranda forest as believing that the real reason for the security operations has to do with opening the area to mining companies. 'There is no reason to have all these troops for such a small population,' observed the

---

[23] 'Govt Fails to Contain Maoists', *Pioneer*, 17 January 2008, available at: http://www.isidelhi.org.in/hrnews/HR_THEMATIC_ISSUES/Naxals/Naxals-08.pdf (accessed 27 August 2015).

[24] 'Police Atrocities on Adivasis of Saranda Forest: A Fact Sheet', Jharkhand Human Rights Movement, 10 October 2011, available at: http://sanhati.com/articles/4230/ (accessed 27 August 2015).

[25] Dungdung, social worker, quoted in 'Horror Tales from Saranda', *Pioneer*, 14 September 2011, available at: http://www.minesandcommunities.org/article.php?a=11185 (accessed 27 August 2015).

official. 'They are trying to establish a corridor for security operations so that mining can begin.'[26]

'Operation Green Hunt' has been in existence for several years as well, launched by the union government to contain the Maoists. It is significant that Operation Green Hunt targeting the Maoists and Naxalites is not operative in all the 216 districts of the country which are said to be 'infested' by these groups, but particularly in those five districts which are especially mineral-rich and where companies like Tata Steel, Essar, Mittal, and Bhushan have interests.[27] Security forces and the police are supplemented by the deadly sounding CoBRA or Commando Battalion for Resolute Action units,[28] armed with extremely sophisticated weapons and with sweeping powers in the forests to kill Naxalites/Maoists.

This information can be interpreted in several ways: that Naxalites/Maoists, operating in mineral-rich states and working among adivasis who inhabit these lands, are as much a political challenge to the state as a grave economic threat to the corporate mining groups; that in the garb of tackling Naxalite/Maoist activities, there can be a legitimate presence of specialized armed forces in such areas so as to 'clear the land' not just of extremists but also of ordinary adivasis; that the presence of such armed forces in these mineral-rich states is evidence of strong resistance by ordinary adivasis against land acquisition or mining projects, which is being sought to be *presented* as a Naxalite threat to internal security, requiring extraordinary force; and that the state is not allowing the FRA to operate in mineral-rich districts, leading to fraudulent land acquisition, as also suggested by aforementioned instances of wilful destruction of land title records of adivasis in these areas.[29]

---

[26] Eric Randolph, 'India Sets Out on a Fight for the Forest', *National*, 28 March 2012, available at: http://www.thenational.ae/news/world/south-asia/india-sets-out-on-a-fight-for-the-forest (accessed 27 August 2015).

[27] Pravin Patel, 'Mukesh Kumar Should Look Within, instead of Throwing Stones at Others', *BizOdisha*, 14 September 2010, available at: http://www.minesandcommunities.org/article.php?a=10379 (accessed 27 August 2015).

[28] 'Maoist Bastions Smashed in Bastar', *Hindu*, 21 September 2009, available at: http://www.isidelhi.org.in/hrnews/HR_THEMATIC_ISSUES/Naxals/Naxals-09.pdf (accessed 27 August 2015).

[29] It is pertinent to note here that to facilitate mining groups to enter mineral-rich areas, the state of Gujarat has gone as far as to remove entire

It is in this context that another strategy by another state government might be understood.

Salwa Judum or 'Land Grab': Chhattisgarh

Quite independently of any union government moves to deal with the Maoists, the Chhattisgarh state government devised in 2005 the violent and divisive strategy of arming civilian adivasis in order to exterminate Maoists and Naxalites. This plan, not officially acknowledged, was institutionalized in the form of what came to be known as 'Salwa Judum'. The most disturbing part of this failed operation was to divide the adivasi population by arming adivasi youth to hunt down 'Maoist' adivasis. Special police officers (SPOs), drawn from among the local adivasi youth, were recruited by the government as part of this operation supposedly for intelligence collection, guarding government-maintained relief camps, and assisting security forces in their operations in remote, forested, hilly regions 'infested by' rebels.[30] When this scheme was put into operation, 13 battalions of central paramilitary forces, including the Central Reserve Police Force (CRPF), were already deployed in Chhattisgarh to assist the state police in anti-Naxal operations.[31] Special police officers were said to be a part of temporary police camps set up to further control Naxalite activities.

There are a few extremely significant pieces of information which ought to be mentioned here in the context of the efforts of the mining companies to enter Bastar, with large opposition growing to the forcible acquisition of land. A most significant report titled 'State Agrarian Relations and Unfinished Task of Land Reforms' by a 15-member committee of the union Rural Development Ministry in January 2008 has devastatingly conclusive evidence of the truth behind Salwa Judum:

---

communities from the ST list so that protective provisions regarding land alienation applicable to Schedule V areas or STs do not apply any more. See the chapter by Rathva et al. in this volume.

[30] 'Chhattisgarh Govt Retrenches 1200 SPOs', *Pioneer*, 4 December 2008, available at: http://www.isidelhi.org.in/hrnews/HR_THEMATIC_ISSUES/Naxals/Naxals-08.pdf (accessed 27 August 2015).

[31] 'Pattern Shows Naxals Gunning for Salwa Judum', *Indian Express*, 16 March 2007, available at: http://www.isidelhi.org.in/hrnews/HR_THEMATIC_ISSUES/Naxals/Naxals-07.pdf (accessed 27 August 2015).

This open, declared war will go down as the biggest land grab ever.... Tata Steel and Essar Steel ... wanted seven villages or thereabouts ... to mine the richest lode of iron ore available in India. [After] initial resistance from the tribals ... the state withdrew its plans. A new approach was necessary.... [It] came about with the Salwa Judum.... Behind them are traders, contractors and miners.... The first financiers of the Salwa Judum were Tata and Essar ... 640 villages ... were laid bare, burnt to the ground and emptied with the force of the gun and the blessings of the state. [Some] 3,50,000 tribals, half the total population of Dantewada district, are displaced, their womenfolk raped, their daughters killed and their youth maimed. Those who could not escape into the jungle were herded together into refugee camps run and managed by the Salwa Judum.... 640 villages are empty. Villages sitting on tons of iron ore are effectively de-peopled and available for the highest bidder. The latest information being circulated is that both Essar Steel and Tata Steel are willing to take over the empty landscape and manage the mines.[32]

A lawyer active in the Chhattisgarh region further added to details of the situation in the following way: In 2005, Salwa Judum started. It was typical strategic hamleting, moving people out of the villages and into camps. In Chhattisgarh, they emptied 644 villages, by the government's admission, 350,000 people. About 50,000 were brought to the camps, and in 2013, these camps still had about 10,000 people. Some fled to neighbouring states, particularly Andhra Pradesh. The rest seem to have gone even deeper into the forest, probably 200,000 people.[33] The

---

[32] 'State Agrarian Relations and Unfinished Task of Land Reforms', quoted by Smita Gupta, 'Mind the drill', *Outlook*, 16 November 2009, available at: http://www.outlookindia.com/article/Mind-The-Drill/262704 (accessed 27 August 2015).

[33] 'The Bastar Land Grab: An Interview with Sudha Bharadwaj of Chhattisgarh Mukti Morcha Conducted by Justin Podur in Raipur on 5 March 2013', *Kafila*, 20 April 2013, available at: http://www.minesandcommunities. org/article.php?a=12256 (accessed 27 August 2015). See also 'Salwa Judum a Disaster for Chhattisgarh', available at: www.isidelhi.org.in/hrnews/HR_ THEMATIC_ISSUES/.../Naxals-07.pdf, p. 43 (accessed 11 November 2014). According to the Asian Indigenous and Tribal People's Network, from two districts alone, a large number of adivasis were reported to have fled to Andhra Pradesh because of bloodshed precipitated by Salwa Judum. About 1.2 lakh members of the Gutti Koya tribes of Bastar and Bijapur districts of Chhattisgarh fled to Andhra Pradesh's Khammam district between January and June 2008 to escape violence by the Maoists and the Salwa Judum activists. See 'Maoists Activities Displaced 4 Lakh Tribals: Report', *Hindustan Times*, 25 May 2009,

Chhattisgarh government announced its decision to permanently settle about 57,000 tribals living in 23 Salwa Judum camps by relocating all the 640 odd villages, 'as the state police would not be able to provide them security if they return to their native villages'.[34] While the adivasis were huddled away in these camps, with their appalling lack of amenities, and kept there for their 'protection', Tata and Essar who had been trying to enter the very same districts where Salwa Judum is operating were able to do so successfully. 'The period of Salwa Judum correlates with the MOUs and the land grab ... some 2200 ha were granted to Tata and a similar amount to Essar, for iron ore prospecting.'[35] The connection between Salwa Judum and steel companies which had 'stealthily' entered the mineral-rich forests was also speculated upon by a report in the *Guardian* while the operation was still on.[36]

The displacement of lakhs of adivasis due to Salwa Judum led to spiralling violence. Thousands of adivasis became homeless as their villages were looted and burnt,[37] and migrated to neighbouring states, since those who did not join Salwa Judum were branded as Maoists and targeted by the authorities. This strategy in Chhattisgarh was finally declared illegal by the Supreme Court due to a public interest litigation filed by concerned citizens to stop the massacres of adivasis caught in the crossfire.

Salwa Judum, then, can reasonably be construed as having been designed to serve several purposes simultaneously: to make ore-rich

---

available at: www.isidelhi.org.in/hrnews/HR_THEMATIC_ISSUES/Naxals/Naxals-09.pdf (accessed 27 August 2015).

[34] 'Raman Govt to Settle Tribals Living in Salwa Judum Camps', *Indian Express*, 9 November 2007, available at: www.isidelhi.org.in/hrnews/HR_THEMATIC_ISSUES/Naxals/Naxals-07.pdf (accessed 27 August 2015).

[35] 'The Bastar Land Grab'.

[36] 'Inside India's Hidden War', *Guardian*, 9 May 2006, available at: http://www.theguardian.com/world/2006/may/09/india.randeepramesh (accessed 27 August 2015).

[37] The Campaign for Peace and Justice in Chhattisgarh, and other such civil society groups, organized public hearings on this in Delhi. These clearly brought out the atrocities committed against the people under Salwa Judum, with women being raped for not joining the government-backed operations and young boys being forced with the threat of violence to join the operations. The security forces had assumed extraordinary powers in the remote areas of the state despite the armed confrontation between the Salwa Judum militia and the deemed Naxalites. See 'Salwa Judum a Disaster for Chhattisgarh'.

village land available for the steel companies; to kill any Maoists, but largely ordinary adivasis who resisted the entry of these companies by dubbing them Maoists; to terrorize, make destitute and homeless, and thus dislocate and disperse out of the state of Chhattisgarh whole adivasi communities who were resisting land acquisition (facilitating hand over of the vacated land to the corporates); and to make a deep fissure in the adivasi community in the region so as to undermine the unity of adivasi movements resisting land acquisition.[38]

The remarkable cynicism of a state government which through an undeclared policy can subject its adivasi citizens to such systematic violence, in order to collude with powerful corporate groups, speaks for itself.

Police and Paramilitary Forces: Kashipur, Odisha

The preceding section discussed the extra-legal ways of acquiring land for companies who aspired to it, from those who are unwilling to part with it. This section will document the situation of those adivasis who live in areas where mining companies have already entered, started mining, and are trying to get deeper into the ore-rich areas.

There are several ways in which the adivasis and their allied groups come under fire from the state, literally, while protesting against mining and other industrial projects, and against further land acquisition. This can be illustrated through various case studies. The issue of excesses by the police, including firing on those protesting against corporate projects, is highlighted by several investigations and reports by concerned individuals.[39]

---

[38] Pitting adivasis against adivasis to realize an aim, one would have thought, was an unusual, one-off strategy adopted by a misguided state government. However, recent report show that now PVTGs, some of the most deprived adivasi communities, are being recruited by the central government, again to fight the 'Maoists'. 'Tribals to Be Trained in Guerrilla Warfare to Fight Maoists in State', *Hindustan Times*, Ranchi edition, 30 June 2014, quoted at http://www.jesaonline.org/index.php?option=com_content&view=article&id=719:adivasis-to-fightkill-adivasis&catid=916:adivasis-and-dalits&Itemid=123 (accessed 27 August 2015).

[39] PUCL 'Police Firing at Kalinganagar'; see also 'Visit Report by Vidhya Das'. Angana Chatterji, 'Open Letter to Shri Navin Patnaik, Chief Minister of Orissa', 6 December 2004, available at: http://www.minesandcommunities.org/article.php?a=3936 (accessed 27 August 2015); 'From an Orissa activist',

Wherever the mining projects are in progress and there is resistance, the government sets up new police posts to suppress the movement. The Odisha government in particular has been strengthening the police set-up in upcoming industrial hubs, as local administrations have failed to contain people's opposition to development projects. New police stations are commissioned, existing police outposts are upgraded into full-fledged police stations, and staff is added to existing police stations wherever there are steel plants, aluminia refineries, or mining of other minerals.[40] Platoons of police are deployed at a time, to the extent that sometimes police outnumber the protestors.[41]

Moreover, human rights organizations have been concerned about the collusion between goons hired by the companies and the police, on the one hand, and 'the dangerous consequences of the use of state-sponsored informal militias' to tackle 'the dramatic rise of conflicts' over forcible acquisition of land, on the other.[42]

The Indian People's Tribunal (IPT) personnel went to investigate the situation arising from adivasi protests against the bauxite mining company, Utkal Alumina International Limited, in Kashipur, Odisha.[43] Going by the available material on a number of other adivasi protests against mining, their narrative is a representative one, as the IPT personnel too state in their report: 'Unfortunately, the violence that is

---

2 December 2004, available at: http://www.minesandcommunities.org/article.php?a=3930 (accessed 27 August 2015); 'From an Observer in the Vedanta Area', 5 December 2004, available at: http://www.minesandcommunities.org/article.php?a=3931 (accessed 27 August 2015).

[40] 'Orissa to Strengthen Police Setup in Industrial Hubs', *Kalinga Times*, Bhubaneswar, 5 May 2007, available at: http://www.minesandcommunities.org/article.php?a=4465 (accessed 27 August 2015).

[41] 'Opposition to Jindal Mounts', *Hindu*, Vizianagaram, 11 July 2007, available at: http://www.thehindu.com/todays-paper/tp-national/tp-andhrapradesh/opposition-to-jindal-mounts/article1870790.ece (accessed 27 August 2015).

[42] 'Refugees Are Human Too: India's Failed National Rehabilitation and Resettlement Policy, 2007', *Asia Centre for Human Rights Weekly Review*, 19 December 2007, available at: http://www.minesandcommunities.org/article.php?a=8377 (accessed 27 August 2015).

[43] The next few paragraphs on the police are drawn from the following report: 'Kashipur: An Enquiry into Mining and Human Rights Violations in Kashipur, Orissa', Report of the IPT on Environment and Human Rights, New Age Printing Press, October 2006, pp. 56–63 (henceforth 'IPT Kashipur Report').

a hallmark of the struggle in Kashipur is not unique. State repression has been the hallmark of bauxite-mining projects in Odisha and this underscores a coordinated effort to ensure that bauxite-mining projects proceed as planned, with or without the consent of the local people.'[44]

Extracts from the IPT Kashipur report are included in the next few paras, almost verbatim, because the description is so graphic and captures so clearly the grim situation facing protestors against corporate groups everywhere.[45]

The police and paramilitary forces along with goondas hired by [the mining company], have consistently disrupted peaceful democratic meetings, conducted village raids and carried out widespread and arbitrary arrests in the area. Intimidation and harassment by these forces have included shootings, beatings, lathi charges, threats, humiliation, and the use of tear gas. Three people have died and many more have been injured.

The number of police and paramilitary forces in the mining areas has been rising dramatically since 2004. The government not only increased the number of local police platoons, but in some cases also deployed two paramilitary groups: the CRPF and the India Reserve Battalion (IRB). To intimidate protestors, it has also been constructing new police outposts and barracks where the companies are operating. The police and paramilitaries only target those opposing the project, while allowing company goondas to openly attack protesters with impunity.

IPT personnel when they visited the mining site noted that the area was 'teeming with armed policemen' and that their team was 'struck by the number of guns they saw'. The area seemed to be under siege and people were living in a perpetual climate of fear. The armed police and reserve battalions were reported to march past villages and conduct regular patrol, as a way of instilling fear in villagers and extorting their consent.[46]

---

[44] 'IPT Kashipur Report', pp. 62, 63.
[45] According to the authors of this report, these accounts are substantiated and supplemented by information from five separate and independent fact-finding investigations conducted by credible civil society organizations in 2005: People's Union for Civil Liberties (PUCL), People's Union for Democratic Rights (PUDR), Association for Protection of Democratic Rights (APDR), Human Rights Forum (HRF), and Indian Social Action Forum (INSAF).
[46] 'IPT Kashipur Report', p. 56.

The large number of armed forces patrolling the area forced residents to restrict their movements and limit excursions outside their homes, even at the expense of neglecting their fields, simply to avoid intimidating encounters with armed forces. The armed forces return again and again to the villages, threatening villagers with arrests or even death in case they continue to oppose the company. These raids have sometimes succeeded in their objective. For example, the Sarpanch of Maikanch surrendered after his village was inundated by 100 CRPF troops for over a month; under duress, he signed a statement vowing not to oppose the mining project.[47]

There is not just the issue of threat of rapes, arrests or murder by the armed police who constantly fire in the air to terrify people meeting to discuss issues regarding land in a bid to disperse them. False charges of a serious nature are foisted by the police against adivasi activists and whoever opposes the companies and arrests made. No one could reach the weekly village markets for fear of being arrested. In the courts, the prosecution vigorously opposes bail for those arrested to lengthen their period of detention. The strategy is to prevent anti-mining activists and community leaders from organizing and participating in protests by keeping them behind bars, thereby weakening the opposition struggle.[48]

Following were the final conclusions of the Tribunal: 'The influx of police and paramilitary forces to the area, village raids by armed forces, the violation of the right to peaceful assembly, and the widespread and arbitrary arrests indicate that there is large-scale repression of dissent in the area, involving disproportionate force, intimidation and harassment. The collusion of the Government of Odisha and Utkal Alumina International (UAIL) in repressing the voices and desires of the local people explains the culture of impunity surrounding incidences of violence.'[49]

The killings of 13 adivasis in Kalinganagar, Odisha, in 2006 happened at the same time as the IPT report on Kashipur was being written, showing the extent to which police violence on protestors can escalate. The continuing protests by adivasis in the last decade have led to repeated bouts of brutal police violence, the entire scenario being similar to the one just recorded. In 2013, deployment of several platoons of police to acquire land and the resulting violence on anti-POSCO (a Korean

---

[47] 'IPT Kashipur Report', p. 56.
[48] 'IPT Kashipur Report', p. 61.
[49] 'IPT Kashipur Report', p. 62.

company) protestors drew sharp protests from civil society organizations in India as well as from Korean trade unionists and human right groups.[50]

Protests against the Jindal steel plant in Angul, Odisha, too have recently led to barbaric violence by the state police and the security guards of the company against the protestors, especially women.[51] These instances can be multiplied ad nauseam, and are only illustrative of the fact that even peaceful protests against land acquisition are met with extreme aggression by the state as well as by company-hired armed militia.

The large-scale, indiscriminate, and systematic violence of the Indian state to which the adivasis have thus been subjected in recent decades shall remain a matter of both disgrace as well as deep concern for any democracy. Emphatically, however, state repression is not a one-way street—this is a dialectical process by which the adivasi communities all over the country have become conscious of their situation and problems, and of possible solutions, and in turn they influence and precipitate some of the reactions and strategies by powerful players opposed to their interests. The affected communities have built a powerful movement on the ground to safeguard their interests, an example of which is given in what follows.

PROTESTS AND REBELLION

Nature of the Movement

The adivasis are not alone in their fight against state policies of development, because these policies have aspects to them which cause concern to a number of individuals and organizations.

---

[50] 'An Open Letter to the Chief Minister of Odisha against the Forceful Acquisition of Land for the POSCO Project', 7 February 2013, available at: http://www.indiaresists.com/an-open-letter-to-the-chief-minister-of-odisha-against-the-forceful-acquisition-of-land-for-the-posco-project/ (accessed 27 August 2015); 'Urgent Appeal from South Korean Trade Unions and Human Rights Organisations, 'No More Death for Odisha People Who Are Opposed to POSCO Project!', available at: http://miningzone.org/archives/2041 (accessed 27 August 2015). 'India and POSCO Must End Abuses Linked to Steel Project: Rights Groups Urge Suspension of Project, Prevention of Forced Evictions', 27 June 2013, available at: http://www.minesandcommunities.org/article. php?a=12363 (accessed 27 August 2015). POSCO stands for Pohang Steel Company Ltd.

[51] 'India: Brutal Violence by Jindal Steel Company against Protestors in Orissa, Protest Statement, Open Letter and Reportage', South Asia Citizens Web, 20 February 2012, available at: http://www.sacw.net/article2543.html (accessed 27 August 2015).

Staunchly opposed to corporate entry into forest areas are the countless NGOs, both adivasi and non-adivasi, national and international in their scale and operations. These organizations are sometimes devoted primarily to adivasi interests and well-being, or they could be an alliance of various individual organizations addressing issues pertaining to different constituencies of people, including adivasis. These organizations could be primarily concerned with, for instance, human rights or civil liberties, or they could be explicitly against displacement, demanding relief, and rehabilitation of those already displaced following land acquisition.

And then there are organizations whose activities directly impact adivasi interests. Amongst these are the ones committed to conservation of environment, including spaces which constitute the primary habitat of the adivasis, that is, the forests; those against alienation of land held by marginalized communities, be it in the forests or outside; and grassroots political organizations including those led by self-proclaimed Maoist and Naxalite groups operating primarily in adivasi areas. There are also anti-globalization and anti-SEZ organizations which oppose land acquisition and mining by transnational companies in adivasi areas, and are opposed to foreign direct investment in mineral-rich states where a large proportion of the adivasis reside.

The base, scale, issues, members, and numbers involved in protests against land acquisition—all have escalated over the last three decades or so, partially because of repression by the state of any legitimate protest against what has been repeatedly termed as 'adivasi land grab' on the part of government and corporate groups. Whether it is a story of success or defeat, brutal repression by the state machinery seems to be a common occurrence.

As far back as in 1987, hundreds of protestors endured police beatings and arrest but managed to stop mining in Gandhamardan, Odisha, by the Bharat Aluminium Company. Bharat had already built a colony for several thousand workers, which had to be abandoned, and is now derelict (Padel and Das 2006). In 1996, the people of Kalinganagar successfully stopped the establishment of a plant by Bhushan Steel in the Kalinganagar industrial complex. In 1997, there was police firing at Sindhigaon, Gopalpur, when people protested against the proposed steel plant by the Tatas, and police firing at Maikanch of Kashipur region led to the loss of three adivasi lives in 2000. Another major protest was held in 2005, where adivasis foiled the proposed Bhumi Pooja of Maharashtra Seamless Steel limited.[52]

[52] PUCL, 'Police Firing at Kalinganagar'; 'Visit Report by Vidhya Das'.

A study of the adivasi protests against forcible land acquisition for industrial projects shows that all over the country, distinct movements against acquiring of land for SEZs have given an impetus to adivasi protests.[53] These anti-land acquisition movements were not confined to one region—they were precipitated wherever the industrial projects were sought to be set up. Organizations with quite diverse perspectives participated. For instance, an umbrella organization Jibika Bachao Andolan (literally, Movement for Saving Livelihoods), though opposed to acquiring of land for corporates, voiced demands like a job for each and every displaced family in the project; land for land and means of livelihood; and homestead land for all landless people within three months.[54] However, movements like Jamin Bachao Andolan (literally, Movement for Saving Land) were less compromising, and coined a slogan 'Jan Denge Par Jamin Nahi Denge' (We will lay down our lives, but will not give up our land). Along with other organizations, it imposed 'people's curfew' in the areas likely to be affected, not allowing entry of company or government officials.[55] In spite of differences among organizations regarding aims and strategies, what united them was their agreement that land acquisition for industrial projects ought not to lead to loss of livelihoods.

Expanding Concerns, Widening Base, and Broader Alliances

From project to project, the battle cry of the protests has been determined by specific territorial, ecological issues or larger issues of displacement and lack of rehabilitation. There are issues of drying up and contamination of the rivers and destruction of livelihoods of fisherfolk as a result of this; pollution of drinking water resources; intensive air pollution in the so-called iron ore belt of the country where suspended particulate matter causes intense respiratory diseases like tuberculosis;[56] new health hazards

---

[53] 'Final Report on the Public Hearing and the Further Investigation on the Struggle by the People of Singur', National Alliance of People's Movements, Mumbai, 17 December 2006, available at: http://www.minesandcommunities.org/article.php?a=4597 (accessed 27 August 2015).

[54] 'Land Acquisition Decried', Statesman News Service, Bhubaneswar, 26 September 2006, available at: http://www.minesandcommunities.org/article.php?a=2564 (accessed 27 August 2015).

[55] 'Gathering Protests over Tribals' Eviction in Jharkhand', IANS, Ranchi, 8 November 2005, available at: http://www.minesandcommunities.org/article.php?a=3325 (accessed 27 August 2015).

[56] 'Adivasis of Bansapal Protest against Expansion of Mining—Public Hearing Disrupted and Cancelled', press note from Keonjhar Suraksha Parishad,

like prospects of an 'ash pond' in the vicinity of villages;[57] diversion of arable land; destruction of the rich agricultural economy of an area;[58] diversion of scant water resources to newly upcoming smelters rather than for irrigation; and loss of precious biodiversity and wildlife. Some or all of these issues converge in areas where mining is already in progress and an expansion is contemplated, or new plants are threatening to be established. Common villagers join the protest when they find that their grazing lands, ponds, cremation grounds, and connecting roads are taken over by steel companies, and especially when they are held legally guilty of trespassing in case they happen to use these roads even in emergencies.[59]

What is interesting to note is the snowballing of these anti-land acquisition and adivasi displacement movements into larger protests by wider sections. Given the brutality which these protests are dealt with by the state machinery with paramilitary forces and police frequently opening fire on protestors, some of these protests, like the ones in Kalinganagar for instance, have caught national and even international attention. The following news item captures some of the widening base of these movements:

> The civil society groups, trade unions, women's groups, peace and justice movements, and students, protested in Mumbai outside the Churchgate station against the Kalinganagar killing of Orissa, which took place on January 2, 2006. People demanded immediate closure of the Tata steel plant of Orissa and (demanded) justice to the deceased and affected adivasi communities. On January 2, 2006 about 21 adivasis were killed when police opened fire against the tribals protesting the takeover and seizure of their land by district administration, for the proposed TATA Steel plant at Kalinganagar in Orissa.

---

15 February 2006, available at: http://www.minesandcommunities.org/article. php?a=5773 (accessed 27 August 2015).

[57] 'Farmers Resist Ash Pond', Statesman News Service, Jajpur, 13 March 2006, available at: http://www.minesandcommunities.org/article.php?a=2457 (accessed 27 August 2015); also see 'Fear of Fresh Stir in Steel Hub', Times News Network, 11 April 2007, available at: http://www.minesandcommunities. org/article.php?a=3041 (accessed 27 August 2015).

[58] 'Patkar Joins in Protests against POSCO', NDTV, 13 February 2006, available at: http://www.minesandcommunities.org/article.php?a=2470 (accessed 27 August 2015).

[59] 'Displaced Villagers Protest Land Grabbing by Bhushan Steel', Pioneer News Service, Dhenkanal, 25 May 2006, available at: http://www. minesandcommunities.org/article.php?a=2438 (accessed 27 August 2015).

There were posters that screamed justice for the adivasis who had sacrificed their lives and stood against the exploitative multinationals. The protesters lighted candle in memory of the martyred and expressed their solidarity with the struggle. The protesters questioned the economic logic of profit by appropriating and displacing the indigenous people and communities from their land and resources for the development of a few. They also condemned the violence of the state and its policies of Globalisation and Privatisation.

The organizations that were part of the protest were National Alliance of Peoples Movements, Lok Raj Sangathan, Kashipur Support Group, India Centre for Human Rights and Law Initiative, Forum against Violence on Women, Shoshit Jan Andolan, Samajwadi Janparishad, Girangaon Rozgar Haq Samiti, Peoples Political Front, Ladaku Garment Mazdoor Sangh, Narmada Solidarity Group, Zhopadi Bachao Andolan, Hind Navjawan, Chemical Mazdoor Sabha, Committee for the Rights to Housing, Focus on Global South, AITUC, CITU, Workers Federation.[60]

In 2008, on the second anniversary of the 'Kalinganagar massacre', a gathering of six to eight thousand people collected at the site. Various anti-displacement movements came together from across India, pledging not to allow any kind of dislocation of inhabitants from their soil.[61] Leaders of various organizations from different parts of the state as well as from West Bengal, Jharkhand, Chhattisgarh, Bihar, and elsewhere vowed to battle the acquisition of farm and forest land by transnational companies.[62] The representatives of those opposing displacement at Nandigram and Singur in West Bengal also participated in the protest. The leaders who addressed the rally strongly opposed the SEZs as well. Interestingly, the leaders of the farmers' movement against diversion of irrigation water from Hirakud reservoir for industrial use also took part in the rally.[63]

[60] 'Mumbai Protests against the Orissa Killing: Report from Orissa Mining', 19 January 2006, available at: http://www.minesandcommunities.org/article.php?a=5779 (accessed 27 August 2015).

[61] 'Resistance Grows to India's Rural Invasions', 2 January 2008, available at: http://www.minesandcommunities.org/article.php?a=8331 (accessed 27 August 2015).

[62] 'Anniversary Pledge to Fight Land-Grab', Statesman News Service, Jajpur, 2 January 2007, available at: http://www.minesandcommunities.org/article.php?a=8331 (accessed 27 August 2015).

[63] 'Kalinganagar Tribals Vow to Continue Stir against Displacement', Hindu, 2 January 2007, available at: http://www.minesandcommunities.org/article.php?a=8331 (accessed 27 August 2015).

More recently, in 2013, the protests against adivasi land alienation required by POSCO attracted brutal police action on the men, women, and children of the area. Anguished that a corporation from their own country was the cause of so much suffering and pain, as many as 10 Korean civil society organizations, including lawyers, human rights activists, trade unionists, conservationists, and academics wrote to the Prime Minister of India against the violence and coercion perpetrated by the Indian state in connection with the POSCO project.[64]

The demands of this expanding movement have escalated too. Agitators in favour of the FRA, 2006 began to protest against adivasis not being treated as the owners of the land which they have been cultivating for generations, and against their being ousted from forests for development projects or mining without their consent or permission. Thousands who were agitating for the forest rights bill to be instituted also pointed out that adivasis have been treated as 'encroachers' and 'criminals' on their own land and forced to leave by forestry officials and mining and logging companies.[65] When civil society activists and representatives of NGOs organized a human chain in the national capital to press the government to notify the rules for the Scheduled Tribes and Other Forest Dwellers (Recognition of Forest Rights) Act, 2006, the protestors added more demands. Apart from protesting against corporate seizure of tribal land in the name of SEZs, and demanding that the authority and effectiveness of the real gram sabhas in determining rights be respected, they insisted that the government bring all adivasi areas under Schedule V and empower the communities to defend and protect the forests against mafias, the government, and companies. They also demanded an end to 'militarization'.[66]

All this shows that the forest rights movement has increasingly become part of a larger movement against land acquisition, against SEZs, against transnational entry into forests under policies of globalization, as well as against increasing police presence to deal with conflicts between protestors and companies. Because of brutality on the part of the armed forces of the Indian state, the support of human rights organizations,

---

[64] 'Urgent Appeal from South Korean Trade Unions and Human Rights Organisations'.

[65] 'Thousands Protest for Rights over India's Forests'.

[66] 'Activists Demand Notification of Tribal Act', *Hindu*, 1 December 2007, available at: http://www.minesandcommunities.org/article.php?a=8317 (accessed 27 August 2015).

both at the national and international levels, has been firm and consistent in this movement.[67]

The concern for rampant land acquisition has, then, brought diverse interest groups together. An umbrella organization protesting against adivasi displacement has come to include all those who will be affected by the acquisition of land for a project, including dalit land in the villages as well as other small or medium landholders whose land also happens to come within the ambit of that project. An organization which might join a protest against a mining project could simply consist of landowners of the region coming together to protest against diversion of irrigation water from their land for a smelter in the area. Protests would also be joined by those concerned primarily with environment issues, like activists belonging to organizations like Green Kalahandi.[68] These latter kinds of organizations found they had a lot in common with the adivasi protestors. This point about the concerns of the conservation movement and adivasi interests will be discussed a little later in more detail, along with its wider implications.

Women Lead: Kalinganagar, Odisha

Women seem to have been active in all contemporary anti-mining protest movements since their inception. When the Bharat Aluminium Company wanted to mine the summit of Gandhamardan, Odisha, with its exceptional wealth of forest cover, a movement arose to prevent this, representing an alliance of local adivasis, dalits, and many others. Women are reported to have actively stopped the passage of mining vehicles by laying their children in front of them to maintain the blockade, saying: 'What future do they have if you destroy our mountain?' This was one of the early successes of the resistance movement as a whole, and the planned bauxite mine on the ridge was finally declared illegal on environmental grounds in 1987 (Padel and Das 2006).

---

[67] The impression of this author, while scanning available data from the last decade, is that the support of international indigenous people's organizations is not much in evidence as far as adivasi struggles against mining and other corporate groups are concerned.

[68] 'People Rise against Vedanta', Statesman News Service, Bhubaneswar, 10 July 2007, available at: http://www.minesandcommunities.org/article.php?a=5576 (accessed 27 August 2015).

The watershed, however, was the police firing of 2006 on adivasis protesting against land acquisition for the Tata company in Kalinganagar, Odisha. After this firing in which 13 adivasi protestors were killed, a group of adivasi women took up the reins of the agitation against industrialization in Kalinganagar.[69] This had a snowballing effect as several organizations from different districts joined the meetings held by women.[70]

After the firing and killings, the anger and resentment against land acquisition and displacement further escalated. Medha Patkar, who was up to then primarily involved in anti-dam protests, joined the movement against the POSCO steel plant and against the Odisha state government's agreement to give 4,000 acres of land to this company, which would lead to large-scale displacement of thousands of adivasi families.[71] Over 10,000 women took a resolution to protect their land from being taken up for the POSCO project a year later, in 2007.[72] 'We are prepared to face bullets, because we will not forsake our source of livelihood for the steel plant,' the women's action committee declared.[73]

---

[69] 'The men may choose to go on the backfoot but women from the 16 villages have resolved to continue our fight for survival and human dignity,' Bini Soye, president, Women's Action Committee, is reported to have said. 'We don't fear death. We have lost 13 lives and are ready to sacrifice another 1300. But we will not allow any industry to come up here. That's a promise.' Sampad Mahapatra, 'Women Lead Kalinganagar Agitation', 2 May 2006, available at: http://www.minesandcommunities.org/article.php?a=3915 (accessed 27 August 2015); also see 'K Nagar Tribal Women Vow to Intensify Stir', Pioneer News Service, Jajpur, 25 May 2006, available at: http://www.minesandcommunities.org/article.php?a=2449 (accessed 27 August 2015).

[70] 'Outrage against Displacement Spreads', Statesman News Service, Bhubaneswar, 23 May 2006, available at: http://www.minesandcommunities.org/article.php?a=2431 (accessed 27 August 2015).

[71] 'Patkar Joins in Protests against Posco', NDTV, 13 February 2006, available at: http://www.minesandcommunities.org/article.php?a=2470 (accessed 27 August 2015).

[72] See 'Naveen Reluctant to Use Force to Acquire Land for Posco Project; PMO Steps Up Pressure; Meeting with Orissa CM This Week', *Financial Express*, Bhubaneswar, 16 April 2007, available at: http://www.minesandcommunities.org/article.php?a=2681 (accessed 27 August 2015).

[73] 'Women Lead Kalinganagar Agitation'. Also see 'K Nagar Tribal Women Vow to Intensify Stir'; 'Naveen Reluctant to Use Force to Acquire Land for Posco Project'.

It is against a specific backdrop that this activism flourishes. Adivasi women maintain some degree of autonomy in their families because they earn their livelihood through collection of minor forest produce from the forests, which is used for family consumption as well as sold or exchanged. At a public hearing organized to give environment clearance to Kalinga Coal Mines, women came out in large numbers to protest and pointed out that they had been protecting the forest for more than 30 years and they would not allow it to be destroyed as it was their most important source of livelihood.[74] The battle against POSCO not only continues, but has intensified in the intervening years.[75] The women's anger and determination, as also the poignancy and desperation of the situation, is clear from the fact that these women managed to stop land acquisition for POSCO temporarily by threatening to take out a semi-nude protest on Women's Day in 2013.[76]

What stand out in this very limited survey of protests, then, are alliances forged by a large number of disparate groups in determined opposition to corporate groups all over the country, especially in adivasi-dominated areas. However, the active participation of women has to be

---

[74] They said they made sal plates and cups, and sold forest produce like lac, resin, *amla* (*Phyllanthus emblica*, *haridra* (turmeric/ *Curcuma longa*), and *bihada* (*Terminalia belliric*) in the market, and would not allow the mining to be done. Sambad, 'The Forest Feeds Us, We Won't Allow Its Destruction', 24 January 2006, available at: http://www.minesandcommunities.org/article.php?a=3803 (accessed 27 August 2015).

[75] Freny Manecksha, 'Against All Odds, a Struggle Continues', *Hindu*, 22 June 2012, available at: http://www.minesandcommunities.org/article.php?a=11768 (accessed 27 August 2015); 'Anti-Posco Brigade Holds Black Day', *Times of India*, 23 June 2013, available at: http://www.minesandcommunities.org/article.php?a=12363 (accessed 27 August 2015); 'India and POSCO Must End Abuses Linked to Steel Project: Rights Groups Urge Suspension of Project, Prevention of Forced Evictions', 27 June 2013, available at: http://www.minesandcommunities.org/article.php?a=12363 (accessed 27 August 2015).

[76] 'Semi-nude Protest at Posco Site Rocks Odisha Assembly', *Hindu*, 8 March 2013, available at: http://www.thehindu.com/news/national/other-states/seminude-protest-at-posco-site-rocks-odisha-assembly/article4488321.ece (accessed 27 August 2015); Minati Dash, 'Dhinkia and Govindpur Mothers Go Naked to Protest against Forcible Land Acquisition for POSCO', 15 March 2013, available at: http://kafila.org/2013/03/15/dhinkia-and-govindpur-mothers-go-naked-to-protest-against-forcible-land-acquisition-for-posco-minati-dash/ (accessed 27 August 2015).

highlighted as a very important component of the movement, because, somewhat like the Chipko movement to save trees (in Uttarakhand), it also represents the spontaneous activism of adivasi women to save their forests, in the process also building an effective opposition to mining.

Because the forests have traditionally provided livelihoods to entire communities, a threat to these livelihoods puts adivasis and all forest-dependent communities at the forefront of saving their habitats from total devastation. The brief preceding discussion thus indicates that a necessary set of practices for the conservation of forests and a respect for ecology would have in any case existed quietly in the forests for centuries, whose aims would not be very different from those of an overt, self-proclaimed environment movement. It is in this context that a conflict of interests between a section of the conservationists and the adivasis, is to be discussed.

ADIVASI RESISTANCE AND THE CONSERVATION MOVEMENT: CONFLICT AND ALLIANCE

Artificial Contradiction?

The contradiction between the concerns of some Indian environmentalists and adivasi communities' well-being is, admittedly, sometimes too glaring and obvious to ignore. This powerful movement has certainly influenced, if not actually guided, central government policies and laws to conserve the environment. These laws, briefly outlined in this section, have adversely affected the lives of adivasis and other forest dwellers for decades.

A number of conservation laws have been instituted in independent India, like the WLPA, 1972, last amended in 2006, and the Forest (Conservation) Act, 1980, amended in 1988. These laws have opposed the very presence of the adivasi in the forests, and drastically affected their access to sources of food. They have curtailed their practices of *jhum*, that is, shifting cultivation, which was a very major source of sustenance for forest communities; the collection of minor forest produce which is consumed as food, and numerous other items sold or exchanged in outlying villages to make a livelihood; and fishing in the rivers or lakes in forests as well as the hunting of small game (both major sources of protein for these communities). Restrained under conservation laws from carrying on these practices, which were often the only or major means of nutrition for these communities, many adivasis, especially Particularly Vulnerable Tribal Groups (PVTGs), began to witness a large-scale incidence of starvation deaths, which were subsequently widely reported(see Radhakrishna 2012).

Further, the legal declaration of large areas in the forests as Reserved Forests, PAs, bird sanctuaries, wildlife sanctuaries or parks, tiger reserves, or elephant habitats was meant to keep the adivasi out of these newly designated zones. All this was done on the premise that the human presence in forests destroys ecological balance. Indigenous communities have been living in those very spaces for centuries, and the section of the environment 'movement' which holds this belief was instrumental in causing permanent displacement of these populations from their homelands. This extensive dislocation, in scale, is second only to that caused by corporate groups who set up industrial projects in adivasi-dominated areas on the grounds that they were 'developing' the region. Without a resettlement or rehabilitation policy worth its name in place, those who helped frame these conservation laws, and continue to support their implementation, have knowingly or inadvertently caused unspeakable misery to hundreds of thousands of adivasis.

Some sections of the environment movement have also strenuously opposed investing residence and 'property' rights in the adivasis through the FRA, 2006. They were, and remain, convinced that for forests in general, and for increasingly extinct species like tigers in particular to survive, the adivasis *must* leave the forests. Guided by this notion, determined and even fraudulent action to get adivasis out by the Forest Department continues to be reported even as this text is being written.[77]

All these factors, and the resulting ambivalence towards adivasis, must be the reason why some otherwise active environment groups have not always been present during the raging protests against land acquisition led largely by adivasis, since such protests invariably dovetail into demands for forest rights.[78] The environment groups are united against

---

[77] Jatindra Dash, 'Tribes People in Odisha Duped into Leaving Forest Homes for Tigers—Rights Group', 27 October 2014, available at: http://in.reuters.com/article/2014/10/27/foundation-india-tigers-idINKBN0IG1HG20141027 (accessed 27 August 2015).

[78] The environment movement is divided on this issue. From the very inception of the entry of these companies, and the resultant people's protests and state repression, a number of organizations have been simultaneously engaging with environment as well as communities, and carrying out important research. To name just two, the Indian People's Tribunal on Environment and Human Rights has been releasing investigative reports on land acquisition in Bastar,

the government and corporate groups over harm industrial projects do to the forests[79], but they are not always sure whether the interests of conservation and the rights of adivasis are coterminous.

It is in this context that a major disagreement within the environment movement needs to be discussed. While the majority of the Indian environmentalists are in favour of the rights of forest-based communities, an influential section of the environmentalists continues to oppose the FRA, as it has been consistently doing from its very inception. A petition has also been filed in the Supreme Court in early 2014 by three prominent conservationists/organizations, seeking to declare the FRA unconstitutional on conservation grounds. This petition, of course, was opposed by another much larger section which understands that this position will only play into the hands of the development lobby and hasten the 'loot' by mining and other companies.[80]

Annulling the critical clauses of the FRA, which is precisely what the government is already indicating its plans to do, is just going to make the forests that much more accessible for ruthless mining companies.[81]

Chhattisgarh; aluminium mining in Kashipur, Odisha; and the Sardar Sarovar Project, among others. See http://www/iptindia.org. (For some reason, lately the organization has modified its nomenclature and now calls itself the Indian Independent People's Tribunal, as revealed by the last report just mentioned, published in 2010.) Kalpavriksh, an Environment Action Group, is committed to conservation as well as community livelihoods, and pioneered the concept of 'community-conserved areas' in South Asia. See http://www.kalpavriksh.org/index.php/conservation-livelihoods1 (accessed 27 August 2015).

[79] In 2011, 27 environmental groups, wildlife researchers, and social activists wrote to the Prime Minister urging classification of areas in nine forests as 'no go' zones for coal mining. 'Support "No Go" Forest Zones for Coal Mining: Activists to PM', *Times of India*, 4 February 2011.

[80] See 'Joint Statement on Anti-FRA Case in SC', http://www.forestrightsact.com/statements-and-news/135-joint-statement-on-anti-fra-case-in-sc (accessed 27 August 2015).

[81] The central government's recent attempts at banning the activities of bodies like the Green Peace may well be because this organization has been consistently opposing mining in adivasi areas. Green Peace vehemently opposed violations of FRA, felling of 500,000 trees in cases like Singrauli (MP), loss of livelihoods of thousands of adivasis, and adverse impact of mining on dozens of forest dwellers' villages. 'What is the point of passing the Forest Rights Act if the same government then prevents its implementation?', they asked. http://www.greenpeace.org/india/en/Press/Moily-stoops-to-favour-Essar-Hindalco-grants-Mahan-forest-clearance/ as accessed on 7 December 2015.

The firm belief on the part of a section of our environmentalists, that large tracts must be human-free for biodiversity to survive, and that the FRA spells the destruction of our forests, is challenged by the opinion of a number of Indian as well as international conservation bodies. Throughout the years 2006 and 2007, the government faced agitations by forest-based communities and others demanding that fair FRA rules be framed, and that the law be effectively put into operation on the ground. At the end of 2007, as many as 15 international organizations working in the field of environment appealed to the then Prime Minister and chairperson of the United Progressive Alliance to implement the FRA, 2006, as in their judgment this Act could become an important model for the rest of the world.

According to the signatories to this appeal, the FRA could crucially help implement India's UN commitments and the World Conservation Union recommendations on conversation of biodiversity, which did not materialize with India's earlier forest and biodiversity laws. The FRA would, in their opinion, fulfil India's international commitments on sustainable use and management of forest diversity, and at the same time 'protect and encourage customary use of biological resources and knowledge, innovations and practices of indigenous and local communities'. They also pointed out that 'indigenous forest communities are the most experienced in terms of what kind of human activities can sustain regeneration and biodiversity'. The 15 international signatories to the appeal included, among others, the Forest and Biodiversity Programme, Friends of the Earth International, World Rainforest Movement, New Wind, Finnish Association for Nature Conservation, and Ecoforestry Union.[82]

---

[82] 'Implement Forest Rights Act, PM Urged', *Hindu*, 27 December 2007, available at: http://www.thehindu.com/todays-paper/implement-forest-rights-act-pm-urged/article1975556.ece (accessed 27 August 2015). The news item which reported this appeal also revealed that a Task Force on Social and Economic Aspects of Conservation for the Environment and Forests Sector was set up by the government, which agreed with the opinion just cited when it said that 'ecosystem services that Indian forests provide are essentially due to conservation efforts by the traditional communities, but … [the way] prevailing laws and administration have treated indigenous forest communities' life and practices, causes unfortunately, near total delegitimisation and non-recognition of the wealth of biodiversity knowledge which has been adapted to local ecosystem[s].'

To a layperson like this author, then, even from the unidimensional point of view of conservation, forests seem much safer in the hands of the forest dwellers, and the FRA seems to have the potential to prevent them from being ousted from forests.[83]

The contradiction between the concerns of the environment movement, and the well-being of the forest communities, then, is an artificial one. What needs to be tackled to conserve the forests is the recognition of the real situation prevailing in forests. The process of vacating the forests of adivasis through declaration of special, human-free zones,[84] in effect, also gave the Forest Department extraordinary powers over vast regions in the forests. This, over the decades, has only facilitated possibilities of undisturbed collusion of individual members of this department with the illegal, organized trade involved in exploitation of forest produce, notably wood and paper and other items worth crores.[85] There is also an international mafia which operates in the forests for body parts and skins of specific wild animals for all manner of commercial purposes. All this would imply that the interests of those members of the Forest Department who are corrupt, and the concern of the Indian environmentalists to empty the forests of adivasis, are, inadvertently, in perfect harmony with interests of the unscrupulous elements relating to natural wealth in the forests.

So in some ways, a process of much more intense and systematic wreckage of the forests has been in motion for decades, contradicting the very aims of the environment movement, once large-scale eviction

---

[83] Driving more and more forest communities *out* of the forests is going to put an end to all vigilance and surveillance by these communities over their habitats.

[84] The latest avowal of this is visible in 'State Pushes for Human-Free Tiger Habitat', available at: http://www.newindianexpress.com/states/odisha/State-Pushes-for-Human-free-Tiger-Habitat/2014/05/08/article2212181.ece (accessed 27 August 2015). See also Dash, 'Tribes People in Odisha Duped into Leaving Forest Homes for Tigers—Rights Group'.

[85] Kanna Kumar S. and Sweta Mishra, 'Foundations of Community-Based Forest Governance Systems in Odisha', http://www.academia.edu/2228317/FOUNDATIONS_OF_COMMUNITY-BASED_FOREST_GOVERNANCE_SYSTEMS_IN_ODISHA (accessed 27 August 2015). Also see Colchester and Erni (1999), which discusses the corruption amongst Forest Department officials and their collusion with the timber mafia. On the powerful timber mafia in the forests, see http://www.theweekendleader.com/Heroism/1380/firmly-rooted.html (accessed 11 November 2014).

of the adivasis took place from the spaces which they knew intimately, cherished, and guarded.[86]

The point to be emphasized is that the forest communities are a part of the conservation movement, if not the movement itself. The contradictions between the designated environment movement and these communities are artificial, and can be resolved.

Grounds for Affinity

Large sections of the environment movement have displayed remarkable affinity with adivasis over opposition to environment-damaging projects, especially mining.[87] Sufficient common ground seems to exist between their own concerns and those of the adivasis, and as far as a position on industrial projects in forest areas, mining companies in particular, is concerned.

[86] At Budhabahal in Odisha, it is reported by researchers that an all-women executive body has been constituted to tackle the timber mafia. See Kanna Kumar and Mishra, 'Foundations of Community-Based Forest Governance Systems in Odisha'. It is a recurring theme in this author's discussions with individual forest community members and adivasi organization representatives, that in parts of the forests where there are no people left, there is now no one to guard the forests against large-scale logging and illegal killing of select wild animals commissioned by influential merchants. See Rashid H. Raza et al., 'Illuminating the Blind Spot: A Study on Illegal Trade in Leopard Parts in India (2001–2010)', a TRAFFIC Report, available at: http://www.conservationindia.org/wp-content/files_mf/traffic_species_mammals68.pdf (accessed 27 August 2015).

Specific wild animals' body parts can fetch the concerned merchant lakhs of rupees in the international market while he operates from a metropolitan city, without taking any of the risks involved either in killing a dangerous wild animal, or in breaking the law. What is really tragic is that the foot soldiers employed for all the work involved in illegal killing of wild animals are individual forest dwellers, who are paid a pittance, sometimes as little as a hundred rupees for their trouble. These individual forest dwellers, sometimes victims of starvation, sometimes simply unscrupulous, mercenary elements from forest communities, get severe punishments under conservation laws in case they are caught. Whatever their excuse, such individuals can be boycotted and punished by the community itself in case they are suspected of being involved in illegal activities such as these, as such actions are seen as harming the wildlife as well as interests of the larger community.

[87] 'Greens See Red over Proposed Mining near Karlapat Sanctuary', *Pioneer*, Bhubaneswar, 10 November 2005, available at: http://www.minesandcommunities.org/article.php?a=3323 (accessed 27 August 2015).

Over the last few years, environment groups have made some of the most successful representations against the entry of mining companies in adivasi areas to the MoEF and to the courts, including the Supreme Court, and have succeeded in raising public awareness through the media on the threat to conservation posed by these companies. The numerous studies provided by conservation groups on the dangers posed by mining to the ecological equilibrium of mineral-rich regions have considerably strengthened the overall struggle by adivasis to keep these companies out of their land. These groups, sometimes with direct international links, can have a tremendous influence with the MoEF of the Government of India. Their personnel are often, though not always, consulted about important decisions that the ministry takes, and wherever there is an environment issue deemed to be involved, they frequently act as experts on various committees, boards, or enquiries set up by the government (or the courts when there is a dispute).[88]

Some of these individuals have consistently opposed mining near sanctuaries or rivers and repeatedly quoted the Supreme Court–empowered environment committees to prove that mining in such areas is extremely dangerous for maintaining an ecological balance.[89] By 2007, the 'growing clout of activist groups in India and the bigger role the judiciary is taking in enforcing the country's environment rules' was noted by the *Wall Street Journal*.[90]

---

[88] Of course, as the earlier briefly alluded to case of Green Peace shows, such organizations have been recently facing intense hostility from the Indian state for opposing its support to corporate groups in mineral-rich areas.

[89] For instance, in the case of Vedanta's plans to mine close to the Karlapat Sanctuary, they warned: 'Mining-related deforestation has led to shrinkage of elephant corridors and an increase in man-elephant conflicts in Keonjhar. The district has seen 61 elephant deaths in the past three years. Almost all these mine areas are forested and are major perennial sources of water. It is apprehended that open-cast mining would lead to the disappearance of the streams and pollute the major drinking water sources for the tribal people. The Niyamgiri hills, with a huge bauxite deposit, have 32 known perennial springs which feed the Vamsadhara and Nagabali rivers.' Prafulla Das, 'Mines of Conflict', available at: http://www.frontline.in/static/html/fl2224/stories/20051202002304000.htm (accessed 27 August 2015); also available at: http://www.minesandcommunities.org/article.php?a=3319 (accessed 27 August 2015).

[90] Jackie Range, 'Indian Activists' Rising Clout: U.K. Company's Plan for Mine Is Threatened by Environmentalist Ire', *Wall Street Journal*, 16 August 2007, available at: http://www.minesandcommunities.org/article.php?a=4585 (accessed 27 August 2015).

It ought to be also mentioned that sections of the Indian environment movement (like several others who joined the adivasi protests against mining, in particular), perhaps for the first time in the movement's own history in India, engaged with adivasis as *people* and with their agonizing predicament in a way they had not thought necessary in the past. Such individuals were forced to engage with issues larger than that of conservation in the process of lending support to the adivasi-led anti-displacement, anti-land acquisition movement, and witnessed what they had had no occasion to witness in the past: the appalling loss of every conceivable human right which forcible ousting from traditional hearths and homesteads brings; the distressing scale of poverty of populations inhabiting resource-rich areas; the sophistication of state intelligence, and machinery for violently suppressing non-violent and legitimate protests in which these individuals too sometimes got beaten or arrested; frank and unabashed collusion between transnational companies and the state in the name of inviting foreign direct investment for 'development'; and most importantly, irrefutable evidence that while the state can be totally indifferent to issues regarding conservation, for the concerned communities it is now a matter of life or death.

Perhaps therein lies the potential for a leap of faith as far as future, rewarding alliances for both movements are concerned.

* * *

The heavy odds that the adivasis continue to face, therefore, are quite overwhelming. There is the appalling determination of corporate groups to enter adivasi areas, flouting every law in sight; the increasing sophistication of the armed machinery of the government, and the readiness to employ it against its own citizens; the hardening of the administrative mindset about what constitutes development or a remedy for insurgency or poverty. There is also constant experimentation with new divisive strategies, including communal ones, to break the adivasi unity.

The successes and gains too have been equally remarkable, especially in the legal domain. Public interest litigation initiated by concerned citizens brought an end to the violence unleashed by Salwa Judum in 2011. The case against the entry of the Vedanta mining group into the Niyamgiri hills of Odisha was finally won in the Supreme Court in 2013, bringing to a conclusion the decade-old struggle on the ground by a large number of groups. Adivasis have some legal weapons in their armoury which are potentially useful.[91] However, legal recourse alone did not suffice in the past, nor is it going to be sufficient in the future, especially since the progressive component of laws affecting the adivasis can be manipulated, or done away with altogether, by a hostile state at any point in time.

There is a full-fledged movement on the ground which these communities have created with wide alliances, passionately committed to preventing the takeover of adivasi lands for private gain. The battle is going to be long and, literally, bloody. This remarkable movement, which will be an ongoing one for the foreseeable future, has entrusted itself with the historic task of watching over not just the rich ecology of adivasis' habitats, but over their very identity and dignity.

REFERENCES

Colchester, Marcus and Christian Erni. 1999. *Indigenous Peoples and Protected Areas in South and Southeast Asia: From Principles to Practice*. Copenhagen: International Work Group for Indigenous Affairs.

Padel, Felix and Samarendra Das. 2006. 'Double Death: Aluminium's Links with Genocide Revealed', 22 March. Available at: http://www.minesandcommunities.org/article.php?a=40 (accessed 29 August 2014).

Radhakrishna, Meena. 2012. 'Thought for Food: Endemic Hunger among Forest Dependent Communities', in Dev Nathan and Virginius Xaxa (eds), *Social Exclusion and Adverse Inclusion*. New Delhi: Oxford University Press, pp. 145–55.

---

[91] A brief survey of these, as also the proposed dilution of some of them under the new government which came to power in May 2014, are discussed in the Appendix.

Appendix
A Brief Review of Laws Impacting Adivasis

Meena Radhakrishna

While Narendra Modi was still the chief minister of Gujarat, a few months before his party came to power at the centre, an important study by Rathva et al. (included in this volume) appeared in *Economic and Political Weekly*. It concluded that 'the Indian state and particularly the Gujarat government is now creating legal ways to intervene in the scheduled areas to exploit natural resources. The Fifth Schedule and the Panchayats (Extension to Scheduled Areas) Act (PESA) are proving to be significant hurdles.' The obstacles referred to were for 'corporate loot' in the mineral-rich area of Chhota Udepur. In Gujarat, the solution was to remove communities who were STs from the scheduled list, so that they lost the protection offered under the Indian constitution to adivasi communities.

The adivasi situation all over the country has become more tenuous and precarious since the Modi government took power in May 2014. There have been a number of news items in the press since then which cause concern regarding changes in existing laws as well as policies of this government in the name of development, which will not only adversely impact environment and conservation, but would grievously harm adivasi interests. It is important to mention here that Prime Minister Modi, who has come to power on the platform of 'development', has often been quoted as saying that he believes in action, not Acts, and that inconvenient pieces of legislation ought to be done away with.[1] This is a clear indication that a number of pieces of legislation, critical for fighting for adivasi rights, are going to be diluted. There was, in any case, a policy of aggressive pushing ahead with development and infrastructure projects even under Prime Minister Manmohan Singh, especially before the elections, in a bid to get corporate support.[2] The new political dispensation has decided to take a number of steps which go much further, and have had a relatively low key coverage in the media.

These include, to name a few: clearing a number of development projects indiscriminately without proper environmental clearance, and diluting the National Green Tribunal to this end; allowing coal mining to take place within 5 rather than 10 kilometres of a sanctuary; allowing expansion of mining up to 50 per cent for mines under a certain capacity without a public hearing; and giving 'fast-track green clearance' to several border roads and defence projects which frequently used to run into trouble with the MoEF (as many of these not only propose to traverse through forest land but also through reserved parks and sanctuaries).[3]

---

[1] 'Action Not Acts—Narendra Modi', 7 June 2014, available at: http://www.narendramodi.in/acts-not-action-living-the-dream-and-fulfilling-the-promises-from-raisina-hill/ (accessed 27 August 2015); 'Govt to cleanse 'the jungle of laws', says PM Modi', PTI, 23 September 2014, available at: http://www.indiatvnews.com/politics/national/govt-to-cleanse-the-jungle-of-law-says-pm-modi-20310.html (accessed 27 August 2015).

[2] Stan Swamy, 'India: Red Carpet Rolled Out for Corporates on Adivasi Land', 26 April 2014, available at: http://www.minesandcommunities.org/article.php?a=12630 (accessed 27 August 2015).

[3] Jay Mazoomdaar, '11 Environmental Disasters Narendra Modi Blessed in His First 100 Days', available at: http://qz.com/255772/the-11-environmental-disasters-narendra-modi-blessed-in-his-first-100-days (accessed 27 August 2015); Aesha Datta, 'Easing of Green Norms for Mining May Face Resistance', available at: http://www.thehindubusinessline.com/economy/policy/easing-of-green-norms-for-mining-may-face-resistance/article6292420.ece (accessed 27 August 2015); Manu Pubby and Anubhuti Vishnoi, 'Defence Projects near China Border in Fast Lane', available at: http://indianexpress.com/article/india/india-others/environment-ministry-to-ease-norms-on-defence-projects-along-china-border/ (accessed 27 August 2015); Chetan Chauhan, 'For Biz Push, Govt to Relax Green Laws', *Hindustan Times*, New Delhi, 1 September 2014, available at: http://www.hindustantimes.com/business-news/for-biz-push-govt-to-relax--green-laws/article1-1258614.aspx (accessed 27 August 2015); Somesh Jha, 'In 50 days, Modi Govt Gives Environment Clearance to 5 Projects', available at: http://www.business-standard.com/article/economy-policy/in-50-

Since the present government took power, there has been a lot of activity within the administration on this account. The Ministry of Environment and Forests (MoEF), which seemed often to be at loggerheads with other powerful ministries dealing with steel, mining, coal, transport, roads and other such 'development'-prone ministries or departments, is the one which is actively seeking clearance for potentially polluting projects. MoEF also used to invite experts to its various bodies, including the National Green Tribunal and other committees, which it seems to be unwilling to do any more, since their reports and recommendations might advocate non-compliance with the development-at-all-costs agenda.

There is every indication that the environmentalists as a body are going to be very inconvenient to the present government, and the experts who had a modest influence earlier on the government's development or conservation policies are going to be ignored or marginalized at best. All these proposed or already operational moves imply that the present government is fully prepared to flout all previous injunctions regarding conservation, followed in however faltering a way (Kothari 2014).

This apprehension emerges in a specific context in which the previous administration, already by 2013, was making overt moves to dilute the Forest Rights Act (FRA), which was seen as a hurdle in clearing development projects.[4] As discussed earlier in the Introduction to this volume, and also in the Epilogue, since the new government came to power in May 2014, there have been fresh moves, based on 'studies', to 'revisit' the FRA, which is now being projected not just as an obstacle to development, but as leading to loss of precious biodiversity.[5] The Ministry of Tribal Affairs, which is meant to be the prime body to oversee the implementation of the FRA, is itself recommending its dilution to clear the way for infrastructure projects on the plea that it will benefit the communities too. Even the

---

days-modi-govt-gives-environment-clearance-to-5-projects-114071800109_1.html (accessed 27 August 2015).

[4] Nitin Sethi, 'PMO Pushes for Dilution of Environmental Clearance Norms', *Times of India*, 11 January 2013, available at: http://www.timesofindia.indiatimes.com/india/PMO-wants-tribalsconsent-in-giving-forests-for-projects-diluted/articleshow/17975932.cms (accessed 27 August 2015).

[5] Vijay Pinjarkar, 'FRA Rights Have Destroyed Forests, Says Study', *Times of India*, 19 September 2014, available at: http://timesofindia.indiatimes.com/city/nagpur/FRA-rights-have-destroyed-forests-says-study/articleshow/42838425.cms (accessed 27 August 2015).

most critical provision about gram sabha consent being required before clearance of projects is under threat, and may be abandoned any time.[6]

It is significant that the MoEF, the Ministry of Tribal Affairs, the Ministries of Steel and Mining—all these no longer 'quarrel' any more, as they nominally used to earlier, as they are all agreed now on one single mission: to clear as many projects as soon as possible.[7]

The proposed changes in policy are sufficiently far-reaching for them to be noticed and opposed by an international human rights forum, since these changes in policy and laws will seriously threaten adivasi rights.[8] At the same time, it ought to be also recorded that the resistance of the people on the ground might lead to some rethinking amongst sections of policymakers and industry leaders as well, since this battle is a two-way, dialectical process.[9]

---

[6] Nitin Sethi, 'Taking away Forests: Tribal Consent Regulations to Be Diluted', *Business Standard*, 31 October 2014, available at: http://www.business-standard.com/article/economy-policy/taking-away-forests-tribal-consent-regulations-to-be-diluted-114103100022_1.html#.VFMw6ll5apY.gmail (accessed 27 August 2015).

[7] Under the new government, it appears that powerful ministries concerned with development or infrastructure projects can overrule what MoEF earlier recommended, as can cabinet committees of various sorts. A proposal for a hydel project in Arunachal Pradesh was cleared in September 2014, although the Forest Advisory Committee of MoEF had been rejecting it up to April 2014 on grounds of loss of precious biodiversity and unacceptable social cost to the tribals of the area. Once the Cabinet Committee on Investment decided that the MoEF 'may grant the requisite clearance for diversion of forest land expeditiously' to this project, it was cleared by the Forest Advisory Committee. *Of the six Forest Advisory Committee members who cleared the project, four were also part of the panel that had unanimously rejected the project in April 2014.* Jay Mazoomdar, '6 years, 2 Rejections Later, India's Largest Hydro Project Cleared', *Indian Express*, 24 September 2014, available at: http://indianexpress.com/article/india/india-others/6-years-2-rejections-later-indias-largest-hydro-project-cleared/ (accessed 27 August 2015).

[8] Amnesty International India, 'Changes to Environment, Land Acquisition Laws Jeopardise Human Rights', press release, 5 November 2014, available at: http://www.minesandcommunities.org/article.php?a=12810 (accessed 27 August 2015).

[9] A news item which appeared in mid-November 2014 describes a round table organized in Odisha with industry heads and policymakers as participants. It reports that though Odisha was the 'El Dorado' for investors in minerals, the participants expressed 'growing concerns over the ecological fallout, negative

There are certain progressive laws, themselves direct gains of pressure on the state from below, which have been used for decades by activists against land alienation, and which in principle help forest communities to retain autonomy and control over resources in their habitats. A few are selectively and briefly explained here in the language of activists, with reasons for their failure in practice. Also included are those proposed pieces of legislation which are threatening to dilute or completely do away with hard-won rights.

PANCHAYATS (EXTENSION TO SCHEDULED AREAS) ACT (PESA), 1996

The first and foremost is PESA, 1996, which prevents the purchase of tribal lands by non-tribals by insisting on a process of proper, democratic consultation with tribal communities, even in the case of major projects considered to be of national importance. The authority of local panchayats has been extended into Schedule V areas to gram sabhas (Padel and Das 2006). The gram sabha is a local decision-making body composed of community members, and PESA empowers this body to make decisions to manage resources in accordance with customary practices.[10]

PESA stipulates a strict requirement of not just consultation prior to land acquisition for development projects, but also in the formulation

---

externalities of mineral-based industries, and resistance offered by affected people'. These factors, the report says, have made both the industry leaders and policymakers treat the 'land conundrum' as a difficult one due to 'the deep emotional bond' the tribals seem to have to their land. As a result of this understanding, moves for focusing on sectors not dependent on natural resources, such as agribusiness, tourism and information technology, fishery, and poultry sectors are afoot. See also 'Business Standard Odisha Round Table: Call for Holistic Vision to Tackle Land Challenge', *Business Standard*, 15 November 2014, available at: http://www.business-standard.com/article/economy-policy/business-standard-odisha-round-table-call-for-holistic-vision-to-tackle-land-challenge-114111501582_1.html (accessed 27 August 2015); 'Odisha Keen to Tap Investments in Non-mineral Sectors', *Business Standard*, 15 November 2014, available at: http://www.business-standard.com/article/economy-policy/odisha-keen-to-tap-investments-in-non-mineral-sectors-114111501332_1.html (accessed 27 August 2015).

[10] *Resource Rich Tribal Poor: Displacing People, Destroying Identity in India's Indigenous Heartland*, report by ActionAid, Indian Social Institute (New Delhi), and LAYA, New Concept Information Systems Pvt. Ltd, 2008, p. 79.

of relief and rehabilitation packages. The PESA is not merely an Act of Parliament, but is in fact a *constitutional provision* based on the recommendations of the Bhuria Committee on implementation of the 73rd Amendment. Consultations must be done in a language intelligible to the gram sabha members, and during mutual deliberations differences of opinion and objections ought to be discussed.

Consultation under PESA is meant to enable local people to express their views on the desirability or propriety of a proposed project, so that the administration and/or corporation is able to reassess or modify the project in response to local concerns.[11] PESA also makes the gram sabha competent to safeguard and preserve the traditions and customs of the people, their cultural identity, community resources, and customary mode of dispute resolution.[12]

In practice, however, there are several issues which defeat this important provision, which have been highlighted by investigative agencies.[13]

1. There is a multiplicity of state agencies at the local level, including panchayati raj agencies and those for local governance, which prevents coherent and strong local self-governance from emerging.
2. Government and company officials forge consent, or the sabhas are not informed of their rights, or the language used is such that it is not always understood—in other words, uninformed consent by gram sabhas is obtained.
3. States like Jharkhand had not notified PESA even years after its enactment,[14] laying the door open to corporate entry.
4. The meetings of the gram sabhas are manipulated to the advantage of the administration, and the police machinery is employed to silence the dissent of people.

[11] 'Kashipur: An Enquiry into Mining and Human Rights Violations in Kashipur, Orissa', report of the IPT on Environment and Human Rights, New Age Printing Press, October 2006, p. 21 (henceforth 'IPT Kashipur Report').

[12] Indian People's Tribunal on Environment and Human Rights Report, 'Nagarnar: An Investigation into Land Acquisition and State Repression in Nagarnar, Bastar, Chhattisgarh, 2003', p. 21 (henceforth 'IPT Nagarnar Report'), available at: http://www/iptindia.org.

[13] 'IPT Kashipur Report', p. 21; 'IPT Nagarnar Report', p. 21; *Resource Rich Tribal Poor*, p. 80.

[14] *Resource Rich Tribal Poor*, p. 80.

5. Gram or palli sabhas can be held, and projects cleared, without the involvement of the local people.[15]

At the same time, this constitutional provision remains a powerful tool in the hands of the adivasis to retain control over their land. Through education and experience, the communities are increasingly becoming aware of their rights under PESA, and have even succeeded in throwing the powerful, persistent, and ruthless mining company Vedanta out of their habitat through the use of this provision.

SCHEDULE V AREAS AND LAWS OPERATING THEREIN

According to the Ministry of Tribal Affairs website, the following are the criteria for declaration of a Scheduled Area: 'preponderance of tribal population; compactness and reasonable size of the area; under-developed nature of the area; and marked disparity in economic standard of the people'.[16] The Fifth Schedule, on the other hand, is the provision for the administration and control of Scheduled Areas and STs.[17] The laws operational in Schedule V areas 'prohibit or restrict the transfer of land by or among members of the Scheduled Tribes in such area'. This is a very important provision, which, along with a landmark Supreme Court judgment (known popularly as the Samatha judgment), has become a potent way to neutralize adivasi land alienation.

---

[15] This happened in the case of the permission obtained by Hindalco for starting mining activity in Mali Parvata in Odisha. An armed demonstration by affected which had adivasis subsequently demanded the scrapping of the resolution of the palli sabha which allowed the company to begin mining. 'Outrage against Displacement Spreads', Statesman News Service, Bhubaneswar, 23 May 2006, available at: http://www.minesandcommunities.org/article.php?a=2431 (accessed 27 August 2015).

[16] Ministry of Tribal Affairs, 'Definition of Scheduled Area', available at: http://www.tribal.nic.in/Content/DefinitionofScheduledAreasProfiles.aspx (accessed 27 August 2015).

[17] Article 244(1), available at: http://www.tribal.nic.in/WriteReadData/userfiles/file/cp/Fifth%20Schedule7615085295.pdf (accessed 27 August 2015).

SAMATHA JUDGEMENT

Samatha, an NGO, first filed a case in the local courts and in the high court in 1993 against the Government of Andhra Pradesh for leasing tribal lands to private mining companies in the scheduled areas.[18] After a four-year battle, and a public interest litigation petition in the Supreme Court, a historic judgment was delivered by the Supreme Court which had the following most important features:

1. 'Every Gram Sabha shall be competent to ... prevent alienation of land in the Scheduled Areas and to take appropriate action to restore any unlawful alienation of land of a scheduled tribe.'
2. Minerals shall be exploited by tribals themselves either individually or through cooperative societies with the financial assistance of the state.
3. Transfer of land in scheduled areas by way of lease to non-tribals, corporation aggregates, and others stands prohibited to prevent their exploitation in any form.
4. Transfer of mining lease to non-tribals, company, corporation aggregates, partnership firm, and so on, is unconstitutional, void, and inoperative.

The court however stated that 'state instrumentalities' (that is, public sector units) like the AP Mineral Development Corporation stand excluded from prohibition. This last fragment of the judgment has been misused by state governments to allow exploitation by corporate mining groups of scheduled areas. This has been done by turning units like the AP Mineral Development Corporation into subsidiaries of large private

---

[18] *Samatha vs State of Andhra Pradesh*, 1997 8 SCC 191. Samatha, an advocacy and social action group working in the southern state of Andhra Pradesh, struggles for the rights of tribal communities and for the protection of the environment in the Eastern Ghats region. In 1992, Samatha was involved in what seemed like a local dispute over adivasi lands being leased out to private mining industries while the government denied the adivasi people grant of title deeds. 'Little did we understand at that point of time that the issue had global implications and was a direct impact of the liberalization process under the new economic policy. The people were forced to work as wage labourers in their own lands where small private companies were extracting minerals like mica and limestone.' See 'The Fifth Schedule of the Constitution and the Samatha Judgement', available at: http://www.samataindia.org.in/documents/SAMATA_EDIT1.PDF (accessed 27 August 2015).

companies. As the concerned NGO points out, the instrumentality of the state has been defined by the court as organizations which are completely owned by the government, or where the government or its agencies are the majority shareholders.[19] This, however, is not respected in practice.

Nevertheless, the Samatha judgment remains one of the most potent weapons in the hands of the adivasis to protect their lands from being alienated to mining companies.

SOME ENVIRONMENT PROTECTION LAWS

Interestingly, in the middle of the 1990s, as the Indian state went about acting on its policies of inviting foreign direct investment into mining and other industrial projects, the MoEF set up procedures to prevent damage to environment by such projects. The MoEF seemed to recognize the threat posed by mining corporates to vast, thickly forested regions, and opposed them off and on, though not very consistently in practice. There are a number of laws and procedures which act as safeguards against corporate entry into adivasi lands, but which are flouted routinely. These procedures have been effectively used by environment groups to stall the progress of specific mining groups' entry.

A host of environment laws prohibit projects in forest areas on grounds of pollution of rivers or water bodies, or threat to the biodiversity of regions where mining or irrigation projects are planned. Clauses from these laws can and have been used by advocacy groups to stall development projects which lead to adivasi land alienation. These include the Environment (Protection) Act, the WLPA, the Forest (Conservation) Act,[20] and also the Water and Air Pollution Prevention and Control Acts. Occasionally, even individual, conscientious forest officers (working under the jurisdiction of the MoEF) have taken measures to keep the 'mining giants' out by exercising the limited powers they have and blocking particular projects.[21]

---

[19] 'The Fifth Schedule of the Constitution and the Samatha Judgement'.
[20] Ironically enough, some of these laws can and have also been used against adivasi interests, as discussed earlier.
[21] Very early in the opposition to the Vedanta company, the divisional forest officer in Rayagada refused forest clearance to the company for the project on the grounds that the reserved forest at the top of the ridge (4,000 feet) was of prime importance. 'From an Observer in the Vedanta Area', 5 December

A notification passed in 1997 requires that an Environment Impact Assessment (EIA) should be given by the MoEF before an industrial project can be launched. This ensures a systematic appraisal of the cost to the environment and also the socio-economic costs of a developmental project in a geographic area.[22] The EIA report has to be submitted by the company to the regional pollution control board authorities, and a *mandatory public hearing* has to be organized in the area by the state pollution board where the project is proposed. Among others, company officials, the district Rural Development Officer if the hearing is held in a village, and state pollution control board officials are required to be present at these meetings. The potentially affected people give their points of view about the desirability of the project, especially as far as environment issues are concerned. These public hearings, if they are held in an open and non-coercive manner, apart from official recording of grievances against the proposed project, frequently act as platforms for the exchange of information between adivasi communities and villagers; for education about and understanding of the issues regarding the impact of a project on the environment; and generally for protests and resistance.[23]

Of course, the EIA clearance *in practice* may not always be acquired at all, and the project may be put into motion, as in the case of a major steel plant in Chhattisgarh which was investigated by the IPT for Environment and Human Rights.[24] An EIA clearance can also be obtained through coercion. The public hearing, which is the crucial component in applying for this clearance, can be held under threatening circumstances so that people do not speak up or are not allowed to.

The court may also instruct the MoEF to conduct studies or investigations regarding the impact of specific projects on the environment before it gives a ruling. Such a study was carried out by

---

2004, available at: http://www.minesandcommunities.org/article.php?a=3931 (accessed 28 August 2015).

[22] 'IPT Nagarnar Report', p. 23.

[23] 'Adivasis of Bansapal Protest against Expansion of Mining—Public Hearing Disrupted and Cancelled', press note from Keonjhar Suraksha Parishad, 15 February 2006, available at: http://www.minesandcommunities.org/article.php?a=5773 (accessed 28 August 2015).

[24] 'IPT Nagarnar report', p. 23.

the Wildlife Institute of India, regarding the impact of bauxite mining in Niyamgiri.[25] Generally speaking, in a staggered or in a serial manner, depending on the nature of the project, environment clearances are required from state pollution boards, from the National Board for Wildlife, earlier the National Environment Appellate Authority, and, since 2010, the National Green Tribunal, and from the MoEF in general.[26]

It is worth mentioning here, however, that all these bodies and laws have been under the unfriendly scrutiny of the new government since May 2014, already arousing considerable discussion and concern at the way they are being ignored in order to give wholesale clearances to projects (Kothari 2014).[27]

FOREST RIGHTS ACT, 2006

The FRA, 2006, has the potential to safeguard adivasi land alienation. The law recognizes three kinds of traditional rights of forest communities, including those of Scheduled Tribes: land rights, use rights, and the right to protect and conserve the forest.[28] The clause with the most potential in this Act, which gives rights to adivasis over their land in the forests, is the reiteration of the clause relating to PESA.

Again, this law, even after nine years, is not working effectively on the ground because of the intense opposition by commercial interests

---

[25] See the report by Wildlife Institute of India, Dehradun, ordered by the MoEF on the instructions of the Supreme Court: 'Studies on Impact of Proposed Lanjigarh Bauxite Mining on Biodiversity including Wildlife and Its Habitat', Wildlife Institute of India, Dehradun, August 2006, available at: http://www.minesandcommunities.org/article.php?a=6044 (accessed 27 August 2015). Also see, 'Niyamgiri Mining Fraught with Danger', Statesman News Service, Bhubaneswar, 18 July 2006, available at: http://www.minesandcommunities.org/article.php?a=1649 (accessed 27 August 2015).

[26] Recently renamed the Ministry of Environment, Forests and Climate Change.

[27] Sreetha Banerjee, 'NDA Government Further Eases Environment Clearances for Projects', *Down to Earth*, 4 August 2014; Meena Menon, 'Clearance without Compliance', *Hindu*, 9 September 2014; Gopi Krishna Warrier, 'Clearance Mela', *Frontline*, 19 September 2014.

[28] See http://www.forestrightsact.com/what-is-this-act-about (accessed 29 August 2015).

as well as the Forest Department which is ironically a party to its implementation. This Act has been discussed in detail by a number of authors in this volume, and in the Introduction to this book.

RIGHT TO FAIR COMPENSATION AND TRANSPARENCY IN LAND ACQUISITION, REHABILITATION, AND RESETTLEMENT ACT, 2013

This piece of legislation, in principle, recognizes some of the basic rights of adivasis and other marginalized sections. However, with the new political dispensation at the centre, there are serious concerns about the impending changes in this law. The following excerpt from an editorial in *Economic and Political Weekly* discusses some of these likely changes.

> The first relates to a watering down of the 'consent clause'. [Capitalists are] upset that the prior consent of at least 80% of the affected families is required for private sector projects and 70% for public-private partnership projects, and want this proportion to be brought down very significantly. Indeed, at the meeting with revenue ministers of the states that the Union Minister for Rural Development, Nitin Gadkari, called in late June [2014], this was a demand made both by BJP- and Congress-governed states.
>
> The other demand was to do away with the requirement of a social impact assessment (SIA), except for 'large' projects. Quite simply, big business finds the SIA 'inconvenient'. It does not seem to want any transparent assessment of whether its proposed projects serve 'public purpose' or whether the extent of the land proposed for acquisition is in excess of what is needed for such projects.
>
> Further, big business wants a redefinition of 'affected families', especially those who would be eligible for rehabilitation and resettlement benefits. Frankly, it seems to want to exclude the non-propertied livelihood losers, for instance, landless labourers—those who have been working in the project area and who would lose their livelihoods with the project coming into being.[29]

The Modi government also plans to introduce an ordinance to bring about amendments in the Land Act. 'Likely amendments include cutting

---

[29] 'Land and Livelihoods Once More', Editorial, *Economic and Political Weekly*, vol. 49, no. 42, 18 October 2014, available at: http://www.epw.in/editorials/land-and-livelihoods-once-more.html (accessed 27 August 2015).

down on the consent process and doing away with the mandatory preparation of the Social Impact Assessment (SIA) Study.'[30]

THE MINES AND MINERALS (DEVELOPMENT AND REGULATION) AMENDMENT ACT (MMDRAA), 2015

This crucial law on the mining sector, which has replaced the MMDR Act, 1957, was initially termed historic because it proposed sharing of mining profits with adivasi and other local communities. In effect, however, it overrides many of the gains of the legislations discussed in this section. It has been analysed as legislation which will promote privatization and override the Samatha judgment as well as protection provided to Fifth Schedule areas. 'Seen together with the ... Land Acquisition Bill which specifically excludes [from its ambit] the issue of leasing tribal land, this Bill not only buries the ownership rights of tribal communities but facilitates the easy entry of international and domestic corporates to Fifth Schedule and tribal dominated mineral-rich areas to plunder the natural resources of our country.'[31]

REFERENCES

Kothari, Ashish. 2014. 'A Hundred Days Closer to Ecological and Social Suicide', *Economic and Political Weekly*, vol. 49, no. 39, pp.10–13. Available at: http://www.epw.in/commentary/hundred-days-closer-ecological-and-social-suicide.html (accessed 9 December 2015).

Padel, Felix and Samarendra Das. 2006. 'Double Death: Aluminium's Links with Genocide Revealed', *Economic and Political Weekly*, 22 March.

---

[30] Shishir Sinha, 'Ordinance to Amend Land Law Soon after Jharkhand, J&K Polls', 17 November 2014, available at: http://www.thehindubusinessline.com/news/ordinance-to-amend-land-law-soon-after-jharkhand-jk-polls/article6605320.ece#.VGmYJHi_jgM.gmail (accessed 27 August 2015). Since the writing of these lines, however, the central government has been forced to withdraw its earlier stated stand under combined, unrelenting pressure from political parties, farmers' organizations, and civil society activists.

[31] Brinda Karat, 'Of Mines, Minerals and Tribal Rights', *Hindu*, 15 May 2012. For a discussion for the adverse impact of this law on local communities, see Sarma, E.A.S., 'Lack of Clarity and Vision in New Mines and Minerals Act, *Economic and Political Weekly*, 11 April 2015 vol l, no 15.

Index

aboriginal
  aborigines 2, 9, 45
  Australian aborigines 14–15
  tribes 128
Acts
  Agency Tracts, Interest, and Land Transfer Act of (1917) 56
  Biological Diversity Act 352, 359
  Chota Nagpur Tenancy Act, 1908 (CNTA) 269–70
  Environment (Protection) Act 417
  Factories Act (1948) 222
  Forest Conservation Act (1980) 272, 285–7
  Forest Settlement Act 268
  Government of India, Act of (1935) 56
  Indian Forest Act (1865, 1878, 1927) 55, 214, 266–7, 282
  Industrial Disputes Act (1947) 222
  Inland Emigration Act (1863) 210
  Land Acquisition Act (1894) 282, 378
  Mines and Minerals (Development and Regulation) Amendment Act (MMDRAA) (2015) 421
  Panchayats (Extension to Scheduled Areas) Act (PESA) 18, 23, 56, 174, 283–4, 413–15
  Plantation Labour Act (PLA) of (1951) 222
  Right to Fair Compensation and Transparency in Land Acquisition, Rehabilitation and Resettlement (LARR) Act (2013) 420–1
  Right to Information (RTI) Act 346
  Santhal Parganas Tenancy Act 270
  Scheduled Districts Act of (1874) 56
  Scheduled Tribes and Other Traditional Forest Dwellers (Recognition of Forest Rights) Act (2006) 18, 20, 255, 259, 279, 325, 339, 396. *See also* Forest Rights Act, 2006
  Water and Air Pollution Prevention and Control Act 417

Index

Wild Life Protection Act, 1972 (WLPA) 280, 282, 286, 339, 358, 417, 441–2
Workmen's Breach of Contract Act (1858 and 1859) 210, 216
Adivasi Vikas Parishad 225
adimjati 5
Adimjati Sewak Sangh 44
adivasi 3–11
   British classification 3–4
   categories 4–5
   classified as Scheduled Caste (SC) category 7–8
   concept of 34–6
   conservation-related dislocation 18–19
   conversion to Christianity 6–7
   emergence of consciousness 42–5
   forced migration and displacement 15–17
   forest 5, 128
   hill. *See* hill tribes
   ideas and processes for shaping identity 48–51
   ideological concept of 129
   legitimacy of cultivators 272
   meaning of 127–8, 164
   national and regional identities 45–8
   plains 115, 119–20, 122
   primitive 5
   racial category 35–6
   and rule of law 264–6
   sensibility and labour potentiality 65–73
   struggle and resistance movements by 23–9
   tea plantations 119–20, 122, 188
   wandering 128
      nomadic 7–8
      semi-nomadic 184
   wild 105
   working-class 25
adivasi consciousness
   class-based politics and 313–17
   community-based politics and 310–13
adivasi labour, in tea plantations 207–26. *See also* tea plantations of West Bengal, tribal labour in
adivasi labour migration
adivasi women's migration 188–95 (*see also* adivasi women; gender)
   historical context of 179–88
   overview 178–9
Adivasi Mahasabha 164, 311–12, 333
adivasi male migrant workers 19, 191
   changing values and lifestyles 243–5
   from middle India 94–5
   seasonal 181, 186–7
   short-term 191
adivasi minorities 141–2
   contribution and response of 145–7
   identity of 142–8
   integration of 142–8
   isolation and assimilation of 143–5
adivasi politics
   apogee of 318–22
   class/community and 330–4
   trajectory of 307–34
Adivasi Pragati Mandal 333
Adivasi Revolt: The Story of the Struggle of the Warlis 314
Adivasi Solidarity Council (ASC) 10
adivasi territoriality 68–9
adivasi voices 167–8
adivasi women (*see also* gender)
   adivasi women's migration (*see also* adivasi labour migration)

concentration of 191, 193–4, 196
contemporary India 188–95
for domestic work 230–5
economic condition and 195–203
historical context of 179–88
migrant workers, distribution of 192
for non-agricultural employment 196–203
overview 178–9
purpose of migration 19
type of, 192
Ahom 98–104, 121–2
Ahom Swargadeos 100, 102
akharas 321
alienation 279
adivasi 257
of adivasi raja and kinsfolk 211
land (*see* land alienation)
of local people 339
of resource-dependent people 310
of traditional adivasi rights 134
alliances 14, 36, 84, 288
among rajas of different dangs 105
broad-based 71
broader 393–7
conflict and 400–8
forged by adivasi movements 26, 27
issue-based 70
between peasants and workers 314
strategic 25
All India Kisan Sabha 317
American Baptists 108–11
Andhra Pradesh 17, 197, 283, 295, 303
Mineral Development Corporation 416
Polavaram Dam in 296
struggle for community forest resource rights 297
animists 86, 103, 128
Annual Report of Dooars Planters' Association 219

Anthropological Survey of India 137
arkatis 211, 217, 218
Arunachal Pradesh 105
Chakma community in 48
Lower Subansiri project in 345
Arya, Shachi 55
Arya Samaj 77
Ashoka Trust for Research in Ecology and Environment 344
Assam Labour Enquiry Report 211
assimilation 13–14, 59, 84, 143–6, 148
argument against 312
cultural 5–6
de-culturated 144
forced 171
ILO Convention 107 62
integrative 144
isolation and 143–5
during National Democratic Alliance regime 323
resistance to 70–1
autonomy 21, 23, 27, 48
and adivasi women 399 (*see also* gender)
community 275
cultural 145, 147–8
and economic equity 144
and ethnicity 140
of forest dwellers 274
of governance 49
local 110
and movements 310–11
political 117, 281, 310
and self-rule 71
success of FRA and 275

backward 166–7
communities 140
districts 374
Backward Classes Commission 128
banajati 312
Banerjee, Narayan 178

Index

banvasi 313
Baptists in Assam 109
barter economy 134
bauxite-mining 296, 330, 389, 397, 419
*bawih*s 113
Bengal Assam Railroad Workers Union 223
Beyond Developmentality 165
Bhuria, Dileep Singh 174
Bhuyan, S. K. 100
Bihar 16, 47, 104, 152, 187, 217, 261, 269, 373, 381, 395
　adivasi society in 211
　brick kilns of 197
　Chota Nagpur region of 9, 126, 212
　communities from, working in tea plantations 164
　High Court 270
　indigo production in 186
　non-adivasi women from dalit and OBC families of 201 (*see also* gender)
　State Electricity Board 72
Bijoy, C. R. 170
Biligiri Sanctuary 344–5, 358
Binjhals 85
biodiversity 358, 366, 403
　adivasi areas and 163
　Biological Diversity Act 352, 359
　conservation of 18, 145, 255, 289, 304, 356, 357, 403
　convention 364–5
　*gram sabha*s for 289–90
　loss of precious 394, 411–12
　management committee 359
　natural resource-related conflicts and 354–5
Birsa Commando Force 120
Bodoland Territorial Council 120
bonded labour 135, 239, 285, 375
Bordoloi, Gopinath 116, 312

Brahminical Hinduism 81, 89
Brahmins 82, 85–6
Brandis, Dietrich 55
British Assam, 106–8 117, 122
British commercial interests 104–5
BRT Tiger Reserve 309
Brundtland Report 162
Burma
　Kon-baung 98, 103–4
　Upper 102–3

Cachar 98, 101–2, 105, 109, 121, 210
Calvinistic Christianity 115
Cambridge World History of Food 184
Campaign for Survival and Dignity (CSD) 257–60, 267, 274, 287–9
capital 59, 241
　concentration of 314
　corporate 324, 326–7, 331, 333
　globalization of 66
　neoliberal 57
　primitive accumulation of 53, 55, 63, 66, 73
　social and cultural 65
　social production and reproduction of 8, 54
　trading and industrial 313
capital accumulation 57, 65, 201–2, 314
capitalism
　corporate 307, 325, 327–8, 331
　Nehruvian state 319
capitalist rule, legitimacy of 265–6
capitalist ruling class 265
caste 139–41
　polarization 83
Castes and Tribes of Southern India 3
Central Reserve Police Force (CRPF) 389
Centre for Women's Development Studies (CWDS) 179, 191–6, 199, 201, 231, 233–4
chain migration 233–5

Chakma community 48
Chaube, S. K. 117
Cheitharon Kumpapa 102
Chhattisgarh 16, 17, 19, 47, 56, 185, 230, 233, 236, 293, 328, 373–4, 395
    Bodhghat in 355
    Chota Nagpur region of 207
    corporate penetration in resource-rich areas 327
    Dantewada 329, 385
    Maoist expansion in 329
    Naxalite/Maoist adivasi in 381–4
    proposed Bhopalpatnam-Ichhampalli dam in 355
    Salwa Judum 384–7
    self-determination of people 320
    steel plant in 418
    struggles for creation of 322
Chhattisgarh Mukti Morcha 320
Christian community 26, 28, 235
Christian Dalits 26, 28, 93–4, 324
Christianity 5, 44, 91, 111, 121, 325
    Calvinistic 115
    colonial exploitation and association with 78
    under colonial rule 121
    conversions to 6–7, 88–9, 92, 154
    local form of 110
    Naga conversion to 110, 112
    vs. Hinduism 78
Christian Missionaries 9, 44, 45, 93, 106, 107, 113, 232, 323
church-based institutions 234, 242, 249
churches
    Anglican Church 108
    Baptist 109
    earliest writings on, in north-east India 109
    Naga 110
    placement agencies association with 239, 249
    role in migration of women 234–5 (*see also* gender)
    rural–urban migration and 237
    vandalization of 92
citizens 266, 353, 370–1, 387, 407
citizenship 98, 120, 156, 275, 287
citizenship rights 2, 156, 283
civil liberties 392
    activists/human rights organizations 27, 370
class-based politics 313–17
class consciousness
    development of 140–1
    formation of 317
    negative 67–9
class(es) 68, 86, 135–6, 139–41, 330–4
    criminal 86
    depressed 7, 128
    dominant class hegemony 140
    inequalities 142
    middle 66
    polarization 83
    of society 66
    working (*see* working class)
Cobo Report 40
collective tenurial systems 272
colonial exploitation 78
colonial forest policy 280
colonization 10, 12–13, 38–40, 45, 49, 59
    British 15
    European 33
    Orissa's 84
Commando Battalion for Resolute Action units (CoBRA) 383
commercial
    establishments 236
    exploitation 8, 279–80
    forestry 54
    large-scale agriculture 55
    monocultural plantations 280
    necessity 55

placement agencies 237
tourism 345
commercialization
 of agriculture 83
 development of 194–5
 of forests 134
 of regional economy 135
communalism 91–2
communist movement 315–17, 332–3
Communist Party of India 147, 223, 317
communists 159, 223, 313–14, 316–17
community 111, 330–4
 Ahom 98–104, 121–2
 baganiya 119
 Chakma 48
 Christian 26, 28, 235
 conserved areas 338–9, 348–54
 dongar 85
 dongariah 85
 Dongria Kondh 396
 Durvas 164
 empowerment to protect and conserve 291
 forest management rights 263
 forest resource 289, 291
 Garo 363
 Hindu 83
 Jhoria 164
 Khandayats 6, 84–5, 87
 Majhi 178
 Maldhari pastoral 301
 Meitei 103, 122
 Mizo 114
 Oriya Kandha 83
 ownership 168–70
 pahariah 85
 politics 310–13
 Rathva 152
 reserves 340, 348, 352
 rights 20–1, 23, 72, 274, 295, 300–1, 348, 355, 357, 364

 ST 119
 Vaishya 82
 Warli 132, 314–16
compensation 27, 266, 268–9, 271, 285, 341, 376, 378–80
consciousness, of indigenous people/ adivasis 42–5
conservation (*see also* environment; ecology)
 of biodiversity 18, 145, 255, 289, 356, 357, 403
 community-based 364–5
 community-conserved areas 348–54
 and development 345–6
 and development threats 354–6
 historical aspects of 338–9
 inclusive 21
 legitimacy for forest resources 55
 legitimacy of state claims to 256–7
 National Environment Policy 347
 overview 337–8
 policy and practice 339–45, 359–64
 related dislocation of adivasis 18–19
 and rights equation (in 2025) 365–6
 wildlife-people conflicts 346–8
conservation reserves 340
Constitution of India 128, 141, 145, 156, 356
 scheduled tribes in 308
 Schedule VI of 278, 281
 Schedule V of 278, 281–3, 291, 376
 74th Amendment 147
Convention on Biological Diversity 347, 354
conversion 5–6
 adopted 6
 of dalits 92–4

to Christianity 6–7, 88–9, 92, 154
to Hinduism 78
Khasi-Jaintia 6
Meitei 103
Naga 110–12
Vaishnavite 103
corporate groups 25–6, 28, 380–91
'criminal tribes' 128
critical tiger habitats 361
Cult of Jagannatha, The 92
culture
  cultural boundaries 318–22
  cultural genocide 170–5
  de-culturated 144
  deculturation 139
customary practices 57–8, 115, 166, 413
customary tenurial regime 269

Dalhousie Memorandum (1855) 55
Dalit 15, 26–7, 29, 92, 196, 201, 307, 378–9, 397
  Christian 26, 28, 93–4, 324
  converts to Christianity 92–4
  delegation in UNWGIP annual sessions 15
  Polavaram 296
  rural working class 327
dam 17, 72, 160
  Polavaram 296
  Sardar Sarovar 168
Dandekar, Ajay 36
Deeper Roots of Historical Injustice: Trends and Challenges in the Forests of India 337
democracy 25, 322, 391
  capitalist 169
  definition of 155
  movements for 20
  rule of law in 260
denotification, of Rathvas 151–6
Denotified Tribe 4

depeasantization 134
Devalle, Susana 127, 322
devaluation
  of domestic service 242
  of women's economic status 250
  (*see also* gender)
development
  of class consciousness 140–1
  commercialization and 194–5
  conservation dilemma and 27
  economic 283
  Mahatma Gandhi's view on 175
  sustainable 159–75 (*see also* sustainable development)
  threats 354–6
  tribal 164–7
Development Dictionary The 164
Development of Primitive Tribal Groups, The 166
Dictionary of Anthropology 127
displacement/dislocation
  conservation related 18–19
  forced migration and 15–17
  investment-induced 160
dispossession 13, 14, 17, 18, 314
  Brahminical Hinduism and 89
  Forest Conservation Act 1980 and, 318
  history of 24, 61, 314–15
  illegal 266–73
  indigenous people and 61
  livelihood 326–7
*dobasi*s 118
doloi 118
dongar 85
dongariah 85
Dongria Kondh Development Agency 166
Dongria Konds 162
Dooars
  recruitment system in 216–19
  tea plantations in, growth of 215–16

Index

dramatis personae 371
Dube, S. C. 138

Eaton, R. M. 82, 111–12, 114
Ecological History of India, An 136
ecology 61, 64–5, 162–3, 167,
    171, 375, 400, 408 (*see also*
    environment; conservation)
ecodevelopment 346–7, 353
ecotourism 345
Economic and Political Weekly 151,
    161, 420
economic development 283
economic blockage 106
economic necessity, for
    conservation 55
economic transformation 127
and globalization 63
economic inequality
economic marginalization, 50
    146
economic vulnerabilities 249
socio-economic inequality 140
economy 59, 64, 73, 75, 159, 161–3,
    167, 184
agrarian 184, 195, 394
colonized 104, 189
economic backbone 19, 232
economic domination 139
economic empowerment 248–50
economic equity 144
economic independence 245
economic non-conformity 134
foreign direct investment (FDI)
    373, 392, 407, 417
globalized 63–4, 66, 121, 345,
    359, 366, 372, 396
industrial modernization 61–2
market 15–17, 107, 135, 163,
    340
natural 57, 134, 184, 195–203
political 65, 141, 144–5, 154–5

of rates of profit 73
regional 135
economy, informal
informality 236, 240
informal labour (*see* informal
    labour)
economy, natural
feudalization 81, 83
ecotourism 345
Elwin, Verrier 172
eminent domain 266–73
employer–employee relations 223 (*see
    also* paid domestic labour)
employer households 5, 231,
    248–9
employment relations 240–1
feminization, of domestic service
    242
empowerment, of domestic workers
    248–50
encroachment 21, 133, 257, 259,
    266, 268, 272, 284–5, 287, 340
and encroachers 255, 257, 259,
    280–1, 283, 285, 287–9, 306,
    318, 396
Engels, Friedrich 165
environment (*see also* conservation;
    ecology)
environmentalism 286–7
and environmentalists 20, 161,
    263, 325, 370, 400, 402–4,
    411
Environment Impact Assessment
    418
movement 258
protection laws 417–19
Environment Impact Assessment
    (EIA) 418
Essar 383, 385, 386
Esteva, Gustavo 164
ethnicity 137–41
ethnic identities 139
minority 142

and tribes of North-East India 118–22
Everybody Likes a Good Drought 160
exclusion
familial 229
social 93, 229, 250
from without 142

family life/homecoming 245–8
female labour migration. *See* adivasi women's migration; gender
folklore metaphors and symbols 129
forest and wildlife conservation laws
background of 279–81
community empowerment 291
Environment (Protection) Act 417
environmentalism impact on 286–7
environment protection laws 417–19
judicial interventions, impact of 286–7
overview 278–9
tribal-forest conflicts, framework for resolving 284–6
tribal rebellions against 281–4
Forest Department 22, 200, 256–60, 262–6, 272–3, 275, 344, 353, 363, 381, 401, 404, 420
Andhra Pradesh 297, 298
Gujarat 301
Jharkhand 300
Karnataka 301
Maharashtra 298–9
Odisha 298
Tamil Nadu 302
Uttar Pradesh 301
West Bengal 55, 300
forest governance
changes in 260
commercial forestry 54, 61
committees 300

community 291
democratizing 279, 286
existing 258
Forest Protection Groups 71
forestry, 360
forest settlement, 267–8, 273, 284
*gram sabha*s and 300
local 287
officials/staff 302, 396
structures of 256
sustainable forestry 72
Forest Protection Groups 71
forest rights 168–70, 291, 293, 295–6, 298, 304, 353
forest rights, struggle for 297–302
Andhra Pradesh 297
in Gujarat 301
in Jharkhand 300
in Maharashtra 298–9
in Odisha 298
in other states 301–2
in West Bengal 300
Forest Rights Act, 2006 (FRA), 19–23, 255–60. *See also* Schedule Tribes and Other Traditional Forest Dwellers (Recognition of Forest Rights) Act 2006
communities eligible for claiming rights 292
forest rights/community ownership and 168–70
*gram sabha*s under 22–3
implementation of 21–2, 260–4
key provisions of 289–90
making of 278–30
National Forest Rights Act Committee 260
National Committee on FRA 262–3
official implementation of 292–5
origins of 287–9
political-economic context 272–3

pushback risk 302–6
recognizing rights under 291
relocation from protected areas 291
Schedule V 20, 23
successes and failures of 273–5
forests
Saranda 167, 382
forests, reserved 18, 238, 267, 271, 283, 353, 401
forest tribes 5, 128
Fuchs, Stephen 128, 134

gairmazrua aam 272
gairmazrua khas 272
Ganamukti Parishad 314, 316, 333
Gandhi, Indira 359
Gandhi, Mahatma 92, 175
gaonburas 118
Garibniwaz 101–2, 104
Garo hills 105, 107, 118
gender 112, 179, 199, 229, 232–3, 242, 244–6, 248, 250, 275
  relations 229, 232, 244–6, 248
  segmentation 201
  and wage inequalities 202
genocide 170
ghatwals 183
Ghurye G. S., 41
girijan 134
Girijan Sangham 333
Glossary of the Tribes and Castes of the Punjab and North-West Frontier Province, A 3
Goalpara 107
Godelier, M. 136
Goodland, Robert 145
Government of India Act of, (1935) 56
*gram sabha*s 22. See also Panchayats (Extension to Scheduled Areas) Act (PESA)
grassroots assertion, of rights 26, 295–7

Guardian 386
Guha, Ranajit 67–9
Gujarat
  community forest resource rights, struggle for 301
  denotification of Rathvas 151–6

Haeckel, Ernst 161
Hardiman, David 43
Harvest in the Hills 109
hegemony 140, 196, 256, 265
heritage site 352
Hidimba 98
highland 351
Hill of Flutes, The 172
hill tribes 5, 49, 97, 119, 122
  Aka and Dufl 104–5
  of Khasi-Jaintia hills, Naga hills, and Lushai hills 115–16
  of Manipur and Tripura, Sixth Schedule and 117
Hindu/Hinduism 77–94
  Brahminical Hinduism 78, 81
  and conversions to Christianity 88–9
  Hindu adivasis 26, 28
  in Orissa 81–8, 90–2
  Rajputization 84
  re-Hinduization 7
  Sanskritization 80, 99–103
  vs. adivasi 153–4
Hindutva 323–6
history
  of Christian conversion 107–8
  de-historization, of subordinate peoples 139
  of dispossession 24, 61, 314–15
  of Indian forestry 279–81
  for indigenous people 13
  mythic 132
  oral 131–2
  of primitive accumulation 53–74

of religious change 28
of term indigenous 12–13
History of British India 54
Horton, Robin 114
House of Commons Papers 187
Human Development Report 183
human traffickers 375
Hutton, J. H. 56

IDCO. *See* Infrastructure Development Corporation of Orissa Limited (IDCO)
identity, of indigenous people/ adivasis
of adivasi minorities 142–8
collective 138–9
constructed 33–8, 48–51, 136–9
ideas and processes for shaping 48–51
international contexts 36–8
national and regional contexts of 45–8
overview 33–4
search for 136–7
terminologies 34–6
Illustrated Weekly of India 79
ILO. *See* International Labour Organization (ILO)
Imam, Bulu 167
Indian Confederation of Indigenous and Tribal Peoples 45
Indian Constitution. *See* Constitution of India
Indian Forest Act
(1865) 55
(1927) 266–7, 282
official implementation of 292–5
VII of (1878) 214
Indian People's Tribunal (IPT) 388–90, 418
India Reserve Battalion (IRB) 389

indigenous communities 15, 39, 45, 47, 49, 51, 278, 401
indigenous peoples
concept of 34–40
definition of 12
emergence of consciousness 42–5
ideas and processes for shaping identity 48–51
identity of 36–8, 45–8
ILO's and UN's concept of 12, 38–40
indigeneity 10–15
inter-tribal marriage 222
marginalization and articulation of rights 51
national governments and 40–1
North-East India 97–122
indigenous peoples, in North-East India 97–122
Ahom 98–104, 121–2
ethnicity of 118–22
Hidimba 98
Judeo-Christian faith 99
Meitei 103, 122
Naga-Kuki conflict 118
overview 97–9
scheduled tribes 115–18
wild tribes 103–15
Indigenous Peoples Working Group 319
indigenous workers 13
indirect rule 99, 105–7, 115–16, 118, 122
Indravati Tiger Reserve 355
inequalities
class 142
cumulative 140
dispersed 140
gender and wage 202
informal labour 27, 298 (*see also* paid domestic work)
agents 193, 195, 218, 234, 238

autonomous agents 121
chief agent 110
contract 104, 210, 237
in brick kilns 200
marginalized wage 60
middlemen 229, 238–9
minimum wages 195
recruiting agents 17, 186, 217–18, 235–9, 245, 248
recruitment for tea plantations 209–11
recruitment in Dooars 216–19
time-expired coolies 104
Infrastructure Development Corporation of Orissa Limited (IDCO) 378
Inland Emigration Act (1863) 210
Inner Line Regulation 106
insurgency (*see also* Maoism)
mode of 70
peasant, 67–8
International Encyclopedia of the Social Sciences 127, 141
International Labour Organization (ILO) 12–13
Convention (107) 59, 62
Convention (169) 62
Islam 5, 78, 82–3, 154
Iyer, L. K. A. 3

*jaherthan*s 272
Jainism 154
Jaintia-Khasi hills 105
jhadi/jhanti 272
Jharkhand
community forest resource rights, struggle for 300
formation of 71
Jharkhand Mukti Morcha (JMM) 320–1
Jindal 167, 378, 382, 391
Joint Forest Management (JFM) 263, 281, 294

Judeo-Christian faith 99

Kalinganagar (Odisha) 174, 372, 377, 394, 397–400
firing 171
killings of adivasis in 2006 390–1
land acquisition in 377–8, 398
prevention of Bhushan Steel plant establishment 392
Kalinganagar Complex 377–8
firing 372, 378, 389, 392
killing 394
massacre 395
kamin 178
Kandhas 83–4, 91, 93
Kashipur (Odisha) 387–91
Kashtkari Sangathana 316
Khadi and Village Industries Commission 323
Khanda 84
Khandayats 6, 84–5, 87
Khasi hills 109, 118
khatian 271
*khawhring*s 113
Koel Karo Jan Sangathan 72–3
Kol insurrection 214
Kosambi D. D., 130
*koyta*s 195
Kshatriyas 6, 82, 84, 87–8

labour
in brick kilns 200
contract 104, 210, 237
informal (*see* informal labour)
nomadic form of 196
ontology of 73–4
potential 73–4
social-cultural background of 60
wage payments 240
labour alterity 59–65
labour market 36, 53, 202, 242, 310. *See also* informal labour

labour potentiality 65–73
labour relations
  capitalist 240
  domestic 240, 242
laiming louba 102
land acquisition 380–9 (*see also* land alienation)
  for industrial projects 377–80
  transparency in 420–1
land alienation 23–4, 185, 232, 275, 326, 396, 413, 415–17, 419
  in Gujarat 27
  illegal dispossession 266–73
  investment-induced displacement 160
  migration to Jalpaiguri and 215
  relocation, from protected areas 291
  and resettlement 18, 291, 380, 401
  Schedule V to prevent 23–4
liberal democratic state, legitimacy of 264
liberalization 17, 372, 416
lifestyles, of adivasi women migrants 243–5. See also gender
livelihood
  dispossession 326–7
  rights of local communities 279
  valued agricultural 199
local communities 97, 172, 343–4, 355–6, 364, 403, 421
  alienation from PAs 346
  conservation traditions and practices of 339
  NTFP views on 300
  participation in management of wildlife conservation 348, 365
  representatives 347
  resource and livelihood rights of 279
  self-reliant 147
Lushai hills 99, 105, 109, 113, 115, 116

Luxemburg, Rosa 54

Madhya Pradesh 16, 47, 152, 196–8, 217, 257, 279, 295, 324, 343, 352, 373
Malwa 186
  Rathvas of 154
*mahajan*s 183
Maharashtra 166, 195–6, 303, 343, 351, 355, 357, 359
  Bhils of Khandesh 186
  Forest Department 21, 298–9
  Garchiroli 72, 298–9
  Nandurbar 196
  Pench National Park 346
  struggle for community forest resource rights 298–9
  Warlis in coastal 132
Maikanch police firing 171
Majhi 178
Manipur 98–9, 101–5, 107, 109, 114, 117–18, 121–2, 310
Maoism
  expansion in Chhattisgarh 329
  in Garchiroli 72
    Integrated Action Plan for Maoist-affected districts 174
  legitimacy to Maoist activities 328
  liberated zone 329
Maoists, 174, 381–4
  in mineral-rich states 381–4
  in neoliberal times 326–30
market economy 15–17
  exchange value 59, 73–4
  of hill–valley exchanges 107
  informal 15–17
  monetization 135
  urban 6
  wage 189
Marx, Karl 165
Massey, James 15
Meitei 103, 122
*mel*s 119

Mendha-lekha 72
MESCO 378
middle class 66, 92, 117–18
middle-class Bengalis 224–5
middle-class environmentalism 286
Midnapur Zamindary Company 182
Mighty Works of God, The 109
migrant 50
migrant households 190
migration
  adivasi women's (*see* adivasi women's migration)
  chain 233–5
  forced 15–17
  networks for 234–5, 238, 245
  rural-to-urban 230
migration, labour
  of adivasi women 188–95 (*see also* gender)
  forced 15–17
  to Jalpaiguri 215
  for non-agricultural employment 196–203
  rural-to-urban 230, 237
  to tea districts 211–13
Mill, James 54
mineral-rich states
  Naxalite/Maoist adivasi in 381–4
  poverty in 372–6
  protests and rebellion in 391–400
Mines and Minerals (Development and Regulation) Amendment Act (MMDRAA) (2015) 421
mining 17, 19, 27, 61, 147, 167, 228, 232, 296, 327–31, 340, 346, 355, 360, 374–7, 387–402, 405–7
  aluminium 372–3
  bauxite 330, 389
  coal 181, 410
  in Gandhamardan 392
  land acquisition for 379
  Maoism and 381–4

mining companies 23, 155, 327, 372, 375–6, 381–2, 384, 387–9, 402, 405–7, 416
Ministry of Environment and Forests (MoEF) 22, 257–60, 262, 281, 283–90, 296, 298, 302–5, 342–3, 345–6, 353, 356, 359, 361–2, 365, 406, 410–12, 417–19
Ministry of Tribal Affairs (MoTA) 21–2, 258–60
MMDRAA. *See* Mines and Minerals (Development and Regulation) Amendment Act (MMDRAA), 2015
MoEF. *See* Ministry of Environment and Forests (MoEF)
Moody, Roger 61
Morris, J. H. 109
Movements. *See also* Maoism; rights
  autonomy of 310–11
  communist 315–17, 332–3
  struggle and resistance 23–9
mukaddam 196
Munda, Birsa 214
Mundari khuntkattidar 269–70
Munshi, K. M. 312
Muria and Their Ghotul, The 172
Mysore: Tribes and Castes 3
mythomoteurs 133

Naga hills 105, 109–11, 115–16, 118
National Advocacy Council for the Development of Indigenous People (NACDIP) 10
National Aluminium Company 166
National Biodiversity Authority 352
National Biodiversity Strategy and Action Plan (NBSAP) 347–8
National Board for Wildlife 419
National Commission for Scheduled Castes and Scheduled Tribes 282
National committee on FRA 262–3

National Democratic Alliance 323–4
National Environment Appellate Authority 419
National Environment Policy (NEP) 347–8
National Forest Rights Act Committee 260
National Green Tribunal 419
nationalism, ecological 320
national parks (NP) 339–40, 342
National Rural Employment Guarantee Act (NREGA) 358–9
National Sample Survey Organisation (NSSO) 120
National Tiger Conservation Authority 303, 355
National Wildlife Action Plan (NWAP) 347, 348, 360
native, concept of 34–6
natural economy 57
Naxalite/Maoist adivasi, in mineral-rich states 381–4. *See also* insurgency; Maoism
Nazi genocide 60
Neelachal Ispat Nigam 378
Nehruvian state
  capitalism 319
  tribal welfare programmes by 313
Neo Liberal State
networks for migration 234–5, 238, 245
NGO. *See* non-governmental organizations (NGOs)
Ningthouja 98, 101–3, 107
Niyamgiri Hills 26, 166, 169, 331, 355, 407 (*see also* Odisha; Vedanta mining group)
  Dongria Konds in 162–3
  impact of bauxite mining on 418–19
  Supreme Court's verdict on 407–8
nokma 118
nomadic forest communities 146

nomadic tribes 7–8
non-governmental organizations (NGOs) 93, 225, 236, 249, 260, 323–4, 343, 351, 359, 361, 370, 392, 396, 416–17
non-timber forest products (NTFPs) 286
North-East India 97–122
  colonial state in 103–15
  ethnicity and tribes of 118–22
  improvement of 103–15
  modernization in 115–18
  nation-state of 115–18
  overview 97–9
  paddy states of 99–103
  religious change in 99–103
  Sanskritization in 99–103
  scheduled tribes of 115–18
  Sixth Schedule for 117–18
  wild tribes of 103–15

occupation (work)
  concentration in 241
  feminized 193
  labour rights and 229
  religious identity in 235
  skills 65, 115, 117, 203, 241–2, 245, 248
occupation, of territory
  colonial, of Assam 106, 108
  forest land 288, 290, 295
  of hill countries 105
Odisha 6, 16–17, 19, 22, 26, 28, 47, 77, 152, 230, 233, 236, 293, 295–6, 298, 301, 327–8, 330, 340, 343, 357, 378, 380 (*see also* Orissa)
  colonial/post-colonial 79
  community forestry movement in 353
  conversion to Christianity in 6
  forest departments in 303
  Gandhamardan 392

Hinduization in 85
Jajpur district of 378
Jhorias and Durvas in 164
Kalinganagar 377, 397–400
Kashipur 387–91
Kashipur movement in, 168
Niyamgiri Hills of 26, 166, 169, 331, 355, 407
police and paramilitary forces in 387–91
Pohang Steel Company Ltd (POSCO) 296, 303, 391, 396, 398–9
poverty in 372–4
protests against plantations 303–4
struggle for community forest resource rights 298
urban/coastal 78
western 87, 185, 197, 201
oikologia 161
oikonomia 161
Operation Anaconda 382
Operation Green Hunt 137, 167, 328, 383
original dwellers 164
  early medieval 81
  Foreign Debt 373
  Gandhian politics 89–90
  Kalinganagar killing of 394
  post-colonial 90–2
Orissa 81–4, 86, 88, 90–2, 373, 375. *See also* Odisha
Orissa Forest Development Corporation 298
Orissa Jungle Manch 298
Oriyaization 83–4
Oriya Kandhas 83
Other Backward Classes (OBC) 42, 164
Outside the Fold: Conversion, Modernity and Belief 80

paddy state(s) 99–103

pahariah 85
paid domestic work
  adivasi female migration for 230–5
  ideal housekeeper for 241–3
  live-in domestics 194, 203, 229, 230–1, 235–6, 239
  placement agencies provide entry into 235–9
  trafficking of 239
  24x7 domestic labour service 240–1
panchayati raj 287, 414
Panchayats (Extension to Scheduled Areas) Act (PESA) 18, 23, 56, 174, 283–4, 413–15. *See also gram sabha*s
Panchsheel 137, 144
Pandita Ramabai's Feminist and Christian Conversions: Focus on Stree Dharma-Neeti 80
Paradigm Wars 62
paramilitary forces 387–91
Particularly Vulnerable Tribal Group (PVTG) 166, 401
Parulekar, Godavari 314
Pathy, Jagannath 127
Patkar, Medha 398
Patnaik, Dinabandhu 87
pauperization 135, 201
Pawsey, Charles 116
peasant 50, 54–6, 109, 135, 145, 189, 201, 311, 314, 337
  Chota Nagpur's 184
  consciousness 316, 332
  dispossessed 315, 317, 333
  farmers 145
  indebted 186
  insurgency 67–8
  non-tribal 183
  rich 84
  sedentary 311
  tribal 183
peasantization 82, 134

Peel, J. D. Y. 115
Periyar Tiger Reserve 346, 360
Permanent Settlement of 1793 55
PESA. *See* Panchayats (Extension to Scheduled Areas) Act (PESA)
Philosophy for NEFA 137
Phulbani 91
placement agencies 235–9
plains tribes 115, 119–20, 122
Plantation Labour Act (PLA) of (1951) 222
plantations. *See* tea plantations of West Bengal, adivasi labour in
Pohang Steel Company Ltd (POSCO) 296, 303, 391, 396, 398–9
Polavaram Dam 296
police, in Odisha 387–91
political economy 65, 141, 144–5, 154–5
political legitimacy 103, 121
political mobilization 307–34 (*see also* communist movement; movements; rights; insurgency; Maoism; revolutionary politics)
  adivasi politics 318–22, 330–4
  class-based politics 313–17
  community-based politics 310–13
  complementary hegemonies 323–6
  cultural boundaries and 318–22
  Hindutva politics 323–6
  Maoism in neoliberal times, rise of 326–30
  overview 307–10
  regionalism and 318–22
  resistance movement and 24–6, 28, 72, 331, 355, 397
POSCO. *See* Pohang Steel Company Ltd (POSCO)
poverty
  concentration of 287
  in mineral-rich states 272–6

Pradhan Mantri Gram Sadak Yojana 327
Prajatantra 91
primitive accumulation 13, 68–9
  adivasi sensibility and labour potentiality of 65–72
  counter insurgency against 54–9
  indigenous perspective against 59–65
  labour potential and 73–4
  overview 53–4
  ST category and 54–9
primitive tribes 5, 128
Progressive Plantation Workers Union 225
Project Tiger 170, 258, 359
protected areas (PAs) 282
  Programme of Work on Protected Areas 364
  relocation from 281
Pruett, G. E. 110
public sector 319, 416
PVTG. *See* Particularly Vulnerable Tribal Group (PVTG)

Queen's Proclamation of (1858) 55–6

race, concept of 34–6
Ramesh, Jairam 161
Ramnath, Madhu 169
ranipaja 134
Rashtriya Swayamsevak Sangh 77
Rath, Gauri Prasad 325
Rathvas, denotification of 151–6
Rebellious Prophets 134
recruiting agents 17, 186, 217–18, 235–9, 245, 248. *See also* labour; migration; informal labour
recruitment (*see also* tea plantations) of adivasi labour for tea plantations 209–11
  in Dooars 216–19
Redfield, Robert 147

Reducing Emissions through Degradation and Deforestation (REDD+) 304
regionalism 318–22
resistance movement 24–6, 28, 72, 331, 355, 397
revolutionary politics 68–70
Revolutionary Socialist Party 223
Re-writing History: Life and Times of Pandita Ramabai 80
rights
  articulation of 51
  authorities and procedures for recognition of 290
  citizenship 2, 156, 283
  community 20–1, 23, 72, 274, 295, 300–1, 348, 355, 357, 364
  community forest resource, struggle for 297–302
  creative grassroots assertion of 26, 295–7
  forest 168–70
  human, 64
  marginalization of 51
  recognized under FRA 291
Risley H. H., 3
Rose, H. A. 3
Roy, A. K. 320
Roy, J. J. M. N. 118, 312
ruling class 100, 140, 265, 314, 322
rural-to-urban migration 230
Russell, G. E. 162
Russell, R. V. 3

Sahlins, Marshall 163
Sahu, B. P. 78, 81
sakhu 272
Salwa Judum 26, 28, 384–7
Samatha Judgment 330–1, 415–17, 421
sanctuary 342, 345, 410
  Abohar 351
  Askot 351
  Biligiri 344–5, 358
  Ghoshu 350
  Karlapat 406
  Kumbalgarh 343–4
  Satkosia Gorge 343
  Sunabeda 343
Sanskritization 80
  in North-East India 99–103
*sarana*s 272
Saranda Forest 167, 382
Sardar Sarovar dam 168
Sariska (Rajasthan) 358
Scheduled Area 152, 185, 415
Scheduled Caste (SC) 7–8, 42, 143, 324
Scheduled Tribe (ST) 1, 2, 4, 8, 18, 20, 41–3, 50–1, 54, 57–8, 119, 127–9, 141, 164, 253
  counter-insurgency functions 54–9
  legal regimes of 57
Scheduled Tribes, The 144
Schedules V and VI 278–9, 281
Schedule V 281, 291, 396
Schedule V areas 20, 22–3, 282–3, 285, 376, 413, 415
Scott, David 106
Scott, J. C. 98
self-help groups (SHGs) 173
Seminar 326
semi-nomadic tribes 184
Sen, Binayak 167
SEZ. *See* special economic zone (SEZ)
Shaktism 100–1, 122
Sharma, B. D. 165
Shiva, 100 107
shuddhi 79
shuddhi karan 7, 93
Simmel, George 147
Singer, Milton 147
Singh, Jaipal 164

Singh, K. S. 183
Sinha, Surajit 138
Skaria, Ajay 105
Snaitang, O. L. 115
social evolutionism 164
social impact assessment (SIA) 420–1
social isolation 248–50
special economic zone (SEZ) 353, 381
Spencer, Herbert 165
Srinivas, M. N. 80
state of nature 53, 55, 57–9, 66, 69, 73
stereotyped 194, 241, 250
stereotypes 139
   ethnocentric 139
   implicit 167
   jobs reinforce 239, 249
   negative 164
Subaltern School 105
subsistence 53–4, 56, 61, 64, 66, 73, 232, 286, 340, 342, 375
subsistence economy 163
Sudras 82
Supplement to Calcutta (Government) Gazette 212
Supreme Court 342
   Central Empowered Committee 343
   Godavarman case 272
sustainable development 159–75
   adivasi voices and realities 167–8
   aim of 161–3
   cultural genocide and 170–5
   forest rights and community ownership 168–70
   of forests and other ecosensitive regions 145–6
   overview 159–60
   three pillars of 162
   tribal development 164–7
Sustainable Development Reports 173
Swargadeo 102

Sword, V. H. 109
syiems 118

Tata 167, 171, 330, 382–3, 385–6, 392, 394, 398
Tata Steel Rural Development Society 71
Tauli-Corpuz, Victoria 62–3
Tea Districts Labour Association (TDLA) 217–18
tea plantations of West Bengal, adivasi labour in 207–26
   adivasi leadership in 224–6
   adivasis' protest movement 213–15
   data collection 208–9
   early problems of 209
   enticement to workers/labour 219–21
   growth in Dooars 215–16
   migration to Jalpaiguri 215
   migration to tea districts 211–13
   overview 207–8
   recruitment of adivasi labour 209–11
   recruitment system in Dooars 216–19
   sociological consequences 221–4
   trade union movement 224–6
tea tribes 119–20, 122, 188
temple 87, 91
tenurial claims 267
tenurial conflicts 284
tenurial security 284, 305, 357
territory 35, 40, 48, 51, 55, 133, 169, 194, 292
   European colonization and demography change in 33–4
   expansion by East India Company 8
   expansion of forests in 55
   indigenous status, in 46
   indigenous with respect to 47

original inhabitants and their
  descendants in 61
people/population born in 34
Thakkar, A. V. 9, 126
Thane 315–16
Thompson, E. P. 264
Thurston, Edgar 3
tiger reserves 340, 345, 361, 401
  2006 amendment to WLPA
    341–2, 358, 360
  BRT 301
  Indravati 355
  management plans for 303
  notification of 362
  Periyar 346, 360
  Sariska 358
Times of India 23
tipkur tipkha 115
Todorov, Tzvetan 131
trafficking, for domestic work 239
tribal development 164–7
tribal-forest conflicts 281–6
Tribal Identity and Minority Status: The Kathkari Nomads in Transition 127
tribal kingships 173
tribal(s) 11, 164
  administrative category 128–9
  characteristics 6–7
  colonial penetration of 133–5
  evolutionary patterns of 136
  historical perspective 129–37
  identifying 127–9
  oral history of 131–2
  representational technology and 130–1
  search for identity 136–7
  traditional sources for history of 132–3
tribe–caste continuum 144
Tribes and Castes of Bengal, The 3
Tribes and Castes of Central Provinces of India, The 3

Tripura 102, 105, 107
  communist movement and adivasi consciousness 316
  Ganamukti Parishad in 314, 316
  Sixth Schedule for 117
  upjati consciousness 315

unemployment 92, 215, 232, 234, 324, 343
United Nations (UN) 11–12
  Declaration on Rights of Indigenous Peoples 42
  General Assembly 13
  Permanent Forum on Indigenous Issues 45, 62
  Sub-Commission on Prevention of Discrimination and Protection of Minorities 37
  UNESCO Declaration on Ethnocide and Ethno-development 60
  UN-sponsored Indigenous Peoples Working Group 319
  Working Group on Indigenous Populations (WGIP) 11, 15, 18, 38
United Progressive Alliance 289
untouchability 7
urban areas 191, 193
urban economy 6
use value 73
Utkala Dipika 88
Utkal Alumina International Limited 388

Vaishnavism 99, 101–3, 121–2
Vaishyas 82
valued agricultural livelihoods 199
Van Raksha Dals (VRD) 71
Vanvasi Kalyan Ashrams 323
vanyajati 134
varna system 3, 6–7, 82, 84–6
Vasundhara 343–4

Vedanta mining group 22, 26, 30, 163, 166, 172–3, 296, 303, 328, 330–1, 355, 407, 415
victims
　families, support to 72–3
　ghatwals 183
　in Lushai village 113
　modernization process of 228
　of conquest and colonization 40
　of sexual exploitation 245
　of starvation 405
　of untouchability 7
Vidyarthi, L. P. 136
Vishva Hindu Parishad (VHP) 26, 92–4
voluntary
　agencies 235
　missionary work 235
　sector organizations 323–4

Wall Street Journal 406
wandering tribes 128
Warlis 132, 314–16
Web of Poverty, The 165
Welsh Calvinistic faith 6
Welsh Calvinistic Methodists 109
　mission 108–9
West Bengal
　Forest Department 55, 300
　struggle for community forest resource rights 300
　tea plantations of 207–26
WGIP. *See* Working Group on Indigenous Populations (WGIP)
Wildlife Crime Bureau 358
Wildlife Institute of India 419

wildlife-people conflicts, in conservation areas 346–8
Wild Life Protection Act (1972) 280
　(*see also* Acts)
　enactment of 280
　informal 19
　leadership from within 224–5
　led movements 9
　rural 318, 327
　Tiger Amendment 169–70
　working class 71, 222, 319–20
wildlife sanctuaries (WLS) 285, 339–40, 342
　Abohar Sanctuary 351
　adivasis rights in 282–3
　Askot Wildlife Sanctuary 351
　establishment of 18
　human habitation in 342
　of Nagaland 350
wild tribes 105
working-class adivasis 24–5, 316
working-class consciousness 314, 326
working-class unity 314, 333–4
Working Group on Indigenous Populations (WGIP) 38. *See also* United Nations (UN)
Workmen's Breach of Contract Act (1858) 210
Workmen's Breach of Contract Act (1859) 216
World Conference on Human Rights (Vienna) 37
World Wide Fund for Nature (WWF) 341

Young India 92

Editor and Contributors

Sharit K. Bhowmik is Adjunct Faculty, Rajiv Gandhi Centre for Contemporary Studies, University of Mumbai, India.

Neema Pathak Broome is a member of Kalpavriksh Environment Action Group, Pune, India.

Rudolf C. Heredia is an independent researcher based in Mumbai, India.

Ashish Kothari is founder-member of Kalpavriksh Environment Action Group, Pune, India.

Indrani Mazumdar is Senior Fellow, Centre for Women's Development Studies, New Delhi, India.

Neetha N. is Senior Fellow (Professor), Centre for Women's Development Studies, New Delhi, India.

Felix Padel is an independent researcher and a former visiting professor at the North East India Study Programme, Jawaharlal Nehru University, New Delhi, India (July–December 2015).

Biswamoy Pati is Senior Fellow, Nehru Memorial Museum and Library, New Delhi, India.

Archana Prasad is Professor, Centre for Informal Sector and Labour Studies, Jawaharlal Nehru University, New Delhi, India.

Meena Radhakrishna is an independent researcher and former faculty at Delhi School of Economics, Department of Sociology, University of Delhi, India.

Dhananjay Rai is Assistant Professor, Centre for Gandhian Thought, Central University of Gujarat, Ahmedabad, India.

N. Rajaram is Professor, Department of Sociology, Central University of Gujarat, Ahmedabad, India.

Arjun Rathva is a social activist based in Gujarat, India.

Madhu Sarin is Fellow, Rights and Resources Initiative, Washington DC, USA and a member of the Campaign for Survival and Dignity.

Savyasaachi is Professor, Department of Sociology, Jamia Milia Islamia, New Delhi, India.

Sudha Vasan is Associate Professor, Department of Sociology, Delhi School of Economics, University of Delhi, India.

Virginius Xaxa is Professor and Deputy Director, Tata Institute of Social Sciences, Guwahati, India.

David Vumlallian Zou is Assistant Professor, Department of History, University of Delhi, India.